Dedication

To my parents, Maxine, Rachel, Kate, William, Ren, and Tai

BRIEF CONTENTS

PREFACE

A Brief Background

In 1995 financial statements and notes for large publicly traded firms filled 10–20 pages. An investor or analyst who was reasonably knowledgeable about a firm could understand its newly issued financial statements and notes in 30 minutes. Since then, accounting has undergone five or six revolutions, among them the Internet bubble and the related circumvention of accounting rules; aggressive and widespread accounting manipulation at such firms as Adelphia, Cendant, Computer Associates, Enron, HealthSouth, Parmalat, Tyco, WorldCom, and many others; the passage of the Sarbanes-Oxley Act in 2002 and the establishment of the Public Company Accounting Oversight Board (PCAOB), which led to hundreds of financial restatements and far stricter compliance with accounting rules; the development of increasingly detailed accounting rules by the Financial Accounting Standards Board (FASB) to avoid the widespread innovation, manipulation, and outright fraud in financial reporting of the previous decade. While those changes led to improvements, there are no absolutes in business. Old rules cannot account for new innovations, and managers develop new ways to circumvent rules. Almost as soon as those corrections were in place, new problems arose, such as the subprime mortgage crisis that began in 2007.

An equally sweeping array of changes is the ongoing convergence of U.S. generally accepted accounting principles (GAAP) and international accounting standards that began at least five years ago. As a result of all these changes, one note in small print can now exceed 10 pages and can be more complex than an entire set of financial statements from 1995.

Balanced Perspective and Broad Outlook

The cases in this series are designed to expose students to the major financial reporting issues and events of the period and help them prepare to assume management and professional leadership roles in the global economy. Most cases relate to the period after the Internet bubble and the Enron-WorldCom-HealthSouth scandals because those events occurred in what is almost ancient history. The problems a financial reporting regulator, standard setter, auditor, preparer, or user faces today are far different from problems they faced even six or seven years ago.

The lesson of these cases is that there continues to be a clear need for accounting rules and auditing because there are widespread instances of accounting manipulation, fraud, and embezzlement. There is also a need for balance because there are also widespread instances where rules are so burdensome and costly that they interfere with a firm's operations, where the rules produce misleading results, and where firms incur high costs to restate financial statements for items that seem subjective, inconsequential, or both. I have tried to include cases that cover a wide range of these situations and issues and to make the cases as nonjudgmental as possible. Regulators, standard setters, auditors, financial statement preparers, and users all have different goals and perspectives; I have tried to include their different views, to the extent possible.

Cases Based on Five Perspectives

The United States has more than 20,000 pages of highly detailed accounting rules that are in a constant state of flux, particularly with the Accounting Standards Codification project and the work toward convergence of U.S. GAAP and International Financial Reporting Standards (IFRS). Each of the four largest accounting firms (Deloitte, Ernst & Young, KPMG, and PwC) has a technical support group of between 100 and 200 highly trained managers and partners at a New York City or New Jersey office. They answer technical questions from their firm's engagement (audit) partners and managers. The accounting rules are so complex and detailed, and change so often, that many highly competent engagement partners call their technical support group almost daily.

Given that complexity, there is no way a case or a book can capture all of the intricacies in financial reporting. There is also no way that general concepts alone can qualify a reader to prepare or understand real financial statements. The cases in this book cover a wide range of financial reporting topics, and they are written at a wide range of technical complexity. Some are very basic and cover only the most fundamental accounting principles. Others are highly technical and cover one or a few very complex issues. In general, the cases are selected or designed from five perspectives:

1. Case structure and design
2. Complexity
3. Managerial/strategic versus technical accounting perspective
4. Regulatory source: IFRS versus U.S. GAAP
5. Regulatory environment

1. Case structure and design

The cases cover a wide range of financial reporting topics. They cover most of the major income statement and balance sheet items, most financial statement notes, and selected topics related to the statements of cash flows and statements of owners' equity. For some topics, it is difficult to find financial statements from a single firm that cover a topic in enough detail, so some cases include information from several firms; examples include revenue recognition (Cases 3.3 and 3.9), impairment charges (Case 4.1), and depreciation (Case 4.3). In other instances, a case about one company covers many different accounting issues because they are all related to one incident. Examples include Microsoft (Case 2.2), Dell (Case 3.6), and Mitchells & Butlers (Case 4.5).

2. Complexity

The cases also cover a wide range of depth and challenge. Some are well suited for an introductory course, such as the first few class sessions of a first-year MBA or EMBA financial accounting course. A few highly technical accounting cases are best suited to a graduate course in financial reporting, financial statement analysis, or valuation. However, most cases are only moderately complex and are suitable for a wide range of undergraduate and graduate accounting courses and for executive education.

3. Managerial/strategic versus technical accounting perspective

MBA courses typically focus more on managerial and strategic issues, while undergraduate and graduate accounting courses focus more on technical issues. Most cases include both managerial/strategic issues and technical financial reporting issues. An MBA class or executive seminar can focus on management or strategy but still spend some time on technical issues, since it is often not possible to understand the managerial or strategic issues in a case unless one knows something about the technical accounting issues. Most cases also include enough information about the technical accounting issue(s) so that accounting students can focus more on that aspect of the case and refer to U.S. GAAP or IFRS pronouncements for more information.

4. Regulatory source: IFRS versus U.S. GAAP

Five years ago U.S. GAAP was the world's dominant set of financial accounting standards. By 2011, most countries have adopted International Financial Reporting Standards (IFRS), and for at least the last five years the FASB and International Accounting Standards Board (IASB) have worked toward convergence of their standards. The cases in this book cover both U.S. GAAP and IFRS. Section 3, "Financial Reporting—U.S. GAAP," includes some references to IFRS; Section 4, "Financial Reporting—IFRS," includes some references to U.S. GAAP; Section 6, "Valuation," includes the InBev (Belgium) acquisition of Anheuser-Busch, a U.S. company.

5. Regulatory environment

Financial reporting regulation is far more extensive than in the past, and the SEC, PCAOB, FASB, and IASB are far more active. Many cases include information about the regulation of financial reporting, and some of them focus on reporting standards. The FASB's Accounting Standards Codification (ASC) project is the first time the United States has had a single source and nomenclature for all its financial reporting standards and rules. Cases with technical accounting information make reference to the ASC.

For students interested in the technical aspects of financial reporting, it is essential to know which rules apply. For MBA students and executives interested in managerial or strategic issues, it is essential to know that the rules exist and must be followed.

Cases Available Online

The cases in this series are available in print and online, in the following forms:

1. The cases printed in this book are also available for purchase from CengageBrain on an individual basis. Go to **www.cengagebrain.com** and search by author, title or ISBN for details.

2. Certain cases are discussed in the synopses below as "online only" and appear in the table of contents; these cases do not appear in the printed book. New cases will be added on a continuing basis and will be posted to the companion website for access by instructors and students.

3. A printed casebook can also been created that includes only the cases you decide to include. Please visit **www.cengage.com/custom/makeityours/sandretto** to select the cases for your casebook. Please refer to the website or inside front cover for more information.

An Overview of the Cases

When reviewing this casebook or the individual cases for inclusion in a course, instructors should refer to the case synopses in the upcoming section. Also, instructors can visit the Instructor Resources page online and consult a table that provides an overview of all the cases in this series by number of pages, level of difficulty, and the primary course(s) for which the case is recommended.

Suggested Cases for Selected Accounting Courses

Additional support for instructors comes in the form of a series of **suggested cases for five accounting courses:** Intermediate Accounting I and II, Financial Reporting, Financial Statement Analysis, and MBA or Executive MBA Financial Accounting. Go to the Instructor Resources page to view and download these tables.

Resources for Students

All resources available to students can be found at **www.cengagebrain.com**. Direct students to search for this casebook by author, title, or ISBN and click on the link to access **Study Tools**.

Case Notes for Instructors

Detailed Case Notes are available to instructors for each case in the series. These are available under password protection at the Instructor Resource page at login.cengage.com.

Acknowledgments

I would first like to thank my daughter, Rachel Sandretto, for heavily editing earlier versions of many of the cases. She also introduced me to the editing process.

I would like to especially thank Brittany Cadwalader (Deloitte), my former teaching and research assistant at Illinois. She heavily edited nearly all of the cases and notes for grammar, writing style, accuracy, and content—in many instances, several times. Her work made the material clearer, more interesting, and far easier to read and understand. She also shortened nearly all of the cases by deleting large amounts of material that, to be charitable, were ancillary to the case focus.

The Department of Accountancy at the University of Illinois provided funding for teaching and research assistants who provided excellent editing and research for many of the cases. Ira Solomon, department head, encourages interactive teaching with Project Discovery, strongly supports the faculty, and maintains outstanding relations with the dozens of accounting firms who regularly visit and otherwise support the University of Illinois.

I would like to thank partners and faculty at the Ernst & Young IFRS seminar (Cleveland, 2009), partners at the PwC year-end technical training seminar (Chicago, 2010), and the following firms for presentations they made to my classes and to students and faculty at the University of Illinois: BDO Seidman; Crowe Horwath; Deloitte; Ernst & Young; Grant Thornton; KPMG; McGladrey & Pullen; and PwC. They provided many new case ideas and were a continual source of technical information.

Several thousand University of Illinois students used earlier versions of these cases; their suggestions and corrections significantly improved them. That is particularly true for Executive MBA students, whose extensive business experience in a wide range of industries was especially helpful in expanding the case perspectives.

Paulo Camasmie spent dozens of hours explaining how he built Big Cat HPV into the world's largest recumbent trike manufacturer and dozens of additional hours improving the Big Cat HPV, LLC case. He particularly wanted students to understand the challenges, risks, and excitement of a new venture. Mr. Gary Tseng, CFO of Semiconductor Manufacturing International Corporation (Shanghai), provided extensive industry background, cost information, and business strategy about the semiconductor industry.

Two of my former students, Nisa Agrawal (PwC) and Jessica Tarica (PwC and Wharton), were particularly helpful with technical accounting issues.

The following business associates, guest speakers, former students, or former teaching assistants helped edit cases, provided case ideas, and offered other invaluable assistance: Douglas Black (Seaton Corp.); Kevin Brower (Ernst & Young); Suzanne Brindise (Houlihan Lokey); Allison Busse (Duff and Phelps); Christina Fertl; Loren Friedman (BDO Consulting); Eric Hiller (founder, aPriori and endaround.org); Angela Jiang; Margaret Kaczor (William Blair); David Kidd (Lincoln International and Adirondack Growth Capital); Alyson Kirkpatrick (PwC); Lerry Knox (Loop Capital); John Kosir; John Levitske (Duff and Phelps); Lisa Luckman (KPMG); Mary McNicholas (Lincoln International); Christina Tseng; Amit Vaishampayan; Mathieu Vincent (PwC); Kevin Wydra (Crowe Horwath); and Pamela Zhang (Deloitte and NYU School of Law).

Matthew Filimonov (senior acquisitions editor, Cengage Learning) and Craig Avery (senior developmental editor, Cengage Learning) managed and directed this project. Karunakaran Gunasekaran (content project manager, PreMediaGlobal) led the editing and typesetting process. Their highly professional work simplified what could have been a burdensome process and also significantly improved the quality of this book.

Michael Sandretto
December 2010

CASE SYNOPSES

Case 1.1 Dublin Small Animal Clinic, Inc. 3

This brief case covers the accounting cycle for a start-up veterinarian practice. The first section includes cash transactions; the second section includes accruals. Students make simple journal entries and then prepare an income statement and balance sheet. This is a good introduction to financial accounting for first-year MBA or Executive MBA students.

KEY TOPICS: The accounting cycle; journal entries; income statement; balance sheet.

Case 1.2 Verona Springs Mineral Water 5

This case covers the accounting cycle for a start-up water bottling firm. It is similar to *Dublin Small Animal Clinic, Inc.* but slightly more complicated. It also asks students to prepare a statement of cash flows. This is a good follow-up to *Dublin Small Animal Clinic, Inc.*

KEY TOPICS: The accounting cycle; journal entries; income statement; balance sheet; statement of cash flows.

Case 1.3 Holton-Central Holdings Inc. 7

Holton-Central Holdings covers the accounting cycle for a manufacturer acquired out of bankruptcy. It is more advanced than *Dublin Small Animal Clinic, Inc.* or *Verona Springs Mineral Water* because the acquisition includes goodwill and the case covers accounting for raw material, work in process, and finished goods inventory.

KEY TOPICS: The accounting cycle; accounting for inventories; goodwill; journal entries; income statement; balance sheet; statement of cash flows.

Case 1.4 Chang Medical Electronics 11

A private equity partner evaluates three possible bond issues for a potential acquisition. The case covers (a) the basics of bond pricing, bond yields, zero-coupon bonds, and bond refinancing and (b) accounting for issued bonds, including the effective interest method. This case can supplement *Sirius XM Radio, Inc., Faces Bankruptcy* (Case 3.5); *Harley-Davidson, Inc. (A)* (Case 5.1); or *Knowles Electronics, Inc.* (Case 6.5). It can be used with *Discounted Cash Flows and the Time Value of Money* (Case 7.4), *Bonds* (Case 7.6), or *Fixed Income Securities (Bonds)* (Case 8.5).

KEY TOPICS: Introduction to bonds; bond valuation; zero-coupon bonds; bond refinancing.

Case 1.5   Janet O'Brien   15

I often pass out this case the first day of class to help students become comfortable talking in class. The case covers cost-based Medicaid nursing home reimbursements, which are managed by individual states but funded about equally by each state and the federal government. Because the state in this case did not audit nursing homes for several years, the homes grew increasingly aggressive in billing the state for high and possibly unallowable costs. The case can be used to consider why we have accounting rules and audits, why cost-based reimbursement is so difficult to control, and why alleged fraud is so common.

KEY TOPICS: Cost-based reimbursements; the need for rules; the need for auditing.

Case 1.6   Big Cat HPV LLC   21

This case covers the first 10 years of operations for a start-up recumbent tricycle manufacturer. The case covers distribution, marketing, sales, product design, production control, cost control, product features, and competitive analysis. That can all be related to the firm's income statements from 2000 through 2007 (later years are omitted for confidentiality). The case can be used in a wide range of courses including managerial and financial accounting, new ventures, production, marketing, or strategy/policy because it covers everything the founder considered important during the first 10 years of Big Cat's operations.

KEY TOPICS: Start-ups; financial statements; product costs; product features; product pricing; strategy; competitive analysis; product design; production control.

SECTION 2   Governance and Regulation   47

Case 2.1   Accounting Irregularities at Xerox   49

This case focuses on Xerox's use of low discount rates for its sales-type (capital) leases in South America. The issues arose when an assistant controller raised questions about Xerox's lease accounting in August 2000. He was fired two days later, which led to an SEC investigation. The case discusses seven accounting issues raised by the SEC. The case can be used in conjunction with *Lease Restatements in the Restaurant Industry, 2004–2005* (Case 3.2) and may be supplemented with *Leases* (Case 8.6)

KEY TOPICS: Corporate governance; sales-type leases; understated discount rates; SEC investigation.

Case 2.2   Financial Reporting Issues at Microsoft Corp   57

This case covers Microsoft's consent decree with the SEC over unsupported accounting accruals. Microsoft had well-designed systems at the operating level to prepare and monitor accruals, but senior management made large, unsupported accrual journal entries each quarter, allegedly to reach earnings targets. When SEC officials aligned the unsupported adjustments with relevant accounts, they discovered that for one quarter Microsoft had negative inventory.

KEY TOPICS: Accruals; corporate governance; materiality; documentation; SEC consent decree.

Case 2.3   Beazer Homes USA, Inc.   73

Beazer Homes was the sixth largest U.S. home builder during the 1998–2006 housing boom. The SEC alleged that Beazer's chief accounting officer understated reported profits in every quarter but one from 2000 through 2005 by understating Beazer's "land inventory" account and overstating its "cost to complete" reserve. The SEC further alleged that during each of the four quarters in 2006, and in the first quarter of 2007, he increased Beazer's reported profits by increasing the "land inventory" account, decreasing the "cost to complete" reserve, and fraudulently recording sale and leaseback transactions for model homes. The cumulative alleged profit understatement for 2000–2005 was about $72 million when Beazer had about $2 billion of total operating profits. However, during nine quarters from 2007 to 2009, Beazer recorded about $1 billion of impairment charges, so the alleged manipulation seems small compared with the uncertainty about Beazer's real financial performance.

KEY TOPICS: Accruals; corporate governance; materiality; documentation; SEC investigation; impairment charges.

Case 2.4   Corporate Governance at IBM and Google   93

IBM and Google are highly profitable and in many ways among the world's most ethical companies. Both have impressive corporate value statements (included in the case), but IBM and Google are publicly traded and employ tens of thousands of employees; they are not charitable organizations. As they react to competitive challenges, they must sometimes reduce salaries or benefits or engage in actions that seriously harm their competitors. This case includes instances in which IBM and Google face complicated decisions.

KEY TOPICS: Corporate values statements; corporate governance; business judgment and competing interests.

Case 2.5   Chrysler LLC Bankruptcy   109

Chrysler and General Motors received large U.S. government loans and needed additional funding to continue operating. A bankruptcy would be extraordinarily costly and might put thousands of employees out of work as the U.S. economy entered its worst recession since the Great Depression. It seemed highly unlikely any private investor would fund either firm. In response, the government proposed a rapid exit through a Chapter 11 bankruptcy reorganization that would seemingly circumvent the legal priority of creditors in bankruptcy. That led some to question whether the plan might lead to a lack of faith in contract law and the courts. This case can be supplemented with *Retiree Benefits in the United States* (Case 7.7).

KEY TOPICS: Bankruptcy; governance; priority in bankruptcy; national policy and competing interests.

Case 2.6   General Growth Properties   119

This case covers a bankruptcy court ruling that seemed to circumvent securitization trust law. General Growth Properties (GGP) owned about 225 malls funded with debt issued by a separate securitization trust for each mall. During the 2008–2009 recession, commercial real estate financing was nearly impossible to obtain.

GGP's malls were financially sound, but GGP was about to declare bankruptcy. GGP changed the independent directors on many securitization trusts, and when it filed for bankruptcy, so did more than 200 of the financially sound trusts. A court ruling let GGP withdraw funds from the trusts, which saved GGP. The case also raises conflict-of-interest issues about a trust fund established for the benefit of the daughter of GGP's deceased cofounder.

KEY TOPICS: Securitization; piercing a securitization trust; corporate governance; business judgment and competing interests; conflicts of interest.

Intel values its inventory at the lower of cost or market. Intel's inventory primarily consists of semiconductors that rapidly decline in value as newer products enter the market. Product demand is difficult to estimate because demand for end products that use Intel semiconductors is highly volatile. As a result, it is difficult to determine whether Intel has excess inventory and difficult to estimate the current value of its inventory. This case discusses those issues and includes Intel's quarterly inventory disclosures from quarter 1, 1996, through quarter 3, 2009.

KEY TOPICS: Inventory write-downs; financial disclosure; accounting estimates.

This case discusses four detailed operating lease rules that many restaurant chains failed to follow. After the PCAOB released its first inspection reports in mid-2005, about 35 restaurant chains restated their financial statements for failing to follow those rules even though, in most instances, the errors were minor. This case is excellent for considering the difference between rules-based U.S. GAAP and principles-based IFRS, which includes none of these four rules. The case includes a letter from the SEC's Chief Accountant to the AICPA in response to an AICPA letter asking if it was necessary for firms to restate their financial statements. Because of the potential criminal liability under Sarbanes-Oxley, most firms restated their financial statements even for immaterial amounts. This case may be supplemented with *Leases* (Case 8.6).

KEY TOPICS: Operating leases; financial restatements; materiality; principles-based versus rule-based accounting.

Revenue Recognition Disclosures (A) includes revenue recognition notes for seven companies, and most notes discuss several different revenue recognition issues. This case may be supplemented with *Revenue Recognition (A)* (Case 8.2) or *Revenue Recognition (B)* (Case 8.3). It is similar to Revenue Recognition Disclosures (B) (Case 3.9).

KEY TOPICS: Revenue recognition disclosures; accruals; principles-based versus rules-based accounting standards.

This case covers securitization by one of the first firms to go bankrupt because of subprime lending. The case gives an overview of an out-of-control mortgage securitization industry. The case is interesting because New Century classified some securitized mortgages as investments; instead of including only its retained interests on its balance sheet, New Century included the entire value of the pool's assets (mortgages) and liabilities (issued notes). The case is difficult but provides a good example of how detailed accounting rules have become and how firms circumvent the rules. This case can be supplemented with *Securitization* (Case 8.9).

KEY TOPICS: Subprime loans and the beginning of the subprime loan crises; securitization; accounting rules for off-balance sheet financing; retained interests; bankruptcy.

This case covers Sirius Radio's 2008 acquisition of XM Radio and the combined firm's near bankruptcy in early 2009. The case can be used to cover three issues: (a) an unusual business combination that resulted in an immediate $4.8 billion impairment charge, (b) an unusual loan that gave the lender 40% of the firm's equity, and (c) the value of Howard Stern to the firm.

KEY TOPICS: Liquidity crises in the recession of 2008; industry analysis; capital structure and leverage; bonds; cash flows; business combinations and goodwill; bankruptcy.

In response to allegations that senior management manipulated accounting numbers to maximize their bonuses, Dell delayed its 2006 annual report by 10 months and then restated four years of financial statements. The restatements decreased net income by $100 million for the four years 2003–2006. That equaled one-tenth of one percent of Dell's after-tax income for the period, and the investigation cost $205 million. The case covers 20–25 different accounting issues; students can evaluate numerous accounting rules in a real setting and then discuss whether the rules should even exist, since most do not exist under IFRS.

KEY TOPICS: Accruals; financial restatements; judgment and accounting errors; materiality; corporate governance; principles-based versus rules-based accounting standards.

This case covers Boeing's defined benefit pension plan and its retiree benefit health-care plan. Boeing's pension fund went from being $5 billion overfunded in 2007 to $9 billion underfunded in 2008 because of wide swings in its investment returns. Boeing's retiree health-care fund has nearly $8 billion in liabilities and almost no assets (less than $100 million). This case can be supplemented with *Retiree Benefits in the United States* (Case 7.7) and *Defined Benefit Retirement Plans* (Case 8.8).

KEY TOPICS: Accounting for defined benefit retirement plans; accounting for retiree health-care benefits.

Online Cases

Case 3.8   Bethlehem Steel Corporation's Deferred Taxes

Bethlehem Steel, for many years the nation's second largest steel company, was marginally profitable in 2000. In both 1999 and 2000, Bethlehem had about $1.3 billion of deferred tax assets on its balance sheet, reduced by a valuation allowance of $325–$340 million. In the second quarter of 2001, Bethlehem wrote off its entire $984 million of deferred tax assets. In a note to its second quarter 10-Q (July 2001), Bethlehem's management stated that the write-off was needed because of technical accounting rules, but management expected to utilize the deferred tax assets in the future. In response, many analysts stated that they expected Bethlehem's stock price to increase. Bethlehem declared bankruptcy a few months later. The case includes a basic explanation of deferred tax accounting.

KEY TOPICS: Valuation allowance; deferred taxes; financial disclosures; bankruptcy.

Case 3.9   Revenue Recognition Disclosures (B)

This case includes revenue recognition notes for six companies, and most notes cover several different revenue recognition issues. This case may be supplemented with *Revenue Recognition (A)* (Case 8.2) or *Revenue Recognition (B)* (Case 8.3). It is similar to Revenue Recognition Disclosures (A) (Case 3.3).

KEY TOPICS: Revenue recognition disclosures; accruals; principles-based versus rules-based accounting standards.

Case 3.10   Carton Medical Devices

This case describes a standard cost system for a discrete part manufacturer. The case is far more of a cost accounting case than a financial reporting case. However, most students will not take a cost accounting course, so this case can be used to explain the types of systems needed to compute a reasonably accurate cost number for inventory valuation and cost analysis.

KEY TOPICS: Inventory valuation; standard cost systems for discrete-part production.

SECTION 4   Financial Reporting—IFRS   241

Case 4.1   Asset Impairments in the Recession of 2008–2009   243

This case begins by discussing the various cost methods under U.S. GAAP and IFRS. These include historical cost, lower of cost or market, lower of cost or net realizable value, fair value, the revaluation method, and impairment testing for goodwill and other assets. The case then provides impairment notes for three IFRS reporting firms (Nestle, Swatch Group, and Royal Bank of Scotland) and two U.S. GAAP reporting firms (News Corp. and CBS Corporation). The case can be used with *Vivendi Group's Goodwill Impairment Test* (Case 4.2) and supplemented with *Impairments and Restructurings* (Case 8.4).

KEY TOPICS: Impairment charges; accounting estimates; financial disclosures.

This case includes Vivendi Group's impairment disclosure note. It discloses by how much assumptions would need to change before Vivendi Group would need to record an impairment charge. This disclosure is more detailed than the notes in *Asset Impairments in the Recession of 2008–2009* (Case 4.1). It can be used with that case and supplemented with *Impairments and Restructurings* (Case 8.4).

KEY TOPICS: Impairment charges; accounting estimates; financial disclosures.

This case provides depreciation disclosures for six semiconductor manufacturers, two in Europe (STMicroelectronics NV and Infineon Technologies), two in Taiwan (Taiwan Semiconductor Manufacturing Company [TSMC] and United Microelectronics Corporation [UMC]), and two in the United States (Intel and Texas Instruments). Although depreciation is one of the two largest costs for a semiconductor manufacturer (together with R&D), some disclosures are very limited, particularly for the two U.S.-based firms.

KEY TOPICS: Depreciation expense; fixed assets; financial disclosures.

This (A) case introduces business combinations and the fair value of acquired assets and liabilities. The case can be used to consider the validity of fair value accounting, since Thomson valued four intangibles whose value is highly subjective: trade names; customer relationships; developed technology; and other. The case also describes how Thomson grew its newspaper business through acquisitions and then entirely transformed itself by selling off nearly all of its newspaper operations and then acquiring firms in the electronic publishing industry. This case may be supplemented with *Business Combinations* (Case 7.2).

KEY TOPICS: Business combinations; divestitures; pro forma results; valuation.

Mitchells & Butlers is a British pub-restaurant chain that uses the revaluation method to value its land and buildings. The case describes IFRS cost and revaluation rules and also includes the firm's fixed asset note. Mitchells & Butlers also reported losses on two hedges as exceptional items. IFRS specifically prohibits extraordinary items, and does not even mention exceptional items, but there appears to be no difference between extraordinary and exceptional items, other than the name. Mitchells & Butlers also reported a $500 million loss on derivatives contracts and uses its land and buildings as collateral for a securitization issue that included 10 different tranches.

KEY TOPICS: Revaluation model for fixed assets; securitization of fixed assets (pubs and restaurants); losses on hedges of anticipated transactions.

Case 4.6   Barclays' Acquisition of Lehman Brothers   321

This case covers Barclays' acquisition of the U.S. operating assets of Lehman Brothers. The case provides background information on the collapse of the subprime mortgage market, and its effect on firms such as Bear Stearns, Citigroup, Merrill Lynch, AIG, Fannie Mae, and Freddie Mac. The case then describes Barclays' emergency acquisition of Lehman Brothers over the period of a few days.

The case includes the note describing how Barclays' recorded the acquisition of Lehman Brothers and, for comparison, includes notes that describe how J.P. Morgan recorded its acquisitions of Bear Stearns, Washington Mutual Bank, and Bank One. The case then considers a lawsuit filed by Lehman Brothers charging Barclays with fraud in its acquisition of Lehman Brothers. This case can be supplemented with *Deposition of Harvey R. Miller Examination by David M. Boies* (Case 4.8) and with *Business Combinations* (Case 7.2).

KEY TOPICS: Financial crises of 2008; bankruptcy; acquisition out of bankruptcy; business combinations; valuation; fair value reporting.

Online Cases

Case 4.7   Thomson's Acquisition of Reuters (B)

This case shows reported net income and shareholders' equity under both Canadian GAAP and IFRS. It also explains the rules for each item that Thomson Reuters would report differently under IFRS. The case can be used in combination with *Thomson's Acquisition of Reuters (A)* (Case 4.4) to consider differences between Canadian GAAP (which is similar to U.S. GAAP) and IFRS. It can also be used to discuss how difficult it would be to change from either Canadian or U.S. GAAP to IFRS.

KEY TOPICS: Change to IFRS reporting; accounting disclosures; differences between IFRS and Canadian GAAP.

Case 4.8   Deposition of Harvey R. Miller Examination by David M. Boies

Many students will be deposed in their careers. This case provides an example of a deposition, although rarely are the questions this carefully crafted or so penetrating, and rarely are the responses this complete or precise. Mr. Boies may be the nation's leading corporate litigator; Mr. Miller may be the nation's leading bankruptcy and restructuring attorney. This case may be supplemented with *Business Combinations* (Case 7.2) *or Business Valuation* (Case 7.3).

KEY TOPICS: Depositions; bankruptcy; valuation; fair value reporting.

Case 4.9   SAP's Alternate Financial Reporting Methods

Although it is a German company, SAP's financial statements use U.S. GAAP (in euros) to make those statements comparable to its primary competitors, who use U.S. GAAP. SAP also reports results in non-U.S. GAAP (in euros), because it disagrees with some U.S. GAAP rules, and in non-U.S. GAAP with constant currency rates (same exchange rate as the previous year), because it believes that is more reflective of its year-to-year performance. The case is technical, but it lets students consider whether there is a correct accounting method for complex firms with international operations.

KEY TOPICS: IFRS versus U.S. GAAP reporting; non-IFRS versus non-U.S. GAAP reporting; adjustments to financial statements for the effect of changes in exchange rates.

SECTION 5   Financial Statement Analysis   347

Case 5.1   Harley-Davidson, Inc. (A)   349

Until the recession of 2008–2009, Harley-Davidson financed most retail motorcycle sales through Harley-Davidson Credit; its customers are highly loyal, so credit defaults were rare. Buyers paid 10–12% interest but were so reliable that Harley-Davidson could contribute $1 billion of receivables and $35 million in cash to a securitization trust, and the trust could then issue $1 billion of 6% notes. In early 2008, the securitization market collapsed. To fund retail sales, Harley-Davidson issued long-term debt, but by the end of 2008 it was near its debt capacity, so it could no longer finance customer receivables at the same level as in the past. The case also describes several accrual accounts, and describes investment losses in Harley-Davidson pension and retiree health benefit fund investments.

KEY TOPICS: Liquidity crises in the recession of 2008–2009; freeze of the securitization market; debt capacity; accruals; retiree fund losses.

Case 5.2   Harley-Davidson, Inc. (B), February 2010   369

This case is an extension of *Harley-Davidson, Inc. (A)*. It includes financial statements through the end of 2009, when Harley-Davidson reported its first loss in at least 15 years. Harley-Davidson resumed securitization in late 2009, but at far less favorable terms than in the past. In a 2008 securitization, Harley's trust issued notes equal to about 96.5% of the combined collateral deposited into the trust; in the 2009 securitization, the trust issued notes equal to about 70% of the combined collateral deposited into the trust. The case can be used with *Harley-Davidson, Inc. (A)* (Case 5.1) to discuss how the availability of financing influences Harley-Davidson's operations and its market value. It can be supplemented with *Securitization* (Case 8.9).

KEY TOPICS: Debt-to-equity ratios; accounting for securitized receivables; valuation.

Case 5.3   Apple Inc. and Retrospective Adoption of Revenue Recognition Rules   381

AICPA Statement of Position 97-2 required that if a firm made a multiple element sale that included software, revenue must be pro-rated over the life of the contract unless the firm had vendor-specific evidence as to the value of each element of the sale. Apple recorded iPhone revenue equally over a 24 month period, but since the iPhone's software value is trivial relative to its hardware value, nearly everyone ignored Apple's reported net income and treated the sale as if all revenue was recognized on the sale date. Apple had nearly $12 billion of deferred revenue at year-end September 26, 2009. In October 2009, the FASB issued two Accounting Software Updates that substantially changed reporting rules for sales with multiple elements that include software. Apple retrospectively restated its 2009 financial statements; the restatements increased Apple's 2009 pretax net income by $4.1 billion and its 2008 pretax net income by $2.1 billion. The revised financial statements had no discernible effect on Apple's share price.

KEY TOPICS: Revised revenue recognition rules for multiple-element sales; financial restatements; retrospective adoption of a new accounting rule; valuation; financial disclosures.

Case 5.4   Merrill Lynch & Co., Inc.   393

This case covers three topics in detail: fair value, the fair value option, and segment disclosures. Those topics are closely related in this case and, although complex, help the reader understand why Merrill Lynch collapsed and understand its value after the collapse. The reader can also estimate profitability by business segment for the 18-month period from June 30, 2007, to December 31, 2008. Merrill has four major business segments: retail and institutional brokerage; investment banking; investment management, including mutual funds; and proprietary trading. During that period the first three business segments remained highly profitable; after expenses, Merrill's proprietary trading group may have lost $70–$80 billion. This case can be supplemented with *Fair Value Reporting* (Case 7.1).

KEY TOPICS: Fair value reporting; the fair value options; fair value reporting of Merrill Lynch's own debt; business segment disclosures; valuation.

Online Cases

Case 5.5   Arby's Potential Bid for Wendy's

This case covers Arby's acquisition of Wendy's. Arby's was far smaller than Wendy's and far less profitable. Arby's was controlled by two individuals who owned a majority of the firm's class A common stock, which had one vote per share. The public owned class B common stock, which had one-tenth of a vote per share. The case can be used to discuss capital structure, corporate governance, and the acquisition process.

KEY TOPICS: Hostile takeover; corporate governance; divestitures; capital structure with multiple classes of common stock.

Case 5.6   General Motors Co. Bankruptcy

This case covers GM's then-proposed bankruptcy and its pension and retiree health-care funds. In late 2008, GM and Chrysler received government loans. In early 2009, the U.S. government proposed a bankruptcy plan that would preserve GM's liability to the UAW pension and retiree health-care fund. Bondholders were to receive 8 cents in cash for each dollar in bonds, plus 16 cents in new unsecured debt and 90% of GM's equity. The case includes a letter from advisers to the creditors that challenges that offer. This case can be supplemented with *Retiree Benefits in the United States* (Case 7.7).

KEY TOPICS: Defined benefit pension plans; retiree health-care plans; bankruptcy; national interest and competing interests; corporate governance.

Case 5.7   Cisco Systems, Inc. Employee Stock Options

This case covers Cisco Systems' employee stock options disclosures. It includes Cisco's 2008 income statement, balance sheet, statement of cash flows, a disclosure note for Cisco's employee stock incentive plans, and a disclosure note for its income taxes. The case covers Cisco's employee stock options plan from two perspectives. First, it considers how Cisco computes its employee stock option costs and how it reports them in its financial statements. Second, the case compares Cisco's relatively clear 2000 disclosures with its comparatively opaque 2008 disclosures.

KEY TOPICS: Employee stock options; income tax reporting for nonqualified employee stock options; financial reporting for nonqualified employee stock options.

On June 12, 2008, InBev made an unsolicited $65 per-share bid for Anheuser-Busch that was subsequently accepted at $70 per share. This case presents information that can be used to consider whether the offer was too high, since Anheuser-Busch had large pension obligations and significant outstanding employee stock options, which were offset by several highly valuable investments that were understated on Anheuser-Busch's balance sheet. This case can be supplemented with *Business Combinations* (Case 7.2).

KEY TOPICS: Hostile takeovers; business acquisitions; segment reporting; valuation; corporate cultures.

This case lets students prepare a preliminary analysis of whether InBev's Anheuser-Busch acquisition was successful. The case includes debt repayment schedules for 2008 and 2009, selected Anheuser-Busch and InBev financial disclosures for 2007, and selected 2009 financial disclosures for the combined Anheuser-Bush InBev. The case also describes how Anheuser-Busch InBev almost immediately dismissed many Anheuser-Busch executives, converted lavish St. Louis executive offices to executive cubicles, reduced charitable contributions, and unilaterally informed vendors that payment would be made in 120 days instead of 30 days.

KEY TOPICS: Corporate restructurings; business acquisitions; IFRS reporting; valuation; corporate cultures.

This case considers unauthorized financial transactions at Koss Corporation, a small publicly traded speaker headset manufacturer headquartered in Milwaukee, Wisconsin. In late December 2009, a federal complaint charged Koss's CFO with embezzling as much as $4.5 million from the company, which had 2009 revenues of only $38.2 million. Two days later, Koss issued a press release stating that the embezzlement might be as high as $20 million. On January 4, 2010, Koss issued a press release stating that the embezzlement may have exceeded $31 million. The case takes the perspective of a hedge fund manager who is analyzing Koss' financial condition with no more information than previously issued financial statements and the knowledge that the CFO may have embezzled $31 million during the previous 10 years (eventually estimated at $50 million).

KEY TOPICS: Unauthorized financial transactions; embezzlement; corporate governance; audits; forensic accounting.

This case covers a Delaware Chancery Court ruling on the value of a privately held business. In 1997, majority shareholders acquired a minority shareholder's stock at a price the minority shareholder felt was far too low. The minority shareholder sued for relief, and in 2010 the Delaware Chancery Court ruled primarily in favor of the minority shareholder. The case discusses in detail the three primary valuation methods used to value a company. This case can be supplemented with *Business Valuation* (Case 7.3) or *Business Valuation Methods* (Case 8.10).

KEY TOPICS: Business valuations; fair value and fair market value; litigation; competing interests.

Online Cases

Case 6.5   Knowles Electronics, Inc.

The case describes how the founder built his firm into one of the world's most exceptional manufacturing firms. Knowles Electronics had a nearly 100% market share of the hearing aid microphone and speaker market and sold products off the shelf to NASA in the 1960s because its products and quality control systems exceeded NASA's lunar program requirements. The case then describes a private equity firm's acquisition of Knowles Electronics.

KEY TOPICS: Leveraged buyouts; private equity; capital structure; financial projections; loan covenants; valuation.

Case 6.6   Asher Associates' Acquisition Targets

This case includes information from offering documents for two privately-held software firms that are for sale. The information includes detailed financial information and add-backs to adjust reported net income to EBITDA (earnings before interest, taxes, depreciation, and amortization). The case includes estimated accounts receivable for one firm, which had minimal accounts receivable records because it used the cash method of accounting. That firm also was an S corporation, which made it more attractive because it would be an asset sale.

KEY TOPICS: Leveraged buyouts; valuation; accounts receivable; EBITDA valuation; adjustments for nonrecurring and unnecessary expenses.

SECTION 7   Background Notes   501

Case 7.1   Fair Value Reporting   503

This note explains current FASB and IFRS fair value reporting rules and the FASB's fair value option rules. It also discusses how fair value and fair value option rules are related to the business valuation industry, which developed many of the concepts behind the FASB and IFRS fair value rules. This case can supplement *Merrill Lynch & Co., Inc.* (Case 5.4).

KEY TOPICS: Fair value; the fair value option.

Case 7.2   Business Combinations   513

This note explains business combination reporting, including rules for recording identifiable intangible assets at their fair value, and rules for computing goodwill or the gain on acquisition. This case can supplement *Thomson's Acquisition of Reuters (A)* (Case 4.4), *Barclays' Acquisition of Lehman Brothers* (Case 4.6), or *InBev and the Anheuser-Busch Acquisition* (Case 6.2).

KEY TOPICS: Financial reporting for business combinations.

Case 7.3   Business Valuation   525

This note discusses business valuation from both an academic view and from the view of a business valuation expert who may follow the methods specified by a business valuation certifying organization. The note introduces the idea of discounts, such as lack-of-control discounts, lack-of-marketability discounts, key employee discounts, and concentration risk discounts. These concepts are widely used in business valuation but are rarely discussed in accounting classes. This case can supplement numerous cases in this book, particularly *Sunbelt Beverage Corp. and Fair Value Litigation* (Case 6.4) and *Asher Associates Acquisition Targets* (Case 6.6).

KEY TOPICS: Business valuation; fair value and fair market value.

Online Cases

Case 7.4   Discounted Cash Flows and the Time Value of Money

This note explains discounted cash flow calculations using Excel™. It covers the Payment function (PMT), the Net Present Value function (NPV), and the Future Value function (FV). This case can supplement *Chang Medical Electronics* (Case 1.4).

KEY TOPICS: Discounted cash flows using Excel.

Case 7.5   Ratio Analysis

This note explains 17 different ratios classified according to five categories: profitability and cost ratios; short-term liquidity ratios; long-run solvency ratios; operating efficiency ratios; and growth measure ratios.

KEY TOPICS: Ratio analysis.

Case 7.6   Bonds

This note discusses bond mathematics. It includes a discussion of bond valuation and bond yields. It also covers conventions for bond pricing and accrued interest. This case can supplement *Chang Medical Electronics* (Case 1.4).

KEY TOPICS: Bond valuation; bond yield conventions; bond pricing conventions; accrued interest conventions.

Case 7.7   Retiree Benefits in the United States

This note explains accounting rules for pensions and other retiree benefits. It also includes a discussion of the Employee Retiree Income Security Act of 1974 (ERISA) and of the Pension Benefit Guarantee Corporation (PBGC). This case can supplement *Chrysler LLC Bankruptcy* (Case 2.5), *The Boeing Company's Retiree Benefits, 2008* (Case 3.7), *Harley-Davidson, Inc. (A)* (Case 5.1), or *General Motors Co. Bankruptcy* (Case 5.6).

KEY TOPICS: Defined benefit plans; retiree health-care plans; Employment Retirement Income Security Act of 1974 (ERISA); Pension Benefit Guarantee Corporation (PBGC).

SECTION 8   Brief Excel Cases

Online Cases

Case 8.1   Discounted Cash Flows

This problem set includes examples of NPV and PMT calculations, plus two required problems. The first problem is to determine which low-cost auto loan interest option is preferable. The second problem is to determine the cash flows associated with a potential bond issue.

KEY TOPICS: Discounted cash-flow analysis using Excel.

Case 8.2   Revenue Recognition (A)

This case requires that students record revenue and notes receivable for a land sale where the buyer pays 10% down and signs a note for the remaining 90% of the purchase price. This case can supplement *Revenue Recognition Disclosures (A)* (Case 3.3) or *Revenue Recognition Disclosures (B)* (Case 3.9).

KEY TOPICS: Revenue recognition problems using Excel.

Case 8.3   Revenue Recognition (B)

The first part of this case requires that students prepare financial statements for a direct-response marketing firm where direct-response marketing costs might be recognized immediately, or over an extended period. Students must then compare the two methods. The second part of this case requires that students prepare financial statements for a retail firm that sells extended warranties. Warranty revenues are first recorded at the time of sale; they are then recorded during the extended warranty period. Students must then compare the two methods. This case can supplement *Revenue Recognition Disclosures (A)* (Case 3.3) or *Revenue Recognition Disclosures (B)* (Case 3.9).

KEY TOPICS: Revenue recognition problems using Excel.

Case 8.4   Impairments and Restructurings

This problem set has three separate problems. The first requires that students prepare a discounted cash flow test for a potentially impaired division. The second and third problems require that students record restructuring costs for a firm that revises its restructuring cost estimates. This case can supplement *Asset Impairments in the Recession of 2008–2009* (Case 4.1).

KEY TOPICS: Accounting for asset impairments; goodwill impairments; accounting for restructurings.

Case 8.5 Fixed Income Securities (Bonds)

This problem set includes three bond problems. The first requires that students calculate the amount received for bonds issued at a premium or a discount. The second requires that students calculate the cost of acquiring those bonds at a later date, and then to show the journal entries needed to record the acquisition/retirement of those bonds. The third requires that students compute the amount received for a zero-coupon bond issue and to show the journal entries for that issue. This case can supplement *Chang Medical Electronics* (Case 1.4).

KEY TOPICS: Accounting for bond issues using Excel; valuing bonds using Excel; early retirement of bonds.

Case 8.6 Leases

This problem set requires students to prepare a table showing annual lease payments and outstanding balances for a manufacturer that leases its construction equipment with sales-type capital leases. Students must also show related journal entries and must calculate how different discount rates determine when income is reported. This case can supplement *Accounting Irregularities at Xerox* (Case 2.1).

KEY TOPICS: Valuing leases using Excel; accounting for sales-type leases; accounting for operating leases; the effect of discount rates on reported revenues.

Case 8.7 Investments in Derivative Securities

This problem requires that students compute the gain or loss from an investment in two derivative securities, one of which trades on the Chicago Mercantile Exchange (CME) and one of which trades on the Chicago Board of Trade (CBOT). The problem is simple, but students learn how fixed-income derivatives are priced and about contract specifications.

KEY TOPICS: Pricing conventions for fixed-income derivative securities.

Case 8.8 Defined Benefit Retirement Plans

This problem set requires that students compute service costs, interest costs, and the cost of changes to a discount rate. This is a relatively straightforward calculation, but it does help students understand what influences a firm's pension liability. This case can supplement *The Boeing Company's Retiree Benefits, 2008* (Case 3.7).

KEY TOPICS: Valuing pension liabilities using Excel; accounting for defined benefit retirement plans; service costs; interest costs; cost of changes in actuarial assumptions.

Case 8.9 Securitization

This case is both a note and a problem set. It explains the basics of securitization and then asks students to compute a firm's gain or loss from securitizing receivables, and calculate gains or losses when the estimated default rate and discount rate change. This case can supplement *New Century Financial Corporation* (Case 3.4) or *Harley-Davidson, Inc. (B), February 2010* (Case 5.2).

KEY TOPICS: Accounting for securitizations using Excel; retained interests; discount rates; assumed default rates.

Case 8.10 Business Valuation Methods

This case requires that students modify market multiple valuations and a discounted cash-flow valuation and then consider which calculations are the most reliable. The required calculations are quite simple, but the exercise helps students understand that most valuations are highly subjective. This case can supplement *Sunbelt Beverage Corp. and Fair Value Litigation* (Case 6.4) and *Asher Associates Acquisition Targets* (Case 6.6).

KEY TOPICS: Discounted cash flow valuation using Excel; market comparable/market multiple valuations.

SECTION 1

INTRODUCTORY CASES

Dublin Small Animal Clinic, Inc.

Rachel Saunders graduated from The Ohio State University College of Veterinary Medicine in 2001. She then worked as a staff veterinarian in a medium-size veterinary practice in Worthington, Ohio, until 2009, when she opened her own practice in nearby Dublin, Ohio.

Dr. Saunders established Dublin Small Animal Clinic (DSAC) on July 1, 2009, by purchasing all of its common stock for $125,000. That same day DSAC paid $2,500 to an attorney who prepared DSAC's legal documents and filed incorporation documents with the State of Ohio; paid $90,000 for medical instruments, furniture, and equipment; and signed a three-year lease on office space for $5,000 per month, payable the first day of each month, and paid that amount.

During July 2009, DSAC received $18,500 from clients for office visits, surgery, medical supplies, and drugs. During July, DSAC also paid $1,500 for drugs and medical supplies, $500 for office supplies, and $13,750 for wages and benefits (which included $6,500 for Dr. Saunders). At the end of July, DSAC had negligible drugs, medical supplies, or office supplies in inventory.

Required

1. Record the above activity, and then prepare an income statement for July 2009 and a balance sheet as of July 31, 2010.

2. Was DSAC successful during its first month of operation? Explain.

Accrual Accounting

In mid-August Dr. Saunders asked an accountant to evaluate her financial statements. The accountant learned that DSAC had billed clients an additional $6,500 for care delivered in July but did not receive payments until August. DSAC also purchased and used an additional $500 of drugs and medical supplies in July but did not pay for them until August. The accountant estimated the instruments, furniture, and equipment would last about five years and decided to depreciate those assets over a 60-month period using straight-line depreciation with no salvage value.

Required

1. Record the additional activity. Prepare a revised income statement for July 2009 and a revised balance sheet as of July 31, 2009.

2. Reevaluate whether DSAC was successful during its first month of operation.

Verona Springs Mineral Water

In February 2009, Mr. Alan Pickering contracted to purchase a mineral spring in the Missouri Ozarks. The property, known locally as Verona Springs, included a 6 million gallon-per-day spring that produced exceptionally pure water. Mr. Pickering planned to bottle the water and sell it in the nearby cities of Springfield, Columbia, St. Louis, and Kansas City.

On March 1, 2009, Mr. Pickering and several relatives purchased 500,000 shares in the company for $1 per share. On that same day, the corporation borrowed $300,000 from the local bank. The bank note required five annual $60,000 principal repayments beginning March 1, 2010. Interest payments of 6% of the outstanding balance on the previous March 1 were required on March 1 of each year, also beginning March 1, 2010. The firm then wrote a check for $525,000 to buy the 65 acres of land that included Verona Springs.

The water was nearly free of pollutants, but it arose into a small pond before flowing to a nearby stream. In the pond, the water was exposed to falling leaves and other contaminants. To maintain purity, Mr. Pickering hired a local firm to drill a flowing artesian well near the spring (in a flowing artesian well, pressure from an underground aquifer forces water to flow naturally to the surface). The company paid $1,000 cash for the drilling on March 10, 2009. Mr. Pickering expected the well to last at least 10 years before redrilling would be needed.

During March, Verona Springs had a building constructed above and around the well. Inside the building, the firm installed filtration, purification, and bottling equipment and a holding tank. The company paid the $240,000 cost by check on March 31, 2009, when the equipment became operational. The firm expected the building and equipment to last 10 years. On April 5, the firm purchased a truckload of 18,200 one-gallon plastic water bottles and lids for $3,200, and 3,100 shipping boxes for $3,100 ($1.00 per box). The $6,300 for those purchases was payable in 30 days. During April, the firm also purchased miscellaneous supplies for $500 and paid in cash.

The firm began bottling water by hiring three local residents to work part-time. During April, they bottled and shipped 18,000 gallons of mineral water (3,000 cases that each contained six 1-gallon bottles). Verona sold the 3,000 cases to regional supermarkets for $5.00 per case. One chain paid for 1,000 cases by check upon receipt; the others purchased on account, payable in 30 days. In late April, the firm paid the three employees a total of $1,500 in cash for their work and also paid a trucking firm $900 in cash to deliver the water. On April 30, the firm had negligible quantities of bottles, lids, boxes, and supplies in inventory.

Required

1. For the two-month period March 1, 2009, to April 30, 2009, prepare (a) journal entries, (b) an income statement, (c) a balance sheet, and (d) a statement of cash flows.

2. Evaluate the company's performance.

3. Is the large decline in cash a concern?

4. How would the three financial statements change if Verona Springs bought 5,100 boxes for $5,100 ($1.00 per box) and if 2,000 boxes remained in inventory?

5. How would the three financial statements change if, in addition to paying a total of $5,100 for boxes, Verona Springs also spent a total of $4,800 for bottles and lids (a total of $9,900 for boxes, bottles, and lids, instead of $6,300), $2,500 instead of $1,500 for labor, $1,600 instead of $900 for shipping, and then shipped a total of 5,000 cases at $5.00 per case (1,000 cases for cash; 4,000 cases on credit)? Also assume negligible quantities of boxes, bottles, lids, and supplies in inventory.

6. Identify costs that may not have been included in the case.

Holton-Central Holdings Inc.

Holton Chairs had been an innovative designer and producer of quality office chairs since Arnold Holton founded the firm in Grand Rapids, Michigan, in 1938. In 1947, Holton purchased Central Chairs and renamed itself Holton-Central Inc. When Mr. Holton died in 1994, long-time executives managed the firm for his heirs. Through a variety of circumstances, including foreign competition, outdated production equipment and processes, expensive wage contracts, and low quality, Holton-Central gradually became unprofitable. In early 2009, Holton-Central Inc., declared bankruptcy and closed its doors. Because of concerns about chemical contaminants at Holton-Central's original factory (no longer in use), no one would buy the corporation as a going concern. Instead, one bidder offered to buy Holton-Central's assets, except for the original factory, and resume operations at the current production facility under the Holton-Central name.

That bidder, Belmont Office Furniture, produced high-quality office desks. Peter Cardell purchased Belmont Office Furniture's assets out of bankruptcy in 2003; within four years he increased revenues by 65% and returned Belmont to profitability. By 2009, Mr. Cardell decided to acquire another office furniture company. On July 1, 2009, the Holton-Central bankruptcy judge accepted Belmont's $4,765,000 offer for Holton-Central's assets and accounts payable. The $4,765,000 purchase price equaled the market value of the tangible assets, minus $875,000 of accounts payable, plus $265,000, which Mr. Cardell considered goodwill:

Raw material inventory	$175,000
Work-in-process inventory	$220,000
Finished goods inventory	$115,000
Equipment (5-year life)	$450,000
Building (20-year life)	$3,600,000
Land	$815,000
Total tangible assets	$5,375,000
Less: Accounts payable	$875,000
Net tangible assets	$4,500,000
Goodwill	$265,000
Total purchase price	$4,765,000

On July 1, 2009, the acquisition was completed as follows:

1. Belmont Office Furniture formed Holton-Central Holdings and paid $3.9 million for all 3,900,000 shares of Holton-Central Holdings' $.01 par value common stock.
2. Holton-Central Holdings borrowed $6,000,000 to help Holton-Central exit from bankruptcy; the principal would be repaid in six $1 million payments each July 1,

beginning July 1, 2010. Also due each July 1, beginning July 1, 2010, was 10% interest on the unpaid balance as of the previous July 1.

3. Holton-Central Holdings paid $4,765,000 cash for the assets of Holton-Central Inc., and assumed the firm's $875,000 of accounts payable.

July 2, 2009–December 31, 2009

Mr. Cardell's first action was to close four furniture showrooms in Chicago, Los Angeles, New York, and Atlanta, because the leases had been cancelled in bankruptcy. These closures would save $950,000 annually; Mr. Cardell believed sales would decline only marginally. He also negotiated a more favorable labor contract with former employees, which would save another $750,000 annually. On July 2, 2009, the firm reopened for business. The following is a summary of Holton-Central's activity for the second half of 2009:

1. Paid the $875,000 of accounts payable.

2. Paid $154,500 for utilities, professional services, and other administrative expenses.

3. Paid $1,408,000 for office wages and related payroll taxes and benefits.

4. Paid $2,785,000 for selling and marketing expenses.

5. Paid $900,000 for production machinery. The machinery was purchased October 1, 2009. The machinery had a useful life of five years with no salvage value.

6. Paid $228,000 for various one-year insurance policies.

7. Purchased $5,345,000 of raw material; $835,000 was unpaid as of December 31, 1998.

8. Manufacturing records showed $4,935,000 of raw material transferred to work in process.

9. Paid $7,878,000 in cash for production wages and charged the costs to work-in-process inventory.

10. Charged $6,662,000 to work-in-process inventory for manufacturing overhead items, including $6,400,000 paid in cash and $262,000 for depreciation on manufacturing facilities.

11. Manufacturing records showed $19,123,000 of work-in-process inventory transferred to finished goods inventory.

12. Sold chairs for $25,563,000. Of that, $4,587,000 had not been paid as of December 31, 2008.

13. Manufacturing records showed cost of goods sold of $18,593,000.

14. Recorded depreciation expense of $86,000.

15. Recorded accrued interest expense.

16. Recorded insurance expense of $95,000.

17. In late December, Mr. Cardell received a call from Holton-Central's largest customer. To cut costs, previous management had substituted a low-grade fabric on 1,800 chairs that the customer purchased in 2008 and 2009. Repairing those chairs would cost $360,000. Mr. Cardell estimated that customers would request repairs to another several thousand chairs, which would cost another $560,000. Although that liability was discharged in bankruptcy, Mr. Cardell believed failure to repair the chairs would irreparably damage the firm's reputation. He notified customers that Holton-Central would repair the chairs at no cost.

18. Computed income tax expense of $365,000 for 2009, payable in 2010.

Required

1. Prepare and record journal entries for Holton-Central's sale of stock, incurrence of debt, and the 18 activities listed above.

2. Prepare a balance sheet as of December 31, 2009, and an income statement and statement of cash flows for the period July 1, 2009, through December 31, 2009.

3. Evaluate Holton-Central's performance during its first six months of operations.

Chang Medical Electronics

In 1972, Dr. Ahn Chang, an MIT physics professor, moved to Portland, Oregon, to provide consulting services to West Coast electronics firms. Within three years, Dr. Chang developed a proprietary health-care product, and his consulting firm evolved into Chang Medical Electronics (CME). Neither his son nor daughter was interested in working at the firm, so in mid-2008 Dr. Chang agreed to sell CME to LaSalle Capital, a private equity group.

LaSalle Capital proposed to acquire CME by paying CME $10 million for 1,000,000 newly issued common shares at $10 per share and $50 million for mandatorily redeemable preferred stock that paid a 10% cumulative annual dividend. CME would then sell about $140 million of bonds to financial institutions through Rainier International, a West Coast investment bank. The $60 million investment from LaSalle Capital, plus the $140 million from newly issued debt, would be used to buy Dr. Chang's 1,825,000 shares of common stock for $102 per share ($186,150,000). Because CME would have adequate cash after the transaction closed, LaSalle Capital was unconcerned about the exact size of the debt issue.

On May 1, 2008, five-year Treasuries yielded 3.1%, AAA-rated five-year corporate bonds yielded 5.57%, and Baa five-year corporate bonds yielded 6.93%. John Tilden, the LaSalle partner managing the CME acquisition, hoped to pay no more than 7.5%. Susan Hupp, the Rainier International banker managing the deal, believed the market yield to maturity would be between 8.15% and 8.5% for a small issue from a highly leveraged firm, depending on the terms.

"I put together three proposals (Exhibit 1)," Ms. Hupp said. "(1A) is a six-year 8.5% bond; (1B) is a six-year 8% bond; (1C) is a six-year zero-coupon bond. Your yield to maturity should be about 8.14% with the 8.5% bond, 8.23% with the 8% bond, and 8.41% with the zero-coupon bond. I rounded each issue to the nearest $5 million so the amounts you receive under each issue differ slightly."

Required

1. For each proposed issue, prepare journal entries to record the initial bond sale and the November 30, 2008, interest payment.

2. Explain why the net bond payable changes with each interest payment. For example, explain why the net bond payable for the zero-coupon bond increases from $137,252,361 to $143,023,822 between May 31, 2008, and November 30, 2008.

3. Why are there different interest rates on the different bonds, even though they mature on the same date? Explain in detail.

4. If LaSalle needed to raise about $200 million, approximately how many $1,000 zero-coupon bonds would it issue?

5. Suppose CME issued $140 million of 8% coupon bonds on May 31, 2008, for $138,499,036, as in Exhibit 1(B). Also suppose that on May 31, 2010, immediately after it paid the $5.6 million interest payment, CME reacquired the entire bond issue for $141,275,000. Show the required journal entry. Show the journal entry if CME instead re-acquired the entire bond issue for $137,250,000.

EXHIBIT 1

CHANG MEDICAL ELECTRONICS

PROPOSED BOND ISSUES, MAY 31, 2008

Quoted yield is the yield to maturity (ytm), assuming ytm equals the semi-annual discount rate x 2

1A. 10% Coupon, 6-year bonds

Principal (face value of bonds): $135,000,000
Amount received (present value): $137,271,338

Coupon rate   :   8.50%
Yield to maturity: 8.14%
Semi-annual
discount rate   :   4.07%

	Payments	Interest expense	Change in bond premium	Unamortized premium	Net bond payable
31-May-08	$ -			$ 2,271,338	$ 137,271,338
30-Nov-08	5,737,500	$ 5,586,943	$ (150,557)	$ 2,120,782	$ 137,120,782
31-May-09	5,737,500	$ 5,580,816	$ (156,684)	$ 1,964,097	$ 136,964,097
30-Nov-09	5,737,500	$ 5,574,439	$ (163,061)	$ 1,801,036	$ 136,801,036
31-May-10	5,737,500	$ 5,567,802	$ (169,698)	$ 1,631,338	$ 136,631,338
30-Nov-10	5,737,500	$ 5,560,895	$ (176,605)	$ 1,454,734	$ 136,454,734
31-May-11	5,737,500	$ 5,553,708	$ (183,792)	$ 1,270,941	$ 136,270,941
30-Nov-11	5,737,500	$ 5,546,227	$ (191,273)	$ 1,079,669	$ 136,079,669
31-May-12	5,737,500	$ 5,538,443	$ (199,057)	$ 880,611	$ 135,880,611
30-Nov-12	5,737,500	$ 5,530,341	$ (207,159)	$ 673,452	$ 135,673,452
31-May-13	5,737,500	$ 5,521,910	$ (215,590)	$ 457,862	$ 135,457,862
30-Nov-13	5,737,500	$ 5,513,135	$ (224,365)	$ 233,497	$ 135,233,497
31-May-14	$ 140,737,500	$ 5,504,003	$ (233,497)	$ 0	$ 135,000,000

1B. 9% coupon, 6-year bonds

Principal (face value of bonds): $140,000,000
Amount received (present value): $138,499,036

Coupon rate   :   8.00%
Yield to maturity: 8.23%
Semi-annual
discount rate   :   4.12%

	Payments	Interest expense	Change in bond discount	Unamortized discount	Net bond payable
31-May-08	$ -			$ (1,500,964)	$ 138,499,036
30-Nov-08	5,600,000	$ 5,699,235	$ 99,235	$ (1,401,729)	$ 138,598,271
31-May-09	5,600,000	$ 5,703,319	$ 103,319	$ (1,298,410)	$ 138,701,590
30-Nov-09	5,600,000	$ 5,707,570	$ 107,570	$ (1,190,840)	$ 138,809,160
31-May-10	5,600,000	$ 5,711,997	$ 111,997	$ (1,078,843)	$ 138,921,157
30-Nov-10	5,600,000	$ 5,716,606	$ 116,606	$ (962,237)	$ 139,037,763
31-May-11	5,600,000	$ 5,721,404	$ 121,404	$ (840,833)	$ 139,159,167
30-Nov-11	5,600,000	$ 5,726,400	$ 126,400	$ (714,434)	$ 139,285,566
31-May-12	5,600,000	$ 5,731,601	$ 131,601	$ (582,833)	$ 139,417,167
30-Nov-12	5,600,000	$ 5,737,016	$ 137,016	$ (445,816)	$ 139,554,184
31-May-13	5,600,000	$ 5,742,655	$ 142,655	$ (303,162)	$ 139,696,838
30-Nov-13	5,600,000	$ 5,748,525	$ 148,525	$ (154,637)	$ 139,845,363
31-May-14	$ 145,600,000	$ 5,754,637	$ 154,637	$ (0)	$ 140,000,000

(continued)

EXHIBIT 1—*continued*

CHANG MEDICAL ELECTRONICS

1C. Zero coupon, 6-year bonds

Principal (face value of bonds): $225,000,000   Coupon rate   :   0.00%
Amount received (present value): $137,252,361   Yield to maturity: 8.41%
                                                       Semi-annual
                                                       discount rate   :   4.21%

	Payments	Interest expense	Change in bond discount	Unamortized discount	Net bond payable
31-May-08	$ -			$ (87,747,639)	$ 137,252,361
30-Nov-08	-	$ 5,771,462	$ 5,771,462	$ (81,976,178)	$ 143,023,822
31-May-09	-	$ 6,014,152	$ 6,014,152	$ (75,962,026)	$ 149,037,974
30-Nov-09	-	$ 6,267,047	$ 6,267,047	$ (69,694,979)	$ 155,305,021
31-May-10	-	$ 6,530,576	$ 6,530,576	$ (63,164,403)	$ 161,835,597
30-Nov-10	-	$ 6,805,187	$ 6,805,187	$ (56,359,216)	$ 168,640,784
31-May-11	-	$ 7,091,345	$ 7,091,345	$ (49,267,871)	$ 175,732,129
30-Nov-11	-	$ 7,389,536	$ 7,389,536	$ (41,878,335)	$ 183,121,665
31-May-12	-	$ 7,700,266	$ 7,700,266	$ (34,178,069)	$ 190,821,931
30-Nov-12	-	$ 8,024,062	$ 8,024,062	$ (26,154,007)	$ 198,845,993
31-May-13	-	$ 8,361,474	$ 8,361,474	$ (17,792,533)	$ 207,207,467
30-Nov-13	-	$ 8,713,074	$ 8,713,074	$ (9,079,459)	$ 215,920,541
31-May-14	$ 225,000,000	$ 9,079,459	$ 9,079,459	$ (0)	$ 225,000,000

Janet O'Brien

In early 2007, Janet O'Brien, a manager with Andersen Young Consulting, was about to start resolving reimbursement disputes between her state's nursing home bureau and 525 individual nursing homes for 2005 and 2006. The state, short of funds, failed to audit the homes since 2000, so Ms. O'Brien was ignoring 2001–2004 because of the statute of limitations. She planned to begin by negotiating separately with the administrators of four 100-bed homes later that day. Because nursing homes worked closely with their industry lobbyists, Ms. O'Brien knew that the initial negotiations would set the tone for negotiations with the remaining 521 homes. If Ms. O'Brien and a home failed to reach an agreement, the state would be forced to file a lawsuit against the firm and take the matter to court. Exhibit 1 contains financial statements for those four homes for the year 2005.

Under the federal Medicaid program, U.S. and state governments each pay about 50% of nursing home costs for patients who are unable to pay. Each state administers its own plan and sets its own reimbursement rules, subject to federal regulations. This state reimbursed nursing homes for the sum of (1) reasonable and necessary patient care costs, (2) a 7% return on equity, and (3) $2.00 per patient per day. However, the total of costs plus allowable profits was limited to a maximum of $92.00 per day for each nursing home patient. Administrators were also limited to a $125,000 annual salary.

Peaceful Valley

Ms. O'Brien was concerned with three items. First, vehicle expense included all costs for a van and a pickup truck, which seemed necessary for patient care. The owner's Buick Park Avenue did not seem reasonable, and the $275,000 motor home did not seem related to patient care. Second, interest expense of $232,000 on a $1,450,000 note payable seemed high. The loan was from the owner's wife with a 16% interest rate; comparable loans seemed to be at 8%. Finally, laundry expense seemed high. Most nursing homes did their own laundry, but Peaceful Valley used an independent laundry located in the nursing home and owned by the owner's son-in-law. When Ms. O'Brien questioned the owner about those items he became quite hostile.

"Who are you to tell me what kind of car to drive? I work 90-hour weeks; I pick up food, equipment, and supplies whenever needed. If a patient needs a prescription at midnight, I drive to the pharmacy and get it! If the state wants to restrict the type of car I drive, let them write rules—don't come here three years after the fact and write your own. As for the loan, that was 20 years ago when 16% was a modest interest rate. We have a debt-to-equity ratio of 24 to 1; try getting a bank loan with that. Finally, if you would like to help with the laundry, feel free to pick it up and do it yourself!"

The Golden Years

Ms. O'Brien also questioned The Golden Years' vehicle expense. The station wagon and van seemed related to patient care; the Corvette and S500 Mercedes did not. Ms. O'Brien also enquired about the owner's $310,000 salary, his wife's $115,000 salary, and $32,000 paid to their daughter, a full-time student at a nearby college.

Finally, Ms. O'Brien asked about educational costs, including $23,500 for a trip the owner, his wife, and their daughter took to a nursing home convention in Hawaii.

The Golden Years' owner was no more pleasant than Peaceful Valley's. "There are no rules on what kind of vehicles we can buy. You don't have a leg to stand on with that issue. As for my salary, that is none of your business. I am not just an administrator; I do maintenance; I cook; I pick up groceries. If it needs to be done, I do it! My wife and I have worked in nursing homes for 30 years. If I were an Andersen Young partner, I would earn far more, work fewer hours, and have far less responsibility. Have you ever cared for a hundred sick, elderly patients? It isn't quite as pleasant as pushing a pencil in an expensive new office building. Perhaps the state can send someone to Andersen Young to tell your partners how much they can earn and what kind of car to drive.

"As for the educational trip, as I recall, consulting firms send their staff to seminars. Are they held in the local Motel 6? The state shouldn't waste taxpayers' money sending a young consultant to tell me how to run this place. The state should pay higher rates. You may have noticed my costs are $94.32 a day—the state pays me $92.00. I'm losing money. Maybe you can find a motel for the state that will feed their guests three meals a day and provide around-the-clock nursing care for $92.00 a day! Also, about every three years the state has a so-called fiscal crisis and delays payments for six or seven months. Try to run your firm by letting clients decide when to pay."

Lake Placid

Ms. O'Brien had four concerns about Lake Placid. First, the nursing home owned a $365,000 houseboat the state was being billed for. Second, the administrator rented the land and building from his mother, and the rent seemed high. Third, a consulting firm provided administrative services to Lake Placid and eight other nursing homes. Consulting costs seemed high, and the person who owned the consulting firm also owned or administered all nine nursing homes. Fourth, the home charged the state for federal income tax expense. Ms. O'Brien asked about those items and asked to see the consulting firm records to determine the owner's salary. Lake Placid's owner was quite civil.

"We're on a lake; we own a houseboat so patients can get on and off easily. There's nothing wrong with that. With regard to who owns the nursing home, it was my father's. He died, so I formed a corporation to run it; I couldn't afford to buy it. I like managing homes so I never did buy the home. As for the consulting firm, I run homes in three states, and the consulting firm is in a fourth. All three states ask to see the consulting records. I can't allow that; I can't ship records all over the country. I also have no idea why you are questioning federal income tax expense. That is an obvious cost; try not paying the internal revenue service and see what happens."

Quiet Acres

Quiet Acres was owned and operated by a religious order whose members took a vow of poverty. They refused any salary, choosing only to eat meals at the nursing home while at work. Their work in patient care, laundry, cleaning, maintenance, and the kitchen made Quiet Acres among the highest quality and lowest cost homes in the state. However, state regulations required that workers who eat meals at a nursing home pay for those meals, so the state had disallowed $225,000 of meal costs. Ms. O'Brien told Quiet Acres' administrator that the state would gladly pay the home $745,000 in 'equivalent wages,' but that regulations specifically required that Quiet Acres reimburse the state for meal costs. Unfortunately, Quiet Acres' administrator believed that equivalent wages violated their poverty vow and refused the offer. As a result, the state notified Quiet Acres that unless it reimbursed the state for the $225,000 of improper meal charges, the state would reduce future payments to Quiet Acres to offset that amount and would disallow such future meal costs.

Summary of Reimbursement Rules

The following is Ms. O'Brien's summary of the rules for the disputes, aside from the general rule that costs be reasonable and necessary for patient care:

1. **Vehicle expense.** There were no dollar limits on total vehicle expense, on what a single vehicle could cost, or on the type of vehicles a home could own.

2. **Loans between related parties.** There were no restrictions on loans from related parties.

3. **Laundry services.** If a nursing home did its own laundry, the state limited laundry cost to $1.65 per patient per day. There were no limits on outside laundry costs and no restrictions on whether an outside laundry could be owned by related parties.

4. **Salaries.** The state placed a $125,000 limit on nursing home administrator salaries for 2005 and 2006 but did not state that administrators could only be paid for one job. The owner of The Golden Years claimed he also did accounting, maintenance, cooking, and driving. There was no limit on salaries to related parties.

5. **Travel and education.** There was no limit on travel and education costs.

6. **Rent from related parties.** There were no restrictions on rent paid to related parties.

7. **Administrative services.** There were no specific limits on administrative costs, other than the $125,000 limit on nursing home administrator salaries. There were no regulations that required a home to provide salary records for a related-party consulting firm.

8. **Food costs.** The state limited food cost to $12.50 per patient per day. The state also required that workers pay for any meals eaten at a nursing home.

Required

1. How would you propose to resolve the various disputes for each home?

2. Why did the disputes arise?

3. How can these and similar disputes be prevented in the future?

EXHIBIT 1

Janet O'Brien, Certified Public Accountant

Balance Sheets

Assets	Peaceful Valley	The Golden Years	Lake Placid	Quiet Acres
Cash	$ 60,000	$ 38,000	$ 58,000	$ 135,000
Receivables	450,000	420,000	485,000	545,000
Vehicles and equipment, net	525,000	570,000	545,000	380,000
Land & buildings, net	760,000	705,000	–	985,0 00
Total Assets	$1,795,000	$1,733,000	$1,088,000	$2,045,000
Liabilities and owners' equity				
Wages payable	$ 40,000	$ 54,000	$51,000	$ 20,000
Accounts payable	245,000	260,000	322,000	255,000
Notes payable	1,450,000	1,300,000	615,000	850,000
Total Liabilities	$1,735,000	$1,614,000	$ 988,000	$1,125,000
Common stock	$ 25,000	$ 100,000	$ 45,000	$ 400,000
Retained earnings	35,000	19,000	55,000	520,000
Total Equity	$ 60,000	$ 119,000	$ 100,000	$ 920,000
Total Liabilities and Owners' Equity	$1,795,000	$1,733,000	$1,088,000	$2,045,000

Income Statements

	Peaceful Valley		The Golden Years		Lake Placid		Quiet Acres	
	Total	Per day	Total	Per day	Total	Per day	Total	Per day
Revenues	$3,450,000	$ 92.00	$3,404,000	$ 92.00	$3,312,000	$ 92.00	$2,485,400	$ 68.09
Expenses								
Nursing & rehabilitation	$1,245,000	$ 33.20	$1,215,000	$ 32.84	$1,225,000	$ 34.03	$ 735,000	$ 20.14
Dietary (food and preparation)	425,000	11.33	322,000	8.70	315,000	8.75	454,000	12.44
Administration	525,000	14.00	873,000	23.59	815,000	22.64	315,000	8.63
Maintenance, cleaning & laundry	293,000	7.81	256,000	6.92	218,000	6.06	162,000	4.44
Utilities	115,000	3.07	108,000	2.92	118,000	3.28	110,000	3.01
Real estate & miscellaneous taxes	205,000	5.47	198,000	5.35	35,000	0.97	172,000	4.71
Lease payments	115,000	3.07	123,000	3.32	325,000	9.03	83,000	2.27
Supplies & medication	107,000	2.85	117,000	3.16	122,000	3.39	132,000	3.62
Depreciation	150,000	4.00	148,000	4.00	45,000	1.25	105,000	2.88
Interest expense	218,000	5.81	130,000	3.51	-	-	80,000	2.19
Total Expenses	$3,398,000	$ 90.61	$3,490,000	$ 94.32	$3,218,000	$ 89.39	$2,348,000	$ 64.33
Net income before income tax	$ 52,000	$ 1.39	$ (86,000)	$ (2.32)	$ 94,000	$ 2.61	$ 137,400	$ 3.76
State and Federal Income Taxes					$ 19,000	$ 0.53		
Net income					$ 75,000	$ 2.08		

(continued)

EXHIBIT 1—*continued*

JANET O'BRIEN, CERTIFIED PUBLIC ACCOUNTANT

Reimbursement ($92 per day max)	Peaceful Valley		The Golden Years		Lake Placid		Quiet Acres	
	Total	Per day	Total	Per day	Total	Per day	Total	Per day
Reimbursement Calculations								
Cost per patient day	$3,398,000	$ 90.61	$3,490,000	$ 94.32	$3,237,000	$ 89.92	$2,348,000	$ 64.33
7% return on equity	$ 4,200	0.11	$ 8,330	0.23	$ 7,000	0.19	$ 64,400	$ 1.76
Profit ($2.00 per patient day)	$ 75,000	2.00	$ 74,000	2.00	$ 72,000	2.00	$ 73,000	2.00
Reported Costs		**$92.73**		**$96.55**		**$92.11**		**$68.09**
Total Patient days	37,500		37,000		36,000		36,500	
Actual Reimbursement per Day		**$ 92.00**		**$ 92.00**		**$ 92.00**		**$ 68.09**

Big Cat HPV[1] LLC

Paulo Camasmie first became interested in cycling when, as a young boy in Sao Paulo, Brazil, he received a high-quality five-speed Caloi road bike. He also loved music and asked his father for a drum set for his 10th birthday. His father agreed, but because of the cost said Paulo would need to wait a year. The following year, 1980, Paulo had lost interest in drums and instead asked for a Sinclair ZX80, one of the world's first personal computers. His model came with 2 kb of RAM, which he upgraded with a 64-kb extension. He then took courses in Basic programming, advanced Basic, and assembly language.

As he developed his math skills on his ZX80, Paulo also developed an interest in designing and building things, particularly functional products that made life simpler, easier, and better. At age 16, by then a competitive water skier, Paulo traveled to California to attend a water ski camp. He was amazed at how advanced the ski boats were compared to those in Brazil. When he returned home, he told his father and brother about the new designs and the three of them formed a boat-building company. Paulo was only a high school student, but his father and brother relied on him to manage production. When Paulo was accepted to the mechanical engineering department at one of Brazil's leading universities, Fundacao Armando Alvares Penteado (FAAP), he left the business to concentrate on his studies, and his brother ran the firm.

When he completed his mechanical engineering degree at FAAP in 1991, Paulo accepted a six-month internship at Chrysler's international operations in Detroit, Michigan. There he worked on developing low-volume production lines, including a minivan production line for China, a Plymouth Horizon line for Egypt, and a Jeep Comanche line for Argentina. He enjoyed the work and received a full-time offer from Chrysler, but Paulo returned to Brazil and his then-girlfriend and now wife, Rafaela.

Because of his international experience at Chrysler, a friend introduced Paulo to the owner of a large Brazilian cookie, candy, and biscuit producer. The owner, who planned to expand internationally, hired Paulo to sell the firm's products to grocery chains and other retailers in France, Germany, the United States, and Russia. Paulo did that for several years but then returned to Brazil to start his own candy company. With his industry contacts, Paulo located an Argentinean firm to produce the bulk candy, a Brazilian firm to package it, and a second Brazilian firm to distribute packaged candy to customers that Paulo obtained as the firm's only salesperson. Although Paulo enjoyed sales, and considered expanding his confectionary business, the cost of expansion was steep—a candy machine, alone, would cost $1 million. Paulo had also long dreamed of designing and producing his own products using his mechanical engineering training and his math skills, although he had no idea what he wanted to design or produce.

The Epiphany

Although the Camasmie family had lived in Sao Paulo for 120 years, Paulo and his wife often talked about moving to a less polluted and smaller city than Sao Paulo, a city of 17 million. One day, as he walked his infant daughter, Maria, through the

---

1. Human-powered vehicle.

streets of Sao Paulo, the noise and the crowds were particularly tiresome. When he returned to their apartment, he saw a Diamondback cruiser bicycle parked inside a garage of their apartment building. The bike had balloon tires and a large, comfortable saddle. As he looked at the bike's frame, he said to himself, "I can do this; I can make a better and more comfortable bike than this." He quickly decided he could move to the United States, build two bikes and sell two; build four, sell four, and grow a company. He rushed upstairs and asked Rafaela to come downstairs. He showed her the bike and said, "let's move to the United States and I'll make bikes." She came from a family of doctors and entrepreneurs; she believed in the value of both education and innovation, and she was supportive. She asked if he knew what he was doing. Paulo really did not have any idea, but simply said, "Sure!", so Rafaela agreed to the plan.

That night he searched the Internet for "comfort" bike and came across a word he had never heard, *recumbent*. Trek, a large U.S. bicycle manufacturer, was producing the R200 bike. Its padded seat was similar to a car's bucket seat, with the back reclined slightly. The pedals were in front of the rider, above the front wheel, and 4 inches lower than the seat. The bike had under-seat steering and looked incredibly comfortable and easy to ride. That it was produced by one of the world's largest bicycle manufacturers gave him confidence that he was not alone in wanting a more comfortable bike.

As he searched the Internet for *recumbent*, Paulo came across six or seven small firms that sold recumbent bicycles. He also came across Web sites for Greenspeed (Australia) and Inspired Cycle Engineering (UK), two firms that made tadpole recumbent tricycles (two wheels in the front and one in the rear; see Exhibit 1). A tadpole trike's front wheels had engineering dynamics similar to a car and had far more design variables than a two-wheel recumbent. Paulo could use his experience at Chrysler to innovate and improve the design. Inspired Cycle Engineering's "Trice" sold for $3,500 and the Greenspeed for $4,000 (before upgrades); WizWheelz sold recumbent trikes but at a far lower price. There seemed room in the middle for a quality product at an affordable price. He thought, "I'll build a tadpole trike. I can build one people will want to own."

Paulo considered what it would take to start a recumbent tricycle company. He was confident he could design and engineer a superior tadpole trike, but he lacked the experience to build one. He called recumbent manufacturers throughout the world to see if one would build a trike to his specifications. He also called the largest dealers and human powered vehicle (HPV) clubs in the United States to learn their views on recumbents. Based on those phone conversations, Paulo learned that California had by far the most recumbent bicycle manufacturers, dealers, and customers, so in 1998 he traveled to Los Angeles to meet with many of them.

Testing the Concept

In California, Paulo found the recumbent community extremely helpful and encouraging. Recumbent manufacturers gladly showed him their operations—many of which were in a garage in a private home. Manufacturers, dealers, and riders let him try dozens of different recumbent bikes and trikes. He was particularly fond of the $4,000 Greenspeed tadpole, which was solid and fast, with a go-cart-like feel. As he became familiar with the dozens of different recumbents, Paulo grew even more confident he could build a tadpole with a polished appearance compared to the homemade look of many recumbents.

At the time, Easy Racer, founded by Gardner Martin, was the world's largest recumbent manufacturer (with eight production and five office employees). Gardner was revered as the guru of recumbent design because his Gold Rush recumbent was the first streamlined bicycle (enclosed in a fairing) to travel faster than 65 miles per hour.[2] It was also comfortable and could hold panniers for long-distance travel. When they met, Gardner asked Paulo why he wanted to make trikes. Paulo described a large delta trike he had ridden that was comfortable but heavy and poorly engineered. He also explained how he had ridden far better designed and built tadpole trikes but was still confident he could build an improved tadpole. Gardner asked Paulo if he knew what the best-selling trike in the world. Paulo answered that it was a kid's trike, which is a delta trike, but he thought that tadpoles were more fun due to their go-cart feel.

Gardner then asked if Paulo knew about the "triangle of stability." Paulo did not and asked Gardner to explain. Gardner explained that when a rider turns the front wheel(s) on a trike, there are two forces on the rider. If the rider turns to the left, one force is downward (gravity), and the other force is to the right of the trike. The rider's forward momentum moves the rider in a straight line, as the trike itself moves left. If the sum of the two vectors on a rider falls within the triangle formed by the trike's wheels, the bike is stable and will not tip over. If the sum of the two vectors falls outside that triangle, the trike becomes unstable and will tip over. By widening the adjacent wheels, lowering the seat, or moving the center of gravity forward, the vector moves toward the center of the triangle and the trike becomes more stable. That kind advice saved Paulo weeks of research.

Paulo was interested in whether Gardner used computer-aided design (CAD) software. Gardner told Paulo that instead of software, he just grabbed tubes and put them together until they felt right and then put them on a jig to see how they fit. Intuition was the key. Gardner seemed to be able to visualize the forces on the tubes, an ability that comes with years of experience.

Paulo Designs a Prototype

When Paulo asked the recumbent manufacturers he visited if they would build a tadpole he designed, all said no except Steve Delaire of Rotator Recumbent Cycles. The other manufacturers all worried about a conflict of interest or else they lacked experience building bikes for others. Mr. Delaire had experience building titanium frames for Easy Racer. He and Paulo got along well, prompting Mr. Delaire to agree to produce tadpoles for Paulo. Paulo would fund his entry into the recumbent trike market with $40,000 of savings from his candy firm's earnings.

Paulo returned to Brazil and sketched a design for a high-quality, premium-priced tadpole recumbent. He refined the design on CAD software and sent the drawings to Mr. Delaire, together with a $10,000 check for tooling, jigs, and a prototype. He then applied for a U.S. executive visa, which would take 18 months to obtain. Six months later he returned to California to view the prototype. Paulo's design was highly refined but would have been costly to build as a prototype. Instead, Mr. Delaire built a far simpler, relatively crude trike based on his own two-wheel recumbents.

Paulo took his prototype to a recumbent rally at People Movers, the Orange County, California, recumbent dealer that had encouraged him to build a tadpole (and the country's first recumbent dealer). More than 100 riders came to the rally, and many looked at Paulo's crude prototype, partially held together by radiator hose clamps. One of them asked, "are you president of a hose clamp manufacturer?" However, based on their encouragement, Paulo asked Mr. Delaire for permission to contact

---

2. Easy Racer Web site, http://www.easyracers.com.

Rotator Recumbent Cycles dealers to see if they would sell trikes that Mr. Delaire built for Paulo; Mr. Delaire readily agreed.

Big Cat HPV LLC, Recumbent Trike Manufacturer

Paulo ordered five trikes from Rotator Recumbent Cycles and committed to a small Orlando, Florida, apartment, which he chose because it would be a nice place to raise Maria and one-year old Antonio and because it had direct flights to Brazil. The night before they left for the United States, Paulo wondered whether he should have listened to everyone who said it was crazy to move. He woke up in the middle of the night in a cold sweat and almost decided to stay. However, the following day he regained his courage and rolled the dice. He, Rafaela, Maria, and Antonio flew to Orlando.

With his marketing background, Paulo wanted a brand name people would remember and a logo they could easily associate with the name. The front wheels of his trikes resembled a cat's front paws so he called his firm Big Cat HPV LLC. He called his bikes Catrike and developed a logo with a drawing of a stylized jaguar encased within an aerodynamic teardrop above the word *Catrike*.

Paulo quickly sold those first trikes, the model C2000, at a retail price of $1,500. People liked them, and there seemed to be little competition. The leading recumbent trike producers sold trikes that were both heavier and more expensive than the C2000. Paulo's C2000 had an advanced design and lower retail price, allowing him to enter this relatively new market. Paulo ordered five more trikes from Rotator Recumbent Cycles, sold those, and then placed a third order. However, Mr. Delaire said that he was too busy with his own products to produce more trikes.

Rafaela asked Paulo what he would do, and Paulo simply said he would build them himself. He did not know how to build trikes, but knew he could figure it out. Rafaela believed in Paulo and supported his decision. Paulo could have found another production source but had always wanted his own production capability. He believed marketing was important, but had no interest in being just a distributor. To build a sustainable company, he wanted in-house research and development, product design, production, and marketing. Paulo wanted production to provide employment for people, but he also believed it made sense strategically. Without control of production, he believed that whoever produced his products would eventually become a competitor with a huge advantage—the producer could always sell for less. In addition, as he would later observe, it is critical for product designers to work with production.

In 2001, Paulo rented a 1,500 square foot factory space in the Orlando Pine Hills area and bought a drill press, a manual tube bender, an inexpensive band saw, some chrome moly steel tubing, and a $100 copy of Turbo CAD at the local Office Depot. He also purchased a tube notcher and a set of hole saws. He then flew to Colorado Springs for a two-week course in bicycle assembly, bicycle maintenance, and wheel building at the Barnett Bicycle Institute. When he returned, he needed a bicycle jig to properly align and hold the tubes together for welding, but had never seen one. He purchased a book on building jigs and fixtures and two days later made a jig out of wood.

Paulo built a prototype of his revised design but decided it was not special. He decided he needed an aluminum frame to build the trike he wanted. Paulo asked some of his contacts if there were reasons why recumbents were not made of aluminum. They told him aluminum was far too difficult to weld and that no one did it. However, because aluminum was common in high-end road bikes, Paulo contacted suppliers about what was needed to weld aluminum.

Paulo found a supplier who sold welding equipment and asked him whether it was difficult to weld aluminum. The vendor said it was easy, and he could teach Paulo to weld aluminum in an hour. He offered to sell Paulo a tungsten inert gas (TIG) welder for $1,500, with a free welding hood and a bottle of argon included. Paulo agreed, and an hour later the vendor arrived with Paulo's welder, hood, and welding supplies. He quickly and easily demonstrated how to weld aluminum tubes by holding an aluminum welding rod in the left hand, the electric arc welding torch in the right hand, and controlling the temperature with a foot pedal. The weld was nearly perfect. He told Paulo that if the aluminum was burning, he should reduce the heat. He then had Paulo try the technique.

Paulo quickly burned through the tube and produced an ugly weld. The vendor said, Good—keep trying until you stop burning through the tubes," and started to leave. Paulo said, "Herbie, come back here you . . . ." The vendor, who is now a friend, laughed and left.

After two weeks of shocking himself, burning himself, and burning through tubes, Paulo learned how to weld aluminum tubes. At that point he was confident he could weld frames for his prototype bikes—not good enough to weld frames for production bikes, but good enough that he could now design a bike, weld the frame himself, and then test ride the bike. He was determined to refine the design, build a better frame than the competition did, and include better components, such as standard disc brakes, which competitors offered as a $200 upgrade.

The First Year

With his sales background, Paulo was aware that the four Ps of marketing are product, price, place, and promotion. He decided that to initially sell his new recumbent the four Ps would be distribution, distribution, distribution, and distribution. He decided to become the first recumbent dealer to sell exclusively through dealers. Competitors seemed interested in keeping the profit margin for themselves. Those that did use dealers usually offered them only a 20–25% margin on retail price. From the start, Big Cat offered dealers much higher margins:

Bronze dealers (no Catrikes in stock)	30% margin
Silver dealers (two Catrikes in stock)	33% margin
Gold dealers (full product line in stock; 40 unit sales per year)	35% margin

Big Cat's first year as a manufacturer was 2002, when it sold 67 units of its only model, the Road, at a retail price of $2,750 and dealer cost of about $1,850, for total revenue of slightly less than $110,000 (Exhibit 2). Paulo realized that he was far from an expert aluminum welder, so he called the head of welding at Westside Tech, a division of the Orlando high school system, and requested the best aluminum welder in Orlando. The head of welding informed Paulo that the best welder was Sharon "Sherry" Little, who happened to be his sister, and who was hearing impaired. Paulo's only concern was how they would communicate, but he was assured she could read lips and that she was the best. Paulo wanted her.

When Ms. Little interviewed for the job, she commented that Paulo had an accent—his lips moved differently—but she assured him she would quickly learn to read them. A week later she and Paulo could easily communicate. Ms. Little had more than 20 years experience as a welder when she joined Big Cat as its second employee (after Paulo). She was so skilled that she welded all the available frames in two days. During the following six weeks, Paulo would assemble the welded frames into bikes and then cut tubes for the next batch of frames. Ms. Little would then return and weld for two more days.

Paulo was able to keep costs low by assembling the trikes and lacing (building) the wheels himself. The firm was marginally profitable in 2002, after a modest salary for Paulo. However, at 67 trikes, Big Cat was a marginal firm. The Road was similar to other tadpole trikes, so even though it was exceptionally well-designed, well-built, and sold for far less than other trikes, the product generated little interest.

Being the firm's only factory worker other than Ms. Little, Paulo gained the experience to become a far better designer and engineer. As he built the frames, he realized he had not designed the product for ease of production. He asked himself why the frame had so many brackets, small tubes, welded joints, nuts, bolts, and moving parts. He had read books on designing products for ease of manufacture and assembly. He knew the rule that better design can lead to better quality and lower cost. However, he now realized that if you make something with your own hands, you think about those issues all of the time: you observe every detail, and you think about the product from the point of view of your vendors and your production operators. One thing he observed was that if the frame had one more bend, it would have one less bracket with bolts and nuts or one less weld. That would make the bike lighter, stronger, more reliable, and easier to build.

He also observed that his frames, and all other tadpole frames, flexed as a rider applied force to the pedals, and the rear wheel twisted. That flexing and twisting was a waste of energy. From his mechanical engineering background, Paulo knew that torsional stiffness, as in a sports car, leads to better handling and less wasted energy. Paulo observed that his seat stays, the tubes that connect the back of the seat to the dropouts (hub) of the rear wheel, were parallelograms, a shape free to move. He redesigned the seat stays as a triangle. Paulo also realized that if he designed a part with more than one function, he could increase strength and reduce weight. Throughout a Big Cat recumbent, parts serve two, three, or even four functions. Once he had a refined design, Paulo built a model out of wood, hung weights on it to observe the deflection, and used a freeware version of a finite element analysis software program, FEA, to verify the deflections.

He built a prototype of his second model, the Catrike Speed. The bike weighed only 29 pounds and the ride felt like a low-flying, flying carpet. Paulo polished the bike by hand, added a neck rest made from a triathlon bike part, and rented a small booth at the 2003 InterBike sales convention in Las Vegas, the national convention for bicycle manufacturers and retailers (dealers). Dealers who stopped by his booth were amazed by the Speed's clean design and build quality—there was nothing else like it in the market. When they asked the price, Paulo responded $1,995. They asked for the retail price, and when he said that was the retail price, they asked if it was built in Taiwan. When he said the United States, they asked if the frame was made in Taiwan. When Paulo said that both the frame and trike were made in the United States, many of them immediately signed on as Catrike dealers and placed orders. By the end of the 2003 convention, Big Cat HPV had signed 60 new dealers.

Prior to the Catrike Speed, most recumbents had a homemade look. Even in 2010, some high-end production recumbents have components held together with hose clamps, and very few use bends. Dealers and others in the trade told Paulo his design revolutionized the recumbent world.

Both dealers and customers loved Paulo's new Catrike Speed. However, he had not yet built the jigs needed to produce the newly redesigned frames. The frame design seemed clean and simple, but the tubes had multiple three-dimensional placed notches and bends. As a result, Paulo spent four months building the jigs and fixtures needed to build the seemingly simple frames. Once those were complete, Big Cat HPV built and shipped 200 Catrike Speeds during the remainder of 2003. That was the turning point—the first time Paulo believed his firm would be a success. He knew he would need to work hard, but before the Speed, he did not know if hard work would be enough.

Production

When Big Cat HPV was large enough to hire its first assembly workers in 2003, Paulo introduced a batch and queue production system (although Paulo continued to lace many of the wheels). When the firm had nine orders for the same model trike, workers cut all the tubes needed for nine trikes. The cut tubes were sent to the welding cell, where a welder produced nine frames. Workers then sent the nine frames to a powder-coating vendor. When the vendor returned the painted frames, Big Cat workers picked the parts needed to complete the batch of nine trikes, assembled various components, such as the handlebar and seat assemblies, and then packed each partially assembled trike, together with additional components and wheels, into a box for shipping.

In July 2004, as sales rapidly increased, Big Cat moved to a 6,000-square foot rented manufacturing facility next door to its powder-coating vendor. Batch size increased from 9 to 18 trikes, and finally to 24 trikes at a time. That reduced powder-coating costs because the vendor charged a relatively high fixed baking cost per order because it used a large oven. That limited Big Cat to offering only one color for each trike and to large batch sizes.

Shortly after Big Cat moved to a larger manufacturing facility, for no particular reason, orders nearly came to a complete halt. With no cash inflow and higher overhead, Paulo was running out of cash. He borrowed heavily on his line of credit and even on his personal credit card. Shortly before he would have been forced to close, orders resumed at a higher level than ever. However, because of the slowdown, sales were only 300 units for all of 2004, compared to 200 units in 2003, when Paulo spent four months designing jigs and fixtures.

Also in 2004, Paulo purchased Solid Works, a three-dimensional computer-aided design (3D CAD) software normally used by far larger manufacturing firms. Big Cat was short of cash, so Paulo financed the purchase. In 2009, Solid Works was so impressed with the products Big Cat designed with its software that it became a Big Cat sponsor. Solid Works invited Big Cat to display its products at Solid Works' annual show, gave Big Cat a free version of its high-end product, and Big Cat includes the name Solid Works on the side of the Catrike cycling jerseys it sells.

In 2005, sales growth continued, and Big Cat sold 700 units. The redesigned trikes were highly popular, and the firm soon had a four-month backlog. To handle the rapid growth, Paulo hired accounting and sales managers and doubled the number of factory workers. However, Big Cat went from a reasonable profit in 2004, to significant operating losses in 2005 (Exhibit 2) and to more debt. With a $1,550 retail price, the new "Pocket" model was highly popular but had no profit margin. Big Cat also had twice as many production employees, but output was no higher than it was before the new hires. The 24-unit batch size also caused serious inventory, production, and delivery problems.

Big Cat sold far more trikes than in the past but had more models. If Big Cat sold only 24 units of a model in a month, it could paint frames only once a month and ship only once a month. It needed to hold considerably more inventory than with small batch sizes, and production bottlenecks became common. Shipping lead time also grew from three or four weeks in 2004 to six months in 2005 (time from when a customer placed an order at a dealer to the date Big Cat shipped the trike).

With the firm's recent success, Paulo focused on designing new products and on marketing. He grew distracted from finance and production, but with the rapid growth, production was soon out of control. Employees were disorganized and wasted time because of the disorder. The factory shipped four, five, or six trikes a day, or sometimes none. As demand grew, dealers were so desperate for products that they sent Big Cat checks with their orders, although they had not been invoiced for the products. There was no system to record those orders, no system to tell if orders had been shipped, and no system to tell if a dealer had paid for a trike: that led to chaos. At that point, Paulo returned to basics. He terminated the sales and accounting managers and laid off half the workforce. He personally called every dealer to apologize and take personal responsibility for the errors. He told them that because of the long delay, he would return any cash they sent as prepayments.

Paulo met with a friend who had a strong mergers and acquisition and valuation background and experience with many successful and failed firms. His friend pointed out that Paulo spent most of his time designing new products and tweaking old designs, was great at it, and that his products were now hot. Big Cat had won Trike of the Year awards in 2003, 2004, and 2005, and there was a large order backlog. His friend told him to stop designing products and spend time learning about production processes. His friend said it was not enough to just have good products; he needed to be able to deliver them as well. His friend's parting tip was to "keep it simple."

Paulo thought his friend was probably correct, so he began to read everything he could about manufacturing. He read *The Goal* by Goldratt and Cox about the theory of constraints, he read about six sigma quality assurance, and read all he could about Toyota's lean manufacturing, which is where he focused most of his efforts because lean manufacturing made sense to him. Paulo would read about a technique at night and then introduce it to his factory the next morning. He became a production engineer. Paulo realized that if you have excellent production systems, with rapid growth there is just more of the same; if you have weak production systems, with rapid growth you have chaos.

Several years earlier, Paulo had read *Trading Up: The New American Luxury*, by Michael Silverstein and Neil Fiske, and realized that he wanted to focus on quality. The recumbent market consisted of a very wide range of quality. As Paulo revised his production operations, he focused on building a premium quality but affordable product and avoided both the low-price and luxury segments. With his improved production processes, he would have control over quality and cost.

Paulo decided his products were suited for single piece flow production, not batch mode production. He moved powder coating in-house and purchased low-volume production equipment. Over a two- or three-year period, Paulo spent most of his time refining Big Cat's production systems. He visited Toyota's Georgetown, Kentucky, auto plant. He also attended numerous manufacturing and quality assurance seminars, but after three years of refining his firm's production processes, he believed he could develop Big Cat's production systems better than outsiders could.

Delegation

Paulo was working long hours but refused to give up the weekends he spent relaxing with his family. He believed he got his best ideas swimming or playing the piano, activities that triggered his creativity and gave him time to think through complex issues and ways to simplify Big Cat's products and operations. Delegating did not work when he initially tried it, but Paulo knew it was necessary in order to grow the firm. Paulo had read *The Fifth Discipline* by Peter M. Senge, who argued it was best to be the ship's builder, not its captain. If the ship is built wrong, there is little a captain can do to correct the problem. As a result, Paulo first made certain the work in an area was well-designed. He then hired someone he trusted to manage and improve the area.

In 2005, he hired Lynn Bradbury to do Big Cat's drafting. Lynn quickly became a Solid Works professional, which gave Paulo time for free-hand drawing, which he loves. He believed that another key to Big Cat's success was the hiring of Mark Egeland in 2007. Mark, a friend of many years, was an avid cyclist, and he raced bicycles and owned trikes. He also earned considerably more than Paulo could pay him. Paulo offered Mark a job as head of marketing for less than he was currently earning but with a minority equity interest. Mark agreed and brought his expertise in marketing and detailed knowledge of the cycling industry and cycling culture to the position. Mark quickly developed a strong rapport with Big Cat's dealers, which gave Paulo time to work on a vision for Big Cat's future. Mark also brought excitement to Big Cat and renewed Paulo's passion for the business.

To maintain a smooth operation, Paulo believed he needed to keep sales, the supply chain, production, and finances in balance. He now had the tools to monitor various indicators for those four areas, much as a driver scans a car's dashboard. He can predict and react to changes in any of those four areas and thus ensures that Big Cat is under control. By 2009, Big Cat had five people working in one large office handling key areas: sales, marketing, supply chain and production, engineering, and administration. Paulo currently handles supply chain and production but plans to hire someone for that position soon. During the firm's first several years in business, employee turnover was nonstop. Paulo's focus on both systems and people has reduced employee turnover to zero.

Production, 2008–2010

From 2008 through mid-2009, Paulo followed each trike model through the production process from beginning to end, recording each of the 750 production steps and the time (in seconds) needed for each step. He also took pictures of each part and each piece of equipment used in the process. He created a database that contains a bill of materials and a process routing sheet for each product, linked to a spreadsheet, so he can predict the time needed to produce each product as well as keep the line in balance.

The lead time in 2010 is now one to two weeks, and the firm ships an average of about 9 trikes each day (about 2,000 trikes each year), for annual revenues of between $2 million and $3 million. Although sales are higher in summer months, Paulo does not want to lay off team members during the winter, so he modified the strict demand-pull philosophy of lean manufacturing. Big Cat has facilities with peak production capacity of 12 trikes a day. Rather than produce only when it receives an order, Big Cat keeps a steady production flow, allowing small fluctuations in output. If demand is greater than the average of nine trikes a day, Big Cat produces to demand; if demand is much below nine trikes per day, it produces to inventory, which avoids peaks and valleys in output.

Total assembly time for a trike, including frame bending, notching, welding, powder coating, component assembly, and packing, is about six and a half hours. All products go through the same flexible production line, with a batch size of one (single-piece flow). Beginning at 6:30 a.m. each day, a worker begins with what Paulo coined a "shop walker" (a rack on wheels that eventually contains all tubes, parts, and components needed to produce one trike). From a rack of precut tubes, a worker pulls the tubes needed to produce a specified model. The worker then moves the shop walker through equipment arranged in an optimal sequence to make the product (a process-based layout).

Tubes are welded at three welding stations, then pass through five additional process stations: degreasing, water rinsing, etching, distilled water rinsing, and priming/sealing. These processes are designed so each operator has 45 minutes of work content so the line pace, or takt time,[3] is 45 minutes. At the end of the day, finished frames are placed in the firm's oven and are heat treated overnight for 10 hours at various temperatures. The following day, frames are powder coated one unit at a time. The bikes are then assembled and packed in about 90 minutes through a series of assembly stations, with 45 minutes of work for each of two workers. A team leader oversees the production and assembly areas and fills in for workers who are ill or on vacation.

In mid-2009, 12 Six-Sigma Black Belt engineers from Lockheed Martin visited Big Cat's production facilities. One of them stated that Big Cat's systems were some of the best they had seen. In November 2009, the Manufacturers Association of Florida named Big Cat HPV the Florida Small Manufacturer of the year and said they were particularly impressed with the firm's human resource practices.

The Environment, Late 2009

For years, Big Cat has had an enviable market position. Since 2005, it has held a popular rally at its factory each winter, started at the request of a Big Cat riders' group from Virginia. That turned into an all-day event and over the years grew to a gathering of more than 200 owners from as far away as Seattle, Washington, and Canada. Big Cat is also widely known in the industry for providing exceptional service. Although Big Cat's warranty is limited to the initial owner, Paulo and his team have honored the warranty for the second and third owners, a fact noted on Big Cat's message board, which routinely draws 5,000 visitors each day.

In early 2010, Paulo was considering what to do next. Big Cat HPV was the largest recumbent tricycle manufacturer in the world. Readers of *BentRider Online*, the leading industry Web publication, voted a Big Cat trike model "Trike of the Year" every year since 2003. His manufacturing processes were state of the art for any industry, despite operating in an industry notorious for unsophisticated manufacturing operations.

In the summer of 2009, Paulo and his family traveled throughout France, Germany, the Netherlands, Switzerland, and Spain for a month. Although the trip was primarily to visit Big Cat's European dealers, Paulo asked his dealers to arrange visits to leading European manufacturers. He also asked them to arrange visits that might help him design products, including visits to architectural sites and motorcycle, furniture, and art dealers or producers. One French dealer (Paulo speaks French) and one German dealer (Rafaela speaks German) became country distributors. Paulo expects sales to grow throughout Europe, and Big Cat is making a similar expansion in both Japan and Australia.

He did have several concerns. Three large recumbent bicycle manufacturers recently entered the trike market: Challenge (the Netherlands); HP Velotechnik (Germany); and Rans (United States). Paulo wondered if he should enter the recumbent bicycle market, which is several times larger than the trike market. There are, however, many established recumbent bicycle firms, including Rans, Easy Racers, and Bacchetta; all are reasonably large with excellent brand recognition.

---

3. Takt time is the maximum time allowed to complete an action in a production line. The term is widely used in lean manufacturing and is derived from the German word *taktzeit*, or cycle time. The word originally referred to the beat of a conductor's baton or a metronome's ticking.

Competition from Taiwan

Paulo also monitored outsourcing to Taiwan. Most of the world's medium-priced bicycles are produced in Taichung, Taiwan, as are many high-end bicycles and most high-end bicycle frames (most low-priced bicycles are built in China). Taiwan-based Giant, the world's largest bicycle manufacturer, produces some of the world's highest-quality bicycles. Giant sponsors the Rabobank Cycling Team, a leading Tour de France team; a Rabobank Team model retails for $12,999.

In the 1990s, some Taichung bicycle manufacturers entered the recumbent market, and by 2005, most U.S. and European recumbent bike or trike producers bought recumbent frames from Taiwan. Some Taichung bicycle plants also produce complete recumbent bicycles and tricycles. TW-Bents (twbents.com.tw) and Performer (performer.com.tw), two of the largest Taiwanese recumbent manufacturers, both offer a range of tadpole recumbent tricycles and short-wheel recumbent bicycles. Most fully assembled Taiwanese recumbents sold in the United States are sold by distributors. ActionBent, based in a Redmond, Washington, industrial park, is the largest distributor of complete Taiwan-built recumbents.[4] It may sell 1,000–1,500 recumbents annually through its Web site and eBay. Getitbent.com, based in a Lake Zurich, Illinois, industrial park, is the second largest distributor of complete Taiwan-built recumbents.[5] It may sell 500–700 recumbents through its Web site, eBay, and recumbent dealers.

Most WizWheelz TerraTrikes are also made in Taiwan. TerraTrikes probably has the widest range of trikes, beginning with models that sell for as little as $899 up to a carbon fiber frame trike for $4,499. WhizWheelz, which sells its TerraTrikes at a very attractive price, may sell 1,500–2,000 trikes annually.

Big Cat HPV pays its employees 20–30% above the $12.00 Central Florida average manufacturing hourly wage rate (2009).[6] All Big Cat HPV employees also have health and dental insurance, which adds another $3 to $4 per hour to wage costs. Manufacturing wage rates are approximately $3.50 per hour (USD) in Taiwan and approximately $1.25 per hour in China (USD).

Component cost may also be 15–30% lower on recumbents built in Taiwan. Most recumbent manufacturers use mountain bike components, although Big Cat now offers road bike components on some models. Shimano (Japan) and SRAM (Chicago) are currently the only firms that produce a complete group of mountain bike components (brakes, brake levers, derailleurs, crank set, chain, shifters, and rear cassette). A complete group retails for between $75 and $2,000, but most U.S. recumbent manufacturers use SRAM X.9 or X.7 or Shimano Deore LX or Deore groups:

SRAM		Shimano	
X.0	$1,000	XT 770	$1,050
X.9	$ 600	Deore LX	$ 500
X.7	$ 300	Deore	$ 300
X.5	$ 150	Alivio	$ 150

---

4. Actionbent Web site, http://www.actionbent.com.
5. Getitbent Web site, http://www.getitbent.com.
6. Bureau of Labor Statistics, May 2008. Metropolitan and nonmetropolitan area occupational employment and wage estimates, Orlando-Kissimmee, Fl: 51-0000 Production Occupations, Team Assemblers (51-2092) and Assemblers and Fabricators; all others (51-2099). http://www.bls.gov/oes/2008/may/oes_36740.htm#b51-0000.

Recumbent producers receive 50–60% component discounts from list prices; Taiwanese firms also produce diamond-frame bikes in high volume, so they may receive discounts of up to 70%. Taiwan producers sometimes buy excess components from previous years from liquidators, which they use on lower-priced bicycles and recumbents. A U.S. distributor of complete Taiwan-built recumbents can specify whether it wants low-cost or medium-cost components. However, the component may be produced by SRAM or Shimano, may be from earlier years, and may be a discontinued version. As a result, unlike most U.S. recumbent manufacturers, U.S. distributors of complete Taiwan-built recumbents do not specify which components are included on a particular model (WhizWheelz, which is not just a distributor, does specify components for all its trikes, including those made in Taiwan).

Although labor costs are lower in Taiwan, shipping costs are far higher. Ocean freight from Taichung to the U.S. West Coast is $5,000 to $6,000 for a 40-foot container, plus $1,000 to $2,000 for ocean or truck freight to a location other than the west coast. A 40-foot container holds 50–60 fully assembled recumbent trikes, 120–150 partially assembled recumbent bikes, 200 recumbent trike frames, or several hundred recumbent bike frames. U.S. distributors order both recumbent bikes and trikes, so a shipping container will include a mix of products. According to Paulo, production quality on Taiwan-built recumbents can be high but is variable: quality may be high in one shipment and low in the next. The primary disadvantages of Taiwanese built recumbents are as follows:

1. **Lead time.** Time between placing an order and receiving a shipment is 3–4 months from Taiwan and 1–2 weeks for Big Cat.

2. **Order size.** There are 50–120 complete recumbents or 200–300 frames in a shipment from Taiwan; Big Cat's production size is 1.

3. **Uniformity.** Big Cat's Web site shows exact component specifications (manufacturer and model). Taiwan recumbent manufacturers often include components from different manufacturers, and recumbents in the same shipment may have different components.

4. **Weight.** Most Taiwan-built recumbents are heavier than U.S.-built recumbents and, because of lack of component uniformity, weight varies from bike to bike of the same model.

A lesser worry is China. Chinese manufacturers now produce recumbents that are such close copies of European and U.S. recumbents that it is unlikely they could be sold anywhere but China. One, produced by Big Camel, is a near exact copy of a Big Cat model.[7] Other Chinese-built recumbents sell on eBay for 40% of the price of U.S.-built recumbents but are of questionable quality.

Supply Chain Modifications

After observing advanced supply-chain management systems at Mercedes Benz and Porsche on his European trip, Paulo decided to eliminate Big Cat's buffer inventory. Big Cat now buys weekly from U.S. suppliers, with weekly shipments on demand. Big Cat buys biweekly from overseas suppliers, even those with a three-month lead time. That allows Big Cat to turn its inventory 30 times per year, which led to a 50% reduction in inventory.

---

7. See http://www.flickr.com/photos/45824734@N03/; http://www1.biketo.com/bbs/thread-91202-1-1.html.

Pricing/Product Offerings

Near the end of 2009, Paulo developed a new pricing/product offering strategy. Prior to 2010, Big Cat offered one standard component group on each model. More expensive models included better components, but if a customer wanted more expensive components than the standard, the only option was to have a dealer buy a frame from Big Cat. The dealer then ordered components from a distributor and charged the customer a markup on parts and labor.

Paulo believed the firm's policy of offering no component choice limited Big Cat two ways. First, when a dealer added components, Big Cat's profit was lower and the customer's price was higher because Big Cat had larger component discounts and lower installation costs: bicycle dealers only occasionally built bikes up from a frame. Second, he also believed that if a customer wanted higher or lower cost components, the customer was less likely to buy a Big Cat because it was slow, expensive, and inconvenient to have a dealer order and install components.

Paulo spent two months developing Exhibit 3. He wanted a price list that offered customers excellent values and greater choice and that would improve profit margins for Big Cat and its dealers. He wanted it logical, simple, fair, and limited to one page. By offering greater value at the high end, he was confident he could sell more high-end trikes. By offering a wider component choice at an attractive price on lower-priced trikes, he was confident he could increase margins on those trikes.

The new pricing scheme offered four different component groups, although no model offered more than three groups and three models offered only two component groups. The Villager offered a 9-speed twist grip group, a 27-speed twist grip group for $150 more, and a bar-end shift component group for $200 more than the 27-speed group. The Road offered the 27-speed group and bar-end group, plus the R (Rival) component group for $300 more than the bar-end group.

Paulo spent considerable time selecting components for each group and determining the price to charge for each upgrade. He believed that attention to detail would limit the number of frames dealers ordered and would also make Big Cat models more attractive relative to competitors' bikes. Some competitors offered models with a few components that were better than those on Big Cat models. Potential customers could now see that a higher-end component group would have better components than those offered by competitors, yet cost less.

Debt

Paulo developed a strong aversion to debt during Big Cat's several phases, from start-up, to rapid growth, to substantial debt, and finally to debt reduction. As Big Cat grew rapidly, it was hurt by debt, and Paulo learned how quickly a business can turn sour. In general, especially in the current economy, banks will not lend to small firms, so Paulo assumes that banks do not exist. He believes Big Cat must develop a positive cash flow; if a business constantly loses money, it should not continuously borrow. It should instead stop, evaluate, and determine what is wrong.

Big Cat had significant debt, including credit card debt, following its rapid growth and operating losses in 2005 (Exhibit 2). It has repaid all credit card debt and expects to repay all other debt within three years. Paulo will lease production equipment that pays for itself over a few years but will no longer borrow to expand. He also changed financial relations with dealers. In the past, dealers paid with credit cards, but the merchant fees were high. When Paulo realized that his dealers are highly reliable, he began offering credit to his top dealers, although he instituted that gradually to cover the gap from instant credit card funding to the 30-day terms. Big Cat now has a healthy accounts receivable, and the reduced merchant fees have increased profits.

Although Exhibit 2 stops at 2007 for proprietary reasons, Big Cat had steady growth in 2008 and 2009. Advertising expenditures are up significantly, and Big Cat now advertises in major cycling journals, including *Bicycling Magazine, Outside Magazine, Bicycle Retailer & Industry News,* and *BentRider Online.*

The Future

Paulo considered a number of alternatives for the future.

Suspended Recumbent Trikes

Suspension systems (shock absorbers) were first added to the front fork and rear triangle of mountain bicycles. Because many roads in Europe are made of cobblestones, suspended recumbent bikes have been sold throughout Europe for at least 15 years. In the past three years, Challenge and HP Velotechnik expanded from the recumbent bike market to the recumbent trike market, and HP Velotechnik trikes are suspended. Although there is currently a strong market for Big Cat trikes in Europe, Europeans call them extreme trikes because they are so light and fast compared to European trikes. If Big Cat adds suspension to its trikes, it will access a large market segment in Europe. Suspension typically adds 2 or 3 pounds to a trike's weight and may increase cost by between $100 and $200. It might take Paulo a year to design suspension systems for his trike line.

Folding Recumbent Trikes

Recumbent trikes are difficult to transport. They will not fit in a car trunk or most hatchbacks, nor on a bike rack attached to a car's trunk. Special roof racks will hold a trike, but it is difficult to lift one onto a roof rack. It is also difficult to transport a recumbent trike on a bus or train. It is common in Europe for a rider to travel on a train with a recumbent, but there is a €10 charge for a nonfolding bike on European trains. Both HP Velotechnik and Challenge sell folding recumbent trikes. A folding trike weighs 2 or 3 pounds more than a nonfolding trike and adds about $250 to the cost. Folding trikes are also slower and more prone to failure. It would take Paulo at least a year and possibly two, to design a folding trike because a Big Cat's seat is welded to its frame.

Recumbent Bicycles

Once a rider decides to buy a diamond-frame road bicycle, the only major decision is how much to spend. A professional or enthusiast may prefer a $7,000 Trek brand bicycle to a $7,000 bike from Bianchi, Cannondale, Giant, or Specialized, but differences between leading brands are minimal. In the recumbent bike market, however, there are major differences between each model. Exhibit 1 describes four general categories, but there are hundreds of different recumbent bikes and most have at least one unusual advantage or disadvantage. If Paulo decides to enter the recumbent bike market, he would consider several factors:

1. **Market segment size.** The high racer/low racer segment, the long-wheelbase segment, and the short-wheelbase comfortable market segment are the three largest U.S. recumbent markets. Estimated annual sales for those segments are high racers/low racers, 2,500 units; long-wheelbase comfortable, 4,000–6,000 units; and short-wheelbase comfortable, 6,000–10,000 units.

2. **Big Cat's in-house production capabilities.** U.S. recumbent bicycle producers sometimes have lengthy delays from Taiwanese suppliers and must order large batches three or four months in advance. Producers have lost sales from

insufficient inventory of popular models during the summer and have excess inventory when a model fails to sell. They also usually offer only one color in each model because of the relatively large-order volumes their Taiwanese suppliers require. By producing any model in any color with a two-week lead time, Big Cat has a significant marketing advantage over competitors that use Taiwan-built frames. Taiwanese frames cost less than Big Cat's in-house frames, but that advantage may be small or nonexistent after shipping costs.

3. **Big Cat's bent-tube production capabilities.** Big Cat may be the only recumbent manufacturer outside of Taiwan with the ability to build bent-tube recumbents (aside from a few very high-end producers). A bent tube does add to a recumbent's cost, but Big Cat's production process is refined enough that it can produce bent-tube recumbent bikes for only $15–$25 more than a straight-tube recumbent bike. Bent-tube recumbent bikes have a more cushioned ride and can have lower seat heights than straight-tube bikes. Paulo may be also able to develop an innovative bike that quickly gains market share.

4. **Europe's value added tax (VAT).** Most countries other than the United States have value added taxes (VAT). The VAT throughout the European Union (EU) is currently 19% and only applies to items consumed in the European Union. When a manufacturer from another country ships to the United States, it is exempt from its own country's VAT, and the United States has no VAT. As a result, when a foreign producer exports to the United States, it is exempt from a large portion of its own country's taxes and is not assessed taxes by the United States. When a U.S. manufacturer exports to the EU, the U.S. firm pays normal taxes in the United States and pays an additional 19% for a VAT.

The Musashi Catbike

Before considering market size, competition, pricing, or strategy, Paulo returned to his first love, product design. He decided to learn how to design a recumbent bicycle. He had never bought one because they are so difficult to ride—it might take a reasonably athletic rider a month or more to learn. On his trip to Europe, Paulo rode some of the world's most sophisticated and expensive recumbents. M-5 and Challenge models from the Netherlands and Velokraft models from Poland are probably the fastest bikes in the world. Paulo thought their bikes were exceptionally well-made but difficult to ride. He returned to basics.

He reread *Bicycling Science*, by David Gordon Wilson, the MIT professor who returned recumbent bicycles to prominence by riding one he built to work each day through the streets of Cambridge, Massachusetts. He also visited Professor Wilson at his home and looked at various recumbents Wilson had built over the years. Paulo began to work through the math and product design and to conduct additional library research. At some point, after thoroughly crunching the numbers and evaluating the steering geometry and steering dynamics, he asked himself why recumbents are made the way they are. To Paulo, the designs seemed fundamentally wrong— they were inherently unstable, based on the physics as he understood it.

A child's bike is easy to ride with no hands; with a recumbent, a highly skilled rider can do that, but only under ideal circumstances. A reasonably skilled rider would not even consider riding a recumbent without using the hands. Paulo wanted a recumbent bike most people could ride with no hands and it seemed that would be possible with a different design. Paulo believed several factors determined how a recumbent bike handled: (1) the head tube angle (angle of the steering post relative to vertical); (2) the front fork rake (offset of the front axle relative to the fork); (3) the wheelbase (distance between the front and rear wheel); (4) weight distribution; (5) seat height;

(6) seat angle; and (7) handlebar tiller (the distance between the handle bars and the axis of the front fork).

Bicycle dynamics, the relationship between these variables, are complex, multidimensional, and nonlinear. All variables are interrelated, and bicycle designers do not agree on how. However, Paulo believed that existing recumbent bikes had design parameters well outside the range of stability. To test his theory, he built a recumbent that allowed him to adjust the head tube angle, the fork rake, and the wheelbase. He then rode and refined. One day, Paulo had two setups within one degree of each other that let him both ride and turn corners with no hands.

From the bike trail, Paulo called Mark Egeland, Big Cat's marketing manager, and asked him to come try the setups. Mark is a hardcore cyclist who can ride a unicycle. He rode the first setup down a hill with no hands and said it was incredible. He tried the second setup and said it was also amazing. Paulo asked Mark which bike they should build. They spent several days riding both models before Mark decided that one of them was perfect—it would be Big Cat's first Catbike.

On February 3, 2010, Big Cat announced that the Musashi was a mid-racer with a 15-inch high seat and a 29-degree seat angle from the horizontal (see Exhibit 4). It would weigh about 27 pounds and retail for $2,350, although it might be offered with component upgrades. There are a few competing mid-racers, but none have remotely the same ease of handling as the Musashi, and they are probably not as fast because of Big Cat's rear triangulation. Big Cat began selling the Musashi in March 2010. Although the first Musashis would only fit riders who were taller than about 5'10", Big Cat sold about 100 Musashis in the first month they were available.

Paulo believed that his ability to delegate and the team he hired were critical to his ability to develop new products. When Lynn Bradbury became proficient on Solid Works, Paulo was able to spend time conceptualizing, understanding the market, and sketching possible new products. As a result, Paulo has now standardized the R&D process. Once he has a free-hand drawing he likes, he crunches the numbers and then passes the project off to Lynn, who manages the prototype. She works with people in fabrication who build the prototype, and the team then refines the design. Lynn builds tooling, Paulo develops the supply chain, and Big Cat then launches the product. Although it was hard for Paulo to let go—to delegate—he believes it renewed his passion for new ideas and gives him the time to develop those ideas.

Paulo expects to introduce a more recreational recumbent bicycle soon (higher seat and less reclined seat back), but he decided to begin with the Musashi to showcase Big Cat's technology and engineering. As with recumbent tricycles, Paulo does not expect to gain market share with sophisticated marketing or low prices. He expects to gain a market share with a far superior product, excellent engineering, high quality, and in-house production, that is, provide a premium product at an affordable price.

The Musashi and Big Cat's follow-on recumbent bikes may change the recumbent bicycle market even more than Big Cat changed the recumbent trike markets. Recumbent trikes will probably always be a niche market—their low height makes them difficult to be seen in traffic. Big Cat's recumbent bikes may be so easy to ride that they become a mainstream product. They may be the first major improvement to bicycle frame design since the 1890s. The worldwide annual recumbent market is probably 50,000–60,000 units; the worldwide annual bicycle market is about 100 million units.[8] Paulo's next problem may be to grow into a far larger company.

---

8. Bicycles Produced in the World—Sources and Methods. Worldometers. http://www.worldometers.info/bicycles/.

Required

1. Evaluate Big Cat's financial performance from 2000 to 2007 (Exhibit 2). As part of your analysis, prepare balance sheets using information from the case and from the following two videos (Big Cat's most expensive piece of equipment is a $40,000–$60,000 Mandrel tube bender):

   http://bikeblips.dailyradar.com/video/it-s-a-catrike-part-1/

   http://bikeblips.dailyradar.com/video/it-s-a-catrike-part-2/

2. Evaluate Paulo's performance in: (a) product design; (b) production process design; (c) entrepreneurship; and (d) strategy.

3. How successful was Paulo at adapting to problems? At seeing and exploiting opportunities?

4. Was the revised price list in Exhibit 3 worth Paulo's effort? Explain.

5. How will the VAT tax influence Paulo's decision to expand in Europe?

6. What actions should Paulo take in the next two years? In the next five years? Explain.

This case was prepared with the cooperation of and considerable assistance from Mr. Paulo Camasmie, founder, Big Cat HPV. Reprinted by permission of Paulo Camasmie.

EXHIBIT 1

Bicycle Designs

Road Bicycles

Traditional bicycles, or diamond frames, were developed gradually during the 1800s and early 1900s. The first bicycles, developed in England, Germany, and France, had no pedals, and some had no steering. A rider propelled the bicycle by pushing his or her feet along the ground. In 1864, Pierre and Ernest Michaux, French father and son carriage makers, invented the first bicycle with pedals attached to a crank.[9]

In the last decade of the 1800s, at least one third of the patents filed at the U.S. Patent and Trademark Office were related to bicycles.[10] Inventors introduced hundreds of designs and materials to increase speed, safety, comfort, and durability. Early bikes had at least one very large wheel (a big wheel is faster than a small one). By the early 1900s, nearly all bikes used a diamond frame with equal-size wheels.[11]

By 1950, bicycle manufacturers built two basic styles of the diamond-frame bicycle. Cruisers had balloon tires, hub brakes, and usually one gear, although some had a three-speed rear hub. Road bicycles had thin tires, caliper brakes, and 10-speeds (a 5-speed derailleur in the rear and a 2-speed derailleur in the front). Both bicycles had steel frames and, until 1980, bicycle design changed only marginally.

Since 1980, frame material evolved from steel to aluminum, titanium, and finally carbon fiber. Components, such as brakes, hubs, wheels, and derailleurs, also improved dramatically. Many components are partially or completely made of titanium or carbon fiber; rear derailleurs can have 11 speeds and shift electronically. However, the frame geometry of a 2010 road bicycle is nearly identical to that of a 1901 Pierce bicycle.[12]

Recumbent Bicycles

On a diamond-frame bicycle, pedals are directly below a rider's body; on a recumbent, the pedals are in front of the seat, resembling a car seat. Recumbents were developed in the early 1900s, and by 1930 the design evolved to where an amateur on a recumbent could beat a professional cyclist on a regular bicycle in the bike races popular throughout Europe. In 1934 the Union Cycliste International (UCI) established design limitations for all UCI sanctioned bicycle races, thereby eliminating all recumbents from UCI races. Recumbents grew nearly extinct after the racing ban. However, in the 1970s and 1980s, MIT professor David Gordon Wilson reintroduced them by riding recumbents he designed and built through the streets of Cambridge, Massachusetts.[13] Over the years, two-wheel recumbents evolved into four designs: (1) long wheelbase, (2) short wheelbase, (3) high racer, and (4) low- or mid-racer.

Unlike upright bicycles, there are major differences in frame geometry between the four recumbent groups and even within each group. New designs are introduced each year offering major improvements over existing designs. Recumbent designs proliferate because pedals can range from 12 inches above or below a rider's seat, and the front wheel can be located in front of or beneath a rider's feet. This offers great flexibility in design, but each design comes with its own advantages and disadvantages.

(continued)

---

9. *Encyclopedia Britannica* Online, see "Development of bicycle."

10. The Franklin Institute Web page, http://www.fi.edu/learn/sci-tech/bicycle-tech/bicycle-tech.php?cts=instrumentation.

11. Called a diamond frame because the frame consists of a triangle in front of the rider, a triangle behind the rider, and the two triangles together form a diamond.

12. History of Buffalo, George N. Pierce, http://www.buffaloah.com/h/pierce/pierce/index.html#bicycles.

13. MIT Emeritus Faculty, David Gordon Wilson, http://meche.mit.edu/people/emeritus/index.html?id=98.

EXHIBIT 1—
continued

BICYCLE
DESIGNS

APPROXIMATE SPECIFICATIONS, BY RECUMBENT TYPE (Note: Designs vary widely)

Design	Seat height	Bottom bracket above/below seat*	Tire size		Wheelbase	Weight	Seat angle from horizontal	Price, U.S. $
			Rear	Front				
Long wheelbase	18"–25"	4"–12" below	26", 700c	20"	60"–70"	35–45 lbs	50°–75°	$1,200–$5,000
Short wheelbase								
Comfort/touring	22"–26"	4" below–6" above	26"	20", 26"	42"–47"	25–40 lbs	45°–70°	$1,000–$3,500
High racer	20"–27"	8–12" above	26", 650c, 700c	Same as rear	42"–49"	18–28 lbs	20°–35°	$1,500–$6,000
Low racer	7"–12"	8–12" above	650c, 700c	20"	44"–55"	18–30 lbs	16°–30°	$1,500–$10,000
Trikes								
Tadpole	4"–12"	1"–10" above	20", 26", 700c	16", 20"	35"–45"	28–38 lbs	20°–50°	$1,000–$5,000
Delta	18"–28"	2"–12" below	20"	20"	45"–65"	35–55 lbs	55°–80°	$1,200–$6,000

*A bottom bracket holds the crankset/pedal assembly.

(continued)

EXHIBIT 1—
continued

BICYCLE DESIGNS

Long-wheelbase recumbents

Comfortable long-wheelbase recumbents usually weigh 35–45 pounds and sell for $1,200–$2,500. Fast long-wheelbase recumbents include the Easy Racer Gold Rush and Rans Xstream. They weigh 25 pounds or less, can be nearly as fast as the fastest short-wheelbase recumbents, and range in price from $2,500 to $5,000.

Comfort/touring short-wheelbase recumbents

The rider's position is similar to that in long-wheelbase recumbents but is more reclined. The pedals are higher relative to the seat, making short-wheelbase recumbents more difficult to learn to ride than long-wheelbase recumbents. Because they have shorter wheelbases, they transmit more shock to the rider. Most U.S. recumbents are not suspended. Some European recumbents are suspended because of the rougher roads common in Europe. Unsuspended models usually weigh 30 pounds; suspended models can weigh 40 pounds. Prices range from $1,200 to more than $5,000 for suspended models.

High racers

These recumbents are difficult to ride because a rider is reclined with the rider's feet high above the seat. Examples include the Bacchetta Corsa, the Volae Team, Rans F5, and numerous models from Challenge. They weigh between 18 and 28 pounds and range in price from about $2,000 to $6,000.

Low racers

A recumbent with a low seat height is inherently less stable than one with a higher seat. Because of the low seat height, reclined seat, and high pedals relative to seat height, low racers are the most difficult recumbents to ride. They can also be unsafe in traffic and are extremely fast. Examples include the Challenge Fujin (Netherlands), M5 Low Racer (Netherlands), and VeloKraft (Poland). They are often made of titanium or carbon fiber, weigh less than 20 pounds, and range in price from $3,000 to $10,000.

Recumbent Trikes

Recumbent trikes are available in a wide range of designs, but there are two basic designs. A delta trike has two wheels in the rear and one in the front; a tadpole trike has two wheels in the front and one in the rear. The third wheel adds both weight and additional rolling resistance, so recumbent trikes are usually at least 2–3 miles per hour slower than recumbent bicycles, but they are safer because they will not tip over.

Tadpole trikes

The seat on a tadpole trike is usually 6"–12" above the ground, and as a consequence tadpoles are difficult to see in traffic, making them popular for use on bike paths. On more comfortable models, the seat may recline 40 degrees from the vertical; on faster models the seat may recline 70 degrees from the vertical. Although a rider's feet are 1"-10" above the seat, it is easy to ride a trike because they do not tip over unless a rider turns sharply. Tadpole trikes can be very fast, turn quickly, are nearly as comfortable as a delta trike, and are similar to riding a go-cart.

Big Cat produces a wide range of tadpole trikes and is the world's largest recumbent trike producer. Greenspeed (Australia) produces a wide range of heavier touring tadpole trikes. Inspired Engineering (England) produces several tadpole trikes that can be purchased with suspension and a folding feature. Tadpole trikes range in price from about $1,200 to $5,000.

Delta trikes

A delta trike's seat is usually at least 18" high, reclined 10–35 degrees from the vertical, and the front wheel is in front of the rider's feet, which are 2"–12" below the seat. The position is similar to a long wheelbase recumbent, but the seat is lower. These trikes are stable and extremely comfortable, but they are long, heavy, and slow. Hase Bikes (Germany) produces numerous long-wheelbase recumbents, including suspended models. The rider is high enough to be seen in traffic, but some riders consider delta trikes too wide to ride safely in traffic. They weigh 35–50 pounds and sell for between $2,000 and $5,000.

EXHIBIT 2

BIG CAT HPV P&L, 2000–2007

BIG CAT PROFIT AND LOSS STATEMENTS, 2000 START-UP THROUGH 2007								
	2000	**2001**	**2002**	**2003**	**2004**	**2005**	**2006**	**2007**
Revenues	$7,075	$32,486	$108,390	$409,201	$642,732	$967,793	$1,099,454	$1,508,783
Cost of goods sold	$4,360	$20,021	$46,923	$281,755	$517,100	$786,913	$659,199	$964,939
Gross margin	$2,715	$12,465	$61,467	$127,446	$125,632	$180,880	$440,255	$543,844
Rent	$4,752	$7,651	$7,860	$10,768	$41,332	$38,956	$37,062	$37,154
Advertising	$3,285	$2,588	$4,783	$6,211	$13,373	$7,794	$10,348	$9,677
Salary, wages, & other	$22,722	$15,188	$36,877	$89,859	$104,473	$225,843	$357,031	$402,923
Admin expenses	$30,759	$25,427	$49,520	$106,838	$159,178	$272,593	$404,441	$449,754
Net income before tax	($28,044)	($12,962)	$11,947	$20,608	($33,546)	($91,713)	$35,814	$94,090

EXHIBIT 3

2010 PRODUCT SPECIFICATIONS

2010 PRODUCT
BIG CAT HPV, LLC

IN LIGHT GRAY (NEW) ITEMS FOR 2010	IN DARK GRAY: STANDARD CONFIGURATIONS		
	DASH	**VILLAGER**	**TRAIL**
GROUP	**MSRP WITH FREIGHT INCLUDED**		
ROLLING CHASSIS (NO GROUP)			
KID	$1,350.00		
9 SP TWIST		$1,650.00	
27 SP TWIST (+$150)		$1,800.00	$1,850.00
BAR END (+$200)		$2,000.00	$2,050.00
"R" (+$300)			
WHEELS FRONT/REAR	349/406	406/406	406/406
SCHWALBE TIRES	KOJAK	RACER	RACER
	*R GROUP: DURANO		
	GEOMETRY		
SEAT ANGLE	43°	50°	45°
TRACK	27.5" (699mm)	31" (787mm)	29" (737mm)
WHEELBASE	33.5" (851mm)	37" (940mm)	36" (914mm)
SEAT HEIGHT	8.5" (215mm)	12.5" (318mm)	9.25" (235mm)
SEAT WIDTH	12" (305mm)	14" (355mm)	14" (355mm)
GROUND CLEARANCE	2.75" (70mm)	5.5" (140mm)	3.5" (89mm)
WEIGHT	28 lb. (12.75Kg)	31 lbs (14.1kg)	32 lbs (14.5kg)
TOTAL WIDTH	31.5" (800mm)	35" (889mm)	33" (838mm)
TOTAL HEIGHT	20.25" (515mm)	27" (686mm)	23.5" (597mm)
TOTAL LENGTH	63" (1600mm)	72" (1829mm)	71" (1803mm)
BB HEIGHT	13.5 (342mm)	14.5" (368mm)	15" (381mm)
TURNING CIRCLE	13' 8" (4.17m)	14' (4.27m)	14'4" (4.37m)
TURNING RADIUS	82" (2083mm)	84" (2134mm)	86" (2184mm)

*HEIGHT WITH NECK REST FOLDED DOWN   ** TOTAL LENGTH, BB HEIGHT, AND TURNING CIRCLE / RADIUS ARE AVERAGES AND VARY BY RIDER

	FEATURES		
BRAKE LEVER VELCRO STRAP (NEW)	☑	☑	☑
STRUCTURAL FRONT BOOM	☑	☑	☑
INDEXING CLAMP	☑	☑	☑
FLAG MOUNT	☑	☑	☑
LEFT MIRROR	☑	☑	☑
CLIPLESS PEDALS	☐	☑	☑
COMPUTER SENSOR MOUNT	☐	☑	☑
DOUBLE BEND FRAME	☐	☐	☐
ERGO SEAT	☐	☐	☐
SPACE NECK REST	☐	☐	☐
VERTEBRAE FRAME	☐	☐	☐
SEAT MESH	DASH	STANDARD	SPORT
PULLEY	STANDARD	STANDARD	SPORT
STANDARD COLORS	ORANGE	SILVER	SILVER
		WHITE	YELLOW
OPTIONAL COLORS	SINGLE COAT COLORS $100 (WHITE, YELLOW, ORANGE, RED, BLUE,		
			R GROUP STANDARD COLORS

EXHIBIT 3—continued

2010 PRODUCT SPECIFICATIONS

SPECIFICATIONS
REV:01/05/10

	POCKET	ROAD	SPEED 2010	EXPEDITION	700
MSRP WITH FREIGHT INCLUDED					
	$1,700.00	$1,750.00	$1,950.00	$2,150.00	$2,350.00
	$1,900.00	$1,950.00		$2,350.00	
	$2,100.00	$2,150.00	$2,350.00	$2,550.00	$2,750.00
		$2,450.00	$2,650.00	$2,850.00	$3,050.00
	349/406	406/406	349/451 (NEW)	406/559	349/700c
	RACER/MARATHON	RACER	KOJAK/DURANO	RACER	KOJAK/DURANO
*R GROUP: DURANO					
GEOMETRY					
	45°	37°	29° (NEW)	37°	27°
	27.5" (699mm)	29" (737mm)	27.5" (699mm)	29" (737mm)	27.5" (699mm)
	35" (889mm)	39" (991mm)	39" (991mm)	43" (1092mm)	45" (1143mm)
	8.25" (210mm)	8" (203mm)	7" (178mm)	10" (254mm)	7" (178mm)
	14" (355mm)	14" (355mm)	14" (355mm)	14" (355mm)	14" (355mm)
	2.75" (70mm)	3" (76mm)	2.25" (57mm)	4.25" (108mm)	2.25" (57mm)
	29 lbs (13.2kg)	33 lbs (15.0kg)	30 lbs (13.6kg)	35 lbs (15.9kg)	33 lbs (15.0kg)
	31.5" (800mm)	33" (838mm)	31.5" (800mm)	33" (838mm)	31.5" (800mm)
	22" (559mm)	24" (610mm)*	22" (559mm)*	26" (660mm)*	26.75" (675mm)*
	70" (1778mm)	74" (1880mm)	75" (1905mm)	79" (2007mm)	83" (2108mm)
	14.5" (368mm)	15" (381mm)	16" (406mm)	16" (406mm)	16" (406mm)
	14' (4.27m)	16' (4.88m)	16'6 (5.03m)	18' (5.49m)	18'4 (5.59m)
	84" (2134mm)	96" (2438mm)	99" (2515mm)	108" (2743mm)	110" (2794mm)
FEATURES					
	☑	☑	☑	☑	☑
	☑	☑	☑	☑	☑
	☑	☑	☑	☑	☑
	☑	☑	☑	☑	☑
	☑	☑	☑	☑	☑
	☑	☑	☑	☑	☑
	☑	☑	☑	☑	☑
	☑	☑	☐	☑	☑
	☐	☑	☑	☑	☑
	☐	☑	☑	☑	☑
	☐	☐	☐	☐	☑
	SPORT	SPORT	SPORT	SPORT	700
	SPORT	SPORT	SPORT	Z-IDLER	Z-IDLER
	SILVER	SILVER	ORANGE	SILVER	SILVER
	LIME GREEN	BLUE	GRAPHITE	RED	BLACK

BLACK, LIME GREEN, PINK) DOUBLE COAT $150: CANDY RED/BLUE/PURPLE, SPARKLE ORANGE/GREEN

GRAPHITE OR BLACK WITH CANDY RED TIE ROD & DUST CAPS

EXHIBIT 3—*continued*

2010 PRODUCT SPECIFICATIONS

GROUP COMPONENTS	KID	9SP	27SP TWIST (+$150)	BAR END (+$200)	"R" (+$300) AVAILABLE 02/01/2010
BRAKE LEVER				AVID FR5	
CHAIN			KMC		KMC 10SP DX10SC
CASSETTE			SRAM		SRAM RIVAL 10SP 11-32
FRONT DERAILLEUR		N/A	MICROSHIFT		SRAM RIVAL
FRONT DERAILLEUR POST		N/A		YES	
DISC BRAKE		AVID BB5			AVID BB7
SHIFTERS		SRAM SX5 HALF PIPE REAR ONLY	SX5 HALF PIPE PAIR	SHIMANO DURA-ACE BAR END	SRAM TT500 10SP
REAR DERAILLEUR		SRAM SX5 REAR DER		SHIMANO DEORE LX SGS	SRAM RIVAL 10 SP
BOTTOM BRACKET		TRUVATIV BB POWER SPLINE		TRUVATIV GXP	SRAM RIVAL GXP TEAM BB
CHAIN RING GUARD		ECONOMY		SUPER GUARD 130BCD	SUPER GUARD 110BCD
CRANK	KID	TRUVATIV	TRUVATIV	TRUVATIV	SRAM
CHAIN RINGS	36T	38T	30/42/52	30/39/52	34/50
ARM LENGTH	152mm	ISOFLOW 170mm	TOURO TRIP 165mm	ELITA TRIP 165mm	RIVAL 10SP 165mm

EXHIBIT 4

MUSASHI: THE FIRST
CATBIKE

SECTION 2

GOVERNANCE AND REGULATION

Accounting Irregularities at Xerox

Chester Carlson was born on February 8, 1908, the only child of an itinerant barber. As a youth, Chester was fascinated with graphics arts and chemistry. His father was crippled with arthritis, and his mother died when he was 17. By the age of 14, he was the family's main source of income, as he worked odd jobs after school and on weekends. As a teenager, Chester worked for a printer, and even printed two issues of a small magazine for amateur chemists using a discarded printing machine he received partially in exchange for his work.[1]

After graduating from high school, Mr. Carlson worked his way through a local junior college, where he received a degree in chemistry. Two years later, in 1930, he received a degree in physics from the California Institute of Technology. In the worsening depression, Mr. Carlson applied for 82 positions and received only two replies, one of which was from Bell Laboratories in New York City, which offered him a job. He was laid off from Bell Labs but then was hired by an electronics firm in New York. He studied law at night and earned a degree from New York Law School, an independent law school in lower Manhattan. While working as the manager of the electronics firm's patent department, Mr. Carlson observed that there were never enough copies of patents and no quick way of getting more.[2] At the time, corporations prepared document copies by using carbon paper in a typewriter or else typing on a mimeograph master and running low-quality copies on a mimeograph machine.

Mr. Carlson began researching copying in the New York Public Library and testing his ideas in the kitchen of his small apartment. By 1937, Mr. Carlson realized he had a very big idea. He filed a fundamental xerography patent in October 1937, opened a small laboratory in nearby Astoria, and hired Otto Kornei, an unemployed German refugee physicist, to help. In 1938, they produced their first copy, and Mr. Carlson filed a second patent for a copying machine, which was granted in 1942. Mr. Carlson worked tirelessly to sell his machine, but from 1939 through 1944 he was turned down by more than 20 companies. Finally, in 1944, the Battelle Memorial Institute, a nonprofit research institute headquartered in Columbus, Ohio, signed a royalty-sharing arrangement with Mr. Carlson. Three years later, in 1947, Battelle signed an agreement with Haloid Corporation, later renamed Xerox, to develop a copying machine. However, it was not until 1959 that Haloid introduced its first significant product, the 914. The 914 quickly gained acceptance throughout the corporate world, Mr. Carlson was soon wealthy, and Battelle became one of the world's largest independent research organizations, with facilities and offices throughout the world.[3]

For years, Xerox held a monopoly on that copying process and became one of the world's most profitable companies. Xerox only offered its machines through leases, which allowed it to capture profit on each copy. When Xerox lost its basic patent

---

1. Xerox, The Story of Xerography, Xerox Company History. www.xerox.com/downloads/usa/en/s/Storyofxerography.pdf.
2. Ibid.
3. Ibid.

protection in the 1960s, IBM and Kodak entered the market. Xerox had 10 years experience producing copiers and had developed a highly specialized manufacturing process. IBM was one of the few companies in the world that could match Xerox's highly polished business sales force, but IBM's copiers were less reliable. In contrast, manufacturing processes for Kodak's photographic printmaking machines were similar to those for Xerox's copiers. Kodak introduced a copier that matched or exceeded Xerox's in quality and reliability, but Kodak lacked a strong business sales force.

IBM and Kodak both suffered large losses in their copying divisions and eventually exited the market. In the 1980s, several Japanese electronics giants, including Canon, entered the copying market. Their machines produced copies comparable in quality to those from Xerox machines, and the Japanese machines were more reliable. The Japanese firms had the technology and financial resources to take market share from Xerox, and by the early 1990s Xerox was in financial trouble.

By the late 1990s, Xerox made a remarkable turnaround when it became one of the few U.S. companies to regain market share from the powerful Japanese electronics firms. Xerox introduced new machines that matched the reliability and quality of the Japanese copiers and included new features not found on other copiers. By 1999, when Xerox reported an after-tax profit of $1.34 billion, it was the *Forbes* magazine's seventh-most admired corporation in America.

In August 2000, Xerox assistant treasurer Mr. James Bingham met with Xerox's CFO and other financial executives to explain what he believed were serious accounting irregularities within the firm, particularly within its South American operations. After considering Mr. Bingham's allegations, Xerox's senior management found them to be without merit and fired Mr. Bingham for unrelated reasons later that week. Mr. Bingham, the son of a prominent Connecticut judge, sued Xerox for wrongful termination. Xerox denied any accounting improprieties and stated that Mr. Bingham was simply a disgruntled former employee.[4]

In a *New York Times* interview, prominent Xerox chairman, Paul A. Allaire, stated, "We are aware of Jim Bingham's allegations, we investigated them, we found there was no basis, and I see no need for an independent investigation now."[5] However, on April 3, 2001, Xerox filed Form 12B-25 with the SEC stating it would be unable to file its annual report on time because its auditor, KPMG, notified Xerox that it needed time to conduct a fuller auditing review than previously anticipated.[6] On June 7, 2001, Xerox filed its 2000 10-K with the SEC and reported a $257 million loss, compared with the $1.34 billion profit in 1999.

On October 5, 2001, Xerox filed Form 8-K notifying the SEC that Xerox Corporation would replace KPMG as its independent auditor (with PricewaterhouseCoopers). On April 11, 2002, the SEC filed a civil action complaint against Xerox Corporation alleging fraudulent accounting. That same day the SEC announced that Xerox Corporation had agreed to pay a $10 million monetary penalty.[7] Two months later, the SEC filed a civil action against Xerox CEO Paul A. Allaire and five other Xerox

4. *Russell Carlson and others v. Xerox Corporation and others*, Case No. 3:00-CV-1621AWT, United States District Court for the District of Connecticut, April 16, 2001. http://securities.stanford.edu/1017/XRX01/2001416_r01c_001621.pdf.

5. Deutsch, Claudia H., and Reed Abelson, "Xerox facing new pressures over auditing," *The New York Times,* February 9, 2001.

6. Xerox, Form 12b-35, Notification of Late Filing, April 3, 2001.

7. For the Complaint: Civil Action No. 02-272789 (DLC), *SEC, Plaintiff, v. Xerox Corporation, Defendant,* U.S. District Court for the Southern District of New York, April 11, 2002. For the settlement announcement: Securities Exchange Act of 1934, Release No. 45730, April 11, 2002.

executives, and on October 3, 2003, it filed a civil action against KPMG LLP and five of its partners.[8] The following are allegations in the SEC's Xerox complaint:

- Xerox signed long-term leases with many customers. Under ASC 840 (FAS 13), *Leases*, Xerox was required to record the transactions as sales-type leases if the lease terms were for three years or more. Bundled with the monthly lease payment was a payment to cover supply costs and the cost of equipment maintenance and repair. The portion of the monthly payments related to future maintenance, service, and supplies should have been recognized as revenue later, when those services were provided. The portion of the monthly payment related to the copier was separated into two parts, revenue that should be recognized when the copier was delivered, and interest costs, which should have been recognized over the lease period. The revenue recognized immediately should only have been the fair value of the equipment being leased.

- Xerox said it was too difficult to estimate a copier's fair value. Instead, Xerox assumed financing operations should earn a 15% return on equity, based on comparable independent finance companies. It established a method for its units to implement the method, although the method was not allowed by U.S. GAAP. The SEC complaint charged that near the end of each quarter, Xerox executives changed assumptions to meet earnings expectations. When a firm computes lease revenue to recognize at lease inception, it specifies a discount rate, as in Exhibit 1. The discount rate should be based on the lessee's incremental borrowing rate because, in effect, Xerox provides its customer with a loan. Exhibit 1 shows a lease calculation at a 6% discount rate and a 25% discount rate (to conserve space, the example is for 24 months instead of the minimum 36 months). In both examples, the monthly lease payment is $27,500 and payment is at the beginning of each month. The present value equals $27,500 plus the present value of the remaining 23 lease payments, discounted at an annualized rate of 6% (.487% monthly) and 25% (1.877% monthly). For the 6% lease, the $624,508 present value is immediately reduced by $27,500, so the lease receivable becomes $597,008 (column 3). The one-month interest at .487% is $2,906 (column 4). Of the $27,500 second monthly payment, $2,906 is interest expense; the remaining $24,594 reduces the lease receivable to $572,414.

- The present value of lease payments is recorded as lease revenue. At the bottom of Exhibit 1, with a copier cost of $500,000, Xerox would report $124,508 of gross margin at time of sale and $35,492 as interest income over the lease term. If Xerox used a 25% annualized discount rate, as in Exhibit 1, it would report only $37,358 of gross margin at lease inception, with $122,642 reported as interest income over the lease term.

- The SEC charged that Xerox consistently used unrealistically low discount rates to compute lease revenue. From 1997 to 1999, Xerox's own average local borrowing rate in Brazil was always more than 25%; most of Xerox's customers would have had much higher borrowing rates. Xerox began using an 8% discount rate in 1997, dropped it to 7% in the third quarter of 1997, and then

---

8. For Xerox: Civil Action No. 03 CV 4087, Complaint Securities Fraud, *SEC, Plaintiff, v. Paul A. Allaire, G. Richard Thoman, Barry D. Romeril, Philip D. Fishbach, Daniel S. Marchibroda and Gregory B. Tayler, Defends,* U.S. District Court of Southern District of New York, June 5, 2003. For KPMG: Civil Action No. CV 0671 (DLC), First Amended Complaint Securities Fraud, *SEC, Plaintiff, v. KPMG LLP, Joseph Boyle, Michael A. Conway, Anthony P. Dolanski, Ronald A. Safran, and Thomas J. Yoho, Defendant.* U.S. District Court for the Southern District of New York.

dropped it to no more than 6% from 1998 to 2000. The SEC complaint alleged that Xerox even dropped the rate to 0% in certain periods of 2000.

- As competition increased, the margin on leased Xerox copiers decreased outside the United States. In response, Xerox used a normalized margin so that margins outside the United States would approximate those in the United States. To accomplish that, Xerox management simply recognized some service revenue (for future repairs, maintenance, and supplies) immediately as lease revenue, without recognizing any of the future costs of those services. In some cases, management even made retroactive adjustments: for example, in 1999, it might compute how much service revenue it could have shifted to lease revenue in 1998 using the new method and then recognize that amount in 1999.

- At times, Xerox imposed price increases on leases, principally Brazil. ASC 840 (FAS 13) and FAS 27 require that price increases be recognized over the remaining lease life. The SEC complaint alleges that Xerox recognized the present value of price increases immediately.

- For simplicity, Exhibit 1 does not show residual values of the leased equipment, but Xerox properly included residual value calculations when it recorded its leases. If equipment that cost $500,000 was expected to be worth $100,000 at lease end, Xerox properly reduced initial cost of goods sold by the present value of that residual value. The SEC complaint alleged that finance executives repeatedly increased residual values without justification.

- Xerox maintained large contingency reserves, accruals, and liabilities (accruals) for lapsed contingencies. Xerox should have debited the accrual and reduced (credited) an expense account. The SEC alleged that Xerox maintained accruals until it needed earnings to meet analysts' expectations. Then, without justification, it reduced approximately 20 excess reserve accounts by $396 million to improve earnings from 1997 to 2000.

- Xerox units signed long-term leases with poor credit risks. Those leases called for low monthly payments for a year and lease payments several times higher in later years. The SEC alleged that Xerox knew customers would be unable to make higher lease payments in later years, so the leases were operating leases, not sales-type leases.

- When Xerox received defective equipment from customers, its accounting department recorded an expense and a liability to the customer. The SEC complaint alleged that a Xerox unit had defective equipment shipped to a rented warehouse, so Xerox accountants were not aware of those returns and never recorded the expense and liability.

On April 19, 2005, the SEC announced that KPMG LLP settled the SEC's charges against it for a total payment of $22.475 million, including disgorgement of $9,800,000, representing 1997–2000 audit fees, plus interest, and a $10 million civil penalty.[9] On June 5, 2003, the SEC announced that six former Xerox senior executives agreed to settle an SEC Enforcement Action by paying more than $22 million in penalties, disgorgement, and interest without admitting or denying the SEC's allegations. The penalties were for accelerating the recognition of equipment revenues by about $3 billion and increasing pre-tax earnings by about $1.4 billion from 1997 to 2000.[10]

---

9. SEC press release 2005-59, April 19, 2005.

10. SEC Litigation Release No. 18174, June 5, 2003.

Prior to the April 11, 2002 complaint and settlement, a Xerox spokesperson repeatedly defended Xerox's accounting methods. With respect to using a 6% discount rate, recording revenue for future services immediately, and reducing accruals, the spokesperson insisted there was absolutely no difference in Xerox's total revenues or total net income. It was simply a matter of timing. The spokesperson stated that the timing of revenues and net income was a minor technical accounting issue that had nothing to do with how Xerox operated its business or with how successful Xerox was at operating its business.

During 2001 and 2002, some analysts wondered whether Xerox would survive. However, Xerox had many valuable subsidiaries and divisions. It sold many of them, avoided serious liquidity or solvency problems, and is again profitable. On January 27, 2003, Xerox filed Form 10-K/A (Amendment No. 5), its fifth amended 10-K. The amendment restated Xerox financial statements for 1997–2001 and included the details on restated revenue and net income (Exhibit 2).

Required

1. Was the spokesperson correct when stating there was no difference in total revenues and total net income using Xerox's original accounting methods versus the revised methods? Do you agree that this was a timing issue that had nothing to do with how successful Xerox was at operating its business? Should revenue timing matter to an investor?

2. Evaluate the alleged accounting errors. Were they material? Were they fraudulent?

EXHIBIT 1

DISCOUNTING
A LEASE AT 6%
AND 25%

Monthly lease payment	$27,500
Cost of leased copiers	$500,000
Annual discount rate	6.00%
Monthly discount rate $\{(1 + \text{annual})^{\wedge}(1/12) - 1\}$	0.487%
Present value of lease payments	$624,508

Beginning of month	Lease payments	Lease receivable	Interest income	Reduction to receivable
		$624,508		
1	$27,500	$597,008		$27,500
2	$27,500	$572,414	$2,906	$24,594
3	$27,500	$547,700	$2,786	$24,714
4	$27,500	$522,866	$2,666	$24,834
5	$27,500	$497,911	$2,545	$24,955
6	$27,500	$472,835	$2,424	$25,076
7	$27,500	$447,636	$2,302	$25,198
8	$27,500	$422,315	$2,179	$25,321
9	$27,500	$396,871	$2,056	$25,444
10	$27,500	$371,302	$1,932	$25,568
11	$27,500	$345,610	$1,807	$25,693
12	$27,500	$319,792	$1,682	$25,818
13	$27,500	$293,849	$1,557	$25,943
14	$27,500	$267,779	$1,430	$26,070
15	$27,500	$241,582	$1,303	$26,197
16	$27,500	$215,258	$1,176	$26,324
17	$27,500	$188,806	$1,048	$26,452
18	$27,500	$162,225	$919	$26,581
19	$27,500	$135,515	$790	$26,710
20	$27,500	$108,674	$660	$26,840
21	$27,500	$81,703	$529	$26,971
22	$27,500	$54,601	$398	$27,102
23	$27,500	$27,367	$266	$27,234
24	$27,500	$0	$133	$27,367

Total interest income:			$35,492	
Reduction to lease receivable				$597,008

At lease inception

Lease receivable	$624,508	
Lease revenue		$624,508
Cash	$27,500	
Lease receivable		$27,500
Cost of goods sold	$500,000	
Inventory		$500,000

Month 1

Cash	$27,500	
Interest income		$2,906
Lease receivable		$24,594

Net income summary

Initial revenue	$624,508
Gross margin	$500,000
Initial net income	$124,508
Total interest income	$35,492
Total	$160,000

(continued)

EXHIBIT 1—
continued

DISCOUNTING
A LEASE AT 6%
AND 25%

				$27,500
Monthly lease payment				$27,500
Cost of leased copiers				$500,000
Annual discount rate				25.00%
Monthly discount rate $\{(1 + \text{annual})^{(1/12)} - 1\}$				1.877%
Present value of lease payments				$537,358

Beginning of month	Lease payments	Lease receivable	Interest income	Reduction to receivable
		$537,358		
1	$27,500	$509,858		$27,500
2	$27,500	$491,928	$9,570	$17,930
3	$27,500	$473,661	$9,233	$18,267
4	$27,500	$455,051	$8,890	$18,610
5	$27,500	$436,092	$8,541	$18,959
6	$27,500	$416,777	$8,185	$19,315
7	$27,500	$397,100	$7,823	$19,677
8	$27,500	$377,053	$7,453	$20,047
9	$27,500	$356,630	$7,077	$20,423
10	$27,500	$335,824	$6,694	$20,806
11	$27,500	$314,627	$6,303	$21,197
12	$27,500	$293,032	$5,905	$21,595
13	$27,500	$271,032	$5,500	$22,000
14	$27,500	$248,619	$5,087	$22,413
15	$27,500	$225,786	$4,666	$22,834
16	$27,500	$202,524	$4,238	$23,262
17	$27,500	$178,825	$3,801	$23,699
18	$27,500	$154,681	$3,356	$24,144
19	$27,500	$130,084	$2,903	$24,597
20	$27,500	$105,026	$2,442	$25,058
21	$27,500	$79,497	$1,971	$25,529
22	$27,500	$53,489	$1,492	$26,008
23	$27,500	$26,993	$1,004	$26,496
24	$27,500	$0	$507	$26,993
			$122,642	
				$509,858

At lease inception

Lease receivable			$537,358	
Lease revenue				$537,358
Cash			$27,500	
Lease receivable				$27,500
Cost of goods sold			$500,000	
Inventory				$500,000

Month 1

Cash			$27,500	
Interest income				$9,570
Lease receivable				$17,930

Net income summary

Initial revenue			$537,358	
Cost of goods sold			$500,000	
Gross margin			$37,358	
Total interest income			$122,642	
Total			$160,000	

EXHIBIT 2

RESTATED
REVENUES AND
NET INCOME

REVENUES	2001	2000	1999	1998	1997
Revenue, previously reported	$16,502	$18,701	$19,567	$19,593	$18,225
Application of SFAS No. 13:					
Revenue allocations in bundled arrangements	65	(78)	(257)	(284)	(87)
Latin America—operating lease accounting	187	(58)	57	(358)	(461)
Other transactions not qualifying as sales-type leases	73	57	(60)	(119)	(152)
Sales of equipment subject to operating leases	197	124	(243)	67	(44)
Subtotal	$522	$45	$(503)	$(694)	$(744)
Other revenue restatement adjustments:					
Sales of receivables transactions	42	61	(6)	—	—
South Africa deconsolidation	(66)	(72)	(71)	(60)	—
Other revenue items, net	8	16	8	(62)	(24)
Subtotal	−16	5	−69	−122	−24
Increase (decrease) in total revenue	$506	$50	$(572)	$(813)	$(786)
Revenues, restated	$17,008	$18,751	$18,995	$18,777	$17,457

PRE-TAX (LOSS) INCOME	2001	2000	1999	1998	1997
Pre-tax (loss) income, previously reported (1)	$(71)	$(384)	$1,908	$579	$2,005
Revenue restatement adjustments:					
Revenue allocations in bundled arrangements	68	(74)	(252)	(281)	(87)
Latin America—operating lease accounting	335	80	39	(238)	(354)
Other transactions not qualifying as sales-type leases	54	12	(50)	(74)	(100)
Sales of equipment subject to operating leases	91	11	(162)	19	(35)
Sales of receivables transactions	12	18	(32)	—	—
South Africa deconsolidation	(10)	(11)	(8)	(6)	—
Other revenue items, net	10	12	22	(31)	(21)
Subtotal	$560	$48	$(443)	$(611)	$(597)
Other restatement adjustments:					
Purchase accounting reserves	(2)	(7)	(20)	—	—
Restructuring reserves	(87)	65	(12)	138	—
Tax refunds	—	—	(14)	(97)	(42)
Other, net	31	(89)	(131)	(22)	(79)
Subtotal	$(58)	$(31)	$(177)	$19	$(121)
Restatement of interest expense	(37)	—	—	—	—
Increase (decrease) to pre-tax income (loss)	$465	$17	$(620)	$(592)	$(718)
Pre-tax income (loss), restated	$394	$(387)	$1,288	$(13)	$1,287

Financial Reporting Issues at Microsoft Corp

In the spring of 1995, Microsoft's chief of internal audits, Charles Pancerzewski, reported suspicious accounting entries to his two direct supervisors, CFO Mike Brown and COO Bob Herbold. Soon afterward, Mr. Pancerzewski, who had previously received stellar performance reviews, received an unsatisfactory performance review and was forced to resign from the firm.[1]

In 1996, Mr. Pancerzewski filed a wrongful termination lawsuit claiming he was terminated because he reported questionable accounting practices to his superiors. His lawsuit mentioned that Microsoft illegally set aside accounting reserves during highly profitable quarters and then reduced those reserves during less profitable quarters.[2]

The *Seattle Weekly* reported that in the fall of 1998, U.S. District Judge Carolyn Dimmick denied Microsoft's final plea for a summary judgment in Mr. Pancerzewski's lawsuit, finding credible evidence that Microsoft may have violated SEC rules as Pancerzewski alleged. Shortly thereafter, Microsoft and Pancerzewski settled out of court under terms that were sealed by court order but that may have been for $4 million.[3] The *Seattle Weekly* article included the following quote from an alleged e-mail that Mr. Brown sent to Mr. Pancerzewski:

> . . . all of the audit reports you have created so far would generally be discoverable in the U.S. . . . and could be fertile ground for an astute litigator.

Shortly after that article appeared in the *Seattle Weekly*, an expanded article appeared in *The Wall Street Journal*, which may have led to an SEC investigation.

Consent Decree

After the SEC investigated Microsoft's accounting practices for two years, Microsoft offered settlement terms to which the SEC agreed. Those terms are set forth in the June 3, 2002, consent decree (Exhibit 1). A consent decree states that the respondent (Microsoft, in this instance), neither admits nor denies guilt. That statement is set forth in Section II of the Consent Decree in Exhibit 1.

Section II states that Microsoft, "without admitting or denying the findings set forth below (section IV) . . . respondent (Microsoft) consents to the entry of this Order. . . ."

The body of the consent decree, Section IV, lists the SEC findings. They are the findings that Microsoft neither admits nor denies in Section II. They are also the findings that in Section VIII Microsoft is ordered to cease-and-desist from engaging in, and to which Microsoft agrees to cease-and-desist from engaging in.

---

1. Romano, Mike, "Microfraud?" *Seattle Weekly News*, January 6, 1999. http://www.seattleweekly.com/1999-01-06/news/microfraud/.

2. Ibid.

3. Ibid.

Section IV states ". . . Microsoft cease-and-desist from committing or causing any violations of, and committing or causing any future violations of, Sections 13(a), 13(b)(2)(A), and 13(b)(2)(B) if the Exchange Act, and Rules 12b-20, 13a-1, and 13a-13 promulgated thereunder."

Findings

Section IV of Exhibit 1 lists SEC findings with regard to the Microsoft investigation. Exhibit 1 is taken directly from the SEC Web site. Unfortunately, numbering within Section IV is highly confusing. There is no Section III, but there are three sections numbered 4. As a result, this case refers to paragraphs by SEC section heading. The following is a discussion of Section IV.

Overview

In "Summary" and "Microsoft Recorded Reserves without a Properly Documented or Substantiated Basis," the SEC provided an overview of the issues. From 1995 until 1998, Microsoft maintained undisclosed reserves, accruals, allowances, and liability accounts that the SEC collectively calls "reserves" or "reserve accounts." These accounts ranged from $200 million to $900 million at quarter end during those four years. At the operating level, divisional controllers maintained reserve accounts in accordance with generally accepted accounting principles (GAAP). The reserves were properly documented and were systematically reviewed by Microsoft's internal audit department.

At the senior corporate level, however, journal entries were made to various reserve accounts without using factually based formulas, analysis, or statistics. There was also little or no documentation to support the adjustments to these reserves. The primary justification was based upon judgment of the likelihood of future events. "As a result, these reserves did not have the documented support as required by the federal securities laws and lacked sufficient substantiation under GAAP.[4]"

Cyclical accrual for marketing expenses

Microsoft prepared a quarterly marketing budget at the beginning of each fiscal year. Microsoft also recorded marketing expenses during each quarter as they occurred. During the first three quarters of each year, Microsoft generally recorded marketing expenses that were lower than budgeted marketing expenses, which were typically a fixed percent of revenues. During a typical quarter when actual marketing expenses were lower than budgeted expenses, Microsoft would debit marketing expenses for the difference and credit an account named "accrued marketing expenses." At the end of each fiscal year, the "accrued marketing expenses" account would be debited and marketing expenses would be credited. There was insufficient support for this entry so it did not satisfy either SEC recordkeeping requirements or GAAP.

OEM sales reserve

Microsoft derives substantial revenue for licensing agreements with personal computer manufacturers such as Dell. For example, Dell includes Microsoft's Windows operating system with most computers it sells. Dell includes that in the price of its computers and must pay Microsoft a licensing fee for each such sale. Under

---

4. SEC, Administrative Proceeding File No. 3-10789, Section IV. A. 12, June 3, 2002.

the agreement, Dell must periodically report the number of copies of Microsoft's operating system it has preinstalled on computers it has sold.

Dell is not required to make daily reports to Microsoft because it must resolve various issues, such as computer returns. As a result, at the end of each quarter Dell will owe Microsoft for preinstalled software it has not yet reported. At the operating level, Microsoft accounting personnel estimate this "unbilled revenue" using formulas and documentation that meet SEC and GAAP requirements. They debit unbilled receivables and credit unbilled but earned revenue (or similar accounts) for that amount. At the corporate level, Microsoft adjusted the unbilled receivables and unbilled but earned revenue accounts without proper documentation.

Accelerated depreciation

In 1996 and 1997, for external financial reporting, Microsoft reduced the useful lives of its computers from three years to one year and reduced the lives of its buildings from 30 to 15 years. Although Microsoft could justify those changes, the changes must be made prospectively. For example, suppose Microsoft had a building that cost $30 million that it had been depreciating for five years using straight line depreciation of $1 million per year. Under GAAP, at the beginning of year six, when Microsoft reduced the life from 30 to 15 years, it would have an asset with a book value of $25 million and a remaining asset life of ten years. As a result, in year six it would record $2.5 million of depreciation expense.

Instead, Microsoft recorded the change retrospectively. That is, Microsoft treated the change as if it had occurred when it acquired the building. With that method, Microsoft would have recorded $2 million each year and at the end of year five it would have recorded $10 million total depreciation expense, not $5 million. Using this example, at the beginning of year six, when Microsoft made the change, it would have debited depreciation expense for an additional $5 million, so that total depreciation was $10 million. At the end of year six, and each year thereafter, it would debit depreciation expense for $2 million, instead of the $2.5 million required under GAAP.

Inventory obsolescence

FASB Topic 450 20 (SFAS No. 5) requires that a loss contingency be probable before it can be recorded. One long-standing accounting rule is that inventory is recorded at the lower of cost or market. The entry is a debit to "cost of sales" and a credit to "inventory reserve," "obsolete inventory reserve," or a similar account. However, firms must document that inventory value has declined before inventory cost can be reduced. At the operating level, Microsoft documented its inventory reserve, maintained proper internal controls over the calculations, and complied with SEC regulations and GAAP.

At the corporate level, Microsoft recorded undocumented inventory write-offs. On some occasions, Microsoft debited "cost of sales" and credited a miscellaneous "reserve" account. On other occasions, Microsoft debited a "reserve" account and credited "cost of sales." When the SEC combined Microsoft's inventory account with the reserve accounts from both the operating levels and the corporate level, the SEC determined that Microsoft's 1997 year-end inventory was negative.

Impaired long-term assets

Microsoft made numerous equity investments in technology companies, many of which were privately held. Microsoft routinely debited an expense account and credited its investment account to allow for a possible decline in the value of these investments. The entries were made without documentation, and there appeared to have been no basis for the entries.

Interest rate fluctuations

Microsoft invested billions of dollars in fixed-income securities (bonds and notes). When interest rates decline, those investments increase in value; when interest rates increase, those investments decline in value. Microsoft adjusted the value of its fixed income investments by debiting an expense account and crediting the investment account or by crediting a gain account and debiting the investment account. The stated reason for these entries was "interest rate fluctuations." The entries were made without documentation, and there appeared to have been no basis for the entries.

Manufacturing facilities

In 1996, Microsoft was considering outsourcing some of its manufacturing operations. Microsoft debited an impairment expense account and credited building accounts for possible impairment. The entry was made without documentation and appeared to have been made without justification.

Summary of the Above Seven Items

The SEC summarized its findings in Table 1, which is shown in Exhibit 2 of this case. The first column shows the quarter and the year end (Microsoft uses a June 30 fiscal year end). The second through eighth columns show the undocumented adjustments by quarter for each of the seven undocumented corporate adjustments, as discussed above. The next-to-last column shows the total of the seven items by quarter (and for year end), whereas the last column shows the total of the seven items as a percent of pre-tax net income. For example, during the quarter ended December 31, 1995, the adjustments reduced expenses by $169.149 million, or 19.11% of pre-tax net income.

Exhibit 3 summarizes those findings. It also shows a graph of reported net income before tax and reported net income before tax plus SEC adjustments.

Unearned Revenues

Microsoft also reported unearned income from the sale of its operating systems (Windows) and the sale of its Office products (Word, Excel, Outlook, and PowerPoint). When a firm sells a product that includes post-sale support, the firm is required to defer some revenue to cover the cost of that post-sale support. Although at the time Microsoft employed many of the world's best programmers, large programs contain a large number of errors. A 1998 *Scientific American* article estimated that operating systems contained about 1.3 million programming errors because of their size and complexity.[5] Office is about as complex as Windows and probably has a similar number of errors.

Once Microsoft sells a copy of Windows or Office, it provides the buyer with limited free support. Microsoft also provides numerous bug fixes or Service Packs that require significant after-sale expenditures. To properly match revenues and expenses, beginning in 1995 Microsoft began to record Unearned Revenues whenever it sold a copy of Windows or Office. For example, if Microsoft received $200 from the sale of Windows, it might defer 25% of the revenue by debiting Cash for $200, crediting Revenue for $150, and crediting Unearned Revenue for $50. Microsoft might then

---

5. Jones, Capers, "Sizing up software," *Scientific American,* December 1998, pp. 104–109.

realize the Unearned Revenue over five quarters by debiting Unearned Revenue and crediting Revenue for $10 each of the next five quarters.

Exhibit 4 shows Unearned Revenues by Quarter and the change in Unearned Revenues by Quarter. Although there are valid reasons for deferring revenue, if Microsoft had not recorded unearned revenues, reported revenues and net income before tax for each quarter would have been higher by the amount that Unearned Revenues increased for that quarter. Exhibits 5 and 6 show how revenues and net income before tax would have been reported had Microsoft not started recording Unearned Revenues in 1995.

Required

1. Explain the accounting issues involved in each of the seven items in the consent decree between the SEC and Microsoft. As part of your explanation, explain why it was or was not valid to record an accrual, allowance, or liability at the operating level for each of the seven items.

2. What, if anything, could have been done to prevent the alleged accounting errors at the corporate level?

3. Be prepared to record a journal entry for each of the seven items.

4. Did the adjustments at the corporate level harm investors, help investors, or have little effect on investors? Explain in detail.

5. Explain unearned revenues. Why did the SEC not include them in its consent decree?

EXHIBIT 1

UNITED STATES OF
AMERICA BEFORE
THE SECURITIES
AND EXCHANGE
COMMISSION

SECURITIES EXCHANGE ACT OF 1934
Release No. 46017 / June 3, 2002

ACCOUNTING AND AUDITING ENFORCEMENT
Release No. 1563 / June 3, 2002

ADMINISTRATIVE PROCEEDING
File No. 3-10789

In the Matter of	:	ORDER INSTITUTING PUBLIC ADMINISTRATIVE
	:	PROCEEDINGS PURSUANT TO SECTION 21C
	:	OF THE SECURITIES EXCHANGE ACT OF 1934,
MICROSOFT CORPORATION,	:	MAKING FINDINGS AND IMPOSING
Respondent.	:	CEASE-AND-DESIST ORDER

I.

The Securities and Exchange Commission ("Commission") deems it appropriate that public administrative proceedings be, and hereby are, instituted pursuant to Section 21C of the Securities Exchange Act of 1934 (the "Exchange Act") to determine whether Microsoft Corporation ("Respondent") violated Sections 13(a), 13(b)(2)(A), and 13(b)(2)(B) of the Exchange Act and Rules 12b-20, 13a-1 and 13a-13 thereunder.

II.

In anticipation of the institution of these administrative proceedings, Microsoft has submitted an Offer of Settlement ("Offer") that the Commission has determined to accept. Solely for the purposes of these proceedings, and for any other proceeding brought by or on behalf of the Commission, or to which the Commission is a party, and without admitting or denying the findings set forth below, except as to jurisdiction of the Commission over it and over the subject matter of these proceedings, which Respondent admits, Respondent consents to the entry of this Order Instituting Public Administrative Proceedings Pursuant to Section 21C of the Securities Exchange Act of 1934, Making Findings and Imposing Cease-and-Desist Order (the "Order"). The Commission has determined that it is appropriate to accept the Offer and accordingly is issuing this Order.

III.

Accordingly, IT IS HEREBY ORDERED, that administrative proceedings pursuant to Section 21C of the Exchange Act be, and they hereby are, instituted.

IV.

FINDINGS

On the basis of this Order and the Offer of Settlement submitted by Respondent, the Commission finds that:

A. Respondent

Microsoft Corporation is a Washington corporation with its principal place of business in Redmond, Washington. Since its initial public offering in 1986, Microsoft's common stock has been registered with the Commission pursuant to Section 12(g) of the Exchange Act [15 U.S.C. § 78l(g)] and is listed on the NASDAQ Stock Market, Inc. At all times relevant herein, Microsoft was required to make and file certain periodic reports with the Commission. Microsoft's principal lines of business consist of providing software for personal computers, office systems and the Internet.

(continued)

EXHIBIT 1—
continued

UNITED STATES OF
AMERICA BEFORE
THE SECURITIES
AND EXCHANGE
COMMISSION

1 Facts

1. Summary

During Microsoft's fiscal years[1] ended June 30, 1995, June 30, 1996, June 30, 1997 and June 30, 1998 (the "relevant period"), Microsoft maintained undisclosed reserves, accruals, allowances and liability accounts (collectively "reserves" or "reserve accounts") that (a) were not in conformity with generally accepted accounting principles ("GAAP") to a material extent, and/or (b) lacked properly documented support and substantiation, as required by the federal securities laws. Moreover, Microsoft failed to maintain internal controls that were adequate under the federal securities laws. Specifically, during the relevant period, Microsoft maintained between approximately $200 million and $900 million in unsupported and undisclosed reserves, a significant portion of which did not comply with GAAP, which resulted in material inaccuracies in filings made by Microsoft with the Commission.

2. Microsoft Recorded Reserves Without a Properly Documented or Substantiated Basis

At the end of each fiscal quarter, certain of Microsoft's senior financial personnel reviewed its reserves. The controllers of the operating units of Microsoft would provide these senior financial personnel with estimates for reserves for their units. These operational reserves represented contingencies faced by each individual operating unit and were described in Microsoft's internal documents as "hard contingencies supported by analysis," "transaction-based," and "systematic." Microsoft's internal accounting policies dictated that operating-level controllers use formulas and documented analyses to estimate and calculate operating reserves each quarter. Additionally, Microsoft's stated policy was to periodically reconcile the operational reserves to the general ledger to ensure that a documented basis existed for the journal entries underlying the operational reserve balances.

By contrast, Microsoft created and maintained certain other reserves that existed only at the corporate level. These corporate reserves were not determined from factually based formulas, analysis or statistics. They were described in Microsoft's records as "based, in part, on judgment regarding the likelihood of future business events." They were also exempted from Microsoft's account reconciliation process for operational reserves described above, which was part of Microsoft's ordinary accounting procedures and was designed to ensure that there was a substantiated basis for the company's financial statements.

In addition, senior Microsoft financial personnel who reviewed reserve estimates from operating units frequently added additional amounts to the reserve estimates of the operating units, without the analysis or support that Microsoft required of its operating units. These corporate level additions were not determined from factually based formulas, analysis or statistics. Microsoft's records also described them as "based, in part, on judgment regarding the likelihood of future business events." These corporate level additions were also exempted from the company's account reconciliation process.

These senior Microsoft financial personnel did not obtain sufficient information concerning Microsoft's historical or actual experience with respect to the reserves being accrued for at the corporate level, nor did they rely on the documentation that was prepared by Microsoft's operating subsidiaries or units. Instead, they relied on their subjective judgments in making adjustments to those reserves that existed at the corporate level, without any significant factual support or analysis, and similarly made additions to the operating level reserves, without any significant factual support or analysis, such that these reserves significantly exceeded the amounts that would have been supported by the information from the

(continued)

---

1. Microsoft's fiscal year begins on July 1 and ends on June 30.

EXHIBIT 1—
continued

UNITED STATES OF
AMERICA BEFORE
THE SECURITIES
AND EXCHANGE
COMMISSION

operational level. As a result, these reserves did not have the documented support as required by the federal securities laws and lacked sufficient substantiation under GAAP. Senior financial personnel used the results of the review to prepare Microsoft's publicly filed financial statements and to cause journal entries to be made to Microsoft's general ledger reflecting the corporate level adjustments to the above-described reserves.

4. Reserves Maintained or Used Without Proper Support or Basis

a. Cyclical Accrual For Marketing Expenses

Marketing expenses represented the largest expense item on Microsoft's statement of operations. For management purposes, Microsoft established budgets for marketing expenses for each fiscal quarter and fiscal year. Management generally determined these budgets as a percentage of forecasted revenue.

Microsoft typically recorded budgeted marketing expenses as its reported marketing expenses when preparing its quarterly reports filed with the Commission, even though it did not have a documented factual basis for believing that its marketing budget was a reasonable estimation of its marketing expenses. In order to account for the difference between the marketing expenses recorded in its books and records, and its budgeted marketing expenses, Microsoft maintained a "marketing accrual," to which these differences were recorded. Microsoft generally budgeted quarterly marketing expenses as a substantially constant percentage of revenue and the effect of this practice was to depict marketing expense as a substantially constant percentage of revenue on a quarterly basis throughout the year. During the first three quarters of a fiscal year, recorded expenses typically were less than budgeted expenses. Microsoft treated the difference between recorded expenses and budgeted expense as incurred but unbilled expenses. At the end of each of the first three fiscal quarters, Microsoft adjusted recorded marketing expense by increasing recorded expenses to the budgeted amount. The difference between recorded expenses and budget were credited to the marketing accrual. Because Microsoft had insufficient support for recording its marketing expenses as the budgeted amount, this practice did not satisfy the requirement of GAAP that marketing expenses be recorded as and when they are actually incurred.

Microsoft's marketing accrual (*i.e.,* the account containing the difference between recorded expenses and its budgeted marketing expenses) tended to increase during the first three fiscal quarters because, during each of these quarters, the difference between recorded and budgeted marketing expenses would be added into reported expenses. At the end of each fiscal year, Microsoft reversed the marketing accrual and released it into income.[2] The following chart shows the quarterly balances of the marketing accrual.

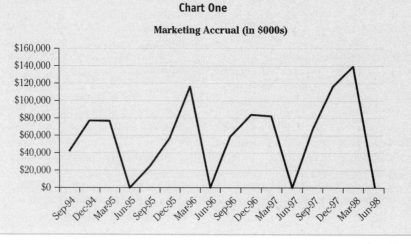

Chart One

Marketing Accrual (in $000s)

(continued)

---

2. As a consequence of this reversal, the marketing accrual did not affect fiscal year-end results.

EXHIBIT 1—
continued

UNITED STATES OF
AMERICA BEFORE
THE SECURITIES
AND EXCHANGE
COMMISSION

The marketing accrual was not documented as required by the federal securities laws and, to a significant extent, was not in conformity with GAAP. Because Microsoft did not analyze and document the use of budgeted amounts as a proxy for actual marketing expenditures, its quarterly financial statements filed with the Commission during the first three quarters of its fiscal years 1995, 1996, 1997 and 1998 did not comply with the requirements of the federal securities laws.

b. Non-Cyclical Reserves

In addition to the annual cyclical accrual for marketing expenses, Microsoft maintained six other reserve accounts that failed to comply with the federal securities laws. These reserve accounts, along with the marketing accrual discussed above, were not in conformity with GAAP to a material extent and/or lacked properly documented support and substantiation as required by the federal securities laws.

i. OEM Sales Reserve

Microsoft derives a significant amount of revenues from licensing agreements with manufacturers of personal computers. These manufacturers were referred to as original equipment manufacturers ("OEMs"). The OEMs installed Microsoft software on new computers that they sold. Under the licensing agreements, the OEMs were required to report in arrears on a periodic basis the number of computers shipped with pre-installed software and the amount of net royalties due to Microsoft from the sales. In accounting for OEM revenue, Microsoft maintained certain accounts, including a so-called OEM GAAP accrual, which was accrued for earned but unbilled revenue, and a so-called OEM sales reserve.

The OEM GAAP accrual was estimated by OEM accounting specialists at the staff-level of Microsoft and was based upon forecasts having a substantial factual and analytical basis. By contrast, however, the OEM sales reserve was determined by the senior Microsoft financial personnel responsible for the corporate level reserve accounts. However, Microsoft had no substantiated basis for the corporate level OEM sales reserve or any methodology by which the balance in the OEM sales reserve was calculated. Accordingly, the OEM sales reserve was not documented as required by the federal securities laws and, to a significant extent, was not in conformity with GAAP. From time to time, as shown in Table 1, Microsoft released portions of the OEM sales reserve into income.

ii. Accelerated Depreciation

Microsoft maintained a corporate reserve for accelerated depreciation. In fiscal years 1996 and 1997, Microsoft, for external reporting purposes, reduced the useful lives of its personal computers from three years to one year and the useful lives of its buildings from thirty years to fifteen years. These changes in depreciable lives were made because: (a) in the day-to-day management of the company, Microsoft treated personal computers as consumable supplies, and (b) buildings and related improvements were routinely gutted and refitted as groups moved freely about the Microsoft campus.

Without regard to the GAAP requirement that changes in depreciable lives of assets be accounted for *prospectively* rather than retrospectively,[3] Microsoft accounted for the impact of the new asset lives cumulatively. In other words, Microsoft accounted for its personal computers and buildings in fiscal years 1996 and 1997 as if they had always had useful lives of one and fifteen years, respectively. This resulted in these assets having net book values that were less than they would have been in the absence of the changes in useful lives.

(continued)

---

3. *See,* APB Opinion No. 20; Accounting Changes, which requires changes in estimates (such as depreciable lives of fixed assets) to be accounted for prospectively.

EXHIBIT 1—
continued

UNITED STATES OF
AMERICA BEFORE
THE SECURITIES
AND EXCHANGE
COMMISSION

The difference in value generated by the old and new useful lives was charged to depreciation expense and credited to an account that Microsoft called "accelerated depreciation."

Microsoft failed to disclose (a) the changes in asset lives and their effect, and (b) the use of the improper method of accounting for the accelerated depreciation reserve. The accelerated depreciation account was not in compliance with GAAP.

iii. Inventory Obsolescence

Statement of Financial Accounting Standards No. 5 ("SFAS 5") requires that certain conditions exist before loss contingencies representing liabilities or asset impairments may be determined and the amount of a reserve accrued. The loss must be probable as of the balance sheet date and reasonably estimable; significantly, the loss must have occurred prior to the creation of the loss contingency and must not be in the future.[4] Furthermore, SFAS 5 prohibits the accrual of reserves for general or unspecified risks.[5] As discussed below, Microsoft did not comply with SFAS 5 because the company's senior financial personnel did not properly assess whether inventory losses had occurred, and made no effort to reasonably estimate the losses.

Microsoft maintained a corporate level reserve account for inventory obsolescence that supplemented the inventory obsolescence reserve accounts determined at the operating level. Microsoft maintained factually supported inventory reserve accounts at the operating level, where operations personnel evaluated and documented the need for such accounts. The corporate level inventory obsolescence reserve had no substantiated basis, as required by SFAS 5. This corporate reserve was not associated with any specific inventory nor was it supported by any statistical or documented analysis during the fiscal years ended June 30, 1995 through June 30, 1998. The corporate reserves, when combined with operating level reserves, caused the net book value of Microsoft's consolidated inventory to be *negative* at the end of the fiscal year ended June 30, 1997. This reserve was, to a significant extent, not in compliance with GAAP, and was not documented as required by the federal securities laws.

iv. Impaired Long Term Assets

Microsoft maintained a corporate reserve account for the valuation of financial assets. According to internal documents, the reserve's purpose was to "allow for potential losses, upon disposition, of Microsoft's financial assets." These financial assets consisted of equity investments made in various technology companies. Microsoft amortized the cost of these financial assets with monthly charges to income without any basis for the charges. The appropriate treatment under GAAP would have been to carry the assets at cost or write down the assets to their fair value in the event that the assets had suffered other than temporary declines in fair value.[6] Microsoft did not have a proper basis under GAAP for the amounts of the monthly charges in the account during its fiscal years 1995 through 1998.

v. Interest Rate Fluctuations

According to internal documents, the reserve account for interest income was designed to "provide for shifts in interest rates or other economic events which may adversely impact Microsoft's return on its portfolio." Adjustments to the interest income reserve were made at the "discretion" of senior financial personnel, and Microsoft did not have any factual analysis or statistical support for the balance in this account. This reserve was determined in a

(*continued*)

---

4. Statement of Financial Accounting Standards No. 5, Paragraph 8.

5. *Id.* at Paragraph 14.

6. Accounting Principles Board Opinion No. 18, Paragraph 6a.

EXHIBIT 1—
continued

UNITED STATES OF
AMERICA BEFORE
THE SECURITIES
AND EXCHANGE
COMMISSION

manner that did not comply with GAAP, and its balance and the adjustments thereto lacked a proper basis under GAAP.[7]

vi. Manufacturing Facilities

Microsoft created a reserve in 1996 because it believed that the value of certain of its manufacturing facilities would be impaired because it was taking steps to outsource certain of its manufacturing activities and dispose of its own facilities that had been engaged in this manufacturing. Microsoft established a reserve account to provide for expenses associated with the disposition of its own plant and equipment, and associated employee-related expenses. Microsoft had no analysis or other factual basis supporting the balance in this account and, consequently, could not establish whether this account pertained to probable losses arising from an event or circumstance that had already occurred or whether it pertained to losses arising from future contingencies. This account therefore was not documented as required by the federal securities laws, and the balances in the account were not determined in a manner that was in conformity with GAAP.

c. Cumulative Balances of Non-Cyclical Reserves

The cumulative balance of the six non-cyclical reserve accounts discussed above is depicted in the chart below:

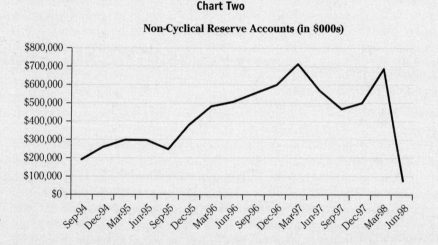

Chart Two

Non-Cyclical Reserve Accounts (in $000s)

Moreover, the amounts of quarterly adjustments to the above described six accounts, together with the amounts of the marketing expenses accrual, are depicted below [see Exhibit 2]:

The balances and adjustments displayed in Chart Two and Table 1 [see Exhibit 2] did not have the documentary support required by the federal securities laws, and a material portion thereof lacked a proper basis under GAAP.

4. Microsoft's Filings with the Commission

As a result of the foregoing, Microsoft filed with the Commission periodic reports and other filings during fiscal years 1995, 1996, 1997, and 1998 that included, directly or by

(continued)

---

7. Statement of Financial Accounting Standards No. 115, Paragraph 2; 16, provides that individual securities classified as either available-for-sale or held-to-maturity shall be written down to fair value if the enterprise determines that declines in fair value are other than temporary.

EXHIBIT 1—
continued

UNITED STATES OF
AMERICA BEFORE
THE SECURITIES
AND EXCHANGE
COMMISSION

incorporation, financial statements that misrepresented Microsoft's financial results by sometimes overstating income and on other occasions understating income.

5. Microsoft's Failure to Maintain Accurate and Complete Books and Records

In connection with its corporate reserve accounts, Microsoft failed to apply its own internal controls requiring a reconciliation of accounts to the general ledger. As noted above, the corporate reserve accounts were excepted from the company-wide policy that required all accounts be reconciled to the general ledger at least once per quarter.

Microsoft's accounting policies required the reconciliation of accounts as part of an extensive process to close the company's books each quarter. Among other things, the controllers and members of the corporate controllers' group reviewed activity in each general ledger account and reconciled the account balances to the general ledger, attaching supporting documentation for all activity and account balances. The reconciliation policy and process were part of a process designed to help ensure the accuracy and integrity of Microsoft's internally and externally reported financial information. However, Microsoft failed to include the corporate reserve accounts in this reconciliation process. As a result, Microsoft lacked an important safeguard for helping ensure that the adjustments to the corporate reserve accounts and the account balances themselves were appropriate or accurately reported in conformity with GAAP.

V. (Omitted)

VI.

Based on the foregoing, the Securities and Exchange Commission finds that Microsoft violated Sections 13(a), 13(b)(2)(A) and 13(b)(2)(B) of the Exchange Act, and Rules 12b-20, 13a-1 and 13a-13 promulgated thereunder.

VII.

In view of the foregoing, it is appropriate to impose the sanction specified in Respondent's Offer of Settlement.

VIII.

ORDER

ACCORDINGLY, IT IS HEREBY ORDERED THAT, pursuant to Section 21C of the Exchange Act, Microsoft cease-and-desist from committing or causing any violations of, and committing or causing any future violations of, Sections 13(a), 13(b)(2)(A), and 13(b)(2)(B) of the Exchange Act, and Rules 12b-20, 13a-1, and 13a-13 promulgated thereunder.

By the Commission.

Jonathan G. Katz
Secretary

Source: http://www.sec.gov/litigation/admin/34-46017.htm.

EXHIBIT 2

MICROSOFT UNSUPPORTED ADJUSTMENTS TO RESERVE ACCOUNTS (IN $000)

	OEM sales reserve	Reserve for accel depr	Marketing accrual	Corporate reserve for inventory obso.	Reserve for mfg facilities	Reserve for valuation of financial assets	Reserve for interest income	Total	% Pre-tax net income
06/30/95	185	-	82,800	(6,000)	-	1,096	(5,000)	73,081	13.36%
09/30/95	40,500	-	(33,956)	-	(4,000)	(3,000)	-	(456)	−0.06%
12/31/95	(83,000)	-	(32,649)	-	(45,000)	(3,500)	(5,000)	(169,149)	−19.11%
03/31/96	26,000	8,515	(58,203)	(30,000)	(5,000)	(3,000)	(5,000)	(66,688)	−7.72%
06/30/96	1,000	(8,329)	124,808	(15,000)	-	(3,000)	17,000	116,479	13.54%
1996 Annual	**(15,500)**	**186**	**-**	**(45,000)**	**(54,000)**	**(12,500)**	**7,000**	**(119,814)**	**−3.55%**
09/30/96	-	(47,609)	(77,324)	-	17,100	(3,000)	7,000	(103,833)	−10.99%
12/31/96	(42,300)	(30,906)	(23,191)	-	4,538	(3,000)	(5,000)	(99,859)	−8.76%
03/31/97	(130,233)	18,686	759	110	902	(3,000)	(5,000)	(117,776)	−7.35%
06/30/97	32,500	11,716	99,756	(1)	(5,021)	(3,000)	(5,000)	130,950	8.05%
1997 Annual	**(140,033)**	**(48,113)**	**-**	**109**	**17,519**	**(12,000)**	**(8,000)**	**(190,518)**	**−3.59%**
09/30/97	89,797	2,686	(88,800)	-	-	(6,000)	(8,000)	(10,317)	−0.86%
12/31/97	(85,631)	2,467	(47,041)	(5,000)	-	(6,000)	(5,000)	(146,205)	−8.26%
03/31/98	-	(14,534)	(20,747)	34	-	(13,000)	(5,000)	(53,247)	−2.59%
06/30/98	29,451	5,273	156,588	-	36,481	1,000	-	228,793	10.96%
1998 Annual	**33,617**	**(4,108)**	**-**	**(4,966)**	**36,481**	**(24,000)**	**(18,000)**	**19,024**	**0.27%**

EXHIBIT 3

MICROSOFT
REPORTED
PRE-TAX NET
INCOME AND
PRE-TAX INCOME
ADJUSTED FOR
SEC FINDINGS

Date	Reported pre-tax net income	SEC adjustments	Adjusted pre-tax net income
9/30/1995	$770.0	$0.5	$770
12/31/1995	$885.0	$169.1	$1,054
3/31/1996	$864.0	$66.7	$931
6/30/1996	$860.0	$116.5	$744
9/30/1996	$945.0	$103.8	$1,049
12/31/1996	$1,140.0	$99.9	$1,240
3/31/1997	$1,603.0	$117.8	$1,721
6/30/1997	$1,626.0	$131.0	$1,495
9/30/1997	$1,202.0	$10.3	$1,212
12/31/1997	$1,770.0	$146.2	$1,916
3/31/1998	$2,057.0	$53.2	$2,110
6/30/1998	$2,088.0	$228.8	$1,859

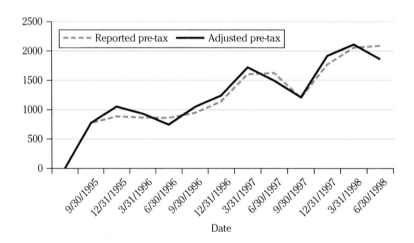

EXHIBIT 4

MICROSOFT REVENUES AND NET INCOME ADJUSTED FOR CHANGE IN UNEARNED REVENUES

Date	Revenue	Pre-tax net income	SEC adjustments	Income adjusted for SEC	Unearned revenues	Change in unearned revenues	Revenue with no unearned	Income with no unearned
9/30/1994	$1,247	$471						
12/31/1994	$1,482	$557						
3/31/1995	$1,587	$592						
6/30/1995	$1,621	$547			$54			
9/30/1995	$2,016	$770	−$0.5	$770	$307	$253	$2,269	$1,023
12/31/1995	$2,195	$885	−$169.1	$1,054	$495	$188	$2,383	$1,242
3/31/1996	$2,205	$864	−$66.7	$931	$545	$50	$2,255	$981
6/30/1996	$2,255	$860	$116.5	$744	$560	$15	$2,270	$759
9/30/1996	$2,295	$945	−$103.8	$1,049	$651	$91	$2,386	$1,140
12/31/1996	$2,680	$1,140	−$99.9	$1,240	$1,013	$362	$3,042	$1,602
3/31/1997	$3,208	$1,603	−$117.8	$1,721	$1,285	$272	$3,480	$1,993
6/30/1997	$3,175	$1,626	$131.0	$1,495	$1,418	$133	$3,308	$1,628
9/30/1997	$3,130	$1,202	−$10.3	$1,212	$1,671	$253	$3,383	$1,465
12/31/1997	$3,585	$1,770	−$146.2	$1,916	$2,038	$367	$3,952	$2,283
3/31/1998	$3,774	$2,057	−$53.2	$2,110	$2,463	$425	$4,199	$2,535
6/30/1998	$3,995	$2,088	$228.8	$1,859	$2,888	$425	$4,420	$2,284

EXHIBIT 5

REVENUES
AND REVENUES
ADJUSTED
FOR CHANGE
IN UNEARNED
REVENUES

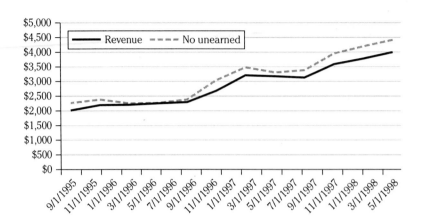

EXHIBIT 6

NET INCOME,
NET INCOME
ADJUSTED FOR
SEC FINDINGS,
AND NET INCOME
ADJUSTED FOR
SEC FINDINGS
AND CHANGE
IN UNEARNED
REVENUES

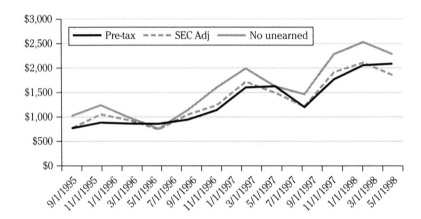

Beazer Homes USA, Inc.

SEC v. Michael T. Rand, Chief Accounting Officer

Beazer Homes, a home builder based in Atlanta, Georgia, was one of the nation's fastest growing homebuilders from 1998 through 2006. As interest rates declined, many Americans bought homes for the first time, and many others bought more expensive homes. This increase in home purchasing led to a rapid growth in new home construction throughout the United States and to the growth of 10 large home builder companies. At the end of 2005, Beazer was the sixth largest home builder in the United States in terms of numbers of homes built (18,401).[1]

Exhibits 1 to 3 show Beazer Homes USA's 2000 income statements, balance sheets, and statements of cash flow from its 2000 10-K; Exhibits 4 to 6 show those same financial statements from its 2007 10-K. As can be seen from Exhibits 1 and 4, Beazer's 2006 revenues were more than five times greater than 1998 revenues, whereas 2006 net income was more than 15 times greater than 1998 net income. Similar increases in revenue and net income were common for the 10 largest home builders as their market values increased by a factor of 10 or more from 1998 to early 2006.

Sales growth for home building began to slow in 2006 as mortgage rates climbed. The following year, 2007, mortgage finance companies began to fail and the market for securitized low-quality mortgages disappeared. Home builders throughout the nation had large inventories of raw land, homes under construction, and completed homes as the housing market collapsed. As shown in Exhibit 4, Beazer's revenues declined from $5.356 million in 2006 to $3.490 million in 2007, and Beazer went from a $369 million profit in 2006 to a $411 million loss in 2007. However, Beazer still had $454 million of cash in 2007 (Exhibit 5), and its cash flows from operating activities in 2007 were $509 million (Exhibit 6).

Department of Justice Investigation

To support their home-building operations, some of the large home builders, including Beazer, offered their customers mortgage financing beginning as early as 2000. On October 11, 2007, Beazer Homes filed a Form 8-K with the SEC reporting that it was under investigation for possible fraud involving mortgage lending at least back to 2000. As part of that investigation, the SEC had questioned certain aspects of Beazer's accounting for reserves and other accrued liabilities and its accounting for model home sale-leasebacks. As a result, Beazer reported that its previously issued financial statements could not be relied upon. On July 1, 2009, the U.S. Department of Justice announced the following settlement with Beazer Homes.[2]

---

1. The Real Estate Bloggers, June 2, 2006. http://www.therealestatebloggers.com/2006/06/02/top-10-largest-home-builders-in-united-states/.

2. Office of Public Affairs, Department of Justice, United States Settles False Claims Allegations Against National Home Builder and Mortgage Lender, July 1, 2009. http://www.justice.gov/opa/pr/2009/July/09-civ-654.html.

Beazer Homes USA Inc. has agreed to pay the United States $5 million dollars, plus contingent payments of up to $48 million dollars to be shared with victimized private homeowners, to resolve allegations that it, and Beazer Mortgage Corp., were involved in fraudulent mortgage origination activities in connection with federally insured mortgages. Beazer Homes, which is headquartered in Atlanta, operates in at least 21 states.

The U.S. Department of Housing and Urban Development's Federal Housing Administration guarantees home mortgage loans for low and low-to-moderate income families. The settlement resolves allegations that when Beazer Mortgage Corp. made Federal Housing Administration (FHA) insured mortgage loans for the purchase of homes built by Beazer Homes USA Inc., the companies fraudulently and improperly: 1) required purchasers to pay "interest discount points" at closing, but then kept the cash and failed to reduce interest rates; 2) provided cash "gifts" to home purchasers through certain charities, so purchasers could come up with minimum required down payments, with assurances the "gifts" would not have to be repaid, and then increased home purchase prices to offset the amount of the gifts; 3) obscured which of its branches made defaulting mortgage loans to avoid FHA detection of excessive default rates, and; 4) ignored "stated income" requirements in making loans to unqualified purchasers.

As a consequence, unqualified home buyers were induced to enter into FHA insured mortgages, interest rates for and the amount of FHA insured mortgages were improperly inflated, and Beazer Mortgage branches involved in fraudulent activity were hidden from the FHA. In some instances, mortgages that resulted from these fraudulent activities defaulted. When they did so, holders of the loans made FHA mortgage insurance claims and the FHA was wrongfully required to pay inflated claims, and to pay for the management, maintenance, rehabilitation, and marketing of defaulted properties.

Financial Accounting Issues

The Department of Justice investigation of Beazer's alleged fraudulent lending practices also led to an investigation of Beazer's financial reporting. That led to an expanded audit and to a restatement of previous financial statements as described in Exhibit 7. Beazer fired Michael T. Rand, its chief accounting officer, and the SEC began an investigation of both Beazer Homes USA and of Mr. Rand. On September 24, 2008, the SEC instituted cease-and-desist proceedings against Beazer Homes USA, Inc., with regard to its improper accounting.[3] A summary of those proceedings is shown in Exhibit 8.

On July 1, 2009, the SEC charged Mr. Rand with conducting a multiyear fraudulent earnings management scheme and with misleading Beazer's outside auditors and internal Beazer accountants to conceal his wrongdoing.[4] That complaint states that Mr. Rand engaged in two primary methods to initially understate earnings and then later overstate earnings.

Beazer has a land acquisition and development inventory account. That account includes the raw land cost and costs for infrastructure items such as roads, recreational areas, and sidewalks. Beazer also has a cost-to-complete liability account to cover specific costs that it expects to incur within four to nine months after a customer purchases a Beazer home. Those items include driveway repairs, paint touch-up, and various repairs to cabinets, doors, electrical systems, and similar adjustments.

3. SEC, In the matter of Beazer Homes USA, Inc., Respondent, September 24, 2008. http://www.sec.gov/litigation/admin/2008/33-8960.pdf.

4. *SEC v. Michael T. Rand.* http://www.sec.gov/litigation/complaints/2009/comp21114.pdf.

With respect to the land acquisition and development inventory account, Beazer estimates the total inventory cost for a subdivision and then allocates that total cost to individual home sites. When the last home is sold, the land acquisition and development inventory account for that subdivision should equal zero. Accountants at Beazer subsidiaries in states such as Texas, Indiana, and Arizona, and at Beazer's Atlanta headquarters, had systems to estimate the total land inventory costs and to allocate those costs to individual home sales. The SEC complaint alleges that Mr. Rand improperly overstated the amounts expensed as land acquisition and development costs, which understated the land acquisition and development inventory account and also understated Beazer profits. However, given the incredibly rapid growth, Mr. Rand may have worried that infrastructure costs might be far higher than in the past because of the costs to correct the work of new employees.

Beazer accountants also had systems in place to estimate the cost-to-complete liability for newly sold homes and systems to reduce that cost-to-complete liability nine months after the homes were sold. The SEC complaint alleges that Mr. Rand overstated the cost-to-complete liability for newly sold homes and failed to reduce the liability set aside for homes that had been sold more than nine months earlier. As with infrastructure costs, Mr. Rand may have worried that with the rapid growth and the influx of new employees, the quality of Beazer Homes might be lower and the cost-to-complete might be significantly higher than in the past.

A final SEC complaint alleges that Beazer sold and then leased back a large number of model or display homes. Beazer recognized the gains on those sale and leaseback transactions even though it had a continuing financial interest in those homes. Under accounting rules, that continuing financial interest prohibited Beazer from recognizing a profit on the sale and leaseback of the homes.

Exhibit 9 summarizes the amount for which the SEC alleges that Mr. Rand understated or overstated profits for those three items for the periods Q1 2000 through Q1 2007:

Column 3 shows the alleged quarterly understatements (Q1 2000 to Q4 2005) and then alleged overstatements (Q1 to Q4, 2006) of net income by quarter for the alleged land inventory understatements. For example, Beazer's first quarter 2000 net income was understated by $902,000 because it overstated the cost of land on homes it sold. Beazer allegedly understated profits from the first quarter 2000 through the fourth quarter 2005 using land inventory adjustments. Beginning in 2006, it began overstating profits with land inventory adjustments.

Column 4 shows the monthly understatements (Q2 2000 to Q2 2005) and then overstatements (Q3 2005 to Q1 2007) of net income by quarter for the alleged cost-to-complete overstatements. Beazer's second quarter 2000 net income was understated by $610,000 because it overstated its liability to make repairs to recently sold homes. Beazer allegedly understated profits from the second quarter 2000 through the second quarter 2005, and then overstated profits with cost-to-complete adjustments.

Column 5 shows that in 2006 Beazer overstated profits by improperly recording profits on the sale and leaseback of display and model homes (Q1 to Q4, 2006).

Column 6 shows the sum of the improper adjustments for the items in columns 3, 4, and 5 by quarter.

Column 7 shows the sum of improper adjustments by year.

Column 8 shows the cumulative alleged improper adjustments. The cumulative alleged improper adjustments reached a maximum of $71,830,000 in the fourth quarter 2005. As Beazer reduced that alleged profit understatement, the cumulative alleged improper adjustment declined to $19,855,000 by the first quarter 2007.

Column 9 shows quarterly income as reported.

Column 10 shows quarterly income from column 9, adjusted for the alleged improper adjustments in column 6.

Column 11 shows the error by quarter as a percent of adjusted quarterly income.

As the housing market deteriorated, Beazer began to record impairment expenses for both goodwill and its inventories of land, partially completed homes, and finished homes. That is also shown in Exhibit 8.

Column 12 shows that in the second quarter 2005 Beazer recorded a $130,255,000 impairment expense for goodwill related to its acquisition of other home builders. Beginning in the first quarter 2007, and continuing through the third quarter 2009, Beazer recorded frequent goodwill and inventory impairment write downs.

Exhibits 10 through 11 show Beazer's income statements, balance sheets, and statements of cash flow from its third quarter 2009 10-Q. Although Beazer suffered losses for the first three quarters of 2008 and 2009, it has had positive cash flow from operations for the first three quarters of 2008 and 2009, it has positive owners' equity, and it has substantial cash on hand.

Wells Notice

Under the Sarbanes-Oxley Act of 2002, if a firm is required to restate its financial statements, the SEC may require the CEO and CFO to return all bonuses they received during the periods for which financial statements were restated. The portion of the act related to bonus repayments does not require the CEO or CFO to have had prior knowledge of the errors. On November 16, 2009, Beazer Homes USA, Inc., filed the following Form 8-K with the SEC announcing it had received a Wells notice to the firm's CEO:

On November 13, 2009, the Staff of the US Securities and Exchange Commission (the "Commission") issued a Wells notice to the Company's Chief Executive Officer, Ian J. McCarthy, indicating that they have preliminarily determined to recommend that the Commission bring a civil action against him to collect certain incentive compensation and other amounts allegedly due under Section 304(a) of the Sarbanes-Oxley Act of 2002. In their Wells notice, the Staff did not allege any lack of due care by Mr. McCarthy in connection with the Company's financial statements or other disclosures. The Commission has taken the position in a recently filed civil action against the chief executive officer of another company that the Commission need not allege misconduct by a CEO to maintain such an action. The Commission Staff has offered Mr. McCarthy an opportunity to make a submission setting forth the reasons why no such action should be filed. Mr. McCarthy intends to respond to the Staff's offer by making such a submission.

The Company is not named in the Wells notice. As disclosed previously, on September 24, 2008, the Company entered into a settlement with the Commission, without admitting or denying wrongdoing, that resolved the Commission's investigation into the financial statement matters that were the subject of the independent investigation conducted by the Audit Committee of the Company's Board of Directors.

Required

1. How serious were the alleged accounting misstatements? As part of your answer, consider whether they were material and whether they were fraudulent.

2. Suppose you were defending Mr. Rand. Could you argue that the impairment charges Beazer made beginning in the second quarter 2005 indicate that accounting is highly imprecise and that his alleged fraudulent adjustments were minor disagreements about estimates? Explain.

3. Evaluate Beazer's financial condition at the end of 2007 (Exhibits 4–7).

4. Evaluate Beazer's financial condition at the end of the third quarter, 2009 (Exhibits 10–12).

5. Were investors harmed by Mr. Rand's alleged fraudulent entries? Explain.

6. What was more serious, the allegations against Beazer Homes for possible mortgage fraud or the allegations against Mr. Rand for possible accounting fraud?

7. Discuss the Wells notice issued to Beazer Homes USA's CEO.

EXHIBIT 1

CONSOLIDATED STATEMENTS OF INCOME 2000 10-K

BEAZER HOMES USA, INC.

| | Year Ended September 30 | | |
	2000	1999	1998
	(in thousands, except per share amounts)		
Total revenue	$1,527,865	$1,394,074	$977,409
Costs and expenses:			
Home construction and land sales	1,255,918	1,153,442	811,203
Amortization of previously capitalized interest	27,704	25,469	19,031
Selling, general and administrative	168,620	153,363	110,259
Operating income	75,623	61,800	36,916
Other (expense)/income, net	(4,138)	(1,256)	578
Income before income taxes	71,485	60,544	37,494
Provision for income taxes	27,879	23,610	14,293
Net income	$43,606	$36,934	$23,201
Dividends and other payments to preferred stockholders	$—	$3,343	$4,000

EXHIBIT 2

CONSOLIDATED
BALANCE SHEETS,
2000 10-K

BEAZER HOMES USA, INC.

	September 30	
	2000	**1999**
	(dollars in thousands, except per share amounts)	
Assets:		
Cash and cash equivalents	$—	$—
Accounts receivable	23,087	21,416
Inventory	629,663	532,559
Deferred tax asset	9,506	5,714
Property, plant, and equipment, net	12,206	13,102
Goodwill, net	7,250	8,051
Other assets	17,167	13,726
Total Assets	$698,879	$594,568
Liabilities and Stockholders' Equity:		
Liabilities:		
Trade accounts payable	$72,212	$54,860
Other liabilities	101,129	90,046
Revolving credit facility	40,000	—
Senior notes	215,000	215,000
Total Liabilities	428,341	359,906
Stockholders' Equity:		
Preferred stock (par value $.01 per share, 5,000,000 shares authorized, no shares issued)	—	—
Common stock (par value $.01 per share, 30,000,000 shares authorized, 12,275,851 and 12,266,149 issued, 8,483,824 and 8,974,122 outstanding)	123	123
Paid in capital	195,134	194,528
Retained earnings	141,094	97,488
Unearned restricted stock	(4,609)	(5,494)
Treasury stock, at cost (3,792,027 and 3,292,027 shares)	(61,204)	(51,983)
Total Stockholders' Equity	270,538	234,662
Total Liabilities and Stockholders' Equity	$698,879	$594,568

EXHIBIT 3

CONSOLIDATED
STATEMENTS OF
CASH FLOWS

BEAZER HOMES USA, INC.

	Year Ended September 30		
	2000	1999	1998
	(in thousands)		
Cash flows from operating activities:			
Net income	$43,606	$36,934	$23,201
Adjustments to reconcile net income to net cash (used)/provided by operating activities:			
Depreciation and amortization	6,852	5,508	3,269
Provision for deferred income taxes	(3,792)	(2,431)	340
Changes, net of effects from acquisitions:			
Increase in inventory	(97,104)	(23,129)	(26,220)
Increase/(decrease) in trade accounts payable	17,352	(17,258)	15,824
Increase in other accrued liabilities	11,083	34,440	18,344
Other	3,277	219	(7,609)
Net cash (used)/provided by operating activities	(18,726)	34,283	27,149
Cash flows from investing activities:			
Capital expenditures	(3,775)	(4,104)	(5,775)
Investment in unconsolidated joint ventures	(8,030)	(2,100)	(1,200)
Acquisitions, net of cash acquired		(91,800)	(16,766)
Net cash used by investing activities	(11,805)	(98,004)	(23,741)
Cash flows from financing activities:			
Proceeds from 8⅞% senior notes			100,000
Net borrowings under revolving credit facility	40,000		(30,000)
Debt issuance costs	(248)	(438)	(3,067)
Cash dividends paid on preferred stock		(3,449)	(4,000)
Stock repurchases	(9,221)		
Net cash provided/(used) by financing activities	30,531	(3,887)	62,933
(Decrease)/increase in cash	—	(67,608)	66,341
Cash and cash equivalents at beginning of year	—	67,608	1,267
Cash and cash equivalents at end of year	$—	$—	$67,608
Interest paid	$29,244	$25,356	$20,379
Income taxes paid	$31,533	$25,909	$14,533

EXHIBIT 4

CONSOLIDATED
STATEMENTS OF
INCOME 2007 10-K

BEAZER HOMES USA, INC.
(in thousands, except share and per share amounts)

	Year Ended September 30		
	2007	**2006**	**2005**
		As Restated, see Note 2	
Total revenue	**$3,490,819**	$5,356,504	$4,992,973
Home construction and land sales expenses	**2,944,385**	4,061,118	3,766,517
Inventory impairments and option contract abandonments	**611,864**	44,175	5,511
Gross (loss) profit	**(65,430)**	1,251,211	1,220,945
Selling, general and administrative expenses	**454,122**	629,322	548,161
Depreciation and amortization	**33,594**	42,425	36,068
Goodwill impairment	**52,755**	–	130,235
Operating (loss) income	**(605,901)**	579,464	506,481
Equity in (loss) income of unconsolidated joint ventures	**(35,154)**	1,343	5,021
Other income, net	**7,775**	2,450	1,712
(Loss) income before income taxes	**(633,280)**	583,257	513,214
(Benefit from) provision for income taxes	**(222,207)**	214,421	237,315
Net (loss) income	**$(411,073)**	$368,836	$275,899

See Notes to Consolidated Financial Statements.

EXHIBIT 5

CONSOLIDATED
BALANCE SHEETS,
2007 10-K

BEAZER HOMES USA, INC.

(in thousands, except share and per share amounts)

	September 30	
	2007	**2006**
		As Restated, see Note 17
ASSETS		
Cash and cash equivalents	$454,337	$167,570
Restricted cash	5,171	4,873
Accounts receivable	45,501	338,033
Income tax receivable	63,981	–
Inventory		
Owned inventory	2,537,791	3,137,021
Consolidated inventory not owned	237,382	471,441
Total Inventory	2,775,173	3,608,462
Residential mortgage loans available-for-sale	781	92,157
Investments in unconsolidated joint ventures	109,143	124,799
Deferred tax assets	232,949	71,344
Property, plant and equipment, net	71,682	76,454
Goodwill	68,613	121,368
Other assets	102,690	109,611
Total Assets	$3,930,021	$4,714,671
LIABILITIES AND STOCKHOLDERS' EQUITY		
Trade accounts payable	$118,030	$140,008
Other liabilities	453,089	557,754
Obligations related to consolidated inventory not owned	177,931	330,703
Senior notes (net of discounts of $3,033 and $3,578, respectively)	1,521,967	1,551,422
Junior subordinated notes	103,093	103,093
Warehouse line	–	94,881
Other secured notes payable	118,073	89,264
Model home financing obligations	114,116	117,079
Total Liabilities	2,606,299	2,984,204
Stockholders' Equity:		
Preferred stock (par value $.01 per share, 5,000,000 shares authorized, no shares issued)	–	
Common stock (par value $0.001, 80,000,000 shares authorized, 42,597,229 and 42,318,098 issued, 39,261,721 and 38,889,554 outstanding)	43	42
Paid in capital	543,705	529,326
Retained earnings	963,869	1,390,552
Treasury stock, at cost (3,335,508 and 3,428,544 shares)	(183,895)	(189,453)
Total Stockholders' Equity	1,323,722	1,730,467
Total Liabilities and Stockholders' Equity	$3,930,021	$4,714,671

See Notes to Consolidated Financial Statements.

EXHIBIT 6

STATEMENTS OF
CASH FLOWS,
2007 10-K

BEAZER HOMES USA, INC.
(in thousands)

	Year Ended September 30		
	2007	**2006**	**2005**
Cash flows from operating activities:		As Restated, see Note 17	
Net (loss) income	**$(411,073)**	$368,836	$ 275,899
Adjustments to reconcile to net cash provided by operating activities:			
Depreciation and amortization	**33,594**	42,425	36,068
Stock-based compensation expense	**11,149**	15,753	11,945
Inventory impairments and option contract abandonments	**611,864**	44,175	5,511
Goodwill impairment charge	**52,755**	–	130,235
Deferred income tax (benefit) provision	**(161,605)**	25,963	(51,186)
Tax benefit from stock transactions	**(2,635)**	(8,205)	11,551
Equity in loss (income) of unconsolidated joint ventures	**35,154**	(1,343)	(5,021)
Cash distributions of income from unconsolidated joint ventures	**5,285**	352	5,844
Changes in operating assets and liabilities:			
Decrease (increase) in accounts receivable	**292,532**	(181,639)	(84,637)
Increase in income tax receivable	**(63,981)**	–	–
Decrease (increase) in inventory	**134,953**	(486,727)	(593,521)
Decrease (increase) in residential mortgage loans available-for-sale	**91,376**	(92,157)	–
Decrease (increase) in other assets	**9,180**	(20,736)	(16,780)
(Decrease) increase in trade accounts payable	**(21,978)**	(1,641)	18,336
(Decrease) increase in other liabilities	**(108,809)**	(83,044)	208,794
Other changes	**1,610**	(8)	806
Net cash provided by (used in) operating activities	**509,371**	(377,996)	(46,156)
Cash flows from investing activities:			
Capital expenditures	**(29,474)**	(55,088)	(48,437)
Investments in unconsolidated joint ventures	**(24,505)**	(49,458)	(42,619)
Changes in restricted cash	**(298)**	(4,873)	–
Distributions and proceeds from sale of unconsolidated joint ventures	**2,229**	4,655	5,597
Net cash (used in) investing activities	**(52,048)**	(104,764)	(85,459)
Cash flows from financing activities:			
Repayment of term loan	**–**	–	(200,000)
Borrowings under credit facilities and warehouse line	**169,888**	1,937,528	439,700
Repayment of credit facilities and warehouse line	**(264,769)**	(1,842,647)	(439,700)
Repayment of other secured notes payable	**(31,139)**	(20,934)	(16,776)
Borrowings under senior notes	**–**	275,000	346,786
Borrowings under junior subordinated notes	**–**	103,093	–
Repurchase of senior notes	**(30,413)**	–	–

(continued)

EXHIBIT 6—
continued

STATEMENTS OF
CASH FLOWS,
2007 10-K

Borrowings under model home financing obligations	**5,919**	117,365	–
Repayment of model home financing obligations	**(8,882)**	(286)	(1,118)
Debt issuance costs	**(2,259)**	(7,206)	(4,958)
Proceeds from stock option exercises	**4,422**	7,298	5,875
Common stock redeemed	**(348)**	(2,624)	–
Treasury stock purchases	**–**	(205,416)	(8,092)
Tax benefit from stock transactions	**2,635**	8,205	–
Dividends paid	**(15,610)**	(16,144)	(13,884)
Net cash (used in) provided by financing activities	**(170,556)**	353,232	107,833
Increase (decrease) in cash and cash equivalents	**286,767**	(129,528)	(23,782)

EXHIBIT 7

RESTATEMENT OF
CONSOLIDATED
FINANCIAL
RESULTS,
2007 10-K

BEAZER HOMES USA, INC.

EXPLANATORY NOTE

In April 2007, the Audit Committee of the Board of Directors initiated an independent investigation of our mortgage origination business through independent legal counsel and independent forensic accountants. During the course of this investigation, the Audit Committee determined that our mortgage origination practices related to certain loans in prior periods violated certain applicable federal and/or state origination requirements. During the course of the investigation, the Audit Committee also discovered accounting and financial reporting errors and/or irregularities that required restatement resulting primarily from (1) inappropriate accumulation of reserves and/or accrued liabilities associated with land development and house costs ("Inventory Reserves") and the subsequent improper release of such reserves and accrued liabilities and (2) inaccurate revenue recognition with respect to certain model home sale-leaseback transactions. In conjunction with the restatement of the items above, we also made corresponding capitalized interest, capitalized indirect costs, and income tax adjustments to our consolidated financial statements as these balances were impacted by the aforementioned adjustments. We also made other adjustments to our consolidated financial statements relating to corrections of accounting and financial reporting errors and/or irregularities, some errors previously identified but historically not considered to be material to require correction and some errors and irregularities discovered as part of the restatement process, consisting of (1) reclassifying model home furnishings and sales office leasehold improvements from owned inventory to property, plant and equipment, net in the amount of $47.0 million at September 30, 2006; (2) reclassifying depreciation and amortization of model home furnishings and sales office leasehold improvements from home construction and land sales expenses to depreciation and amortization in the amount of $32.1 million and $26.8 million for the fiscal years ended September 30, 2006 and 2005, respectively; (3) recognizing total revenue ($11.6 million) and home construction and land sales expenses ($8.7 million) for the fiscal year ended September 30, 2006, related to inappropriate revenue recognition timing in the fiscal year ended September 30, 2005, for certain home closings in California; (4) reclassifying the results of operations from our fiscal 2005 title services from other income, net ($5.9 million) to total revenue ($8.1 million) and selling, general and administrative ("SG&A") expenses ($2.2 million); (5) reclassifying $5.0 million from restricted cash at September 30, 2006 to cash and cash equivalents as such amount was determined not to be restricted; (6) recognizing the reversal of certain warranty accruals related to our captive insurance subsidiary in the fiscal years ended prior to fiscal 2005 ($8.7 million), as reflected in the prior period restatement caption in the Consolidated Statements of Stockholders' Equity, instead of the previously presented reversal of $8.7 million in warranty accruals through

(continued)

home construction and land sales expenses for the fiscal year ended September 30, 2005; (7) certain other miscellaneous immaterial adjustments; and (8) the related tax effects of the adjustments described in (1) through (7) above.

As discussed in Note 17 to the accompanying Consolidated Financial Statements in this Annual Report on Form 10-K for the fiscal year ended September 30, 2007 ("2007 Form 10-K"), we have restated our consolidated financial statements and the related disclosures for fiscal 2006 and 2005. Specifically, we have restated our consolidated balance sheet as of September 30, 2006 and the related consolidated statements of operations, stockholders' equity and cash flows, including related disclosures, for the fiscal years ended September 30, 2006 and 2005. The accompanying Management's Discussion and Analysis of Financial Condition and Results of Operations in Part II, Item 7, has been updated to reflect the effects of the restatement.

In addition, the unaudited quarterly data reflected in this 2007 Form 10-K presents the condensed consolidated financial information included in the amended Quarterly Reports on Form 10-Q/A for the fiscal quarters ended December 31, 2006 and March 31, 2007 and the Quarterly Report on Form 10-Q for the fiscal quarter ended June 30, 2007. These reports, which are being filed concurrently with this 2007 Form 10-K, contain restated condensed consolidated financial statements for the comparative periods of fiscal 2007 and 2006.

As a result of the errors and irregularities discussed above, and for the purpose of the Selected Financial Data included in Item 6 of this 2007 Form 10-K, we have also restated our Balance Sheet Data as of September 30, 2005, 2004 and 2003 and the related Statement of Operations and Supplemental Financial Data for the fiscal years ended September 30, 2004 and 2003. In addition, the cumulative effect of the errors and irregularities attributable to periods prior to October 1, 2002 have been reflected in the Balance Sheet Data as an increase to retained earnings at September 30, 2002 of $24.8 million for fiscal years 1998–2002.

The following table reconciles net income "as previously reported" to net income "as restated" (in thousands):

Fiscal Year	Net Income, as Previously Reported	Adjustments	Net Income, as Restated
2003	$172,745	$(971)	$171,774
2004	235,811	10,365	246,176
2005	262,524	13,375	275,899
2006	388,761	(19,925)	368,836

EXHIBIT 8

CEASE-AND-DESIST
PROCEEDINGS,
BEAZER HOMES

The Improper Accruals and Reversals

Between approximately 2000 and 2007, Beazer created, and later reversed, improper accruals and reserves by, among other ways, manipulating the amounts recorded in two series of accounts in order to manage earnings. These accounts were the land inventory accounts and the house cost to complete accounts.

7. *The Land Inventory Accounts.* As part of its homebuilding and sales operations, Beazer regularly acquired large parcels of land upon which it constructed houses. Beazer recorded this purchased land as an asset on its balance sheet in accounts denoted as "land inventory accounts." Also recorded in these accounts were capitalized costs for the common development of the parcel, such as costs for sewer systems and streets. Each Beazer subdivision under construction had at least one land inventory account associated with it in Beazer's general ledger.

8. As subdivisions were built, Beazer allocated the land acquisition cost, as well as past and future common development costs, to individual home lots which were then offered for sale. When a home sale was recorded in Beazer's general ledger, all associated homebuilding costs, including the costs of the land recorded in the land inventory account, were expensed to cost of sales. As part of these journal entries, the land inventory account was reduced and a cost of sales expense account increased to reflect the value of the land and improvements that Beazer sold with the house. Because Beazer sold houses within a subdivision as the development of that subdivision progressed, the land expense recorded for any particular house sale was necessarily an estimate. As individual houses in a development were sold, the land inventory accounts were decreased by an amount representing the amounts of the land and development costs allocated to each individual house. Shortly after the final house in a development had been sold, the balance in the land inventory account would be at or near zero.

9. In certain quarters between 2000 through 2007, however, Beazer, acting through certain officers and employees, manipulated the amounts recorded in the land inventory accounts in order to manage earnings. Specifically, in various quarters during fiscal years 2000 through 2005, Beazer over-allocated land inventory expense to individual properties sold. This over-allocation caused Beazer to report more expense and less profit on each sold house in certain subdivisions. When all or most of the houses in a development were eventually sold, these over-allocations resulted in the affected land inventory accounts having negative (or credit) balances. The credit balances that resulted from the intentional over-allocation were then improperly held open in Beazer's general ledger—acting, in effect, as improper reserves. By these actions, Beazer understated its net income by a total of $42 million for fiscal years 2000 through 2005.

10. Beginning at least by the second quarter of 2006, Beazer, acting through certain officers and employees, began to reverse the excess reserves existing in the land inventory accounts, which increased then-current period earnings. The credit balances in land inventory accounts were debited, *i.e.*, zeroed out, and a cost of sales expense credited, *i.e.*, reduced. This improperly reduced expenses and increased Beazer's earnings. During 2006, Beazer overstated its cumulative reported net income of $389 million by $16 million by "zeroing out" credit balances in its land inventory accounts. For the first two quarters of fiscal 2007, Beazer understated its cumulative reported net loss of $102 million by $1 million due to the reversal of improper land inventory reserves.

11. *The House Cost to Complete Accounts.* Under its accounting policies, Beazer recorded revenue and profit on the sale of a house after the close of the sale of that house to a third party. In the journal entries to record the sale, Beazer typically reserved a portion

(continued)

EXHIBIT 8—
continued

CEASE-AND-DESIST
PROCEEDINGS,
BEAZER HOMES

of its profit earned on the house. This reserve, called a " house cost to complete"
reserve, was established to cover any known and unknown expenses that Beazer might
incur on the sold house after the close, such as outstanding invoices, unbudgeted
cost overruns, minor repairs or final cosmetic touchups. Although the amount of this
reserve varied by region, it was typically $2,000 to $4,000 per house, above known
outstanding invoices. Beazer's policy was to reverse any unused portion of the house
cost to complete reserve within four to nine months after the house's close, taking any
unused portion into income at that time. Although creation of such a house cost to
complete reserve is proper, in some instances, Beazer, acting through certain officers
and employees, utilized these reserves to manage improperly its earnings. In various
quarters between 2000 and 2005, Beazer over-reserved house cost to complete expenses
in order to defer profit to future periods. In later periods, Beazer eliminated these cost
to complete reserves, resulting in inflated profits for those periods. In certain instances,
Beazer also purposefully did not recognize certain current period house cost to complete
expenses, again resulting in inflated profits for those periods.

12. Between fiscal years 2000 and 2005, Beazer understated its net income by $6 million
due to excess house cost to complete accruals. During fiscal year 2006, when Beazer
began to reverse some of the excess accruals, Respondent overstated its net income
by over $1.2 million. Beazer also understated its cumulative net loss for the first two
quarters of fiscal 2007 by $1 million.

The Sale-Leaseback Transactions

13. As part of its marketing activities, Beazer typically builds and furnishes between one and
five model homes for each of its housing developments. Prior to 2006, Beazer typically
retained ownership of the large majority (upwards of 70–80%) of its model homes and
entered into sale-leaseback arrangements with third parties for the remaining ones.
Beginning in fiscal 2006, Beazer significantly increased the number of model homes it
leased. At the end of fiscal 2006, Beazer had leased 557 of its 793 model homes or 70%.
Beazer improperly accounted for more than half of these leased model homes as sale-
leasebacks in order to improve Beazer's financial results.

14. Specifically, beginning near the end of fiscal 2005, Beazer, acting through certain of its
officers and employees, engaged in negotiations with the third party entity representing
the Investor Pools concerning possible sale-leaseback transactions for Beazer's model
homes. Pursuant to the transaction terms under discussion, the Investor Pools would
purchase certain Beazer model homes at 92% of the homes' appraised value. Beazer
would then lease the model homes, at monthly lease payments equal to the Investor
Pools' purchase price multiplied by the current 30 day LIBOR rate plus 450 basis points
(prorated on a monthly basis). Beazer would also retain a right to receive a percentage
of the appreciation of the model home upon its sale at the end of the lease term (the
"Appreciation Rights").

15. However, Beazer's outside auditor informed certain Beazer officers and employees that
any Appreciation Rights represented a "continuing interest" that, pursuant to Generally
Accepted Accounting Principles ("GAAP"), required Beazer to record the transactions
as financing, not as sale-leasebacks. This proper accounting treatment would not have
permitted Beazer to record the model home sales revenue and profit at the beginning of
the lease term.

16. In order to circumvent GAAP, and deceive its outside auditor, Beazer, acting through
certain officers and employees, caused the model home sale-leaseback written

(continued)

EXHIBIT 8—
continued

CEASE-AND-DESIST
PROCEEDINGS,
BEAZER HOMES

agreements with the Investor Pools to omit any reference to Appreciation Rights and recorded the model home transactions as sale-leasebacks, recognizing home sales revenue in fiscal 2006. Based upon the terms of the written agreements, the outside auditor agreed that the transactions qualified for sale-leaseback accounting. However, unbeknownst to the outside auditor, Beazer, acting through certain officers and employees, and the Investor Pools had also entered into oral side agreements which contained the Appreciation Rights and allowed Beazer to receive a percentage of the model homes' price appreciation upon their sale at the end of the lease term.

17. As a result of Beazer's improper recording of these transactions as sale-leasebacks, Beazer overstated its fiscal year 2006 revenues by $117 million and net income by $14 million. For the first two quarters of fiscal 2007, Beazer understated its cumulative revenue by $2.6 million and overstated its cumulative net loss by $3.9 million due to the improper sale-leasebacks accounting.

		BEAZER HOMES USA, INC.				
1	2	3	4	5	6	7
		(Overstated) Understated expenses or Overstated Sale-leaseback Revenues[1]				
Year	Quarter	Land inventory cost	Cost to complete reserve	Fraudulent sale-leaseback transactions	Total change, operating income	Change to operating inc for the year
2000	Q-1	−$902,000			−$902,000	
	Q-2	−$791,000	−$610,000		−$1,401,000	
	Q-3	−$727,000	−$5,000		−$732,000	
	Q-4	−$987,000	−$2,288,000		−$3,275,000	−$6,310,000
2001	Q-1	−$1,455,000	−$1,138,000		−$2,593,000	
	Q-2	−$584,000	−$543,000		−$1,127,000	
	Q-3	−$1,322,000	$0		−$1,322,000	
	Q-4	−$2,571,000	$0		−$2,571,000	−$7,613,000
2002	Q-1	−$1,827,000	−$2,184,000		−$4,011,000	
	Q-2	−$2,761,000	−$813,000		−$3,574,000	
	Q-3	−$1,270,000	$0		−$1,270,000	
	Q-4	−$2,586,000	$0		−$2,586,000	−$11,441,000
2003	Q-1	−$2,440,000	−$1,380,000		−$3,820,000	
	Q-2	−$1,422,000	$0		−$1,422,000	
	Q-3	−$1,086,000	$0		−$1,086,000	
	Q-4	$0	$0		$0	−$6,328,000
2004	Q-1	−$3,996,000	−$1,057,000		−$5,053,000	
	Q-2	−$4,253,000	$0		−$4,253,000	
	Q-3	−$5,963,000	−$1,137,000		−$7,100,000	
	Q-4	−$2,227,000	−$2,051,000		−$4,278,000	−$20,684,000
2005	Q-1	−$3,388,000	−$805,000		−$4,193,000	
	Q-2	−$4,443,000	−$1,427,000		−$5,870,000	
	Q-3	−$5,122,000	$200,000		−$4,922,000	
	Q-4	−$4,469,000	$0		−$4,469,000	−$19,454,000
2006	Q-1	$100,000	$183,000	$8,306,000	$8,589,000	
	Q-2	$301,000	$0	$4,179,000	$4,480,000	
	Q-3	$14,278,000	$2,130,000	$1,583,000	$17,991,000	
	Q-4	$10,816,000	$209,000	$8,341,000	$19,366,000	$50,426,000
2007	Q-1		$1,549,000		$1,549,000	1549000
	Q-2					
	Q-3					
	Q-4					
2008	Q-1					
	Q-2					
	Q-3					
	Q-4					
2009	Q-1					
	Q-2					
	Q-3					
	Q-4					

1. Note 1: SEC Complaint for Injunctive and other relief, *SEC v. Michael T. Rand*, July 1, 2009.
http://www.sec.gov/litigation/complaints/2009/comp21114.pdf.

EXHIBIT 9—
continued

SEC
ADJUSTMENTS
AND IMPAIRMENT
CHARGES

BEAZER HOMES USA, INC.				
8	9	10	11	12
Cumulative change to operating inc	Operating income, as reported	Restated operating income	Error as a % of restated operating inc	Goodwill and inventory impairments[2]
−$902,000	$13,201,000	$14,103,000	−6.4%	
−$2,303,000	$14,979,000	$16,380,000	−8.6%	
−$3,035,000	$20,943,000	$21,675,000	−3.4%	
−$6,310,000	$26,500,000	$29,775,000	−11.0%	
−$8,903,000	$22,992,000	$25,585,000	−10.1%	
−$10,030,000	$29,074,000	$30,201,000	−3.7%	
−$11,352,000	$31,885,000	$33,207,000	−4.0%	
−$13,923,000	$38,278,000	$40,849,000	−6.3%	
−$17,934,000	$37,098,000	$41,109,000	−9.8%	
−$21,508,000	$38,225,000	$41,799,000	−8.6%	
−$22,778,000	$53,721,000	$54,991,000	−2.3%	
−$25,364,000	$64,130,000	$66,716,000	−3.9%	
−$29,184,000	$59,066,000	$62,886,000	−6.1%	
−$30,606,000	$61,487,000	$62,909,000	−2.3%	
−$31,692,000	$65,968,000	$67,054,000	−1.6%	
−$31,692,000	$92,634,000	$92,634,000	0.0%	
−$36,745,000	$75,652,000	$80,705,000	−6.3%	
−$40,998,000	$77,844,000	$82,097,000	−5.2%	
−$48,098,000	$96,238,000	$103,338,000	−6.9%	
−$52,376,000	$128,201,000	$132,479,000	−3.2%	
−$56,569,000	$110,878,000	$115,071,000	−3.6%	
−$62,439,000	−$58,114,000	−$52,244,000	11.2%	$130,235,000
−$67,361,000	$178,637,000	$183,559,000	−2.7%	
−$71,830,000	$255,517,000	$259,986,000	−1.7%	
−$63,241,000	$139,752,000	$131,163,000	6.5%	
−$58,761,000	$164,702,000	$160,222,000	2.8%	
−$40,770,000	$155,895,000	$137,904,000	13.0%	
−$21,404,000	$108,724,000	$89,358,000	21.7%	
−$19,855,000	−$94,259,000	−$95,808,000	−1.6%	$119,923,000
	$64,317,000			$79,854,000
	−$181,815,000			$154,244,000
	−$264,113,000			
	−$199,267,000			$168,512,000
	−$290,215,000			$235,965,000
	−$141,344,000			$99,847,000
	−$116,952,000			
	−$ 62,326,000			$28,852,000
	−$102,699,000			$51,755,000
	−$50,693,000			$11,856,000

2. Note 2: All other financial data, including goodwill and inventory impairment charges, taken from Beazer Homes USA, Inc., 10-Q and 10-K reports filed with the SEC.

EXHIBIT 10

STATEMENTS OF
OPERATIONS, 2009
Q-3 10-Q

BEAZER HOMES USA, INC.				
(in thousands, except per share data)				
	Three Months Ended June 30		Nine Months Ended June 30	
	2009	2008	2009	2008
Total revenue	$224,653	$455,578	$645,340	$1,361,649
Home construction and land sales expenses	207,176	407,512	580,920	1,223,252
Inventory impairments and option contract abandonments	11,856	95,482	76,320	451,854
Gross profit (loss)	5,621	(47,416)	(11,900)	(313,457)
Selling, general and administrative expenses	51,357	83,517	174,596	245,696
Depreciation and amortization	4,957	6,046	13,079	18,250
Goodwill impairment	—	4,365	16,143	52,470
Operating loss	(50,693)	(141,344)	(215,718)	(629,873)
Equity in loss of unconsolidated joint ventures	(4,041)	(18,568)	(13,795)	(75,069)
Gain on extinguishment of debt	55,214	—	58,788	—
Other expense, net	(22,370)	(13,489)	(59,958)	(20,907)
Loss from continuing operations before income taxes	(21,890)	(173,401)	(230,683)	(725,849)
Provision for (benefit from) income taxes	5,990	(63,707)	(7,981)	(249,771)
Loss from continuing operations	(27,880)	(109,694)	(222,702)	(476,078)
Loss from discontinued operations, net of tax	(96)	(148)	(472)	(1,893)
Net loss	$(27,976)	$(109,842)	$(223,174)	$(477,971)

EXHIBIT 11

CONSOLIDATED
BALANCE SHEETS,
2009 Q-3 10-Q

BEAZER HOMES USA, INC.
(in thousands, except share and per share data)

	June 30, 2009	September 30, 2008
ASSETS		
Cash and cash equivalents	$464,949	$584,334
Restricted cash	11,902	297
Accounts receivable (net of allowance of $6,129 and $8,915, respectively)	26,185	46,555
Income tax receivable	13,957	173,500
Inventory		
Owned inventory	1,397,181	1,545,006
Consolidated inventory not owned	58,542	106,655
Total inventory	1,455,723	1,651,661
Investments in unconsolidated joint ventures	29,905	33,065
Deferred tax assets	22,109	20,216
Property, plant and equipment, net	30,071	39,822
Goodwill	—	16,143
Other assets	53,788	76,206
Total assets	$2,108,589	$2,641,799
LIABILITIES AND STOCKHOLDERS' EQUITY		
Trade accounts payable	$76,461	$90,371
Other liabilities	248,973	358,592
Obligations related to consolidated inventory not owned	31,764	70,608
Senior notes (net of discounts of $2,013 and $2,565, respectively)	1,407,486	1,522,435
Junior subordinated notes	103,093	103,093
Other secured notes payable	34,122	50,618
Model home financing obligations	46,908	71,231
Total liabilities	1,948,807	2,266,948
Stockholders' equity:		
Preferred stock (par value $.01 per share, 5,000,000 shares authorized, no shares issued)	—	—
Common stock (par value $0.001 per share, 80,000,000 shares authorized, 42,605,804 and 42,612,801 issued and 39,248,648 and 39,270,038 outstanding, respectively)	43	43
Paid-in capital	565,037	556,910
Retained earnings (accumulated deficit)	(221,329)	1,845
Treasury stock, at cost (3,357,156 and 3,342,763 shares, respectively)	(183,969)	(183,947)
Total stockholders' equity	159,782	374,851
Total liabilities and stockholders' equity	$2,108,589	$2,641,799

See Notes to Unaudited Condensed Consolidated Financial Statements.

EXHIBIT 12

STATEMENTS OF
CASH FLOWS, 2009
Q-3 10-Q

BEAZER HOMES USA, INC.
(in thousands)

	Nine Months Ended June 30	
	2009	**2008**
Cash flows from operating activities:		
Net loss	**$(223,174)**	$(477,971)
Adjustments to reconcile net loss to net cash provided by operating activities:		
Depreciation and amortization	**13,079**	18,415
Stock-based compensation expense	**8,865**	8,694
Inventory impairments and option contract abandonments	**76,320**	451,854
Goodwill impairment	**16,143**	52,470
Deferred income tax benefit	**(1,893)**	(118,817)
Excess tax benefit from equity-based compensation	**2,267**	454
Equity in loss of unconsolidated joint ventures	**13,795**	75,069
Cash distributions of income from unconsolidated joint ventures	**2,991**	2,096
Gain on extinguishment of debt	**(58,788)**	—
Provision for doubtful accounts	**(2,786)**	3,349
Changes in operating assets and liabilities:		
Decrease (increase) in accounts receivable	**23,156**	(8,996)
Decrease (increase) in income tax receivable	**159,543**	(80,563)
Decrease in inventory	**90,833**	261,324
Decrease in other assets	**21,832**	41,324
Decrease in trade accounts payable	**(13,910)**	(28,176)
Decrease in other liabilities	**(126,760)**	(169,673)
Other changes	**(13)**	(6,354)
Net cash provided by operating activities	**1,500**	24,499
Cash flows from investing activities:		
Capital expenditures	**(5,484)**	(7,949)
Investments in unconsolidated joint ventures	**(9,042)**	(11,137)
Changes in restricted cash	**(11,605)**	4,268
Net cash used in investing activities	**(26,131)**	(14,818)
Cash flows from financing activities:		
Repurchase of Senior Notes	**(54,836)**	—
Repayment of other secured notes payable	**(11,995)**	(100,472)
Repayment of model home financing obligations	**(24,323)**	(27,728)
Debt issuance costs	**(1,311)**	(21,135)
Common stock redeemed	**(22)**	(27)
Excess tax benefit from equity-based compensation	**(2,267)**	(454)
Net cash used in financing activities	**(94,754)**	(149,816)
Decrease in cash and cash equivalents	**(119,385)**	(140,135)
Cash and cash equivalents at beginning of period	**584,334**	454,337
Cash and cash equivalents at end of period	**$464,949**	$314,202

See Notes to Unaudited Condensed Consolidated Financial Statements.

Corporate Governance at IBM and Google

IBM and Google are two of the most successful firms in the history of business. Since the demise of Bell Laboratories following the breakup of AT&T, IBM has had the world's leading corporate research labs. Five IBM scientists have won Nobel Prizes in physics (compared with 12 from Bell Labs), and every year since at least 1992 IBM employees have been granted more patents than employees at any other firm in the world.[1] More importantly, some technology analysts consider IBM's research more fundamental, yet more practical, and its patents more valuable, than those of most competitors.

Google was founded in 1998 by two Stanford computer science graduate students, Larry Page and Sergey Brin, at the start of the Internet boom. Google quickly became the world's dominant search engine and gained widespread fame for its corporate culture. Google offered employees free healthy lunches and dinners, and snack tables were spread throughout the firm's offices. Google buildings included space for bicycles, pets, pool and foosball tables, volleyball courts, and gyms. The firm offered employees free massages, meditation classes, and yoga sessions. Employees were encouraged to spend 20% of their time at work on projects of their choice, which led to innovative developments and motivated employees.

IBM

Back in 1890, the U.S. Census Bureau estimated it would need 10 years to compile the information obtained in the 1890 census.[2] The Census Bureau sponsored a contest for an improved way to process that data. In response, Henry Hollerith invented a three-part system that included (1) a keypunch machine with an alpha-numeric keyboard used to punch holes into a card; (2) the Hollerith code, which associated various hole sequences with the 10 Arabic numerals and the 26 letters of the English alphabet; and (3) a machine that read the punched cards and tabulated the results. His machines were used to complete the census in three months. Mr. Hollerith then founded the Tabulating Machine Company in 1896. For that work, Mr. Hollerith received a patent in 1889 and a Columbia University PhD in 1890. In 1911, his firm merged with two others to form the Computing-Tabulating-Recording Company, which changed its name to International Business Machines Company in 1924.[3]

In both 1992 and 1993, IBM reported operating losses of about $9 billion (Exhibit 1). There were calls for IBM to sell unprofitable business units, and there was even concern that IBM might be forced into bankruptcy. In 1993, IBM hired Louis V. Gerstner, Jr., who dramatically changed IBM's operations and focus.[4] Within a year, he returned IBM to

---

1. "IFI patent intelligence analysis of 2008's top U.S.-patent recipients suggests America may be losing dominance," Wolters Kluwer Health. http://www.ificlaims.com/IFIPatents010909.htm.

2. Information for this section from IBM Archives: Valuable Resources on IBM's History. http://www-03.ibm.com/ibm/history/.

3. See Columbia University history, http://www.columbia.edu/acis/history/hollerith.html. Also see IBM history, http://www-03.ibm.com/ibm/history/documents/pdf/1885–1969.pdf.

4. Lagace, Martha, Gerstner: Changing Culture at IBM—Lou Gerstner Discusses Changing the Culture at IBM. Harvard Business School. Archive. http://hbswk.hbs.edu/archive/3209.html.

profitability and soon transformed IBM from primarily a computer manufacturer into a firm that provided information technology (IT) services throughout the world. In the mid-1990s, data processing became so complex that many large organizations outsourced their entire IT departments. IBM was one of the few firms in the world large enough and skilled enough to manage those projects. That work was highly profitable, but by the late 1990s IBM's service operations faced severe competition, first from large Indian IT firms such as Infosys Technologies and Wipro Limited and then from Hewlett Packard.

For at least the past 40 years IBM has been one of the world's most respected companies. However, because it faced various competitive challenges from Microsoft, Indian IT firms, and Hewlett Packard, IBM was forced to take actions to reduce costs, and many of those actions were widely criticized (see below). In July 2003, IBM invited all 319,000 of its employees throughout the world to engage in an open "values jam" on its global intranet. Tens of thousands of employees offered comments about the company over a three-day period. That discussion produced IBM's current corporate value statement (Exhibit 2).[5] According to that value statement, employees were brutally honest, and some of what they wrote was painful for management to read.

Exhibit 2 states that IBM's stock price must increase by 10% before IBM's 300 most senior executives benefit from their employee stock options. In addition, the executives must first invest their own funds in IBM stock before they can buy stock under IBM's executive stock option plan. The corporate values statement mentions that this requirement is unique in the computer industry and possibly in all of U.S. business. Although IBM's value statement is more restrictive than most values statements for U.S. companies, IBM has received criticism for some of its actions during the past 10 years.

Pension dispute

Like most large companies founded prior to the 1990s, IBM included a defined benefit pension plan for all employees as part of its compensation package.[6] IBM terminated its defined benefit pension plan in 1999 and transferred all employees to a cash balance pension plan.[7] Employees filed a class action lawsuit against IBM claiming the plan discriminated against older workers. In 2003, a lower court ruled that IBM's revised pension plan did discriminate against older employees. IBM appealed the case, but to limit its maximum exposure it agreed to pay plaintiffs $320 million. If IBM lost on appeal, it agreed to pay an additional $1.4 billion (i.e., plaintiffs agreed to a $1.4 billion additional payment as a cap). In 2007, IBM won its appeal, although the $320 million payment was not returned because of the contractual agreement.[8]

Overtime dispute

Under the U.S. Department of Labor's Fair Labor Standards Act, employees in the United States are classified as either exempt or nonexempt employees. Exempt employees are professional or managerial employees who are exempt from the minimum wage laws and from the requirement to be paid at least one and one-half times

---

5. IBM, Our Values at Work on Being an IBMer. http://www.ibm.com/ibm/values/us/.

6. A defined benefit plan pays employees a fixed monthly pension based on years worked, average earnings over the last few years of employment, and retirement age. If the pension fund suffers investment losses, IBM must contribute additional cash to make up for the shortfall. In contrast, with a defined contribution plan, such as a 401k plan, an employer's only obligation is to make a specified contribution each year to each employee's retirement fund.

7. Some companies began offering a third option in the mid-1990s, called a cash balance plan. It is similar to a defined contribution plan, but the employer guarantees a specified annual return on its contributions.

8. Taub, Stephen, "IBM pension ruling stands," January 16, 2007. *CFO.* http://www.cfo.com/article.cfm/8546414.

the regular rate of pay if they work more than 40 hours during a seven-day period. Nonexempt employees must be paid at least the federal minimum wage ($7.25 per hour as of July 24, 2009) and must be paid overtime.[9]

In late 2007 IBM reclassified several thousand technical employees from non-exempt status to exempt status, which eliminated the requirement that they be paid for overtime (work in excess of 40 hours per week). In a class action lawsuit, employees claimed IBM illegally reclassified them as exempt workers to avoid paying them over-time. As part of a negotiated settlement, IBM agreed to reclassify 8,000 workers back to nonexempt status but to reduce their base salaries by 15% to make IBM salaries competitive with other salaries in the computer industry.[10]

IBM mainframes

Computers that use either Microsoft Windows or versions of the UNIX operating sys-tem are widely used by businesses, governmental organizations, and individuals throughout the world. However, IBM mainframe computers are still the computer of choice and necessity at many large organizations that must maintain data integrity and near-zero downtime. IBM sells both the mainframes and the operating systems that run those mainframes. The mainframe computers are highly profitable because there is no real alternative for many large-scale organizations.

Several large Japanese firms and a few U.S. start-ups developed mainframe computers that could run IBM's mainframe operating systems. Because IBM has such a high markup on its mainframes, those potential competitors could sell their products at substantially lower prices than those from IBM.

However, IBM continues to dominate the mainframe computing market because it refuses to sell its mainframe operating systems to firms that do not also purchase IBM mainframes. In October 2009, the U.S. Department of Justice (DOJ) began an investigation into whether IBM abused its monopoly position in the mainframe computer market. As part of its investigation, the DOJ may investigate IBM's purchase of Platform Solutions, a firm that developed software to mimic IBM's mainframe operating system. IBM first sued Platform Solutions but then acquired the firm for $150 million and discontinued Platform Solution's software.[11]

Google

Google began in a proverbial Silicon Valley garage.[12,13] As Google built what is by far the world's most popular search engine, it concurrently developed a way to sell advertising through its search results. Google earned $184 million in pre-tax profits in 2002 and $5.85 billion in pre-tax profits in 2008, the most rapid profit growth in the history of business by a wide margin.

Google is widely praised as one of the world's most ethical and socially respon-sible firms. Its motto, "Don't be evil," seemed to be a mantra for the firm's young employees, many of them highly idealistic. Google's value statement (Exhibit 3) was more than a listing of the firm's values. It was almost a call to improve the world.

---

9. U.S. Department of Labor Web site.

10. McDougall, Paul, "IBM responds to overtime lawsuits with 15% salary cuts," *InformationWeek,* January 23, 2008. http://www.informationweek.com/news/global-cio/compensation/showArticle. jhtml?articleID=205917177.

11. Vance, Ashlee, and Steve Lohr, "U.S. begins antitrust inquiry of IBM," *The New York Times,* October 7, 2009.

12. Google Corporate Information, Google Milestones. http://www.google.com/corporate/history.html.

13. Owned by Susan Wojcicki, now a Google VP of product management. Her sister, Anne, and Mr. Brin married in 2007.

Google's 2008 revenues increased by 31% from 2007 but, partially because of a $1.1 billion impairment charge for Clearwire and AOL equity investments, Google's 2008 operating income exceeded 2007 operating income by only 3.2%.

Revenues for the first three quarters of 2009 were only 5.5% higher than the first three quarters of 2008. However, because of firm-wide cost cuts, including Google's first ever employee count reduction (by only 2.3%), Google's operating income before tax increased by 22%. Like IBM, Google has recently been criticized for some of its actions.

Dual classes of stock

Google first issued stock to the public in August 2004. Google separated its equity ownership into two classes of stock. The A shares, which were sold to the public, have one vote per share; the B shares, primarily owned by cofounders Sergey Brin and Larry Page—and CEO Eric Schmidt—have 10 votes per share. Dual class common stock has been relatively common in the newspaper industry (*The New York Times* and, prior to its acquisition by News Corp, *Dow Jones/The Wall Street Journal*). It has also been used by some family-controlled firms, such as Molex Inc.

Google's founders stated that they wanted to control the firm to avoid quarterly earnings pressure from security analysts.[14] In 2006, shareholders proposed that Google eliminate its two classes of stock, but the founders rejected that proposal.

Google rankings

One of the most popular and important features of Google's search engine is its ranking system, which ranks sites by popularity. However, if a site competes with Google, Google has the ability to lower the ranking of that site when a user enters a term related to the other site. In March 2006, KinderStart, a directory and search engine for information related to children, which competed with Google in some areas, sued Google for anticompetitive acts. KinderStart had been ranked in the top 10 results when users entered terms related to children. Google reduced KinderStart's ranking to zero, and KinderStart's advertising business declined by approximately 70%. The judge dismissed that lawsuit in July 2006 but gave KinderStart an option to amend and then refile its lawsuit against Google.[15]

Google Books

Google Books is a project to scan, digitize, and preserve all of the world's written knowledge. As part of that project, Google entered into agreements with many of the world's major libraries to scan their entire inventories of printed books.

Copyright laws prevent individuals or organizations from copying material without the written permission of the copyright holder (person or organization). Copyright laws have changed over the years and now vary by type of writing. In general, since January 1, 1978, copyrights last for the author's life, plus 70 years. Since 1922, most copyrights have lasted for about that long.

Of the millions of books in print, most have been published since 1922, and most of those are orphan books. That is, the copyright holder either cannot be located or identified. The copyright may be owned by a publisher long out of business, or a deceased author may have owned the copyright but it may be difficult or impossible to locate

14. Valdmanis, Thor, "Google IPO's two classes of stock raise questions," *USA Today*, May 16, 2004. http://www.usatoday.com/money/industries/technology/2004-05-16-google-nonvoting_x.htm.

15. Mills, Elinor, "Judge dismisses suit over Google ranking," *CNET News*, July 13, 2006. http://news.cnet.com/Judge-dismisses-suit-over-Google-ranking/2100-1030_3-6094132.html.

the heirs. To avoid the potential copyright infringement issues associated with these orphan books, Google entered into a legal settlement with groups representing publishers and authors. Google agreed to pay those groups $125 million and also give identified copyright holders 63% of all revenue from the sale of orphaned works.[16]

Many Google competitors worry that this will give Google a significant advantage in targeting its advertising. The American Civil Liberties Union (ACLU) and various other organizations objected to the settlement because of privacy concerns. They worry Google Books will give Google unique insight into the reading habits of those who download books.

The U.S. Department of Justice, several European countries, and some members of the U.S. Senate and House of Representatives are concerned that this legal settlement circumvents U.S. and foreign government copyright laws. The U.S. DOJ stated that the settlement would provide benefits to the public but also raises significant issues regarding class action, copyright, and antitrust laws.[17]

The agreement has been widely criticized throughout Europe, including in a speech by German Chancellor Angela Merkel, who said the German government strongly opposed Google Books, a project so secret that Google will not allow anyone to observe how it scans books.[18]

In response, Google cofounder Sergey Brin published an editorial, "A Library to Last Forever," in *The New York Times* on October 8, 2009.[19] Mr. Brin passionately argued that Google Books is primarily an altruistic effort by Google to make books available to the public that would otherwise be lost forever. He strongly defended the settlement because it allows payment to authors who would otherwise receive nothing for their work and because it allows any other company an equal opportunity to scan orphan books.

On December 18, 2009, a French court ruled that Google Books violates France's copyright laws. A French court fined Google €300,000 ($431,000), plus €10,000 ($14,300) per day until it stops providing viewers with portions of the scanned books. The lawsuit, brought by French publishing houses, accused Google of offering free searchable portions of copyrighted books. In doing so, Google earns advertising revenues without adequately compensating copyright holders.[20]

Google Voice

Google developed an iPhone application to let iPhone owners use Google Voice, a voice over Internet protocol (VoIP) that provides free instant messaging and low-cost long distance calling over Google voice lines. Apple initially rejected the application, which would directly reduce AT&T revenues and indirectly reduce Apple revenues because the iPhone is apparently heavily subsidized by AT&T.

---

16. Gain, Bruce, Opposition to Aspects of Google Book Project Settlement Mounts, Intellectual Property Watch, September 18, 2009. http://www.ip-watch.org/weblog/2009/09/18/opposition-to-aspects-of-google-book-project-settlement-mounts/.

17. Helft, Miguel, "Government urges changes to Google Books deal," *The New York Times*, September 18, 2009. http://www.nytimes.com/2009/09/19/technology/internet/19google.html.

18. Doward, Jamie, and Paul Harris, "Google digital library plan opposed by Angela Merkel," *The Observer*, Sunday 11 October 2009. http://www.guardian.co.uk/technology/2009/oct/11/google-digital-library-merkel-opposition.

19. Brin, Sergey," A library to last forever," (opinion), *New York Times*, October 8, 2009. http://www.nytimes.com/2009/10/09/opinion/09brin.html.

20. Reuters, "Google fined by French court," *CNNMoney.com*, December 18, 2009. http://money.cnn.com/2009/12/18/news/international/google_france.reut/index.htm.

In July 2009 the U.S. Federal Communications Commission (FCC) announced it would investigate Apple's rejection of the Google application. In response, in October 2009, AT&T stated it would not object to third-party VoIP applications such as Skype and Google Voice.[21] However, AT&T did file a complaint with the FCC against Google Voice. The FCC announced it would investigate whether Google Voice violates telecommunications laws because it blocks calls to some rural areas and call services with high fees, fees that AT&T and other telephone companies must pay.[22]

Google Street View

Google Street View is a project to eventually show street views of nearly any street in the world. For example, a user can obtain directions from one location to another using Google Maps. The directions are shown by number on the left of the resulting Web page. To the right of each direction, when available, is a camera icon. Clicking on the icon shows a photograph of a street view at that location. Below the photograph is a map with a person icon. By moving the person icon, the street view photograph moves along the street, as it would be seen by a person standing where the person icon is located.[23]

The street view feature can be very useful to individuals in an unfamiliar location and to businesses that wish to provide directions for their customers. However, many individuals and governments complained about the invasion of privacy. In the United States, Google initially removed identifiable faces of individuals at their request. In some countries, it is illegal to show an identifiable face, which is considered an invasion of privacy.[24] Switzerland filed a suit to block all Google Street Views; other countries, including England, Germany, Greece, and Japan, have asked or forced Google to hide faces, building numbers, license plates, or views inside residences.[25]

Nexus One

Google introduce the Android operating system for mobile phones in 2007. It is an open-source operating system that can be modified and upgraded by programmers throughout the world, is based on the Linux operating system, and is free. In February 2009, HTC, a major Taiwanese electronics manufacturer, introduced the first mobile phones based on Android.[26] On September 10, 2009, Motorola introduced its first Android-based mobile phone, the Cliq.[27] Motorola introduced its second Android-based phone, the Droid, in October 2009, the first mobile phone to use Google's Android 2.0 operating system.[28]

---

21. Reuters, "AT&T allows Internet voice calls on Apple's iPhone," October 6, 2009. http://www.reuters.com/article/technologyNews/idUSTRE5956SA20091007?feedType=RSS&feedName=technologyNews.

22. Kang, Cecilia, "FCC begins inquiry into Google Voice," *The Washington Post*, October 9, 2009. http://voices.washingtonpost.com/posttech/2009/10/fcc_begins_inquiry_into_google.html.

23. See Google Maps and Google Street View directions on Google's Web site.

24. "Google faces 'Street View Block'," *BBC News,* July 4, 2008. http://news.bbc.co.uk/2/hi/7488524.stm.

25. The Associated Press, "Swiss privacy agency top sue Google over street view," *The New York Times,* November 13, 2009. http://www.nytimes.com/2009/11/14/technology/companies/14google.html?ref=global-home.

26. Culpan, Tim, "Google Android may run Asus Netbook, Rival Microsoft," Bloomberg Press, February 20, 2009. http://www.bloomberg.com/apps/news?sid=a070KzBQtm_U&pid=20601080.

27. "Motorola introduces Android phone," Bloomberg UTV, September 11, 2009. http://www.bloomber-gutv.com/utvilife/latest-electronic-gadgets/31801/motorola-introduces-android-phone.html.

28. Reardon, Marguerite, "Can the Droid save Motorola?", *CNET News*, October 30, 2009.

On January 7, 2010, Google announced it would sell its own mobile phone, the Nexus One produced by HTC, through its Web site for an unbundled price of $529, or $179 with a T-Mobile phone contract. That announcement drew immediate criticism for several reasons. Motorola licensed the name *Droid* from George Lucas, who had trademarked "Droid" from his Star Wars movies. The family of Philip K. Dick planned to file suit against Google because it claimed Google had taken the name *Nexus* from Dick's novel *Do Androids Dream of Electric Sheep?* That novel, the basis of the movie *Blade Runner,* featured a series of Nexus 6 model robots. In its defense, Google claimed it was using Nexus in the more general sense of a place where things converge.[29]

Google also received criticism because it was competing against mobile phone manufacturers who developed the market for Android. They were now being undercut by Google, which was offering the first mobile phone to use Android 2.1, an operating system upgrade announced the same day as Nexus One, although Google's Android Web site stated that "Android 2.1 does not add significant user features . . . ."[30] The Nexus One could only be purchased through Google's Web site. The prominent ad placement, just below the search field on Google's home page, seemed to give the Nexus One a significant advantage over other Android-based mobile phones, such as Motorola's.

Users could buy the Nexus One for $179 bundled with T-Mobile service, but only for new T-Mobile customers, which upset existing T-Mobile customers. Finally, there were widespread complaints about customer service. Service was available only through Google online, primarily through Google-monitored user help forums. Users who called HTC or T-Mobile were directed to Google's Web site, with no option to talk to a live operator. The Nexus One was considered a potent competitor to Apple's iPhone, but Apple has excellent iPhone customer service through its stores, live support, online support, and through AT&T.

Google China

On January 12, 2010, Google filed a Form 8-K with the SEC that contained the following announcement (see Exhibit 4).

> On January 12, 2010, Google posted on the Official Google Blog an announcement that it was the target of a cyber attack and that it will be reviewing the feasibility of its business operations in China. A copy of the blogpost is filed as Exhibit 99.1 to this Form 8-K and is incorporated herein by reference.

Required

1. Would IBM's value statements have caused IBM to act differently in the three situations described in the case? Explain.

2. Are Google's actions in the situations described in the case consistent with Google's value statements? Explain.

3. Compare and contrast the IBM and Google value statements. Do the two values statements have different purposes? Are they appropriate for IBM and Google?

4. Should a for-profit organization have a values statement? If so, what should be its purpose?

---

29. Raphael, F.R., "Google's Nexus One faces new woes," *PC World*, January 8, 2009.

30. Google, Android 2.1, Release 1, January 2010. http://developer.android.com/sdk/android-2.1.html.

INTERNATIONAL BUSINESS MACHINES CORPORATION
(millions)

Year ended Dec 31	Revenue*			Total revenue	Income from continuing ops before tax
	Services	Sales	Financing		
1991	$12,996	$47,591	$4,179	$64,766	($118)
1992	$14,987	$44,858	$4,678	$64,523	($9,026)
1993	$17,006	$41,544	$4,166	$62,716	($8,797)
1994	$16,937	$43,690	$3,425	$64,052	$5,155
1995	$20,123	$48,257	$3,560	$71,940	$7,813
1996	$22,854	$49,368	$3,725	$75,947	$8,587
1997	$25,166	$47,794	$5,548	$78,508	$9,027
1998	$28,916	$47,282	$5,469	$81,667	$9,040
1999	$32,172	$49,703	$5,673	$87,548	$11,757
2000	$33,152	$47,068	$4,869	$85,089	$11,411
2001	$34,956	$43,532	$4,579	$83,067	$11,450
2002	$36,360	$40,530	$4,296	$81,186	$7,524
2003	$42,635	$42,550	$3,946	$89,131	$9,417
2004	$46,213	$46,248	$3,832	$96,293	$10,669
2005	$47,357	$40,067	$3,710	$91,134	$12,226
2006	$48,328	$40,716	$2,379	$91,423	$13,317
2007	$54,057	$42,202	$2,526	$98,785	$14,489
2008	$58,892	$42,156	$2,582	$103,630	$16,715

*Revenue breakdown may not always be consistent from year-to-year

GOOGLE INC.
(thousands)

	Total revenue	Income from continuing ops before tax
2002	$439,508	$184,915
2003	$1,465,934	$346,654
2004	$3,189,223	$650,234
2005	$6,138,560	$2,141,677
2006	$10,604,917	$4,011,040
2007	$16,593,986	$5,673,980
2008	$21,795,550	$5,853,596

Business Value, and a Company's Values

We've been spending a great deal of time thinking, debating and determining the fundamentals of this company. It has been important to do so. When IBMers have been crystal clear and united about our strategies and purpose, it's amazing what we've been able to create and accomplish. When we've been uncertain, conflicted or hesitant, we've squandered opportunities and even made blunders that would have sunk smaller companies.

It may not surprise you, then, that last year we examined IBM's core values for the first time since the company's founding. In this time of great change, we needed to affirm IBM's reason for being, what sets the company apart and what should drive our actions as individual IBMers.

Importantly, we needed to find a way to engage everyone in the company and get them to speak up on these important issues. Given the realities of a smart, global, independent-minded, 21st-century workforce like ours, I don't believe something as vital and personal as values could be dictated from the top.

So, for 72 hours last summer, we invited all 319,000 IBMers around the world to engage in an open "values jam" on our global intranet. IBMers by the tens of thousands weighed in. They were thoughtful and passionate about the company they want to be a part of. They were also brutally honest. Some of what they wrote was painful to read because they pointed out all the bureaucratic and dysfunctional things that get in the way of serving clients, working as a team or implementing new ideas. But we were resolute in keeping the dialog free-flowing and candid. And I don't think what resulted—broad, enthusiastic, grass-roots consensus—could have been obtained in any other way.

In the end, IBMers determined that our actions will be driven by these values:

- Dedication to every client's success
- Innovation that matters, for our company and for the world
- Trust and personal responsibility in all relationships

I must tell you, this process has been very meaningful to me. We are getting back in touch with what IBM has always been about—and always will be about—in a very concrete way. And I feel that I've been handed something every CEO craves: a mandate, for exactly the right kinds of transformation, from an entire workforce.

Where will this lead? It is a work in progress, and many of the implications remain to be discovered. What I can tell you is that we are rolling up our sleeves to bring IBM's values to life in our policies, procedures and daily operations.

I've already touched on a number of things relating to clients and innovation, but our values of trust and personal responsibility are being managed just as seriously—from changes in how we measure and reward performance, to how we equip and support IBMers' community volunteerism.

Our values underpin our relationships with investors, as well. In late February, the board of directors approved sweeping changes in executive compensation. They include innovative programs that ensure investors first receive meaningful returns—a 10 percent increase in the stock price—before IBM's top 300 executives can realize a penny of profit from their stock option grants. Putting that into perspective, IBM's market value would have to increase by $17 billion before executives saw any benefit from this year's option awards. In addition, these executives will be able to acquire market-priced stock options only if they first invest their own money in IBM stock. We believe these programs are unprecedented, certainly in our industry and perhaps in business.

EXHIBIT 2

OUR VALUES AT
WORK ON BEING AN
IBMER

(continued)

EXHIBIT 2—
continued

OUR VALUES AT
WORK ON BEING AN
IBMER

Clearly, leading by values is very different from some kinds of leadership demonstrated in the past by business. It is empowering, and I think that's much healthier. Rather than burden our people with excessive controls, we are trusting them to make decisions and to act based on values—values they themselves shaped.

To me, it's also just common sense. In today's world, where everyone is so interconnected and interdependent, it is simply essential that we work for each other's success. If we're going to solve the biggest, thorniest and most widespread problems in business and society, we have to innovate in ways that truly matter. And we have to do all this by taking personal responsibility for all of our relationships—with clients, colleagues, partners, investors and the public at large. This is IBM's mission as an enterprise, and a goal toward which we hope to work with many others, in our industry and beyond.

Samuel J. Palmisano
Chairman, President and Chief Executive Officer

From: Our Values at Work on Being an IBMer. http://www.ibm.com/ibm/values/us/.

EXHIBIT 3

GOOGLE: OUR
PHILOSOPHY

Never Settle for the Best

"The perfect search engine," says Google co-founder Larry Page, "would understand exactly what you mean and give back exactly what you want." Given the state of search technology today, that's a far-reaching vision requiring research, development and innovation to realize. Google is committed to blazing that trail. Though acknowledged as the world's leading search technology company, Google's goal is to provide a much higher level of service to all those who seek information, whether they're at a desk in Boston, driving through Bonn, or strolling in Bangkok.

To that end, Google has persistently pursued innovation and pushed the limits of existing technology to provide a fast, accurate and easy-to-use search service that can be accessed from anywhere. To fully understand Google, it's helpful to understand all the ways in which the company has helped to redefine how individuals, businesses and technologists view the Internet.

Ten Things Google has found to be true

1. Focus on the user and all else will follow.

From its inception, Google has focused on providing the best user experience possible. While many companies claim to put their customers first, few are able to resist the temptation to make small sacrifices to increase shareholder value. Google has steadfastly refused to make any change that does not offer a benefit to the users who come to the site:

- The interface is clear and simple.
- Pages load instantly.
- Placement in search results is never sold to anyone.
- Advertising on the site must offer relevant content and not be a distraction.

By always placing the interests of the user first, Google has built the most loyal audience on the web. And that growth has come not through TV ad campaigns, but through word of mouth from one satisfied user to another.

2. It's best to do one thing really, really well.

Google does search. With one of the world's largest research groups focused exclusively on solving search problems, we know what we do well, and how we could do it better. Through continued iteration on difficult problems, we've been able to solve complex issues and provide continuous improvements to a service already considered the best on the web at making finding information a fast and seamless experience for millions of users. Our dedication to improving search has also allowed us to apply what we've learned to new products, including Gmail, Google Desktop, and Google Maps. As we continue to build new products* while making search better, our hope is to bring the power of search to previously unexplored areas, and to help users access and use even more of the ever-expanding information in their lives.

3. Fast is better than slow.

Google believes in instant gratification. You want answers and you want them right now. Who are we to argue? Google may be the only company in the world whose stated goal is to have

---

*Full-disclosure update: When we first wrote these "10 things" four years ago, we included the phrase "Google does not do horoscopes, financial advice or chat." Over time we've expanded our view of the range of services we can offer—web search, for instance, isn't the only way for people to access or use information—and products that then seemed unlikely are now key aspects of our portfolio. This doesn't mean we've changed our core mission; just that the farther we travel toward achieving it, the more those blurry objects on the horizon come into sharper focus (to be replaced, of course, by more blurry objects).

(continued)

EXHIBIT 3—
continued

GOOGLE: OUR
PHILOSOPHY

users leave its website as quickly as possible. By fanatically obsessing on shaving every excess bit and byte from our pages and increasing the efficiency of our serving environment, Google has broken its own speed records time and again. Others assumed large servers were the fastest way to handle massive amounts of data. Google found networked PCs to be faster. Where others accepted apparent speed limits imposed by search algorithms, Google wrote new algorithms that proved there were no limits. And Google continues to work on making it all go even faster.

4. Democracy on the web works.

Google works because it relies on the millions of individuals posting websites to determine which other sites offer content of value. Instead of relying on a group of editors or solely on the frequency with which certain terms appear, Google ranks every web page using a breakthrough technique called PageRank™. PageRank evaluates all of the sites linking to a web page and assigns them a value, based in part on the sites linking to them. By analyzing the full structure of the web, Google is able to determine which sites have been "voted" the best sources of information by those most interested in the information they offer. This technique actually improves as the web gets bigger, as each new site is another point of information and another vote to be counted.

5. You don't need to be at your desk to need an answer.

The world is increasingly mobile and unwilling to be constrained to a fixed location. Whether it's through their PDAs, their wireless phones or even their automobiles, people want information to come to them. Google's innovations in this area include Google Number Search, which reduces the number of keypad strokes required to find data from a web-enabled cellular phone and an on-the-fly translation system that converts pages written in HTML to a format that can be read by phone browsers. This system opens up billions of pages for viewing from devices that would otherwise not be able to display them, including Palm PDAs and Japanese i-mode, J-Sky, and EZWeb devices. Wherever search is likely to help users obtain the information they seek, Google is pioneering new technologies and offering new solutions.

6. You can make money without doing evil.

Google is a business. The revenue the company generates is derived from offering its search technology to companies and from the sale of advertising displayed on Google and on other sites across the web. However, you may have never seen an ad on Google. That's because Google does not allow ads to be displayed on our results pages unless they're relevant to the results page on which they're shown. So, only certain searches produce sponsored links above or to the right of the results. Google firmly believes that ads can provide useful information if, and only if, they are relevant to what you wish to find.

Google has also proven that advertising can be effective without being flashy. Google does not accept pop-up advertising, which interferes with your ability to see the content you've requested. We've found that text ads (AdWords) that are relevant to the person reading them draw much higher clickthrough rates than ads appearing randomly. Google's maximization group works with advertisers to improve clickthrough rates over the life of a campaign, because high clickthrough rates are an indication that ads are relevant to a user's interests. Any advertiser, no matter how small or how large, can take advantage of this highly targeted medium, whether through our self-service advertising program that puts ads online within minutes, or with the assistance of a Google advertising representative.

Advertising on Google is always clearly identified as a "Sponsored Link." It is a core value for Google that there be no compromising of the integrity of our results. We never manipulate

(*continued*)

EXHIBIT 3—
continued

GOOGLE: OUR
PHILOSOPHY

rankings to put our partners higher in our search results. No one can buy better PageRank. Our users trust Google's objectivity and no short-term gain could ever justify breaching that trust.

Thousands of advertisers use our Google AdWords program to promote their products; we believe AdWords is the largest program of its kind. In addition, thousands of web site managers take advantage of our Google AdSense program to deliver ads relevant to the content on their sites, improving their ability to generate revenue and enhancing the experience for their users.

7. There's always more information out there.

Once Google had indexed more of the HTML pages on the Internet than any other search service, our engineers turned their attention to information that was not as readily accessible. Sometimes it was just a matter of integrating new databases, such as adding a phone number and address lookup and a business directory. Other efforts required a bit more creativity, like adding the ability to search billions of images and a way to view pages that were originally created as PDF files. The popularity of PDF results led us to expand the list of file types searched to include documents produced in a dozen formats such as Microsoft Word, Excel and PowerPoint. For wireless users, Google developed a unique way to translate HTML formatted files into a format that could be read by mobile devices. The list is not likely to end there as Google's researchers continue looking into ways to bring all the world's information to users seeking answers.

8. The need for information crosses all borders.

Though Google is headquartered in California, our mission is to facilitate access to information for the entire world, so we have offices around the globe. To that end we maintain dozens of Internet domains and serve more than half of our results to users living outside the United States. Google search results can be restricted to pages written in more than 35 languages according to a user's preference. We also offer a translation feature to make content available to users regardless of their native tongue and for those who prefer not to search in English, Google's interface can be customized into more than 100 languages. To accelerate the addition of new languages, Google offers volunteers the opportunity to help in the translation through an automated tool available on the Google.com website. This process has greatly improved both the variety and quality of service we're able to offer users in even the most far flung corners of the globe.

9. You can be serious without a suit.

Google's founders have often stated that the company is not serious about anything but search. They built a company around the idea that work should be challenging and the challenge should be fun. To that end, Google's culture is unlike any in corporate America, and it's not because of the ubiquitous lava lamps and large rubber balls, or the fact that the company's chef used to cook for the Grateful Dead. In the same way Google puts users first when it comes to our online service, Google Inc. puts employees first when it comes to daily life in our Googleplex headquarters. There is an emphasis on team achievements and pride in individual accomplishments that contribute to the company's overall success. Ideas are traded, tested and put into practice with an alacrity that can be dizzying. Meetings that would take hours elsewhere are frequently little more than a conversation in line for lunch and few walls separate those who write the code from those who write the checks. This highly communicative environment fosters a productivity and camaraderie fueled by the realization that millions of people rely on Google results. Give the proper tools to a group of people who like to make a difference, and they will.

(continued)

EXHIBIT 3—
continued

GOOGLE: OUR
PHILOSOPHY

10. Great just isn't good enough.

Always deliver more than expected. Google does not accept being the best as an endpoint, but a starting point. Through innovation and iteration, Google takes something that works well and improves upon it in unexpected ways. Search works well for properly spelled words, but what about typos? One engineer saw a need and created a spell checker that seems to read a user's mind. It takes too long to search from a WAP phone? Our wireless group developed Google Number Search to reduce entries from three keystrokes per letter to one. With a user base in the millions, Google is able to identify points of friction quickly and smooth them out. Google's point of distinction however, is anticipating needs not yet articulated by our global audience, then meeting them with products and services that set new standards. This constant dissatisfaction with the way things are is ultimately the driving force behind the world's best search engine.

From: Google Corporate Information page, http://www.google.co.uk/corporate/tenthings.html.

EXHIBIT 4

A New Approach
to China

1/12/2010 03:00:00 PM

Like many other well-known organizations, we face cyber attacks of varying degrees on a regular basis. In mid-December, we detected a highly sophisticated and targeted attack on our corporate infrastructure originating from China that resulted in the theft of intellectual property from Google. However, it soon became clear that what at first appeared to be solely a security incident—albeit a significant one—was something quite different.

First, this attack was not just on Google. As part of our investigation we have discovered that at least twenty other large companies from a wide range of businesses—including the Internet, finance, technology, media and chemical sectors—have been similarly targeted. We are currently in the process of notifying those companies, and we are also working with the relevant U.S. authorities.

Second, we have evidence to suggest that a primary goal of the attackers was accessing the Gmail accounts of Chinese human rights activists. Based on our investigation to date we believe their attack did not achieve that objective. Only two Gmail accounts appear to have been accessed, and that activity was limited to account information (such as the date the account was created) and subject line, rather than the content of emails themselves.

Third, as part of this investigation but independent of the attack on Google, we have discovered that the accounts of dozens of U.S.-, China- and Europe-based Gmail users who are advocates of human rights in China appear to have been routinely accessed by third parties. These accounts have not been accessed through any security breach at Google, but most likely via phishing scams or malware placed on the users' computers.

We have already used information gained from this attack to make infrastructure and architectural improvements that enhance security for Google and for our users. In terms of individual users, we would advise people to deploy reputable anti-virus and anti-spyware programs on their computers, to install patches for their operating systems and to update their web browsers. Always be cautious when clicking on links appearing in instant messages and emails, or when asked to share personal information like passwords online. You can read more here about our cyber-security recommendations. People wanting to learn more about these kinds of attacks can read this Report to Congress (PDF) by the U.S.-China Economic and Security Review Commission (see p. 163-), as well as a related analysis (PDF) prepared for the Commission, Nart Villeneuve's blog and this presentation on the GhostNet spying incident.

We have taken the unusual step of sharing information about these attacks with a broad audience not just because of the security and human rights implications of what we have unearthed, but also because this information goes to the heart of a much bigger global debate about freedom of speech. In the last two decades, China's economic reform programs and its citizens' entrepreneurial flair have lifted hundreds of millions of Chinese people out of poverty. Indeed, this great nation is at the heart of much economic progress and development in the world today.

We launched Google.cn in January 2006 in the belief that the benefits of increased access to information for people in China and a more open Internet outweighed our discomfort in agreeing to censor some results. At the time we made clear that "we will carefully monitor conditions in China, including new laws and other restrictions on our services. If we determine that we are unable to achieve the objectives outlined we will not hesitate to reconsider our approach to China."

(continued)

EXHIBIT 4

A NEW APPROACH
TO CHINA

These attacks and the surveillance they have uncovered—combined with the attempts over the past year to further limit free speech on the web—have led us to conclude that we should review the feasibility of our business operations in China. We have decided we are no longer willing to continue censoring our results on Google.cn, and so over the next few weeks we will be discussing with the Chinese government the basis on which we could operate an unfiltered search engine within the law, if at all. We recognize that this may well mean having to shut down Google.cn, and potentially our offices in China.

The decision to review our business operations in China has been incredibly hard, and we know that it will have potentially far-reaching consequences. We want to make clear that this move was driven by our executives in the United States, without the knowledge or involvement of our employees in China who have worked incredibly hard to make Google.cn the success it is today. We are committed to working responsibly to resolve the very difficult issues raised.

From: Google Blog, January 12, 2010, 3:00 p.m. http://googleblog.blogspot.com/2010/01/new-approach-to-china.html.

Chrysler LLC Bankruptcy

Walter P. Chrysler joined General Motors as manager of its Buick manufacturing plant in 1912 and became president of the Buick division four years later. In 1919, he left GM to join the Maxwell Motor Corporation, a failing GM competitor. Under his leadership, Maxwell Motor Corporation returned to profitability and was renamed the Chrysler Corporation. In 1928, Chrysler acquired Dodge Brothers and became the third of Detroit's Big Three automakers.[1]

Chrysler continued to expand until the late 1970s, when Chrysler's financial condition deteriorated and it received a $1.5 billion loan through the federal Chrysler Corporation Loan Guarantee Act of 1979. In 1984, Chrysler developed the enormously popular minivan, repaid its government-backed loans, and returned to profitability.[2] Although Chrysler's profitability fluctuated during the 1980s and 1990s, by late 1990 its profitability was high and steady. In 1997, Daimler Benz acquired Chrysler and renamed itself Daimler Chrysler. During the following decade, Chrysler lost market share, its quality deteriorated, and it suffered major losses. In 2007, Daimler Chrysler sold a majority interest in Chrysler to Cerberus Capital Management, LP, a large New York City-based private equity firm.[3] A year earlier Cerberus had acquired a 51% interest in GMAC, GM's financial subsidiary, which was also in financial difficulty.[4]

Under Cerberus's ownership and the leadership of Robert Nardelli, Chrysler's market share, product quality, and financial condition all quickly improved.[5] However, the worldwide recession, which began in the United States in late 2007, led to a significant decline in auto sales at every major auto manufacturer, including Chrysler. GM and Chrysler both suffered sales declines in excess of 40%, both were on the verge of bankruptcy, and both received U.S. government loans in late 2008 ($9.4 billion to GM and $4 billion to Chrysler).[6]

As the economy worsened in 2009, the U.S. federal government provided Chrysler with an additional $4 billion loan. Given the magnitude of their operating losses, it was clear that both Chrysler and GM would require additional government loans to avoid bankruptcy. However, the federal government demanded significant concessions from both the United Auto Workers (UAW) and Chrysler and GM creditors before it would provide additional funding.

---

1. Chrysler, LLC, One Man's Car Company, The Walter P. Chrysler Story. http://www.chryslerllc.com/en/about_us/our_history/.

2. Ibid.

3. Landler, Mark, and Micheline Maynard, "Chrysler Group to be sold for $7.4 billion," *The New York Times,* May 14, 2007.

4. Press release, Cerberus Capital Management, P.P., GM Reaches Agreement to Sell Controlling Stake in GMAC. http://www.cerberuscapital.com/news_press_release_040306.html

5. Taylor, Alex, III, "The Chrysler steamroller," *Fortune,* February 8, 2008. http://money.cnn.com/2008/02/08/news/companies/taylor_nardelli.fortune/index.htm.

6. Isidore, Chris, "Bush announces auto rescue," *CNNMoney,* December 19, 2008. http://money.cnn.com/2008/12/19/news/companies/auto_crisis/index.htm.

Chrysler Debt

Chrysler was privately held (80.1% by Cerberus and 19.9% by Daimler), so its financial statements are unavailable.[7] However, when Cerberus acquired Chrysler for $7.4 billion in 2007, it apparently did so with only a $500 million equity investment; to complete the funding, Chrysler also issued $6.9 billion of debt secured by all of Chrysler's buildings and equipment.

That debt would have initially been bought by institutional investors such as major banks, pension funds, hedge funds, and university endowments. Some investors, such as some state retirement funds, are only allowed to own investment quality bonds, based on ratings from one of the three major rating agencies (Standard & Poor's, Moody's, and Fitch). Investment grade bonds are those rated BBB or better for Standard & Poor's, the largest rating agency.[8] Those funds must resell the downgraded bonds through the secondary market; lower-rated bonds sold in the secondary market are often acquired by hedge funds or high-yield debt funds (sometimes called junk bond funds), although pension funds and university endowments sometimes buy these lower-rated securities to increase their investment returns.

In the case of Chrysler's secured debt, most was held by the major banks and investment banks that financed Cerberus's acquisition of Chrysler. However, three state of Indiana retiree funds (Indiana State Teachers Retirement Fund, Indiana State Police Pension Trust, and Indiana Major Movers Construction Fund) bought a $100 million Chrysler face value note from JP Morgan Chase for $43.9 million through the secondary market in August 2007, three months after Cerberus acquired Chrysler.[9]

Proposed Sale of Chrysler

Prior to bankruptcy, the U.S. government had demanded that secured bondholders accept a cash payment equal to 29% of the face value of their bonds. The federal government agreed to guarantee existing and future warranties on all Chrysler automobiles and provide up to $8 billion in additional loans to Chrysler. Without the guarantee, many of Chrysler's buildings and much of its equipment would have been worth little because the entire auto industry had collapsed in the worsening recession. Thus, without that guarantee, it seemed highly likely that Chrysler would declare bankruptcy, the warranties on all Chrysler autos would have been cancelled, and secured bondholders might have received less than 29% of the face value of their bonds.

Under the government's proposed reorganization plan, Chrysler would be owned by the U.S. government, the United Auto Workers (UAW), and Fiat. Fiat would acquire 20% of Chrysler's common stock in exchange for Fiat's small car technology, which Chrysler CEO Robert Nardelli estimated to be worth up to $10 billion.[10] Fiat's market capitalization at the time, however, was only about $5.2 billion. The UAW's retiree health-care fund would receive 55% of Chrysler's common stock in exchange for cancelling Chrysler's liability to that fund. The U.S. and Canadian governments would receive the remaining 25% equity in exchange for their loans to Chrysler.

---

7. BBC News, "Chrysler bankruptcy deal revealed," April 30, 2009. http://news.bbc.co.uk/2/hi/8027109.stm.

8. Standard & Poor's RatingsDirect, Understanding Standard & Poor's Rating Definitions, June 3, 2009. http://www2.standardandpoors.com/spf/pdf/fixedincome/Understanding_Rating_Definitions.pdf.

9. Vellequette, Larry P., "Analysis: Indiana pension funds' loss tiny compared to Chrysler's," ToledoBlade.com, June 10, 2009. http://toledoblade.com/apps/pbcs.dll/article?AID=/20090610/BUSINESS02/906100326/-1/BUSINESS07.

10. Reuters, "Chrysler estimates Fiat deal value at up to $10 bln," March 16, 2009. http://www.reuters.com/article/idUSN1651806520090316.

Most Chrysler debt was owned by large financial institutions that had received billions of dollars from the U.S. government's Temporary Asset Relief Program (TARP). The large financial institutions quickly agreed to the offer, as did several hedge funds that may have indirectly received government funds when the United States prevented AIG and other financial intuitions from going bankrupt. However, the three Indiana funds rejected the offer. On May 1, 2009, Chrysler entered into bankruptcy proceedings.[11]

Bankruptcy

Under Section 1129 of the U.S. Bankruptcy Code, secured lenders must be given absolute priority over unsecured lenders and equity holders to have a confirmable bankruptcy plan (see paragraph (b) (2) (A) of Exhibit 1). Bankruptcy judges have considerable flexibility to restructure a bankrupt firm's debt, but it is very rare for unsecured lenders to receive better terms than secured lenders. When Chrysler entered bankruptcy, the U.S. government provided $4.5 billion of debtor in possession (DIP) financing. That is, Chrysler's new equity owners, the debtors, would be allowed to operate Chrysler using a new $4.5 billion loan from the U.S. government (i.e., $4.5 billion of DIP financing, which may have prevented the loss of tens of thousands of jobs in the U.S. auto industry). The U.S. government also agreed to provide $6 billion of financing after Chrysler exited bankruptcy and to fund GMAC for four years to provide wholesale and retail financing for GM and Chrysler.[12]

When Chrysler entered bankruptcy, it had large auto inventories due to the recession. To save cash, it closed its factories and reduced the pay of laid-off UAW members to 80% of their base pay. Even with those reduced costs, Chrysler was still losing $100 million each day.[13] On May 14, Chrysler notified 789 of its 3,181 dealers that they were being terminated and that after Tuesday, June 9, they would no longer have the right to sell new Chrysler vehicles. In many cases, at Chrysler's request, those dealers had upgraded their facilities, acquired other Chrysler dealers, and bought unneeded new Chrysler vehicles to help Chrysler through the recession. Chrysler also stated that it would not repurchase any new vehicles, tools, or parts inventories from terminated dealers but would help them find buyers for those inventories.[14]

Chrysler could have asked the bankruptcy judge to cancel its liabilities to the UAW retiree health-care fund and terminate the defined benefit pension plan for UAW workers, but did not. Federal officials argued that had they terminated the UAW retiree health-care fund liability, Chrysler retirees would have switched to Medicaid, which could have been even more expensive than funding the retiree health-care fund.

On June 1, 2009, highly respected U.S. Bankruptcy Judge Arthur Gonzalez, who handled the Enron and WorldCom bankruptcies, approved the sale of Chrysler to the UAW, Fiat, and the U.S. and Canadian governments, free and clear of all liens and interests. Judge Gonzalez agreed that Chrysler's secured debt holders would receive $2 billion cash in exchange for forgiving $6.9 billion of loans. The bankruptcy-emergent Chrysler left behind all liabilities other than its Chrysler warranty liabilities, pension fund liabilities, and UAW health-care liabilities (replaced by equity in the new

---

11. Rutenbert, Jim, and Bill Vlasic, "Chrysler files to seek bankruptcy protection," *The New York Times*, April 30, 2009. http://www.nytimes.com/2009/05/01/business/01auto.html.

12. The Bankruptcy Litigation Blog. http://www.bankruptcylitigationblog.com/uploads/file/38-41.pdf.

13. De la Merced, Michael J., and Micheline Maynard, "Fiat completes acquisition of Chrysler," *The New York Times,* June 20, 2009.

14. Gupta, Poornima, "Chrysler to terminate 25 percent of U.S. dealers," Reuters, May 14, 2009. http://www.reuters.com/article/idUSTRE54D3FM20090514.

Chrysler) and the DIP financing it received from the U.S. government (in bankruptcy, DIP financing takes precedence even over secured debt).

Three Indiana State pension funds (the Indiana State Police Pension Trust, the Indiana Teachers Retirement Fund, and the Major Moves Construction Fund) and several groups of the terminated Chrysler dealers filed a lawsuit to block the proposed sale. The Indiana State pension funds alleged that the approved sale could not occur without its consent, as it had an interest in the collateral.[15] Judge Gonzales, however, overruled their objection. He held that as the Indiana State pension funds were parties to a prepetition syndicated credit facility that appointed J.P. Morgan as its administrative agent, the pension funds were bound by the acts of their agent, which in this case acted in accordance with the wishes of the syndicate as a whole, who supported the sale (i.e., received the consent of the majority of the holders of syndicated loans, most of whom were recipients of federal bailout payments). Judge Gonzalez held that the Indiana State pension funds had "contracted away their right to act inconsistently."

The Indiana State pension funds and a group of auto dealers immediately appealed the decision. On June 3, Judge Gonzalez said that the appeal could be directly heard by the United States Court of Appeals for the Second District. Normally, bankruptcy court appeals are heard by a Federal District Court, but Judge Gonzalez said the matter was of public importance because Fiat could walk away from the deal if it did not close by June 15.[16]

On Friday, June 5, after hearing two hours of arguments, the United States Court of Appeals for the Second District took a 10-minute recess and affirmed Judge Gonzalez's ruling and allowed the sale to proceed on Monday, June 8. Attorneys for the state of Indiana and groups of auto dealers appealed to the United States Supreme Court. On Monday, June 8, without comment, Justice Ruth Bader Ginsburg delayed the sale pending a review of the appeal, but on Tuesday the United States Supreme Court rejected the appeal and allowed the sale to proceed.[17] On Wednesday, June 10, Chrysler exited bankruptcy, and Fiat CEO Sergio Marchionne was named Chrysler CEO.

When Chrysler exited bankruptcy, it left behind all liabilities and many unneeded assets. Although the remaining assets could be used to pay unsecured creditors, most were not retained by Chrysler because they had little or no value or had negative value because of environmental damage. Among the left-behind potential liabilities were thousands of unsettled lawsuits against Chrysler because of injuries that allegedly occurred from defective Chrysler vehicles. The new Chrysler also had no liability for future injuries caused by defective Chrysler vehicles sold prior to the date Chrysler exited bankruptcy. In the case of GM, after extensive negotiations with state attorneys general, GM and the U.S. government agreed that, although GM will not assume liabilities for injury claims or accidents that occurred prior to the date GM exits bankruptcy, it will assume liability for all damages caused by GM vehicles sold after the date GM exits bankruptcy, including all GM vehicles produced prior to the date GM exits bankruptcy.[18]

15. Staff (Legal), "Indiana Pensioners Object to Chrysler Sale," *The New York Times*, May 20, 2009.

16. De la Merced, Michael J., "A ruling may speed new plans for Chrysler," *The New York Times*, June 3, 2009. http://www.nytimes.com/2009/06/03/business/03chrysler.html?ref=michael_j_de_la_merced.

17. On June 3, 2009, the Indiana State pension funds filed a petition with the United States Supreme Court for reconsideration of their objections and in an attempt to recover some of the losses they sustained in the sale. See de la Merced, Michael J., "As Court Clears Path, Chrysler is Set to Exit Bankruptcy," *The New York Times*, June 9, 2009. http://www.nytimes.com/2009/06/10/business/global/10chrysler.html.

18. De La Merced, Michael J., "G.M. to Maintain Legal Liability for Claims," *The New York Times* online, June 28, 2009. http://www.nytimes.com/2009/06/28/business/28gm.html?ref=michael_j_de_la_merced.

Chrysler is privately held so its liabilities on the date of bankruptcy are not readily available. However, Chrysler almost certainly has many of the same liabilities as General Motors Corp., which was publicly traded at the time. Exhibit 2 lists GM's accrued liabilities as of December 31, 2008 (Chrysler's was about half the size of GM). The part of Chrysler that exited bankruptcy has no liability for those accruals. To the extent that Chrysler assets remaining in bankruptcy had value, they could be used to pay the accrued liabilities; however, it is unlikely any of those liabilities will be paid.

Some attorneys believed the bankruptcy, appellate, and Supreme Court completely disregarded Section 1129 when they approved the government's bankruptcy plan for Chrysler. Others were concerned that the rulings could lead to uncertainty in how courts would handle future bankruptcies. A recent article by Roe and Skeel stated that[19]

Chrysler's operations entered and exited bankruptcy in forty-two days, making it one of the fastest major industrial bankruptcies in memory. It entered as a company widely thought to be ripe for liquidation if left on its own, obtained massive funding from the United States Treasury, and exited through a pseudo-sale of its main assets to a new government-funded entity. Most creditors were picked up by the purchasing entity, but some were not. The unevenness of the compensation to prior creditors raised considerable concerns in capital markets. . . .

The informal, makeshift checks that courts had previously required when there were strong section 1129 implications were in Chrysler weak or nonexistent. The courts did not even see fit to discuss section 1129 in their opinions. There was de facto consent from a majority of the bank lenders (although not from products-liability claimants), but that consent came from parties afflicted with serious conflicts of interest. . . .

For minority creditors, there's a century of bankruptcy and equity-receivership law designed to balance protection from the majority's potential to encroach on the minority and squeeze them out perniciously. These are neither small nor simple fairness-based considerations: capital markets depend on effective mechanism that prevent financial majorities from ousting financial minorities from their ratable position in an enterprise. That's what's at stake.

It's in that light that the Chrysler bankruptcy was pernicious. It failed to comply with good bankruptcy practice, reviving practices that were soundly rejected nearly a century ago. Going forward, the extent of Chrysler's damage to bankruptcy practice and financial markets will depend either on congressional action or on how Chrysler is construed by other courts, and whether they will limit its application, as they should.

Even before the final Supreme Court ruling on June 10, 2009, attorneys for Jim Balsillie, co-CEO of Research in Motion, seemingly attempted to circumvent bankruptcy laws, and they referenced the Chrysler case in their filings. Mr. Balsillie offered to purchase the Phoenix Coyotes, a National Hockey League (NHL) franchise, out of bankruptcy. However, as part of the bankruptcy plan, Mr. Balsillie would have the right to move the team to Hamilton, Ontario, even though franchise rules specifically prohibit such moves without compensation to the NHL and to nearby NHL teams in Toronto (Maple Leafs) and Buffalo (Sabres).[20]

---

19. Roe, Mark J. and Skeel, David A., "Assessing the Chrysler Bankruptcy," *Michigan Law Review,* Vol 108, pp. 27, 2010.

20. Vanderbilt Journal of Entertainment & Technology Law, Team's Bankruptcy Filing Challenges Traditional Sports League Authority, JET Blog, June 2, 2009. http://jetl.wordpress.com/2009/06/02/teams-bankruptcy-filing-challenges-traditional-sports-league-authority/.

In contrast, on June 13, 2009, lenders for Six Flags, the theme park company, filed a prenegotiated reorganization plan with the bankruptcy court in which the company would eliminate about $1.8 billion in debt and a $300 million payment due to preferred equity shareholders. Secured lenders holding about $1.13 billion in debt would receive about 90% of the equity in the postbankruptcy company and holders of about $1.29 billion in unsecured debt would receive the remaining 10% of equity—existing equity holders would receive nothing.[21] That postbankruptcy equity split between secured and unsecured lenders is a relatively normal division of equity. Secured lenders accept less than 100% of what they are legally entitled to, and unsecured lenders agree to not challenge the terms in court.

Required

1. One alternative to the sale of Chrysler was to cease operations and then liquidate (sell) the firm's remaining assets. Chrysler did have a potentially valuable Auburn Hills, Michigan, headquarters building (although there is little demand for office space in the Detroit area). Discuss whether Chrysler should have been liquidated.

2. In its lawsuit, attorneys for the state of Indiana stated that the harm from showing preference to unsecured creditors such as the UAW, over secured creditors such as the state of Indiana pension funds, might do far more long-run damage to the U.S. economy than any short-term harm from the loss of jobs from liquidating Chrysler. Do you agree or disagree with that statement? As part of your analysis, discuss the harm that would arise from showing preference to unsecured creditors over secured creditors.

3. Were there alternatives to the government's preferred bankruptcy structure that would have satisfied the state of Indiana pension funds? Explain.

4. Chrysler exited bankruptcy with all its debt cancelled, and GM may soon follow suit. Will that give GM and Chrysler an unfair advantage over Ford? Explain.

---

21. Spector, Mike, and Jeffrey McCracken, "Six Flags files for Chapter 11 in accord with lenders," *The Wall Street Journal*, June 15, 2009.

EXHIBIT 1

U.S. BANKRUPTCY
CODE SECTION
1129,
CONFIRMATION OF
THE PLAN[22]

Release date: 2005-07-12

(a) The court shall confirm a plan only if all of the following requirements are met:

(1) The plan complies with the applicable provisions of this title.

(2) The proponent of the plan complies with the applicable provisions of this title.

(3) The plan has been proposed in good faith and not by any means forbidden by law.

(4) Any payment made or to be made by the proponent, by the debtor, or by a person issuing securities or acquiring property under the plan, for services or for costs and expenses in or in connection with the case, or in connection with the plan and incident to the case, has been approved by, or is subject to the approval of, the court as reasonable.

(5)

   (A)

      (i) The proponent of the plan has disclosed the identity and affiliations of any individual proposed to serve, after confirmation of the plan, as a director, officer, or voting trustee of the debtor, an affiliate of the debtor participating in a joint plan with the debtor, or a successor to the debtor under the plan; and

      (ii) the appointment to, or continuance in, such office of such individual, is consistent with the interests of creditors and equity security holders and with public policy; and

   (B) the proponent of the plan has disclosed the identity of any insider that will be employed or retained by the reorganized debtor, and the nature of any compensation for such insider.

(6) Any governmental regulatory commission with jurisdiction, after confirmation of the plan, over the rates of the debtor has approved any rate change provided for in the plan, or such rate change is expressly conditioned on such approval.

(7) With respect to each impaired class of claims or interests—

   (A) each holder of a claim or interest of such class—

      (i) has accepted the plan; or

      (ii) will receive or retain under the plan on account of such claim or interest property of a value, as of the effective date of the plan, that is not less than the amount that such holder would so receive or retain if the debtor were liquidated under chapter 7 of this title on such date; or

   (B) if section 1111 (b)(2) of this title applies to the claims of such class, each holder of a claim of such class will receive or retain under the plan on account of such claim property of a value, as of the effective date of the plan, that is not less than the value of such holder's interest in the estate's interest in the property that secures such claims.

(continued)

22. Chicago Bankruptcy Lawyers & Attorneys, 2009. http://www.bankruptcy-lawyers-chicago.com/uscode11/usc_sec_11_00001129----000-.html.

EXHIBIT 1—
continued

U.S. BANKRUPTCY
CODE SECTION 1129,
CONFIRMATION OF
THE PLAN

(8) With respect to each class of claims or interests—

(A) such class has accepted the plan; or

(B) such class is not impaired under the plan.

(9) Except to the extent that the holder of a particular claim has agreed to a different treatment of such claim, the plan provides that—

(A) with respect to a claim of a kind specified in section 507 (a)(1) or 507 (a)(2) of this title, on the effective date of the plan, the holder of such claim will receive on account of such claim cash equal to the allowed amount of such claim;

(B) with respect to a class of claims of a kind specified in section 507 (a)(3), 507 (a)(4), 507 (a)(5), 507(a)(6), or 507 (a)(7) of this title, each holder of a claim of such class will receive—

(i) if such class has accepted the plan, deferred cash payments of a value, as of the effective date of the plan, equal to the allowed amount of such claim; or

(ii) if such class has not accepted the plan, cash on the effective date of the plan equal to the allowed amount of such claim; and

(C) with respect to a claim of a kind specified in section 507 (a)(8) of this title, the holder of such claim will receive on account of such claim deferred cash payments, over a period not exceeding six years after the date of assessment of such claim, of a value, as of the effective date of the plan, equal to the allowed amount of such claim.

(10) If a class of claims is impaired under the plan, at least one class of claims that is impaired under the plan has accepted the plan, determined without including any acceptance of the plan by any insider.

(11) Confirmation of the plan is not likely to be followed by the liquidation, or the need for further financial reorganization, of the debtor or any successor to the debtor under the plan, unless such liquidation or reorganization is proposed in the plan.

(12) All fees payable under section 1930 of title 28, as determined by the court at the hearing on confirmation of the plan, have been paid or the plan provides for the payment of all such fees on the effective date of the plan.

(13) The plan provides for the continuation after its effective date of payment of all retiree benefits, as that term is defined in section 1114 of this title, at the level established pursuant to subsection (e)(1)(B) or (g) of section 1114 of this title, at any time prior to confirmation of the plan, for the duration of the period the debtor has obligated itself to provide such benefits.

(b)

(1) Notwithstanding section 510 (a) of this title, if all of the applicable requirements of subsection (a) of this section other than paragraph (8) are met with respect to a plan, the court, on request of the proponent of the plan, shall confirm the plan notwithstanding the requirements of such paragraph if the plan does not discriminate unfairly, and is fair and equitable, with respect to each class of claims or interests that is impaired under, and has not accepted, the plan.

(continued)

EXHIBIT 1—
continued

U.S. BANKRUPTCY
CODE SECTION 1129,
CONFIRMATION OF
THE PLAN

(2) For the purpose of this subsection, the condition that a plan be fair and equitable with respect to a class includes the following requirements:

   (A) With respect to a class of secured claims, the plan provides—

      (i)

      (I) that the holders of such claims retain the liens securing such claims, whether the property subject to such liens is retained by the debtor or transferred to another entity, to the extent of the allowed amount of such claims; and

      (II) that each holder of a claim of such class receive on account of such claim deferred cash payments totaling at least the allowed amount of such claim, of a value, as of the effective date of the plan, of at least the value of such holder's interest in the estate's interest in such property;

      (ii) for the sale, subject to section 363 (k) of this title, of any property that is subject to the liens securing such claims, free and clear of such liens, with such liens to attach to the proceeds of such sale, and the treatment of such liens on proceeds under clause (i) or (iii) of this subparagraph; or

      (iii) for the realization by such holders of the indubitable equivalent of such claims.

   (B) With respect to a class of unsecured claims—

      (i) the plan provides that each holder of a claim of such class receive or retain on account of such claim property of a value, as of the effective date of the plan, equal to the allowed amount of such claim; or

      (ii) the holder of any claim or interest that is junior to the claims of such class will not receive or retain under the plan on account of such junior claim or interest any property.

   (C) With respect to a class of interests—

      (i) the plan provides that each holder of an interest of such class receive or retain on account of such interest property of a value, as of the effective date of the plan, equal to the greatest of the allowed amount of any fixed liquidation preference to which such holder is entitled, any fixed redemption price to which such holder is entitled, or the value of such interest; or

      (ii) the holder of any interest that is junior to the interests of such class will not receive or retain under the plan on account of such junior interest any property.

(c) Notwithstanding subsections (a) and (b) of this section and except as provided in section 1127 (b) of this title, the court may confirm only one plan, unless the order of confirmation in the case has been revoked under section 1144 of this title. If the requirements of subsections (a) and (b) of this section are met with respect to more than one plan, the court shall consider the preferences of creditors and equity security holders in determining which plan to confirm.

(d) Notwithstanding any other provision of this section, on request of a party in interest that is a governmental unit, the court may not confirm a plan if the principal purpose of the plan is the avoidance of taxes or the avoidance of the application of section 5 of the Securities Act of 1933. In any hearing under this subsection, the governmental unit has the burden of proof on the issue of avoidance.

EXHIBIT 2

NOTE 14, ACCRUED
EXPENSES, OTHER
LIABILITIES AND
DEFERRED INCOME
TAXES, GENERAL
MOTORS CORP.,
DEC 31, 2008

The following table summarizes the components of accrued expenses, other liabilities and deferred income taxes:

	December 31	
	2008	**2007**
	(Dollars in millions)	
Automotive and Other—Current		
Dealer and customer allowances, claims and discounts	$8,939	$9,833
Deposits from rental car companies	6,142	7,758
Deferred revenue	1,493	1,242
Policy, product warranty and recall campaigns	3,792	4,655
Delphi contingent liability	150	924
Payrolls and employee benefits excluding postemployment benefits	1,591	1,680
Self-insurance reserves	355	351
Taxes (other than income taxes)	1,276	1,421
Derivative liability	2,718	587
Postemployment benefits including facility idling reserves	1,727	901
Interest	775	812
Pensions	430	446
Postretirement benefits	4,002	335
Deferred income taxes	87	116
Other	2,444	2,963
Total accrued expenses	**$35,921**	**$34,024**
Automotive and Other—Noncurrent		
Dealer and customer allowances, claims and discounts	$1,578	$912
Deferred revenue	1,260	1,933
Policy, product warranty and recall campaigns	4,699	4,960
Delphi contingent liability	1,570	1,870
Payrolls and employee benefits excluding postemployment benefits	2,314	2,082
Self-insurance reserves	1,324	1,483
Derivative liability	817	264
Postemployment benefits including facility idling reserves	1,626	1,145
Deferred income taxes	563	1,034
Other	1,212	1,217
Total other liabilities and deferred income taxes	**$16,963**	**$16,900**

The following table summarizes activity for policy, product warranty, recall campaigns and certified used vehicle warranty liabilities:

	2008	2007
	(Dollars in millions)	
Balance at January 1	$9,615	$9,064
Warranties issued in period	4,277	5,135
Payments	(5,068)	(4,539)
Adjustments to preexisting warranties	294	(165)
Effect of foreign currency translation	(627)	223
Liabilities transferred in the sale of Allison (Note 4)	—	(103)
Balance at December 31	$8,491	$9,615

We review and adjust these estimates on a periodic basis based on the differences between actual experience and historical estimates or other available information.

General Growth Properties

Crises in Securitization

On April 16, 2009, General Growth Properties (GGP) filed for bankruptcy protection. At the time, GGP owned 254 shopping malls, 25 office complexes, 10 planned communities, and had 10 properties under development.[1] Although GGP had $28.9 billion of assets at the time of its filing, other aspects of the bankruptcy filing were far more significant than its size.

GGP had transferred ownership of most of its properties to special purpose entities (SPEs). Institutional investors purchased notes issued by each SPE and collateralized by the properties transferred to each SPE. That process supposedly isolated the properties from the reach of GGP creditors because SPEs are considered bankruptcy-remote entities. Since the first securitization in the early 1980s, that bankruptcy protection veil had never been pierced.

In the two weeks prior to filing for bankruptcy, GGP replaced many independent directors of its SPEs. When GGP filed for voluntary bankruptcy protection, the directors of 158 GGP bankruptcy-remote SPEs simultaneously voted to file for bankruptcy protection although none of the SPEs were in default and each had adequate cash flows to service its debt. The SPE directors appeared to file for bankruptcy protection for the benefit of GGP, not for the benefit of the SPE's creditors. That simultaneous filing, known as substantive consolidation, could potentially allow the bankruptcy court to pool all of the assets and liabilities of GGP and its SPEs. In effect, GGP might be able to repay its creditors using cash that had been set aside by contract as protection for SPE creditors. Many investors and attorneys believed that a ruling in favor of substantive consolidation might be the end of securitization as we know it.

Background

In 1954, Martin Bucksbaum (33) and his younger brother Matthew (28) sold the grocery stores their parents owned in and near Marshalltown, Iowa (population 25,000). They used the funds, and debt, to build Iowa's first shopping center in Cedar Rapids, 70 miles to the east of Marshalltown. By 1964, the Bucksbaum brothers owned five commercial real estate properties, and in 1970 they formed General Growth Properties (GGP) to hold their properties. In 1972, GGP went public on the New York Stock Exchange (NYSE) as a real estate investment trust (REIT). Twelve years later, in 1984, GGP sold its 19 shopping malls to Equitable Life Insurance for $800 million. GGP was liquidated, and the brothers formed General Growth Management (GGM) to manage a majority of those sold properties.[2]

In 1989, GGM acquired The Center Companies to become the nation's second largest regional shopping center management company. In 1993, GGM reopened GGP, again as an REIT, and again went public on the NYSE. The Bucksbaum brothers

---

1. GGP 2008 10-K.

2. Company history, GGP Web site, http://www.ggp.com/company/CompanyHistory.aspx.

retained 45% ownership and sold the remaining 55% to the public for $418 million, valuing GGP at $760 million and their interest at $342 million.[3]

In June 1995, Martin Bucksbaum, GGP's chairman and CEO, returned to Marshalltown from Chicago, where he had negotiated a deal to acquire regional malls and community shopping centers from Sears, Roebuck & Co. for $1 billion. The acquired properties would be included in GGP/Homart, a new entity owned by GGP and four institutional investors. A month later, Martin Bucksbaum died of a heart attack and his brother Matthew was named chairman and CEO. GGP completed the GGP/Homart acquisition in December 1995 and moved the firm's headquarters to Chicago.[4]

Expansion

In 1996, GGP acquired GGM; the following year GGP announced that, together with Ivanhoe Inc., a leading Canadian institutional real estate investor, it had purchased the Oaks Mall in Florida and the Westroads Mall in Nebraska. Those two malls, and 11 others owned by GGP, were pooled into a single collateralized mortgage-backed securitization (CMBS) financing that included 10- and 15-year tranches (i.e., the pools issued some notes that matured in 10 years and some that matured in 15 years). Those notes would need to be refinanced because the lease cash inflows were insufficient to cover balloon payments due at the end of years 10 and 15.[5]

In the first half of 1998, GGP acquired shopping malls worth more than $1.5 billion, so that by June 1998, it owned or managed 121 malls in 37 states. In May 1999, John Bucksbaum was appointed as CEO, succeeding his father, Matthew, who retained his position as chairman of the board of directors. Under John Bucksbaum, GGP continued its rapid growth.[6] From 2005 to 2008, *Forbes* magazine consistently included Mathew Bucksbaum and his family in the Forbes 400, a list of the 400 wealthiest families and individuals in the United States. In 2008, they came in at number 205 on the list with a net worth of $2.2 billion.[7]

Exhibit 1 provides selected GGP financial information from 1994, shortly before the death of Martin Bucksbaum, through December 31, 2008, shortly before GGP filed for bankruptcy protection. According to Exhibit 1, GGP remained profitable from 1994 through 2008; cash flow from operating activities grew steadily and was substantial, even in 2008, when GGP began to anticipate a bankruptcy filing. Because REITs are required to pay out at least 90% of their earnings as distributions, GGP's net change in cash was near zero each year. Cash distributions per share grew every year from 1994 through 2008, and GGP's stock price grew steadily during that period. However, as the U.S. recession worsened, and credit markets froze, it became obvious that GGP would be unable to refinance its debt that would come due in 2009 and 2010. GGP discontinued its dividends in the fourth quarter, 2008, and its stock price dropped from $44.23 to $.24 per share.

GGP's acquisition of GGP/Homart in 1995, the year of Matthew Bucksbaum's death, increased GGP's debt as a percent of assets to 74.9%. Debt as a percent age of assets gradually declined to 60.2% in 2001. However, in the fourth quarter of 2004, GGP acquired The Rouse Company, a Maryland-based mall owner, for $14.3 billion ($6.8 billion in cash, the assumption of $5.1 billion in Rouse debt, plus purchase price

---

3. Ibid.

4. Strom, Stephanie, "Martin Bucksbaum, 74, pioneer in shopping center development," (Obituaries), *The New York Times*, July 10, 1995.

5. Company history, GGP Web site.

6. Ibid.

7. *Forbes* 400 List, 2005–2008.

adjustments, and acquisition costs). That increased GGP's debt-to-asset percentage to 88%, a very high percent relative to others in the industry. At the time of GGP's Rouse acquisition, the Simon Property Group, the only mall owner larger than GGP, had debts equal to 73.6% of assets. Even on September 30, 2009, when debt financing was very limited, and when GGP's debts were 92.3% of assets, the Simon Property Group debts were only 78.3% of assets.

The Resignation of John Bucksbaum

On October 27, 2008, GGP filed a Form 8-K with the SEC that announced:

> (b) Effective October 21, 2008, Bernard Freibaum resigned as a director of General Growth Properties, Inc. ("GGP"). Effective October 26, 2008, John Bucksbaum resigned as Chief Executive Officer and Robert Michaels resigned as President and as a director.

> (c) Effective October 26, 2008, Adam Metz was appointed interim Chief Executive Officer of GGP and Thomas Nolan was appointed interim President. Messrs. Metz and Nolan will continue to serve as directors of GGP. . . . The compensation of Messrs. Metz and Nolan has not yet been determined.[8]

GGP took the aforementioned action after the board of directors learned that an affiliate of the Bucksbaum family trust had advanced Mr. Michaels, its former president, a $10 million unsecured loan and Mr. Freibaum, its former CFO, a $90 million unsecured loan. The loans allowed Mr. Michaels and Mr. Freibaum to repay personal margin debt related to their purchases GGP stock, which had fallen from a high of $44.23 earlier in 2008, to $1.97 on October 27, 2008. Mr. Michaels had repaid his $10 million loan, but $80 million of Mr. Freibaum's loan was still outstanding.

Because the loans were from a family trust rather than GGP, no security laws (such as Sarbanes-Oxley) were violated. A November 3, 2008, SEC letter to GGP requested additional information:

> We note from your disclosure that affiliates of the Bucksbaum family trust advanced an unsecured loan to Mr. Friebaum (sic), your former Director and Chief Financial Officer, and that $80 million of the original $90 million unsecured loan is presently outstanding. It appears a principal stockholder of the company has settled the personal margin debt related to the company's common stock on Mr. Friebaum's (sic) behalf generating the original $90 million unsecured loan. As such, please tell us whether the company has considered, and provide us with your analysis of SAB Topic 5.T. Within your response, please provide support detailing how you believe Mr. Friebaum (sic) will be able to repay the outstanding amount due.[9]

Potential Bankruptcy

Even though GGP was profitable in 2008 (Exhibit 2), its assets exceeded its liabilities by nearly $1.8 billion (Exhibit 3), and it had positive cash flows from operating activities of $556 million (Exhibit 4), GGP received the following "Going Concern" opinion (excerpt) from its auditors, Deloitte & Touche:

> The accompanying financial statements have been prepared assuming that the Company will continue as a going concern. As discussed in Note 1 to the consolidated financial statements, as of February 26, 2009, the Company has $1.18 billion in past due debt, an additional $4.09 billion of debt that could be accelerated by its lenders,

---

8. GGP 8-K, October 27, 2008 (Date of earliest reported event: October 21, 2008).

9. Woody, Kevin, Accounting Branch Chief, Securities and Exchange Commission, letter dated November 3, 2008 (see SEC, Edgar, General Growth Properties, UPLOAD, 2008-11-03).

and $2.29 billion in other debt scheduled to mature in 2009. . . . These matters, which could result in the Company seeking legal protection from its lenders, raise substantial doubt about the Company's ability to continue as a going concern. Management's plans concerning these matters are also discussed in Note 1 to the consolidated financial statements. The consolidated financial statements do not include any adjustments that might result from the outcome of this uncertainty.[10]

The problem arose because GGP financed the purchase of long-term assets with medium-term debt. In the early 1980s, investment banks developed a form of financing known as securitization. Relatively unmarketable assets with cash inflows (such as home mortgages or auto loans) were used to collateralize newly issued marketable securities. The first securitizations were for home mortgage pools called collateralized mortgage obligations (CMOs). A bank or mortgage finance company (the loan originator) loaned money to home buyers in exchange for a mortgage. In a two-step process, the loan originator first sold residential mortgages to one legal entity, which resold them to an SPE (a securitization trust). That two-step process isolated the mortgages so creditors of the loan originator would be unable to gain access to mortgages in the trust (the securitization trust was bankruptcy remote).

Because the mortgages were isolated from the originator and its creditors, they could be used as collateral for notes the trust sold to institutional investors. A loan originator might transfer $500 million of 8% mortgages to a trust; the trust might then sell $480 million of 6% notes to institutional investors. The $20 million difference between the $500 million of mortgages in the trust and the $480 million of mortgage-backed notes the trust issued, plus the 2% interest rate spread (8% minus 6%), gave institutional investors a cushion against mortgage defaults.

A home mortgage is self-amortizing; contractual monthly payments from the home buyer are sufficient to repay the borrowed amount, plus interest. If the notes the trust sells to institutional investors are for a sufficiently long period, the securitization pool is also self-amortizing. That is, monthly payments from home buyers will be sufficient to repay notes issued by the securitization pool, plus interest.

The earliest securitization pools were considered very safe. The cushion between collateral and notes issued was adequate, and the mortgages and the notes were both self-amortizing. Securitization trust-backed notes typically received AAA or AA credit ratings.[11]

In the mid-1980s, investment banks introduced commercial mortgage-backed securities (CMBS).[12] Various classes of commercial real estate, such as shopping malls or office towers, were transferred to a securitization trust, which then sold notes to institutional investors. Tenant lease payments to the trust were sufficient to pay interest on notes sold to institutional investors and to repay some but not all of the loan principal. As a result, the debt on the property was not self-amortizing, so the securitization trusts were not self-amortizing.

A shopping mall built for $500 million might be financed with $450 million of debt issued by a CMBS trust. The mall operator might initially sign 3-year leases with small tenants and 15-year leases with anchor tenants. Those lease payments would not be sufficient to repay the $450 million debt, but mall operators expect to resign many existing tenants and find replacement for tenants that leave. As a result, although

---

10. Deloitte & Touche, audit report dated February 26, 2009, GGP 10-K, 2008.

11. Standard & Poor's, Moody's, and Fitch provide bond ratings that are used throughout the world. Many organizations are prohibited by statute or internal policies from investing in anything but investment-grade fixed income securities, which are typically the top several ratings from those rating agencies.

12. Wheeler, Darrell, Mitch Wasterlain, and Jeff Prince, "In turbulent times CMBS and CDOs remain complementary," *CBMS World*, Summer 2007, p. 41.

initial lease payments are insufficient to pay interest and repay the $450 million principal, renewal and replacement leases are expected to eventually cover all interest payments, plus principal repayments, possibly over 20–25 years.

CMBS notes issued in the 1980s were usually 10-year fixed-rate notes, with balloon payments due in year 10. Lease receipts during the initial 10-year period, even for fully occupied commercial real estate, were far too low to repay the entire principal plus interest. Instead, as the debt neared maturity, borrowers refinanced their properties with a second or third CMBS pool.

From their inception in the early 1980s until 2006, very few securitization trusts defaulted on their notes. In late 2006, however, the subprime mortgage securitization market began to collapse. Several mortgage finance companies either failed or were acquired by larger institutions in the first half of 2007. In October 2007, Merrill Lynch and Citigroup reported $5–$6 billion losses from subprime mortgage-backed investments, and a month later each reported additional $10 billion losses. By the first quarter 2008, the entire U.S. securitization market had effectively closed. Investors no longer trusted ratings from the rating agencies, nor the quality of assets in securitization pools.

With the securitization markets closed, commercial real estate firms such as GGP, even though they might be highly profitable, could no longer refinance their maturing debt. None of GGP's securitization trusts were in any danger of defaulting on its notes. However, GGP was far more leveraged than many of its competitors. It had $6.6 billion of unsecured debt that it would probably not be able to refinance, and much of its $18.3 billion of fixed-rate and variable-rate collateralized debt was for shorter periods than the collateralized debt issued by its competitors, sometimes for as little as five or even three years, as shown in Note 6 to GGP's 2008 10-K:

Note 6 Mortgages, Notes and Loans Payable		
Mortgages, notes and loans payable are summarized as follows (see Note 14 for the maturities of our long term commitments):		
	December 31, 2008	**December 31, 2007**
	(In thousands)	
Fixed-rate debt:		
Collateralized mortgages, notes and loans payable	$15,538,825	$16,943,760
Corporate and other unsecured term loans	3,798,351	3,895,922
Total fixed-rate debt	19,337,176	20,839,682
Variable-rate debt:		
Collateralized mortgages, notes and loans payable	2,732,437	819,607
Credit facilities (unsecured)	—	429,150
Corporate and other unsecured term loans	2,783,700	2,193,700
Total variable-rate debt	5,516,137	3,442,457
Total Mortgages, notes and loans payable	$24,853,313	$24,282,139

Bankruptcy

On April 16, 2009, GGP filed for voluntary bankruptcy protection, and the New York Stock Exchange suspended trading in its common stock. Shortly before GGP declared bankruptcy, it replaced many of the independent directors of its SPEs. Concurrently with GGP's bankruptcy filing, 158 of GGPs 273 affiliated SPEs simultaneously filed for voluntary bankruptcy protection even though they were in no danger of imminent default.[13] Most of the SPEs had significant excess cash that was held in the SPE for the protection of the institutional investors who purchased the SPE's notes. That excess cash would have eventually been transferred to GGP, assuming the SPEs could be refinanced. If the bankruptcy filings were successful, however, the excess cash might be immediately transferred to GGP.

Residential mortgages or auto loan SPEs are operationally simple. They have three purposes: (1) collect receivables, (2) pay interest and repay principal on notes issued by the SPE, and (3) return the excess funds, if any, to the loan originator. In their first-day pleadings before the bankruptcy court, Adam S. Metz, GGP's new CEO, and James A. Mesterharm, its advisor, both argued that GGP's SPEs are far more complex than residential mortgage or auto loan SPEs and are also far more integrated:[14]

5. While our properties have a significant economic and social impact on each of the local communities they serve, the shopping center business is a national one and many of our tenants operate nationwide. To meet their needs, we operate a highly-integrated and centrally managed national platform of properties in major and middle markets in 44 states. GGP has close relationships with national retailers in virtually every retail category. A critical element of our business strategy is to create synergies for both GGP and its tenants by our ability to provide retailers with multiple, desirable locations for their stores and a regional or nationwide footprint.

6. The company's senior management, based in Chicago, makes all key strategic decisions regarding GGP's properties. For example, property management functions are centralized in our Chicago headquarters, which provides accounting, business development, cash management, construction, contracting, design, finance, forecasting, human resources and employee benefits, insurance and risk management, facility services, marketing, legal, leasing, tax, treasury, and other similar functions for all of the company's properties. The details of our integrated management structure and operations, and its benefits and efficiencies, are discussed further in the Declaration of James A. Mesterharm, our restructuring consultant.

11. . . . The circumstances that compelled GGP to file for Chapter 11, however, can be summarized succinctly: GGP has approximately $18.4 billion in outstanding debt obligations that have matured or will mature between now and the end of 2012, including past due maturities of $2.0 billion, $1.3 billion more coming due in the remainder of 2009, and $6.4 billion in 2010.

Independent Directors

Standard & Poor's established, and other rating agencies and institutional lenders have followed, that for an SPE to maintain bankruptcy-remote status at least one director of the SPE must be "independent."[15] An independent director is defined as an individual who is unrelated or unaffiliated and has no current or prior relationship

---

13. Westlaw Business, "General growth: Bankruptcy and the downfall of securitization as we know it? Legal currents," *The Legal Lens on Business News*, May 5, 2009.

14. Metz, Adam S., Declaration of Adam S. Metz, United States Bankruptcy Court Southern District of New York, In re *General Growth Properties, Inc., et al., Debtors.* April 15, 2009.

15. Rowell, Robert, "Practice aids: Single purpose entities (SPEs)," Debt3, July/August 2005. http://www.debt3online.com/?page=article&article_id=54; SMC Global, Independent Directors for Bankruptcy Remote Entities, Services page. http://www.smcglobal.net/bankruptcyremote.htm.

with either a lender or borrower of the SPE.[16] The independence of directors ensures that there is not an overlap of directors at the parent and subsidiary levels, as well as provides for the independent judgment of a director without an economic interest in the SPE or affiliate and the relevant transaction(s).[17]

The consent of the independent director is required for the SPE to file for bankruptcy and, thus, provides the lender and borrower "an assurance of 'independence' on a bankruptcy vote as [n]o bankruptcy action can be declared without the approval of the independent director."[18] In "In re *Kingston Square Associates*," the Bankruptcy Court for the Southern District of New York "suggested that the standard for an independent director to follow in deciding whether to consent to a voluntary bankruptcy filing is that of a fiduciary whose responsibility includes secured creditors, equity holders, and unsecured creditors."[19]

Motion to Dismiss the Filing of Certain Debtors

On May 4, 2009, ING Clarion Capital Loan Services, LLC (ING Clarion), as special servicer for the lenders, filed a motion to dismiss the jointly administered GGP bankruptcy cases of Bakersfield Mall LLC, RASCAP Realty, Ltd., Visalia Mall, L.P., GGP-Tucson Mall L.L.C., Lancaster Trust,[20] HO Retail Properties II Limited Partnership, RS Properties Inc., Stonestown Shopping Center L.P., and Fashion Place, LLC.[21] In the motion, ING Clarion argued that inclusion of the above referenced entities as debtors in the GGP bankruptcy case was "[i]n contravention of the fundamental premise of asset isolation upon which the commercial real estate lending market (including, but not limited to the market for which the commercial mortgage backed securities) is based."[22] ING Clarion went on to state that if GGP is allowed to bring in the aforementioned special purpose entities into its bankruptcy, it would have tremendous impact on commercial real estate lending as well as the structured finance market.[23] It was argued that the bankruptcy remoteness of these entities was a fundamental

---

16. Sargent, Patrick C., Charles T. Marshall and Peter K. McKee, Jr., "Round 1 of General Growth Properties Bankruptcy: SPE Structure survives," June 24, 2009. http://www.andrewskurth.com/pressroom-publications-640.html.

17. Sargent, Patrick, In re *Kingston Square Associates*: Questioning Independent Director Provisions, Andrews Kurth, LLP, Web page, http://www.andrewskurth.com/pressroom-publications-InReKingston SquareAssociatesQuestioningInd.html (discussing In re *Kingston Square Associates*, 214 B.R. 713 (Bankr. S.D.N.Y. 1997).

18. SMC Global, Independent Directors for Bankruptcy Remote Entities.

19. McKune, Kathleen O., Esq.,"SPE's—Who, what, why, where, when and how?" A:\#353112v2–ABA Seminar SPE's.doc, January 29, 2004, Page 7. http://www.abanet.org/rppt/meetings_cle/spring2004/rp/Mindingpandq/mckune2.pdf.

20. ING Clarion contends that Lancaster Trust is not eligible to be a debtor under Section 109 of the Bankruptcy Code because a trust is not explicitly included as a "person" under the Section, and as such, should not be able to be a debtor.; Motion of ING Clarion Captital Loan Services LLC, Pursuant to 11 U.S.C. § 1112(b), to Dismiss the Cases of Bakersfield Mall LLC; RASCAP Realty, Ltd., Visalia Mall, L.P.; GGP-Tucson Mall L.L.C., Lancaster Trust, HO Retail Properties II Limited Partnership, RS Properties Inc., Stonestown Shopping Center, L.P., and Fashion Place, LLC. (Docket No. 334); In re *General Growth Properties, Inc., et al.* (Jointly Administered), Case No. 09-11977 (ALG); pages 16–17.

21. Motion of ING Clarion Capital Loan Services LLC, Pursuant to 11 U.S.C. § 1112(b), to Dismiss the Cases of Bakersfield Mall LLC; RASCAP Realty, Ltd., Visalia Mall, L.P.; GGP-Tucson Mall L.L.C., Lancaster Trust, HO Retail Properties II Limited Partnership, RS Properties Inc., Stonestown Shopping Center, L.P., and Fashion Place, LLC. (Docket No. 334); In re *General Growth Properties, Inc., et al.* (Jointly Administered), Case No. 09-11977 (ALG).

22. Ibid., page 2.

23. Ibid., page 3.

premise on which the commercial real estate market relied, and if held invalid by enabling debtors such as GGP to include such entities, "investors as well as more traditional real estate lenders will no longer be able to rely on the bankruptcy remoteness of their special purpose entity borrowers, and the infusion of badly needed capital [would be] be chilled."[24]

ING Clarion felt that GGP "took advantage" of the more favorable terms and financing that it was able to obtain because the special purpose entities were an isolated asset, yet because of its own financial problems, was now attempting, in "bad faith," to consolidate its assets in an effort to apply maximum operational and financial leverage within bankruptcy.[25] All the special purpose entities in question were not in default, provided positive monthly cash flows (exceeding the amounts required under their respective loan documents), and displayed "no imminent threats to their respective financial stability."[26]

ING Clarion's motion for dismissal was premised on Section 1112(b) of the Bankruptcy Code, which provides that a movant may request dismissal of a bankruptcy case for "cause."[27] Bankruptcy Code Section 1112(b)(4) providing examples of what constitutes "cause" for purposes of conversion or dismissal.[28]

On May 29, 2009, Wells Fargo Bank, N.A., as a trustee for the registered holders of securities and noteholders, filed a similar motion to that of ING Clarion, but for the Faneuil Hall Marketplace, LLC, and Saint Louis Galleria, LLC.[29] On that same date, Metropolitan Life Insurance Company filed two motions for dismissal of the bankruptcy filings of certain special purpose entities. The first motion was to have the cases of Providence Place Holdings LLC and Rouse Providence LLC dismissed.[30] The second motion was to dismiss the cases of Howard Hughes Properties, Limited Partnership, 10000 West Charleston Boulevard LLC, 9901-9921 Covington Cross, LLC, and 1120/1140 Town Center Drive, LLC.[31] In addition, Metropolitan Life Insurance filed a motion with JBC Bank N.V. to dismiss the Chapter 11 cases of White Marsh Mall LLC, White Marsh Mall Associates, White Marsh Phase II Associates, and White Marsh General Partnership.[32] In all of these motions, the movants argued that bankruptcy filings of the respective special purpose entities were not filed in good faith or for a "reorganization purpose."[33] Rather, it was believed that they were filed "merely to

---

24. Ibid., page 3.

25. Ibid., pages 2, 11.

26. Ibid., pages 5–10.

27. 11 U.S.C.§ 1112(b)(1).

28. 11 U.S.C.§ 1112(b)(4).

29. Motion of Wells Fargo Bank, N.A., as Trustee, et al., To Dismiss the Cases of Faneuil Hall Marketplace, LLC and Saint Louis Galleria LLC; (Docket No. 429); In re *General Growth Properties, Inc., et al.* (Jointly Administered), Case No. 09-11977 (ALG).

30. Motion of Metropolitan Life Insurance Company to Dismiss the Cases of Providence Place Holdings LLC and Rouse Providence LLC Pursuant to Section 1112(b) of the Bankruptcy Code; (Docket No. 629); In re *General Growth Properties, Inc., et al.* (Jointly Administered), Case No. 09-11977 (ALG).

31. Motion of Metropolitan Life Insurance Company to Dismiss the Cases of Howard Hughes Properties, Limited Partnership, 10000 West Charleston Boulevard LLC, 9901-9921 Covington Cross, LLC, and 1120/1140 Town Center Drive, LLC Pursuant to Section 1112(b) of the Bankruptcy Code; (Docket No. 630); In re *General Growth Properties, Inc., et al.* (Jointly Administered), Case No. 09-11977 (ALG).

32. Motion of Metropolitan Life Insurance Company and KBC Bank N.V. to Dismiss the Cases of White Marsh Mall, LLC, White Marsh Mall Associates, White Marsh Phase II Associates, and White Marsh General Partnership Pursuant to Section 1112(b) of the Bankruptcy Code; (Docket No. 631); In re *General Growth Properties, Inc., et al.* (Jointly Administered), Case No. 09-11977 (ALG).

33. Ibid., page 3.

obtain leverage and tactical advantage in future efforts" for GGP, whose "unrelated financial problems" were the basis for the bankruptcy filings.[34]

Bankruptcy Court Ruling

On August 11, 2009, United States Bankruptcy Judge Allan L. Gropper rendered a Memorandum of Opinion with regard to five aforementioned motions to dismiss. In his Memorandum of Opinion, Judge Gropper considered the nature of special purpose entities and agreed that "there [was] no question that this structure was designed to make each subject debtor 'bankruptcy remote.'"[35] He, however, held that the interests of GGP as entire group needed to be considered.[36] Specifically, Judge Gropper referred to the fact that those who lend to a special purpose entity are aware that they are "extending credit to a company that [is] part of a much larger group, and that there [are] benefits as well as possible detriments from this structure."[37] Cited were the large amount of fixed debt that was not contingent; cross-default provisions of loans, which would cause defaults under the loans of its affiliates; and hyper-amortization provisions of the loans.[38] "If the ability of [GGP] to obtain refinancing became impaired, the financial situation of the [special-purpose entities] would inevitably be impaired."[39] Judge Gropper explained that GGP is attempting to reorganize its capital structure and refinance its debt based on future cash flows and earnings of subsidiaries and could not do so "responsibly" without including its subsidiaries and affiliates.[40]

Judge Gropper, however, held that "the interests of the subsidiaries or their creditors should [not] be sacrificed to the interests of the parents or their creditors" and that the filing of the bankruptcy would not "sacrifice [or impair their] fundamental rights."[41] Though the movants were only currently receiving interest on the loans and would not receive amortization payments, as secured creditors, they still possessed "a panoply of rights, including adequate protection and the right to postpetition interest and fees if they are oversecured."[42] In addition, there remained "continuance maintenance of the properties encumbered by their liens, a replacement lien on the cash from the properties of the [movants] that is paid upstream to the GGP parent, and a second priority lien on other properties."[43]

Though the cash flows were partially interrupted and special servicers were appointed for the respective entities, the movants were secured creditors and the protections negotiated through the special purpose entity remained in place and would continue to exist within in the Chapter 11 bankruptcy.[44] Most importantly, the assets of the special purpose entities would not be substantively consolidated with the other Debtors.

Based on this, Judge Gropper denied all five of the motions to dismiss.

---

34. Ibid., page 3.

35. Memorandum of Opinion, page 28.

36. Ibid.

37. Ibid.

38. KattenMuchinRosenman, LLP, "GGP opinion leaves unanswered questions," Client Advisory. www.kattenlaw.com/.../GGP_Opinion_Leaves_Unanswered_Questions.pdf; page 2.

39. Memorandum of Opinion, page 28.

40. Ibid., page 30.

41. Ibid., pages 30, 41.

42. Ibid., page 41.

43. KattenMuchinRosenman, LLP, "GGP opinion."

44. Memorandum of Opinion, page 42.

Complaint of Mary Bucksbaum Scanlan, Daughter of Martin Bucksbaum

On August 17, 2009, Mary Bucksbaum Scanlan, Martin's daughter, and the niece of Matthew Bucksbaum and cousin of John Bucksbaum, filed a complaint against the General Trust Company, the law firm Neal, Gerber & Eisenberg, and attorneys Marshall Eisenberg and Earl Melamed. Ms. Scanlan's complaint alleged various acts of attorney malpractice and breaches of fiduciary duty.[45]

1. This is an action to redress repeated acts of attorney malpractice and breaches of the fiduciary duties owed to Mary by her attorneys at Neal, Gerber & Eisenberg, LLP (NGE) and the actions by those attorneys that unlawfully assisted General Trust Company (GTC) in breaching the fiduciary duties that it owed to Mary as the trustee of the trusts that once held over two billion dollars in assets for Mary's benefit.

2. Mary was born in 1969 and she is the only natural born child of Melva and Martin Bucksbaum (Martin). Martin, along with his brother, Matthew Bucksbaum (Matthew), was responsible for the creation over several decades of a vast real estate empire, with their efforts culminating in the creation of General Growth Properties, Inc. (GGP). When Martin died in 1995, GGP was publicly traded on the New York Stock Exchange and was one of the largest real estate investment trusts in the United States.

3. Beginning when Mary was a child, Martin established a series of trusts for her benefit (which are described below and are referred to collectively herein as Mary's Trusts or the Trusts). Martin's brother, Matthew, similarly established a series of trusts for his family, including trusts for the benefit of his daughter, Ann Friedman, and his son, John Bucksbaum (John).

4. Beginning by at least the 1980s, NGE, through Eisenberg, simultaneously represented both Martin and Matthew individually and the business entities that Martin and Matthew established in connection with their real estate ventures and other investments.

5. NGE, acting primarily through Eisenberg, created a situation in which NGE simultaneously represented (1) GGP and its affiliates, (2) Mary's Trusts, which were heavily invested in GGP, (3) the myriad entities that were created by NGE as investment vehicles for both Mary's Trusts and the trusts established for the benefit of other Bucksbaum family members, (4) Mary as an individual and (5) other members of the Bucksbaum family, who held top executive level positions at GGP. Eisenberg also served as GGP's Corporate Secretary from at least 1992 to 2004.

6. In addition to these conflicting attorney-client representations, NGE established GTC in the late 1980s to serve as the corporate trustee for Mary's Trusts and as the trustee for other trusts that had been established for the benefit of other Bucksbaum family members. NGE also acts as counsel for GTC. While NGE was counsel to both GTC and Mary individually, NGE systematically implemented a series of transactions in which GTC replaced the existing trustees of Mary's

---

45. In re *Mary Bucksbaum Scanlan, Plaintiff, v. Marshall Eisenberg, Earl Melamed, Neal, Gerber & Eisenberg, LLP, an Illinois limited liability partnership, and General Trust Company, a South Dakota corporation*, Defendants. Case 1: 09-cv-05026, Filed 08/17/2009 In the United States District Court for the Northern District of Illinois.

Trusts, transactions that furthered the self-interests of Eisenberg, Melamed and NGE. As a result, GTC now acts as the sole corporate trustee for all of Mary's Trusts and it controls the vast majority of her assets. Eisenberg and Melamed, who are both partners in NGE, also personally control GTC. Eisenberg is the majority owner of GTC, the President of GTC, a member of GTC's Board of Directors and one of the three members of GTC's Trust Committee. Melamed also serves on GTC's Board of Directors, as GTC's Secretary and as the second member of GTC's three member Trust Committee.

7. In addition to these conflicting roles, Eisenberg and Melamed also individually own stock in GGP—a fact that gives rise to yet another conflict of interest.

8. As a result of these conflicts, NGE, Eisenberg and Melamed placed themselves in a situation in which they were rendered incapable of satisfying their professional obligations to render independent, objective legal advice in their role as Mary's counsel and ensuring that GTC satisfied its fiduciary responsibilities to properly manage the assets of Mary's Trusts for her benefit. For example, in addition to the significant legal fees that have been paid to NGE by GGP, Mary's Trusts and Mary individually over the past several decades, Eisenberg placed himself in a position to gain additional remuneration as a result of his ownership interest in GTC. In addition, as GGP's stock price plummeted during 2008—from an all time high of $64.43 in 2007 to below $1.00 per share in November 1008—NGE, Eisenberg and Melamed, acting through GTC, sacrificed hundreds of millions of dollars of the non-GGP assets held by Mary's Trusts, without disclosure to Mary, to satisfy loan obligations that GTC, NGE, Eisenberg and Melamed undertook through M.B. Capital Partners III (hereinafter referred to as MB Capital Partners) to buy more GGP stock in 2008. MB Capital Partners is one of the partnership entities that had been established by NGE to act as an investment vehicle for Mary's Trusts and the trusts of other members of the Bucksbaum family. Furthermore, without disclosure to Mary, GTC, NGE, Eisenberg and Melamed caused assets owned by Mary's Trusts to be used to make personal unsecured loans totaling at least $90 million dollars to two officers of GGP for the purpose of allowing those officers to meet margin calls associated with their holdings of GGP stock as GGP teetered toward insolvency.

9. As a result of the defendants' wrongful conduct, the value of Mary's Trusts has been reduced by more than three hundred million dollars.

General Growth Properties May Exit Bankruptcy

GGP stock reached a low of approximately $.10 per share when it filed for bankruptcy protection. By freeing much of the excess cash in its SPEs, GGP operated within bankruptcy protection successfully enough that on December 1, 2009, it filed a 607 proposed reorganization plan that would allow GGP and many of its SPEs to exit bankruptcy.[46] On December 18, 2009, GGP announced that the bankruptcy court had authorized the company to pay a dividend to common stockholders.[47] Although

---

46. In re *General Growth Properties, Inc., et al, Debtors.* Disclosure Statement for Plan Debtors' Joint Plan of Reorganiation Under Chapter 11 of the Bankruptcy Code; Case No. 09-11977 (ALG), Docket #3659, filed 12/1/2009.

47. EX-99.1, GGP Form 8-K, *"General Growth Properties, Inc., Announces Common Stock Dividend,"* December 21, 2009, Press Release dated December 18, 2009. http://www.sec.gov/Archives/edgar/data/895648/000095012309072159/c55176exv99w1.htm.

GGP was still in bankruptcy as of early August 2010, GGP's stock was relisted on the New York Stock Exchange in May 2010. GGP's market price in early August 2010 had risen from its low of about $.10 per share to above $14.00 per share.

Required

1. Evaluate governance issues in relation to:

    a. Loans to GGP executives to cover margin losses on GGP common stock purchases.

    b. The replacement of independent directors.

    c. The Mary Bucksbaum Scanlon's Trusts.

2. Why was GGP the only major mall owner/manager to file for bankruptcy protection during the financial crises of 2008–2009?

3. Many analysts expected GGP equity holders to lose most or all of their financial interests in GGP. The joint bankruptcy filing of GGP and most of its SPEs has apparently allowed GGP to successfully reorganize much of its debt and repay all of its obligations, while retaining substantial value for its equity holders. Do you agree or disagree with the court's decision to allow GGP's SPEs to enter bankruptcy protection? Explain.

4. What are the implications of the GGP bankruptcy for the securitization markets? Explain.

EXHIBIT 1

GENERAL GROWTH PROPERTIES, SELECTED FINANCIAL INFORMATION ($ MILLIONS)

	2008	2007	2006	2005	2004	2003	2002	2001	2000	1999	1998	1997	1996	1995	1994
Revenue	$3,362	$3,262	$3,256	$3,073	$1,800	$1,271	$977	$804	$699	$612	$426	$291	$217	$167	$153
Net income	$26	$288	$59	$76	$268	$263	$209	$92	$138	$101	$66	$90	$60	$43	$14
Revenue growth (%)	3.07%	0.18%	5.96%	70.72%	41.62%	30.09%	21.52%	15.02%	14.22%	43.66%	46.39%	34.10%	29.94%	9.15%	
Total Assets	$29,294	$28,814	$25,241	$25,307	$25,719	$9,583	$7,281	$5,647	$5,284	$4,955	$4,027	$2,098	$1,758	$1,456	
Total Debt	$27,294	$26,885	$23,046	$22,738	$22,621	$7,009	$4,901	$3,398	$3,244	$3,120	$2,649	$1,276	$1,235	$1,091	
Debt as a % of Assets	92.3%	93.3%	91.3%	89.8%	88.0%	73.1%	67.3%	60.2%	61.4%	63.0%	65.8%	60.8%	70.3%	74.9%	
Cash flow from															
Operating activities	$556	$707	$816	$842	$719	$578	$460	$207	$287	$206	$85	$94	$53	$61	$49
Investing activities	−$1,209	−$1,781	−$210	−$160	−$9,022	−$1,745	−$949	−$367	−$357	−$1,238	−$1,480	−$176	−$15	−$469	−$145
Financing activities	$722	$1,076	−$611	−$619	$8,311	$1,124	$382	$294	$71	$1,039	$1,389	$92	−$40	$421	$96
Net change in cash	$69	$2	−$5	$63	$28	−$43	−$107	$134	$1	$7	−$6	$10	−$2	$13	$0
Cash distributaion/share*	$1.50	$1.85	$1.68	$1.49	$1.26	$1.02	$0.89	$0.75	$0.69	$0.66	$0.63	$0.60	$0.57	$0.55	$0.53
Stock price—low*	$0.24	$39.31	$41.92	31.38	$24.31	$15.90	$12.67	$10.93	$8.79	$8.33	$10.96	$10.08	$6.88	$6.17	$6.42
Stock price—high*	$44.23	$67.43	$52.32	48.27	$26.90	$28.03	$17.43	$13.50	$12.17	$12.88	$12.90	$12.75	$10.92	$7.25	$7.54
Cash distribution as a % of average stock price	6.75%	3.47%	3.57%	5.82%	5.74%	4.64%	5.91%	6.11%	6.55%	6.22%	5.25%	5.26%	6.44%	8.25%	7.55%

*Adjusted for 3–1 stock split in 2003.

EXHIBIT 2

GENERAL GROWTH
PROPERTIES,
INCOME
STATEMENTS

	Years Ended December 31		
	2008	**2007**	**2006**
	(dollars in thousands, except for per share amounts)		
Revenues:			
Minimum rents	$2,085,758	$1,933,674	$1,753,508
Tenant recoveries	927,332	859,801	773,034
Overage rents	72,882	89,016	75,945
Land sales	66,557	145,649	423,183
Management and other fees	85,773	106,584	115,798
Other	123,223	127,077	114,815
Total revenues	3,361,525	3,261,801	3,256,283
Expenses:			
Real estate taxes	274,317	246,484	218,549
Repairs and maintenance	234,987	216,536	199,078
Marketing	43,426	54,664	48,626
Other property operating costs	436,804	418,295	368,706
Land sales operations	63,441	116,708	316,453
Provision for doubtful accounts	17,873	5,426	22,078
Property management and other costs	184,738	198,610	181,033
General and administrative	57,972	37,005	18,800
Provisions for impairment	116,611	130,533	4,314
Litigation (recovery) provision	(57,145)	89,225	—
Depreciation and amortization	759,930	670,454	690,194
Total expenses	2,132,954	2,183,940	2,067,831
Operating income	1,228,571	1,077,861	1,188,452
Interest income	3,197	8,641	11,585
Interest expense	(1,299,496)	(1,174,097)	(1,117,437)
(Loss) income before income taxes, minority interest and equity in income of Unconsolidated Real Estate Affiliates	(67,728)	(87,595)	82,600
(Provision for) benefit from income taxes	(23,461)	294,160	(98,984)
Minority interest	(9,145)	(77,012)	(37,761)
Equity in income of Unconsolidated Real Estate Affiliates	80,594	158,401	114,241
(Loss) income from continuing operations	(19,740)	287,954	60,096
Discontinued operations, net of minority interests - gain (loss) on dispositions	46,000	—	(823)
Net income	$26,260	$287,954	$59,273

EXHIBIT 3

GENERAL GROWTH
PROPERTIES,
BALANCE SHEETS

	Years Ended December 31	
	2008	2007
	(dollars in thousands)	
Assets		
Investment in real estate:		
Land	$3,354,480	$3,310,634
Buildings and equipment	23,609,132	22,653,814
Less accumulated depreciation	(4,240,222)	(3,605,199)
Developments in progress	1,076,675	987,936
Net property and equipment	23,800,065	23,347,185
Investment in and loans to/from		
Unconsolidated Real Estate Affiliates	1,869,929	1,857,330
Investment land and land held for		
development and sale	1,823,362	1,639,372
Net investment in real estate	27,493,356	26,843,887
Cash and cash equivalents	168,993	99,534
Accounts and notes receivable, net	385,334	388,278
Goodwill	340,291	385,683
Deferred expenses, net	333,901	290,660
Prepaid expenses and other assets	835,455	806,277
Total assets	$29,557,330	$28,814,319
Liabilities and stockholders' equity		
Mortgages, notes and loans payable	$24,853,313	$24,282,139
Investment in and loans to/from		
Unconsolidated Real estate affiliates	32,294	53,964
Deferred tax liabilities	868,978	860,435
Accounts payable, accrued expenses and	1,539,149	1,688,241
other liabilities		
Total liabilities	27,293,734	26,884,779
Minority interests:		
Preferred	121,232	121,482
Common	387,616	351,362
Total minority interests	508,848	472,844
Commitments and contingencies	—	—
Preferred stock: $100 par value;		
5,000,000 shares authorized; none issued		
and outstanding	—	—
Stockholders' equity		
Common stock: $.01 par value;		
875,000,000 shares authorized, 270,353,677		
and 245,704,746 shares issued as of		
December 31, 2008 and 2007, respectively	2,704	2,457
Additional paid-in capital	3,337,657	2,601,296
Retained earnings (accumulated deficit)	(1,452,733)	(1,087,080)
Accumulated other comprehensive (loss) income	(56,128)	35,658
Less common stock in treasury, at cost,		
1,449,939 and 1,806,650 shares as of		
December 31, 2008 and 2007, respectively	(76,752)	(95,635)
Total stockholders' equity	1,754,748	1,456,696
Total liabilities and stockholders' equity	$29,557,330	$28,814,319

EXHIBIT 4

GENERAL GROWTH PROPERTIES, CASH FLOW STATEMENTS

	2008	2007	2006
		(in thousands)	
Cash Flows from Operating Activities:			
Net income	$26,260	$287,954	$59,273
Adjustments to reconcile net income to net cash provided by operating activities:			
Minority interests	9,145	77,012	37,761
Equity in income of Unconsolidated Real Estate Affiliates	(80,594)	(158,401)	(114,241)
Provision for doubtful accounts	17,873	5,426	22,078
Distributions received from Unconsolidated Real Estate Affiliates	68,240	124,481	111,864
Depreciation	712,522	635,873	663,523
Amortization	47,408	34,581	26,671
Amortization of debt market rate adjustment and other non-cash interest expense	28,410	(11,073)	(13,570)
Gains on dispositions, net of minority interest	(46,000)	—	—
Provisions for impairment	116,611	130,533	4,314
Participation expense pursuant to Contingent Stock Agreement	2,849	31,884	110,740
Land/residential development and acquisitions expenditures	(166,141)	(243,323)	(200,367)
Cost of land sales	24,516	48,794	175,184
Deferred income taxes including tax restructuring benefit	(4,144)	(368,136)	58,252
Straight-line rent amortization	(27,827)	(24,334)	(34,176)
Amortization of intangibles other than in-place leases	(5,691)	(20,945)	(41,668)
Glendale Matter deposit	(67,054)	—	—
Net changes:			
Accounts and notes receivable	12,702	(21,868)	(23,091)
Prepaid expenses and other assets	26,845	53,819	28,165
Deferred expenses	(62,945)	(37,878)	(46,741)
Accounts payable and accrued expenses	(94,188)	135,980	(30,733)
Other, net	17,644	27,037	23,113
Net cash provided by operating activities	556,441	707,416	816,351

EXHIBIT—4 continued

GENERAL GROWTH PROPERTIES, CASH FLOW STATEMENTS

Cash Flows from Investing Activities:

Acquisition/development of real estate and property additions/improvements	(1,187,551)	(1,495,334)	(699,403)
Proceeds from sales of investment properties	72,958	3,252	23,117
Increase in investments in Unconsolidated Real Estate Affiliates	(227,821)	(441,438)	(285,747)
Distributions received from Unconsolidated Real Estate Affiliates in excess of income	110,533	303,265	627,869
Loans (to) from Unconsolidated Real Estate Affiliates, net	15,028	(161,892)	67,821
(Increase) decrease in restricted cash	(12,419)	(11,590)	12,017
Other, net	20,282	22,805	43,926
Net cash used in investing activities	(1,208,990)	(1,780,932)	(210,400)

Cash Flows from Financing Activities:

Proceeds from issuance of mortgages, notes and loans payable	3,732,716	4,456,863	9,366,183
Principal payments on mortgages, notes and loans payable	(3,314,039)	(2,692,907)	(9,383,378)
Deferred financing costs	(63,236)	(28,422)	(38,916)
Cash distributions paid to common stockholders	(389,528)	(450,854)	(403,831)
Cash distributions paid to holders of Common Units	(78,255)	(96,978)	(88,992)
Cash distributions paid to holders of perpetual and convertible preferred units	(8,812)	(13,873)	(17,546)
Proceeds from issuance of common stock, including from common stock plans	829,291	60,625	49,267
Redemption of minority interests—preferred	—	(60,000)	—
Purchase of Treasury stock	—	(95,648)	(85,925)
Other, net	13,871	(2,895)	(8,465)
Net cash provided by (used in) financing activities	722,008	1,075,911	(611,603)
Net change in cash and cash equivalents	69,459	2,395	(5,652)
Cash and cash equivalents at beginning of period	99,534	97,139	102,791
Cash and cash equivalents at end of period	$168,993	$99,534	$97,139

Supplemental Disclosure of Cash Flow Information:

Interest paid	$1,342,659	$1,272,823	$1,170,929
Interest capitalized	66,244	86,606	58,019
Taxes paid	43,835	96,133	34,743

FINANCIAL REPORTING— U.S. GAAP

3

Intel Corporation and Inventory Write-downs

Both the International Financial Reporting Standards (IFRS) and U.S. Generally Accepted Accounting Principles (GAAP) require that inventory be valued at the lower of cost or some measure of what that inventory can be sold for in the market. Under U.S. GAAP, the rule is usually called *lower of cost* or *market*; under IFRS it is called *lower of cost* or *net realisable value*.

Inventory cost includes the purchase price, import duties, shipping costs, and similar items. It also includes conversion costs such as direct labor and an allocation of indirect labor and both variable and fixed production overhead.

In many instances, the cost of inventories may not be recoverable. Electronics manufacturers, such as Dell and Palm, purchased large inventories of chips that were in short supply. When chip manufacturers drastically reduced the price on those chips, Dell and Palm wrote down their inventories. Similarly, when demand for Intel's products decline, Intel must write down its inventories. Firms also write down damaged goods, and the fashion industry will write down goods toward the end of a season, when items may sell for less than their cost.

Under IFRS, inventories must be written down to lower of cost or "net realisable value" (IAS 2, par. 28), where *net realisable* value is defined as:

> *Net realisable value refers to the net amount that an entity expects to realize from the sale of inventory in the ordinary course of business. Fair value reflects the amount for which the same inventory could be exchanged between knowledgeable and willing buyers and sellers in the marketplace. The former is an entity-specific value; the latter is not. Net realizable value for inventories may not equal fair value less costs to sell (IAS 2, par. 7).*

Suppose a retailer using IFRS buys a television from its supplier for $325 and expects to sell the television for $425. A week later the supplier drops the price to $275, and in response, the retailer drops its retail price to $375. If the retailer's selling cost is $35, its net realizable value will be $340 ($375 selling price, less $35 selling cost). Its $340 net realizable value is greater than its $325 cost, so the retailer would continue to value the item at its $325 original cost.

Here is a typical IFRS inventory disclosure from The Swatch Group's 2008 annual report:

> *Inventories are stated at the lower of cost and net realizable value. Cost is determined using the weighted average price method. Some companies, particularly those in the Production segment, value their inventories using the standard cost method. As these costs are regularly reviewed and adjusted, this method approximates the results of the weighted average price method. The valuation of spare parts for customer service is confined to those units that are considered likely to be used, based on historical demand.*

> *Net realizable value is the estimated selling price in the ordinary course of business, less estimated costs of completion and the applicable variable selling expenses.*

Under U.S. GAAP, inventory is written down to the lower of cost or market, but the market is subject to both a ceiling and a floor. The ceiling is net realizable value, and the floor is net realizable value less a normal profit margin. In most cases, the differences between U.S. GAAP and IFRS lower of cost or market rules are minimal.

Firms are required to disclose inventory write-downs if they are material, but those disclosures often provide limited information about the write-down. Inventory write-downs are particularly common at firms that sell seasonal goods such lawn mowers, winter coats, or swim suits. They are also common at technology firms where new products depress the price of older products as prices drop rapidly, following Moore's Law.[1]

Intel is the world's leading semiconductor producer. The number of devices on Intel's semiconductors has increased by about 50% every 18 months since about 1971, so Intel continually introduces new products, which make obsolete existing products. Because the cost of Intel products declines rapidly, and because Intel introduces new products every quarter, Intel probably has inventory write-downs every quarter. In many quarters, the write-downs have been significant enough to merit at least some disclosure. In other quarters, Intel only disclosed that there is uncertainty in the valuation of obsolete or excess inventory. Most of Intel's 10-Q reports contain a statement similar to the following from Intel's first quarter 2009 10-Q.

Management Discussion and Analysis of Financial Condition and Results of Operations
Inventory

The valuation of inventory requires us to estimate obsolete or excess inventory as well as inventory that is not of saleable quality. The determination of obsolete or excess inventory requires us to estimate the future demand for our products. The estimate of future demand is compared to work in process and finished goods inventory levels to determine the amount, if any, of obsolete or excess inventory. As of March 28, 2009, we had total work-in-process inventory of $1,448 million and total finished goods inventory of $1,217 million. The demand forecast is included in the development of our short-term manufacturing plans to enable consistency between inventory valuation and build decisions. Product-specific facts and circumstances reviewed in the inventory valuation process include a review of the customer base, the stage of the product life cycle of our products, consumer confidence, and customer acceptance of our products, as well as an assessment of the selling price in relation to the product cost. If our demand forecast for specific products is greater than actual demand and we fail to reduce manufacturing output accordingly, or if we fail to forecast the demand accurately, we could be required to write off inventory, which would negatively impact our gross margin.

Notes to Consolidated Condensed Financial Statements—Unaudited
Note 6: Inventories

Inventories at the end of each period were as follows:

(In millions)	March 28, 2009	Dec. 27, 2008
Raw materials	$380	$608
Work in process	1,448	1,577
Finished goods	1,217	1,559
Total inventories	**$3,045**	**$3,744**

1. Intel cofounder Gordon Moore observed in 1965 that the number of transistors on a chip approximately doubles every two years. That rule, known as Moore's Law, has been extended to the cost of electronics components such as CPU and memory chips, LCD monitors, and hard drives, and to the cost of consumer electronics products. See www.intel.com/technology/mooreslaw/index.htm.

The valuation of inventory requires us to estimate obsolete or excess inventory as well as inventory that is not of saleable quality. The determination of obsolete or excess inventory requires us to estimate the future demand for our products. It is reasonably possible that our estimate of future demand for our products could change in the near term and result in additional inventory write-offs, which would negatively impact our gross margin.

Exhibit 1 summarizes Intel's deferred tax asset from inventory. Intel must record an inventory write-down expense for financial reporting but is not allowed to report inventory write-downs for tax reporting. For example, suppose Intel wrote inventory down by $100 million in Q2 2009. Also suppose Intel was subject to an average income tax rate of 30%. For financial reporting, Intel would record the following entry to write down inventory:

Cost of sales—inventory write-down	$100,000,000	
Allowance for obsolete inventory		$100,000,000

Because this reduces reported financial accounting income by $100 million, it will reduce the provision for income taxes (income tax expense) by $30 million (because of the 30% tax rate). However, because this does not reduce income taxes payable to the IRS, the offsetting debit will be to deferred tax assets, not to taxes payable:

Deferred tax assets	$30,000,000	
Provision for income taxes		$30,000,000

As a result, when Intel's deferred tax asset for inventory valuation in Exhibit 1 increases by $30 million, Intel has increased its allowance for obsolete inventory by about $100 million.

Exhibit 2 shows all of Intel's 10-Q inventory write-down disclosures from Q1 1996 through Q3 2009, except for the general statement that inventory write-downs require estimates. Over the years, some analysts suggested that Intel may use excessive inventory write-downs to lower net income in quarters when profit is higher than expected. In subsequent quarters, when profit is lower than expected, those analysts suggested that Intel might sell the written-down inventory at abnormally high profit margins to increase reported profits.

Required

1. Evaluate this statement from Intel's Q1 2004 10-Q footnote disclosure (Exhibit 2): "In addition, Q1 2003 benefited from the unusually high level of sales of microprocessor and chipset inventory that had been previously reserved."

2. Evaluate this statement from Intel's Q2 2007 10-Q footnote disclosure: "Sales of desktop microprocessor inventory that had been previously written off further offset the effect of the revenue decline."

3. Evaluate this statement from Intel's Q2 2008 10-Q: These increases were partially offset by sales in the first half of 2007 of desktop microprocessor inventory that had been previously written off.

4. How much flexibility does Intel have in writing down excess inventories? Explain.

5. Evaluate the quality of the inventory disclosures in Exhibit 2.

EXHIBIT 1

INTEL CORP.
2008 10-K TAX
FOOTNOTE

The following deferred tax assets are taken from the Taxes note to Intel Corp.'s annual 10-K reports. They are the deferred tax asset that results from inventory write-downs for financial reporting purposes that were not yet allowed for tax reporting (inventory write-downs are not permitted for tax reporting until the written-down inventory is sold to a third party or destroyed).

The inventory write-down depends on the cumulative amount written off for financial reporting that has not been written off for tax purposes, adjusted for Intel's effective rate, which has averaged about 30% over the past two decades. The amount Intel has written off for financial reporting purposes but not for tax purposes is probably about 3.5 times as large as its deferred tax asset for inventory reserves.

DEFERRED TAX ASSET, INVENTORY VALUATION

	Millions
1994	$255
1995	$104
1996	$187
1997	$163
1998	$106
1999	$91
2000	$120
2001	$209
2002	$184
2003	$156
2004	$193
2005	$251
2006	$268
2007	$315
2008	$602

EXHIBIT 2

INTEL CORP.
QUARTERLY
INVENTORY
WRITE-DOWN
DISCLOSURES, 1996
TO Q3, 2009

10-Q INVENTORY WRITE-DOWN DISCLOSURES

1996

Q1

Cost of sales rose by 50% from Q1 1995 to Q1 1996 primarily due to increased unit volumes. Gross margin declined from 55% in Q1 1995 to 48% in Q1 1996 due primarily to increased sales of Pentium processor related board level products at lower margins, factory start-up costs and inventory reserves, including continuing reserves related to inventories of certain purchased components.

Q2

Cost of sales rose by 19% from Q2 1995 to Q2 1996, primarily due to increased unit volumes. Gross margin was 53% in Q2 1996 versus 54% in Q2 1995. Although the Company's gross margin percentage had been declining since Q2 1995, it returned to the prior year's level, primarily due to lower memory inventory write offs than the Company has been experiencing recently.

(continued)

EXHIBIT 2—
continued

INTEL CORP.
QUARTERLY
INVENTORY
WRITE-DOWN
DISCLOSURES, 1996
TO Q3, 2009

1997

Q1

Cost of sales declined by 5% from Q1 1996 to Q1 1997 due to shifts in product mix and factory efficiencies due to increased volume. Costs for Q1 of 1996 also included unusually high inventory reserves, including reserves related to inventories of certain purchased components. Gross margin increased from 48% in Q1 1996 to 64% in Q1 1997 due to the more favorable product mix and the reduced costs discussed above.

1998

Q2

Cost of sales increased by 29% from Q2 1997 to Q2 1998 due to the shift in product mix to the Pentium(R) II processor, reflecting the cost of purchased components for the Single Edge Contact ("SEC") cartridge, higher unit volumes, and higher fixed costs. In addition, in Q2 1998 reductions in product costs on the highest volume processors caused inventories to be written down to the new lower costs. Gross margin decreased to 49% in Q2 1998 from 61% in Q2 1997 primarily due to the lower processor prices, the impact of the SEC cartridge, the inventory write-downs and higher fixed costs.

1999

Q2

Cost of sales decreased by 8% in Q2 1999 compared to Q2 1998 primarily due to lower unit costs for microprocessors in Q2 1999 partially offset by higher unit sales volumes. In addition, cost of sales in Q2 1998 included unusually high inventory write-downs. The lower unit costs in Q2 1999 were achieved primarily through redesigned microprocessor products with lower-cost packaging, including packaging using fewer purchased components, as well as factory efficiencies and lower purchase prices on the purchased components. The gross margin percentage increased to 59% in Q2 1999, up from 49% in Q2 1998. The improvement in gross margin was primarily a result of lower unit costs in the Intel Architecture Business Group operating segment in Q2 1999, as well as the absence of the unusually high inventory write-downs recognized in Q2 1998, partially offset by the impact of lower prices in Q2 1999.

Q3

Cost of sales decreased by 3% in the first nine months of 1999 compared to the first nine months of 1998. In the Intel Architecture Business Group operating segment, lower unit costs for microprocessors in the first nine months of 1999 and the absence in 1999 of the unusually high inventory write-downs recognized in the first nine months of 1998 were partially offset by higher unit sales volumes in the first nine months of 1999.

2001

Q1

Although the total cost of sales increased 8% in Q1 2001 compared to Q1 2000, the cost of sales within the Intel Architecture Group operating segment decreased slightly for the same period. The decrease was primarily due to lower sales volume as well as lower unit costs of microprocessors as a result of lower cost packaging, partially offset by increased start-up costs related to 300-millimeter wafer manufacturing and 0.13-micron process technology. Within the "all other" category for segment reporting, higher costs due to higher sales volume of flash memory and the impact of higher inventory reserves in the flash memory and networking and communications businesses more than offset the decreased costs from the Intel Architecture Group.

(continued)

EXHIBIT 2—
continued

INTEL CORP.
QUARTERLY
INVENTORY
WRITE-DOWN
DISCLOSURES, 1996
TO Q3, 2009

Q2

Total cost of sales was essentially flat in Q2 2001 compared to Q2 2000, and the cost of sales within the Intel Architecture Group operating segment was also flat for the same period. Lower cost of sales due to a lower sales volume of microprocessors was offset by a higher average cost per unit and higher start-up costs related to the 0.13-micron process technology ramp and 300-millimeter wafer manufacturing. Within the "all other" category for segment reporting, cost of sales increased slightly primarily due to the impact of higher inventory reserves in the flash memory and networking and communications businesses, partially offset by the impact of lower unit volumes.

Q3

Net operating results decreased by $683 million to a loss of $236 million in the first nine months of 2001 from a profit of $447 million in the first nine months of 2000 primarily due to the impact of underutilized factory capacity, lower flash memory unit sales volume and higher inventory reserves.

2002
Q1

Despite the decline in net revenues for ICG, net operating results were approximately flat, with a loss of $150 million in Q1 2002 compared to a loss of $153 million in Q1 2001. This was primarily due to the impact of lower inventory write-downs in Q1 2002 compared to higher-than-normal write-downs in Q1 2001, as well as lower operating expenses, offset by the impact of lower revenues across all product lines in Q1 2002.

Q2

Our gross margin percentage decreased to 47% for Q2 2002 from 48% in Q2 2001, primarily due to the Web hosting business wind down charge. Excluding the impact of this charge, the gross margin percentage increased to 49%, primarily due to better overall factory capacity utilization and lower ICG inventory write-downs in Q2 2002, compared to higher than normal ICG inventory write-downs in Q2 2001.

Q3

Cost of sales for the first nine months of 2002 was approximately flat compared to the first nine months of 2001. In the Intel Architecture business, lower start-up manufacturing costs were more than offset by higher costs related to significantly higher volumes and higher unit costs of microprocessors, including microprocessors for the Microsoft Xbox. Cost of sales was lower due to the impact of lower unit volumes in ICG, as well as lower inventory write-downs for both ICG and WCCG.

2003
Q1

Operating income increased to $1,913 million in Q1 2003, compared to $1,802 million in Q1 2002. The increase was primarily due to the Q1 2002 impact of a charge of $155 million related to a settlement agreement with Intergraph Corporation and, in Q1 2003, higher unit volumes of microprocessors and an unusually high level of sales of microprocessor and chipset inventory that had previously been reserved.

(continued)

EXHIBIT 2—
continued

INTEL CORP.
QUARTERLY
INVENTORY
WRITE-DOWN
DISCLOSURES, 1996
TO Q3, 2009

Q2

The operating loss increased to $143 million in Q2 2003 from a $127 million loss in Q2 2002 primarily due to the mix shift to lower-margin wired Ethernet connections. In the current competitive environment, sales of wireless Ethernet connections sold in conjunction with processors and chipsets comprising the Intel Centrino mobile technology also increased the operating loss. These negative impacts were partially offset by lower inventory write-downs, as well as lower operating expenses in Q2 2003 as we continued our efforts to streamline operations and refocus on our core strategic areas.

2004
Q1

Operating income increased $1.1 billion, or 58%, in Q1 2004 compared to Q1 2003. The increase was primarily due to the impact of higher revenue and lower unit costs for microprocessors. These increases were partially offset by a $162 million charge in Q1 2004 relating to a settlement agreement with Intergraph Corporation. In addition, Q1 2003 benefited from the unusually high level of sales of microprocessor and chipset inventory that had been previously reserved.

Q2

The operating loss decreased to $126 million in Q2 2004, from a loss of $255 million in Q2 2003. Higher revenue, as well as the absence of costs incurred in Q2 2003 for underutilized factory capacity for flash memory products, improved the operating results. In addition, due to improved demand, sales of flash memory product inventory that had been previously reserved contributed to the lower operating loss. These improvements were partially offset by higher costs for flash memory products as we sold higher density products, as well as the impact of higher inventory write-offs primarily for certain applications and cellular processors.

Q3

Operating income decreased $109 million, or 4%, in Q3 2004 compared to Q3 2003. The decrease was primarily due to higher operating expenses as well as higher inventory write downs, partially offset by higher revenue from sales of microprocessors (see "Operating Expenses" below for further discussion on operating expense fluctuations).

2006
Q1

Operating income decreased $1.0 billion, or 42%, in Q1 2006 compared to Q1 2005. The significant decrease was primarily due to lower microprocessor revenue, the impact of increased write-downs of chipset inventory and higher operating expenses. These decreases were partially offset by approximately $190 million of lower start-up costs in Q1 2006.

Q2

Operating income decreased $250 million, or 11%, in the first half of 2006 compared to the first half of 2005. The decline was primarily caused by an increase in operating expenses, and to a lesser extent, higher write-down of inventory. A majority of the decline was offset by the effects of higher revenue, and to a lesser extent, by approximately $170 million of lower start-up costs in the first half of 2006.

(continued)

EXHIBIT 2—
continued

INTEL CORP.
QUARTERLY
INVENTORY
WRITE-DOWN
DISCLOSURES, 1996
TO Q3, 2009

2007

Q2

Operating income decreased by $178 million, or 9%, in the first half of 2007 compared to the first half of 2006. The decrease in operating income was primarily due to the revenue decline. Approximately $400 million of higher start-up costs, primarily related to our 45-nm process technology, as well as approximately $180 million of higher factory underutilization charges, were offset by lower operating expenses. Sales of desktop microprocessor inventory that had been previously written off further offset the effect of the revenue decline.

2008

Q1

Gross margin as a percentage of revenue was lower in the first quarter of 2008 as compared to the fourth quarter of 2007 as a result of lower microprocessor unit sales, chipset inventory write-offs, [and] higher microprocessor unit costs as we transition to products using our 45-nm process technology, and higher start-up costs associated with that transition.

Operating income decreased by $197 million, or 14%, in Q1 2008 compared to Q1 2007. The decrease in operating income was primarily due to higher operating expenses related to process development and advertising. Higher chipset unit costs and sales in Q1 2007 of mobility microprocessor inventory that had been previously written off were more than offset by lower microprocessor unit costs and higher microprocessor and chipset revenue.

Q2

Operating income increased by $1.7 billion, or 100%, in the first half of 2008 compared to the first half of 2007. The increase in operating income was primarily due to higher microprocessor revenue and approximately $330 million of lower start-up costs, primarily related to our 45-nm process technology. Lower unit cost for microprocessors and chipsets and $180 million of lower factory underutilization charges also contributed to the increase in operating income. These increases were partially offset by sales in the first half of 2007 of desktop microprocessor inventory that had been previously written off.

2009

Q3

Our gross margin percentage for the third quarter compared to the second quarter was positively impacted by higher microprocessor sales volume, lower microprocessor unit costs, lower factory underutilization charges, and lower startup costs as we transition into production using our 32-nm process technology. These improvements to our gross margin percentage were partially offset by inventory write-offs of our new 32-nm microprocessor products that were not yet qualified for sale. As we move into the fourth quarter we expect our gross margin percentage to increase further as 32-nm products built in the fourth quarter are qualified for sale. In addition, our gross margin percentage is expected to increase due to higher microprocessor sales volume and lower factory underutilization charges on increased production.

Lease Restatements in the Restaurant Industry, 2004–2005

Prior to 1970, most U.S. firms used leasing for short-term needs. A small firm might lease an office, copier, or manufacturing space for one or two years to limit the risk if the business failed. If a larger firm needed expensive equipment or a building, it often financed the asset by borrowing from a bank, using the asset as collateral. No lease accounting rules existed and none were necessary. Firms simply recorded lease expense when they made each month's rent or lease payment.

Beginning in about 1970, U.S. firms realized they could structure long-term lease agreements that were equivalent to buying an asset with debt. A firm might purchase a $50 million building with a $50 million bank loan to be repaid over a 20-year period at $410,000 per month (an effective annual interest rate of about 8%). Instead, the firm might ask its bank to structure the transaction as a $410,000 per month 20-year lease, with the additional stipulation that at the end of 20 years the firm must purchase the building for $1. The firm would also maintain and insure the building.

Except for the additional $1 after 20 years, the terms are identical, thus the bank should be indifferent as to whether the transaction is called a loan or a lease. With a lease, however, the firm would not record the building as an asset or record the present value of lease payments as debt. Using the example in the previous paragraph, suppose the firm had $150 million of assets, $50 million of debt, and $100 million of equity prior to the transaction, its debt-to-equity ratio would have been 0.5. With $50 million of added assets and debt, the debt-to-equity ratio would increase to 1.0; with a lease, the ratio would remain at 0.5. Firms began to use leasing as one of the first forms of off-balance sheet financing. Leasing became so common that in November 1976 the newly established Financial Accounting Standards Board (FASB) issued guidance on how to account for leases (Section 840, previously FAS 13).

ACS 840 (FAS 13), *Accounting for Leases*

The FASB classified leases into two categories, shorter-term operating leases and longer-term capital leases. For an operating lease, the lessee records lease expense each month when it pays the rent or lease cost. The journal entry is a debit to lease or rent expense and a credit to cash, although as discussed later in this case, in practice the journal entries are more complex.

With a capital lease, the lessee records the lease so it is equivalent to buying an asset with debt. Thereafter, the lessee separates lease payments into an interest component and a partial principal repayment. The lessee also depreciates the leased asset over the lease term, as if it bought the asset with borrowed funds.

Capital Lease Example

Exhibit 1 provides a simple example of a two-year capitalized lease. Typically, capital leases are for much longer periods, but conceptually they are identical to this example. The lessee makes a $10,000 lease payment at the beginning of each month, starting January 1, 2008 (second column). The lessee computes the lease's present value, which requires a discount rate. FASB's guidance on accounting for leases requires that the rate be the lessee's incremental borrowing rate, or the rate the lessee could have borrowed the funds it needed to purchase the leased asset.[1]

Exhibit 1 assumes an 8% effective annual borrowing rate, or a .643% monthly rate.[2] The present value of the 24 $10,000 monthly payments is $223,155.73 (the $10,000 initial payment, plus the net present value [NPV] of the remaining 23 payments, discounted at .643% monthly). That amount is recorded as a lease asset and a lease liability at the lease inception. Because the lessee pays $10,000 at the beginning of the month, the present value of the lease liability immediately declines to $213,115.73.

During January, the lessee incurs $1,371.45 of interest expense (.643% monthly interest rate, multiplied by the $213,115.73 lease payable at the beginning of January). The journal entries to record those transactions are shown at the lower left of Exhibit 1. The lessee also records straight-line depreciation expense each month over the 24-month lease term. The journal entries to record the activity for February are shown in the lower right of Exhibit 1.

Each month the $10,000 lease payment is separated into two components: interest expense and principal repayment (repayment of the lease liability). At the end of the lease, the lease liability declines to zero and accumulated depreciation increases to $223,155.73 (the value of the leased asset at inception). Interest expense plus accumulated depreciation equals the $240,000 of lease payments.

Had this been recorded as an operating lease, the lessee would have debited lease expense and credited cash for $10,000 each month. Total expenses would still be $240,000, but the lessee would not have recorded a lease asset or a lease liability at lease inception.

Test for Operating or Capital Lease

Operating leases are short-term leases with few ownership characteristics. If a realtor leases 750 square feet of office space for a year, with no requirement or incentive to renew the lease, there is no reason to believe the lease is equivalent to buying the office space. In contrast, capital leases have substantial ownership characteristics. The guidance on accounting for leases established four tests for a capital lease; if a lease passes any of the following four tests (slightly simplified), then it is classified as a capital lease:

1. The lease transfers ownership to the lessee at the end of the lease.
2. The lease contains a bargain purchase option.
3. The lease term is equal to 75% or more of the economic life of the leased property.
4. The present value at the lease inception of the minimum lease payments equals 90% or more of the fair value of the leased property.[3]

The first two tests are relatively straightforward; the last two are not. If the lease term is equal to 75% or more of the economic life of the leased property, then the lease is a capital lease. An asset's economic life, however, is highly subjective. In some instances, such as semiconductor production, equipment becomes obsolete in 2 or 3 years; in other instances, equipment may be used for 50 or 75 years. As a result, firms can often justify an economic life far beyond the lease term and thereby circumvent the third test.

---

1. ACS 840; previously FAS 13, *Lease Accounting, Financial Accounting Standards Board, November 1976, paragraph 7.*

2. $1.08 \wedge (1/12) - 1 = 0.00643$.

3. FAS 13, paragraph 5, subparagraph L.

The fourth test, although far less subjective than the third, is subject to manipulation. Sometimes a firm's incremental borrowing rate is readily determined, but often it is not. As a result, some firms have assumed unrealistically high borrowing rates to circumvent the fourth test. There are also many subtleties that the last test does not address. For example, suppose the lease term for a building is 10 years and the present value of the lease payments is only 60% of the building's fair value. That clearly does not equal or exceed the 75% requirement of the fourth test, so the transaction seems to qualify as an operating lease.

However, suppose that if the lessee fails to renew the lease for a second 10-year period, the lessee must pay a $15 million penalty. As another alternative, suppose there is no failure-to-renew penalty, but that the lessee guarantees the building will have a fair value of at least $30 million at the end of the 10-year lease. Over the years, a large number of issues arose that were not fully addressed by the guidance on accounting for leases. As a result, the FASB, Securities and Exchange Commission (SEC), and American Institute of Certified Public Accountants (AICPA) issued about 100 additional leasing guidelines, clarifications, and rules.

As the rules for leases and other accounting issues became more complex, large CPA firms established technical groups to provide guidance to engagement partners (partners responsible for conducting an audit). Technical groups include senior partners and managers who are experts in fields such as revenue recognition, leasing, derivatives, hedging, employee compensation, taxes, and international operations. In these areas, accounting rules are detailed, complex, and unsettled.

Each of the four large accounting firms (Deloitte & Touche, Ernst & Young, KMPG, and PwC) has a technical group of at least 100 partners and managers. The groups receive several thousand relatively formal inquiries each month from engagement partners and managers, although many partners call their technical groups almost daily with less formal questions. Technical groups can sometimes answer a question with little or no research but usually research a topic and then provide an answer. In many instances they must contact technical groups of the other big four firms or, if necessary, the FASB and SEC.

In contrast, the International Financial Reporting Standards (IFRS) has only one leasing standard, International Accounting Standard (IAS) 17, *Leases.* The IFRS standard has five tests for whether a lease is a finance (the IFRS term for capital lease) or operating lease. The first two are very similar to those under U.S. GAAP. IFRS takes a more general view on the next two. Instead of a lease term that is 75% or more of the asset's life, IAS 17 requires that "the lease term is for the major part of the economic life of the asset even if title is not transferred." Instead of 90% or more of the asset's present value, IAS 17 requires that "at the inception of the lease, the present value of the minimum lease payments amounts to at least substantially all of the fair value of the leased asset." In practice, at least some of the large accounting firms simply use the 75% and 90% bright-line tests from the lease accounting guidance under U.S. GAAP when applying lease accounting to firms that report under IFRS. The IFRS also requires that a lease be capitalized (reported as a finance lease) if "the leased assets are of such a specialized nature that only the lessee can use them without major modification."

Leasing Problems in the Restaurant Industry

Prior to 2002, the AICPA administered peer reviews in which CPA firms reviewed the work of similar-size firms. In response to perceived widespread financial manipulation, in 2002 the U.S. Congress passed the Sarbanes-Oxley Act. Part of that act established the Public Company Accounting Oversight Board (PCAOB), which replaced peer reviews with a far more rigorous PCAOB inspection process. In 2003, the

PCAOB conducted limited inspections of the four remaining large CPA firms. In 2004, the PCAOB began conducting complete inspections annually for all CPA firms with 100 or more publicly traded clients and every three years for those with at least 1, but fewer than 100, publicly traded clients.

During the initial PCAOB inspections of the accounting firm audits, PCAOB accountants identified numerous problems with how publicly traded companies accounted for operating leases. The PCAOB discovered four main issues (all now covered by ACS 840-20 [*Operating Leases*]):

1. FASB Technical Bulletin 85-3 requires that payments under operating leases with scheduled rent increases must be expensed on a straight-line basis over the lease term. Suppose a three-year operating lease requires monthly lease payments of $10,000 in 2008 and, to cover anticipated inflation, payments of $10,400 in 2009 and $10,800 in 2010. Under this rule, the firm records monthly lease expense of $10,400 for each of the 36 months. During the first year, the firm debits rent expense for $10,400, credits cash for $10,000, and credits lease liability for $400. During the last year, the firm debits rent expense for $10,400 and lease liability for $400 and credits cash for $10,800. Many firms simply recorded their monthly cash payment as lease expense.

2. Tenants often modify leased space before moving into the property. These leasehold improvements are usually capitalized and then amortized over the shorter of the asset life or the lease term. Landlords often provide tenants with cash incentives to offset the cost of modifying rental space. A retail clothing store may wish to construct changing rooms, a fitting room, check-out counters, and display areas using a corporate-wide design theme. Suppose the construction cost and cash incentive are each $300,000 and the lease term is 60 months. FASB Technical Bulletin 88-1 (and other rules) requires that firms record the $300,000 cash received as a liability and the $300,000 paid as an asset. Thereafter, each month the tenant debits the liability for $5,000 and credits rent expense for $5,000. Assuming the improvements have a 60-month life, the tenant also debits depreciation expense for $5,000 and credits accumulated depreciation for $5,000. Many firms simply offset the cash incentive against the cost of leasehold improvements at the lease inception, so no additional accounting was needed other than to debit lease expense and credit cash each month.

3. FAS 98, *Accounting for Leases,* requires that leasehold improvements be amortized on a straight-line basis over the shorter of either the lease term or the estimated useful life of the leasehold improvement. If a lease contains a renewal option, the lease term should include both the initial lease term, plus the renewal period, only if the renewal is reasonably assured. For example, if the lessee must pay a substantial penalty for failing to renew, then the renewal may be reasonably assured. Many firms included the renewal period as part of the period over which leasehold improvements were amortized, even though renewal was not reasonably assured under the FASB definition. In other instances, lessees amortized leasehold improvements only over the initial lease period even though, under FASB rules, renewal seemed to be reasonably assured.

4. Landlords often provide tenants with a rent holiday; for example, no rent due while the space is being modified. Suppose a tenant signs a 60-month lease at $10,000 per month, but the landlord waives rent for the first 2 months while the tenant constructs leasehold improvements. Under ACS 840-20 (previously Technical Bulletin 85-3), the lessee must spread the $580,000 of lease expense over the entire 60-month period on a straight-line basis ($9,666.67 per month). Many firms recorded no lease accounting entries during the first 2 months and then recorded $10,000 of rent expense for each of the remaining 58 months.

Partially in response to the PCAOB inspection findings, numerous companies filed restated financial statements with the SEC to correct some or all of the above errors. Because lease accounting errors were so widespread, the AICPA asked the SEC whether it was necessary for firms to restate their previously issued financial statements to correct their lease accounting. In response, the SEC sent the AICPA the letter in Exhibit 2.

Although the above problems were not restricted to restaurant and retail chains, the larger chains have hundreds of or thousands of leases, so their problems were often significant. The following is a partial list of restaurants and other retailers with lease accounting issues for 2004 or 2005:

Abercrombie & Fitch	Applebee's	Benihana
Big Lots	Borders Group	Brinker International
Buca di Beppos	CKE Restaurants	Cracker Barrel
Darden Restaurants	Dollar General	Jack in the Box
Kohl's	Krispy Kreme Doughnuts	Lone Star Steakhouse
Lowe's	McDonald's	Pep Boys
Rubios Restaurants	Ruby Tuesday	Sears
Starbucks	Target	Total Entertainment
Restaurant	Toys 'R Us	Tully's Coffee

Brinker International

Brinker International owns Chili's, On the Border, Maggiano's Little Italy, and Romano's Macaroni Grill. On December 22, 2004, Brinker filed a Form 8-K with the SEC detailing the following problems with its lease accounting:

Following a review of its accounting policy and in consultation with its independent registered public accounting firm, KPMG LLP, the company has corrected its computation of straight-line rent expense and the related deferred rent liability. This move is similar to recent restatements announced by other KPMG client restaurant companies.

Historically, when accounting for leases with renewal options, rent expense has been recorded on a straight-line basis over the initial non-cancelable lease term. Buildings and leasehold improvements on those properties are depreciated over a period equal to the shorter of the term of the lease—including option periods provided for in the lease—or the useful life of the assets. Brinker will recognize rent expense on a straight-line basis over sufficient renewal periods to equal the depreciable life of 20 years, including cancelable option periods where failure to exercise such options would result in an economic penalty.

For the year ended June 30, 2004, correcting the errors in lease accounting, and another minor item, reduced after-tax net income from $153.961 million to $150.918 million.

Starbucks Corporation

Starbucks determined in 2005 that its then-current method of accounting for leasehold improvements under operating leases (tenant improvement allowances) and its then-current method of accounting for rent holidays were not compliant with GAAP. The company restated its financial statements for fiscal years 2004, 2003, and 2002.

Starbucks included the following in Item 6. Selected Financial Data, in the Management Discussion and Analysis section of its 2004 10-Q:

> *The Company had historically accounted for tenant improvement allowances as reductions to the related leasehold improvement asset on the consolidated balance sheets and capital expenditures in investing activities on the consolidated statements of cash flows. Management determined that Financial Accounting Standards Board ("FASB") Technical Bulletin No. 88-1,* Issues Relating to Accounting for Leases, *requires these allowances to be recorded as deferred rent liabilities on the consolidated balance sheets and as a component of operating activities on the consolidated statements of cash flows. Additionally, this adjustment results in a reclassification of the deferred rent amortization from "Depreciation and amortization expenses" to "Cost of sales including occupancy costs" on the consolidated statements of earnings.*

> *The Company had historically recognized rent holiday periods on a straight-line basis over the lease term commencing with the initial occupancy date, or the opening date for Company-operated retail stores. The store opening date coincided with the commencement of business operations, which corresponds to the intended use of the property. Management reevaluated FASB Technical Bulletin No. 85-3,* Accounting for Operating Leases with Scheduled Rent Increases, *and determined that the lease term should commence on the date the Company takes possession of the leased space for construction purposes, which is generally two months prior to a store opening date. Excluding tax impacts, the correction of this accounting requires the Company to record additional deferred rent in "Accrued occupancy costs" and "Other long-term liabilities" and to adjust "Retained earnings" on the consolidated balance sheets as well as to correct amortization in "Costs of sales including occupancy costs" on the consolidated statements of earnings for each of the three years in the period ended October 3, 2004. The cumulative effect of these accounting changes is a reduction to retained earnings of $8.6 million as of the beginning of fiscal 2002 and decreases to retained earnings of $1.3 million, $1.5 million and $1.2 million for the fiscal years ended 2002, 2003 and 2004, respectively (Note: Starbuck's retained earnings were restated downward from $2.487 billion to $2.474 billion at the end of fiscal 2004.)*

Required

1. Suppose you were advising the CEO and CFO of Brinker International or Starbucks Corporation about whether to restate financial statements for the errors discussed in this case. After reading SEC Chief Accountant Donald T. Nicolaisen's letter to the AICPA, what would you recommend?

2. Evaluate the four operating lease rules discussed in this case. Are the rules needed? How difficult are the lease rules to implement in a large restaurant chain or retail chain, with hundreds or thousands of leases? As part of your answer, would it be reasonable for these chains to force landlords to enter into leases with standard terms that would simplify their lease accounting?

3. U.S. firms may soon shift to International Financial Reporting Standards (IFRS), where accounting standards are based far more on general principles than on highly detailed rules. For example, the International Accounting Standards Board has one standard on leases (IAS 17, *Leases*), and two lease interpretations (IFRIC 4, *Determining Whether an Arrangement Contains a Lease,* and SIC-15, *Operating Leases—Incentives*). Discuss the advantages and disadvantages of far less detailed rules.

4. The IASB is considering a highly simplified lease accounting rule that would require firms to capitalize all leases with a term of more than two or three years. Discuss the advantages and disadvantages of such a simple rule.

EXHIBIT 1

CAPITAL LEASE EXAMPLE: LESSEE

	Lease payment, beginning of month	Lease payable, beginning of month	Interest expense for month	Reduction to lease payable	Depreciation expense
Annualized interest rate		8.000%			
Monthly interest rate		0.643%			
Present value of lease payments		$223,155.73			
January-08	$10,000	$213,155.73	$1,371.45	$8,628.55	$9,298.16
February-08	$10,000	$204,527.18	$1,315.93	$8,684.07	$9,298.16
March-08	$10,000	$195,843.11	$1,260.06	$8,739.94	$9,298.16
April-08	$10,000	$187,103.17	$1,203.83	$8,796.17	$9,298.16
May-08	$10,000	$178,307.00	$1,147.23	$8,852.77	$9,298.16
June-08	$10,000	$169,454.23	$1,090.27	$8,909.73	$9,298.16
July-08	$10,000	$160,544.50	$1,032.95	$8,967.05	$9,298.16
August-08	$10,000	$151,577.45	$975.25	$9,024.75	$9,298.16
September-08	$10,000	$142,552.71	$917.19	$9,082.81	$9,298.16
October-08	$10,000	$133,469.89	$858.75	$9,141.25	$9,298.16
November-08	$10,000	$124,328.64	$799.93	$9,200.07	$9,298.16
December-08	$10,000	$115,128.58	$740.74	$9,259.26	$9,298.16
January-09	$10,000	$105,869.32	$681.17	$9,318.83	$9,298.16
February-09	$10,000	$96,550.49	$621.21	$9,378.79	$9,298.16
March-09	$10,000	$87,171.69	$560.87	$9,439.13	$9,298.16
April-09	$10,000	$77,732.56	$500.13	$9,499.87	$9,298.16
May-09	$10,000	$68,232.69	$439.01	$9,560.99	$9,298.16
June-09	$10,000	$58,671.70	$377.50	$9,622.50	$9,298.16
July-09	$10,000	$49,049.20	$315.58	$9,684.42	$9,298.16
August-09	$10,000	$39,364.78	$253.27	$9,746.73	$9,298.16
September-09	$10,000	$29,618.06	$190.56	$9,809.44	$9,298.16
October-09	$10,000	$19,808.62	$127.45	$9,872.55	$9,298.16
November-09	$10,000	$9,936.07	$63.93	$9,936.07	$9,298.16
December-09	$10,000	$0.00	$0.00		$9,298.16
Depreciation expense				$223,155.73	$223,155.73
Interest expense			$16,844.27		$16,844.27
Total expense					$240,000.00
Reduction to lease payable				$213,155.73	
Total lease payments	$240,000				

Lessee Journal Entries

January 1, 2008

Lease asset	$223,156	
Lease liability		$223,156
Lease asset and liability at inception		

Lease liability	$10,000	
Cash		$10,000
First lease payment		

January 31, 2008

Interest expense	$1,371.45	
Accrued interest (liability)		$1,371.45
Interest expense, January		

Depreciation expense	$9,298.16	
Accumulated dep, leased asset		$9,298.16
Depreciation expense, January		

February 1, 2008

Accrued interest (liability)	$1,371.45	
Lease liability	$8,628.55	
Cash		$10,000.00
Second lease payment		

February 28, 2008

Interest expense	$1,315.93	
Accrued interest (liability)		$1,315.93
Interest expense, February		

Depreciation expense	$9,298.16	
Accumulated dep, leased asset		$9,298.16
Depreciation expense, February		

EXHIBIT 2

SEC STAFF LETTER
TO THE AICPA:
LEASES

Robert J. Kueppers
Chairman
Center for Public Company Audit Firms
American Institute of Certified Public Accountants
Harborside Financial Center
201 Plaza Three
Jersey City, NJ 07311-3881

February 7, 2005

Dear Mr. Kueppers:

In recent weeks, a number of public companies have issued press releases announcing restatements of their financial statements relating to lease accounting. You requested that the Office of the Chief Accountant clarify the staff's interpretation of certain accounting issues and their application under generally accepted accounting principles relating to operating leases. Of specific concern is the appropriate accounting for: (1) the amortization of leasehold improvements by a lessee in an operating lease with lease renewals, (2) the pattern of recognition of rent when the lease term in an operating lease contains a period where there are free or reduced rents (commonly referred to as "rent holidays"), and (3) incentives related to leasehold improvements provided by a landlord/lessor to a tenant/lessee in an operating lease. It should be noted that the Commission has neither reviewed this letter nor approved the staff's positions expressed herein. In addition, the staff's positions may be affected or changed by particular facts or conditions. Finally, this letter does not purport to express any legal conclusion on the questions presented.

The staff's views on these issues are as follows:

Amortization of Leasehold Improvements—The staff believes that leasehold improvements in an operating lease should be amortized by the lessee over the shorter of their economic lives or the lease term, as defined in paragraph 5(f) of FASB Statement 13 ("SFAS 13"), Accounting for Leases, as amended. The staff believes amortizing leasehold improvements over a term that includes assumption of lease renewals is appropriate only when the renewals have been determined to be "reasonably assured," as that term is contemplated by SFAS 13.

Rent Holidays—The staff believes that pursuant to the response in paragraph 2 of FASB Technical Bulletin 85-3 ("FTB 85-3"), Accounting for Operating Leases with Scheduled Rent Increases, rent holidays in an operating lease should be recognized by the lessee on a straight-line basis over the lease term (including any rent holiday period) unless another systematic and rational allocation is more representative of the time pattern in which leased property is physically employed.

Landlord/Tenant Incentives—The staff believes that: (a) leasehold improvements made by a lessee that are funded by landlord incentives or allowances under an operating lease should be recorded by the lessee as leasehold improvement assets and amortized over a term consistent with the guidance in item 1 above; (b) the incentives should be recorded as deferred rent and amortized as reductions to lease expense over the lease term in accordance with paragraph 15 of SFAS 13 and the response to Question 2 of FASB Technical Bulletin 88-1 ("FTB 88-1"), Issues Relating to Accounting for Leases, and therefore, the staff believes it is inappropriate to net the deferred rent against the leasehold improvements; and (c) a registrant's statement of cash flows should reflect cash received from the lessor that is accounted for as a lease incentive within operating activities and the acquisition of leasehold improvements for cash within investing activities. The staff recognizes that evaluating when improvements should be recorded as assets of the lessor or assets of the lessee may require significant judgment and factors in making that evaluation are not the subject of this letter.

(continued)

EXHIBIT 2—
continued

SEC STAFF LETTER
TO THE AICPA:
LEASES

To the extent that SEC registrants have deviated from the lease accounting standards and related interpretations set forth by the FASB, those registrants, in consultation with their independent auditors, should assess the impact of the resulting errors on their financial statements to determine whether restatement is required. The SEC staff believes that the positions noted above are based upon existing accounting literature and registrants who determine their prior accounting to be in error should state that the restatement results from the correction of errors or, if restatement was determined by management to be unnecessary, state that the errors were immaterial to prior periods.

Registrants should ensure that the disclosures regarding both operating and capital leases clearly and concisely address the material terms of and accounting for leases. Registrants should provide basic descriptive information about material leases, usual contract terms, and specific provisions in leases relating to rent increases, rent holidays, contingent rents, and leasehold incentives. The accounting for leases should be clearly described in the notes to the financial statements and in the discussion of critical accounting policies in MD&A if appropriate. Known likely trends or uncertainties in future rent or amortization expense that could materially affect operating results or cash flows should be addressed in MD&A. The disclosures should address the following:

Material lease agreements or arrangements.

The essential provisions of material leases, including the original term, renewal periods, reasonably assured rent escalations, rent holidays, contingent rent, rent concessions, leasehold improvement incentives, and unusual provisions or conditions.

The accounting policies for leases, including the treatment of each of the above components of lease agreements.

The basis on which contingent rental payments are determined with specificity, not generality.

The amortization period of material leasehold improvements made either at the inception of the lease or during the lease term, and how the amortization period relates to the initial lease term.

As you know, the SEC staff is continuing to consider these and related matters and may have further discussions on lease accounting with registrants and their independent auditors.

We appreciate your inquiry and further questions about these matters can be directed to Tony Lopez, Associate Chief Accountant in the Office of the Chief Accountant (202-942-7104) or Louise Dorsey, Associate Chief Accountant in the Division of Corporation Finance (202-942-2960).

Sincerely,

Donald T. Nicolaisen
Chief Accountant

cc:	Carol Stacey, Chief Accountant, Division of Corporation Finance Robert Herz, Chairman, Financial Accounting Standards Board AICPA SEC Regulations Committee

http://www.sec.gov/info/accountants/staffletters/cpcaf020705.htm

Revenue Recognition Disclosures (A)

By 2008, U.S. Generally Accepted Accounting Principles (GAAP) included more than 200 different revenue recognition guidelines, rules, and regulations. The most straightforward sale is a retail sale for cash, such as a consumer paying cash for groceries. There is a slight chance the customer will return the goods because they are unsatisfactory, but in most cases there is clearly a sale. There is no uncertainty about the price, no uncertainty about whether the customer will pay for the purchase, no uncertainty about whether the customer has taken possession of the goods, and very low probability that the goods will be returned. The store would almost certainly recognize revenue on the date the transaction occurred by debiting cash and crediting revenue.

As business became more complicated, so did revenue recognition. Transactions involving multiple elements are common. A computer manufacturer may sell a package of hardware, software, warranties, and telephone support. It is unclear how a one-time initial payment should be allocated among those four elements and unclear how an initial payment—combined with a monthly fee over some period—should be allocated between the four elements.

Sometimes products or contracts cover several years, such as large infrastructure projects or ships, so revenue may be recognized gradually over the production period. Sometimes there is a question as to whether a credit customer will pay the amount due. Sometimes there is a question about price because it may depend on the performance a product delivers. Sometimes revenue is recognized before a product is shipped because a customer wishes to secure a supply of a scarce item. There are also dozens of technical revenue recognition issues related to specific industries.

During the late 1990s' Internet boom, many Internet start-ups devised highly unusual revenue recognition methods. Some firms recognized revenue long before cash would be collected; others recognized revenue although no cash would ever be exchanged. In response, in December 1999, the SEC issued Staff Accounting Bulletin (SAB) 100 to express the SEC accounting staff's views on revenue recognition. In December 2003, the SEC issued a revised and expanded version of that bulletin, SAB 104, *Revenue Recognition, Corrected Copy.* Because it was issued by the SEC, SAB 104 is probably the most authoritative document on revenue recognition in the United States. The following is an overview of the general concepts covered by SAB 104. The selected text from SAB 104 includes four revenue recognition criteria that are widely quoted by U.S. firms in the revenue recognition note of their 10-Q and 10-K reports (see Exhibit 1) and are also widely quoted by other accounting rule-making bodies.

Selected text, SAB 104: Revenue recognition—general

The accounting literature on revenue recognition includes both broad conceptual dis-cussions as well as certain industry-specific guidance.[1] If a transaction is within the scope of specific authoritative literature that provides revenue recognition guidance, that literature should be applied. However, in the absence of authoritative literature addressing a specific arrangement or a specific industry, the staff will consider the existing authoritative accounting standards as well as the broad revenue recognition criteria specified in the FASB's conceptual framework that contain basic guidelines for revenue recognition.

Based on these guidelines, revenue should not be recognized until it is realized or realizable and earned.[2] Concepts Statement 5, paragraph 83(b) states that "an entity's revenue-earning activities involve delivering or producing goods, rendering services, or other activities that constitute its ongoing major or central operations, and rev-enues are considered to have been earned when the entity has substantially accom-plished what it must do to be entitled to the benefits represented by the revenues". Paragraph 84(a) continues "the two conditions (being realized or realizable and being earned) are usually met by the time product or merchandise is delivered or services are rendered to customers, and revenues from manufacturing and selling activities and gains and losses from sales of other assets are commonly recognized at time of sale (usually meaning delivery)". In addition, paragraph 84(d) states that "If services are rendered or rights to use assets extend continuously over time (for example, interest or rent), reliable measures based on contractual prices established in advance are commonly available, and revenues may be recognized as earned as time passes."

The staff believes that revenue generally is realized or realizable and earned when all of the following criteria are met:

1. Persuasive evidence of an arrangement exists,

2. Delivery has occurred or services have been rendered,

3. The seller's price to the buyer is fixed or determinable, and

4. Collectability is reasonably assured.

Some revenue arrangements contain multiple revenue-generating activities. The staff believes that the determination of the units of accounting within an arrangement should be made prior to the application of the guidance in this SAB topic by reference to the applicable accounting literature.

Revenue recognition in practice

The FASB Codification project now covers all U.S. revenue recognition rules—ACS 650 (Revenue Recognition). However, the FASB substantially simplified its revenue recognition rules for multiple-element sales that include software with Accounting Standards Update (ASU) 13, *Multiple-Deliverable Revenue Arrangements*—ASC Topic 650 (Revenue Recognition) and ASU 14, *Certain Arrangements that Include Software*

---

1. The February 1999 AICPA publication *Audit Issues in Revenue Recognition* provides an overview of the authoritative accounting literature and auditing procedures for revenue recognition and identifies indicators of improper revenue recognition.

2. Concepts Statement 5, paragraphs 83–84; ARB 43, Chapter 1 A, paragraph 1; Opinion 10, paragraph 12. The citations provided herein are not intended to present the complete population of citations where a particular criterion is relevant. Rather, the citations are intended to provide the reader with additional reference material.

Elements—ACS Topic 985 (Software). Both ASUs became effective for firms whose fiscal year began after June 15, 2010, although early adoption was permitted for both ASUs.

Exhibit 1 contains selections from the revenue recognition note for seven publicly traded U.S. firms. Those notes cover a wide range of revenue recognition issues.

Required

For each note in Exhibit 1:

1. Explain the revenue recognition rules for each firm. As part of your explanation, prepare journal entries for each described method.

2. For each firm, are the revenue recognition methods described in the note reasonable? Explain in detail.

3. In most cases, IFRS accounting rules provide only general revenue recognition guidelines. For each firm, discuss whether detailed revenue recognition rules are needed.

EXHIBIT 1

GENERAL
MOTORS REVENUE
RECOGNITION
NOTES

General Motors

Automotive Revenue Recognition

We recorded an adjustment to correct deferred revenue related to data disks provided to customers to update their vehicle's navigational system. We did not compute deferred revenue using fair value as determined by vendor specific objective evidence as required by EITF 00-21, *Revenue Arrangements with Multiple Deliverables*. Additionally, we did not defer revenue on the correct number of 2006 models containing navigation systems. As part of our restatement, pre-tax earnings were decreased, through a reduction of Automotive sales, by $33.1 million ($21.5 million after tax) in 2005.

In addition, we incorrectly recognized revenue for our sponsorship of the GM Card program, which offers rebates that can be applied primarily against the purchase or lease of GM vehicles. We corrected this accounting by deferring and recognizing additional revenue over the average utilization period of points earned by retail customers. As part of our restatement, pre-tax earnings were increased, through an increase to Automotive sales, by $42.3 million ($27.5 million after tax) and $19.7 million ($12.8 million after tax) in 2005 and 2004, respectively, and retained earnings was decreased at January 1, 2004 by $147 million.

Deere & Company

Revenue Recognition

Sales of equipment and service parts are recorded when the sales price is determinable, and title and all risk of ownership are transferred to independent parties based on the sales agreements in effect. In the U.S. and most international locations, this transfer occurs primarily when goods are shipped. In Canada and some other international locations, certain goods are shipped to dealers on a consignment basis under which title and risk of ownership are not transferred to the dealer. Accordingly, in these locations, sales are not recorded until a retail customer has purchased the goods. In all cases, when a sale is recorded by the company, no significant uncertainty exists surrounding the purchaser's obligation to pay. No right of return exists on sales of equipment. Service parts returns are estimable and accrued at the time a sale is recognized. The company makes appropriate provisions based on experience for costs such as doubtful receivables, sales incentives and product warranty.

Financing revenue is recorded over the lives of related receivables using the interest method. Deferred costs on the origination of financing receivables are recognized as a reduction in finance revenue over the expected lives of the receivables using the interest method. Income from operating leases is recognized on a straight-line basis over the scheduled lease terms.

Target Corporation

Revenues

Our retail stores generally record revenue at the point of sale. Sales from our online business include shipping revenue and are recorded upon delivery to the guest. Total revenues do not include sales tax as we consider ourselves a pass through conduit for collecting and remitting sales taxes. Generally, guests may return merchandise within 90 days of purchase. Revenues are recognized net of expected returns, which we estimate using historical return patterns. Commissions earned on sales generated by leased departments are included within sales and were $16 million in 2007, $15 million in 2006 and $14 million in 2005.

Revenue from gift card sales is recognized upon redemption of the gift card. Our gift cards do not have expiration dates. Based on historical redemption rates, a small and relatively stable percentage of gift cards will never be redeemed, referred to as "breakage." Estimated breakage revenue is recognized over a period of time in proportion to actual gift card redemptions and was immaterial in 2007, 2006 and 2005.

(continued)

EXHIBIT 1—
continued

General
Motors Revenue
Recognition
Notes

Credit card revenues are recognized according to the contractual provisions of each applicable credit card agreement. When accounts are written off, uncollected finance charges and late fees are recorded as a reduction of credit card revenues. Target retail store sales charged to our credit cards totaled $4,105 million, $3,961 million and $3,655 million in 2007, 2006 and 2005, respectively. We offer new account discounts and rewards programs on our REDcard products, the Target Visa, Target Card and Target Check Card. These discounts are redeemable only on purchases made at Target. The discounts associated with our REDcard products are included as reductions in sales in our Consolidated Statements of Operations and were $108 million, $104 million and $97 million in 2007, 2006 and 2005, respectively.

Apple Inc.
Revenue Recognition

Net sales consist primarily of revenue from the sale of hardware, software, music products, digital content, peripherals, and service and support contracts. For any product within these groups that either is software, or is considered software-related in accordance with the guidance in Emerging Issues Task Force ("EITF") No. 03-5, *Applicability of AICPA Statement of Position 97-2 to Non-Software Deliverables in an Arrangement Containing More-Than-Incidental Software* (e.g., Mac computers, iPod portable digital music players and iPhones), the Company accounts for such products in accordance with the revenue recognition provisions of American Institute of Certified Public Accountants ("AICPA") Statement of Position ("SOP") No. 97-2, *Software Revenue Recognition*, as amended. The Company applies Staff Accounting Bulletin ("SAB") No. 104, *Revenue Recognition,* for products that are not software or software-related, such as digital content sold on the iTunes Store and certain Mac, iPod and iPhone supplies and accessories.

The Company recognizes revenue when persuasive evidence of an arrangement exists, delivery has occurred, the sales price is fixed or determinable, and collection is probable. Product is considered delivered to the customer once it has been shipped and title and risk of loss have been transferred. For most of the Company's product sales, these criteria are met at the time the product is shipped. For online sales to individuals, for some sales to education customers in the U.S., and for certain other sales, the Company defers revenue until the customer receives the product because the Company legally retains a portion of the risk of loss on these sales during transit. If at the outset of an arrangement the Company determines the arrangement fee is not, or is presumed not to be, fixed or determinable, revenue is deferred and subsequently recognized as amounts become due and payable and all other criteria for revenue recognition have been met.

Revenue from service and support contracts is deferred and recognized ratably over the service coverage periods. These contracts typically include extended phone support, repair services, web-based support resources, diagnostic tools, and extend the service coverage offered under the Company's one-year limited warranty.

The Company sells software and peripheral products obtained from other companies. The Company generally establishes its own pricing and retains related inventory risk, is the primary obligor in sales transactions with its customers, and assumes the credit risk for amounts billed to its customers. Accordingly, the Company generally recognizes revenue for the sale of products obtained from other companies based on the gross amount billed.

The Company accounts for multiple element arrangements that consist only of software or software-related products in accordance with SOP No. 97-2. If a multiple-element arrangement includes deliverables that are neither software nor software-related, the Company applies EITF No. 00-21, *Revenue Arrangements with Multiple Deliverables,* to determine if those deliverables constitute separate units of accounting from the SOP No. 97-2 deliverables. If the Company can separate the deliverables, the Company applies

(continued)

EXHIBIT 1—
continued

GENERAL
MOTORS REVENUE
RECOGNITION
NOTES

SOP No. 97-2 to the software and software-related deliverables and applies other appropriate guidance (e.g., SAB No. 104) to the deliverables outside the scope of SOP No. 97-2. Revenue on arrangements that include multiple elements such as hardware, software, and services is allocated to each element based on the relative fair value of each element. Each element's allocated revenue is recognized when the revenue recognition criteria for that element have been met. Fair value is generally determined by vendor specific objective evidence ("VSOE"), which is based on the price charged when each element is sold separately. If the Company cannot objectively determine the fair value of any undelivered element included in a multiple-element arrangement, the Company defers revenue until all elements are delivered and services have been performed, or until fair value can objectively be determined for any remaining undelivered elements. When the fair value of a delivered element has not been established, the Company uses the residual method to recognize revenue if the fair value of all undelivered elements is determinable. Under the residual method, the fair value of the undelivered elements is deferred and the remaining portion of the arrangement fee is allocated to the delivered elements and is recognized as revenue.

The Company records reductions to revenue for estimated commitments related to price protection and for customer incentive programs, including reseller and end-user rebates, and other sales programs and volume-based incentives. The estimated cost of these programs is accrued as a reduction to revenue in the period the Company has sold the product and committed to a plan. The Company also records reductions to revenue for expected future product returns based on the Company's historical experience. Revenue is recorded net of taxes collected from customers that are remitted to governmental authorities, with the collected taxes recorded as current liabilities until remitted to the relevant government authority.

In 2007, the Company began shipping Apple TV and iPhone. For Apple TV and iPhone, the Company indicated it may, from time-to-time, provide future unspecified features and additional software products free of charge to customers. Accordingly, Apple TV and iPhone handsets sales are accounted for under subscription accounting in accordance with SOP No. 97-2. As such, the Company's policy is to defer the associated revenue and cost of goods sold at the time of sale, and recognize both on a straight-line basis over the currently estimated 24-month economic life of these products, with any loss recognized at the time of sale. Costs incurred by the Company for engineering, sales, marketing and warranty are expensed as incurred.

Allowance for Doubtful Accounts

The Company records its allowance for doubtful accounts based upon its assessment of various factors. The Company considers historical experience, the age of the accounts receivable balances, credit quality of the Company's customers, current economic conditions, and other factors that may affect customers' ability to pay.

Shipping Costs

For all periods presented, amounts billed to customers related to shipping and handling are classified as revenue, and the Company's shipping and handling costs are included in cost of sales.

Warranty Expense

The Company generally provides for the estimated cost of hardware and software warranties at the time the related revenue is recognized. The Company assesses the adequacy of its preexisting warranty liabilities and adjusts the amounts as necessary based on actual experience and changes in future estimates. For products accounted for under subscription accounting pursuant to SOP No. 97-2, the Company recognizes warranty expense as incurred.

(continued)

EXHIBIT 1—
continued

GENERAL
MOTORS REVENUE
RECOGNITION
NOTES

Perini Corporation

(d) Method of Accounting for Contracts

Revenues and profits from the Company's contracts and construction joint venture contracts are generally recognized by applying percentages of completion for the period to the total estimated profits for the respective contracts. Percentage of completion is determined by relating the actual cost of the work performed to date to the current estimated total cost of the respective contracts. However, on construction management contracts, profit is generally recognized in accordance with the contract terms, usually on the as-billed method, which is generally consistent with the level of effort incurred over the contract period. When the estimate on a contract indicates a loss, the Company's policy is to record the entire loss during the accounting period in which it is estimated. In the ordinary course of business, at a minimum on a quarterly basis, the Company prepares updated estimates of the total forecasted revenue, cost and profit or loss for each contract. The cumulative effect of revisions in estimates of the total forecasted revenue and costs, including unapproved change orders and claims, during the course of the work is reflected in the accounting period in which the facts that caused the revision become known. The financial impact of these revisions to any one contract is a function of both the amount of the revision and the percentage of completion of the contract. An amount equal to the costs incurred which are attributable to unapproved change orders and claims is included in the total estimated revenue when realization is probable. Profit from unapproved change orders and claims is recorded in the period such amounts are resolved.

In accordance with normal practice in the construction industry, the Company includes in current assets and current liabilities amounts related to construction contracts realizable and payable over a period in excess of one year. Billings in excess of costs and estimated earnings represents the excess of contract billings to date over the amount of contract costs and profits (or contract revenue) recognized to date on the percentage of completion accounting method on certain contracts. Costs and estimated earnings in excess of billings represents the excess of contract costs and profits (or contract revenue) recognized to date on the percentage of completion accounting method over the amount of contract billings to date on the remaining contracts. Costs and estimated earnings in excess of billings results when (1) the appropriate contract revenue amount has been recognized in accordance with the percentage of completion accounting method, but a portion of the revenue recorded cannot be billed currently due to the billing terms defined in the contract and/or (2) costs, recorded at estimated realizable value, related to unapproved change orders or claims are incurred. Costs and estimated earnings in excess of billings related to the Company's contracts and joint venture contracts at December 31, 2007 and 2006, consisted of the following (in thousands):

	2007	2006
Unbilled costs and profits incurred to date*	$8,982	$33,011
Unapproved change orders	9,313	8,369
Claims	56,102	54,961
	$74,397	$96,341

*Represents the excess of contract costs and profits recognized to date on the percentage of completion accounting method over the amount of contract billings to date on certain contracts.

Of the balance of "Unapproved change orders" and "Claims" included above in costs and estimated earnings in excess of billings at December 31, 2007 and December 31, 2006, approximately $45.3 million and $48.2 million, respectively, are amounts subject to pending

(continued)

EXHIBIT 1—
continued

GENERAL
MOTORS REVENUE
RECOGNITION
NOTES

litigation or dispute resolution proceedings as described in Note 2, "Contingencies and Commitments". These amounts are management's estimate of the probable cost recovery from the disputed claims considering such factors as evaluation of entitlement, settlements reached to date and experience with the customer. In the event that future facts and circumstances, including the resolution of disputed claims, cause a reduction in the aggregate amount of the estimated probable cost recovery from the disputed claims, the amount of such reduction will be recorded against earnings in the relevant future period.

Granite Construction
Revenue Recognition

We use the percentage of completion accounting method for construction contracts in accordance with the American Institute of Certified Public Accountants Statement of Position 81-1, "Accounting for Performance of Construction-Type and Certain Production-Type Contracts." Revenue and earnings on construction contracts, including construction joint ventures, are recognized on the percentage of completion method in the ratio of costs incurred to estimated final costs. Revenue in an amount equal to cost incurred is recognized prior to contracts reaching 25% completion. The related profit is deferred until the period in which such percentage completion is attained. It is our judgment that until a project reaches 25% completion, there is insufficient information to determine what the estimated profit on the project will be with a reasonable level of assurance. In the case of large, complex design/build projects we may continue to defer profit recognition beyond the point of 25% completion based on evaluation of specific project risks. The factors considered in this evaluation of risk associated with each design/build project include the stage of design completion, the stage of construction completion, status of outstanding purchase orders and subcontracts, certainty of quantities, certainty of schedule and the relationship with the owner.

Revenue from contract claims is recognized when we have a signed settlement agreement and payment is assured. Revenue from contract change orders, which occur in most large projects, is recognized when the owner has agreed to the change order in writing. During 2007, we settled various contract issues for which the associated cost was included in prior periods (see Note 2). Provisions are recognized in the statements of income for the full amount of estimated losses on uncompleted contracts whenever evidence indicates that the estimated total cost of a contract exceeds its estimated total revenue. Contract cost consists of direct costs on contracts, including labor and materials, amounts payable to subcontractors, direct overhead costs and equipment expense (primarily depreciation, fuel, maintenance and repairs). Depreciation is provided using accelerated methods for construction equipment. Contract cost is recorded as incurred and revisions in contract revenue and cost estimates are reflected when known. The completion threshold for the start of contract profit recognition is applied to all percentage of completion projects unless and until we project a loss on the project, in which case the estimated loss is immediately recognized.

The New York Times Company
Revenue Recognition

Advertising revenue is recognized when advertisements are published, broadcast or placed on the Company's Web sites or, with respect to certain Web advertising, each time a user clicks on certain ads, net of provisions for estimated rebates, rate adjustments and discounts.

Rebates are accounted for in accordance with Emerging Issues Task Force ("EITF") 01-09, Accounting for Consideration Given by a Vendor to a Customer (including Reseller of the Vendor's Products) ("EITF 01-09"). The Company recognizes a rebate obligation as a reduction of revenue, based on the amount of estimated rebates that will be earned and claimed, related to the underlying revenue transactions during the period. Measurement of the rebate

(continued)

EXHIBIT 1—
continued

GENERAL
MOTORS REVENUE
RECOGNITION
NOTES

obligation is estimated based on the historical experience of the number of customers that ultimately earn and use the rebate.

Rate adjustments primarily represent credits given to customers related to billing or production errors and discounts represent credits given to customers who pay an invoice prior to its due date. Rate adjustments and discounts are accounted for in accordance with EITF 01-09 as a reduction of revenue, based on the amount of estimated rate adjustments or discounts related to the underlying revenue during the period. Measurement of rate adjustments and discount obligations are estimated based on historical experience of credits actually issued.

Circulation revenue includes single copy and home-delivery subscription revenue. Single copy revenue is recognized based on date of publication, net of provisions for related returns. Proceeds from home-delivery subscriptions are deferred at the time of sale and are recognized in earnings on a pro rata basis over the terms of the subscriptions.

New Century Financial Corporation

Background

In the mid-1960s, U.S. 30-year conventional (fixed) mortgage rates were relatively stable in the 5.5% range. Homebuyers typically paid 20% of the purchase price in cash, and followed the rule of thumb that homeowners should not spend more than 25% of their after-tax income on housing costs.

Local banks and savings and loan institutions made mortgage loans only to local buyers because of restrictive banking laws and because most individuals had strong relationships with local financial institutions. Housing prices rose moderately during the 1960s, mortgage default rates were low, and in cases of a mortgage default the house's value often exceeded the mortgage due. Serious problems usually arose only if a bank's region suffered a serious recession, but those occurrences were rare.

In 1983, Solomon Brothers and First Boston developed the first collateralized mortgage obligations (CMOs). A financial institution establishes a CMO by acquiring a group of similar mortgages. It then bundles them into a separate legal entity, a securitization pool, which owns the mortgages. The securitization pool sells notes backed (collateralized) by its mortgages to institutional investors with excess funds, such as insurance firms, commercial banks, pension funds, foundations, and endowments. Those notes trade as marketable securities so the individual mortgages, which cannot trade like securities, are said to have been securitized (converted into marketable securities).

A CMO offers numerous advantages for both borrowers and lenders. Prior to CMOs, borrowers were typically restricted to borrowing from nearby financial institutions, which severely limited competition. In addition, banks sometimes restricted the amounts they would loan by category, such as home loans or auto loans, so at times mortgage funds were not readily available.

With respect to lenders, financial institutions with excess cash, such as insurance companies and pension funds, could not enter the mortgage market without opening large numbers of lending offices, which would have been highly inefficient. With CMOs, they could easily invest funds in mortgages by location, mortgage size, and credit risk. That change provided financial institutions with a highly efficient way to invest in mortgages and diversified across a number of factors. Prior to CMOs, mortgages contained four types of risk.

- *Interest rate risk:* As interest rates fluctuate, so does the value of debt. If interest rates increase, the value of a bond or mortgage declines. Suppose an investor pays $10,000 for a 10-year, $10,000 face value note that pays 8% interest. If interest rates increase to 8.5% later in the day, the note is worth less because it is now possible to pay $10,000 for a $10,000 face value note paying 8.5% interest. Investors will buy the 8% note only if it sells for less than the $10,000 face value 8.5% note.

  Interest rate economics are complex, but interest rate risk increases as maturity increases (a 10-year note is less risky than a 30-year bond because the

10-year note is repaid sooner) and decreases as the interest rate increases (a 10-year, 12% note is less risky than a 10-year, 5% note because a higher percentage of cash payments for the 10-year 12% note will be paid in earlier years).

- *Credit or default risk:* The risk that a borrower will default on payment of interest, principal, or both is called credit or default risk. Interest rates increase with default risk.

- *Prepayment risk:* Nearly all U.S. residential mortgages allow for early mortgage repayment under any circumstances. As interest rates decline, homeowners typically refinance their mortgages to obtain a lower rate; the lenders are paid sooner than required by the mortgage contract, so they are forced to reinvest the proceeds at a lower interest rate. That is called prepayment risk.

- *Concentration risk:* Prior to CMOs, mortgages had significant concentration risk, the risk that too much of a lender's debt is dependent upon a small number of factors; if something negatively impacts one of those factors, the lender may come to harm. Historically, local banks lent to individuals who bought homes in proximity to the bank. If the region had a local recession, the bank might incur significant mortgage-lending losses.

There are many ways to form CMOs, but all CMOs help lenders avoid concentration risk by letting them spread their investments over a wide range of mortgage pools. A CMO may include only one type of note, but most issue many classes of notes, called *tranches* (French for layer or slice). Some CMOs have more than 40 tranches; some notes pay a fixed interest rate whereas others may pay floating interest rates based on some published floating rate, such as LIBOR (London Interbank Offering Rate). Typically, notes in the "A" tranche(s) are the lowest-risk notes and pay the lowest interest rate; notes in riskier tranches pay increasingly higher interest rates. Pools can be structured to limit both prepayment and credit risk. The highest risk tranche, typically the R, or residual, tranche, is usually suitable only for hedge funds, although unscrupulous sellers have sold them to unsophisticated buyers for far more than their fair value.

Mortgage Brokers

The first CMOs were formed by investment banks with residential mortgages obtained from commercial banks and savings and loan institutions. As that market grew in size and sophistication, mortgage brokers entered the market. Mortgage brokers typically represent many different lending institutions, such as mortgage finance companies and commercial banks (called correspondents). A mortgage broker arranges the loan for the correspondent and receives a commission, called a *yield spread premium.* The correspondent usually sells the mortgage, either by securitizing the mortgages, or by selling them to an investment bank that securitizes the mortgages.

By 2005, there were tens of thousands of mortgage brokers in the United States. Many had graduated from college only two or three years earlier and earned commissions in excess of $300,000 annually from fees as high as 9% of the mortgage principal. Some mortgage brokerage firms are relatively large, whereas others consist of only one or a few employees. An advantage for home buyers is that mortgage brokers have access to many different lending institutions. Some lenders make loans only to buyers with high credit ratings, and others make loans to buyers with weak credit ratings. As a result, one mortgage broker may serve a range of clients.

The competition between lending agencies helps to keep lending rates low. However, a mortgage broker's compensation depends on the fees charged to the home buyer and the effective interest rate. Brokers can offer borrowers fixed-rate loans or more risky floating-rate loans that initially require low monthly payments. From about 2000 through 2006, lending institutions offered home buyers increasingly lower initial monthly payments. First, buyers were allowed to pay only the interest costs for several years; after four or five years, monthly payments sometimes doubled when the borrower was required to both pay interest and repay the mortgage balance.

Later, buyers were allowed to pay only a portion of the interest costs for several years, so the mortgage balance increased for four or five years. Monthly payments then increased so the borrower paid the full interest cost for four or five years, during which time the mortgage balance remained constant. Monthly payments then increased so the borrower was both paying interest and repaying the mortgage principal, which could be significantly higher than the amount initially borrowed. In addition, the initial interest rates were often low but could increase significantly in a few years. Those loans were difficult for unsophisticated borrowers to understand.

Mortgage Finance Companies

There were hundreds of mortgage finance companies in the United States. They made (originated) mortgage loans directly to home buyers through their own employees, and they also obtained mortgages from mortgage brokers. The finance companies then securitized the mortgages and sold the associated notes to investment banks for resale to financial institutions or else sold the mortgages they originated to other financial institutions, which then securitized them.

The decision to securitize a mortgage or sell it to another financial institution often depends on the type of mortgage, because a mortgage pool typically consists of mortgages with similar terms. If an institution has enough mortgages to form a pool, it will often form the pool and earn extra fees for servicing it. The servicer earns those fees by collecting mortgage payments and then making payments to those who purchased notes backed by the mortgages. If an institution lacked enough mortgages of a particular type, it typically sold those mortgages to another financial institution.

The U.S. Mortgage Industry

As the costs of the Vietnam War began to affect the U.S. economy during the 1970s, mortgage rates rose from about 7% in 1970 to 9% in the mid-1970s, 14% in 1980, and a high of more than 18% in 1981. They then declined to about 8% by early 2000. The 20% down payment rule held until the mid-1980s; by 2000 many homeowners obtained mortgages with only 10% down.

Beginning in early 2000, mortgage rates began a steady decline from 8% in January 2000 to a low of 5.2% in June 2003; they remained in the 5.5–6.0% range until the end of 2005 (Exhibit 1). The continual decline in interest rates led to a rapid growth in both the residential mortgage and construction industries. Mortgage brokers and mortgage finance companies were particularly successful at convincing homeowners to refinance. They simplified the refinancing process, and savings were nearly immediate for a homeowner. Many refinancings involved little risk, since housing prices rose significantly during the 1990s and early 2000s. A homeowner might seek a $250,000 refinance mortgage on a house purchased five years earlier for $300,000 but with a $500,000 current market value—equivalent to a $250,000 (50%) down payment.

Many homeowners refinanced two or three times between 2000 and 2005. A homeowner might have borrowed $285,000 with an 8%, 30-year mortgage. After monthly payments of $2,036 for 4 years, the homeowner would owe $259,260. If the owner refinanced the home at 5.25% with a 20-year mortgage, the monthly payment would decline from $2,036 to $1,800, and the mortgage would be repaid in 20 more years. With the rapid refinancing growth, the mortgage industry was highly profitable and grew quickly. In 2000, financial institutions originated less than $1 trillion in mortgages, and the United States had $5.1 trillion of mortgages outstanding. Mortgage originations peaked at $3.25 trillion in 2005, and by the end of 2006, the United States had $13.1 trillion of mortgages outstanding (although originations declined to $2.6 trillion).[1]

Interest rates began to stabilize in mid-2003 and remained in the 5.5–6.0% range until the end of 2005. Stable interest rates had a major effect on mortgage finance companies and mortgage brokers. The mortgage refinancing market declined throughout 2003 and the first part of 2004. Many homeowners had been slow to refinance, so some of them refinanced even though interest rates were higher in 2005 than in 2003 or 2004. However, by 2005, the refinancing market nearly disappeared. When interest rates began to rise in 2006, new home sales declined, home builders experienced record cancellations, and new home inventories began to climb. In response, many new home builders began to offer mortgages to their customers. At that point, many large mortgage finance companies had a choice. They could exit the mortgage business, substantially reduce their size, or ease their credit standards. Most chose to ease their credit standards.

Subprime Loans

By 2005, mortgage credit standards plummeted. To maintain sales, mortgage finance companies and some builders began offering loans with very low initial monthly payments (teaser loans) to borrowers with weak credit ratings. They also offered no-documentation mortgages. A homebuyer might be offered a 6.5% rate documented with a tax return or payroll stubs. With no documentation other than a stated but unverified annual income, the rate might be 7.0–8.5%.

These Alt-A (lower than prime A mortgages due to a lower credit rating or lack of documentation) and subprime loans offered initial monthly payments as low as one-third the monthly payment that would be required in 5 years and one-fourth the monthly payment that would be due in 10 years. By 2006, the subprime mortgage market exceeded $1.5 trillion. Several mortgage finance companies and several financial institution subsidiaries originated or purchased at least $40 billion of subprime mortgages annually.

Exhibit 2 provides an example of a common mortgage loan. The heading seemingly offers a $500,000, no down payment, 3% annual interest loan for $1,251 per month. The text provides additional but incomplete information about the loan. By analyzing the text and other material, a potential buyer would learn the following, which is summarized in Exhibit 3:

- The initial annual interest rate is 6.75%, not 3%; the 3% rate is solely for the purpose of calculating the initial $1,251 monthly payment.
- The buyer must pay points of 1.41% at closing ($7,050), added to the $500,000 home price.
- The actual interest expense during the first month is $2,768. Because the borrower pays only $1,251, the principal rises each month. This is a negative or reverse amortization loan.
- In some states, state law prohibits the principal (initial amount borrowed) from increasing by more than 10%; in other states, the principal can increase by

1. Afenberg, Forrest, Office of Federal Housing Enterprise Oversight, July 2005, and Freddie Mac NABE Teleconference, January 17, 2007, Frank E. Northaft, Chief Economist.

considerably more. In month 42, when the principal has grown from $507,040 to $576,545, the loan converts to an interest-only loan and the 6.75% fixed-interest rate loan converts to a variable rate loan. In this example, the rate increases to 7.0% and the monthly payment increases to $3,147. However, the new interest rate (and monthly payment) could be far higher.

- After 5 years (month 61) the interest rate increases by 1.0%, but this is also based on a variable interest rate that could be higher. The monthly payment increases to $3,710.

- After 10 years (month 121), the borrower pays interest and begins repaying the principal over the remaining 20 years of the mortgage; the monthly payment increases to $4,723.

- If the buyer is late on more than two payments, the interest rate increases to 16% and monthly payments increase to $7,043.

New Century Financial Corporation
Overview

New Century Financial Corp. started as a mortgage finance company in 1996. As the mortgage refinance market soared, New Century became one of the fastest growing firms in the nation. The firm originated or purchased $27 billion of mortgage loans in 2003, $42 billion in 2004, and $56 billion in 2005, when it became the nation's second largest subprime mortgage lender. Profits increased from $245 million in 2003 to $376 million in 2004 and $411 million in 2005.

Most mortgages New Century originated or purchased were either Alt-A or subprime loans; however, it did not make the highly aggressive negative amortization loans described in Exhibit 2. Payments for New Century mortgages were always at least equal to the interest, so the mortgage principal never increased, and New Century did not charge excessive penalties or interest rates for late payments. New Century also had a proprietary system to evaluate the credit worthiness of its borrowers. New Century Financial only made loans if the monthly payment did not exceed 28% of a borrower's pre-tax income and total payments (mortgage payments plus other debt) did not exceed 34% of pre-tax income. The following is a description of the firm's lending practices (2005 10K):

Underwriting Standards

Our loan origination standards and procedures are designed to produce high quality loans. These standards and procedures encompass underwriter qualifications and authority levels, appraisal review requirements, fraud prevention, funds disbursement controls, training of our employees and ongoing review of our employees' work. We help to ensure that our origination standards are met by employing accomplished and seasoned managers, underwriters and processors and through the extensive use of technology. In addition, we employ proprietary underwriting systems in our loan origination process that improve the consistency of underwriting standards, assess collateral adequacy and help to prevent fraud.

A qualified independent appraiser inspects and appraises each mortgage property and gives an opinion of value and condition. Following each appraisal, the appraiser prepares a report that includes a market value analysis based on recent sales of comparable homes in the area and, when appropriate, replacement cost analysis based on the current cost of constructing a similar home. All appraisals must conform to the Uniform Standards of Professional Appraisal Practice adopted by the Appraisal Foundation's Appraisal Standards Board and are generally on forms acceptable to

Fannie Mae and Freddie Mac. Our underwriting guidelines require a review of the appraisal by one of our qualified employees or by a qualified review appraiser that we have retained. Our underwriting guidelines then require our underwriters to be satisfied that the value of the property being financed, as indicated by the appraisal, would support the requested loan amount.

Most of our conventional loans conform to Fannie Mae, Freddie Mac, FHA, or VA standards, and our other non-conforming "prime grade" loans meet overall industry standards for loan documentation and borrower characteristics. The underwriting guidelines for conventional conforming loans comply with the guidelines established by Fannie Mae or Freddie Mac. Our underwriting guidelines for FHA-insured or VA-guaranteed mortgage loans comply with guidelines established by the U.S. Department of Housing and Urban Development, or HUD, and the VA, as applicable. Non-conforming "prime grade" mortgage loans originated through our mortgage loan origination platform acquired from RBC Mortgage must also meet overall industry standards for loan documentation and borrower characteristics so that these loans are saleable in the secondary market.

We periodically evaluate and modify our underwriting guidelines. We also adopt new underwriting guidelines appropriate to new loan products we may offer.

Income Documentation

Our underwriting guidelines include three levels of income documentation requirements, referred to as the "full documentation," "limited documentation" and "stated income documentation" programs.

- Under the full documentation program, we generally require applicants to submit two written forms of verification, or 12 or more consecutive monthly bank statements on their individual or business bank accounts, showing stable income for at least 12 months.
- Under the limited documentation program, we generally require applicants to submit six consecutive monthly bank statements on their individual bank accounts.
- Under the stated income documentation program, an applicant may be qualified based upon monthly income as stated on the mortgage loan application if the applicant meets certain criteria.

All of these documentation programs require that, with respect to any salaried employee, the applicant's employment be verified by telephone. In the case of a purchase money loan, we require verification of the source of funds, if any, to be deposited by the applicant into escrow. Under each of these programs, we review the applicant's source of income, calculate the amount of income from sources indicated on the loan application or similar documentation, review the applicant's credit history, and calculate the debt service-to-income ratio to determine the applicant's ability to repay the loan. We also review the type, use and condition of the property being financed. We use a qualifying interest rate that is equal to the initial interest rate on the loan to determine the applicant's ability to repay an adjustable-rate loan. For our interest-only adjustable rate mortgage, or ARM, loans we generally use the initial interest-only payment for determining the borrower's repayment ability.

For the year ended December 31, 2005, full documentation loans as a percentage of total originations totaled $30.4 billion, or 54.2%, limited documentation loans totaled $1.5 billion, or 2.7%, and stated documentation loans totaled $24.2 billion, or 43.1%.

Securitization pools

Institutional investors who purchase notes issued by a securitization pool require assurance that there will be sufficient payments from the borrowers to pay interest and repay principal on the notes they buy. That assurance can come in at least four forms:

1. The quality of the debt;
2. The interest rate spread between the rate borrowers pay to the pool and the rate the pool pays to those who buy the notes it issues;
3. The difference between the face value of mortgages owned by the pool and the face value of the notes sold by the pool; and
4. Insurance to protect bondholders in the event of default.

With very high-quality debt, such as new car financing to borrowers with high credit ratings, institutional investors who purchase notes from the pool may require little protection. If Toyota Financial Services (the loan originator) forms a pool with $500 million of 8% auto receivables, institutional investors may be willing to buy $480 million of 6% notes backed by auto receivables owned by the pool. When individuals who borrow to purchase cars make monthly payments, their payments are first used to pay 6% interest and repay $480 million of principal to the note holders. After the note holders are repaid, the remaining payments from auto buyers are paid to Toyota Finance.

The amount remaining in the pool after note holders are paid is Toyota Finance's "Residual or retained interest" in the pool. Retained interest can be more than the $20 million difference between the $500 million of receivables transferred to the pool and the $480 million notes issued. If most borrowers repay their loans, retained interest will be more because borrowers pay 8% interest on $500 million of receivables, and the pool pays 6% interest on $480 million of notes. The retained interest could be less than $20 million if defaults are high. If defaults are exceptionally high, Toyota's retained interest could be zero and note holders could lose part of their principal and expected interest payments. With lower quality debt, such as used car financing to low credit-rating borrowers, the residual or retained interest might be 25% or more of the receivables transferred to the pool.

Accounting for securitization pools

When a firm (the loan originator) securitizes receivables, it can do so in two ways. First, it can sell the receivables without recourse to a special purpose entity (SPE), which is the securitization trust. The originator has no claim to the receivables (other than a claim to the retained interests, if any) and no liability for the receivables-backed notes issued by the securitization trust. These are securitizations legally structured as a sale.

A second option is for the originator to transfer receivables to a securitization trust, but the originator remains liable for the receivables-backed notes. These are securitizations legally structured as a financing; the securitization trust provides financing for the firm's receivables, but it does not buy them. In nearly all cases, securitizations are legally structured as sales; institutional investors who purchase the notes have no claim against the loan originator if borrowers default in large numbers. If a securitization is legally structured as a financing, it is also structured as a financing for accounting purposes. That is, the loan originator must include on its balance sheet both the receivables in the securitization trust and the trust's liabilities to the note purchasers.

If a securitization is legally structured as a sale, it is not necessarily structured as a sale for accounting. If the sale of receivables to a securitization trust includes a call or a put option, additional rules apply.[2] If the securitization includes a put option, such that institutional investors can require that the originator repurchase the receivables, then the loan originator must include the fair value of that put as a liability on its balance sheet. If the securitization includes a call option, such that the loan originator has the right to buy back the receivables from the securitization trust, then even though, legally, the securitization is structured as a sale, for accounting purposes it is structured as a financing. The loan originator must include on its balance sheet both the receivables owned by the securitization trust and the trust's liabilities to its note holders. In 2002, New Century retained a call option on the mortgages it sold to its securitization trusts. As a result, it recorded those securitized mortgages as financings even though, legally, they were structured as sales. The following is from New Century's September 30, 2006, 10-Q (Exhibit 4 provides additional information about mortgage loans held for investment):

Mortgage Loans Held for Investment

Mortgage loans held for investment represent loans securitized through transactions structured as financings, or pending securitization through transactions that are expected to be structured as financings. Mortgage loans held for investment are stated at amortized cost, including the outstanding principal balance, less the allowance for loan losses, plus net deferred origination costs. The financing related to these securitizations is included in the Company's condensed consolidated balance sheet as financing on mortgage loans held for investment.

Securitizations Structured as Financings

These securitizations are structured legally as sales, but for accounting purposes are treated as financings under SFAS 140. The securitization trusts do not meet the qualifying special purpose entity criteria under SFAS 140 and related interpretations due to their ability to enter into derivative contracts. Additionally, we have the option to purchase loans from the securitization trusts at our discretion. Accordingly, the loans, which we refer to as "mortgage loans held for investment," remain on our balance sheet, retained interests are not created, and financing for mortgage loans held for investment replaces the credit facility debt originally financing the mortgage loans. We record interest income on securitized loans and interest expense on the bonds issued in the securitizations over the life of the securitizations. Deferred debt issuance costs and discount related to the bonds are amortized on a level yield basis over the estimated life of the bonds.

In most cases, loan originators prefer to structure securitizations as sales to keep both the assets (receivables) and liabilities (notes payable) off their balance sheet. Instead, they only report their retained interest in the pool. That disclosure lets analysts and investors see the loan originator's maximum possible loss from its securitization transactions. In addition, a note to the financial statement typically provides information on how the retained interest was computed, such as the estimated default rate on mortgages and the discount rate used to compute the present value of estimated cash payments to the securitization trust.

When a securitization is legally structured as a sale but for accounting purposes is structured as a financing, investors are typically interested only in the loan

---

2. ASC 860.50, *Transfers and Servicing, Servicing Assets and Liabilities* (FAS 140).

originator's retained interest (maximum exposure to loss) and how that retained interest was computed (default and discount rates). New Century could have disclosed its retained interest on its securitizations structured as financings (but legally structured as sales), but it chose not to do so.

In Topic 860, *Transfers and Servicing* (FAS 140), the FASB stated that the key to whether a loan originator should include a trust's assets and liabilities on its balance sheet was whether the loan originator controls the assets (through a call option), not whether it was liable for the securitization trust's debt (through a put option): "an objective in accounting for transfers of financial assets is for each entity that is a party to the transaction to recognize only assets it controls and liabilities it has incurred, to derecognize assets only when control has been surrendered, and to derecognize liabilities only when they have been extinguished (860-10-10-01)." That rule seems to go against traditional accounting. Normally, a firm records a debt because it has a liability, not because it has the option to assume a liability.

In its balance sheet (Exhibit 5), New Century uses the term "mortgage loans held for investment, net of allowance" to describe its assets from securitizations structured as financings; it calls the liability associated with that securitization as "financing on mortgage loans held for investment, net." In a note to its financial statements, New Century stated that it does not disclose the retained interest on securities structured as financings.

In early 2007, several mortgage finance firms declared bankruptcy, several major hedge funds announced losses in excess of $1 billion, and several large commercial banks announced major losses in their subprime lending subsidiaries. Some of those banks closed their mortgage finance subsidiaries. New Century Financial Corp. reported $267.6 million of net earnings through the first three quarters of 2006 (Exhibit 6), and positive cash provided by operating activities for those three quarters of $209.9 million (Exhibit 7), but on April 2, 2007, the firm filed for bankruptcy. The firm later stated that it was unlikely it would ever release its 2006 annual report and that it was being investigated for criminal accounting fraud.

Required

1. Identify the risks in New Century's balance sheet.

2. On September 30, 2005, New Century had $14 billion of mortgage loans held for investment, offset by $13.9 billion of financing on mortgage loans held for investment. Did classifying these securitizations as mortgage loans held for investment, rather than as sales, provide more information to investors, less information to investors, or about the same amount of information to investors? Why did New Century not disclose its retained interest in mortgage loans held for investment?

3. Evaluate the $191.6 million allowance for uncollectible mortgages on September 30, 2006, and the $198.1 million allowance on December 31, 2005 (Exhibit 4).

4. How did New Century earn a profit in 2006 and in prior years? Explain in detail.

5. How did New Century go from a highly profitable firm on September 30, 2006 (Exhibit 6), to filing for bankruptcy on April 2, 2007? From a firm with high cash flows from operations (Exhibit 7) to bankruptcy?

6. What additional information in its 10-Q would help investors better understand New Century's financial condition? Is that information available in financial reports from other firms?

EXHIBIT 1

U.S. 30-YEAR
CONVENTIONAL
(FIXED) MORTGAGE
RATES BY MONTH

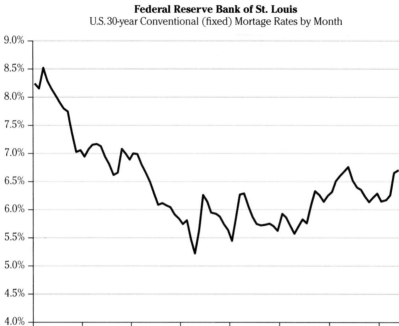

Federal Reserve Bank of St. Louis
U.S. 30-year Conventional (fixed) Mortage Rates by Month

EXHIBIT 2

TYPICAL SUB-PRIME
LOAN: JANUARY
2004 THROUGH
JULY 2007

\$500,000 Mortgage only \$1,251 per month
3% annual interest rate, no down payment

*Rate is variable and subject to change. Credit restrictions may apply. After the initial fixed-rate period, the rate will adjust every 6 months. The initial, minimum monthly payment on a 30-year \$500,000, 5-year Adjustable Rate Loan is \$1,251 with 1.41 points due at closing (which can be added to the \$500,000 mortgage). The minimum payment is based on a rate that is implied solely for the purpose of calculating the minimum payment which in this example is 3.0%. Interest will accrue at a rate of 6.75%. Paying only the minimum payment will result in deferred interest or negative amortization since you will not be paying all the interest charged each month. The unpaid interest is added to the principal balance. Interest can be deferred until the outstanding principal balance is 10 to 15% higher than the original loan amount, depending on the state of residence. If the maximum limit is reached during the first 5 years, the payment automatically converts to an interest only payment. In this example, the maximum limit will be reached in the 41st month, when the loan amount reaches \$575,000.00. At that point, the minimum payment will convert to an interest-only payment of \$3,147. After 5 years, the interest rate increases by .25% (assuming the variable interest based on market rates does not change) and the interest only payment increases to \$3,710. After 10 years, the principal and interest payment is \$4,723 and remains at that amount through year 30, when the loan amount due will have been reduced to zero. The Annual Percentage Rate is beginning after year 10 is 8.00%. Rates could change daily. Actual payments and rates may vary depending on individual client situation and current rates. Other restrictions may apply. For example, any two late payments will be considered a default and will convert the loan from a stated interest only or interest only loan to a principal and interest loan and the annual rate will increase to 16%. If a borrower defaulted in month 30, the loan would become a principal plus interest loan at 16%, with payments due over the following 330 months. Monthly payments would increase from \$1,251 to \$7,042.78.

EXHIBIT 3

PROJECTED PAYMENTS FROM EXHIBIT 2, FIRST 21 MONTHS

Basic Terms

Points due at closing:	1.41%
Initial loan (excluding points):	$5,00,000
Implied annual interest rate:	3.00%
Implied monthly interest rate:	0.25%

Month	Principal	Monthly Pmt	Interest Exp
0	$507,050		
1	$508,567	$1,251	$2,768
2	$510,092	$1,251	$2,776
3	$511,626	$1,251	$2,784
4	$513,168	$1,251	$2,793
5	$514,718	$1,251	$2,801
6	$516,277	$1,251	$2,809
7	$517,845	$1,251	$2,818
8	$519,421	$1,251	$2,826
9	$521,005	$1,251	$2,835
10	$522,598	$1,251	$2,844
11	$524,200	$1,251	$2,852
12	$525,811	$1,251	$2,861
13	$527,430	$1,251	$2,870
14	$529,059	$1,251	$2,879
15	$530,696	$1,251	$2,888
16	$532,342	$1,251	$2,897

Actual Interest Rates

	Until Month 42	Months 42 to 60	Months 61 to 360
Annual rate:	6.75%	7.00%	8.00%
Monthly rate:	0.55%	0.57%	0.64%

Month	Principal	Monthly Pmt	Interest Exp
61	$576,545	$3,710	$3,710
62	$576,545	$3,710	$3,710
63	$576,545	$3,710	$3,710
64	$576,545	$3,710	$3,710
65	$576,545	$3,710	$3,710
66	$576,545	$3,710	$3,710
67	$576,545	$3,710	$3,710
68	$576,545	$3,710	$3,710
69	$576,545	$3,710	$3,710
70	$576,545	$3,710	$3,710
71	$576,545	$3,710	$3,710
72	$576,545	$3,710	$3,710
73	$576,545	$3,710	$3,710
74	$576,545	$3,710	$3,710
75	$576,545	$3,710	$3,710
76	$576,545	$3,710	$3,710
77	$576,545	$3,710	$3,710

17	$533,997	$1,251
18	$535,661	$1,251
19	$537,334	$1,251
20	$539,016	$1,251
21	$540,708	$1,251
22	$542,409	$1,251
23	$544,119	$1,251
24	$545,838	$1,251
25	$547,567	$1,251
26	$549,305	$1,251
27	$551,053	$1,251
28	$552,810	$1,251
29	$554,577	$1,251
30	$556,353	$1,251
31	$558,139	$1,251
32	$559,935	$1,251
33	$561,741	$1,251
34	$563,556	$1,251
35	$565,382	$1,251
36	$567,217	$1,251
37	$569,062	$1,251
38	$570,918	$1,251
39	$572,784	$1,251
40	$574,659	$1,251
41	$576,545	$1,251
42	$576,545	$3,147
43	$576,545	$3,147

78	$2,906	$576,545	$3,710
79	$2,915	$576,545	$3,710
80	$2,924	$576,545	$3,710
81	$2,933	$576,545	$3,710
82	$2,942	$576,545	$3,710
83	$2,951	$576,545	$3,710
84	$2,961	$576,545	$3,710
85	$2,970	$576,545	$3,710
86	$2,979	$576,545	$3,710
87	$2,989	$576,545	$3,710
88	$2,998	$576,545	$3,710
89	$3,008	$576,545	$3,710
90	$3,017	$576,545	$3,710
91	$3,027	$576,545	$3,710
92	$3,037	$576,545	$3,710
93	$3,046	$576,545	$3,710
94	$3,056	$576,545	$3,710
95	$3,066	$576,545	$3,710
96	$3,076	$576,545	$3,710
97	$3,086	$576,545	$3,710
98	$3,096	$576,545	$3,710
99	$3,106	$576,545	$3,710
100	$3,116	$576,545	$3,710
101	$3,126	$576,545	$3,710
102	$3,137	$576,545	$3,710
103	$3,147	$576,545	$3,710
104	$3,147	$576,545	$3,710

EXHIBIT 3—*continued*

PROJECTED PAYMENTS FROM EXHIBIT 2, FIRST 21 MONTHS

Basic Terms

Points due at closing:	1.41%
Initial loan (excluding points):	$5,00,000
Implied annual interest rate:	3.00%
Implied monthly interest rate:	0.25%

Month	Principal	Monthly Pmt	Interest Exp
44	$576,545	$3,147	$3,147
45	$576,545	$3,147	$3,147
46	$576,545	$3,147	$3,147
47	$576,545	$3,147	$3,147
48	$576,545	$3,147	$3,147
49	$576,545	$3,147	$3,147
50	$576,545	$3,147	$3,147
51	$576,545	$3,147	$3,147
52	$576,545	$3,147	$3,147
53	$576,545	$3,147	$3,147
54	$576,545	$3,147	$3,147
55	$576,545	$3,147	$3,147
56	$576,545	$3,147	$3,147
57	$576,545	$3,147	$3,147
58	$576,545	$3,147	$3,147
59	$576,545	$3,147	$3,147
60	$576,545	$3,147	$3,147

Actual Interest Rates

	Until Month 42	Months 42 to 60	Months 61 to 360
Annual rate:	6.75%	7.00%	8.00%
Monthly rate:	0.55%	0.57%	0.64%

Month	Principal	Monthly Pmt	Interest Exp
105	$576,545	$3,710	$3,710
106	$576,545	$3,710	$3,710
107	$576,545	$3,710	$3,710
108	$576,545	$3,710	$3,710
109	$576,545	$3,710	$3,710
110	$576,545	$3,710	$3,710
111	$576,545	$3,710	$3,710
112	$576,545	$3,710	$3,710
113	$576,545	$3,710	$3,710
114	$576,545	$3,710	$3,710
115	$576,545	$3,710	$3,710
116	$576,545	$3,710	$3,710
117	$576,545	$3,710	$3,710
118	$576,545	$3,710	$3,710
119	$576,545	$3,710	$3,710
120	$576,545	$3,710	$3,710
121	$575,532	$4,723	$3,710

3. Mortgage Loans Held for Investment

During the nine months ended September 30, 2006, the Company securitized $3.4 billion in loans through transactions structured as financings. There were no securitizations structured as financings for the three months ended September 30, 2006. A summary of the components of mortgage loans held for investment at September 30, 2006 and December 31, 2005 is as follows (dollars in thousands):

	September 30, 2006	December 31, 2005
Mortgage loans held for investment:		
First trust deeds	$13,560,995	15,877,535
Second trust deeds	570,299	334,689
Allowance for loan losses	(191,561)	(198,131)
Net deferred origination costs	91,266	129,772
	$14,030,999	16,143,865

At September 30, 2006, the Company had mortgage loans held for investment having an unpaid principal balance of approximately $817.8 million on which the accrual of interest had been discontinued. If these mortgage loans had been current throughout their terms, interest income would have increased by approximately $25.5 million for the nine months ended September 30, 2006. At September 30, 2005, the Company had mortgage loans held for investment having an unpaid principal balance of approximately $423.4 million on which the accrual of interest had been discontinued. If these mortgage loans had been current throughout their terms, interest income would have increased by approximately $15.3 million for the nine months ended September 30, 2005.

The following table presents a summary of the activity for the allowance for losses on mortgage loans held for investment for the three and nine months ended September 30, 2006 and 2005 (dollars in thousands):

	Three Months Ended September 30		Nine Months Ended September 30	
	2006	2005	2006	2005
Balance, beginning of period	$209,889	145,565	198,131	90,227
Additions	20,756	38,542	80,906	105,655
Charge-offs, net	(39,084)	(6,348)	(87,476)	(18,123)
Balance, end of period	$191,561	177,759	191,561	177,759

We have historically sold our loans through both whole loan sales and securitizations structured as sales. Since 2003, we have also retained a portion of our loan production for investment on our balance sheet through securitizations structured as financings rather than sales. Our decisions regarding secondary marketing transactions in 2006 will be based on market conditions and our ability to access external sources of capital. We do not currently intend to structure any securitizations as sales in 2006.

EXHIBIT 4

NOTE 3, NEW CENTURY FINANCIAL CORP. SEPTEMBER 30, 2005, 10-Q

EXHIBIT 5

NEW CENTURY
FINANCIAL
CORPORATION AND
SUBSIDIARIES

CONSOLIDATED BALANCE SHEETS, SEPT 30, 2006 AND DEC 31, 2005 ($ 000)

	September 30, 2006	December 31, 2005
	(Unaudited)	
ASSETS		
Cash and cash equivalents	$408,860	503,723
Restricted cash	572,847	726,697
Mortgage loans held for sale at lower of cost or market	8,945,134	7,825,175
Mortgage loans held for investment, net of allowance of $191,561 and $198,131	14,030,999	16,143,865
Residual interests in securitizations—held-for-trading	223,680	234,930
Mortgage servicing assets	59,878	69,315
Real estate owned, net of allowance of $56,318 and $18,196, respectively	84,021	37,642
Accrued interest receivable	109,598	101,945
Income taxes, net	80,551	80,823
Office property and equipment, net	87,736	86,886
Goodwill	95,792	92,980
Prepaid expenses and other assets	360,672	243,109
Total assets	$25,059,768	26,147,090

(*continued*)

EXHIBIT 5—
continued

NEW CENTURY
FINANCIAL
CORPORATION AND
SUBSIDIARIES

LIABILITIES AND STOCKHOLDERS' EQUITY

Credit facilities on mortgage loans held for sale	$8,487,850	7,439,685
Financing on mortgage loans held for investment, net	13,858,940	16,045,459
Accounts payable and accrued liabilities	574,258	508,163
Junior subordinated notes	51,545	—
Convertible senior notes, net	—	4,943
Notes payable	22,826	39,140
Total liabilities	22,995,419	24,037,390
Commitments and contingencies		
Stockholders' equity:		
Preferred stock, $0.01 par value. Authorized 25,000,000 shares at Sep 30, 2006, and 10,000,000 shares at Dec 31, 2005;		
Series A preferred stock; issued and outstanding 4,500,000 shares Sep 30, 2006 and Dec 31, 2005	45	45
Series B preferred stock; issued and outstanding 2,300,000 shares Sep 30, 2006, and none Dec 31, 2005	23	—
Common stock, $0.01 par value. Authorized 300,000,000 shares at Sep 30, 2006 and Dec 31, 2005; issued and outstanding 55,329,184 and 55,723,267 shares at Sep 30, 2006 and Dec 31, 2005	553	557
Additional paid-in capital	1,246,451	1,234,362
Accumulated other comprehensive income	23,450	61,045
Retained earnings	793,827	828,270
	2,064,349	2,124,279
Deferred compensation costs	—	(14,579)
Total stockholders' equity	2,064,349	2,109,700
Total liabilities and stockholders' equity	$25,059,768	26,147,090

See accompanying notes to unaudited condensed consolidated financial statements.

EXHIBIT 6

NEW CENTURY
FINANCIAL
CORPORATION AND
SUBSIDIARIES

CONSOLIDATED INCOME STATEMENTS, ($ 000)

	Three Months Ended September 30		Nine Months Ended September 30	
	2006	**2005**	**2006**	**2005**
Interest income	$514,172	494,621	1,478,288	1,246,553
Interest expense	(375,228)	(290,899)	(1,019,552)	(671,535)
Net interest income	138,944	203,722	458,736	575,018
Provision for losses on mortgage loans held for investment	(20,756)	(38,542)	(80,906)	(105,655)
Net interest income after provision for losses	118,188	165,180	377,830	469,363
Other operating income:				
Gain on sale of mortgage loans	173,045	176,241	497,732	409,797
Servicing income	17,770	10,203	47,424	23,556
Other income (loss)	(20,747)	4,986	18,845	12,257
Total other operating income	170,068	191,430	564,001	445,610
Operating expenses:				
Personnel	112,575	146,575	356,218	378,258
General and administrative	57,498	49,823	170,086	133,922
Advertising and promotion	14,643	25,661	41,197	66,204
Professional services	13,295	11,580	33,588	29,063
Total operating expenses	198,011	233,639	601,089	607,447
Earnings before income taxes	90,245	122,971	340,742	307,526
Income tax expense	23,603	2,867	64,822	7,583
Net earnings	66,642	120,104	275,920	299,943
Dividends paid on preferred stock	3,174	2,567	8,307	2,852
Net earnings available to common	$63,468	117,537	267,613	297,091

See accompanying notes to unaudited condensed consolidated financial statements.

EXHIBIT 7

NEW CENTURY
FINANCIAL
CORPORATION AND
SUBSIDIARIES

CONDENSED CONSOLIDATED STATEMENTS OF CASH FLOWS ($ 000: UNAUDITED)

	Nine months ended September 30	
	2006	**2005**
Cash flows from operating activities:		
Net earnings	$275,920	299,943
Adjustments to reconcile net earnings to net cash provided by operating activities:		
Depreciation and amortization of office property and equipment	22,669	16,048
Amortization of deferred costs related to mortgage loans held for investment	64,984	65,072
Amortization related to mortgage servicing rights and other	15,004	8,634
Stock-based compensation	16,658	5,657
Cash flows received from residual interests in securitizations	2,113	15,021
Accretion of Net Interest Receivables, or "NIR"	(18,986)	(11,949)
NIR gains	—	(34,807)
Servicing gains	(30,026)	(60,927)
Fair value adjustment of residual interests in securitizations	28,123	7,645
Provision for losses on mortgage loans held for investment	80,906	105,655
Provision for repurchase losses	5,261	4,300
Increase in real estate owned, net	(46,379)	(16,558)
Mortgage loans originated or acquired for sale	(42,077,479)	(30,215,340)
Mortgage loan sales, net	40,630,368	25,453,537
Principal payments on mortgage loans held for sale	446,841	209,084
Increase in credit facilities on mortgage loans held for sale	1,048,165	4,513,854
Tax benefit (change) related to non-qualified stock options	(5,037)	—
Net change in other assets and liabilities	(249,179)	77,391
Net cash provided by operating activities	209,926	442,260
Cash flows from investing activities:		
Mortgage loans originated or acquired for investment, net	(3,376,627)	(10,273,642)
Principal payments on mortgage loans held for investment	5,370,993	4,984,710
Sale of mortgage servicing rights	29,479	8,477
Purchase of office property and equipment	(23,519)	(46,761)
Acquisition of net assets	9,795	(80,573)
Net cash provided by (used in) investing activities	2,010,121	(5,407,789)

(continued)

EXHIBIT 7—
continued

NEW CENTURY
FINANCIAL
CORPORATION AND
SUBSIDIARIES

Cash flows from financing activities:		
Proceeds from issuance of financing on mortgage loans held for investment, net	3,280,904	9,792,230
Repayments of financing on mortgage loans held for investment	(5,488,031)	(4,688,033)
(Increase) decrease in restricted cash	153,850	(317,306)
Proceeds from issuance of junior subordinated notes	51,545	—
Net proceeds from issuance of common stock	14,714	25,368
Net proceeds from issuance of preferred stock	55,603	108,664
Increase (decrease) in notes payable, net	(16,314)	7,680
Payment of dividends on common stock	(294,193)	(259,067)
Payment of dividends on preferred stock	(7,700)	(2,852)
Excess tax benefits from stock-based compensation	5,037	—
Purchase of common stock	(70,325)	(13,950)
Net cash provided by (used in) financing activities	(2,314,910)	4,652,734
Net decrease in cash and cash equivalents	(94,863)	(312,795)
Cash and cash equivalents, beginning of year	503,723	842,854
Cash and cash equivalents, end of period	$408,860	530,059
Supplemental cash flow disclosure:		
Interest paid	$1,014,275	652,937
Income taxes paid	60,720	24,746
Supplemental noncash financing activity:		
Restricted stock issued	$8,340	14,866
Restricted stock cancelled	2,478	5,896
Accrued dividends on common stock	102,400	93,183
Accrued dividends on preferred stock	607	—

Sirius XM Radio Inc.
Faces Bankruptcy

On February 10, 2009, Sirius XM Radio Inc. announced that it was working with advisors to prepare for a possible bankruptcy filing.[1] Sirius Radio and XM Radio had been competitors in the satellite radio broadcasting field from 2002 until July 28, 2008, when Sirius acquired XM.

XM Radio had offered the world's first satellite radio service beginning November 12, 2001.[2] Sirius Satellite Radio launched a more limited satellite radio service February 14, 2002, in Denver, Houston, Phoenix, and Jackson, Mississippi, and then expanded nationally in mid-2002.[3] XM and Sirius began with similar operations and funding. By December 31, 2002, XM Satellite Radio had raised about $1.8 billion ($1.5 billion from the sale of common stock and $270 million from long-term debt); Sirius had raised about $2.2 billion ($960 million from the sale of common stock, $670 million from long-term debt, and $530 million from cumulative convertible preferred stock). XM had spent about $815 million for property and equipment; Sirius had spent about $1 billion (primarily for satellites and related equipment). Each had cumulative losses of about $900 million by December 31, 2002.

The following business description is from the combined Sirius XM Radio's third-quarter 2008 10-Q:

(1) Business

We provide satellite radio in the United States. We broadcast music, sports, news, talk, entertainment, traffic and weather for a subscription fee through proprietary satellite radio systems—the SIRIUS system and the XM system. On July 28, 2008, our wholly owned subsidiary, Vernon Merger Corporation, merged (the "Merger") with and into XM Satellite Radio Holdings Inc. and, as a result, XM Satellite Radio Holdings Inc. is now our wholly owned subsidiary. The SIRIUS satellite radio system consists of three in-orbit satellites, approximately 120 terrestrial repeaters that receive and retransmit signals, satellite uplink facilities and studios. The XM satellite radio system consists of four in-orbit satellites, over 700 terrestrial repeaters that receive and retransmit signals, satellite uplink facilities and studios. Subscribers can also receive music channels and certain other channels over the internet.

SIRIUS and XM radios are primarily distributed through retailers; automakers, or OEMs; and through our websites. On September 30, 2008, SIRIUS and XM radios were available at more than 20,000 retail locations. We also have agreements with every major automaker, Acura/Honda, Aston Martin, Audi, Automobili Lamborghini, Bentley, BMW, Chrysler, Dodge, Ford, General Motors, Honda, Hyundai, Infiniti/Nissan, Jaguar, Jeep, Kia, Land Rover, Lincoln, Lexus/Toyota/Scion, Maybach, Mazda, Mercedes-Benz, Mercury, MINI, Mitsubishi, Rolls-Royce, Volvo and Volkswagen, to offer either SIRIUS or XM satellite radios as factory or dealer-installed equipment in their

---

1. Kouwe, Zachery, Sirius XM Prepares Bankruptcy Filing, *The New York Times*, February 10, 2009, *The New York Times* Web site. http://dealbook.blogs.nytimes.com/2009/02/10/sirius-xm-prepares-bankruptcy-filing/?scp=8&sq=Sirius%20Kouwe&st=cse.

2. XM Radio 10-Q, for the quarter ending September 30, 2002, p. 20.

3. Sirius Satellite Radio 10-Q for the quarters ending March 31, 2002 and June 30, 2002.

vehicles. SIRIUS and XM radios are also offered to customers of rental car companies, including Hertz and Avis.

As of September 30, 2008, we had 18,920,911 subscribers compared with 8,321,785 subscribers as of December 31, 2007 and 7,667,476 subscribers as of September 30, 2007. Our current subscriber total includes 9,716,070 XM subscribers that we acquired as a result of the Merger. Our subscriber totals include subscribers under our regular pricing plans; subscribers that have prepaid, including payments received from automakers for prepaid subscriptions included in the sale or lease price of a new vehicle; active SIRIUS radios under our agreement with Hertz; active XM radios under our agreement with Avis; and subscribers to SIRIUS Internet Radio and XM Internet Radio, our Internet services.

Our primary source of revenue is subscription fees, with most of our customers subscribing on an annual, semi-annual, quarterly or monthly basis. We offer discounts for pre-paid and long-term subscriptions as well as discounts for multiple subscriptions. We also derive revenue from activation fees, the sale of advertising on select non-music channels, the direct sale of satellite radios and accessories, and other ancillary services, such as our Backseat TV, data and weather services.

In certain cases, automakers include a subscription to our radio services in the sale or lease price of vehicles. The length of these prepaid subscriptions varies, but is typically three months to one year. In many cases, we receive subscription payments from automakers in advance of the activation of our service. We also reimburse various automakers for certain costs associated with satellite radios installed in their vehicles.

We also have an interest in the satellite radio services offered in Canada. SIRIUS Canada Inc. ("SIRIUS Canada"), a Canadian corporation that we jointly own with Canadian Broadcasting Corporation and Standard Radio Inc., offers a satellite radio service in Canada. Canadian Satellite Radio Holdings Inc. ("XM Canada"), a Canadian corporation in which we have an ownership interest, also offers satellite radio service in Canada. Subscribers to the SIRIUS Canada service and the XM Canada service are not included in our subscriber count.

On August 5, 2008, we changed our name from Sirius Satellite Radio Inc. to Sirius XM Radio Inc. XM Satellite Radio Holdings Inc., together with its subsidiaries, is operated as an unrestricted subsidiary under our existing indebtedness. As an unrestricted subsidiary, transactions between the companies are required to comply with various contractual provisions in our respective debt instruments.

Both XM Radio and Sirius Satellite Radio began by offering customers a wide range of radio channels. Since their merger, customers can continue with XM Everything or Sirius Everything for $12.95 per month, XM Everything plus the best of Sirius or Sirius Everything plus the best of XM for $16.99 per month, or all of XM and all of Sirius for $19.99 per month. Sirius offers more limited packages for as low as $6.99 per month while XM offers limited packages for as low as $9.99 per month.

XM Satellite Radio

The following is a sample of channels currently offered by XM Radio:

Description	Number of channels
Music	98
National Football League (NFL)	13
Family	5
News	16
Sports, other	17
Comedy	4

Oprah	1
Professional Golf Association (PGA)	1
Major League Baseball (MLB)	16
College sports	
ACC	3
Pac 10	3
Big 10	3
SEC	3
Big East	1
Big 12	1
National Hockey League (NHL)	6
Traffic and Weather	12
National Basketball Association (NBA)	5

Sirius Radio and Howard Stern

Exhibit 1 shows subscribers for Sirius Satellite Radio, XM Satellite Radio, and the combined Sirius XM Radio from their 10-Q and 10-K reports (XM Radio stopped reporting subscriber numbers in June 2007). Sirius Radio began with about as many music channels as XM Radio (currently 89 for Sirius; 98 for XM Radio), nearly as many news channels, and more religious and political talk channels. However, with its slightly earlier start, XM Radio signed long-term contracts with every major U.S. professional sports league. XM Radio's current sports offerings (above) are similar to its offerings when it began operations. In contrast, Sirius Radio has only a single NFL channel and a single NASCAR channel.

Because a large percentage of satellite radios are sold to men between the ages of 18 and 49, by June 30, 2004, XM Radio had more than four times as many subscribers as Sirius Radio. With no possibility of expanding into the professional or college sports markets, Sirius Radio seemed to have lost the satellite radio market race. On April 8, 2004, an event seemingly unrelated to satellite radio offered Sirius a chance to compete with XM's sports offerings. Howard Stern, a highly popular, irreverent radio entertainer with nearly 10 million listeners, had, for the first time in six years, violated Federal Communications Commission (FCC) decency standards. The Federal Communications Commission (FCC) fined Mr. Stern's employer, Clear Channel Communications, $495,000 for Mr. Stern's violation and threatened larger fines for future violations.[4] Clear Channel dropped Mr. Stern's program from six of its major stations, and Mr. Stern began discussions with Sirius Radio.

On October 6, 2004, Sirius Satellite Radio's Web site added a press release titled "Howard Stern and Sirius Announce the Most Important Deal in Radio History."[5] That agreement paid Mr. Stern $100 million per year for five years, plus $200 million in Sirius stock. In exchange, Mr. Stern agreed to provide two full stations of programming for the five-year period beginning January 9, 2006. From that announcement, until January 2006, when Mr. Stern began broadcasting on Sirius Radio, Sirius increased its subscriber base from 660,000 to 3.3 million. By June 30, 2006, Sirius increased its subscriber base to 4.7 million and by December 31, 2006, to about 6.0 million.

---

4. Hilden, Julie, "The FCC tries to silence Howard Stern: Can the radio shock jock sue?" April 13, 2004, FindLaw. http://writ.news.findlaw.com/hilden/20040413.html.

5. Sirius Satellite Radio, "Howard Stern and Sirius announce the most important deal in radio history." http://www.sirius.com/servlet/ContentServer?pagename=Sirius/CachedPage&c=PresReleAsset&cid=10 97008921509.

At the time, each subscriber paid a monthly fee of $12.95 for Sirius Radio. To encourage subscribers to pay in advance, Sirius offered lower fees for quarterly or annual subscriptions. On average, Sirius received approximately $11.15 per month per subscriber. (See Exhibit 1.) For the first three quarters of 2004, Sirius Radio reported its average monthly fee. Both XM Radio and Sirius Radio charged $12.95 per month, but both offered discounts to subscribers who paid for a quarter or a year in advance.

Financial Results

Adding Mr. Stern allowed Sirius to rapidly close XM's subscriber lead, but the market did not seem large enough for two competitors in an industry with such high fixed costs for capital equipment and talent. Both firms remained highly unprofitable. On February 19, 2007, Sirius Radio announced it would merge with XM Radio in a stock swap. Exhibit 2 provides details of the merger, which closed July 28, 2008.

The combined firm's 2008 income statements, balance sheets, and cash flow statements are shown in Exhibits 3, 4, and 5. The income statements and cash flow statements show Sirius Radio results for 2006 and 2007, and combined results for 2008. The balance sheet shows Sirius Radio as of December 31, 2007, and the combined firm as of December 31, 2008. At the time of the merger, each firm had a cumulative loss of about $4 billion. The merged firm's 2008 revenues were nearly double the 2007 revenues of Sirius Radio, but the combined firm reported a $5.3 billion loss in 2008.

However, the $5.3 billion 2008 loss included a $4.77 billion goodwill impairment charge at the merger date, when XM Radio immediately wrote off $4.77 billion of the $6.6 billion goodwill it recorded as part of the price it paid for XM Radio (Exhibit 6). Cash flow from operations for 2008 was negative by $153 million, including $51 million of merger-related costs (Exhibit 5).

Exhibit 7 describes accounting policies for revenue recognition and subscriber acquisition costs, and Exhibit 8 provides selected details on its debt. Although Sirius XM had $383 million of cash and equivalents as of December 31, 2008 (Exhibit 4), credit markets were nearly frozen as a result of the worldwide 2008–2009 financial crises. Sirius XM Radio was fully compliant with its debt covenants on December 31, 2008, but it had $1 billion of debt to refinance during 2009 (Exhibit 8). Because that debt would be nearly impossible to refinance, on February 10, 2009, Sirius XM Radio announced it was considering bankruptcy. Seven days later, on February 17, 2009, John Malone's Liberty Media agreed to lend Sirius XM Radio $530 million. Upon completion of the debt financing, Liberty Media would receive 12.5 million shares of preferred stock that would be convertible into 40% of Sirius XM's common stock (Exhibit 9).

Required

1. Explain the acquisition (Exhibit 2). How subjective are the intangible asset valuations? Why did Sirius XM Radio immediately write off $4.77 billion of the acquired goodwill (Exhibit 6)? Did the write-off indicate Sirius overpaid for XM radio? Was the merger a wise one for Sirius? For XM?

2. Assume there were no costs associated with Mr. Stern's contract other than the $500 million cash payment and $200 million of common stock, paid as follows: $300 million January 1, 2006; $100 million January 1 of 2007, 2008, 2009, and 2010. (For this question, assume there is no difference in value between the cash and common stock.)

   a. Assume Sirius Radio's cost of capital was 15%. Should Sirius Radio have entered into the contract with Mr. Stern? What assumptions did you make? Explain your assumptions about revenue per subscriber per month

(Exhibit 1). Explain subscriber acquisition costs (Exhibits 3 and 7), and explain why you did or did not include them in your evaluation.

   b. Should Sirius XM Radio re-sign Mr. Stern when his contract expires on December 31, 2010? If so, how much should it offer to pay him? Explain.

3. Would you have offered Sirius XM Radio the same financing terms on February 17, 2009, as those Liberty Media offered? Explain.

4. What do the Liberty Media investment terms imply for Sirius XM Radio's value? Explain.

	Sirius Radio			XM Radio	
Period ended	Subscribers	Quarterly growth	Average monthly fee	Subscribers	Quarterly growth
December 31, 2001				30,000	
March 31, 2002	412			76,242	154.1%
June 30, 2002	3,347	712.4%		136,718	79.3%
September 30, 2002	11,821	253.2%		201,554	47.4%
December 31, 2002	29,947	153.3%		347,159	72.2%
March 31, 2003	68,059	127.3%		483,075	39.2%
June 30, 2003	105,186	54.6%		692,253	43.3%
September 30, 2003	149,612	42.2%		929,648	34.3%
December 31, 2003	261,061	74.5%		1,300,000	39.8%
March 31, 2004	351,663	34.7%	$11.87	1,680,000	29.2%
June 30, 2004	480,341	36.6%	$11.17	2,100,000	25.0%
September 30, 2004	662,289	37.9%	$11.08	2,500,000	19.0%
December 31, 2004	1,143,258	72.6%		3,250,000	30.0%
March 31, 2005	1,448,695	26.7%		3,700,000	13.8%
June 30, 2005	1,814,626	25.3%		4,400,000	18.9%
September 30, 2005	2,173,920	19.8%		5,000,000	13.6%
December 31, 2005	3,316,560	52.6%		5,950,000	19.0%
March 31, 2006	4,077,747	23.0%		6,500,000	9.2%
June 30, 2006	4,678,207	14.7%		7,000,000	7.7%
September 30, 2006	5,119,308	9.4%		7,200,000	2.9%
December 31, 2006	6,024,555	17.7%		8,000,000	11.1%
March 31, 2007	6,581,045	9.2%		7,900,000	−1.3%
June 30, 2007	7,142,538	8.5%			
September 30, 2007	7,667,476	7.3%			
December 31, 2007	8,321,785	8.5%			
March 31, 2008	8,644,319	3.9%			
June 30, 2008	8,924,139	3.2%			
	Sirius XM				
September 30, 2008	18,920,911				
December 31, 2008	19,003,856				
March 31, 2009	18,599,434				

*10-Q reports: Sirius Radio; XM Radio and; Sirius XM Radio.

EXHIBIT 1

SIRIUS RADIO AND XM RADIO SUBSCRIBERS*

EXHIBIT 2

NOTE 4,
ACQUISITION

On July 28, 2008, Vernon Merger Corporation, a wholly owned subsidiary of SIRIUS, merged with and into XM Satellite Radio Holdings Inc. As a result, XM Holdings became our wholly-owned subsidiary.

The results of operations for XM Holdings have been included in our consolidated results of operations beginning August 1, 2008. The effective date of the Merger was July 28, 2008; however, due to the immateriality of the results of operations for the period July 28, 2008 through July 31, 2008, we have accounted for the Merger as if it had occurred on July 31, 2008, with the results and balances of XM Holdings included as of July 31, 2008. The Merger has been accounted for under the purchase method of accounting pursuant to the provisions of SFAS No. 141, *Business Combinations*. The application of purchase accounting under SFAS No. 141 resulted in the transaction being valued at $5,836,363, based upon the average closing price of $3.79 of our common stock on The NASDAQ Global Select Market for the two days prior to, including, and the two days subsequent to the public announcement of the Merger on February 19, 2007.

On that basis, the table below shows the value of the consideration paid in connection with the Merger:

	Total
Fair value of common stock issued to XM Holdings stockholders	$5,460,853
Fair value of preferred stock issued to XM Holdings stockholders	47,095
Fair value of converted stock options	94,616
Fair value of restricted stock issued to XM Holdings stockholders	66,628
Fair value of converted warrants	115,784
Acquisition costs	51,387
Total	$5,836,363

SFAS No. 141 requires that the total purchase price be allocated to the fair value of assets acquired and liabilities assumed based on their fair values at the acquisition date, with any excess recorded as goodwill. We have allocated the purchase price based on the fair values of assets acquired and liabilities assumed in connection with the Merger.

The table below summarizes the fair value of the XM Holdings assets acquired, liabilities assumed and related deferred income taxes as of the acquisition date.

	July 31, 2008
Acquired assets:	
Current assets	$1,078,148
Property and equipment	912,638
Non-amortizable intangible assets	2,250,000
Amortizable intangible assets	474,460
Goodwill	6,601,046
Other assets	326,948
Total assets	$11,643,240
Assumed liabilities:	
Current liabilities	789,001
Total debt	2,576,512
Deferred income taxes	847,616
Other non-current liabilities and deferred credit on executory contracts	1,593,748
Total liabilities	$5,806,877
Total consideration	$5,836,363

(continued)

EXHIBIT 2—
continued

Note 4,
Acquisition

During the third quarter of 2008, we recorded a preliminary estimate of goodwill in the amount of $6,626,504, which was adjusted to $6,601,046 during the fourth quarter of 2008 upon finalization of the fair value of acquired assets and assumed liabilities in the Merger. During the three months ended December 31, 2008, we recognized an incremental $15,331 of impairment of goodwill as an adjustment to the $4,750,859 goodwill impairment loss recognized in the third quarter of 2008, which was based on our preliminary purchase price allocations (see Note 5, Goodwill).

In connection with the Merger, $2,250,000 of the purchase price was allocated to certain indefinite lived intangible assets of XM Holdings, including $2,000,000 associated with XM Holdings' FCC license and $250,000 associated with trademarks. During the year ended December 31, 2008, no impairment loss was recorded for intangible assets with indefinite lives.

In connection with the Merger, $474,460 of the purchase price was allocated to certain finite-lived intangible assets of XM Holdings which are subject to straight-line amortization, except for the subscriber relationships which are amortized on an accelerated basis. Acquired finite-lived intangible assets included $33,000 associated with a licensing agreement with a manufacturer, $42,000 associated with a licensing agreement with XM Canada, $380,000 associated with subscriber relationships, $16,552 associated with proprietary software, $2,000 associated with developed technology and $908 associated with leasehold interests. During the year ended December 31, 2008, we recorded amortization expense of $35,789.

In connection with the Merger, we identified $74,473 of costs associated with reductions in staffing levels and consolidations, which was comprised of $66,515 in severance and related benefits and $7,958 in lease and other contract termination costs. During 2008, we paid $38,676 in severance and related benefits and the remaining severance and related benefits are expected to be paid by the end of 2009. These costs were recognized in accordance with the EITF No. 95-3, *Recognition of Liabilities in Connection with a Purchase Business Combination*, as assumed liabilities in the business combination. As of December 31, 2008, the balance of this liability was $35,797.

EXHIBIT 3

SIRIUS XM
RADIO, INCOME
STATEMENTS

	For the Years Ended December 31		
	2008	**2007**	**2006**
	(in thousands, except per share data)		
Revenue:			
Subscriber revenue, including effects of rebates	$1,543,951	$854,933	$575,404
Advertising revenue, net of agency fees	47,190	34,192	31,044
Equipment revenue	56,001	29,281	26,798
Other revenue	16,850	3,660	3,989
Total revenue	1,663,992	922,066	637,235
Operating expenses (depreciation and amortization shown separately below) (1)			
Cost of services:			
Satellite and transmission	59,279	27,907	41,797
Programming and content	312,189	236,059	520,424
Revenue share and royalties	280,852	146,715	69,918
Customer service and billing	165,036	93,817	76,462
Cost of equipment	46,091	35,817	35,233
Sales and marketing	231,937	183,213	203,682
Subscriber acquisition costs	371,343	407,642	451,614
General and administrative	213,142	155,863	129,953
Engineering, design and development	40,496	41,343	70,127
Impairment of goodwill	4,766,190	—	—
Depreciation and amortization	203,752	106,780	105,749
Restructuring and related costs	10,434	—	—
Total operating expenses	6,700,741	1,435,156	1,704,959
Loss from operations	(5,036,749)	(513,090)	(1,067,724)
Other income (expense)			
Interest and investment income	9,079	20,570	33,320
Interest expense, net of amounts capitalized	(144,833)	(70,328)	(64,032)
Loss from redemption of debt	(98,203)	—	—
Loss on investments	(30,507)	—	(4,445)
Other (expense) income	(9,599)	31	79
Total other expense	(274,063)	(49,727)	(35,078)
Loss before income taxes	(5,310,812)	(562,817)	(1,102,802)
Income tax expense	(2,476)	(2,435)	(2,065)
Net loss	$(5,313,288)	$(565,252)	$(1,104,867)
Net loss per common share (basic and diluted)	$(2.45)	$(0.39)	$(0.79)
Weighted average common shares outstanding (basic and diluted)	2,169,489	1,462,967	1,402,619

| | As of December 31 | |
	2008	2007
	(in thousands, except share and per share data)	
ASSETS		
Current assets:		
Cash and cash equivalents	$380,446	$438,820
Accounts receivable, net of allowance for doubtful accounts of $10,860 and $4,608, respectively	102,024	44,068
Receivables from distributors	45,950	60,004
Inventory, net	24,462	29,537
Prepaid expenses	67,203	31,392
Related party current assets	114,177	2,161
Restricted investments	—	35,000
Other current assets	58,744	37,875
Total current assets	793,006	678,857
Property and equipment, net	1,703,476	806,263
FCC licenses	2,083,654	83,654
Restricted investments, net of current portion	141,250	18,000
Deferred financing fees, net	40,156	13,864
Intangible assets, net	688,671	—
Goodwill	1,834,856	—
Related party long-term assets, net of current portion	124,607	3,237
Other long-term assets	81,019	90,274
Total assets	$7,490,695	$1,694,149

(*continued*)

EXHIBIT 4

SIRIUS XM RADIO, 2008 Q3 BALANCE SHEETS

EXHIBIT 4—
continued

SIRIUS XM RADIO,
2008 Q3 BALANCE
SHEETS

LIABILITIES AND STOCKHOLDERS' EQUITY (DEFICIT)

Current liabilities:		
Accounts payable and accrued expenses	$877,594	$464,943
Accrued interest	76,463	24,772
Deferred revenue	985,180	548,330
Current maturities of long-term debt	399,726	35,801
Related party current liabilities	68,373	1,148
Total current liabilities	2,407,336	1,074,994
Long-term debt, net of current portion	2,851,740	1,278,617
Deferred revenue, net of current portion	247,889	110,525
Deferred credit on executory contracts	1,037,190	—
Deferred tax liability	894,453	12,771
Other long-term liabilities	43,550	9,979
Total liabilities	7,482,158	2,486,886
Commitments and contingencies (Note 16)	—	—
Stockholders' equity (deficit):		
Series A convertible preferred stock, par value $0.001 (liquidation preference of $51,370 at December 31, 2008); 50,000,000 authorized at December 31, 2008, 24,808,959 shares issued and outstanding at December 31, 2008	25	—
Common stock, par value $0.001; 8,000,000,000 and 2,500,000,000 shares authorized at December 31, 2008 and 2007, respectively; 3,651,765,837 and 1,471,143,570 shares issued and outstanding at December 31, 2008 and 2007, respectively	3,652	1,471
Accumulated other comprehensive loss, net of tax	(7,871)	—
Additional paid-in capital	9,724,991	3,604,764
Accumulated deficit	(9,712,260)	(4,398,972)
Total stockholders' equity (deficit)	8,537	(792,737)
Total liabilities and stockholders' equity (deficit)	$7,490,695	$1,694,149

See accompanying notes to the consolidated financial statements.

EXHIBIT 5

SIRIUS XM RADIO,
STATEMENTS OF
CASH FLOWS

	For the Years Ended December 31		
	2008	2007	2006
	(in thousands)		
Cash flows from operating activities:			
Net loss	$ (5,313,288)	$ (565,252)	$ (1,104,867)
Adjustments to reconcile net loss to net cash used in operating activities:			
Depreciation and amortization	203,752	106,780	105,749
Impairment of goodwill	4,766,190	—	—
Non-cash interest expense, net of amortization of premium	(6,311)	4,269	3,107
Provision for doubtful accounts	21,589	9,002	9,370
Non-cash loss from redemption of debt	98,203	—	—
Amortization of deferred income related to equity method investment	(1,156)	—	—
Loss on disposal of assets	4,879	(428)	1,661
Impairment loss	—	—	10,917
Loss on investments, net	28,999	—	4,445
Share-based payment expense	87,405	78,900	437,918
Deferred income taxes	2,476	2,435	2,065
Other non-cash purchase price adjustments	(68,330)	—	—
Other	1,643	—	—
Changes in operating assets and liabilities, net of assets and liabilities acquired:			
Accounts receivable	(32,121)	(28,881)	(1,871)
Inventory	8,291	4,965	(20,246)
Receivables from distributors	14,401	(13,179)	(20,312)
Related party assets	(22,249)	(1,241)	(1,189)
Prepaid expenses and other current assets	(19,953)	11,118	(42,132)
Other long-term assets	(5,490)	13,691	(18,377)
Accounts payable and accrued expenses	(65,481)	66,169	26,366
Accrued interest	23,081	(8,920)	1,239
Deferred revenue	55,778	169,905	181,003
Related party liabilities	34,646	—	—
Other long-term liabilities	30,249	1,901	3,452
Net cash used in operating activities	(152,797)	(148,766)	(421,702)

(continued)

EXHIBIT 5 —
continued

SIRIUS XM RADIO,
STATEMENTS OF
CASH FLOWS

Cash flows from investing activities:			
Additions to property and equipment	(130,551)	(65,264)	(92,674)
Sales of property and equipment	105	641	127
Purchases of restricted and other investments	(3,000)	(310)	(12,339)
Acquisition of acquired entity cash	819,521	—	—
Merger related costs	(23,519)	(29,444)	—
Purchase of available-for-sale securities	—	—	(123,500)
Sale of restricted and other investments	65,869	40,191	255,715
Net cash provided by (used in) investing activities	728,425	(54,186)	27,329
Cash flows from financing activities:			
Proceeds from exercise of warrants and stock options and from share borrow arrangement	471	4,097	25,787
Long-term borrowings, net of related costs	531,743	244,879	—
Payment of premiums on redemption of debt	(18,693)	—	—
Payments to minority interest holder	(1,479)	—	—
Repayment of long term borrowings	(1,146,044)	(625)	—
Net cash (used in) provided by financing activities	(634,002)	248,351	25,787
Net (decrease) increase in cash and cash equivalents	(58,374)	45,399	(368,586)
Cash and cash equivalents at beginning of period	438,820	393,421	762,007
Cash and cash equivalents at end of period	$380,446	$438,820	$393,421

EXHIBIT 6

NOTE 5, GOODWILL

During the third quarter of 2008, we recorded a preliminary estimate of goodwill in the amount of $6,626,504 in connection with the Merger. Pursuant to the provisions of SFAS No. 141, we have allocated the consideration paid to the fair value of acquired assets and assumed liabilities. These allocations were preliminary at September 30, 2008 and were finalized by December 31, 2008.

SFAS No. 142 requires that we assess goodwill for impairment at least annually or more frequently if indicators of impairment exist. The price of our common stock declined significantly from February 19, 2007, the measurement date for valuation of the Merger through December 31, 2008, indicating a potential impairment. Under SFAS No. 142, the fair value of the entity (based upon market capitalization) is compared to its carrying value, and if the fair value exceeds its carrying value, then goodwill is not impaired. If the carrying value exceeds the fair value then we will compare the implied fair value of goodwill to the carrying value of goodwill. If the implied fair value exceeds the carrying value then goodwill is not impaired; otherwise, an impairment loss will be recorded by the amount the carrying value exceeds the implied fair value. Our impairment analysis indicated that the carrying value of goodwill exceeded the implied fair value of goodwill, resulting in an estimated impairment charge of $4,750,859 in the third quarter of 2008 and an incremental goodwill impairment charge of $15,331 in the fourth quarter of 2008 when the finalization of the purchase price allocations were completed.

The changes in the carrying value of goodwill for the year ended December 31, 2008 were as follows:

Balance at December 31, 2007	$—
Acquisition	6,601,046
Impairment Loss	(4,766,190)
Balance at December 31, 2008	$1,834,856

EXHIBIT 7

NOTE 3, SIGNIFICANT ACCOUNTING POLICIES

Revenue Recognition

We derive revenue primarily from subscribers, advertising and direct sales of merchandise. Revenue from subscribers consists of subscription fees; revenue derived from our agreements with Hertz and Avis; non-refundable activation fees; and the effects of rebates. Revenue is recognized as it is realized or realizable and earned.

We recognize subscription fees as our services are provided. Prepaid subscription fees are recorded as deferred revenue and amortized to revenue ratably over the term of the applicable subscription plan.

At the time of sale, vehicle owners purchasing or leasing a vehicle with a subscription to our service typically receive between a three-month and twelve-month prepaid subscription. Prepaid subscription fees received from certain automakers are recorded as deferred revenue and amortized to revenue ratably over the service period, upon activation and sale to a customer. We reimburse automakers for certain costs associated with the satellite radio installed in the applicable vehicle at the time the vehicle is manufactured. The associated payments to the automakers are included in Subscriber acquisition costs. In the opinion of management, this is the appropriate characterization of our relationship since we are responsible for providing the service to the customers, including being obligated to the customers in the case of an interruption of service.

(continued)

EXHIBIT 7—
continued

NOTE 3,
SIGNIFICANT
ACCOUNTING
POLICIES

Activation fees are recognized ratably over the estimated term of a subscriber relationship, currently estimated to be approximately 3.5 years. The estimated term of a subscriber relationship is based on actual historical experience.

As required by Emerging Issues Task Force ("EITF") No. 01-09, *Accounting for Consideration Given by a Vendor to a Customer (Including a Reseller of the Vendor's Products)*, an estimate of rebates that are paid by us to subscribers is recorded as a reduction to revenue in the period the subscriber activates service. For certain rebate promotions, a subscriber must remain active for a specified period of time to be considered eligible. In those instances, the estimate is recorded as a reduction to revenue over the required activation period. We estimate the effects of mail-in rebates based on actual take-rates for rebate incentives offered in prior periods, adjusted as deemed necessary based on take-rate data available at the time. In subsequent periods, estimates are adjusted when necessary. For instant rebate promotions, we record the consideration paid to the consumer as a reduction to revenue in the period the customer participates in the promotion.

We recognize revenue from the sale of advertising as the advertising is broadcast. Agency fees are calculated based on a stated percentage applied to gross billing revenue for our advertising inventory and are reported as a reduction of Advertising revenue. We pay certain third parties a percentage of Advertising revenue. Advertising revenue is recorded gross of such revenue share payments in accordance with EITF No. 99-19, *Reporting Revenue Gross as a Principal versus Net as an Agent,* as we are the primary obligor in the transaction. Advertising revenue share payments are recorded to Revenue share and royalties during the period in which the advertising is broadcast.

Equipment revenue and royalties from the sale of satellite radios, components and accessories is recognized upon shipment, net of discounts and rebates. Shipping and handling costs billed to customers are recorded as revenue. Shipping and handling costs associated with shipping goods to customers are reported as a component of Cost of equipment.

EITF No. 00-21, *Accounting for Revenue Arrangements with Multiple Deliverables,* provides guidance on how and when to recognize revenues for arrangements that may involve the delivery or performance of multiple products, services and/or rights to use assets. Revenue arrangements with multiple deliverables are required to be divided into separate units of accounting if the deliverables in the arrangement meet certain criteria. Arrangement consideration must be allocated among the separate units of accounting based on their relative fair values.

Subscriber Acquisition Costs

Subscriber acquisition costs include hardware subsidies paid to radio manufacturers, distributors and automakers, including subsidies paid to automakers who include a satellite radio and a prepaid subscription to our service in the sale or lease price of a new vehicle; subsidies paid for chip sets and certain other components used in manufacturing radios; device royalties for certain radios; commissions paid to retailers and automakers as incentives to purchase, install and activate radios; product warranty obligations; provisions for inventory allowance; and compensation costs associated with stock-based awards granted in connection with certain distribution agreements. Subscriber acquisition costs do not include advertising, loyalty payments to distributors and dealers of radios and revenue share payments to automakers and retailers of radios.

Subsidies paid to radio manufacturers and automakers are expensed upon installation, shipment, receipt of product or activation. Commissions paid to retailers and automakers are expensed upon either the sale or activation of radios. Chip sets that are shipped to radio manufacturers and held on consignment are recorded as inventory and expensed as Subscriber acquisition costs when placed into production by radio manufacturers. Costs for chip sets not held on consignment are expensed as Subscriber acquisition costs when the chip sets are installed, shipped, received, or activated by a subscriber.

EXHIBIT 8

NOTE 12, DEBT

(Dollar amounts in thousands, unless otherwise stated)

Our debt consists of the following:

	Conversion Price (per share)	Long-Term Debt December 31	
		2008	2007
SIRIUS Debt			
Senior Secured Term Loan due 2012	N/A	$246,875	$249,375
9 ⅝% Senior Notes due 2013	N/A	500,000	500,000
3 ¼% Convertible Notes due 2011	$5.30	230,000	230,000
2 ½% Convertible Notes due 2009	4.41	189,586	299,998
3 ½% Convertible Notes due 2008	1.38	—	33,301
8 ¾% Convertible Subordinated Notes due 2009	28.46	1,744	1,744
XM and XM Holdings Debt			
Senior Secured Term Loan due 2009	N/A	100,000	N/A
7% Exchangeable Senior Subordinated Notes due 2014	1.88	550,000	N/A
9.75% Senior Notes due 2014	N/A	5,260	N/A
13% Senior Notes due 2013	N/A	778,500	N/A
Less: discount	N/A	(74,986)	N/A
10% Convertible Senior Notes due 2009	10.87	400,000	N/A
Less: discount		(16,449)	
10% Senior Secured Discount Convertible Notes due 2009	0.69	33,249	N/A
Add: premium		34,321	N/A
Senior Secured Revolving Credit Facility due 2009	N/A	250,000	N/A
Add: premium		151	
Other debt:			
Capital leases	N/A	23,215	N/A
Total debt		3,251,466	1,314,418
Less: current maturities		399,726	35,801
Total Long Term		$2,851,740	$1,278,617

Subsequent to December 31, 2008, we have entered into agreements that have had a significant impact on our debt and capital structure as more fully described in Note 19.

SIRIUS Debt (partial)

Senior Secured Term Loan

In June 2007, SIRIUS entered into a term credit agreement with a syndicate of financial institutions. The term credit agreement provides for a Senior Secured Term Loan (the "SIRIUS Term Loan") of $250,000, which has been fully drawn. Interest under the SIRIUS Term Loan is based, at our option, on (i) adjusted LIBOR plus 2.25% or (ii) the higher of (a) the prime rate and (b) the Federal Funds Effective Rate plus 1/2 of 1.00%, plus 1.25%. As of December 31, 2008, the interest rate was 5.44%. LIBOR borrowings may be made for interest periods, at our option, of one, two, three or six months (or, if agreed by all of the lenders, nine or twelve months). The SIRIUS Term Loan amortizes in equal quarterly installments of 0.25% of the initial aggregate principal amount for the first four and a half years, with the balance of the loan thereafter being repaid in four equal quarterly installments. The SIRIUS Term Loan matures on December 20, 2012.

(continued)

EXHIBIT 8—
continued

Note 12, Debt

The SIRIUS Term Loan is guaranteed by our wholly owned subsidiaries, including Satellite CD Radio, Inc. (the "Guarantor"), and is secured by a lien on substantially all of SIRIUS' and the Guarantor's assets, including SIRIUS' three in-orbit satellites and one ground spare satellite and the shares of the Guarantors.

The SIRIUS Term Loan contains customary affirmative covenants and event of default provisions. The negative covenants contained in the SIRIUS Term Loan are substantially similar to those contained in the indenture governing the 9 ⅝% Senior Notes due 2013.

2 ½% Convertible Notes due 2009

In February 2004, SIRIUS issued $250,000 in aggregate principal amount of 2½% Convertible Notes due 2009 (the "2½% Notes") resulting in net proceeds, after debt issuance costs, of $244,625. In March 2004, SIRIUS issued an additional $50,000 in aggregate principal amount of the 2½% Notes pursuant to an option granted in connection with the initial offering of the notes, resulting in net proceeds of $48,975. As of December 31, 2008, $110,414 principal balance of the 2½% Notes were converted into shares of our common stock. During 2009, but prior to the maturity date, an additional $18,000 principal balance of the 2½% Notes were converted into shares of our common stock (see Note 19, Subsequent Events). The remaining principal balance of $171,586 of the 2½% Notes matured on February 15, 2009, and were paid in cash at maturity.

XM and XM Holdings Debt (partial)

On the date of the Merger, XM and XM Holdings had debt in the aggregate amount of $2,600,000. Following the Merger, XM repurchased notes with aggregate principal amounts outstanding of $795,000 in accordance with "change of control put" terms of such indebtedness. In addition, XM satisfied its $309,400 transponder repurchase obligation associated with one of its satellites in accordance with the terms of a sale-leaseback transaction. In order to effect these repurchases, XM issued approximately $1,328,500 in aggregate principal amount of new debt securities.

10% Convertible Senior Notes due 2009

XM Holdings has issued $400,000 aggregate principal amount of 10% Convertible Senior Notes due 2009 (the "10% Convertible Notes"). Interest is payable semi-annually at a rate of 10% per annum. The 10% Convertible Notes mature on December 1, 2009. The 10% Convertible Notes may be converted by the holder, at its option, into shares of our common stock at a conversion rate of 92.0 shares of our common stock per $1,000 principal amount, which is equivalent to a conversion price of $10.87 per share of common stock (subject to adjustment in certain events). As a result of the fair valuation at acquisition date, we recognized an initial discount of $23,700.

10% Senior Secured Discount Convertible Notes due 2009

XM Holdings and XM, as co-obligors, have outstanding $33,249 aggregate principal amount of 10% Senior Secured Discount Convertible Notes due 2009 (the "10% Discount Convertible Notes"). Interest is payable semi-annually at a rate of 10% per annum. The 10% Discount Convertible Notes mature on December 31, 2009. At any time, a holder of the notes may convert all or part of the accreted value of the notes at a conversion price of $0.69 per share. The 10% Discount Convertible Notes rank equally in right of payment with all of XM Holdings' and XM's other existing and future senior indebtedness, and are senior in right of payment to all of XM Holdings' and XM's existing and future subordinated indebtedness. As a result of the fair valuation at the acquisition date, we recognized an initial premium of $57,550.

Senior Secured Revolving Credit Facility

XM is party to a $250,000 Senior Secured Revolving Credit Facility (the "XM Revolving Credit Facility"), which has been fully drawn. The XM Revolving Credit Facility matures on May 5, 2009.

(continued)

EXHIBIT 8—
continued
NOTE 12, DEBT

Borrowings under the XM Revolving Credit Facility bear interest at a rate of LIBOR plus 150 to 225 basis points or an alternate base rate, to be the higher of the JPMorgan Chase prime rate and the Federal Funds rate plus 50 basis points, in each case plus 50 to 125 basis points. For $187,500 of the drawn amount, the interest rate at December 31, 2008 was 3.1875%; and for $62,500 of the drawn amount, the interest rate at December 31, 2008 was 3.9375%. The XM Revolving Credit Facility is secured by substantially all the assets of XM, other than certain specified property.

Covenants and restrictions

The 9⅝% Notes, Loral Credit Agreement, SIRIUS Term Loan, XM Term Loan, 13% Notes and XM Revolving Credit Facility require compliance with certain covenants that restrict our ability to, among other things, (i) incur additional indebtedness, (ii) incur liens, (iii) pay dividends or make certain other restricted payments, investments or acquisitions, (iv) enter into certain transactions with affiliates, (v) merge or consolidate with another person, (vi) sell, assign, lease or otherwise dispose of all or substantially all of our assets, and (vii) make voluntary prepayments of certain debt, in each case subject to exceptions as provided in the applicable indenture or credit agreement. SIRIUS operates XM Holdings as an unrestricted subsidiary for purposes of compliance with the covenants contained in its debt instruments. The XM Term Loan and the XM Revolving Credit Facility also require XM to maintain a level of cash and cash equivalents of at least $75,000. If we fail to comply with these covenants, the 9⅝% Notes, SIRIUS Term Loan, XM Term Loan, 13% Notes, the Revolving Credit Facility and any loans outstanding under the Loral Credit Agreement, the SIRIUS Term Loan and the XM Term Loan could become immediately payable and the Loral Credit Agreement could be terminated.

At December 31, 2008, we were in compliance with all such covenants.

EXHIBIT 9
NOTE 9,
RELATED PARTY
TRANSACTIONS

Liberty Media Corporation and its affiliate, Liberty Media, LLC (collectively, "Liberty Media"), have invested in us an aggregate of $350,000 in the form of loans, and are committed to invest an additional $180,000 in loans as of March 31, 2009. Liberty Media is the holder of our Convertible Perpetual Preferred Stock, Series B (the "Series B Preferred Stock"), has representatives on our board of directors and is considered a related party. See Note 11, Debt, to our unaudited consolidated financial statements for further information regarding indebtedness owed to Liberty Media.

Investment Agreement

On February 17, 2009, we entered into an Investment Agreement (the "Investment Agreement") with Liberty Media. Pursuant to the Investment Agreement, we agreed to issue to Liberty Radio, LLC 12,500,000 shares of Series B Preferred Stock with a liquidation preference of $0.001 per share in partial consideration for certain loan investments. The Series B Preferred Stock was issued on March 6, 2009.

The Series B Preferred Stock is convertible into 40% of our outstanding shares of common stock (after giving effect to such conversion). Liberty Radio, LLC has agreed not to acquire more than 49.9% of our outstanding common stock for three years from the date the Series B Preferred Stock was issued, except that Liberty Radio, LLC may acquire more than 49.9% of our outstanding common stock at any time after the second anniversary of such date pursuant to any cash tender offer for all of the outstanding shares of our common stock that are not beneficially owned by Liberty Radio, LLC or its affiliates at a price per share greater than the closing price of the common stock on the trading day preceding the earlier of the

(continued)

EXHIBIT 9—
continued

NOTE 9,
RELATED PARTY
TRANSACTIONS

public announcement or commencement of such tender offer. The Investment Agreement also provides for certain other standstill provisions during such three year period.

The holder of our Series B Preferred Stock is entitled to appoint a number of our board of directors proportionate to its ownership levels from time to time.

Loan investments
On February 17, 2009, SIRIUS entered into a Credit Agreement (the "LM Credit Agreement") with Liberty Media Corporation, as administrative agent and collateral agent, and Liberty Media, LLC, as lender. The LM Credit Agreement provides for a $250,000 term loan and $30,000 of purchase money loans.

On February 17, 2009, XM entered into a Credit Agreement with Liberty Media Corporation, as administrative agent and collateral agent, and Liberty Media, LLC, as lender. On March 6, 2009, XM amended and restated that credit agreement (the "Second-Lien Credit Agreement") with Liberty Media Corporation. Pursuant to the Second-Lien Credit Agreement, XM may borrow $150,000 of term loans on December 1, 2009. The proceeds of these loans will be used to repay a portion of the 10% Convertible Notes due 2009 of our wholly owned subsidiary, XM Holdings, on the stated maturity date thereof. The Second-Lien Credit Agreement matures on March 1, 2011, and bears interest at 15% per annum. XM pays a commitment fee of 2% per annum on the undrawn portion of the Second-Lien Credit Agreement until the date of disbursement of the loans or the termination of the commitments.

On March 6, 2009, XM amended and restated (i) the $100,000 Credit Agreement, dated as of June 26, 2008, among XM, XM Holdings, the lenders named therein and UBS AG, as administrative agent (the "UBS Term Loan"), and (ii) the $250,000 Credit Agreement, dated as of May 5, 2006, among XM, XM Holdings, the lenders named therein and JPMorgan Chase Bank, N.A., as administrative agent (the "JPM Revolver" and, together with the UBS Term Loan, the "Previous Facilities"). The Previous Facilities were combined as term loans into the Amended and Restated Credit Agreement, dated as of March 6, 2009, among XM, XM Holdings, the lenders named therein and JPMorgan Chase Bank, N.A., as administrative agent (the "First-Lien Credit Agreement"), and Liberty Media, LLC, purchased $100,000 aggregate principal amount of such loans from the existing lenders. XM paid a restructuring fee of 2% to the existing lenders under the Previous Facilities.

We accounted for the Series B Preferred Stock by recording a $227,716 increase to additional paid-in capital, excluding issuance costs, for the amount of allocated proceeds received and an additional $186,188 increase in paid-in capital for the beneficial conversion feature, which was immediately recognized as a charge to retained earnings.

We recognized Interest expense related to Liberty Media of $11,483 for the three months ended March 31, 2009.

Dell Inc. and Financial Restatements

With $1,000 of start-up capital, Michael Dell founded Dell Inc. in his University of Texas dorm room in 1984, three years after International Business Machines launched its first personal computer (PC), which used Microsoft's Disk Operating System (DOS). In 1985, Dell shipped its first PC. Thousands of entrepreneurs began selling personal computers and dozens of them advertised heavily through *PC Magazine* and other computer magazines, but Dell was by far the most successful. It offered risk-free returns, next-day at-home assistance, leading edge technology, and low prices.

In 1988, Dell raised $30 million in its initial public offering (IPO), paving the way for a market value of $85 million. The firm grew rapidly as PCs gained widespread use. By 1989, Dell revenues were $388 million, and net income was $5 million. By 1992, revenues were $2 billion, and net income increased to $101 million. Other firms have grown more rapidly, but they have all been software or Internet firms, which require far less infrastructure. Most manufacturing firms need decades to reach $2 billion in revenues. As they grow, they gradually develop and install control systems for engineering, product development, inventory, manufacturing, quality assurance, sales, customer service, accounting, and finance. They also hire and develop a management team that grows with the firm, so senior executives are highly knowledgeable about their function and have long histories of dealing with executives in other regions and functional areas.

Dell grew far too fast to gradually develop its infrastructure and management team. As a result, throughout the firm's existence, investors worried that Dell might have undetected problems with both operations and accounting records. One such problem arose in 1993. Although revenues increased to $2.9 billion, the 45% growth was less than anticipated. Dell also experienced problems in its notebook business and reported a $40 million loss in 1993. That led to a lawsuit in which plaintiffs accused the company of failing to disclose adverse information and accused Michael Dell of selling securities in Dell Inc. while in the possession of material, nonpublic information.[1]

> *The Company and its Chairman, Michael S. Dell, are defendants in nineteen lawsuits filed between May and November 1993, in the United States District Court for the Western District of Texas, Austin Division. Thomas J. Meredith, the Company's Chief Financial Officer, is also a defendant in seven of the lawsuits. Joel Kocher, Senior Vice President of the Company, is also a defendant in one of the lawsuits, but the plaintiffs have conditionally agreed to dismiss him. The suits have been consolidated, an amended and consolidated complaint has been filed, and the plaintiffs have requested class certification for a class of persons who purchased or held the Company's common stock between February 24, 1993, and July 14, 1993. In general, the plaintiffs allege that the Company made overly optimistic forecasts about the Company's prospects without a reasonable basis and failed to disclose adverse material information about the Company's business (particularly with regard to problems in its notebook*

---

1. Dell 2003 10-K report, Item 3. Legal Proceedings, p. 9. http://www.sec.gov/Archives/edgar/data/826083/0000950134-94-000347.txt

business) on a timely basis, thereby inducing the plaintiffs to buy Company common stock at artificially high prices. The plaintiffs also allege that Mr. Dell sold securities of the Company while in the possession of material, non-public information about the Company. The consolidated complaint asserts that these actions or omissions violated various provisions of the federal securities laws, particularly Section 10(b) of the Exchange Act and Rule 10b-5; that Mr. Dell's trades violated Section 20A of the Exchange Act; and that the defendants violated provisions of Texas statutes and common law principles against negligent misrepresentation and deceit.[2]

In 1993, Michael Dell was only 28. Although he had hired older, more experienced managers, many thought the executive team was too weak for such a large, rapidly growing firm. In response, in 1996 Mr. Dell hired Kevin B. Rollins, a highly successful director and partner at Bain & Company, one of the world's leading strategic consulting firms. Mr. Rollins began as senior vice president, corporate strategy; one month later he was named vice president, general manager—Americas. The following year he was promoted to vice chairman.[3]

In March 2001, Mr. Rollins was named president and chief operating officer, and in July 2004, he replaced Mr. Dell as chief executive officer. At that time, *Forbes* estimated Mr. Dell's net worth at $14.2 billion. Only eight Americans, Warren Buffet, Microsoft cofounders Bill Gates and Paul Allen, and five Sam Walton heirs, had a higher net worth. Although he remained Chairman of Dell's Board of Directors, Mr. Dell began to focus more on philanthropic work.[4]

Dell continued to grow, but by 2006, the company faced growing competition from Hewlett-Packard and Lenovo and was often criticized for weak customer support. In August 2006, Dell announced that the Securities and Exchange Commission (SEC) had launched an informal investigation of Dell's accounting policies one year earlier, possibly as a result of audit inspections conducted by the newly formed Public Company Accounting Oversight Board (PCAOB). A month later, in September 2006, Dell announced that a U.S. attorney in New York had subpoenaed scores of documents dating back to 2002, an indication that a criminal investigation was underway. Dell also announced it would delay issuing its second quarter financial results, cancelled a long-scheduled meeting with financial analysts, and announced it was conducting its own internal investigation.[5]

In November 2006, Dell announced the SEC informal investigation had been upgraded to a formal investigation. By January 2007, Mr. Rollins had resigned as CEO and Dell director, and Michael Dell returned to take his place. In March 2007, Dell reported that it had found evidence of misconduct, had found deficiencies in its financial controls, and would delay its annual report for the year 2006 until it completed its investigation. On October 30, 2007, Dell released its 2006 10-K eight months after its due date. The investigation eventually cost $205 million, according to Dell spokesperson David Frink.[6]

The three Exhibits to this case include selected information from Dell's 10-K for the year ended February 2, 2007, filed October 30, 2007: Exhibit 1, Item 7, Management

---

2. Dell 2003 10-K.

3. Dell 10-K reports, 1996–2006.

4. Hansell, Saul, "Rollins to succeed Dell as chief executive," *The New York Times*, March 5, 2004. http://www.nytimes.com/2004/03/05/technology/05dell.html?scp=5&sq=michael%20dell%202001&st=cse.

5. Darlin, Damon, Dell Accounting Inquiry Made formal by SEC, *The New York Times*," November 16, 2006. http://query.nytimes.com/gst/fullpage.html?res=9F0CE5D6173EF935A25752C1A9609C8B63&sec=&spon=&&scp=1&sq=dell%20is%20conducting%20its%20own%20investigation&st=cse.

6. Ackerman, Ruthie, "Dell climbs out of accounting hell," *Forbes*, Market Scan, October 30, 2007.

Discussion and Analysis; Exhibit 2, Note 2, Audit Committee Independent Investigation and Restatement; and Exhibit 3, Item 9A, Controls and Procedures.

Exhibit 1 summarizes Dell's investigation. Exhibit 2 describes the most significant problems Dell identified during its accounting and financial reporting investigation. Exhibit 2 also includes restated financial statements for 2004 through 2006, and a summary of revisions to Retained Earnings for 2003 through 2006. Exhibit 3 describes the internal control deficiencies that investigation uncovered and describes steps that Dell management is undertaking to correct the problems. The following sections explain in more detail seven accounting problems discussed in Exhibit 2.

Vendor-specific Objective Evidence

Firms often make what are called multiple-element sales. When a vendor sells for one price a bundle consisting of software plus software support, the issue arises as to how to split the revenue between the software sale, which is recognized immediately, and software support, which is recognized evenly over the support period. The same issue arises for a bundle of computer hardware and support for the hardware and for similar products, such as the sale of a complex manufacturing system and support for that system.

The revenue recognition guidance for the software industry (Section 980, previously SOP No. 97-2) establishes rules for allocating the portion of revenue to be recognized immediately as a software sale and the portion to be recognized evenly over the life of the support contract.[7] The entire sales price must be spread equally over the contract life unless the seller has its own specific evidence about the market price of each software product. That is, suppose that Dell sells software developed by a third party as a bundle of software and a three-year support contract for $15,000. Dell may note that other vendors sell the software for $6,000, so it might be reasonable to record $6,000 of revenue at the time of sale and then spread the remaining $9,000 over the three-year period at a rate of $3,000 annually. However, if Dell has not sold the software separately, it has no vendor-specific objective evidence (VSOE) about the value of the software. In that case, Dell must spread the entire $15,000 over the life of a support contract at a rate of $5,000 annually.

In contrast, products other than software are governed by the revenue recognition guidance in the codification (Section 605, previously FASB EITF 00-21), which is far less restrictive.[8] That guidance allows a seller to use evidence from other vendors about the market price of the item being sold, or even to use its own best judgment.

In many instances, such as with the Apple iPhone, revenue deferral under the previous revenue recognition guidance for the software industry seemed completely unreasonable. As a result, in October 2009 the FASB issued two Accounting Standards Updates (ASU) that substantially modify revenue recognition for multiple element sales. ASU 2009-13, *Revenue Recognition* (Topic 605), *Multiple-Deliverable Revenue Arrangements*, and ASU 2009-14, *Software* (Topic 985), *Certain Revenue Arrangements That Include Software Elements*, became effective June 15, 2010.

Reporting Revenue Gross as a Principal vs. Net as an Agent

During the Internet boom, many start-up companies sold products such as watches, industrial products, and chemicals through their Web sites. One issue accountants

---

7. Specifically, the reference is 980-605-25 (980 = Software, 605 = Revenue Recognition, 25 = Recognition).

8. Specifically, the reference is 605-25-25 (605 = Revenue Recognition, 25 = Multiple-Element Arrangements, 25 = Recognition).

had not spent much time considering was whether a reseller should report the net amount of the sale on its income statement (the difference between revenue and the resellers cost) or whether the reseller should report the gross sales amount and then deduct the cost paid to the supplier.

Start-ups often reported sales at net proceeds until just before going public. Shortly before their IPO, many start-ups shifted to reporting gross sales minus cost of sales. Suppose a start-up reports net sales of $1 million in 1998 and net sales double to $2 million in 1999. That is a significant increase but not a large enough dollar increase to generate much interest from potential IPO investors. Suppose the firm's gross profit margin is 10%. Gross revenues were $10 million in 1998 and $20 million in 1999; cost of sales were $9 million in 1998 and $18 million in 1999. Net revenues and gross margin would have been $1 million in 1998 and $2 million in 1999. By changing from net to gross revenue reporting, the firm could report that revenues increased from $1 million in 1998 to $20 million in 1999. Potential investors might infer that the firm might soon be the next eBay or Amazon.

In response, the FASB issued Principal Agent Considerations with Respect to Revenue Recognition (Topic 605, previously EITF No. 99-19).[9] The guidance requires that in order to recognize gross revenue less cost of sales, rather than just net revenue, the reseller must be more than a sales agent. Evidence that the reseller is not an agent would be that the reseller bears risk of nonpayment and takes possession of the goods, in contrast to simply filling orders for the vendor and having the vendor bear all risk of loss.

In response, many Internet resellers agreed to bear some risk of loss. They also took possession, but only legally. Suppose a reseller in California received an order for a product manufactured in Ohio to be shipped to Iowa. The arrangement between the vendor and the reseller might be a legal document stating that the California reseller takes legal possession on the Ohio vendor's loading dock, just before it is handed to a common carrier for shipment to the customer in Iowa. Although that is legal possession that fulfills the requirement of EITF 99-19, the reseller never sees the product.

Warehouse Arrangements

In a warehouse arrangement, a vendor agrees to warehouse goods for a customer until they are needed by that customer. In many cases, these arrangements are legitimate. Suppose a manufacturer's highly profitable product includes a crucial and difficult to manufacture machine part from a small vendor. The manufacturer may order 1,000 units from the vendor but ask the vendor to hold the part until needed. As soon as the vendor produces a batch of the parts, the vendor bills the manufacturer for payment within 30 days, even though the parts may not be shipped for another two months.

Because the vendor has fulfilled the following four requirements of SEC Staff Accounting Bulletin 104, the vendor recognizes revenue when goods are transferred to finished goods inventory:

- Persuasive evidence of an arrangement exists.
- Delivery has occurred or services have been rendered.
- The seller's price to the buyer is fixed or determinable.
- Collectability is reasonably assured.

---

9. Specifically, this is Section 605 (Revenue Recognition), Sub-topic 45 (Principal Agent Considerations).

Firms also use warehousing arrangements to record sales too early. For example, Sunbeam was acquired, and the new owners appointed a well-known executive to improve operations. When revenues declined that fall, Sunbeam sold barbeque grills to its customers in November and December. Customers bought barbeque grills at that time because Sunbeam offered them large discounts, no payment until the following summer, and a right to return the goods at no penalty. Sunbeam also kept the completed barbeque grills at its warehouse for shipping the following spring. In this instance, the warehousing arrangement was not for the benefit of Sunbeam customers, it was for the benefit of Sunbeam in an attempt to report revenues too early.

Deferred Warranty Revenue

Retailers and some manufacturers sell extended warranties on the products they sell. An electronics retailer may sell a television set for $1,000 that costs $950. Most electronics products include a one-year manufacturer's warranty; an extended warranty might cover repair costs for two years after the manufacturer's warranty expires. These extended warranties are often highly profitable. A two-year extended warranty on the $1,000 television might sell for $75. The expected repair cost to the retailer might only be $10, so the expected profit of $65 from the warranty is more than the $50 profit from the sale of the television.

The business model for many retailers was to heavily advertise and sell electronics equipment at a low profit margin. The expectation was that enough customers would purchase the highly profitable extended warranties to make the overall business profitable. Although the equipment and the extended warranty were separate sales, retailers could not remain in business without the accompanying extended warranty sales. As a result, most retailers would recognize the $75 warranty revenue at the time of sale and also record the expected $10 cost as a debit to "cost of sales" and a credit to a liability account, "deferred warranty costs." With that method, the retailer would record the entire $115 profit at the time of sale.

In 1990, the FASB issued *Recognition of Guarantees* (Topic 460, previously FASB Technical Bulletin 90-1).[10] That bulletin requires that the product and the extended warranty be treated as two separate sales and that the revenue for the extended warranty be recognized only during the warranty period (years 2 and 3). In the above example, the $75 cash received for the warranty would be recorded as "deferred revenue" at the time of sale. It would then be recognized as revenue in years 2 and 3. In response, most retailers outsourced their extended warranty business. In this example, they might still sell the extended warranty for $75 but would pay a third party $13 to bear all risks of repairing the product. In response, one FASB Board member stated that the FASB should have not gotten involved.

Sale of Computer Part Commodities

Computer manufacturers maintain inventories of commodity parts such as hard drives, microprocessors, memory chips, and power supplies. Most items are relatively generic, so they can readily be used by other computer manufacturers. Manufacturers routinely sell excess component inventories to other manufacturers or to component resellers, often at a loss. One way to think of this type of transaction is that the firm purchased too much inventory and then suffered a loss on the sale. That transaction is part of the normal purchasing process. Buyers often buy in anticipation of high

10. Specifically, the reference is Section 460 (Guarantees), Sub-topic 10 (Overall), and Section 25 (Recognition).

sales or a shortage of parts. Sometimes they are correct, and their action reduces the cost of products; sometimes they are incorrect, and their action increases the cost of products. With that view, the loss is considered an increase to cost of goods sold, so the net of revenue from the sale and the cost of the products sold are both included in cost of goods sold. However, under current U.S. Generally Accepted Accounting Practices (GAAP), firms are required to record the sales price as revenue and the product cost as cost of goods sold.

Vendor Funding Arrangements

Vendors provide their customers with various funding arrangements, such as allowances for advertising or a rebate based on quantity purchased. Some customers recorded the cash received from vendors for advertising support as a reduction to selling, general, and administrative expenses. However, in 2002, the FASB issued additional revenue recognition guidance (Section 605, previously EITF No. 2-16), which requires that such payments be recorded as a reduction to cost of goods sold.[11]

Restructuring Reserves

Firms are required to record a restructuring expense whenever they incur a liability with regard to restructuring their operations, such as closing a plant, moving operations, or terminating employees. There are two primary issues relating to restructuring expenses. Prior to 2002, the guidance on exit or disposal cost obligations (Topic 420, previously EITF 94-3) required that firms record restructuring expenses on the date they committed to an exit plan. In 2002, the FASB issued additional guidance on exit or disposal cost obligations (Topic 420, previously FAS 146).[12] The primary change is that commitment to a plan is no longer sufficient to recognize a liability. Instead, a firm must have actually incurred the liability, for example, by indentifying the group of employees who will be terminated and by agreeing to a specified payment to such individuals.

The second issue is how firms have implemented restructuring reserve rules. Prior to the Sarbanes-Oxley Act, firms often recorded far larger restructuring expenses than they expected to incur. The resulting liability account, restructuring reserve, would be maintained as a liability on a firm's balance sheet even when all expected restructuring costs had been incurred. In almost all instances, that amount was included in some general liability account, so financial statement readers had no idea of the size of the liability and usually had no idea the liability even existed. Later, when profits were lower than expected, the firm would close the restructuring reserve account and lower some expense category, such as selling, general, and administrative expenses. Currently, U.S. firms provide substantially more detail about restructuring reserves in notes to the financial statements.

---

11. Specifically, the reference is 605-50: Topic 605 (Revenue Recognition), Sub-topic 50 (Customer Payments and Incentives).

12. Specifically, the reference is 420-10: Topic 420 (Exit or Disposal Cost Obligations), Sub-topic 10 (Overall).

Required

1. For each of the accounting issues discussed in the body of the case and in Exhibit 2:

   a. Discuss whether the accounting rule seems reasonable.

   b. Discuss whether it seems likely that Dell recorded the transaction improperly to manipulate results or whether it was more likely an honest mistake (e.g., Dell did not know about the rule; the implementation relied on judgment and the investigators had the benefit of hindsight, or the sheer volume of low-value orders Dell ships, possibly as many as 10,000 to 20,000 each day, makes it very difficult to properly implement these detailed rules.)

   c. Discuss whether the error is material and should have been disclosed.

2. For most of the above items, firms following IFRS will lack detailed guidance, so they will rely on reasonable judgment. Having detailed rules clearly increases consistency, but the United States has such detailed rules that no one knows them all. To ensure compliance, firms need individuals or teams who specialize in various aspects of accounting. One team may specialize in revenue recognition, another in leasing, a third in fair value, and a fourth in hedging rules:

   a. Is the consistency provided by the rules described in this case worth the cost of complying with them? Explain.

   b. Would a senior executive at a firm such as Dell prefer U.S. GAAP rules or IFRS rules? Explain.

   c. Would a user of external financial statements, such as an investment manager, prefer U.S. GAAP rules or IFRS rules? Explain.

3. At the start of the investigation, which cost $205 million, Dell did not know the extent of the problems.[13] Should Dell have been required to undertake this investigation?

4. Exhibit 2 includes income statements for fiscal years 2005 and 2006 with "as reported" and "as restated" numbers, a balance sheet for 2006 with "as reported" and "as restated" numbers, a statement of cash flows with "as reported" and "as restated" numbers for both 2005 and 2006, and a table showing changes in "retained earnings" for 2003 through 2006. Given the accounting issues involved, the cost of the investigation, and the dollar amount of the restatements, were the restatements worth their cost? As part of your answer, discuss whether an analyst would change his or her estimated value of Dell or, equivalently, change his or her estimates of Dell's future prospects as a result of these restated financial statements.

5. Exhibit 3 discusses changes Dell is making to its accounting organization and to its control procedures. Evaluate those changes in terms of their probable costs and benefits. Why is Dell making the changes?

---

13. Ackerman, Ruthie, "Dell climbs out of accounting hell," *Forbes* Market Scan, October 30, 2007.

EXHIBIT 1

ITEM 7,
MANAGEMENT
DISCUSSION AND
ANALYSIS, 10-K,
FEBRUARY 2, 2007

AUDIT COMMITTEE INDEPENDENT INVESTIGATION AND RESTATEMENT

Background

In August 2005, the Division of Enforcement of the United States Securities and Exchange Commission (the "SEC") initiated an inquiry into certain of our accounting and financial reporting matters and requested that we provide certain documents. Over the course of several months, we produced documents and provided information in response to the SEC's initial request and subsequent requests.

In June 2006, the SEC sent us an additional request for documents and information that appeared to expand the scope of the inquiry, with respect to both issues and periods. As documents and information were collected in response to this additional request, our management was made aware of information that raised significant accounting and financial reporting concerns, including whether accruals, reserves, and other balance sheet items had been recorded and reported properly. After evaluating this information and in consultation with PricewaterhouseCoopers LLP, our independent registered public accounting firm, management determined that the identified issues warranted an independent investigation and recommended such to the Audit Committee of our Board of Directors.

On August 16, 2006, the Audit Committee, acting on management's recommendation, approved the initiation of an independent investigation. The Audit Committee engaged Willkie Farr & Gallagher LLP ("Willkie Farr") to lead the investigation as independent legal counsel to the Audit Committee. Willkie Farr in turn engaged KPMG LLP ("KPMG") to serve as its independent forensic accountants.

Scope of the Investigation

The scope of the investigation was determined by Willkie Farr, in consultation with the Audit Committee and KPMG. The investigation involved a program of forensic analysis and inquiry directed to aspects of our accounting and financial reporting practices throughout the world, and evaluated aspects of our historical accounting and financial reporting practices since Fiscal 2002 and, with respect to certain issues, prior fiscal years.

Willkie Farr and KPMG assembled an investigative team that ultimately consisted of more than 375 professionals, including more than 125 lawyers and 250 accountants. Investigative teams were deployed in our three geographic regions — Americas (including our corporate functions), EMEA, and APJ. Information and documents were gathered from company personnel worldwide. Using proprietary search software, the investigative team evaluated over five million documents. Investigative counsel also conducted over 200 interviews of approximately 150 individuals, and the KPMG accountants, in connection with their forensic work, conducted numerous less formal discussions with various company employees. In addition, using a proprietary software tool designed to identify potentially questionable journal entries based on selected criteria (for example, entries made late in the quarterly close process, entries containing round dollar line items between $3 million and $50 million, and liability-to-liability transfers), KPMG selected and reviewed in excess of 2,600 journal entries that were highlighted by the tool or specifically identified by the forensic teams investigating specific issues.

Summary of Investigation Findings

The investigation raised questions relating to numerous accounting issues, most of which involved adjustments to various reserve and accrued liability accounts, and identified evidence that certain adjustments appear to have been motivated by the objective of attaining financial targets. According to the investigation, these activities typically occurred

(continued)

EXHIBIT 1—
continued

ITEM 7,
MANAGEMENT
DISCUSSION AND
ANALYSIS, 10-K,
FEBRUARY 2, 2007

in the days immediately following the end of a quarter, when the accounting books were being closed and the results of the quarter were being compiled. The investigation found evidence that, in that timeframe, account balances were reviewed, sometimes at the request or with the knowledge of senior executives, with the goal of seeking adjustments so that quarterly performance objectives could be met. The investigation concluded that a number of these adjustments were improper, including the creation and release of accruals and reserves that appear to have been made for the purpose of enhancing internal performance measures or reported results, as well as the transfer of excess accruals from one liability account to another and the use of the excess balances to offset unrelated expenses in later periods. The investigation found that sometimes business unit personnel did not provide complete information to corporate headquarters and, in a number of instances, purposefully incorrect or incomplete information about these activities was provided to internal or external auditors.

The investigation identified evidence that accounting adjustments were viewed at times as an acceptable device to compensate for earnings shortfalls that could not be closed through operational means. Often, these adjustments were several hundred thousand or several million dollars, in the context of a company with annual revenues ranging from $35.3 billion to $55.8 billion and annual net income ranging from $2.0 billion to $3.6 billion for the periods in question. The errors and irregularities identified in the course of the investigation revealed deficiencies in our accounting and financial control environment, some of which were determined to be material weaknesses that require corrective and remedial actions. For a description of the control deficiencies identified by management as a result of the investigation and our internal reviews described below, as well as management's plan to remediate those deficiencies, see "Part II—Item 9A—Controls and Procedures."

Other Company Identified Adjustments

Concurrently with the investigation, we also conducted extensive internal reviews for the purpose of the preparation and certification of our Fiscal 2007 and prior financial statements and our assessment of internal controls over financial reporting. Our procedures included expanded account reviews and expanded balance sheet reconciliations to ensure all accounts were fully reconciled, supported, and appropriately documented. We also implemented improvements to our quarterly and annual accounting close process to provide for more complete review of the various business unit financial results. These additional reviews identified issues involving, among other things, revenue recognition in connection with sales of third party software, amortization of revenue related to after-point-of-sale extended warranties, and accounting for certain vendor reimbursement agreements.

Restatement

As a result of issues identified in the Audit Committee investigation, as well as issues identified in the additional reviews and procedures conducted by management, the Audit Committee, in consultation with management and PricewaterhouseCoopers LLP, our independent registered public accounting firm, concluded on August 13, 2007 that our previously issued financial statements for Fiscal 2003, 2004, 2005, and 2006 (including the interim periods within those years), and the first quarter of Fiscal 2007, should no longer be relied upon because of certain accounting errors and irregularities in those financial statements. Accordingly, we have restated our previously issued financial statements for those periods. See Note 2 of Notes to Consolidated Financial Statements included in "Part II—Item 8—Financial Statements and Supplementary Data."

EXHIBIT 2

NOTE 2, AUDIT
COMMITTEE
INDEPENDENT
INVESTIGATION
AND RESTATEMENT,
10-K, YEAR ENDED
FEBRUARY 2, 2007

Summary of Investigation Findings

The investigation raised questions relating to numerous accounting issues, most of which involved adjustments to various reserve and accrued liability accounts, and identified evidence that certain adjustments appear to have been motivated by the objective of attaining financial targets. According to the investigation, these activities typically occurred in the days immediately following the end of a quarter, when the accounting books were being closed and the results of the quarter were being compiled. The investigation found evidence that, in that time frame, account balances were reviewed, sometimes at the request or with the knowledge of senior executives, with the goal of seeking adjustments so that quarterly performance objectives could be met. The investigation concluded that a number of these adjustments were improper, including the creation and release of accruals and reserves that appear to have been made for the purpose of enhancing internal performance measures or reported results, as well as the transfer of excess accruals from one liability account to another and the use of the excess balances to offset unrelated expenses in later periods. The investigation found that sometimes business unit personnel did not provide complete information to corporate headquarters and, in a number of instances, purposefully incorrect or incomplete information about these activities was provided to internal or external auditors.

The investigation identified evidence that accounting adjustments were viewed at times as an acceptable device to compensate for earnings shortfalls that could not be closed through operational means. Often, these adjustments ranged from several hundred thousand to several million dollars, in the context of a company with annual revenues ranging from $35.3 billion to $55.8 billion and annual net income ranging from $2.0 billion to $3.6 billion for the periods in question. The errors and irregularities identified in the course of the investigation revealed deficiencies in Dell's accounting and financial control environment, some of which were determined to be material weaknesses that require corrective and remedial actions.

Other Company Identified Adjustments

Concurrently with the investigation, Dell also conducted extensive internal reviews for the purpose of the preparation and certification of Dell's Fiscal 2007 financial statements and its assessment of internal controls over financial reporting. Dell's procedures included expanded account reviews and expanded balance sheet reconciliations to ensure all accounts were fully reconciled, supported, and appropriately documented. Dell also implemented improvements to its quarterly and annual accounting close process to provide for more complete review of the various business unit financial results.

Restatement Adjustments

As a result of the issues identified in the Audit Committee independent investigation, as well as issues identified in additional reviews and procedures conducted by management, the Audit Committee, in consultation with management and PricewaterhouseCoopers LLP, concluded on August 13, 2007, that Dell's previously issued financial statements for Fiscal 2003, 2004, 2005, and 2006 (including the interim periods within those years), and the first quarter of Fiscal 2007, should no longer be relied upon because of certain accounting errors and irregularities in those financial statements. Accordingly, Dell has restated its previously issued financial statements for those periods. Restated financial information is presented in this report.

The cumulative adjustments required to correct the errors and irregularities in the financial statements prior to Fiscal 2005 are reflected in the restated retained earnings as of the end of Fiscal 2004, as shown in the Statement of Stockholders' Equity. The cumulative effect of those adjustments reduced retained earnings by $52 million at January 31, 2004.

(continued)

EXHIBIT 2—
continued

Note 2, Audit
Committee
Independent
Investigation
and Restatement,
10-K, Year Ended
February 2, 2007

The nature of the restatement adjustments and the impact of the adjustments to Fiscal 2006 are shown in the following table:

	As reported	Revenue recognition		Warranty liabilities	Other reserves and accruals	Provision for income tax[a]	As restated
		Software sales	Other				
			(in millions, except per share data)				
Net revenue	$55,908	$(248)	$130	$—	$(2)	$—	$55,788
Cost of net revenue	45,958	(244)	124	52	7	—	45,897
Gross margin	9,950	(4)	6	(52)	(9)	—	9,891
Operating expenses:							
Selling, general, and administrative	5,140	—	1	—	(90)	—	5,051
R & D and engineering	463	—	—	(1)	(4)	—	458
Total operating exp	5,603	—	1	(1)	(94)	—	5,509
Operating income	4,347	(4)	5	51	85		4,382
Investment and other income, net	227	—	11	(4)	(8)	—	226
Income before income taxes	4,574	(4)	16	(55)	77	—	4,608
Income tax provision	1,002					4	1,006
Net income	$3,572						$3,602

Fiscal 2006 — **Adjustments**

[a]Primarily represents the aggregate tax impact of the adjustments.

The nature of the restatement adjustments and the impact of the adjustments to Fiscal 2005 are shown in the following table:

	As reported	Revenue recognition		Warranty liabilities	Other reserves and accruals	Provision for income tax[a]	As restated
		Software sales	Other				
			(in millions, except per share data)				
Net revenue	$49,205	$(105)	$21	$—	$—	$—	$49,121
Cost of net revenue	40,190	(93)	21	21	(36)	—	40,103
Gross margin	9,015	(12)	—	(21)	36	—	9,018
Operating expenses:							
Selling, general, and admin	4,298	—	—	—	54	—	4,352
Research, development, and engineering	463	—	—	—	(3)	—	460
Total operating expenses	4,761	—	—	—	51	—	4,812

Fiscal 2005 — **Adjustments**

(continued)

EXHIBIT 2—
continued

NOTE 2, AUDIT
COMMITTEE
INDEPENDENT
INVESTIGATION
AND RESTATEMENT,
10-K, YEAR ENDED
FEBRUARY 2, 2007

Operating income	4,254	(12)	—	(21)	(15)	—	4,206
Investment and other income, net	191	—	1	—	5	—	197
Income before income taxes	4,445	(12)	1	(21)	(10)	—	4,403
Income tax provision	1,402					(17)	1,385

(a)Primarily represents the aggregate tax impact of the adjustments.

Revenue Recognition Adjustments

Software Sales—The largest revenue recognition adjustment relates to correcting the timing and amount of revenue recognized on the sale of certain software products. Dell is a reseller of a broad array of third-party developed software. Individually significant categories of software are analyzed for application of the appropriate accounting under American Institute of Certified Public Accountants ("AICPA") Statement of Position No. 97-2, *Software Revenue Recognition* ("SOP 97-2"). However, the allocation of software sales revenue between the software license (recognized at point of sale) and post-contract support (deferred and recognized over time) for other high volume, lower dollar value software products has historically been assessed as a group and the post-contract support revenue was deferred based on an estimate of average "Vendor Specific Objective Evidence" ("VSOE"). During the course of its internal reviews, Dell determined that its application of SOP 97-2 for these high volume software products was not correct. Dell has determined that the most appropriate application of SOP 97-2 is to defer all of the revenue from these "other software" offerings and amortize the revenue over the post-contract support period as VSOE has not been appropriately established. Additionally, during the course of its reviews, Dell identified certain software offerings where it had previously recognized the gross amount of revenue from the sale but where it functions more as a selling agent as opposed to the principal in the sale to the customer. In those cases Dell should have recognized the revenue net of the related cost pursuant to EITF Issue No. 99-19, *Reporting Revenue Gross as a Principal vs. Net as an Agent*.

Other—The other revenue recognition adjustments include cases where Dell recognized revenue in the incorrect periods or recognized the incorrect amount of revenue on certain transactions, and cases where the allocation of revenue among the individual elements of the sale was not correct. The primary categories of other revenue recognition adjustments include the following:

- *SAB 104 Deferrals*—Instances were identified where Dell prematurely recognized revenue prior to finalization of the terms of sale with the customer, or prior to title and/or risk of loss having been passed to the customer. Sometimes these situations involved warehousing arrangements. Additionally, there were situations where revenue was incorrectly deferred to later periods despite title and/or risk of loss having passed to the end customer. Under SAB 104, there were also cases where the in-transit deferral calculation for the period end was not appropriately calculated or was based on incorrect assumptions.

- *Deferred Warranty Revenue*—Pursuant to FASB Technical Bulletin No. 90-1, *Accounting for Separately Priced Extended Warranty and Product Maintenance Contracts*—Dell defers and amortizes the revenue from the sale of extended warranties and enhanced service level agreements over the service period of the associated agreement. In some instances Dell's accounting estimates of the agreement durations were not correct, resulting in revenue being recognized over a shorter time period than the actual contract durations. Additionally, an error was identified in the amount of deferred revenue recognized and amortized during the restatement period.

(continued)

EXHIBIT 2—
continued

NOTE 2, AUDIT
COMMITTEE
INDEPENDENT
INVESTIGATION
AND RESTATEMENT,
10-K, YEAR ENDED
FEBRUARY 2, 2007

- *Customer Rebate Accruals*—Dell's U.S. Consumer segment and small business group historically offered various forms of rebates to stimulate sales, including mail-in rebates. The rebate redemption liability is estimated at the time of sale based on historical redemption rates for the various types of promotions. Dell has determined that this liability was overstated due to a number of factors, including failure to update redemption rates when appropriate, additional amounts accrued for expected customer satisfaction costs, and unsupported incremental accruals recorded in addition to the calculated redemption liability estimate.

- *Japan Services Transactions*—In late January 2007, a Japanese systems integrator with whom Dell's Japanese services division did business, filed for bankruptcy. The bankruptcy trustee publicly indicated that the systems integrator had engaged in fictitious transactions. Dell promptly commenced an internal investigation led by Dell's Ethics Office to determine whether its Japanese business unit had engaged in any fictitious transactions with the systems integrator. Dell hired independent outside counsel who retained independent accountants to lead the investigation. The investigation determined that almost all of the transactions of the Japan services business involving the systems integrator likely were fabricated, as were certain additional smaller transactions involving two other Japanese systems integrators. The impact of the adjustments reduced net revenue and cost of revenue to eliminate the effect of the fictitious transactions.

- *Sales Reflected in Cost of Sales*—There were transactions identified involving the sale of certain computer component commodities and parts where the net proceeds were presented as a reduction of cost of sales rather than as revenue.

Warranty Liabilities

The issues related to Dell's warranty liabilities include situations where certain vendor reimbursement agreements were incorrectly accounted for as a reduction in the estimate of the outstanding warranty liabilities. There were also instances where warranty reserves in excess of the estimated warranty liability, as calculated by the warranty liability estimation process, were retained and not released to the income statement as appropriate. Additionally, certain adjustments in the warranty liability estimation process were identified where expected future costs or estimated failure rates were not accurate.

Other Reserves and Accruals

Many of the restatement adjustments relate to the estimates and reconciliation of various reserves and accrued liabilities, including employee benefits, accounts payable, litigation, sales commissions, payroll, employee bonuses, and supplier rebates. Dell extensively reviewed its accruals and underlying estimates, giving consideration to subsequent developments after the date of the financial statements, to assess whether any of the previously recorded amounts required adjustment. Dell conducted expanded account reviews and expanded balance sheet reconciliations to ensure that all accounts were fully reconciled, supported, and appropriately documented. As a result of this review, Dell determined that a number of its accruals required adjustment across various accounting periods. The largest of these adjustments are described in more detail below:

- *Employee Bonuses*—Certain employee bonuses were not accrued correctly, including the timing of the recording of the accrual for the employee bonuses. Additionally, in certain cases when excess accruals resulted from differences in the actual bonus payments, the excess accruals were not adjusted as appropriate.

- *Vendor Funding Arrangements*—In some instances vendor funding arrangements were not accounted for appropriately under EITF Issue No. 02-16, *Accounting by a Customer (Including a Reseller) for Certain Consideration Received from a Vendor.* Certain amounts received from vendors were recorded as a reduction in operating expenses instead of being correctly recorded as a reduction of cost of goods sold. Additionally, certain amounts received were retained on the balance sheet and released in future periods despite the earnings process having been complete in the earlier period. Finally, there were instances

(continued)

EXHIBIT 2—
continued

NOTE 2, AUDIT
COMMITTEE
INDEPENDENT
INVESTIGATION
AND RESTATEMENT,
10-K, YEAR ENDED
FEBRUARY 2, 2007

where the benefit of certain vendor funding was recorded prior to the completion of the earnings process.

- *Unsubstantiated Accruals and Inadequately Reconciled Accounts*—In some instances accrual and reserve accounts lacked justification or supporting documentation. In certain cases these accounts were used to accumulate excess amounts from other reserve and accrual accounts. However, these excess reserves were not released to the income statement in the appropriate reporting period or were released for other purposes. In some instances accounts had incorrect balances because they had not been properly reconciled or because reconciling items had not been adjusted timely.

The table below summarizes the effects of the restatement adjustments on the Consolidated Statement of Financial Position at February 3, 2006.

| | February 3, 2006 | | |
	As reported	Adjustments	As restated
		(in millions)	
ASSETS			
Current assets:			
Cash and cash equivalents	$7,042	$12	$7,054
Short-term investments	2,016	—	2,016
Accounts receivable, net	4,089	(7)	4,082
Financing receivables, net	1,363	3	1,366
Inventories	576	12	588
Other	2,620	68	2,688
Total current assets	17,706	88	17,794
Property, plant, and equipment, net	2,005	(12)	1,993
Investments	2,691	(5)	2,686
Long-term financing receivables, net	325	—	325
Other non-current assets	382	72	454
Total assets	$23,109	$143	$23,252
LIABILITIES AND STOCKHOLDERS' EQUITY			
Current liabilities:			
Short-term borrowings	$—	$65	$65
Accounts payable	9,840	28	9,868
Accrued and other	6,087	153	6,240
Total current liabilities	15,927	246	16,173
Long-term debt	504	121	625
Other non-current liabilities	2,549	(142)	2,407
Total liabilities	18,980	225	19,205
Redeemable common stock and capital in excess of par value	—	—	—
Stockholders' equity:			
Common stock and capital in excess of par	9,540	(37)	9,503
Treasury stock	(18,007)	—	(18,007)
Retained earnings	12,746	(47)	12,699
Accumulated other comprehensive loss	(103)	2	(101)

(continued)

EXHIBIT 2—
continued

NOTE 2, AUDIT
COMMITTEE
INDEPENDENT
INVESTIGATION
AND RESTATEMENT,
10-K, YEAR ENDED
FEBRUARY 2, 2007

Other	(47)	—	(47)
Total stockholders' equity	4,129	(82)	4,047
Total liabilities and equity	$23,109	$143	$23,252

Statement of Financial Position Adjustments

In addition to the income statement adjustments described above, certain Statement of Financial Position classification adjustments were also identified. These include (i) correcting the classification of advances under credit facilities by DFS from other current and non-current liabilities to short-term borrowings and long-term debt as appropriate; (ii) correcting the presentation of liabilities for estimated litigation settlements by presenting estimated insurance recoveries as a receivable from the insurance carriers rather than as a reduction of the estimated settlement liability; (iii) correcting an error in the calculation and recording of the tax benefit of employee stock options which had an offsetting impact on accrued and other liabilities and stockholders equity; (iv) adjusting the fair value of long-term debt, where the interest rate is hedged with interest rate swap agreements; and (v) adjusting deferred revenue to record professional and deployment services impacting accounts receivable and accrued and other liabilities. These balance sheet corrections in classifications are included in the adjustments column above.

Statement of Cash Flows

The following table presents the major subtotals for Dell's Consolidated Statement of Cash Flows and the related impact of the restatement adjustments discussed above for Fiscal 2006 and 2005:

	Fiscal Year Ended			
	February 3, 2006		January 28, 2005	
	As reported	As restated	As reported	As restated
	(in millions)			
Net cash provided by (used in):				
Net income	$3,572	$3,602	$3,043	$3,018
Non-cash adjustments	912	789	59	643
Changes in working capital	(67)	(53)	1,755	1,772
Changes in noncurrent assets and liabilities	422	413	453	388
Operating activities	4,839	4,751	5,310	5,821
Investing activities	3,878	4,149	(2,317)	(1,678)
Financing activities	(6,226)	(6,252)	(3,128)	(3,129)
Effect of exchange rate changes on cash and equivalents[a]	(196)	(73)	565	46
Net increase in cash and cash equivalents	2,295	2,575	430	1,060
Cash and cash equivalents at beginning of year	4,747	4,479	4,317	3,419
Cash and cash equivalents at end of year	$7,042	$7,054	$4,747	$4,479

[a]The cash flows have been revised to reflect a closer approximation of the weighted-average exchange rates during the reporting periods. For most periods, this revision reduced the previously reported effect of exchange rate changes on cash and cash equivalents with an offsetting change in effects of exchange rate changes on monetary assets and liabilities denominated in foreign currencies and changes in operating working capital included in cash flows from operating activities.

(continued)

EXHIBIT 2—
continued

NOTE 2, AUDIT
COMMITTEE
INDEPENDENT
INVESTIGATION
AND RESTATEMENT,
10-K, YEAR ENDED
FEBRUARY 2, 2007

Comprehensive Income

The following table presents the impact of the restatement adjustments discussed above on Dell's comprehensive income for Fiscal 2006 and 2005:

| | Fiscal Year Ended | | | |
| | February 3, 2006 | | January 28, 2005 | |
	As reported	As restated	As reported	As restated
	(in millions)			
Comprehensive income:				
Net income	$3,572	$3,602	$3,043	$3,018
Unrealized gains on foreign currency hedging instruments	11	9	52	46
Unrealized losses on marketable securities	(24)	(24)	(52)	(52)
Foreign currency translations adjustments	(8)	(8)	1	1
Comprehensive income	$3,551	$3,579	$3,044	$3,013

Cumulative Restatement Adjustments to Previously Reported Beginning Retained Earnings by Category

The following table presents the impact of adjustments on previously reported beginning retained earnings for Fiscal 2006, Fiscal 2005, Fiscal 2004, and Fiscal 2003.

	February 3, 2006	January 28, 2005	January 30, 2004	January 31, 2003
	(in millions)			
Beginning retained earnings as reported	$9,174	$6,131	$3,486	$1,364
Revenue recognition:				
Software	(21)	(9)	(7)	(2)
Other	(216)	(217)	(102)	(64)
Revenue recognition	(237)	(226)	(109)	(66)
Warranty liabilities	202	223	129	31
Restructuring reserves	(18)	(18)	(14)	80
Other	(45)	(35)	(49)	32
(Provision) benefit for income taxes	21	4	11	(18)
Cumulative adjustment to beginning retained earnings	(77)	(52)	(32)	59
Beginning retained earnings as restated	$9,097	$6,079	$3,454	$1,423

This Report includes the certifications of our Chief Executive Officer and Chief Financial
Officer required by Rule 13a-14 of the Securities Exchange Act of 1934 (the "Exchange Act").
See Exhibits 31.1 and 31.2. This Item 9A includes information concerning the controls and
control evaluations referred to in those certifications.

Background

The Audit Committee of our Board of Directors has completed an independent investigation
into certain accounting and financial reporting matters. As a result of issues identified
in that investigation, as well as issues identified in additional reviews and procedures
conducted by management, the Audit Committee, in consultation with management and
PricewaterhouseCoopers LLP, our independent registered public accounting firm, concluded on
August 13, 2007 that our previously issued financial statements for Fiscal 2003, 2004, 2005,
and 2006 (including the interim periods within those years), and the first quarter of Fiscal
2007, should no longer be relied upon because of certain accounting errors and irregularities
in those financial statements. Accordingly, we have restated our previously issued financial
statements for those periods. See "Part II — Item 7 — Management's Discussion and
Analysis of Financial Condition and Results of Operations — Audit Committee Independent
Investigation and Restatement" and Note 2 of Notes to Consolidated Financial Statements
included in "Part II — Item 8 — Financial Statements and Supplementary Data."

As a result of management's review of the investigation issues and its other internal reviews,
we have identified several deficiencies in our internal control over financial reporting,
including our control environment and period-end financial reporting process, which are
discussed more fully below. The control deficiencies failed to prevent or detect a number
of accounting errors and irregularities, which led to the restatement described above. The
control deficiencies represent material weaknesses in our internal control over financial
reporting and require corrective and remedial actions.

Evaluation of Disclosure Controls and Procedures

Disclosure controls and procedures (as defined in Rules 13a-15(e) and 15d-15(e) under the
Exchange Act) are designed to ensure that information required to be disclosed in reports
filed or submitted under the Exchange Act is recorded, processed, summarized, and reported
within the time periods specified in SEC rules and forms and that such information is
accumulated and communicated to management, including the chief executive officer and the
chief financial officer, to allow timely decisions regarding required disclosures.

In connection with the preparation of this Report, Dell's management, under the supervision
and with the participation of the current Chief Executive Officer and current Chief Financial
Officer, conducted an evaluation of the effectiveness of the design and operation of our
disclosure controls and procedures as of February 2, 2007. Based on that evaluation, the
restatement of previously issued financial statements described above, and the identification
of certain material weaknesses in internal control over financial reporting (described below),
which we view as an integral part of our disclosure controls and procedures, our Chief
Executive Officer and Chief Financial Officer have concluded that our disclosure controls and
procedures were not effective as of February 2, 2007. Nevertheless, based on a number of
factors, including the completion of the Audit Committee's investigation, our internal review
that identified revisions to our previously issued financial statements, efforts to remediate
the material weaknesses in internal control over financial reporting described below, and the
performance of additional procedures by management designed to ensure the reliability of
our financial reporting, we believe that the consolidated financial statements in this Report
fairly present, in all material respects, our financial position, results of operations and cash
flows as of the dates, and for the periods, presented, in conformity with generally accepted
accounting principles in the United States of America ("GAAP").

(continued)

EXHIBIT 3—
continued

ITEM 9A, CONTROLS
AND PROCEDURES,
10-K, YEAR ENDED
FEBRUARY 2, 2007

Management's Report on Internal Control Over Financial Reporting

Management, under the supervision of the Chief Executive Officer and the Chief Financial Officer, is responsible for establishing and maintaining adequate internal control over financial reporting. Internal control over financial reporting (as defined in Rules 13a-15(f) and 15d(f) under the Exchange Act) is a process designed to provide reasonable assurance regarding the reliability of financial reporting and the preparation of financial statements for external purposes in accordance with GAAP. Internal control over financial reporting includes those policies and procedures which (a) pertain to the maintenance of records that, in reasonable detail, accurately and fairly reflect the transactions and dispositions of assets, (b) provide reasonable assurance that transactions are recorded as necessary to permit preparation of financial statements in accordance with GAAP, (c) provide reasonable assurance that receipts and expenditures are being made only in accordance with appropriate authorization of management and the board of directors, and (d) provide reasonable assurance regarding prevention or timely detection of unauthorized acquisition, use or disposition of assets that could have a material effect on the financial statements. A material weakness is a deficiency, or a combination of deficiencies, in internal control over financial reporting such that there is more than a remote likelihood that a material misstatement of the annual or interim financial statements will not be prevented or detected.

In connection with the preparation of this Report, Dell's management, under the supervision and with the participation of the current Chief Executive Officer and current Chief Financial Officer, conducted an evaluation of the effectiveness of our internal control over financial reporting as of February 2, 2007 based on the criteria established in *Internal Control — Integrated Framework* issued by the Committee of Sponsoring Organizations of the Treadway Commission ("COSO"). As a result of that evaluation, management identified the following control deficiencies as of February 2, 2007 that constituted material weaknesses:

• *Control environment*—We did not maintain an effective control environment. Specifically:

- We did not maintain a tone and control consciousness that consistently emphasized strict adherence to GAAP. This control deficiency resulted in an environment in which accounting adjustments were viewed at times as an acceptable device to compensate for operational shortfalls, which in certain instances led to inappropriate accounting decisions and entries that appear to have been largely motivated to achieve desired accounting results and, in some instances, involved management override of controls. In a number of instances, information critical to an effective review of transactions and accounting entries was not disclosed to internal and external auditors.

- We did not maintain a sufficient complement of personnel with an appropriate level of accounting knowledge, experience, and training in the application of GAAP commensurate with our financial reporting requirements and business environment.

The control environment, which is the responsibility of senior management, sets the tone of the organization, influences the control consciousness of its people, and is the foundation for all other components of internal control over financial reporting. The control environment material weaknesses described above contributed to the material weaknesses related to our period-end financial reporting process described below.

• *Period-end financial reporting process*—We did not maintain effective controls over the period-end reporting process, including controls with respect to the review, supervision, and monitoring of accounting operations. Specifically:

- Journal entries, both recurring and nonrecurring, were not always accompanied by sufficient supporting documentation and were not always adequately reviewed and approved for validity, completeness, and accuracy;

(continued)

EXHIBIT 3—
continued

ITEM 9A, CONTROLS
AND PROCEDURES,
10-K, YEAR ENDED
FEBRUARY 2, 2007

- Account reconciliations over balance sheet accounts were not always properly and timely performed, and the reconciliations and their supporting documentation were not consistently reviewed for completeness, accuracy, and timely resolution of reconciling items; and

- We did not design and maintain effective controls to ensure the completeness, accuracy, and timeliness of the recording of accrued liabilities, reserves, and operating expenses, primarily related to our accrued warranty obligations, goods and services received but not invoiced, customer rebates, and nonproduction operating expenses.

These material weaknesses resulted in the restatement of our annual and interim financial statements for Fiscal 2003, 2004, 2005, and 2006 and the first quarter of Fiscal 2007, and resulted in adjustments, including audit adjustments, to our annual and other interim financial statements for Fiscal 2007.

Additionally, these material weaknesses could result in misstatements of substantially all of our financial statement accounts that would result in a material misstatement of our annual or interim consolidated financial statements that would not be prevented or detected on a timely basis.

Based on management's evaluation, because of the material weaknesses described above, management has concluded that our internal control over financial reporting was not effective as of February 2, 2007. Our independent registered public accounting firm, PricewaterhouseCoopers LLP, has audited management's assessment of the effectiveness of our internal control over financial reporting as of February 2, 2007, and that report appears in this Report.

Remediation Plan

Our management, under new leadership as described below, has been actively engaged in the planning for, and implementation of, remediation efforts to address the material weaknesses, as well as other identified areas of risk. These remediation efforts, outlined below, are intended both to address the identified material weaknesses and to enhance our overall financial control environment. In January 2007, Michael S. Dell re-assumed the position of Chief Executive Officer and Donald J. Carty assumed the position of Chief Financial Officer. The design and implementation of these and other remediation efforts are the commitment and responsibility of this new leadership team.

- Our new leadership team, together with other senior executives, is committed to achieving and maintaining a strong control environment, high ethical standards, and financial reporting integrity. This commitment will be communicated to and reinforced with every Dell employee and to external stakeholders. This commitment is accompanied by a renewed management focus on decision-making and processes that are intended to achieve maximum shareholder value over the long-term and a decreased focus on short-term, quarter-by-quarter operating results.

- As a result of the initiatives already underway to address the control deficiencies described above, we have effected personnel changes in our accounting and financial reporting functions. Consequently, many of the employees involved in the accounting processes in which errors and irregularities were made are no longer involved in the accounting or financial reporting functions. In addition, we have taken, or will take, appropriate remedial actions with respect to certain employees, including terminations, reassignments, reprimands, increased supervision, training, and imposition of financial penalties in the form of compensation adjustments.

- We are in the process of reorganizing the Finance Department, segregating accounting and financial reporting responsibility from planning and forecasting responsibility, with

(continued)

EXHIBIT 3—
continued

Item 9A, Controls
and Procedures,
10-K, Year Ended
February 2, 2007

a renewed commitment to accounting and financial reporting integrity. We have appointed a new Chief Accounting Officer and have strengthened that position, making it directly responsible for all accounting and financial reporting functions worldwide. In addition, we are implementing personnel resource plans, and training and retention programs, that are designed to ensure that we have sufficient personnel with knowledge, experience, and training in the application of GAAP commensurate with our financial reporting requirements.

- We will continue our efforts to establish or modify specific processes and controls to provide reasonable assurance with respect to the accuracy and integrity of accounting entries and the appropriate documentation, review, and approval of those entries. These efforts include:

  - Centralization of the development, oversight, and monitoring of accounting policies and standardized processes in all critical accounting areas, including areas involving management judgment and discretion;

  - Implementation and clarification of specific accounting and finance policies, applicable worldwide, regarding the establishment, increase, and release of accrued liability and other balance sheet reserve accounts;

  - Creation of a revenue recognition accounting resource function to coordinate complex revenue recognition matters and to provide oversight and guidance on the design of controls and processes to enhance and standardize revenue recognition accounting procedures;

  - Improving the processes and procedures around the completion and review of quarterly management representation letters, in which our various business and finance leaders make full and complete representations concerning, and assume accountability for, the accuracy and integrity of their submitted financial results;

  - Extending the time between the end of a financial reporting period and the public release of financial and operating data with respect to that period, giving our accounting organization more time to appropriately process the close of the accounting records and analyze the reported results prior to public announcement;

  - Enhancing the development, communication, and monitoring of processes and controls to ensure that appropriate account reconciliations are performed, documented, and reviewed as part of standardized procedures; and

  - Increasing the focus by the internal audit function and the Chief Accounting Officer on the review and monitoring of key accounting processes, including journal entries and supporting documentation, revenue recognition processes, account reconciliations, and management representation letter controls and processes.

- We will implement company-wide training (led by the Chief Accounting Officer and other finance executives with appropriate accounting expertise) to enhance awareness and understanding of standards and principles for accounting and financial reporting. This training will include:

  - Development and communication of an accounting code of conduct that will serve as a set of guiding principles emphasizing our commitment to accounting and financial reporting integrity, as well as transparency and robust and complete communications with, and disclosures to, internal and external auditors;

  - Comprehensive programs for all finance personnel globally (with initial focus on personnel directly responsible for accounting and financial reporting) covering all fundamental accounting and financial reporting matters, including accounting policies, financial reporting requirements, income statement classification, revenue recognition, vendor funding, accounting for reserves and accrued liabilities, and account reconciliation and documentation requirements; and

(continued)

EXHIBIT 3—
continued

ITEM 9A, CONTROLS
AND PROCEDURES,
10-K, YEAR ENDED
FEBRUARY 2, 2007

– Appropriate programs for other company personnel, including senior management, to emphasize the importance of accounting and financial reporting integrity.

- We will invest in the design and implementation of additional and enhanced information technology systems and user applications commensurate with the complexity of our business and our financial reporting requirements. It is expected that these investments will improve the reliability of our financial reporting by reducing the need for manual processes, subjective assumptions, and management discretion; by reducing the opportunities for errors and omissions; and by decreasing our reliance on manual controls to detect and correct accounting and financial reporting inaccuracies.

- We will reemphasize and invigorate our communications to all Dell employees regarding the availability of our Ethics Hotline, through which employees at all levels can anonymously submit information or express concerns regarding accounting, financial reporting, or other irregularities they have become aware of or have observed. In addition, these communications will emphasize the existence and availability of other reporting avenues or forums for all employees, such as their management chain, their Human Resources representatives, the Ethics Office, the Ombudsman's Office, the Legal Department, and direct contact with the Chief Financial Officer or the Audit Committee.

The Audit Committee has directed management to develop a detailed plan and timetable for the implementation of the foregoing remedial measures (to the extent not already completed) and will monitor their implementation. In addition, under the direction of the Audit Committee, management will continue to review and make necessary changes to the overall design of our internal control environment, as well as policies and procedures to improve the overall effectiveness of internal control over financial reporting.

We believe the remediation measures described above will remediate the control deficiencies we have identified and strengthen our internal control over financial reporting. We are committed to continuing to improve our internal control processes and will continue to diligently and vigorously review our financial reporting controls and procedures. As we continue to evaluate and work to improve our internal control over financial reporting, we may determine to take additional measures to address control deficiencies or determine to modify, or in appropriate circumstances not to complete, certain of the remediation measures described above.

Inherent Limitations over Internal Controls

Our system of controls is designed to provide reasonable, not absolute, assurance regarding the reliability and integrity of accounting and financial reporting. Management does not expect that our disclosure controls and procedures or our internal control over financial reporting will prevent or detect all errors and all fraud. A control system, no matter how well designed and operated, can provide only reasonable, not absolute, assurance that the objectives of the control system will be met. These inherent limitations include the following:

- Judgments in decision-making can be faulty, and control and process breakdowns can occur because of simple errors or mistakes.

- Controls can be circumvented by individuals, acting alone or in collusion with each other, or by management override.

- The design of any system of controls is based in part on certain assumptions about the likelihood of future events, and there can be no assurance that any design will succeed in achieving its stated goals under all potential future conditions.

- Over time, controls may become inadequate because of changes in conditions or deterioration in the degree of compliance with associated policies or procedures.

- The design of a control system must reflect the fact that resources are constrained, and the benefits of controls must be considered relative to their costs.

(continued)

EXHIBIT 3—
continued

ITEM 9A, CONTROLS
AND PROCEDURES,
10-K, YEAR ENDED
FEBRUARY 2, 2007

Because of the inherent limitations in all control systems, no evaluation of controls can provide absolute assurance that all control issues and instances of fraud, if any, have been detected.

Changes in Internal Control over Financial Reporting

During the third and fourth quarters, and since the end, of Fiscal 2007, we have begun the implementation of some of the remedial measures described above, including (a) communication, both internally and externally, of our commitment to a strong control environment, high ethical standards, and financial reporting integrity; (b) certain personnel actions; (c) the reorganization of the Finance Department to separate accounting and financial reporting responsibility from planning and forecasting responsibility and to strengthen the Chief Accounting Officer role, giving it direct and centralized responsibility for all accounting and financial reporting functions worldwide; (d) the design and implementation of a comprehensive training program for all Finance Department personnel; (e) the implementation of more rigorous period-end financial reporting policies and processes involving journal-entry approval, supporting documentation, account reconciliations, and management representation letters; (f) an increased corporate audit focus on key accounting controls and processes, including documentation requirements; (g) extension of the time between the end of reporting periods and earnings release dates to give the accounting organization more time to close the books and process and analyze results; and (h) the design and implementation of a new internal global ethics awareness campaign, including refreshed tools, resources, and policies.

In addition to continuing the actions we implemented in the third quarter of Fiscal 2007, we took the following specific actions in the fourth quarter of Fiscal 2007: Implemented certain personnel actions; further enhanced of our management representation letter process; and began the centralization of the accounting functions.

The Boeing Company's Retiree Benefits, 2008

Background, Defined Benefit Pension Plans

Many large U.S. industrial firms and most U.S. governmental units (local, state, and federal) provide defined benefit pension plans to their employees. Upon retirement, an employee receives a formula-based monthly retirement benefit (payment) until death. The monthly benefit is typically a function of years of service, final salary over the last few years of employment, retirement age, and whether the employee elects a lower benefit for the life of both the employee and spouse.

The pension plan (plan) is the set of rules that govern eligibility, benefits, and other details. Nongovernmental pension plans must meet standards established by the Employee Retirement Income Security Act of 1974 (ERISA) and are insured by the Pension Benefit Guarantee Corporation, a federal corporation created by ERISA. The pension fund (fund) is a legal entity separate from the employer (sponsor); the fund holds the plan assets and pays retirees their benefits. A fund has trustees who are subject to fiduciary rules. In nearly all cases, pension trustees hire third-party investment advisers to invest pension assets and hire pension consultants to help select and monitor their investment advisers.

The employer contributes to the fund based on ERISA minimum funding requirements.[1] Because contributions to a qualified fund are tax deductible and fund earnings are nontaxable, contributions are also subject to an IRS maximum. The fund's assets are its cash, stocks, bonds, real estate, and other investments; the fund's liabilities are the pension benefits it owes to retirees and future retirees.

For each year an employee works, the employee gains additional benefits, and the fund incurs additional liabilities because the retirement benefit is partially determined by years worked (up to some limit). Under ERISA vesting rules, a sponsor has a choice of Cliff or graduated vesting. With Cliff vesting, the sponsor has no pension obligation until an employee has five years of service. After five years, the employee's retirement benefit is determined using the sponsor's retirement formula (years of service, final salary, retirement age, and spousal election). If an employer elects graduated vesting, there is no liability until the employee works for the employer for three years. After three years, the sponsor's liability to the employee equals its formula-based obligation, multiplied by 20%. That increases to 40% after four years, 60% after five years, 80% after six years, and 100% after seven years.

Actuaries estimate the pension benefits a fund owes to retirees and future retirees. Actuaries then compute the present value of those future obligations using a discount rate that reflects current market interest rates. In the United States, the SEC suggested that the discount rate should be the rate on fixed income securities issued by corporations that receive one of the two highest ratings from a major rating agency—ASC 715 20 S99 (FAS 158). In contrast to a fund's obligations, it is simple to determine fund assets. Fund assets equal the fair value of the fund's investments at the valuation date, which is the date of the sponsor's fiscal year end—ASC 715 (FAS 158).

---

1. None of the ERISA or IRS rules apply to governmental retirement funds. Those funds are only subject to laws and regulations of their own jurisdiction.

Changes in Fund Liabilities

The primary increases in fund liabilities are from service costs and interest costs. Payments to retirees decrease fund liabilities, whereas revised actuarial assumptions can increase or decrease liabilities. The second table in Exhibit 1 shows Boeing's fund liabilities (Change in benefit obligation) and fund assets (Change in plan assets) for 2008 and 2007. Prior to 2008, firms could report pension fund assets and liabilities for up to three months prior to their fiscal year end; as of 2008, they must report them as of the fiscal year end, so the table is for the periods ending September 30, 2007, and December 31, 2008.

Service cost

Employees earn one additional year of service by working another year. Years of service is one determinant of a retiree's pension benefit; the additional year of service increases the fund's liability and is called "Service cost." As shown in Exhibit 1, service cost increased Boeing's pension liability by $1.188 billion for the 15 months ended December 31, 2008, and by $953 million for the 12 months ended September 30, 2007. That table also shows liabilities and assets for "Other Postretirement Benefits" (retiree health-care costs), which will be discussed later.

Interest cost

A fund's liability is computed by discounting estimated future payments at a discount rate. The first table in Exhibit 1's Assumptions section shows that Boeing used a 6.2% discount rate in 2007 to compute its September 30, 2007, $45.734 billion fund liability. As of December 31, 2008, Boeing was one year nearer to paying those future benefits, so the liability's present value is greater. For example, future benefits expected to be paid in 10 years as of September 30, 2007, would be divided by 1.062 raised to the tenth power. As of December 31, 2008, they would be divided by a smaller number (1.062 raised to the ninth power), so the liability is greater. That increased liability is called "interest cost." From Exhibit 1, interest cost was $3.524 billion for the 15 months ended December 31, 2008, and $2.681 billion for the 12 months ended September 30, 2007.[2]

Actuarial gains and losses

From Exhibit 1, Boeing used 5.9%, 6.2%, and 6.1% discount rates in 2006, 2007, and 2008. When Boeing raised its discount rate from 5.9% in 2006 to 6.2% in 2007, it discounted expected future benefits at a higher discount rate, so its pension liability decreased. When it decreased its discount rate from 6.2% in 2007 to 6.1% in 2008, it discounted expected future benefits at a lower discount rate, so its pension liability increased. The lower liability in 2007 and higher liability in 2008 are from one revised actuarial assumption, the discount rate (based on the market interest rate for high-grade corporate bonds). Boeing would have had other revised actuarial assumptions, but they are not disclosed. Boeing reported a $1.172 billion decrease in pension liabilities in 2007 and a $1.255 billion increase in pension liabilities in 2008 from revised actuarial assumption, including the discount rate.

Benefits paid

Boeing's retirees received $3.056 billion in benefit payments in 2008, which reduced liabilities by $3.056 billion.

---

2. This discussion ignores payments made during 2008, but those are bookkeeping issues.

Other items

Other items increase or decrease a fund's liabilities, but they are usually minor or one-time items.

Changes in Fund Assets

Actual return on plan assets

Investment gains or losses are almost always the largest change to a fund's assets. In the 12 months ending September 30, 2007, Boeing's fund earned $6.029 billion on its investments; in the 15 months ending December 31, 2008, it lost $7.296 billion.

Company contributions

Company contributions increase fund assets. Boeing contributed $580 million to its fund in 2007 and $531 million in 2008. Company contributions change significantly from year to year. For funds with assets that exceed liabilities (overfunded), company contributions may be small or zero for many years.

Benefits paid

For both 2007 and 2008, benefits paid in the Plan asset section are lower than benefits paid in the Liabilities section. The Boeing Company apparently paid some pension benefits itself; those payments reduce pension liabilities but not pension assets.

Fund Status

Exhibits 2 and 3 show Boeing's 2008 income statements and balance sheets. Boeing's pension fund had $45.734 billion of liabilities and $50.439 billion of assets in 2007, so it was overfunded by $4.705 billion. In 2008, it had $49.017 billion of liabilities and $40.597 billion of assets, so it was underfunded by $8.42 billion; that is, the fund was $13.125 billion worse off at the end of 2008 than at the end of 2007. Under accounting rules, Boeing reported the underfunded or overfunded amount on its balance sheet. Overfunded amounts appear as an asset; underfunded amounts appear as a liability. The table that shows fund liabilities and assets includes a panel at the bottom; that panel describes where overfunded or underfunded amounts appear on Exhibit 3. On Boeing's 2007 balance sheet, $5.924 billion appears as "Pension plan assets, net"; $8.383 billion appears as "Accrued pension plan liability, net" on its 2008 balance sheet.

Retirement Expense Smoothing

The above discussion focused on the fund's assets and liabilities and where overfunded or underfunded amounts appear on Boeing's balance sheet. Boeing must also record pension expense on its income statement (most U.S. firms, including Boeing, use net periodic benefit cost instead of pension expense). Pension expense is computed using items that change fund liabilities and assets, including: (a) service cost; (b) interest cost; (c) actuarial gains and losses; and (d) investment gains and losses. The first two items are relatively predictable, and Boeing has considerable control over them so they directly determine pension expense. The last two items are unpredictable, and Boeing has only limited control over them, so under accounting rules they indirectly determine pension expense.

When interest rates increase (decrease), fund liabilities decrease (increase); when the stock market rises (drops), fund assets increase (decrease). If Boeing used fund investment gains and losses to compute pension expense, it would use the $6.029 billion gain in 2007 and the $7.296 billion loss in 2008, or a $13.325 billion swing in one year. Because Boeing's 2008 net income was only $2.654 billion (Exhibit 2), the $13.325 billion change in fund earnings would overwhelm net earnings from operating activities. To avoid wide earnings swings, the FASB requires that firms smooth the effects of both actuarial gains and losses and fund earnings and losses—ASC 715 (FAS 158)—although there is some pressure on the FASB and the IASB to include actual results in pension expense. The following are components of Boeing's net periodic benefit cost, which is shown in the first table of Exhibit 1.

Service cost

For 2007, Boeing reported a $953 million service cost in its "Change in benefit obligation" and the same amount ($952 because of rounding) when computing its "Net periodic benefit cost" (pension expense) in the first table in Exhibit 1. The numbers are different for 2008 but only because the "Change in benefit obligation" for 2008 is for a 15-month period and the "Net periodic benefit cost" is for a 12-month period.

Interest cost

Boeing's liabilities increased by $2.681 billion in 2007 because of interest cost; Boeing also included the $2.681 billion interest cost as a component of net periodic benefit cost on its income statement. As with service costs, 2008 interest cost differs because of the 15-month period.

Expected return on plan assets

Boeing's net periodic benefit cost (pension expense) increased because of service costs and interest costs. Boeing's pension fund earnings lower pension expense and, for overfunded pension funds, can be high enough that pension expense is negative. To avoid wide swings in pension expense and reported income, Boeing's pension expense is reduced by the fund's expected long-run earnings, not by actual earnings. The Assumptions section of Exhibit 1 shows that Boeing used an 8.5% expected return on plan assets for 2007 and an 8.00% expected return for 2008. As shown on the first table of Exhibit 1, Boeing used the $3.507 billion expected return on plan assets in 2007 and the $3.811 billion expected return in 2008, not the $6.029 billion actual gain in 2007 or the $7.296 billion actual loss in 2008.

Recognized net actuarial loss

Boeing's pension fund liability decreased by $1.172 billion in 2007 and increased by $1.255 billion in 2008 because of revised actuarial assumptions (partially because of interest rate swings). Rather than use those relatively volatile numbers to compute pension expense, accounting rules proscribe a relatively complex averaging; the first table in Exhibit 1 shows Boeing used a recognized net actuarial loss of $764 million in 2007 and $392 million in 2008, rather than the actual liability changes.

Other

Boeing's pension expense includes amortization of prior service costs. When fund liabilities increase because of plan changes that increase benefits without requiring additional work, the increased liability is called "prior service cost"; it is an additional cost for work performed in the past. Prior service costs are spread over a number of years, rather than recognized in the year they are granted.

Net periodic benefit cost included in earnings from operations

The first table in Exhibit 1 also reports net periodic benefit cost included in earnings from operations. Pension costs are recorded as expenses for employees in functions such as sales, marketing, research and development, finance, and accounting. When pension costs relate to manufacturing employees, including manufacturing executives, they are overhead costs that must be first added to inventory cost and then expensed as a part of cost of goods sold when the inventory is sold.

Other Postretirement Benefits (OPEB)

In most cases, retiree health-care insurance is by far the largest component of an OPEB fund. For accounting purposes, there is little difference between pension benefits and OPEB. For financial statement analysis and valuation, there are major differences. Qualified pension funds are regulated by ERISA and insured by the Pension Benefit Guarantee Corporation (PBGC); OPEB funds are unregulated and uninsured. Employer contributions to pension funds are tax deductible and fund earnings are nontaxable. Employer contributions to OPEB funds are non-tax deductible, and OPEB fund earnings are taxable. As a result, firms have little incentive to contribute to retiree health-care funds, unless they are required to do so by a labor contract.

Boeing's OPEB fund is typical for firms that offer retiree health-care benefits but are not required to contribute to the fund. In 2007, Boeing's OPEB fund had a $7.662 billion liability but only $96 million of assets. Of the $507 million of OPEB benefits paid, the fund paid $19 million and The Boeing Company paid the rest. In 2008, Boeing's OPEB fund had a $7.859 billion liability but only $79 million of assets. Of the $630 million benefits paid, the fund paid only $16 million.

Tax Accounting for Postretirement Benefits

Firms must record an asset for the amount by which a fund is overfunded or a liability for the amount by which it is underfunded. Firms must also smooth investment gains or losses and the effects of revised actuarial assumptions. Boeing's pension fund went from $4,705 billion overfunded in 2007 to $8.42 billion underfunded in 2008, or a $13.125 billion change to its balance sheet. In 2008, Boeing recorded only $562 million of pension expense on its income statement. That $12.563 billion difference is charged to "Accumulated Other Comprehensive Loss," but net of tax because when Boeing pays those costs in the future, it will receive a tax benefit. There is a similar effect for Boeing's OPEB fund. The following note from Boeing's 2008 10-K discloses Boeing's net deferred tax assets:

Significant components of our deferred tax assets, net of deferred tax liabilities, at December 31 were as follows:

	2008	2007
Retiree health-care accruals	$2,970	$2,581
Inventory and long-term contract methods of income recognition and other (net of valuation allowance of $17 and $0)	(604)	638
Partnerships and joint ventures	(500)	(429)
Other employee benefits accruals	1,367	1,476
In-process research and development related to acquisitions	93	108
Net operating loss, credit, and charitable contribution carryovers (net of valuation allowance of $31 and $20)	270	275
Pension asset (liability)	3,026	(1,648)
Customer and commercial financing	(1,604)	(1,587)
Unremitted earnings of non-U.S. subsidiaries	(55)	(48)
Other net unrealized losses (gains)	197	(18)
Net deferred tax assets	$5,160	$1,348

This section of Boeing's 2008 Statement of Owners' Equity shows that for pension and OPEB fund smoothing, and other minor items, Boeing recorded an $8.565 billion charge to "Accumulated Other Comprehensive Loss," (net of a $4.883 billion increase to deferred tax assets):

(Dollars in millions, except per share data)	Common stock	Additional Paid-in capital	Treasury stock	ShareValue trust	Retained earnings	Accumulated other comprehensive loss	Total
Balance December 31, 2007	$5,061	$4,757	($14,842)	($2,752)	$21,376	($4,596)	$9,004
Net earnings					2,672		2,672
Unrealized loss on derivative instruments, net of tax of $93						(159)	(159)
Unrealized loss on certain investments, net of tax of $61						(121)	(121)
Reclassification adjustment for losses realized in net earnings, net of tax of $(2)						4	4
Currency translation adjustment						(180)	(180)
Postretirement liability adjustment, net of tax of $(4,883)						(8,565)	(8,565)
Comprehensive expense							(6,349)
Share-based compensation and related dividend equivalents		243			(8)		235
ShareValue Trust activity		(1,540)		1,452			(88)
Excess tax pools		99					99
Treasury shares issued for stock options exercised, net		(9)	53				44
Treasury shares issued for other share-based plans, net		(94)	65				(29)
Treasury shares repurchased			(2,937)				(2,937)
Treasury shares transfer			(97)	97			
Cash dividends declared ($1.62 per share)					(1,187)		(1,187)
SFAS 158 transition amount, net of tax of $50					(178)	92	(86)
Balance December 31, 2008	$5,061	$3,456	($17,758)	($1,203)	$22,675	($13,525)	($1,294)

From the above information, it is possible to estimate Boeing's 2008 net journal entry for its pension and OPEB Fund activities (with a small unexplained difference):

	Debits	Credits
Deferred tax assets, retiree health care accruals [$2,581 minus $2,970]	$389	
Pension asset (liability) [($1,648) minus $3,026]	$4,674	
Postretirement liability adjustment, net of tax of ($4,883)	$8,565	
Net periodic benefit cost, pensions	$562	
Net periodic benefit cost, OPEB	$570	
Pension benefits paid by Boeing [$3,056 minus $2,991]		$65
OPEB benefits paid by Boeing [$630 minus $16]		$614
Cash, to Pension fund		$531
Cash, to OPEB fund		$19
Pension plan assets, net [$5,924 minus $16]		$5,908
Accounts payable, pensions [$51 minus $53]		$2
Accounts payable, OPEB [$430 minus $458]		$28
Accrued pension plan liability [$1,155 minus $8,383]		$7,228
Accrued retiree health care [$7,007 minus $7,322]		$315
Totals	$14,760	$14,710
Change due to 15 months in 2008:	($86)	
Revised Totals	$14,674	$14,710
Unexplained difference		$36

Required

1. Explain the above journal entry, including the cash flow implications for financial statement analysis and valuation.

2. What would Boeing's pension and OPEB expense have been in 2008 if it did not use smoothing for its investment gains and losses and for revised actuarial assumptions? Would it be less or more confusing if Boeing did not use smoothing for its pension expense? Explain.

3. How subjective are the Boeing's pension assumptions (Exhibit 1)? How subjective are Boeing's retiree health-care assumptions (Exhibit 1)? Are Boeing's pension assumptions more or less subjective than its retiree health-care assumptions?

4. Explain the "Market-Related Value of Assets" paragraph in Exhibit 1.

EXHIBIT 1

NOTE 14, THE
BOEING COMPANY
POSTRETIREMENT
PLANS

We have various pension plans covering substantially all employees. We fund all our major pension plans through trusts. Pension assets are placed in trust solely for the benefit of the plans' participants and are structured to maintain liquidity that is sufficient to pay benefit obligations as well as to keep pace over the long term with the growth of obligations for future benefit payments.

We also have postretirement benefits other than pensions which consist principally of health care coverage for eligible retirees and qualifying dependents, and to a lesser extent, life insurance to certain groups of retirees. Retiree health care is provided principally until age 65 for approximately half those retirees who are eligible for health care coverage. Certain employee groups, including employees covered by most United Auto Workers bargaining agreements, are provided lifetime health care coverage.

The funded status of the plans is measured as the difference between the plan assets at fair value and the projected benefit obligation (PBO). We have recognized the aggregate of all overfunded plans in Pension plan assets, net and the aggregate of all underfunded plans in either Accrued retiree health care or Accrued pension plan liability, net. The portion of the amount by which the actuarial present value of benefits included in the PBO exceeds the fair value of plan assets, payable in the next 12 months, is reflected in Accounts payable and other liabilities.

Effective December 31, 2008, SFAS No. 158 requires us to measure plan assets and benefit obligations at fiscal year end. We previously performed this measurement at September 30 of each year. Beginning in fourth quarter of 2007 in accordance with this Standard, we eliminated the use of a three-month lag period when recognizing the impact of curtailments or settlements and, instead, recognize these amounts in the period in which they occur. As a result of implementing the measurement date provisions of SFAS No. 158, we recorded an additional quarter of pension and other postretirement benefit (OPB) cost as of January 1, 2008 as a $178 decrease to Retained earnings and a $92 decrease to Accumulated other comprehensive loss, which resulted in a net decrease of $86 to Shareholders' equity. The provisions of SFAS No. 158 do not permit retrospective application.

The components of net periodic benefit cost are as follows:

Years ended December 31,	Pension			Other postretirement benefits		
	2008	2007	2006	2008	2007	2006
Components of net periodic benefit cost						
Service cost	$952	$953	$908	$126	$136	$143
Interest cost	2,823	2,681	2,497	459	473	436
Expected return on plan assets	(3,811)	(3,507)	(3,455)	(8)	(8)	(7)
Amortization of prior service costs	206	200	188	(93)	(88)	(90)
Recognized net actuarial loss	392	764	912	86	159	131
Settlement/curtailment loss		10				
Net periodic benefit cost	$562	$1,101	$1,050	$570	$672	$613
Net periodic benefit cost included in Earnings from operations	$696	$1,082	$746	$507	$648	$481

Note: A portion of net periodic benefit cost is allocated to production as product costs and may remain in inventory at the end of each reporting period.

(continued)

EXHIBIT 1—
continued

Note 14, The
Boeing Company
Postretirement
Plans

The following tables show changes in the benefit obligation, plan assets and funded status of both pensions and OPB. Benefit obligation balances presented below reflect the PBO for our pension plans and accumulated postretirement benefit obligations (APBO) for our OPB plans.

	15-Month Period Ending December 31, 2008		12-Month Period Ending September 30, 2007	
	Pension	Other Postretirement Benefits	Pension	Other Postretirement Benefits
Change in benefit obligation				
Beginning balance	$45,734	$7,662	$45,582	$8,334
Service cost	1,188	159	953	136
Interest cost	3,524	574	2,681	473
Plan participants' contributions	12		11	
Amendments	470	(6)	95	(34)
Actuarial gain/(loss)	1,255	135	(1,172)	(753)
Settlement/curtailment/ acquisitions/ dispositions, net	1		(57)	(8)
Benefits paid	(3,056)	(630)	(2,431)	(507)
Exchange rate adjustment	(111)	(35)	72	21
Ending balance	$49,017	$7,859	$45,734	$7,662
Change in plan assets				
Beginning balance at fair value	$50,439	$96	$46,203	$89
Actual return on plan assets	(7,296)	(22)	6,029	10
Company contribution	531	19	580	15
Plan participants' contributions	12	1	11	1
Settlement/curtailment/ acquisitions/ dispositions, net		1	(65)	
Benefits paid	(2,991)	(16)	(2,382)	(19)
Exchange rate adjustment	(98)		63	
Ending balance at fair value	$40,597	$79	$50,439	$96
Reconciliation of funded status to net amounts recognized				
Funded status-plan assets less projected benefit obligation			$4,705	$(7,566)
Adjustment for fourth quarter contributions			13	129
Net amount recognized			$4,718	$(7,437)
Amounts recognized in statement of financial position at December 31, consist of:				
Pension plan assets, net	$16		$5,924	
Accounts payable and other liabilities	(53)	$(458)	(51)	$(430)
Accrued retiree health care		(7,322)		(7,007)
Accrued pension plan liability, net	(8,383)		(1,155)	
Net amount recognized	$(8,420)	$(7,780)	$4,718	$(7,437)

(continued)

EXHIBIT 1—
continued

NOTE 14, THE
BOEING COMPANY
POSTRETIREMENT
PLANS

Amounts recognized in Accumulated other comprehensive loss at December 31, 2008 are as follows:

	Pensions	Other Postretirement Benefits
Net actuarial loss	$18,556	$1,644
Prior service cost/(credit)	1,430	(403)
Total recognized in Accumulated other comprehensive loss	$19,986	$1,241

The estimated amount that will be amortized from Accumulated other comprehensive loss into net periodic benefit cost during the year ended December 31, 2009 is as follows:

	Pensions	Other Postretirement Benefits
Recognized net actuarial loss	$651	$ 92
Amortization of prior service costs	242	(89)
Total	$893	$ 3

The accumulated benefit obligation (ABO) for all pension plans was $45,218 and $41,818 at December 31, 2008 and September 30, 2007. Each of our eight major pension plans have ABOs that exceed plan assets at December 31, 2008. Key information for all plans with ABO in excess of plan assets as of December 31, 2008 and September 30, 2007 is as follows:

	December 31, 2008	September 30, 2007
Projected benefit obligation	$48,658	$1,501
Accumulated benefit obligation	44,863	1,255
Fair value of plan assets	40,225	465

The Medicare Prescription Drug, Improvement and Modernization Act of 2003 reduced our APBO by $491 at December 31, 2008 and $516 at September 30, 2007. These reductions/ actuarial gains are amortized over the expected average future service of current employees.

Assumptions

	December 31 2008	December 31 2007	September 30 2006	September 30 2005
Discount rate: pension and OPB	6.10%	6.20%	5.90%	5.50%
Expected return on plan assets	8.00%	8.25%	8.25%	8.50%
Rate of compensation increase	5.50%	5.50%	5.50%	5.50%

The discount rate for each pension plan is determined by discounting the plans' expected future benefit payments using a yield curve developed from high quality bonds that are rated as Aa or better by Moody's as of the measurement date. The yield curve is fitted to yields developed from bonds at various maturity points. Bonds with the ten percent highest and the ten percent lowest yields are omitted. A portfolio of about 300 bonds is used to construct the yield curve. Since corporate bond yields are generally not available at maturities beyond 30 years, it is assumed that spot rates will remain level beyond that 30-year point. The present value of each plan's benefits is calculated by applying the spot/discount rates to projected benefit cash flows. All bonds are U.S. issues, with a minimum outstanding of $50.

(continued)

EXHIBIT 1—
continued

NOTE 14, THE
BOEING COMPANY
POSTRETIREMENT
PLANS

The disclosed rate is the average rate for all the plans, weighted by the projected benefit obligation. As of December 31, 2008, the weighted average was 6.10%, and the rates for individual plans ranged from 4.25% to 6.60%. As of September 30, 2007, the weighted average was 6.20%, and the rates for individual plans ranged from 5.30% to 6.40%.

The pension fund's expected return on assets assumption is derived from a review of actual historical returns achieved by the pension trust and anticipated future long-term performance of individual asset classes with consideration given to the related investment strategy. While the study gives appropriate consideration to recent trust performance and historical returns, the assumption represents a long-term prospective return. The expected return on plan assets determined on each measurement date is used to calculate the net periodic benefit cost/(income) for the upcoming plan year.

	December 31, 2008	September 30, 2007
Assumed health care cost trend rates		
Health care cost trend rate assumed next year	7.50%	7.50%
Ultimate trend rate	5.00%	5.00%
Year that trend reached ultimate rate	2014	2013

Assumed health care cost trend rates have a significant effect on the amounts reported for the health care plans. To determine the health care cost trend rates we look at a combination of information including ongoing claims cost monitoring, annual statistical analyses of claims data, reconciliation of forecast claims against actual claims, review of trend assumptions of other plan sponsors and national health trends, and adjustments for plan design changes, workforce changes, and changes in plan participant behavior. A one-percentage-point change in assumed health care cost trend rates would have the following effect:

	Increase	Decrease
Effect on postretirement benefit obligation	$640	$(567)
Effect on total of service and interest cost	56	(49)

Market-Related Value of Assets

The expected return on plan assets is determined based on the expected long-term rate of return on plan assets and the market-related value of plan assets (MRVA). Since our adoption of FAS 87, *Employers' Accounting for Pensions*, in 1987, we have determined the MRVA based on a five-year moving average of plan assets. As of December 31, 2008, the MRVA is approximately $7,500 greater than the fair market value of assets.

Plan Assets

Pension assets totaled $40,597 and $50,439 at December 31, 2008 and September 30, 2007. In late 2006, the Company decided to modify the pension asset strategy with the objective of reducing volatility relative to pension liabilities, achieving a competitive investment return, achieving diversification between and within various asset classes, and managing other risks. In order to reduce the volatility between the value of pension assets and liabilities, the Company increased its allocation to fixed income as well as lengthened the duration of its fixed income holdings. The allocation to alternative investments, which include private equity, real estate, real assets, hedge funds, and global strategies, was also increased in order to address the return and diversification objectives. Key risk management areas addressed through this modified strategy include funded status risk, interest rate risk, market risk, counterparty risk, operational risk, and liquidity.

(continued)

EXHIBIT 1—
continued

NOTE 14, THE
BOEING COMPANY
POSTRETIREMENT
PLANS

Asset allocations are monitored and rebalanced on a regular basis. Actual investment allocations vary from target allocations due to periodic investment strategy changes, market value fluctuations, and the length of time it takes to complete investments in asset classes such as private equity, real estate, real assets, and other investments. Additionally, actual and target allocations vary due to the timing of benefit payments or contributions made on or near the measurement date.

Pension investment managers are retained with a specific investment role and corresponding investment guidelines. Investment managers have the ability to purchase securities on behalf of the pension fund and invest in derivatives, such as equity or bond futures, swaps, options, or currency forwards. Derivatives generally are used to achieve the desired market exposure of a security or an index, transfer value-added performance between asset classes, achieve the desired currency exposure, adjust portfolio duration, or rebalance the total portfolio to the target asset allocation.

The actual allocations for the pension assets at December 31, 2008 and September 30, 2007, and target allocations by asset category, are as follows:

| Asset Category | Percentage of Plan Assets | | Target Allocations | |
	December 31, 2008	September 30, 2007	December 31, 2008	September 30, 2007
Equity	28%	38%	28%	28%
Debt	55	46	45	45
Real estate and real assets	4	4	10	10
Private equity	5	4	6	6
Hedge funds	3	3	6	6
Global strategies	5	5	5	5
	100%	100%	100%	100%

Equity includes domestic and international equity securities, such as common, preferred or other capital stock, as well as equity futures, currency forwards and residual cash allocated to the equity managers. Plan assets did not include any of our common stock at December 31, 2008 and September 30, 2007. Equity and currency management derivatives based on net notional amounts totaled 7.9% and 1.9% of plan assets at December 31, 2008 and September 30, 2007.

Debt includes domestic and international debt securities, such as U.S. Treasury securities, U.S. government agency securities, corporate bonds; cash equivalents; and investments in bond derivatives such as bond futures, options, swaps and currency forwards. Bond derivatives based on net notional amounts totaled 5.2% and 16.6% of plan assets at December 31, 2008 and September 30, 2007. Additionally, Debt includes "To-Be-Announced" mortgage-backed securities (TBA) and treasury forwards which have delayed, future settlement dates. Debt included $410 and $2,478 related to TBA securities and treasury forwards at December 31, 2008 and September 30, 2007.

Private equity represents private market investments which are generally limited partnerships. Real estate includes investments in private and public real estate. Real assets include investments in natural resources (such as energy and timber) and infrastructure. Hedge funds include event driven, relative value, long-short and market neutral strategies. Global strategies seek to identify inefficiencies across various asset classes and markets, using long-short positions in physical securities and derivatives.

(continued)

EXHIBIT 1—
continued

NOTE 14, THE
BOEING COMPANY
POSTRETIREMENT
PLANS

We held $79 and $96 in trust fund assets for OPB plans at December 31, 2008 and September 30, 2007. Most of these funds are invested in a balanced index fund which is comprised of approximately 60% equities and 40% debt securities. The expected rate of return on these assets does not have a material effect on the net periodic benefit cost.

Some of our assets, primarily our alternative investments, including private equity, real estate, real assets, hedge funds, and global strategies, do not have readily determinable market values given the specific investment structures involved and the nature of the underlying investments. For the December 31, 2008 plan asset reporting, publicly traded asset pricing was used where possible; where it was not available, estimates were derived from both investment manager discussions that focused on the underlying fundamentals as well as an application of a public market proxy that reasonably correlated to the applicable asset class.

EXHIBIT 2

THE BOEING
COMPANY,
CONSOLIDATED
STATEMENT OF
OPERATIONS

(Dollars in millions)	Years ended December 31		
	2008	**2007**	**2006**
Sales of products	$50,180	$57,049	$52,644
Sales of services	10,729	9,338	8,886
Total revenues	60,909	66,387	61,530
Cost of products	(41,662)	(45,375)	(42,490)
Cost of services	(8,467)	(7,732)	(7,594)
Boeing Capital Corporation interest expense	(223)	(295)	(353)
Total costs and expenses	(50,352)	(53,402)	(50,437)
	10,557	12,985	11,093
Income from operating investments, net	241	188	146
General and administrative expense	(3,084)	(3,531)	(4,171)
Research and development expense, net of credits of $50, $130 and $160	(3,768)	(3,850)	(3,257)
Gain/(loss) on dispositions/business shutdown, net	4	38	(226)
Settlement with U.S. Department of Justice, net of accruals			(571)
Earnings from operations	3,950	5,830	3,014
Other income, net	247	484	420
Interest and debt expense	(202)	(196)	(240)
Earnings before income taxes	3,995	6,118	3,194
Income tax expense	(1,341)	(2,060)	(988)
Net earnings from continuing operations	2,654	4,058	2,206
Net gain on disposal of discontinued operations, net of taxes of $10, $9 and $5	18	16	9
Net earnings	$2,672	$4,074	$2,215

EXHIBIT 3

THE BOEING
COMPANY,
CONSOLIDATED
STATEMENTS
OF FINANCIAL
POSITIONS

(Dollars in millions)	December 31 2008	December 31 2007
Assets		
Cash and cash equivalents	$3,268	$7,042
Short-term investments	11	2,266
Accounts receivable, net	5,602	5,740
Current portion of customer financing, net	425	328
Deferred income taxes	1,046	2,341
Inventories, net of advances and progress billings	15,612	9,563
Total current assets	25,964	27,280
Customer financing, net	5,857	6,777
Property, plant and equipment, net	8,762	8,265
Goodwill	3,647	3,081
Other acquired intangibles, net	2,685	2,093
Deferred income taxes	4,114	197
Investments	1,328	4,111
Pension plan assets, net	16	5,924
Other assets, net of accumulated amortization of $400 and $385	1,406	1,258
Total assets	$53,779	$58,986
Liabilities and shareholders' equity		
Accounts payable and other liabilities	$17,587	$16,676
Advances and billings in excess of related costs	12,737	13,847
Income taxes payable	41	253
Short-term debt and current portion of long-term debt	560	762
Total current liabilities	30,925	31,538
Deferred income taxes		1,190
Accrued retiree health care	7,322	7,007
Accrued pension plan liability, net	8,383	1,155
Non-current income taxes payable	1,154	1,121
Other long-term liabilities	337	516
Long-term debt	6,952	7,455
Shareholders' equity:		
Common shares issued, par value $5.00 – 1,012,261,159 and 1,012,261,159 shares	5,061	5,061
Additional paid-in capital	3,456	4,757
Treasury shares, at cost	(17,758)	(14,842)
Retained earnings	22,675	21,376
*Accumulated other comprehensive loss	(13,525)	(4,596)
ShareValue Trust shares	(1,203)	(2,752)
Total shareholders' equity	(1,294)	9,004
Total liabilities and shareholders' equity	$53,779	$58,986

*Net of tax.

SECTION 4

FINANCIAL REPORTING—IFRS

Asset Impairments in the Recession of 2008–2009

Asset Valuation

From the time double-entry bookkeeping was developed 700 or 800 years ago until the 1980s, firms reported most assets and liabilities at historical cost.[1] Since the mid-1980s, accounting rules in the United States and much of the rest of the world gradually moved away from historical cost, toward fair value or some similar measure of current market price.[2] Although most rules apply to asset valuations, some also apply to liabilities. Over the years, U.S. GAAP (Generally Accepted Accounting Standards) and IFRS (International Financial Reporting Standards) developed the following valuation methods (differences between IFRS and U.S. GAAP are usually small but are sometimes significant):

- Historical cost
- Lower of cost or market inventory valuation
- Historical cost, subject to impairment
- Fair value
- Revaluation

Historical cost

Historical cost is simply the cost to purchase, build, or produce an asset. Typically, that includes all costs to prepare an asset for its intended use, including shipping, testing, and installation costs.

Lower of cost or market

Under IFRS, inventory is valued at the lower of cost or net realizable value, where net realizable value is the net amount an inventory is expected to realize. That definition is not necessarily equal to the current market price or the fair value (defined later) and is far from straightforward. A manufacturer combines parts and components into finished units, so if the market price of an inventory item drops, but the selling price of the finished unit remains unchanged, it is highly unlikely a firm would record an inventory write-down.

Under U.S. GAAP, inventory is valued at the lower of cost or market, where market is subject to a floor and a ceiling. Market cannot be greater than net realizable value and cannot be less than net realizable value reduced by a normal profit margin. Those rules are described in ACS 330.

---

1. Inventory had long been valued at the lower of cost or market.

2. U.S. Generally Accepted Accounting Standards (GAAP) are primarily set by the Financial Accounting Standards Board (FASB) under the authority of the SEC. International Financial Reporting Standards (IFRS) are set by the International Accounting Standards Board (IASB) and are used, or will soon be used, in more than 100 countries.

330-10-35-3: *The rule of lower of cost or market is intended to provide a means of measuring the residual usefulness of an inventory expenditure. The term* market *is therefore to be interpreted as indicating utility on the inventory date and may be thought of in terms of the equivalent expenditure which would have to be made in the ordinary course at that date to procure corresponding utility.*

330-10-35-4: *As a general guide, utility is indicated primarily by the current cost of replacement of the goods as they would be obtained by purchase or reproduction. In applying the rule, however, judgment must always be exercised and no loss shall be recognized unless the evidence indicates clearly that a loss has been sustained. There are therefore exceptions to such a standard. Replacement or reproduction prices would not be appropriate as a measure of utility when the estimated sales value, reduced by the costs of completion and disposal, is lower, in which case the realizable value so determined more appropriately measures utility.*

330-10-35-5: *Furthermore, when the evidence indicates that cost will be recovered with an approximately normal profit upon sale in the ordinary course of business, no loss shall be recognized even though replacement or reproduction costs are lower. This might be true, for example, in the case of production under firm sales contracts at fixed prices, or when a reasonable volume of future orders is assured at stable selling prices.*

Under U.S. GAAP, the decline in value is reported as a loss; written-down inventory cannot later be increased in value. Under IFRS, written-down inventory is reported as a loss, but written-down inventory can later be increased in value up to its original cost; the increase is reported as a gain.[3]

Historical cost subject to impairment

Under historical cost subject to impairment, fixed assets, identifiable intangible assets, and goodwill are periodically revalued. If an asset's value becomes impaired, the asset is written down and the decline in value is reported as a loss. Under U.S. GAAP, when an asset is impaired, the asset is written down to its new (lower) value and the firm debits an impairment expense account. As with inventory, when an asset's value has been reduced for impairment, it cannot be later written up in value.

Under IFRS, as under U.S. GAAP, when an asset is impaired, the asset is written down to its new (lower) value and the firm debits an impairment expense account. If goodwill has been written down for impairment, it cannot be later written up in value. For all other items that have been reduced in value because of impairment, under IFRS the items can later be increased in value up to their original cost and the increase in value is shown as a reversal of (reduction to) impairment expense.

Fair value

Many financial assets and financial liabilities are reported at fair value, a measure of current market price. U.S. GAAP and IFRS differ in how they define fair value; they also differ in which assets and liabilities must or may be reported at fair value.

- IFRS: Fair value is the amount for which an asset could be exchanged, or a liability settled, between knowledgeable, willing parties in an arm's length transaction.[4]

---

3. IAS 36, *Impairment of Assets,* par. 110–116, IASB, January 17, 2008.

4. IAS 32, *Financial Instruments: Presentation,* par. 11, Revised December 2003.

- U.S. GAAP: Fair value is the price that would be received to sell an asset or paid to transfer a liability in an orderly transaction between market participants at the measurement date.[5]

Although the above fair value definitions seem similar, in practice they can be significantly different. The U.S. GAAP definition is an exit price. It is what an asset is worth to an unidentified market participant. As a result, an asset included in a business acquisition that is worthless to the acquirer, such as a trademark for a brand of chewing gum the acquirer has no intention of producing or selling, may be highly valuable to a competitor. The acquirer must value the asset at what a hypothetical competitor would pay. Alternatively, an asset acquired in a business acquisition that is highly valuable to the acquirer, but worthless to anyone else, would have a fair value of zero.

In contrast, the IFRS definition is more flexible. It is usually interpreted to mean an entry price, or what it is worth to the firm that acquires the asset. However, the definition is flexible enough that fair value can also be defined as a recent market transaction price.

Both U.S. GAAP and IFRS require that most financial assets be reported at fair value. U.S. GAAP gives firms an option to use fair value for its own liabilities, such as accounts and notes payable and long-term debt; IFRS does not.[6] IFRS gives firms the option to report investment property (i.e., rental property or property held for investment) at fair value; U.S. GAAP does not.[7]

Revaluation

Revaluation is currently used only under IFRS. It provides firms with an option to value property, plant, and equipment at fair value less accumulated depreciation. If an asset decreases in value, the decline is reported as a loss. If the asset subsequently increases in value, the increase, up to the asset's original cost (less accumulated depreciation), is reported as a gain.[8] If that asset increases in value beyond its original cost (less accumulated depreciation), the asset is reported on the firm's balance sheet at its fair value (less accumulated depreciation), but the increase in value beyond original cost (less accumulated depreciation) is reported as a gain in the other comprehensive income section of owners' equity, not on a firm's income statement.

If a revaluation asset has only increased in value, the gain is reported in the other comprehensive income section of owners' equity, not as a gain on the firm's income statement. Revaluation differs from historical cost, subject to impairment, in that under revaluation, assets can be reported on a firm's balance sheet at an amount that exceeds historical cost, less accumulated depreciation. Unlike fair value, with revaluation reported amounts in excess of cost less accumulated depreciation are reported in the other comprehensive income section of owners' equity, not on a firm's income statement.

---

5. ACS 820 (formerly SFAS 157, *Fair Value*, par. 5, Financial Accounting Standards Board, September 2006).

6. ACS 825 (formerly SFAS 159, *The Fair Value Option for Financial Assets and Financial Liabilities,* FASB, February 2007).

7. IAS 40, *Investment Property*, IASB, January 17, 2008.

8. IAS 16, *Property, Plant, and Equipment*, par. 31, 39, and 40, IASB, January 17, 2008.

Asset Impairment Rules

As the worldwide recession worsened in the last half of 2008, many companies reported substantial impairments to their asset values. Although it is relatively simple to compute asset impairment, the rules are detailed, slightly different for U.S. GAAP and IFRS, and slightly different depending on the type of asset. The calculations are also subjective. ACS 360, formerly SFAS 144, *Accounting for the Impairment or Disposal of Long-lived Assets*, and ACS 350, formerly SFAS 142, *Goodwill and Other Intangible Assets*, are the primary U.S. GAAP asset impairment statements; IAS 36, *Impairment of Assets*, is the primary IFRS impairment statement.

Asset Classes

Asset classes for impairment testing are (1) tangible assets, such as buildings, machinery, and equipment; (2) intangible assets with finite lives, such as patents, copyrights, and customer lists; (3) intangible assets with indefinite useful lives, such as trademarks and newspaper mastheads; and (4) goodwill acquired in an acquisition. Although goodwill is an intangible asset, under both IFRS and U.S. GAAP rules for goodwill are different from those for other intangible assets.

Under both IFRS and U.S. GAAP, the impairment of some assets, such as inventory and financial assets and liabilities, are governed by other rules.

Frequency of Impairment Testing

Under both IFRS and U.S. GAAP, all assets subject to impairment tests must be tested whenever there is an indication an asset may be impaired. Examples of an indication of impairment would include significant revenue declines or operating losses. In addition, goodwill and intangible assets with an indefinite life must be tested for impairment at least annually, regardless of whether there is an indication of impairment.

Impairment tests

IFRS

IAS 36, *Impairment of Assets*, contains all IFRS impairment rules.

Tangible asset; identifiable intangible assets

Under IFRS, an asset is impaired if its carrying amount (book value) is greater than its recoverable amount, where recoverable amount equals the greater of an asset's (1) fair value less cost to sell or (2) value in use, which is generally the present value of the asset's future cash flows. The loss on the impairment is reported as a loss on a firm's income statement. Except for goodwill, if at a later date the firm determines the impairment no longer exists, the asset should be increased in value, up to its original cost, less accumulated depreciation. That is, under IFRS, the impairment is reversed (except for goodwill).

Goodwill

Under IFRS, each cash-generating unit with recorded goodwill (e.g., division or subsidiary) must be tested for impairment at least annually and whenever an impairment indication exists. As with other assets tested for impairment, if the carrying amount exceeds that cash-generating unit's recoverable amount, then the cash-generating unit is impaired. The recoverable amount is defined as the greater of the cash-generating unit's fair value less cost to sell or value in use.

Whenever the cash-generating unit's carrying value is greater than its recoverable amount, the firm must record an impairment expense. A cash-generating unit with goodwill would almost certainly include tangible assets, would likely also include intangible assets with finite lives, and might include intangible assets with indefinite useful lives. Suppose a cash-generating unit had a recoverable value of $2 million and, for example, $1 million of tangible assets, $1 million of intangible assets with finite lives, and $1 million of goodwill. Conceivably, that firm could decide that the fair value of its tangible assets and its intangible assets with finite lives had each declined in value by $500,000, so there was no goodwill impairment. However, IFRS (and U.S. GAAP) require that an impairment loss first be used to reduce goodwill down to zero before the firm can record an impairment loss for other assets. An impairment charge against goodwill cannot be reversed.

U.S. GAAP

ACS 350 (formerly SFAS 142, *Goodwill and Other Intangible Assets*) provides impairment rules for goodwill and for intangible assets that are not subject to amortization (i.e., intangible assets with indefinite useful lives). ACS 360 (formerly SFAS 144, *Accounting for the Impairment or Disposal of Long-Lived Assets*) provides impairment rules for tangible assets and for intangible assets with finite lives.

Intangible assets with indefinite useful lives (not subject to amortization)

If an intangible asset that is not subject to amortization has a carrying value that exceeds its fair value, the asset is impaired. This is similar to the IFRS test, but carrying value is compared to fair value, not to the greater of fair value less cost to sell, or value in use. Impairment charges cannot be reversed under U.S. GAAP.

Tangible assets and intangible assets with finite useful lives

The carrying value of these assets is first subject to a recoverability test. If the carrying value is not recoverable, then the carrying value is compared with fair value. Under the recoverability test, an asset's estimated undiscounted future cash flows are first compared with the asset's carrying amount. If the sum of undiscounted future cash flows exceeds the asset's carrying amount, the asset is not impaired under U.S. GAAP. If the undiscounted cash flows are less than the carrying amount, then the asset is impaired and a second test is used to compute the impairment.

If the asset is impaired, then the impairment equals the carrying amount minus the discounted present value of future cash flows (not the undiscounted future cash flows). The impairment expense cannot be reversed.

Goodwill

One difference between the U.S. GAAP test and the IFRS test is that under U.S. GAAP the test is applied to an operating segment or to one level below an operating segment rather than to a cash-generating unit (as under IFRS). That difference would usually be minor. A second difference is that, under U.S. GAAP, the carrying amount of an operating segment is compared to that segment's fair value, not to the greater of its fair value less cost to sell, or value in use.

Under both U.S. GAAP and IFRS, if the operating segment or cash-generating unit is impaired, the impairment amount is first used to reduce goodwill. If the impairment charge is large enough to reduce goodwill to zero, the remainder of the impairment is used to reduce the value of identifiable tangible and intangible assets in that operating segment or cash-generating unit.

Disclosures

Under IFRS, if a firm uses discounted cash flow analysis to value a cash-generating unit, the firm must disclose the discount rate. If the cash-generating unit includes goodwill or other indefinite-lived intangible assets (such as trademarks), then the firm must also disclose other assumptions made to value that cash-generating unit (such as projected revenue growth rates and projected profit margins). Firms are encouraged but not required to disclose those assumptions even if a cash-generating unit does not include goodwill or identifiable intangible assets with indefinite lives.

Impairment in the Recession of 2008–2009

As the recession of 2008–2009 worsened, firms throughout the world recorded impairment charges or explained why impairment charges were not. The following firms included impairment disclosures in 2008 or 2009 shareholders reports that were interesting because of the size of the impairment, the lack of impairment, or the disclosure itself:

Nestlé (Exhibit 1—IFRS)

Nestlé is one of the world's largest consumer products companies. During the past several years, Nestlé acquired Powwow, a large European water distributor; Ralston-Purina, a large U.S.-based pet food and animal feed producer; Gerber, a U.S.-based baby food manufacturer; and Dryer's, a U.S.-based ice cream producer. Exhibit 1 includes Nestlé's impairment test disclosures for those major acquisitions.

The Swatch Group (Exhibit 2—IFRS)

The Swatch group is one of the world's largest watch manufacturers. Exhibit 2 shows its 2008 impairment test disclosures.

Royal Bank of Scotland (Exhibit 3—IFRS)

The Royal Bank of Scotland (RBS) is one of the world's largest banks. In recent years, RBS recorded significant goodwill when it acquired NatWest, Charter One, ABN Amro and Churchill. Because of the worldwide banking crises, RBS recorded substantial goodwill impairment charges, as disclosed in Exhibit 3.

News Corp. (Exhibit 4—U.S. GAAP)

News Corp., headed by Rupert Murdoch, acquired *The Wall Street Journal* in 2007. Internet advertising drove many newspapers into bankruptcy and others into near bankruptcy. Many analysts and investors thought *The Wall Street Journal's* unique market niche and relatively wealthy readers would isolate the journal from Internet competition. However, in 2008 the News Corp. recorded significant impairment charges, primarily for the WSJ acquisition. Those impairment charges are disclosed in Exhibit 4.

CBS Corporation (Exhibit 5—U.S. GAAP)

The worldwide recession and the Internet hurt most media companies, including CBS Corporation. Exhibit 5 provides CBS's 2008 impairment disclosure.

Required

1. Evaluate the five general valuation rules discussed at the beginning of the case. Is it useful to have those different valuation methods? Explain.

2. Why are the impairment rules for goodwill different than for other assets? Explain.

3. Evaluate the recoverability test used in U.S. GAAP.

4. Are the differences between IFRS and U.S. GAAP significant? Explain.

5. Compare the three IFRS disclosures in Exhibits 1, 2, and 3. How subjective are the impairment calculations? Which assumptions needed to compute impairment are the most subjective? Which are least subjective? Explain.

6. Compare the two U.S. GAAP disclosures, using the same criteria as in question 5.

7. Which of the five disclosures is most informative? Which is least informative? Why?

8. Which disclosures are most informative, the IFRS disclosures, the U.S. GAAP disclosures, or are the differences more company specific? Explain.

EXHIBIT 1

NESTLÉ IMPAIRMENT
NOTE, 2008
ANNUAL REPORT

14.1 Impairment charge during the period

Nestlé Waters Home and Office Delivery business in Europe

Goodwill related to the 2003 acquisition of Powwow has been allocated for the impairment test to the Cash Generating Unit (CGU) defined as the Nestlé Waters Home and Office Delivery (HOD) business in Europe. As at 31 December 2008, the carrying amounts of all goodwill items allocated to this CGU and expressed in various European currencies represent an equivalent of CHF 836 million before 2008 impairment (2007: CHF 1119 million).

According to IFRS requirements an annual impairment test was conducted in the second half of the year. Following further deterioration of the business in various countries since the last impairment test and the foreseen disposal of the Italian and UK HOD operations, the present value of future cash flows was revised downwards.

As the recoverable amount of the CGU was lower than its carrying amount, an impairment of goodwill amounting to CHF 442 million has been recognised in 2008 (2007: CHF 210 million).

The recoverable amount of the CGU has been determined based upon a value-in-use calculation. Deflated cash flow projections covering the next 50 years, discounted at a weighted average rate of 6.2%, were used in this calculation. The cash flows for the first five years were based upon financial plans approved by Group Management; years six to ten were based upon Group Management's best expectations. Cash flows were assumed to be flat for years eleven to 50. Cash flows have been adjusted to reflect the specific business risks.

Main assumptions, based on past experiences and current initiatives, were the following:

- Sales: annual growth between 1.5 and 8.3% for the first three years and between 2.2 and 2.3% in the six years afterwards.
- EBIT margin evolution: consistent with sales growth and enhanced cost management and efficiency, with a higher growth during the first three years and then steadily improving ten basis points per year over the following years.

14.2 Yearly impairment tests

Goodwill impairment reviews have been conducted for more than 200 goodwill items allocated to some 50 Cash Generating Units (CGUs). There are no significant carrying values of goodwill that are allocated across multiple CGUs.

Detailed results of the impairment tests are presented below for the three significant goodwill items, representing more than 50% of the net book value at 31 December 2008. For the purpose of the tests, they have been allocated to the following CGUs: PetCare, Infant Nutrition and Ice Cream USA.

PetCare

Goodwill related to the 2001 acquisition of Ralston Purina has been allocated for the impairment test to the CGU of the product category PetCare on a worldwide basis. As at 31 December 2008, the carrying amounts, expressed in various currencies, represent an equivalent of CHF 9888 million (2007: CHF 10 618 million) for the goodwill and CHF 29 million (2007: CHF 29 million) for the intangible assets with indefinite useful life.

The recoverable amount of the CGU is higher than its carrying amount. The recoverable amount has been determined based upon a value-in-use calculation. Deflated cash flow projections covering the next 50 years, discounted at a weighted average rate of 6.7%, were used in this calculation. The cash flows for the first five years were based upon financial plans approved by Group Management; years six to ten were based upon Group Management's best expectations,

(continued)

EXHIBIT 1—
continued

NESTLÉ IMPAIRMENT
NOTE, 2008
ANNUAL REPORT

which are consistent with the Group's approved strategy for this period. Cash flows were assumed to be flat for years eleven to 50, although Group Management expects continuing growth. Cash flows have been adjusted to reflect the specific business risks.

Main assumptions, based on past experiences and current initiatives, were the following:

- Sales: annual growth between 3.9 and 7.9% for North America and between 3 and 4.5% for Europe over the first ten-year period.
- EBIT margin evolution: steadily improving margin over the period, in a range of 10–30 basis points per year for North America and 10–60 basis points per year for Europe, consistent with sales growth and portfolio rationalisation.

Assumptions used in the calculation are consistent with the expected long-term average growth rate of the PetCare business in the regions concerned.

The key sensitivity for the impairment test is the growth in sales and EBIT margin. Assuming no sales growth and no improvement in EBIT margin over the entire period would not result in the carrying amount exceeding the recoverable amount.

An increase of 100 basis points in the discount rate assumption would not change the conclusions of the impairment test.

Infant Nutrition

Goodwill and intangible assets with indefinite useful life related to the 2007 acquisition of Gerber have been allocated for the impairment test to the CGU of the Infant Nutrition businesses on a worldwide basis. As at 31 December 2008, the carrying amounts, expressed in various currencies, represent an equivalent of CHF 3963 million (2007: CHF 4227 million) for the goodwill and CHF 1405 million (2007: CHF 1497 million) for the intangible assets with indefinite useful life.

The recoverable amount of the CGU is higher than its carrying amount. The recoverable amount has been determined based upon a value-in-use calculation. Deflated cash flow projections covering the next 50 years, discounted at a weighted average rate of 8%, were used in this calculation. The cash flows for the first five years were based upon financial plans approved by Group Management; years six to ten were based upon Group Management's best expectations, which are consistent with the Group's approved strategy for this period. Cash flows were assumed to be flat after, although Group Management expects continuing growth. Cash flows have been adjusted to reflect the specific business risks.

Main assumptions were the following:

- Sales: annual growth between 2 and 5% for North America and between 5.2 and 5.7% for the rest of the world over the first five-year period.
- EBIT margin evolution: steadily improving margin over the period, in a range of 10–50 basis points per year for North America and in a range of 60–90 basis points per year for the rest of the world.

The key sensitivity for the impairment test is the growth in sales and EBIT margin. Assuming no sales growth and no improvement in EBIT margin over the entire period would not result in the carrying amount exceeding the recoverable amount.

An increase of 100 basis points in the discount rate assumption would not change the conclusions of the impairment test.

Ice Cream USA

Goodwill and intangible assets with indefinite useful life related to the Group's Ice cream businesses in the USA (Nestlé Ice Cream Company and Dreyer's) has been allocated for the

(continued)

EXHIBIT 1—
continued

NESTLE IMPAIRMENT
NOTE, 2008
ANNUAL REPORT

impairment test to the Ice Cream USA CGU. As at 31 December 2008, the carrying amounts, expressed in USD, represent an equivalent of CHF 3096 million (2007: CHF 3301 million) for the goodwill and CHF 76 million (2007: CHF 81 million) for the intangible assets with indefinite useful life.

The recoverable amount of the CGU is higher than its carrying amount. The recoverable amount has been determined based upon a value-in-use calculation. Deflated cash flow projections covering the next 50 years, discounted at 6.4%, were used in this calculation. The cash flows for the first five years were based upon financial plans approved by Group Management; years six to ten were based upon Group Management's best expectations, which are consistent with the Group's approved strategy for this period. Cash flows were assumed to be flat for years eleven to 50, although Group Management expects continuing growth. Cash flows have been adjusted to reflect the specific business risks.

Main assumptions, based on past experiences and current initiatives, were the following:

– Sales: annual growth between 2 and 5% over the first ten-year period.

– EBIT margin evolution: steadily improving margin over the period, in a range of 70–270 basis points per year, which is consistent with strong sales growth and enhanced cost management and efficiency.

The key sensitivity for the impairment test is the growth in sales and EBIT margin. Limiting annual growth to only 4% until 2017 and 0% thereafter would not result in the carrying amount exceeding the recoverable amount. Reaching 80% of the expectations in terms of EBIT evolution would not result in the carrying amount exceeding the recoverable amount.

An increase of 100 basis points in the discount rate assumption would not change the conclusions of the impairment test.

EXHIBIT 2

THE SWATCH
GROUP, GOODWILL
IMPAIRMENT
TESTING

Goodwill is allocated to the Group's cash-generating units (CGUs), which correspond to the profit centers for the segment «Watches & Jewelry» and the reportable segments for the business segments «Production» and «Electronic Systems». A segment-level summary of the goodwill allocation is presented below:

(CHF million)	31.12.2008	31.12.2007
Watches & Jewelry	157	155
Production	36	32
Electronic Systems	11	45
Total	**204**	232

The recoverable amount of a cash-generating unit is determined based on value-in-use calculations. These calculations use cash flow projections based on financial budgets approved by management covering a five-year period. Cash flows beyond the five-year period are extrapolated using a steady growth rate. The discount rates used are derived from a capital asset pricing model using data from Swiss capital markets and reflect specific risks relating to the relevant segments. This is then adjusted to a pre-tax rate.

(continued)

Ranges of key assumptions used

	2008			2007		
	Watches & Jewelry	**Production**	**Electronic Systems**	**Watches & Jewelry**	**Production**	**Electronic Systems**
Estimated growth rate beyond five-year period	1%	0.50%	0%	1%	1%	0.50%
Expected gross margin	56%–64%	26%–30%	31%–35%	56%–68%	27%–32%	35%–40%
Pre-tax discount rate	9.1%	10.2%	10.5%	6.5%	7.4%	7.6%

No impairment charge for goodwill had to be recorded in 2008. Management believes that any reasonably possible change in any of the key assumptions would not cause the carrying value of goodwill to exceed the recoverable amount.

EXHIBIT 2—
continued

THE SWATCH
GROUP, GOODWILL
IMPAIRMENT
TESTING

Impairment review

The Group's goodwill acquired in business combinations is reviewed annually at 30 September for impairment by comparing the recoverable amount of each cash generating unit (CGU) to which goodwill has been allocated with its carrying value. In light of the unprecedented market conditions the review has been updated to reflect the latest position as at 31 December 2008.

The Group recognised goodwill of £23.3 billion (€33.5 billion) following the preliminary allocation of fair values since acquiring ABN AMRO on 17 October 2007. On final allocation of fair values, goodwill of £23.9 billion (€34.2 billion) was recognised (see Note 34), of which £17.6 billion (€25.3 billion) was attributable to minority interests. Of the minority interests goodwill, £5.4 billion (€5.7 billion) was in respect of Santander acquired businesses which were subsequently sold during 2008. The remaining goodwill in respect of the State of the Netherlands minority interest of £18.8 billion (€19.6 billion) was reduced in part by £2.7 billion (€2.9 billion) following the sale of the Asset Management business with £14.6 billion (€15.2 billion) of the remainder subsequently impaired following the acquisition by the State of the Netherlands for £6.2 billion (€6.5 billion). In addition, a further £1.1 billion (€1.2 billion) impairment was recognised on other intangible assets attributable to the State of the Netherlands acquired businesses.

On the finalisation of the allocation of fair values, goodwill arising on the acquisition of ABN AMRO attributable to the Group has been allocated to those CGUs which are expected to benefit from the synergies of the combination based on their relative values. In addition, following the reorganisation of the Group reporting structure, NatWest and Citizens goodwill was reallocated to the appropriate CGUs.

EXHIBIT 3

ROYAL BANK OF
SCOTLAND, 2008
ANNUAL REPORT

(continued)

EXHIBIT 3—
continued

ROYAL BANK OF
SCOTLAND, 2008
ANNUAL REPORT

The CGUs where the goodwill arising is significant, principally on the acquisitions of NatWest, Charter One, ABN AMRO and Churchill, are as follows:

2008	Recoverable amount based on:	Goodwill prior to write down £m	Write down £m	Goodwill at 31 December £m
Global Banking & Markets	Value in use	8,946	(8,946)	—
Global Transaction Services	Value in use	3,121	—	3,121
UK Retail & Commercial Banking	Value in use	6,009	—	6,009
US Retail & Commercial Banking	Value in use	7,405	(4,382)	3,023
Europe & Middle East Retail & Commercial Banking	Value in use	1,201	(1,201)	—
Asia Retail & Commercial Banking	Value in use	970	(863)	107
RBS Insurance	Value in use	935	—	935

2007	Recoverable amount based on:	Goodwill at 30 September £m
RBS Insurance	Fair value less costs to sell	1,064
Global Banking & Markets	Fair value less costs to sell	2,346
UK Corporate Banking	Fair value less costs to sell	1,630
Retail	Fair value less costs to sell	4,278
Wealth Management	Fair value less costs to sell	1,100
Citizens – Retail Banking	Value in use	2,067
Citizens – Commercial Banking	Value in use	2,274
Citizens – Consumer Financial Services	Value in use	1,701

17 Intangible assets

In 2007, the recoverable amounts for all CGUs, except Citizens, were based on fair value less costs to sell. Fair value was based upon a price-earnings methodology using current earnings for each unit. Approximate price earnings multiples, validated against independent analyst information, were applied to each CGU. The multiples used were in the range 9.5–13.0 times earnings after charging manufacturing costs. The goodwill allocated to Global Banking & Markets, UK Corporate Banking, Retail and Wealth Management principally arose from the acquisition of NatWest in 2000. The recoverable amount of these cash generating units exceeded their carrying value by over £15 billion. The recoverable amount for RBS Insurance exceeded its carrying value by over £1.5 billion. The multiples or earnings would have to be less than one third of those used to cause the value in use of the units to equal their carrying value.

In light of the unprecedented market turmoil, fair value was increasingly hard to appraise and consequently the Group has generally adopted value in use tests for CGUs in 2008, based upon management's latest five year forecasts. The long-term growth rates have been based on respective country GDP rates adjusted for inflation. The risk discount rates are based on observable market long-term government bond yields and average industry betas adjusted for an appropriate risk premium based on independent analysis.

Goodwill in respect of Global Banking & Markets principally arose from the acquisition of ABN AMRO in October 2007. The failure of a number of banks and severe weakness in the global economy during the second half of 2008 resulted in a fundamental reappraisal of business forecasts, leading to the conclusion that the Global Banking & Markets business at 31 December 2008 could support no goodwill allocated from the ABN AMRO or NatWest

(continued)

EXHIBIT 3—
continued

ROYAL BANK OF
SCOTLAND, 2008
ANNUAL REPORT

acquisitions. In addition, impairments were recognised in respect of intangible assets and certain property, plant and equipment: the customer relationship intangible was impaired by £0.9 billion and capitalised software was impaired by £0.4 billion. The value in use was based on a 3% terminal growth rate and pre-tax discount rate of 19.5%. The result was insensitive to reasonably possible changes in key assumptions.

The recoverable amount of the Global Transaction Services business based on a 3% terminal growth rate and 15.7% pre tax risk discount rate exceeded its carrying value by more than 100% and was insensitive to a reasonably possible change in key assumptions. The goodwill arises principally from the global payments business acquired through the ABN AMRO acquisition along with cash management and corporate money transmission businesses previously in Citizens and Regional businesses.

UK Retail and Commercial Banking was formed at the beginning of 2008 when the Group brought together the businesses that use its UK branch network. It primarily comprised the UK Retail and Corporate banks but excluded their transaction services business. The recoverable amount was equal to the carrying amount including goodwill arising from the NatWest acquisition. This is based on a 4% terminal growth rate and 15.9% pre-tax risk discount rate. A 1% change in discount rate or the terminal growth rate would change the recoverable amount by over £2 billion and £1 billion respectively. In addition, a 5% change in forecast pre-tax earnings would change the recoverable amount by approximately £1 billion.

The goodwill in Europe & Middle East Retail and Commercial Banking arose from the Group's interests in Ulster Bank Group principally arising out of the acquisitions of NatWest and First Active. The Irish economy stalled in 2008, with the Government providing rescue packages to local banks, and forecasts within the eurozone economies have reduced accordingly. The impairment review, based on a 3% terminal growth rate and 14.1% pre-tax risk discount rate, showed all goodwill associated with the business was impaired. The result was insensitive to reasonably possible changes in key assumptions.

The Asia Retail and Commercial Banking business comprises much of the Group's Wealth management business and retail operations in Asia. The outlook in the Asian economies has deteriorated and falling investment values have reduced the yield from managed portfolios. The allocated goodwill principally arising on the acquisition of ABN AMRO was impaired by £862 million based on a 5% terminal growth rate and 14% pre-tax risk discount rate. A 1% change in the discount rate or similar change in the terminal growth rate would change the recoverable amount by approximately £200 million and £100 million respectively. In addition, a 5% change in forecast pre-tax earnings would change the recoverable amount by approximately £50 million.

Further developments in the Group's US businesses have led to the separation of the transaction services business, with the retail and commercial business being managed as a single unit. The 2007 impairment review indicated the recoverable amount of Citizens exceeded its carrying value by over £2.5 billion ($5 billion) using a terminal growth rate of 5% and a pre tax discount rate of 16.5%. In 2008, rates of 5% and 18% were used respectively and the recoverable amount indicated an impairment of £4.4 billion ($6.4 billion). A 1% change in discount rate or the terminal growth rate would change the recoverable amount and hence goodwill impairment by over £1 billion ($2 billion) and £0.7 billion ($1 billion) respectively. In addition, a 5% change in forecast pre-tax earnings would change the recoverable amount by approximately £0.5 billion ($0.8 billion).

The goodwill allocated to RBS Insurance principally arose from the acquisition of Churchill in 2003. The recoverable amount based on a 3% terminal growth rate and 14.6% pre tax risk discount rate exceeded the carrying amount by over £3 billion, and was insensitive to reasonably possible changes in key assumptions.

EXHIBIT 4

NEWS CORPORATION

Note 8—Goodwill, Intangible Assets and Other Long-lived Assets, Q3 10-Q Dated March 31, 2009

In accordance with SFAS No. 142, the Company's goodwill and indefinite-lived intangible assets, which primarily consist of Federal Communications Commission ("FCC") licenses, are reviewed annually for impairment or earlier if events occur or circumstances change that would more likely than not reduce the fair value of the Company's goodwill and indefinite-lived intangible assets below their carrying amount. During the second quarter of fiscal 2009, the Company performed an interim impairment review because the Company believed events had occurred and circumstances had changed that would more likely than not reduce the fair value of the Company's goodwill and indefinite-lived intangible assets below their carrying amounts. These events included: (a) the continued decline of the price of the Class A Common Stock and Class B Common Stock; (b) the reduced growth in advertising revenues; (c) the decline in the operating profit margins in some of the Company's advertising-based businesses; and (d) the decline in the valuations of other television stations, newspapers and advertising-based companies as determined by the current trading values of those companies.

The Company's goodwill impairment review is determined using a two-step process. The first step of the process is to compare the fair value of a reporting unit with its carrying amount, including goodwill. In performing the first step, the Company determines the fair value of a reporting unit by primarily using a discounted cash flow analysis and market-based valuation approach methodologies. Determining fair value requires the exercise of significant judgments, including judgments about appropriate discount rates, perpetual growth rates, relevant comparable company earnings multiples and the amount and timing of expected future cash flows. The cash flows employed in the analyses are based on the Company's estimated outlook and various growth rates have been assumed for years beyond the long-term business plan period. Discount rate assumptions are based on an assessment of the risk inherent in the future cash flows of the respective reporting units. In assessing the reasonableness of its determined fair values, the Company evaluates its results against other value indicators, such as comparable public company trading values. If the fair value of a reporting unit exceeds its carrying amount, goodwill of the reporting unit is not impaired and the second step of the impairment review is not necessary. If the carrying amount of a reporting unit exceeds its fair value, the second step of the goodwill impairment review is required to be performed to measure the amount of impairment loss, if any. The second step of the goodwill impairment review compares the implied fair value of the reporting unit's goodwill with the carrying amount of that goodwill. The implied fair value of goodwill is determined in the same manner as the amount of goodwill recognized in a business combination. That is, the estimated fair value of the reporting unit is allocated to all of the assets and liabilities of that unit (including any unrecognized intangible assets) as if the reporting unit had been acquired in a business combination and the estimated fair value of the reporting unit was the purchase price paid. If the carrying amount of the reporting unit's goodwill exceeds the implied fair value of that goodwill, an impairment loss is recognized in an amount equal to that excess.

The Company performed an impairment review consisting of a comparison of the estimated fair value of the Company's FCC licenses with their carrying amount on a station-by-station basis using a discounted cash flow valuation method, assuming a hypothetical start-up scenario for a broadcast station in each of the markets the Company operates in. The significant assumptions used were the discount rate and terminal growth rates and operating margins, as well as industry data on future advertising revenues in the markets where the Company owns television stations. These assumptions are based on actual historical performance in each market and estimates of future performance in each market. These assumptions take into account the weakening of advertising markets that have affected both the national and local markets in which the Company's stations operate.

(continued)

EXHIBIT 4—
continued

News Corporation

The assumptions noted above take into account the weakening of the economies in the markets where the Company's businesses operate, which the Company expects will continue through at least the remainder of 2009. The assumptions have been adjusted since the Company's annual impairment review conducted in fiscal 2008 to reflect the weakened global economies and, in particular, the advertising markets. Accordingly, the market growth rates and operating profit margin assumptions were lowered to reflect the current general economic trends in the markets where the Company's businesses operate. The potential increase in the goodwill impairment charge resulting from a 10% adverse change in the estimated value of the impaired reporting units would be approximately $900 million. The potential increase in the FCC licenses impairment charge resulting from a 10% adverse change in the assumptions above would be approximately $480 million.

As a result of this impairment review, the Company recorded a non-cash impairment charge of approximately $8.4 billion in the nine months ended March 31, 2009. The charge consisted of a write-down of the Company's indefinite-lived intangibles (primarily FCC licenses) of $4.6 billion, a write-down of $3.6 billion of goodwill and a write-down of Newspapers and Information Services fixed assets of $185 million in accordance with SFAS No. 144, "Accounting for the Impairment or Disposal of Long-Lived Assets." As a result of the continued adverse economic conditions in the markets in which the Company conducts business, the Company will continue to monitor its goodwill, indefinite-lived intangible assets and long-lived assets for possible future impairment.

Intangible assets, net decreased $5.6 billion during the nine months ended March 31, 2009, primarily due to non-cash impairment charges of $4.6 billion related to FCC licenses and newspaper mastheads at the Company's Television and Newspapers and Information Services segments of $4.2 billion and $400 million, respectively. In addition, FCC licenses at the Television segment decreased an additional $430 million due to the sale of the Stations in July 2008. Also contributing to the decreases were unfavorable foreign currency translation adjustments of $378 million.

Goodwill balances decreased $4.1 billion during the nine months ended March 31, 2009. This decrease was primarily due to non-cash impairment charges taken during the nine months ended March 31, 2009 of $3.6 billion. The impairments at the Television and Newspapers and Information Services segments were due to a decline in the advertising-based businesses and lower projected growth. The Other segment impairment was due to higher valuations assigned to recent acquisitions, principally IGN, Photobucket and Jamba, that can no longer be sustained due to the decline in advertising-based businesses and the expected decline in future revenues. Also contributing to this decrease was foreign currency translation adjustments of $600 million and a reduction of $217 million at the Television segment due to the sale of the Stations in July 2008. The finalization of purchase price allocations and new acquisitions offset the decrease in goodwill by $339 million, primarily due to the formation of the Star Jupiter venture in January 2009.

EXHIBIT 5

CBS Corporation
Q3 2008 10-Q

GOODWILL AND INTANGIBLE ASSETS

SFAS No. 142 "Goodwill and Other Intangible Assets" ("SFAS 142") requires the Company to perform a fair value-based impairment test of goodwill and other intangible assets with indefinite lives annually and also between annual tests if an event occurs or if circumstances change that would more likely than not reduce the fair value of a reporting unit below its book value. During the third quarter of 2008, the Company performed an interim impairment test as a result of its assessment of factors such as the continuation of adverse market conditions, which affected the Company's market value and trading multiples for entities within the Company's industry, as well as the continued economic slowdown which has adversely affected the Company's advertising revenues, primarily at the Company's local businesses. The first step of the goodwill impairment test examines whether the book value of each of the Company's reporting units exceeds its fair value. If the book value of a reporting unit exceeds its fair value, the second step of the test requires the Company to then compare the implied fair value of that reporting unit's goodwill with the book value of its goodwill. The Company's reporting units are generally one level below or at the operating segment level.

The estimated fair value of each reporting unit was computed principally based upon the present value of future cash flows (Discounted Cash Flow Method) and both the traded and transaction values of comparable businesses (Market Comparable Method). The Discounted Cash Flow Method and Market Comparable Method resulted in substantially equal fair values.

For the impairment test of intangible assets with indefinite lives, the fair value of the intangible asset is compared with its book value. The estimated fair value of intangible assets was computed using the Discounted Cash Flow Method.

As a result of this impairment test, the Company recorded a non-cash impairment charge of $14.12 billion in the third quarter of 2008 to reduce the carrying value of goodwill by $10.99 billion and intangible assets by $3.13 billion. The charge was reflected as a reduction to goodwill at the Television segment of $5.81 billion, the Radio segment of $2.33 billion and the Outdoor segment of $2.85 billion, as well as a reduction to the carrying value of intangible assets related to FCC licenses at the Television segment of $2.13 billion and the Radio segment of $984.6 million, and franchise agreements at the Outdoor segment of $8.2 million.

Vivendi Group's Goodwill Impairment Test

Exhibit 1 is Vivendi Group's goodwill impairment note from its 2009 annual report. The following is an overview of IFRS Impairment rules from IAS 36, *Impairment of Assets*.

Tangible Asset; Identifiable Intangible Assets

Under IFRS, an asset is impaired if its carrying amount (book value) is greater than its recoverable amount, where recoverable amount equals the greater of an asset's (1) fair value less cost to sell or (2) value in use, which is generally the present value of the asset's future cash flows. The loss on the impairment is reported as a loss in a firm's income statement. Except for goodwill, if at a later date the firm determines the impairment no longer exists, the asset should be increased in value, up to its original cost, less accumulated depreciation. That is, under IFRS, the impairment is reversed (except for goodwill).

Goodwill

Under IFRS, each cash-generating unit with recorded goodwill (e.g., division or subsidiary) must be tested for impairment at least annually and whenever an impairment indication exists. As with other assets tested for impairment, if the carrying amount exceeds that cash-generating unit's recoverable amount, then the cash-generating unit is impaired. The recoverable amount is defined as the greater of the cash-generating unit's fair value less cost to sell or value in use.

Whenever the cash-generating unit's carrying value is greater than the recoverable amount, the firm must record an impairment expense. A cash-generating unit with goodwill would almost certainly include tangible assets, would likely also include intangible assets with finite lives, and might include intangible assets with indefinite useful lives. Suppose a cash-generating unit had a recoverable value of $2 million and, for example, $1 million of tangible assets, $1 million of intangible assets with finite lives, and $1 million of goodwill. Conceivably, that firm could decide that the fair value of its tangible assets and its intangible assets with finite lives had each declined in value by $500,000, so there was no goodwill impairment. However, IFRS (and U.S. GAAP) require that a cash-generating unit's impairment loss first be used to reduce goodwill down to zero before the firm can record an impairment loss for other assets. An impairment charge against goodwill cannot be reversed.

Required

1. Evaluate Vivendi's goodwill impairment note in Exhibit 1. Is it clear? Is it comprehensive?

2. Could Vivendi have reported a goodwill impairment charge for 2009? Explain.

EXHIBIT 1

VIVENDI GROUP'S
GOODWILL
IMPAIRMENT TEST,
2009 ANNUAL
REPORT

Goodwill impairment test

During the fourth quarter of 2009, Vivendi tested the value of goodwill allocated to its cash-generating units (CGU) or groups of CGU applying the same valuation methods used every year. Vivendi ensures that the recoverable amount of CGU or groups of CGU exceed their carrying value (including goodwill). The recoverable amount is determined as the higher of the value in use determined by the discounted value of future cash flows (discounted cash flow method (DCF)) and the fair value (less costs to sell), determined based on market data (stock market prices, comparison with similar listed companies, comparison with the value attributed to similar assets or companies in recent transactions).

The test was performed by Vivendi on the basis of an internal valuation of the recoverable amounts, except in the case of Activision Blizzard (AB) and Universal Music Group (UMG) for which Vivendi required the assistance of independent experts.

Regarding UMG, the recoverable amount was determined using usual valuation methods (DCF and stock market multiples) using financial assumptions consistent with previous years, which are as follows regarding the DCF method: discount rate of 8.50% (compared to 9.30% as of December 31, 2008) and perpetual growth rate of 1.00% (unchanged compared to December 31, 2008) – please refer to the table below. Vivendi's management concluded that the carrying value exceeded the recoverable amount of UMG and consequently recognized an impairment loss of €616 million as of December 31, 2009.

Regarding the remaining cash-generating units (CGU) or groups of CGU, Vivendi's management concluded that the recoverable amount exceeded their carrying value. In addition, as of December 31, 2009, GVT goodwill had not been tested given the recent purchase price allocation date (please refer to note 2.1) and the closing date, together with the fact that no triggering event had occurred that would indicate a decrease in value between those dates.

A description of the methods used to test for impairment is presented in Note 1.3.5.7.

CGU or groups of CGU tested are as follows:

Operating Segments	Cash Generating Units (CGU)	CGU or Groups of CGU
Activision Blizzard	Activision	Activision
	Blizzard	Blizzard
	Distribution	Distribution
Universal Music Group	Recorded music	Universal Music Group
	Artist services and merchandising	
	Music publishing	
SFR	Mobile	Mobile
	Broadband Internet and fixed	Broadband Internet and fixed
Maroc Telecom Group	Mobile	Maroc Telecom
	Fixed and Internet	
	Other entities	Other entities
Canal+ Group	French Pay-TV	Canal+ France
	Canal Overseas	
	StudioCanal	StudioCanal
	Other entities	na*

na*: not applicable.

(continued)

EXHIBIT 1—
continued

Vivendi Group's
Goodwill
Impairment Test,
2009 Annual
Report

Key assumptions used for the determination of recoverable amounts

The value in use of each asset or group of assets is determined as the discounted value of future cash flows (discounted cash flow method (DCF)) by using cash flow projections consistent with the 2010 budget and the most recent forecasts prepared by the operating segments. These forecasts are established for each operating segment on the basis of the financial targets as well as the following main key assumptions: the discount rate, the perpetual growth rate, EBITA as defined in Note 1.2.3, capital expenditures, competitive environment, regulatory environment, technological development and level of commercial expenses.

The main assumptions used are presented in the following table.

Operating Segments	CGU or Groups of CGU	Valuation Method		Discount Rate		Perpetual Growth Rate	
		2009	2008	2009	2008	2009	2008
Activision Blizzard	Activision	DCF, stock market price & comparables model	DCF, stock market price & comparables model	11.50%	11.70%	4.00%	3.00%
	Blizzard	DCF, stock market price & comparables model	DCF, stock market price & comparables model	11.50%	11.70%	4.00%	3.00%
	Distribution	DCF, stock market price & comparables model	DCF, stock market price & comparables model	13.00%	11.70%	4.00%	3.00%
Universal Music Group	Universal Music Group	DCF & comparables model	DCF & comparables model	8.50%	9.30%	1.00%	1.00%
SFR	Mobile	DCF	DCF & comparables model	7.00%	8.00%	0.50%	1.50%
	Broadband Internet and fixed	DCF	DCF	8.00%	9.55%	0.50%	0.50%
Maroc Telecom Group	Maroc Telecom	Stock market price	Stock market price	na*	na*	na*	na*
	Onatel	DCF	DCF	14.00%	14.50%	4.50%	4.50%
	Gabon Telecom	DCF	DCF	15.50%	15.50%	2.50%	2.50%
	Mauritel	DCF	DCF	14.00%	14.00%	2.50%	2.50%
	Sotelma	DCF	na*	14.00%	na*	4.50%	na*
Canal+ Group	Canal+ France	DCF & comparables model	DCF	8.50%	8.80%	1.50%	1.50%
	StudioCanal	DCF	DCF	8.50%–9.00%	8.75%–9.25%	0.00%–1.00%	0.00%–1.00%

na*: not applicable.
DCF: Discounted Cash Flows.

The determination of recoverable amounts using a post-tax discount rate applied to post-tax cash flows provides recoverable amounts consistent with the ones that would have been obtained using a pre-tax discount rate applied to pre-tax cash flows.

(*continued*)

EXHIBIT 1—
continued

VIVENDI GROUP'S
GOODWILL
IMPAIRMENT TEST,
2009 ANNUAL
REPORT

Sensitivity of recoverable amounts

The following tables summarize information about the change in the discount rate and in the perpetual growth rate for each principal CGU or group of CGU used for the tests as of December 31, 2009 and December 31, 2008 that would have been required in order for the recoverable amount to equal the carrying value, except for UMG as the carrying value is equal to the recoverable amount due to the goodwill impairment loss recognized for as of December 31, 2009.

	Discount Rate		**Perpetual Growth Rate**	
	Applied rate (in %)	Change in the discount rate in order for the recoverable amount to be equal to the carrying amount (in points)	Applied rate (in %)	Change in the perpetual growth rate in order for the recoverable amount to be equal to the carrying amount (in points)
Activision Blizzard				
Activision	11.50%	+4.15 points	4.00%	−6.15 points
Blizzard	11.50%	(a)	4.00%	(a)
Universal Music Group	8.50%	na*	1.00%	na*
SFR				
Mobile	7.00%	+6.00 points	0.50%	−33.30 points
Broadband Internet and fixed	8.00%	+1.15 point	0.50%	−2.20 points
Maroc Telecom Group	(b)	na*	(b)	na*
Canal+ Group				
Canal+ France	8.50%	+0.25 point	1.50%	−0.35 point
StudioCanal	9.00%	+1.30 point	0.00%	−1.95 point

Depreciation in the Semiconductor Industry

The semiconductor fabrication industry uses some of the world's most expensive machinery. A semiconductor fabrication plant includes several hundred pieces of equipment that each cost more than $1 million, some cost $50 million. A 2009 state-of-the-art foundry cost from $3 to 4$ billion.[1] Because of technological innovations, a typical facility is obsolete in 18 months to three years.

Background

From the invention of the first practical vacuum tube in 1904 until the 1950s, vacuum tubes were the key element in electronics such as radios, televisions, computers, and other electronic devices. Vacuum tubes provide a switching function (turning an electrical current on or off) and other functions such as signal amplification. Vacuum tubes are bulky, they leak and break, and they have short operating lives. As a result, early computers, with thousands of vacuum tubes, were large and prone to failure.[2]

In December 1947, three Bell Laboratory scientists, John Bardeen, Walter Brattain, and William Shockley, invented a small solid-state (germanium) amplifying device for which they won the 1956 Nobel Prize in Physics. Solid-state technology was soon used to produce other discrete electronic devices, such as diodes, resistors, and capacitors, which led to the birth of the microelectronics industry. Electronic products soon contained relatively small circuit boards filled with these discrete electronic circuits, rather than vacuum tubes.

Discrete solid-state devices were a major improvement over vacuum tubes. However, the sheer number of discrete devices in electronic equipment placed an upper limit on what could be built. In 1959, Jack Kilby, a new Texas Instruments employee, developed the first integrated circuit (IC), a single piece of germanium with five separate electronic components (transistors, diodes, and capacitors).[3] The five separate devices still needed to be connected by wires soldered to each device. That problem was soon overcome by Robert Noyce of Fairchild Semiconductor, who integrated the "wiring" into the germanium, which led to the semiconductor revolution.[4]

---

1. In 2006, Samsung announced its 300-mm wafer fabrication facility in Austin, Texas, would cost about $3.5 billion. See http://www.semiconductor-technology.com/projects/samsung300/. In April 2009, Quimonda, an Infineon spinoff, announced plans to sell its new Sandston, Virginia, 300-nm fabrication facility, recently completed at a cost of $3 billion. See http://www.eetasia.com/ART_8800519717_480200_NT_13918bc1.HTM.

2. See Van Zant, Peter, *Microchip Fabrication*, 5th edition, McGraw-Hill, New York, 2004, for both details about semiconductor manufacturing and a general history of the semiconductor industry.

3. Nobel Prize in Physics 2000. http://nobelprize.org/nobel_prizes/physics/laureates/2000/kilby-autobio.html.

4. William Shockley left Bell Lab to start Shockley Semiconductor, where he hired some of the world's leading semiconductor engineers and scientists. Dr. Shockley was brilliant but abrasive; eight senior employees left to join Fairchild Semiconductors, formed by Fairchild Cameras to employ them. Two of them, Gordon Moore and Robert Noyce, left to form Intel. Eugene Kleiner left to form Kleiner Perkins Caufield & Byers, which has funded Google, Palm, Amazon, Netscape, Flextronics, AOL, Sun Microsystems, Lotus, Genentech, and many other start-ups.

In 1964, Gordon Moore introduced Moore's Law, which states that the number of devices on a semiconductor doubles every two years. Three years later, in 1968, Gordon Moore and Robert Noyce cofounded Intel. In 2009, Intel will introduce an integrated circuit with 2 billion components, a doubling every 21 months since 1959.[5] However, the processes needed to produce integrated circuits have fundamentally changed the industry. The first integrated circuits were built in laboratories by engineers and scientists such as Jack Kilby and Robert Noyce. By the 1970s, they were built in $2–$3 million production facilities. Fabrication facilities cost $100 million in the 1980s, $1–$2 billion in the 1990s, and now cost in excess of $3 billion.

Wafer Fabrication

Integrated circuits (processor or memory chips) are produced on silicon wafers. Fabrication technology has been driven by two factors, wafer size and process width. The silicon wafers gradually increased from 1-inch diameter in the 1970s to 2, 3, and 4 inches; 150 mm (6 inches); 200 mm (8 inches); and the 300-mm (12 inches) wafers used in state-of-the art 2009 fabrication. Wafer size may soon increase to 450 mm (18 inches).

Firms fabricate 200–300 integrated circuits (called dies) on each wafer. Once they are fabricated, dies are separated and then packaged in a protective enclosure that includes connectors. As the size of a wafer increases, the cost and complexity of fabrication equipment increases. However, manufacturers produce more dies on larger wafers, so cost per die decreases, even with more expensive machinery.

As a wafer increases in diameter from 1 inch to 450 mm (12 inches), wafer area increases by a factor of about 144 (larger wafers have less edge waste, so useable area increases even more). Although that is a significant increase, it is trivial compared to the increase in devices per integrated circuit (five in 1959; two billion in 2009). To fabricate the massive increase in devices per integrated circuit, the industry has continually shrunk the size of each device (e.g., transistor) by decreasing the process width.[6] In the early 1970s, state-of-the-art fabrication technology used a 10-μm process technology (10 millionth of a meter); technology moved to a 1-μm process in the 1980s and to a 350-nm process in the mid-1990s. Current state-of-the-art process technology is 32 nm (32 billionths of a meter).

These investments often have a useful life of two years or less. Intel introduced the world's first 45-nm process technology in early 2007. In February 2009, Intel announced it would invest $7 billion over the next two years to expand and transform three U.S. plants to a 32-nm process.[7] Intel recently began fabricating the 32-nm process CPUs and began shipping the CPUs in early 2010. Transistors per CPU increased from about 1 billion to 2 billion, whereas CPU size decreased by 50%.[8]

Semiconductor Manufacturing

The semiconductor industry consists of three primary segments: (1) design and production of the equipment used to fabricate semiconductors; (2) semiconductor design (processor and memory chips); and (3) fabrication, packaging, and sale of

---

5. Moore's Law, 40th Anniversary, Intel Web site. Moore's Law also applies to cost per device and integrated circuit. See http://www.intel.com/pressroom/kits/events/moores_law_40th/index.htm?iid=tech_mooreslaw+body_presskit.

6. Process width generally refers to gate width, but sometimes to device width, such as a transistor.

7. Edwards, Cliff, "Intel invests in the U.S.," *Business Week*, February 10, 2009. Available at www.businessweek.com/technology/content/feb2009/tc20090210_647573.htm.

8. See Intel Web site.

semiconductors. The enormous cost of a single plant has led to a continual decline in the number of firms in the world that produce semiconductors. There are four fundamental types of semiconductor firms:

- Integrated device manufacturers (IDMs) design, produce, and sell integrated circuits. They include Intel, Texas Instruments, STMicroelectronics, AMD, and Infineon, although Infineon and AMD may soon close their manufacturing facilities and outsource their production to pure-play foundries.

- Captive divisions of large firms design, produce, and sell integrated circuits to their parent company and to third parties. Samsung, Toshiba, IBM, and NEC all have significant semiconductor operations that are part of much larger organizations. Their investments in semiconductor manufacturing facilities are not publicly available.

- Pure-play foundries produce integrated circuits for others but do not design and sell their own products. They include TSMC (Taiwan Semiconductor Manufacturing Company) and UMC (United Microelectronics Corporation).

- Fabless firms design and sell their own chips but outsource fabrication to foundries. They include Qualcomm and NVIDIA and may soon include AMD and Infineon.

The two largest semiconductor production costs are research and development (R&D) and machinery and equipment. R&D is exceptionally costly for integrated circuit design, but R&D is also extremely costly for designing and developing the equipment to produce integrated circuits. Until the 1970s, the larger IDMs and captive divisions developed and built much of the equipment needed to produce their own semiconductors. As the time between integrated circuit machinery improvements decreased and the cost to design and build the integrated circuit machinery increased, by the 1980s and 1990s it became impossible for even the largest and most sophisticated IDMs or captive divisions to design and produce their own integrated circuit machinery.

Instead, giant firms such as Intel, IBM, TSMC, and Samsung now work closely with key machinery suppliers such as Applied Materials and KLA to codevelop the latest generation of machinery. That lets the largest IDMs and captive divisions influence machinery design so the machines will better fit the integrated circuits they plan to produce. It also lets them refine their process technology and design their next-generation integrated circuits with future machinery improvements in mind. Because Intel is by far the largest integrated circuit manufacturer, even though it does not develop and produce its own integrated circuit machinery, it was the first to introduce 45-nm technology and is now the first to introduce 32-nm technology.[9]

Depreciation of Buildings, Machinery, and Equipment in the Semiconductor Industry

Semiconductor manufacturers must continually adapt new technology, primarily larger silicon wafers and narrower process widths, although new technologies are frequently introduced in other areas of semiconductor design and production. Because of the constant technological change, most fabrication equipment has a short useful life. As a result, it is helpful when semiconductor manufacturers provide details about how quickly they depreciate their machinery and equipment. However, integrated circuit manufacturing is usually in flux.

---

9. E-mail communications with Mr. Gary Tseng, former CFO of Taiwan Semiconductor Manufacturing Company (TSMC) and United Microelectronics Corporation (UMC), and now CFO of Semiconductor Manufacturing International Corporation (SMIC), December 2009–January 2010.

Fabrication machinery is defined by the generation of the process; the four most recent generations are 90 nm, 65 nm, 45 nm, and 32 nm. A general rule is that machinery is cost-competitive for two or three generations of process technology—cost-competitive in the sense that a one-generation-old machine can reasonably compete with a current-generation machine and in that if an IC manufacturer replaces machinery every time a new generation of machinery is available, its production costs will be too high. When a company buys machinery to produce 65-nm ICs, that same machinery can also produce 45-nm ICs and, for some processes, can produce 32-nm ICs.

IC production machinery that is well-maintained can be used for more than 20 years as long as there are still IC products being sold using the older technology. That is very often the case in the analog and mix-signal IC market, where design rule and process rule migrates at a much slower pace. As a result, when Intel announces that some machinery has been obsoleted, it means Intel no longer produces products using that technology. If Intel is shifting from a 45-nm process to a 32-nm process, it replaces older equipment because the equipment cannot produce the 32-nm product or cannot produce it efficiently.

However, Intel's obsolete machinery is usually in demand by IC manufacturers who produce and sell less-sophisticated ICs than those of Intel and produce them in lower volumes. It is common for logic IC producers such as Intel to depreciate machinery over five years, with a scrap value equal to one year of depreciation. In the past, when demand was very strong, some memory chip manufacturers may have depreciated machinery over three years, with one year of scrap value. In some instances, that depreciation life is too short and the scrap value too low because there is usually an active market for used IC machinery. When the used machinery supply is tight, and demand is very high, resale value can equal 60% of original cost. In a normal situation, the resale value is between 20% and 25% of original cost, depending on the type of machinery and demand. In the past 18 months, during the worldwide recession (mid-2008 through January 2010), many firms cut their capital expenditures budgets and used IC machinery often sold for 10% of its original cost.[10]

Most semiconductor firms produce some advanced process products (65/45 nm) and some lower technology products (350/180 nm). Because depreciation costs are high for the most current equipment, the profit margin on advanced process products is often low. In contrast, profit margins for products produced on old, fully depreciated machinery is often very high. Firms such as Shanghai-based Semiconductor Manufacturing International Corporation (SMIC) create a depreciation rate for fully depreciated machinery that is, for example, based on the equipment's value in the used equipment market. They use that depreciation rate for internal profit reports (but not for financial or tax reporting) to compute more valid product costs, which are then used in product pricing decisions.[11]

A large part of a semiconductor's inventory value is the allocated depreciation on production machinery and equipment. Under both U.S. GAAP and IFRS, firms must allocate production facility depreciation to semiconductors based on some measure of normal production. For example, if a firm expects to record $2 billion of production facility depreciation in 2010 and produce 100 million semiconductors (for simplicity, assume the semiconductors are identical), then the firm will add $20 to inventory for every semiconductor it produces in 2010.

---

10. Communication, Mr. Gary Tseng.

11. Communication, Mr. Gary Tseng.

If the firm has less demand for its products and produces only 80 million units, it will have added only $1.6 billion of depreciation to inventory (much of which will have been shipped and charged to cost of sales). There are two possible ways to account for the $400 million difference between the depreciation recorded in 2010 and the amount added to inventory. One way is to spread the $2 billion of depreciation over the 80 million units actually produced, for a depreciation cost of $25 per unit. Another way is to charge the additional $400 million of depreciation to cost of sales as the cost of excess production capacity in 2010. Under both IFRS and U.S. GAAP, firms must record the $400 million of unallocated depreciation as an excess capacity expense in 2010. It would be helpful if firms disclosed whether they did incur such a charge.

This is a particularly difficult challenge for IC manufacturers when they set prices and evaluate their operations. IDMs, captive divisions, and pure-play foundries all face a constantly changing demand for their products. Pure-play foundries also face a problem of constantly changing customer product designs. When the demand swings and changing designs are combined with the fierce competition between the large IC manufacturers, it is very difficult to estimate whether investments in new machinery will be worth the cost. Furthermore, throughout each year it is difficult to estimate whether a firm is meeting its annual budget plan. As a result, even the best-managed IC manufacturers have problems valuing inventory and problems evaluating performance during each year. In addition, even if an IC manufacturer can reasonably estimate its product costs, competitive forces in a very high fixed-cost industry can lead to wide swings in prices and to prices that far exceed variable production costs but are far too low to cover long-run costs (including R&D and equipment). As a result, the accounting function is far more of a business operation art than a science.[12]

Exhibit 1 provides summary information about six semiconductor firms and Exhibits 2 through 7 provide financial statement disclosures for plant, property, and equipment, and the related depreciation, for those firms. Two are European firms that are reducing their manufacturing capacity by outsourcing some production to foundries, and two are Taiwanese firms that are the world's largest foundries. The remaining two are integrated U.S. semiconductor firms that have been in business from the beginning of the semiconductor age.

European Semiconductor Manufacturers
STMicroelectronics NV

STMicroelectronics NV (STM) is Europe's largest semiconductor firm. Its corporate offices are in the Netherlands, but it is headquartered in Switzerland. STM reports its results in U.S. dollars and its financial statements are prepared using U.S. GAAP. STM is audited by PricewaterhouseCoopers.

From p. 20, 2008 Form 20-F, STM says

> *We are incorporated in the Netherlands and our shares are listed on Euronext Paris and on the Borsa Italiana, and, consequently, we are subject to an EU regulation issued on September 29, 2003 requiring us to report our results of operations and Consolidated Financial Statements using IFRS (previously known as International Accounting Standards or "IAS"). As from January 1, 2008, we are also required to prepare a semi-annual set of accounts using IFRS reporting standards. We use U.S. GAAP as our primary set of reporting standards, as U.S. GAAP has been our reporting standard since our creation in 1987. Applying U.S. GAAP in our financial reporting is designed*

---

12. Communication, Mr. Gary Tseng.

to ensure the comparability of our results to those of our competitors, as well as the continuity of our reporting, thereby providing our investors with a clear understanding of our financial performance.

The obligation to report our Consolidated Financial Statements under IFRS requires us to prepare our results of operations using two different sets of reporting standards, U.S. GAAP and IFRS, which are currently not consistent. Such dual reporting materially increases the complexity of our investor communications. The main potential areas of discrepancy concern capitalization and amortization of development expenses required under IFRS and the accounting for compound financial instruments. Our financial condition and results of operations reported in accordance with IFRS will differ from our financial condition and results of operations reported in accordance with U.S. GAAP, which could adversely affect the market price of our common shares.

From p. 29, Reduced Asset Intensity, STM says

While confirming our mission to remain an integrated device manufacturing company, and in conjunction with our decision to pursue the strategic repositioning of our product portfolio, we have decided to reduce our capital intensity in order to optimize opportunities between internal and external front-end production, reduce our dependence on market cycles that impact the loading of our fabs, and decrease the impact of depreciation on our financial performance. We have been able to reduce the capex-to-sales ratio from a historic average of 26% of sales during the period of 1995 through 2004, to approximately 10% of sales in 2008. Our capital expenditure budget for 2009 is approximately $500 million, representing a 50% reduction compared to 2008.

Infineon Technologies

Infineon is a German-based semiconductor manufacturer that reports its results in Euros, but its financial statements are prepared in accordance with U.S. GAAP. It produces specialized semiconductors for five industries: automotive (number 2 market position); industrial electronics (number 1); chip card and security (i.e., electronic passports and health-care cards, number 1); mobile phone platforms (number 3); and broadband access (number 1). Infineon, which has the option of reporting under U.S. GAAP or IFRS, prepares its financial statements using U.S. GAAP. Infineon is audited by KPMG.

In its 2008 Form 20-F (p. 29), Infineon disclosed that it plans to outsource production of some product lines:

Fixed assets investment and depreciation for Infineon Logic: We are pursuing a differentiated manufacturing strategy for our five operating segments. In the context of this strategy, we will continue to invest in manufacturing capacities for special processes, particularly in the power semiconductor arena. In contrast, we do not plan to invest in our own manufacturing capacities starting with 65-nanometer structure sizes for the standard semiconductor manufacturing process, so-called CMOS technology. We anticipate that our annual investment in property, plant and equipment and intangible assets including capitalized development costs, will fall to approximately €250 million in the 2009 fiscal year. This compares to an investment in property, plant and equipment and intangible assets including capitalized development costs of €370 million in the 2008 fiscal year as recorded under IFRS. In the 2009 fiscal year, depreciation expense is expected to total around €400 million and additional amortization of intangible assets, including capitalized development costs, will be around €50 million, compared to €496 million and €75 million in the prior year, respectively, as recorded under IFRS. In subsequent fiscal years, we will tailor our capital investment to the demand development, but expect to limit such investments to 10 percent or less of our revenues. We expect annual depreciation and amortization expense, including amortization charges for capitalized development costs under IFRS, to decrease further and to fall in line with our capital investment.

From its 2008 Form 20-F, p. 32, Infineon states that

Transition to International Financial Reporting Standards ("IFRS") Beginning with the first quarter of the 2009 fiscal year, we will prepare our financial statements according to IFRS. For the years prior to the 2009 fiscal year, we have prepared our financial statements according to U.S. GAAP. As part of the transition to IFRS, we have published IFRS consolidated financial statements for the 2007 and 2008 fiscal years as supplemental information to the U.S. GAAP consolidated financial statements included elsewhere in this Annual Report on Form 20-F.

Asian Semiconductor Manufacturers
Taiwan Semiconductor Manufacturing Company (TSMC)

Taiwan-based TSMC is the world's largest semiconductor foundry. It reports its results in New Taiwan dollars (NT$). It prepares its financial statements with respect to financial accounting standards and accounting principles generally accepted in Taiwan. Its SEC Form 20-F discloses that there would be no significant differences between its accounting for fixed assets and depreciation had it applied U.S. GAAP. TSMC is audited by Deloitte & Touche.

United Microelectronics Corporation (UMC)

Taiwan-based UMC is the world's second largest semiconductor foundry. It reports its results in New Taiwan dollars (NT$). It prepares its financial statements with respect to financial accounting standards and accounting principles generally accepted in Taiwan. Its SEC Form 20-F discloses that there would be no significant differences between its accounting for fixed assets and depreciation had it applied U.S. GAAP. UMC is audited by Ernst & Young.

United States Semiconductor Manufacturers
Intel

Intel, the world's largest semiconductor firm, reports its results in U.S. dollars and prepares its financial statements in accordance with U.S. GAAP. Intel is audited by Ernst & Young.

Texas Instruments (TI)

Texas Instruments produces a wide range of semiconductor products. It reports its results in U.S. dollars and prepares its financial statements in accordance with U.S. GAAP. Texas Instruments is audited by Ernst & Young.

Required

1. Evaluate the disclosures in the notes that accompany the financial statements of these six firms. Which are the most informative? The least informative? Why?

2. Using the information in the case, or any other information, estimate the length of time over which each of these six firms depreciate their semiconductor production machinery and equipment.

EXHIBIT 1

SELECTED FINANCIAL INFORMATION (MILLIONS OF $U.S., EUROS, OR NT$)

Years ending December 31, except Infineon (years end September 30): For periods shown, approximately .65 to .85 Euros = 1 $ U.S. and 35 NT$ = 1 $ U.S.					
	2008	2007	2006	2005	2004
STMicroelectronics NV					
Net sales	$9,842	$10,001	$9,854	$8,882	$8,760
Cost of sales	$6,282	$6,465	$6,331	$5,845	$5,532
Research & development	$2,152	$1,802	$1,667	$1,630	$1,532
Net income after tax	$(7,486)	$(477)	$782	$266	$601
Property, plant, & equipment	$18,775	$19,181	$19,951	$17,312	$17,981
Accum depreciation	$(14,036)	$(14,137)	$(13,525)	$(11,137)	$(10,539)
Property, plant, & equipment (net)	$4,739	$5,044	$6,426	$6,175	$7,442
Investments, PP&E*	$983	$1,140	$1,533	$1,441	$2,050
Depreciation**	$1,366	$1,413	$1,766	$1,944	$1,837
Infineon Technologies AG****					
Net sales	€4,321	€4,074	€4,114	€7,929	€5,843
Cost of sales	€2,823	€2,702	€2,805	€4,909	€4,670
Research & development	€755	€768	€816	€1,293	€1,219
Net income after tax***	€(3,122)	€(368)	€(268)	€(312)	€61
Property, plant, & equipment	€6,964	€12,908	€13,254	€11,461	€10,763
Accum depreciation	€(5,653)	€(9,261)	€(9,490)	€(7,710)	€(7,176)
Property, plant, & equipment (net)	€1,311	€3,647	€3,764	€3,751	€3,587
Investments, PP&E*	€312	€498	€1,253	€1,368	€1,163
Depreciation**	€542	€609	€1,405	€1,316	€1,320
Taiwan Semiconductor Manufacturing Company (TSMC)—amounts in NT$					
Net sales	$333,158	$322,631	$317,407	$266,565	$257,213
Cost of sales	$191,408	$180,280	$161,597	$158,362	$14,139
Research & development	$21,481	$17,946	$16,076	$14,016	$12,516
Net income after tax	$100,523	$109,932	$127,195	$93,633	$92,329
Property, plant, & equipment	$862,462	$800,352	$717,132	$642,948	$590,165
Accum depreciation (not avail)	$(618,816)	$(540,100)	$(463,038)	$(398,125)	$(331,254)
Property, plant, & equipment (net)	$243,645	$260,252	$245,094	$244,823	$258,911
Investments, PP&E*	$59,223	$84,001	$78,737	$79,879	$81,095
Depreciation**	$81,512	$80,005	$73,715	$75,649	$69,819

(continued)

EXHIBIT 1—*continued*

SELECTED FINANCIAL INFORMATION (MILLIONS OF $U.S., EUROS, OR NT$)

	2008	2007	2006	2005	2004
United Microlectronics Corp. (UMC)—amounts in NT$					
Net sales	$96,814	$113,311	$112,004	$100,316	$129,191
Cost of sales	$81,129	$89,768	$90,638	$90,643	$92,392
Research & development	$8,274	$9,631	$9,419	$9,633	$7,364
Net income after tax	$(22,320)	$16,962	$32,619	$7,027	$31,843
Property, plant, & equipment	$494,947	$484,140	$463,525	$428,622	$415,481
Accum depreciation (not avail)	$(386,537)	$(346,921)	$(311,697)	$(269,508)	−$223,457
Property, plant, & equipment (net)	$108,410	$137,219	$151,828	$159,114	$192,024
Investments, PP&E*	$11,515	$28,299	$33,240	$22,163	$81,110
Depreciation**	$37,197	$37,829	$44,301	$51,366	$45,590
Intel Corp.					
Net sales	$37,586	$38,334	$35,382	$38,826	$34,209
Cost of sales	$16,742	$18,430	$17,164	$15,777	$14,463
Research & development	$5,722	$5,755	$5,873	$5,145	$4,778
Net income after tax	$5,292	$6,976	$5,044	$8,664	$7,516
Property, plant, & equipment	$48,088	$46,052	$47,084	$44,132	$39,833
Accum depreciation (not avail)	$(30,544)	$(29,134)	$(29,482)	$(27,021)	$(24,065)
Property, plant, & equipment (net)	$17,544	$16,918	$17,602	$17,111	$15,768
Investments, PP&E*	$5,197	$5,000	$5,860	$5,818	$3,843
Depreciation**	$4,360	$4,546	$4,654	$4,345	$4,590
Texas Instruments, Inc.					
Net sales	$12,501	$13,835	$14,255	$13,392	$12,580
Cost of sales	$6,256	$4,666	$6,996	$7,029	$6,954
Research & development	$1,940	$2,140	$2,195	$2,015	$1,978
Net income after tax*****	$1,920	$2,657	$4,341	$2,324	$1,861
Property, plant, & equipment	$7,321	$7,568	$7,751	$8,921	$9,573
Accum depreciation (not avail)	$(4,017)	$(3,859)	$(3,801)	$(5,022)	$(5,655)
Property, plant, & equipment (net)	$3,304	$3,609	$3,950	$3,899	$3,918
Investments, PP&E*	$763	$686	$1,272	$1,330	$1,298
Depreciation**	$1,022	$1,022	$1,052	$1,375	$1,479

* From statements of cash flows.

** From statements of cash flows; includes depreciation expense in selling, general, and administrative costs and depreciation in cost of sales.

*** Loss on discontinued operations of €2,987 in 2008.

**** Infineon spun off its Qimonda memory business on May 1, 2006.

**** Net income from discontinued operations in 2006 of $1.703 billion.

EXHIBIT 2

STMICROELECTRONICS,
SELECTED
DISCLOSURES, 2008
FORM 20-F

PP. 62–63: PROPERTY, PLANT AND EQUIPMENT

Our business requires substantial investments in technologically advanced manufacturing facilities, which may become significantly underutilized or obsolete as a result of rapid changes in demand and ongoing technological evolution. We estimate the useful life for the majority of our manufacturing equipment, the largest component of our long-lived assets, to be six years, except for our 300-mm manufacturing equipment as stated below. This estimate is based on our experience using the equipment over time. Depreciation expense is a major element of our manufacturing cost structure. We begin to depreciate new equipment when it is placed into service. In the first quarter of 2008, we launched our first solely owned 300-mm production facility in Crolles (France). Consequently, we assessed the useful life of our 300-mm manufacturing equipment based on relevant economic and technical factors. Our conclusion was that the appropriate depreciation period for such 300-mm equipment is 10 years. This policy was applied starting January 1, 2008.

P. F-18

Buildings	33 years
Facilities & leasehold improvements	5–10 years
Machinery and equipment	3–10 years
Computer and R&D equipment	3–6 years
Other	2–5 years

P. F-38

Property, plant and equipment consisted of the following:

December 31, 2008	Gross Cost	Accumulated Depreciation	Net Cost
Land	89	—	89
Buildings	1,001	(264)	737
Capital leases	68	(53)	15
Facilities & leasehold improvements	3,153	(2,115)	1,038
Machinery and equipment	13,700	(11,037)	2,663
Computer and R&D equipment	528	(440)	88
Other tangible assets	187	(127)	60
Construction in progress	49	—	49
Total	18,775	(14,036)	4,739

December 31, 2007	Gross Cost	Accumulated Depreciation	Net Cost
Land	91	—	91
Buildings	1,036	(344)	692
Capital leases	71	(49)	22
Facilities & leasehold improvements	3,205	(1,975)	1,230
Machinery and equipment	13,938	(11,183)	2,755
Computer and R&D equipment	554	(458)	96
Other tangible assets	185	(128)	57
Construction in progress	101	—	101
Total	19,181	(14,137)	5,044

(continued)

EXHIBIT 2—
continued

STMICROELECTRONICS,
SELECTED
DISCLOSURES, 2008
FORM 20-F

In 2008, as described in Note 21, the Company recorded $77 million impairment charge on long-lived assets of the Company's manufacturing sites in Carrollton, Texas and in Phoenix, Arizona, of which $75 million on Phoenix site which had previously been designated for closure as part of the 2007 restructuring plan.

As at December 31, 2007 property, plant and equipment amounting to $394 million were reported as a component of the line "Assets held for sale" on the consolidated balance sheet as part of the assets to be transferred to Numonyx, the newly created flash memory company upon FMG deconsolidation.

EXHIBIT 3

INFINEON, SELECTED
DISCLOSURES, 2008
FORM 20-F

PROPERTY, PLANT AND EQUIPMENT, NET

A summary of activity for property, plant and equipment for the years ended September 30, 2007 and 2008, is as follows:

	Land and buildings	Technical equipment and machinery	Other plant and office equipment	Construction in progress	Total
			(€ in millions)		
Cost:					
September 30, 2007	687	4,655	1,416	144	6,902
Additions	19	189	63	50	321
Impairments	—	(23)	—	—	(23)
Disposals	(19)	(158)	(109)	(1)	(287)
Reclassifications	7	115	13	(135)	—
Transfers[1]	18	27	(7)	6	44
Foreign currency effects	1	7	(1)	—	7
September 30, 2008	713	4,812	1,375	64	6,964
Accumulated depreciation:					
September 30, 2007	(440)	(3,733)	(1,267)	—	(5,440)
Depreciation	(29)	(365)	(103)	—	(497)
Disposals	19	149	105	—	273
Reclassifications	—	(2)	2	—	—
Transfers[1]	—	9	8	—	17
Foreign currency effects	—	(7)	1	—	(6)
September 30, 2008	(450)	(3,949)	(1,254)	—	(5,653)
Book value September 30, 2007	247	922	149	144	1,462
Book value September 30, 2008	263	863	121	64	1,311

[1] Amounts shown as transfers in the year ended September 30, 2008 relate primarily to assets of the ALTIS disposal group that were reclassified into held and used.

EXHIBIT 4

Taiwan Semiconductor Manufacturing Company Ltd (TSMC), Selected Disclosures, 2008 Form 20-F

PP. 13–14, PROPERTY, PLANT AND EQUIPMENT, ASSETS LEASED TO OTHERS AND IDLE ASSETS

Property, plant and equipment and assets leased to others are stated at cost less accumulated depreciation. When an indication of impairment is identified, any excess of the carrying amount of an asset over its recoverable amount is recognized as a loss. If the recoverable amount increases in a subsequent period, the amount previously recognized as impairment would be reversed and recognized as a gain. However, the adjusted amount may not exceed the carrying amount that would have been determined, net of depreciation, as if no impairment loss had been recognized. Significant additions, renewals and betterments incurred during the construction period are capitalized. Maintenance and repairs are expensed as incurred.

Depreciation is computed using the straight-line method over the following estimated service lives: buildings—10 to 20 years; machinery and equipment—5 years; and office equipment—3 to 5 years.

P. 17, NOTE 12, PROPERTY, PLANT AND EQUIPMENT

	Year Ended December 31, 2008				
	Balance, Beginning of Year	Addition (Deductions)	Disposals	Reclassification	Balance, End of Year
Cost					
Buildings	$101,907,892	$12,115,531	$(8,524)	$(311)	$114,014,588
Machinery and equipment	589,131,625	49,396,313	(3,385,502)	(134,175)	635,008,261
Office equipment	9,167,107	764,414	(182,709)	57	9,748,869
	700,206,624	$62,276,258	$(3,576,735)	$(134,429)	758,771,718
Accumulated depreciation					
Buildings	57,349,828	$8,010,214	$(8,524)	$(4)	65,351,514
Machinery and equipment	422,278,071	63,145,978	(1,258,542)	(119,347)	484,046,160
Office equipment	7,097,120	935,140	(182,706)	26	7,849,580
	486,725,019	$72,091,332	$(1,449,772)	$(119,325)	557,247,254
Advance payments and construction in progress	21,082,953	$(3,324,915)	$-	$-	17,758,038
Net	$234,564,558				$219,282,502

(*continued*)

EXHIBIT 4—continued

TAIWAN SEMICONDUCTOR MANUFACTURING COMPANY LTD (TSMC), SELECTED DISCLOSURES, 2008 FORM 20-F

	Year Ended December 31, 2007				
	Balance, Beginning of Year	Addition	Disposals	Reclassification	Balance, End of Year
Cost					
Buildings	$96,961,851	$5,025,296	$(31,835)	$(47,420)	$101,907,892
Machinery and equipment	527,850,728	61,793,498	(487,386)	(25,215)	589,131,625
Office equipment	8,659,225	936,003	(328,555)	(99,566)	9,167,107
	633,471,804	$67,754,797	$(847,776)	$(172,201)	700,206,624
Accumulated depreciation					
Buildings	49,595,917	$7,783,832	$(30,957)	$1,036	57,349,828
Machinery and equipment	361,401,800	61,492,223	(459,113)	(156,839)	422,278,071
Office equipment	6,469,533	958,315	(328,363)	(2,365)	7,097,120
	417,467,250	$70,234,370	$(818,433)	$(158,168)	486,725,019
Advance payments and construction in progress	12,230,805	$8,268,467	$-	$583,681	21,082,953
Net	$228,235,359				$234,564,558

EXHIBIT 5

UNITED MICROELECTRONICS CORPORATION (UMC), SELECTED DISCLOSURES, 2008 FORM 20-F

PROPERTY, PLANT AND EQUIPMENT (P. F17)

Property, plant and equipment are stated at cost. Interest incurred on loans used to finance the construction of property, plant and equipment is capitalized and depreciated accordingly. Maintenance and repairs are charged to expense as incurred. Significant renewals and improvements are treated as capital expenditures and are depreciated over their estimated useful lives. Upon disposal of property, plant and equipment, the original cost and accumulated depreciation are written off and the related gain or loss is classified as non-operating income or expense. Idle assets are classified as other assets at the lower of net book or net realizable value, with the difference charged to non-operating expenses.

Depreciation is recognized on a straight-line basis using the estimated economic life of the assets:

Buildings	3–55 years
Machinery and equipment	5–6 years
Transportation equipment	4–5 years
Furniture and fixtures	2–20 years
Leased assets and leasehold improvements	The lease period or estimated economic life, whichever is shorter

(continued)

EXHIBIT 5—
continued

UNITED
MICROELECTRONICS
CORPORATION
(UMC), SELECTED
DISCLOSURES, 2008
FORM 20-F

2. PROPERTY, PLANT AND EQUIPMENT(P. F-2*)

As of December 31, 2007

	Cost	Accumulated Depreciation	Book Value
	NT$'000	NT$'000	NT$'000
Land	1,922,230	—	1,922,230
Buildings	22,529,856	(7,944,046)	14,585,810
Machinery and equipment	446,198,339	(336,320,744)	109,877,595
Transportation equipment	85,877	(65,574)	20,303
Furniture and fixtures	3,429,067	(2,549,736)	879,331
Leasehold improvement	42,809	(40,845)	1,964
Construction in progress and prepayments	9,931,551	—	9,931,551
Total	484,139,729	(346,920,945)	137,218,784

As of December 31, 2008

	Cost	Accumulated Depreciation	Book Value
	NT$'000	NT$'000	NT$'000
Land	2,269,237	—	2,269,237
Buildings	24,354,334	(9,897,661)	14,456,673
Machinery and equipment	459,711,569	(373,639,088)	86,072,481
Transportation equipment	76,742	(66,334)	10,408
Furniture and fixtures	3,582,387	(2,891,844)	690,543
Leasehold improvement	53,432	(42,391)	11,041
Construction in progress and prepayments	4,899,607	—	4,899,607
Total	494,947,308	(386,537,318)	108,409,990

EXHIBIT 6

INTEL CORP.,
SELECTED
DISCLOSURES, 2008
10-K

P 64: PROPERTY, PLANT AND EQUIPMENT

Property, plant and equipment, net at fiscal year-ends was as follows:

	2008	2007
	(in millions)	
Land and buildings	$16,546	$15,267
Machinery and equipment	28,812	27,754
Construction in progress	2,730	3,031
	48,088	46,052
Less: accumulated depreciation	(30,544)	(29,134)
Total property, plant and equipment, net	$17,544	$16,918

We state property, plant and equipment at cost, less accumulated depreciation. We compute depreciation for financial reporting purposes using the straight-line method over the following estimated useful lives: machinery and equipment, 2 to 4 years; buildings, 4 to 40 years. We regularly perform reviews if facts and circumstances indicate that the carrying amount of assets may not be recoverable or that the useful life is shorter than we had

(continued)

originally estimated. We assess the recoverability of our assets held for use by comparing the projected undiscounted net cash flows associated with the related asset or group of assets over their remaining estimated useful lives against their respective carrying amounts. Impairment, if any, is based on the excess of the carrying amount over the fair value of those assets. If we determine that the useful lives are shorter than we had originally estimated, we depreciate the net book value of the assets over the newly determined remaining useful lives. For a discussion of restructuring-related asset impairment charges, see "Note 15: Restructuring and Asset Impairment Charges."

We identify property, plant and equipment as held for sale when it meets the criteria of SFAS No. 144, "Accounting for Impairment or Disposal of Long-Lived Assets." We reclassify held for sale assets to other current assets and cease recording depreciation.

We capitalize interest on borrowings related to eligible capital expenditures. We add capitalized interest to the cost of qualified assets and amortize it over the estimated useful lives of the assets. We record capital-related government grants earned as a reduction to property, plant and equipment.

Intel's statements of cash flows reports depreciation in the years 2006, 2007, and 2008 of $4.654 billion, $4.546 billion, and $4.360 billion, respectively.

EXHIBIT 6—
continued

Intel Corp.,
Selected
Disclosures,
2008 10-K

P. 9: PROPERTY, PLANT AND EQUIPMENT AND OTHER CAPITALIZED COSTS

Property, plant and equipment are stated at cost and depreciated over their estimated useful lives using the straight-line method. Leasehold improvements are amortized using the straight-line method over the shorter of the remaining lease term or the estimated useful lives of the improvements. Acquisition-related intangibles are amortized on a straight-line basis over the estimated economic life of the assets. Capitalized software licenses generally are amortized on a straight-line basis over the term of the license. Fully depreciated or amortized assets are written off against accumulated depreciation or amortization.

EXHIBIT 7

Texas
Instruments,
Selected
Disclosures,
2008 10-K

P. 30: PROPERTY, PLANT AND EQUIPMENT AT COST

		December 31	
	Depreciable Lives	2008	2007
Land	—	$83	$82
Buildings and improvements	5–40 years	2,948	2,895
Machinery and equipment	3–10 years	4,290	4,591
Total		$7,321	$7,568

Thomson's Acquisition of Reuters (A)

Background

Roy Thomson, grandfather of Thomson Reuters' current chairman, was born in Toronto in 1894. After a varied background in farming, sales, and radio broadcasting, Mr. Thomson acquired his first newspaper, *The Timmins Press*, Ontario, in 1934. He acquired other Canadian and U.S. newspapers during the following 20 years before acquiring his first UK newspaper in 1953, *The Scotsman*. A year later, already the owner of more newspapers than anyone else in Canada, Mr. Thomson moved to Scotland where he continued his firm's steady growth in the publishing industry.[1]

In 1957, Mr. Thomson formed Scottish Television in central Scotland. In 1959, he acquired the Kemsley Group, a national and regional UK newspaper chain that owned *The Sunday Times* of London. Mr. Thomson formed Thomson Publication (UK) in 1961 to launch and acquire business and consumer magazines and book publishers. By 1964, Thomson was one of the world's largest media companies and Mr. Thomson was awarded the title Baron Thomson of Fleet. The following year, he expanded into the travel industry by acquiring tour companies and Britannia Airways. In 1967, he acquired *The Times of London*, which he combined with *The Sunday Times* to form Times Newspapers. Thomson joined a consortium in 1971 to explore for oil and gas in the North Sea; in 1973 and 1974, that consortium discovered two major oil fields.

Lord Thomson died in 1976 and was succeeded by his son, Kenneth (Ken) Thomson. A year later Thomson Newspaper's daily U.S. circulation numbered more than 1 million. From 1934 through 1976, Lord Roy Thomson built one of the world's largest, most prestigious, and most profitable newspaper chains. Ken Thomson, through dozens of acquisitions and divestitures, managed a business transformation that is probably unmatched in all of business history for size, complexity, and success.

In 1978, Ken Thomson restructured the firm by moving its worldwide headquarters to Toronto and retaining two main operating subsidiaries in the United Kingdom and United States. He also turned over management to professional executives in the firm's Stamford, Connecticut, headquarters, although he and two trusted Canadian lawyers oversaw the work of their U.S. executives.

Thomson acquired Wadsworth in 1978, a college textbook and professional book publisher. In 1980, Thomson Newspapers' daily circulation in Canada passed 1 million but the firm began its move to technical publishing by acquiring Warren, Gorham & Lamont, a major information publisher for finance professionals. A year later, Thomson sold *The Times of London* to News International, Ltd., and acquired Litton, a publisher of high-quality health-care information.

In 1985, Thomson acquired Gale, a leading provider of information for libraries, schools, and businesses, and AutEx, which helps financial traders identify and track liquidity in global securities markets. In 1986, Thomson acquired Compu-Mark, the

---

1. Background information is from the Thomson Reuters company history on the firm's Web site, http://thomsonreuters.com/about/company_history/?view=Standard.

worldwide market leader in trademark research and South-Western Publishing, a leading business textbook publisher. Throughout this acquisition spurt, the Thomson family retained more than a 70% ownership of Thomson common stock, and Ken Thomson became one of the world's wealthiest individuals.

Thomson acquired legal publishers in the UK, Canada, and Australia in 1987 and 1988. In 1988, Thomson also funded ILX Systems, an electronic financial information supplier started by former E.F. Hutton executives. A year later, Thomson disposed of its North Sea oil interests and acquired a large U.S. legal and tax publisher, Research Institute of America (RIA). Thomson acquired additional information providers in the health-care, scientific, and educational fields in 1994 and 1995, and in 1996 it acquired West Publishing (WestLaw), one of the world's two dominant legal information providers.

In 1998, Thomson began its exit from most businesses other than those that electronically provided technical information to professionals. That year it sold Thomson Travel for $2 billion (USD) and one year later acquired Spain's premier legal publisher. In 2000, Thomson acquired legal and financial information providers in Argentina, Brazil, and the United States and sold its North American community newspaper group for $2.5 billion (USD). As a result, Thomson avoided the massive loss in value or bankruptcies suffered by other newspaper chains, such as *The New York Times, The Wall Street Journal,* and the Tribune Companies, as they lost advertising revenue to the Internet.[2]

Thomson acquired additional information providers in 2001 and 2002. In 2002, Lord Kenneth Thomson retired and his son, David K. R. Thomson, was appointed chairman of Thomson Corporation. At the time, Ken Thomson was the ninth wealthiest person in the world ($22 billion USD) and his family was the wealthiest in Canada.

In 2002, Thomson began a more aggressive challenge to Bloomberg and Reuters, the dominant firms in the financial information market. Thomson announced a $300 million plus, five-year deal with Merrill Lynch to develop and implement a new financial workstation to support Merrill Lynch Financial Advisors. By 2005, Merrill Lynch had installed at least 25,000 Thomson terminals. In 2003, Thomson sold its print-based health-care magazines, other print-based information divisions, and the last of its remaining newspapers. It also acquired additional health-care and financial information providers. In 2006, Lord Kenneth R. Thomson, former chairman of the board, died at the age of 82.

A year later, Thomson began what is by far its largest divestiture and acquisition. In 2007, Thomson sold its Thomson Learning division, which included its higher education, career, and library reference assets, to a private equity firm for $7.75 billion (USD). That same year Thomson announced it would acquire Reuters Group PLC for $17.2 billion (USD).

Thomson's 2008 Acquisition of Reuters

Over the years, Thomson acquired or developed dozens of firms in the financial information sector. In 2008, it acquired Reuters, the world's largest financial information provider. Reuters, a London-based firm, was founded in 1851 by Paul Julius Reuter, a German-born immigrant who had operated a news and stock price information service in Germany using telegraph cables and a fleet of carrier pigeons.

---

2. In November 2006, The New York Times Company reportedly rejected a $600 million offer for *The Boston Globe,* a newspaper it acquired for $1.3 billion in 1993; in March 2009, it threatened to close the *Globe,* which was losing $50 million annually. In 2000, when Thomson sold its U.S. newspaper group for $2.5 billion, The New York Times Company had a market value of approximately $6 billion; its market value was $1.2 billion in August 2010.

To acquire Reuters without the Thomson family losing majority control, Thomson sold its book publishing division, Thomson Learning, in the third quarter of 2007. It used those proceeds, together with debt and equity, to acquire Reuters in the second quarter of 2008. Portions of Thomson Reuters's second-quarter 2008 financial statement describe the acquisition.

Exhibit 1 provides selected parts of Thomson Reuters's management discussion and analysis (MD&A). That exhibit (1) describes Thomson Reuters's business operations and how the firm earns a profit, (2) explains why Thomson Reuters evaluates its businesses using free cash flow instead of accounting profit based on generally accepted accounting principles, and (3) explains how Thomson and Reuters are integrating their operations and reducing costs.

Exhibit 2 includes those parts of the MD&A that explain Thomson Reuters's business segments. Exhibit 2 also provides selected financial information for each business unit, including revenues, operating profit, and growth by business segment.

Exhibit 3 provides pro forma financial results as if Thomson and Reuters had been combined for the three months ended June 30, 2007 and 2008, and the six months ended June 30, 2007 and 2008. Those results are unaudited and were prepared using assumptions that may not be indicative of how the combined companies will operate in the future.

Exhibits 4–7 are the 2008 income statements, balance sheets, statements of cash flows, and statement of changes in stockholders' equity. They include Reuters for parts of the second quarter, 2008 but not for earlier periods. For example, the December 31, 2007 balance sheet includes cash from the sale of Thomson Learning to a private equity firm, while the June 30, 2008 balance sheet has far less cash because it was used in the Reuters acquisition. Similarly, capital (common stock) increased from $2.932 billion on December 31, 2007, to $11.020 billion on June 30, 2008, because Thomson issued $8.226 billion of common stock (ordinary shares) to acquire Reuters (Exhibit 7).

Exhibit 8 includes the first four notes to the Thomson Reuters second quarter 2008 financial statements, including Note 4: Acquisition of Reuters Group PLC.

Required

1. Explain how Thomson Reuters accounted for the acquisition (see primarily Exhibit 7, Note 4). Why does Thomson Reuters refer to this as a preliminary purchase price allocation?

2. How reliable are allocations to the different asset and liability accounts (see primarily Exhibit 7, Note 4)? In particular, how reliable are the estimated fair values of $2 billion, $2.4 billion, and $1 billion for trade names, customer relationships, and other? How reliable are the estimated useful lives for customer relationships and other?

3. Compare the pro forma income statement information in Exhibit 2 to the Canadian GAAP income statement in Exhibit 3. Are the pro forma statements useful? How difficult would they be to prepare, and how subjective are they?

4. Evaluate Thomson Reuters' method of evaluating its businesses as described in Exhibit 1.

5. Explain why you believe the Reuters acquisition will or will not be considered a success in five to ten years.

EXHIBIT 1

MANAGEMENT'S
DISCUSSION AND
ANALYSIS

The following management's discussion and analysis is intended to assist you in understanding and evaluating changes in our financial condition and operations for the three-month and six-month periods ended June 30, 2008, compared to the same periods in the preceding year. We recommend that you read this management's discussion and analysis in conjunction with our consolidated financial statements for each of the three-month and six-month periods ended June 30, 2008 and the year ended December 31, 2007, the related notes to those financial statements, and our management's discussion and analysis for the year ended December 31, 2007. Our financial statements are prepared in accordance with accounting principles generally accepted in Canada, or Canadian GAAP. References in this discussion to "$" are to U.S. dollars, references to "£" are to British pounds sterling, references to "€" are to the Euro, references to "¥" are to the Japanese yen and references to "C$" are to Canadian dollars. Unless otherwise indicated or the context otherwise requires, references in this discussion to "we," "our," "us" and "Thomson Reuters" are to Thomson Reuters Corporation, Thomson Reuters PLC and their respective subsidiaries which operate as a unified group under a dual listed company (DLC) structure. In addition to historical information, this management's discussion and analysis contains forward-looking statements. Readers are cautioned that these forward-looking statements are subject to risks and uncertainties that could cause our actual results to differ materially from the forward-looking statements. Some of these factors include those identified in the section entitled "Cautionary Note Concerning Factors That May Affect Future Results" at the end of this management's discussion and analysis and in the "Risk Factors" section of Thomson Reuters PLC's annual report on Form 20-F for the year ended December 31, 2007 filed with the U.S. Securities and Exchange Commission and the Canadian securities regulatory authorities. This management's discussion and analysis is dated as of August 11, 2008.

OVERVIEW

On April 17, 2008, The Thomson Corporation (Thomson) acquired Reuters Group PLC (Reuters) and Thomson Reuters was formed. Thomson Reuters is organized in two divisions:

- *Markets*, which consists of our financial businesses, which are a combination of those operated by Reuters and Thomson Financial prior to the closing of the acquisition; and

- *Professional*, which consists of our Legal, Tax & Accounting, Scientific and Healthcare segments.

By combining Thomson's strength in North America with Reuters's strength in Europe, the Middle East and Asia, we created a business that we believe will allow us to grow faster than either Thomson or Reuters could have on its own. We expect to achieve this by:

- Capitalizing on a global brand and presence to drive international growth

- We currently operate in 93 countries and serve customers in more than 140

- Our first-half 2008 pro forma revenues were 57% from the Americas, 33% from Europe and 10% from Asia

- Delivering greater value to customers through a broader range of electronically delivered critical information and decision support tools

- Our revenues are overwhelmingly digital, which means we can leverage the Internet to deliver services and software rapidly and efficiently

- Our customers depend on our intelligent information, and we are at the center of their daily workflows

- Integrating Thomson and Reuters businesses to accelerate growth and capture synergies

- Our Markets Division recently rolled out a new product strategy, drawing upon the best assets of Reuters and Thomson Financial, and sales, service and product teams are coming together in a unified force to benefit customers with new offerings and enhancements

(continued)

EXHIBIT 1—
continued

MANAGEMENT'S
DISCUSSION AND
ANALYSIS

- Across our organization, we are identifying new opportunities to drive revenue growth and profitability
- Leveraging increased revenue diversity and scale, financial strength and capital deployment to maximize shareholder return
- We have a disciplined capital strategy and strong financial flexibility evidenced by our balanced funding of the Reuters acquisition and retirement of our acquisition credit facility through the issuance of approximately $3 billion of new securities in June 2008
- We continue to maintain strong credit ratings and provide returns to shareholders through dividends and share repurchases

Thomson Reuters operates under a DLC structure, which means that we have two parent companies, both of which are publicly listed:

- Thomson Reuters Corporation, an Ontario, Canada corporation, and
- Thomson Reuters PLC, an English company.

Thomson Reuters Corporation and Thomson Reuters PLC operate as a unified group pursuant to contractual arrangements as well as provisions in their organizational documents. Under the DLC structure, shareholders of Thomson Reuters Corporation and Thomson Reuters PLC both have a stake in Thomson Reuters, with cash dividend, capital distribution and voting rights that are comparable to the rights they would have if they were holding shares in one company carrying on the Thomson Reuters business. The boards of the two parent companies comprise the same individuals, as do the companies' executive management teams.

Our Business and Strategy

What Thomson Reuters does — We are the world's leading source of intelligent information for businesses and professionals. We define intelligent information as information that organizes itself, suggests connections and fits into professionals' workflows. We combine industry expertise with innovative technology to deliver critical information to decision makers in the financial, legal, tax and accounting, scientific, healthcare and media markets, powered by the world's most trusted news organization, Reuters. We believe that our intelligent information provides our customers with a competitive advantage by enabling them to make better decisions faster.

How Thomson Reuters makes money — We generate revenues by supplying knowledge workers with business-critical information solutions and services. We make our information more valuable by adding expert analysis, insight and commentary, and couple it with software tools and applications that our customers can use to search, compare, synthesize and communicate the information. To further enhance our customers' workflows, we deliver information and services electronically, integrate our solutions with our customers' own data and tailor the delivery of information to meet specific customer needs. As we integrate critical information with analysis, tools and applications, we place greater focus on the way our customers use our content, instead of simply selling the content itself and are moving from just informing our customers to enabling their decisions. We believe our ability to embed our solutions into customers' workflows is a significant competitive advantage as it leads to strong customer retention.

Thomson Reuters business environment and trends — As a global organization, we are affected by economic and market dynamics, governmental regulations and business conditions of each market and country in which we operate. Currently, global markets are being impacted by a variety of factors, and the mortgage and credit markets within the financial services markets are being hit particularly hard. While we are not immune to economic cycles, the professional markets that we serve have historically been resilient. Further, our business has increasingly become subscription-based with more customers entering into multi-year commitments for our critical workflow tools and applications, which we believe will help mitigate the impact of a downturn in global markets.

(continued)

EXHIBIT 1—
continued

MANAGEMENT'S
DISCUSSION AND
ANALYSIS

Relative to the financial services industry, while we have observed the industry softening in the Americas, we also see the industry growing in other parts of the world due to the international nature of the banking businesses. Against this backdrop, our Markets Division revenues from Asia increased 15% and from the Middle East increased 30%. The downturn is not impacting all banks or geographic regions equally, and we are not experiencing widespread cancellations or downgrades in service. Within the industry, the fixed income asset class continues to make headlines for significant losses. While this situation has impacted our business, this area comprises only 10% of Markets Division revenue. More than offsetting the impact from the fixed income asset class was the strong continued growth in the remaining 90% of the Markets Division revenue base, including areas such as foreign exchange and other exchange-traded instruments, commodities and energy and corporate.

Consolidated financial statements and accounting standards — Our primary financial statements beginning with the three and six months ended June 30, 2008 are the consolidated financial statements of Thomson Reuters Corporation. Those statements account for Thomson Reuters PLC as a subsidiary and have been prepared in accordance with Canadian GAAP. We are seeking exemptive relief to present Thomson Reuters Corporation's financial statements in accordance with International Financial Reporting Standards (IFRS) in 2009. We have provided a voluntary reconciliation to IFRS in this management's discussion and analysis. See the section entitled "Recently Issued Accounting Standards" for more information.

Results for Reuters are included in our consolidated financial statements beginning April 17, 2008, as we are accounting for the acquisition under the purchase method. For informational purposes, we have also included Thomson Reuters pro forma results in this management's discussion and analysis, which present the hypothetical performance of our business as if Thomson had acquired Reuters on January 1, 2007. See the sections of this management's discussion and analysis entitled "Acquisition of Reuters" and "Unaudited Pro Forma Results" for more information.

Acquisition of Reuters
Consideration

On April 17, 2008, Thomson acquired Reuters for approximately $17 billion. Under the terms of the acquisition:

- All of the issued and outstanding Reuters ordinary shares were cancelled; and
- Reuters shareholders received, for each Reuters ordinary share held:
- 352.5 pence in cash; and
- 0.16 Thomson Reuters PLC ordinary shares.

One Thomson Reuters PLC ordinary share is equivalent to one Thomson Reuters Corporation common share under the DLC structure. As part of the transaction, Thomson shareholders continued to hold their shares of Thomson, renamed as Thomson Reuters Corporation.

Thomson Reuters PLC issued 194,107,278 of its ordinary shares to Reuters shareholders when the transaction closed on April 17, 2008. These shares were valued at approximately $8.2 billion, or $42.38 per share using the average Thomson share price a few days before and after May 15, 2007, the date of the announcement of the acquisition. The par value of Thomson Reuters PLC ordinary shares was changed from £10 to 25 pence shortly after the acquisition closed.

On May 1, 2008, Thomson Reuters paid $8.45 billion in cash to former Reuters shareholders to satisfy the cash consideration component of the transaction. Thomson Reuters funded this cash consideration using proceeds from the sale of its Thomson Learning businesses as well as borrowings under an acquisition credit facility. See the section entitled "Financial Position" for further discussion on acquisition-related borrowings and repayments.

(continued)

EXHIBIT 1—
continued

MANAGEMENT'S
DISCUSSION AND
ANALYSIS

A total of 33,670,064 Reuters options were outstanding as of April 17, 2008. These options will expire during the fourth quarter of 2008. Upon exercise, holders will be entitled to consideration of 352.5 pence in cash and 0.16 Thomson Reuters PLC ordinary shares for each share of Reuters that would have been received. The fair value of outstanding options, determined using the Black-Scholes pricing model, was $195 million and was included in the purchase consideration.

The purchase consideration was as follows (millions of U.S. dollars):

Cash	8,450
Ordinary shares, Thomson Reuters PLC	8,226
Reuters Group PLC options	195
Transaction costs	138
Total purchase consideration	17,009

We have not yet completed the allocation of the purchase price to the Reuters assets acquired and liabilities assumed, but we have included a preliminary purchase price allocation in note 4 of our consolidated financial statements for the six months ended June 30, 2008. We expect to finalize our purchase price allocation within 12 months from the closing date of the acquisition.

Selected Historical and Pro Forma Financial Information

The following table summarizes selected financial information for Thomson Reuters for the three and six-month periods ended June 30, 2008 and 2007.

	Three months ended June 30		Six months ended June 30	
	(unaudited)			
	2008	2007	2008	2007
	(millions of U.S. dollars, except per share amounts)			
Canadian GAAP results:				
Revenues	3,128	1,805	4,962	3,467
Operating profit	295	352	511	577
Earnings from continuing operations	179	262	372	471
Earnings (loss) from discontinued operations, net of tax	(6)	115	(5)	130
Net earnings	173	377	367	601
Diluted earnings per share from continuing operations	$0.22	$0.40	$0.52	$0.73
Diluted earnings per share	$0.22	$0.58	$0.51	$0.93
Pro forma results:				
Pro forma revenues	3,442	3,091	6,696	5,921
Pro forma operating profit	336	409	764	554
Pro forma revenues from ongoing businesses	3,422	3,069	6,654	5,963
Pro forma underlying operating profit	708	618	1,284	1,040
Pro forma underlying operating profit margin	*20.7%*	*20.1%*	*19.3%*	*17.4%*

(continued)

EXHIBIT 1—
continued

MANAGEMENT'S
DISCUSSION AND
ANALYSIS

Please see the "Results of Operations" section of this management's discussion and analysis for commentary on these results. The 2008 results are not directly comparable to 2007 results due to the inclusion of financial results from Reuters beginning with the date of acquisition and certain one-time items. Therefore, we have provided supplemental information and analysis in the section entitled "Unaudited Pro Forma Results" to further explain our operating performance.

Seasonality

Historically, Thomson's revenues and operating profits from continuing operations were proportionately the smallest in the first quarter and the largest in the fourth quarter, as certain product releases were concentrated at the end of the year, particularly in the regulatory and healthcare markets. As costs were incurred more evenly throughout the year, its operating margins historically increased as the year progressed. For these reasons, the performance of its businesses were not comparable quarter to consecutive quarter and were best considered on the basis of results for the whole year or by comparing results in a quarter with the results in the same quarter for the previous year. As Reuters's revenues and profits have not historically fluctuated significantly throughout the year, we anticipate that the seasonality of Thomson Reuters revenues and operating profits will be slightly less pronounced.

USE OF NON-GAAP FINANCIAL MEASURES

In addition to our results reported in accordance with Canadian GAAP, we use certain non-GAAP financial measures as supplemental indicators of our operating performance and financial position and for internal planning purposes. We have historically reported non-GAAP financial results as we believe their use provides more insight into our performance.

The following is a description of our non-GAAP financial measures, including an explanation of why we believe they are useful measures of our performance, including our ability to generate cash flow.

- *Revenue and operating profit from ongoing businesses.* We believe our revenue and profits are best measured based on our ability to grow our ongoing businesses over the long term. Accordingly, we evaluate our revenue and operating profits excluding results from disposals, which are defined as businesses sold or held for sale that do not qualify for discontinued operations classification.

- *Net debt.* We define our net debt as our total indebtedness, including associated fair value hedging instruments (swaps) on our debt, less cash and cash equivalents. Given that we hedge some of our debt to reduce risk, we include hedging instruments as we believe it provides a better measure of the total obligation associated with our outstanding debt. However, because we intend to hold our debt and related hedges to maturity, we do not consider the associated fair market value of cash flow hedges in our measurements. We reduce gross indebtedness by cash and cash equivalents on the basis that they could be used to pay down debt. See the reconciliation of this measure to the most directly comparable Canadian GAAP measure in the "Liquidity and Capital Resources" section of this management's discussion and analysis.

- *Free cash flow.* We evaluate our operating performance based on free cash flow, which we define as net cash provided by operating activities less capital expenditures, other investing activities and dividends paid on our preference shares. We use free cash flow as a performance measure because it represents cash available to repay debt, pay common and ordinary dividends and fund new acquisitions. See the reconciliation of this measure to the most directly comparable Canadian GAAP measure in the "Liquidity and Capital Resources" section of this management's discussion and analysis.

(continued)

EXHIBIT 1—
continued

MANAGEMENT'S
DISCUSSION AND
ANALYSIS

Non-GAAP measures do not have any standardized meaning prescribed by Canadian GAAP and, therefore, are unlikely to be comparable with the calculation of similar measures used by other companies. You should not view these measures as alternatives to measures of financial performance calculated in accordance with Canadian GAAP. Due to the significant impact of the Reuters acquisition on our results, we included pro forma results as if we had acquired Reuters on January 1, 2007 to provide a more meaningful analysis of our performance compared to the prior year. Pro forma results do not reflect the actual results of our business. See the section entitled "Unaudited Pro Forma Results."

INTEGRATION AND SYNERGY PROGRAMS

As a consequence of the Reuters acquisition, we announced an integration and synergy program directed at integrating Thomson and Reuters and capturing cost synergies. Its primary objective is the integration of Thomson Financial with Reuters, which now comprise the new Markets Division, but also includes efforts to integrate both shared services across the whole of Thomson Reuters and corporate departments. Because the objectives of the program are similar to those of the THOMSON*plus* and Core Plus programs, we are managing these initiatives as a single program beginning in the three month period ended June 30, 2008. Because these are corporate initiatives, incremental expenses associated with these programs are reported within the Corporate and Other segment. The integration and synergy initiatives are expected to be completed in 2011 at a total cash cost of $1.2 billion, which excludes expenses associated with THOMSON*plus* and Core Plus incurred prior to 2008. We will incur restructuring costs associated with these efforts, including severance and losses on lease terminations and other cancellations of contracts. Certain costs will qualify to be recorded as part of goodwill and the remainder will be expensed.

We expect the program will generate run-rate savings of approximately $1.2 billion by 2011. In addition to realizing synergies from the creation of the Markets Division, we also expect to realize efficiencies and improve effectiveness across Thomson Reuters, including in areas such as technology procurement, third-party data suppliers, real estate and data center infrastructure. Further savings will be realized by eliminating duplicative corporate functions, consolidating shared service centers, and improving our effectiveness by extending common platforms in back office business systems.

In the three-month period ended June 30, 2008, we incurred $141 million of expenses associated with integration and synergy programs primarily related to severance and consulting costs associated with technology initiatives. In the six-month period ended June 30, 2008, we incurred $154 million of expenses, including legacy spending in THOMSON*plus* as a stand-alone program. These legacy expenses primarily related to consulting fees and severance costs related to efforts to deploy SAP as a company-wide enterprise resource planning (ERP) system.

THOMSON*plus*, as a stand-alone program, achieved annualized run-rate savings of approximately $160 million upon its completion at June 30, 2008. These savings were primarily due to the elimination of certain positions and the relocation of others to lower cost locations, including those resulting from the establishment of a facility in Hyderabad, India to perform certain finance functions.

We have prepared certain unaudited pro forma financial information for Thomson Reuters to illustrate the effect of the acquisition of Reuters and to provide comparable results to measure our performance. These pro forma results for the three-month and six-month periods ended June 30, 2008 and 2007, have been prepared as if the acquisition had occurred on January 1, 2007. This pro forma information:

- has not been audited;

- has been prepared for illustrative purposes only, and because of its nature, addresses a hypothetical situation and, therefore, does not represent Thomson Reuters actual financial position or results;

- does not purport to represent what the consolidated results of operations actually would have been if the acquisition had occurred on January 1, 2007 or what those results will be for any future periods. The pro forma adjustments are based on current information; and

- has not been adjusted to reflect any matters not directly attributable to the acquisition. No adjustment, therefore, has been made to periods prior to the closing date (April 17, 2008) for actions which have or may be taken upon completion of the acquisition, such as any integration plans of Thomson Reuters.

Pro Forma Results

The following tables set forth the pro forma results for Thomson Reuters for the three-month and six-month periods ended June 30, 2008 and 2007:

	Three months ended June 30			Six months ended June 30		
	2008[1]	2007	Change	2008[1]	2007	Change
Pro forma revenues						
Legal	923	852	8%	1,732	1,592	9%
Tax & accounting	189	155	22%	394	315	25%
Scientific	154	140	10%	295	267	10%
Healthcare	109	100	9%	204	192	6%
Professional	1,375	1,247	10%	2,625	2,366	11%
Sales & trading	1,001	901	11%	1,976	1,799	10%
Investment & advisory	593	544	9%	1,189	1,071	11%
Enterprise	338	275	23%	638	530	20%
Media	119	106	12%	233	207	13%
Markets	2,051	1,826	12%	4,036	3,607	12%
Eliminations	(4)	(4)	n/m	(7)	(10)	n/m
Pro forma revenues from ongoing businesses	3,422	3,069	12%	6,654	5,963	12%
Disposals	20	22	n/m	42	44	n/m
Pro forma revenues before purchase accounting normalization	3,442	3,091	11%	6,696	6,007	11%
Purchase accounting normalization	—	—	n/m	—	(86)	n/m
Pro forma revenues	3,442	3,091	11%	6,696	5,921	13%

(continued)

EXHIBIT 2—
continued

UNAUDITED PRO
FORMA RESULTS

Pro forma operating profit						
Legal	321	294	9%	546	500	9%
Tax & accounting	33	31	6%	72	69	4%
Scientific	48	41	17%	77	73	5%
Healthcare	10	9	11%	13	13	0%
Professional	412	375	10%	708	655	8%
Markets	372	286	30%	715	502	42%
Corporate & other	(221)	(98)	n/m	(277)	(208)	n/m
Amortization	(158)	(158)	n/m	(316)	(315)	n/m
Pro forma operating profit from ongoing businesses	405	405	0%	830	634	31%
Disposals	3	4	n/m	6	6	n/m
Impairment of assets held for sale	(72)	—	n/m	(72)	—	n/m
Pro forma operating profit before purchase accounting normalization	336	409	(18%)	764	640	19%
Purchase accounting normalization	—	—	n/m	—	(86)	n/m
Pro forma operating profit	336	409	(18%)	764	554	38%

(1) In the second quarter of 2008, we revised our methodology for corporate expense allocation with respect to Reuters. As a result, we reclassified previously reported pro forma results in arriving at our six-month pro forma results. Our previously reported pro forma segment operating profit for Markets and Corporate and Other for the three months ended March 31, 2008 have been reclassified to $343 million and ($56) million, respectively. Our previously reported pro forma segment operating profit for Markets and Corporate and Other for the three months ended March 31, 2007 have been reclassified to $216 million and ($110) million, respectively. There was no impact on our total operating profit in these periods.

Pro forma revenues. For the three-month and six-month periods ended June 30, 2008, pro forma revenues increased 11% and 13%, respectively. These increases include the effects of revenues from a disposal that could not be classified as a discontinued operation, as well as the impact of a pro forma purchase accounting adjustment on 2007 revenues. In order to present the performance of our ongoing businesses, the effects of the disposals and purchase accounting adjustment, were removed. Total pro forma revenues from ongoing businesses for both the three-month and six-month periods ended June 30, 2008 increased 12%. The primary components of the increase compared to the prior year periods were as follows:

	3 months ended June 30		Percentage change due to			
	2008	2007	Existing businesses	Acquired businesses	Currency translation	Total
Professional	1,375	1,247	6%	3%	1%	10%
Markets	2,051	1,826	7%	0%	5%	12%
Eliminations	(4)	(4)				
	3,422	3,069	7%	1%	4%	12%

(continued)

EXHIBIT 2—
continued

UNAUDITED PRO
FORMA RESULTS

	6 months ended June 30		Percentage change due to			
	2008	**2007**	**Existing businesses**	**Acquired businesses**	**Currency translation**	**Total**
Professional	2,625	2,366	7%	3%	1%	11%
Markets	4,036	3,607	8%	0%	4%	12%
Eliminations	(7)	(10)				
	6,654	5,963	8%	1%	3%	12%

As revenues in both periods for our Professional Division were not impacted by the Reuters acquisition, its pro forma results correspond to the analysis provided in the section entitled "Results of Operations." For both the three months and six months ended June 30, 2008, pro forma revenues in our Markets Division increased 12%. These increases were largely a result of higher revenues from existing businesses and were exhibited in each major geographic area, particularly Asia, and in all the Markets Division's subsegments.

In the three months and six months ended June 30, 2008, Sales & Trading revenues increased 11% and 10%, respectively. Excluding the effects of foreign currency translation, Sales & Trading revenues increased 5% and 6%, respectively. These increases were primarily a result of higher Treasury, Commodity & Energy and cross-asset class trading, offset by slower growth in Fixed Income and Equities. Treasury revenues were driven by foreign exchange volatility and higher transaction volumes. Commodity & Energy revenues increased due to higher demand for our information products resulting from sector activity. Tradeweb's revenues increased due to higher transaction fees from new asset classes, particularly dollar and Euro-denominated interest rate swaps.

In the three months and six months ended June 30, 2008, Investment & Advisory revenues increased 9% and 11%, respectively. Excluding the effects of foreign currency translation, Investment & Advisory revenues increased 8% and 10%, respectively. These increases were primarily a result of increased desktops and datafeed sales, particularly in the investment management and corporate sectors. Investment management revenues benefited from higher sales of advanced analytics. Revenues from the corporate sector increased primarily due to demand in Europe and Asia.

Enterprise revenues increased 23% and 20% for the three months and six months ended June 30, 2008, respectively. Excluding the effects of foreign currency translation, Enterprise revenues increased 14% and 15%, respectively. These increases primarily reflected higher data feed revenues. Trade & Risk Management revenues increased as a result of higher sales of our Kondor+ solution. Additionally, revenues for PORTIA, our portfolio accounting solution, increased due to greater activity for our customers, upgrade releases and demand for new modules.

Media revenues increased 12% and 13% for the three months and six months ended June 30, 2008, respectively. Excluding the effects of foreign currency translation, Media revenues increased 2% and 4%, respectively. These increases were primarily due to the favorable impact of foreign exchange. Additionally, revenues from agency services increased due to higher demand offset by timing of expenses and weakness in the Consumer business.

Pro forma operating profit. For the three months ended June 30, 2008, pro forma operating profit decreased 18%. The decrease was primarily the result of spending on our integration and synergy programs, as well as an impairment on assets held for sale. For the six months ended June 30, 2008, pro forma operating profit increased 38%. The increase was largely due to a purchase accounting adjustment that reduced revenues in the prior year period.

(continued)

EXHIBIT 2—
continued

UNAUDITED PRO
FORMA RESULTS

In both periods, we experienced certain unusual or one-time items that impacted comparability. The following table provides an analysis of our profitability excluding those items to derive our underlying operating profit.

	Three months ended June 30		Six months ended June 30	
	2008	**2007**	**2008**	**2007**
Pro forma operating profit	**336**	409	**764**	554
Adjustments:				
Amortization	**158**	158	**316**	315
Purchase accounting normalization	—	—	—	86
Disposals	**(3)**	(4)	**(6)**	(6)
Impairment of assets held for sale	**72**	—	**72**	—
Fair value adjustments	**4**	28	**(16)**	30
Integration and synergy program costs	**141**	27	**154**	61
Pro forma underlying operating profit	**708**	618	**1,284**	1,040
Pro forma underlying operating profit margin %	***20.7%***	*20.1%*	***19.3%***	*17.4%*

For the three months and six months ended June 30, 2008, pro forma underlying operating profit increased 15% and 23%, respectively. Pro forma underlying operating profit in both periods benefited significantly from the favorable effect of foreign currency translation. These increases also reflected the higher revenues in each period, savings attributable to certain spending which was deferred prior to the Reuters acquisition, and initial synergy savings in the post-acquisition period. Our pro forma underlying operating margin increased in both periods as a result of the impact of foreign exchange translation, effects of scale and the impact of synergy initiatives.

For the three months and six months ended June 30, 2008, pro forma operating profit for the Markets Division increased 30% and 42%, respectively. These increases largely reflected the factors discussed above, including a significant benefit from the effect of foreign currency translation.

Pro forma adjusted earnings and pro forma adjusted earnings per share from continuing operations. The table below presents a reconciliation of pro forma underlying operating profit to pro forma adjusted earnings from continuing operations for the three-month and six-month periods ended June 30, 2008.

	Three months ended June 30, 2008	Six months ended June 30, 2008
Pro forma underlying operating profit	708	1,284
Adjustments:		
Integration and synergy program costs	(141)	(154)
Net Interest expense	(112)	(225)
Income taxes	(73)	(145)
Tradeweb ownership interests	(4)	(6)
Dividends declared on preference shares	(1)	(3)
Pro forma adjusted earnings from continuing operations	377	751
Pro forma adjusted earnings per share from continuing operations	$0.45	$0.90

(continued)

EXHIBIT 2—
continued

UNAUDITED PRO
FORMA RESULTS

Our adjusted earnings from continuing operations for the three-month and six-month periods ended June 30, 2008, were $377 million, or $0.45 per share, and $751 million, or $0.90 per share, respectively. These measures are presented to allow an analysis of our performance on the same basis as our Business Outlook contained in this management's discussion and analysis, which assumes the acquisition of Reuters had occurred on January 1, 2007. We derived our pro forma adjusted earnings by deducting from pro forma underlying operating profit certain normally recurring items appearing below operating profit on the statements of earnings: interest expense, income taxes, Tradeweb ownership interests and dividends declared on preference shares. Additionally, we deduct costs associated with our integration and synergy programs, but exclude "other income and expense" and amortization.

Pro forma interest expense and income taxes reflect assumptions in the "Business Outlook" section. Specifically, interest expense was derived by reflecting in the period a proportional amount of the pro forma full year run rate. Income taxes reflect an estimated pre-amortization effective tax rate. These amounts do not represent the actual amounts in the consolidated financial statements of Thomson Reuters for the three-month and six-month periods ended June 30, 2008.

Pro forma basic weighted average common and ordinary shares outstanding reflected the actual reported weighted average common and ordinary shares outstanding adjusted as if the approximately 194 million Thomson Reuters PLC shares issued to Reuters shareholders on April 17, 2008 were outstanding from the beginning of the period presented, as well as the effect of the approximately 34 million Reuters Group PLC share options assumed. Pro forma adjusted earnings per share from continuing operations do not represent actual earnings per share attributable to shareholders.

Pro Forma Information Calculation

The calculation of pro forma information for the six-months ended June 30, 2008 is set forth below:

Six months ended June 30, 2008	Thomson Reuters	Pro forma adjustments Reuters[1]	Other	Adjustment Note	Pro forma Thomson Reuters
Revenues	4,962	1,699	35	a)	6,696
Cost of sales, selling, marketing, general and administrative expenses	(3,863)	(1,364)	95	b), c), d), e)	(5,132)
Depreciation	(313)	(86)	(13)	d)	(412)
Amortization	(203)	(8)	(105)	d)	(316)
Impairment of assets held for sale	(72)	—	—		(72)
Operating profit	511	241	12		764

Represents Reuters results for the pre-acquisition period January 1, 2008 to April 16, 2008.

(continued)

EXHIBIT 2—
continued

UNAUDITED PRO
FORMA RESULTS

The calculation of pro forma information for the six months ended June 30, 2007 is set forth below:

Six months ended June 30, 2007	Thomson	Pro forma adjustments		Adjustment Note	Pro forma Thomson Reuters
		Reuters	Other		
Revenues	3,467	2,540	(86)	a)	5,921
Cost of sales, selling, marketing, general and administrative expenses	(2,535)	(2,174)	53	b), c), d), e)	(4,656)
Depreciation	(232)	(136)	(28)	d)	(396)
Amortization	(123)	(28)	(164)	d)	(315)
Operating profit	577	202	(225)		554

Pro Forma Adjustments

The pro forma adjustments for the six-month periods ended June 30, 2008 and 2007 reflected adjustments made in the unaudited pro forma financial statements in the Thomson Reuters PLC annual report on Form 20-F for the year ended December 31, 2007, as follows, except as noted in a) below due to additional information made available to us following completion of the acquisition:

(a) To adjust the carrying value of Reuters deferred revenue obligation as of January 1, 2007 to its estimated fair value, revenues were reduced by $86 million for the three months ended March 31, 2007, which carried through to the six months ended June 30, 2007. Because of Reuters contractual quarterly billing cycle, this adjustment was reflected in its entirety in the quarter ended March 31, 2007.

In the Thomson Reuters consolidated financial statements for the six-month period ended June 30, 2008, the first reporting period after the Reuters acquisition, reported revenues were reduced by $35 million. For purposes of the pro forma results, the revenue reduction was reversed, as it is assumed to have occurred in 2007, and therefore should not be recognized again in 2008 pro forma results.

(b) Thomson and Reuters expensed integration planning and other transaction-related costs that do not qualify to be capitalized as part of estimated purchase consideration. For purposes of the pro forma results, $238 million and $44 million of expenses incurred in the six-month periods ended June 30, 2008 and 2007, respectively, were reversed because the pro forma results have been prepared as if the acquisition had occurred on January 1, 2007, and these expenses would have been incurred prior to the closing date. Additionally, these expenses are non-recurring in nature and are not expected to have a continuing impact on the consolidated results.

There was no adjustment taken to reverse integration and synergy program expenses incurred beginning from April 17, 2008, the acquisition date.

(c) For the six-month period ended June 30, 2008, cost of sales, selling, marketing, general and administrative expenses were increased by $140 million (June 30, 2007—decrease of $36 million) to eliminate amortization related to past service costs and net actuarial gains and losses in connection with Reuters pension and other post-retirement benefit plans. These expenses were eliminated as retirement plan assets and obligations would have been reflected at their fair values on January 1, 2007.

(continued)

EXHIBIT 2—
continued

UNAUDITED PRO
FORMA RESULTS

The adjustments to amortization, depreciation and rent expense described in d) and e) below relate to pre-acquisition periods. The adjustments reflect the effects of purchase accounting on operating profit as if the Reuters acquisition had occurred on January 1, 2007. These adjustments were not required from April 17, 2008, the closing date of the acquisition, and after the closing as the Thomson Reuters Corporation consolidated financial statements for the six-month period ended June 30, 2008 reflect application of purchase accounting to the Reuters acquisition beginning from April 17, 2008.

(d) Amortization and depreciation

- Adjustments of $105 million and $164 million were recorded in the six-month periods ended June 30, 2008 and 2007, respectively, to reflect additional amortization attributable to the preliminary fair value increment allocated to identifiable intangible assets.

- Adjustments of $13 million and $28 million were recorded in the six-month periods ended June 30, 2008 and 2007, respectively, to reflect additional depreciation attributable to the preliminary fair value increment allocated to computer hardware and other property, and internal use software.

- Adjustments of $6 million and $12 million were recorded in the six-month periods ended June 30, 2008 and 2007 to decrease and increase, respectively, cost of sales, selling, marketing, general and administrative expenses to reflect amortization attributable to the preliminary fair value increment allocated to capitalized software to be sold externally. Reuters accelerated amortization on certain impaired software assets in the second quarter of 2008. The adjustment to decrease amortization in 2008 is partly due to these accelerated charges and other factors.

(e) Adjustments of $9 million and $15 million were recorded in the six-month periods ended June 30, 2008 and 2007, respectively, to reflect additional rent expense attributable to amortization of the preliminary fair value increment allocated to favorable and unfavorable leases.

Pro Forma Depreciation by Segment
The following table details pro forma depreciation expense by segment and disposals for the three and six-month periods ended June 30, 2008 and 2007:

	Three months ended June 30		Six months ended June 30	
	2008	2007	2008	2007
Professional division	(millions of U.S. dollars)			
Legal	(61)	(52)	(116)	(100)
Tax & accounting	(7)	(5)	(15)	(11)
Scientific	(8)	(7)	(16)	(13)
Healthcare	(6)	(6)	(13)	(11)
Markets division	(121)	(126)	(247)	(254)
Corporate and other	(3)	(3)	(4)	(6)
Disposals	—	—	(1)	(1)
Total	(206)	(199)	(412)	(396)

EXHIBIT 3

THOMSON REUTERS
CONSOLIDATED
STATEMENT
OF EARNINGS
(UNAUDITED)

	Three months ended June 30		Six months ended June 30	
	2008	2007 (note 11)	2008	2007 (note 11)
	(millions of U.S. dollars, except per share amounts)			
Revenues	3,128	1,805	4,962	3,467
Cost of sales, selling, marketing, general and administrative expenses	(2,428)	(1,274)	(3,863)	(2,535)
Depreciation	(192)	(117)	(313)	(232)
Amortization	(141)	(62)	(203)	(123)
Impairment of assets held for sale (note 7)	(72)	—	(72)	—
Operating profit	295	352	511	577
Net other (expense) income (note 8)	(38)	6	(64)	12
Net interest expense and other financing costs (note 9)	(54)	(51)	(15)	(104)
Income taxes (note 10)	(20)	(45)	(54)	(14)
Tradeweb ownership interests (note 17)	(4)	—	(6)	—
Earnings from continuing operations	179	262	372	471
(Loss) earnings from discontinued operations, net of tax (note 11)	(6)	115	(5)	130
Net earnings	173	377	367	601
Dividends declared on preference shares	(1)	(2)	(3)	(3)
Earnings attributable to Thomson Reuters Corporation common shares and Thomson Reuters PLC ordinary shares	172	375	364	598

The related notes form an integral part of these consolidated financial statements.

EXHIBIT 4

THOMSON REUTERS
CONSOLIDATED
BALANCE SHEET
(UNAUDITED)

	June 30, 2008 (note 4)	December 31, 2007
Assets	(millions of U.S. dollars)	
Cash and cash equivalents	789	7,497
Accounts receivable, net of allowances	1,811	1,565
Prepaid expenses and other current assets	801	512
Deferred income taxes	197	104
Current assets	3,598	9,678
Computer hardware and other property, net	1,723	731
Computer software, net	1,903	721
Identifiable intangible assets, net	8,618	3,438
Goodwill	19,994	6,935
Other non-current assets	1,994	1,328
Total assets	37,830	22,831

(continued)

EXHIBIT 4—
continued

THOMSON REUTERS
CONSOLIDATED
BALANCE SHEET
(UNAUDITED)

Liabilities and shareholders' equity		
Liabilities		
Short-term indebtedness	**4**	183
Accounts payable and accruals	**2,560**	1,536
Deferred revenue	**1,235**	1,108
Current portion of long-term debt and finance lease obligations	**667**	412
Current liabilities	**4,466**	3,239
Long-term debt and finance lease obligations (note 18)	**7,733**	4,264
Other non-current liabilities	**1,270**	783
Deferred income taxes	**2,622**	974
Minority interest in equity of consolidated affiliate (note 17)	**73**	—
Shareholders' equity		
Capital	**11,020**	2,932
Retained earnings	**10,341**	10,355
Accumulated other comprehensive income	**305**	284
Total shareholders' equity	**21,666**	13,571
Total liabilities and shareholders' equity	**37,830**	22,831

EXHIBIT 5

THOMSON REUTERS
CONSOLIDATED
STATEMENT OF
CASH FLOW
(UNAUDITED)

	3 months ended June 30		6 months ended June 30	
(millions of U.S. dollars)	**2008**	**2007**	**2008**	**2007**
Cash provided by (used in):				
Operating activities				
Net earnings	**173**	377	**367**	601
Remove loss (earnings) from discontinued operations	**6**	(115)	**5**	(130)
Add back (deduct) items not involving cash:				
Depreciation	**192**	117	**313**	232
Amortization	**141**	62	**203**	123
Net gains on disposals of businesses and investments	**—**	(2)	**—**	(8)
Impairment of assets held for sale (note 7)	**72**	—	**72**	—
Deferred income taxes	**(77)**	(19)	**(130)**	(61)
Other, net	**96**	71	**184**	135
Changes in working capital and other items (note 19)	**283**	5	**170**	(96)
Discontinued operations (note 11)	**(6)**	(53)	**(20)**	(66)
Net cash provided by operating activities	**880**	443	**1,164**	730

(*continued*)

Investing activities				
Acquisitions, less cash acquired (note 16)	**(8,147)**	(29)	**(8,270)**	(183)
Proceeds from (payments for) disposals of discontinued operations, net of income taxes paid (note 11)	**—**	438	**(53)**	473
Proceeds from other disposals	**—**	5	**154**	11
Capital expenditures, less proceeds from disposals	**(232)**	(142)	**(340)**	(240)
Other investing activities	**(11)**	(13)	**(23)**	(23)
Capital expenditures of discontinued operations (note 11)	**—**	(58)	**—**	(95)
Acquisitions by discontinued operations (note 11)	**—**	—	**—**	(54)
Other investing activities of discontinued operations	**—**	(2)	**(7)**	(6)
Net cash (used in) provided by investing activities	**(8,390)**	199	**(8,539)**	(117)
Financing activities				
Proceeds from debt	**5,921**	—	**7,600**	—
Repayments of debt	**(4,679)**	(20)	**(5,079)**	(20)
Net repayments under short-term loan facilities	**(1,426)**	(380)	**(1,072)**	(136)
Repurchase of common and ordinary shares (note 12)	**(458)**	(20)	**(458)**	(75)
Dividends paid on preference shares	**(1)**	(2)	**(3)**	(3)
Dividends paid on common and ordinary shares	**(390)**	(153)	**(516)**	(306)
Other financing activities, net	**192**	5	**194**	15
Net cash (used in) provided by financing activities	**(841)**	(570)	**666**	(525)
Translation adjustments	**(82)**	—	**1**	—
(Decrease) increase in cash and cash equivalents	**(8,433)**	72	**(6,708)**	88
Cash and cash equivalents at beginning of period	**9,222**	350	**7,497**	334
Cash and cash equivalents at end of period	**789**	422	**789**	422

EXHIBIT 5—
continued

THOMSON REUTERS
CONSOLIDATED
STATEMENT OF
CASH FLOW
(UNAUDITED)

EXHIBIT 6

CONSOLIDATED STATEMENT OF CHANGES IN SHAREHOLDERS' EQUITY (UNAUDITED)

(millions of U.S. dollars)	Stated Share Capital[(1)]	Contributed Surplus	Total Capital	Retained Earnings	Accumulated Other Comprehensive Income ("AOCI")	Total Retained Earnings and AOCI	Total
Balance, December 31, 2007	2,727	205	2,932	10,355	284	10,639	13,571
Comprehensive income:							
Net earnings				367	—	367	367
Unrecognized net gain on cash flow hedges				—	1	1	1
Foreign currency translation adjustments				—	20	20	20
Comprehensive income				367	21	388	388
Issuance of Thomson Reuters PLC shares	96	8,130	8,226	—	—	—	8,226
Dividends declared on preference shares				(3)	—	(3)	(3)
Dividends declared on common shares and ordinary shares				(378)	—	(378)	(378)
Shares issued under Dividend Reinvestment Plan ("DRIP")	108	—	108	—	—	—	108
Repurchases of shares	(8)	(471)	(479)	—	—	—	(479)
Effect of stock compensation plans	24	209	233	—	—	—	233
Balance, June 30, 2008	2,947	8,073	11,020	10,341	305	10,646	21,666

Balance, December 31, 2006	2,642	157	2,799	7,169	513	7,682	10,481
Opening balance adjustment for income tax accounting change (note 5)	—	—	—	(33)	—	(33)	(33)
Balance, January 1, 2007	2,642	157	2,799	7,136	513	7,649	10,448
Comprehensive income:							
Net earnings				601	—	601	601
Unrecognized net loss on cash flow hedges				—	(20)	(20)	(20)
Foreign currency translation adjustments				—	88	88	88
Net gain reclassified to income				—	(38)	(38)	(38)
Comprehensive income				601	30	631	631
Dividends declared on preference shares				(3)	—	(3)	(3)
Dividends declared on common shares				(314)	—	(314)	(314)
Shares issued under DRIP	8	—	8	—	—	—	8
Repurchases of shares	(7)	—	(7)	(68)	—	(68)	(75)
Effect of stock compensation plans	48	26	74	—	—	—	74
Balance, June 30, 2007	2,691	183	2,874	7,352	543	7,895	10,769

(1) Includes common, ordinary and preference share capital.

The related notes form an integral part of these consolidated financial statements.

EXHIBIT 7

NOTES TO
CONSOLIDATED
FINANCIAL
STATEMENTS
(UNAUDITED)

(Unless otherwise stated, all amounts are in millions of U.S. dollars)

Note 4: Acquisition of Reuters Group PLC

Preliminary purchase price allocation

The acquisition has been accounted for using the purchase method and the results of Reuters have been included in the consolidated statement of earnings for the three-month and six-month periods ending June 30, 2008, beginning from April 17, 2008, the closing date of the acquisition. The purchase consideration was as follows (millions of U.S. dollars):

Cash	8,450
Ordinary shares, Thomson Reuters PLC	8,226
Reuters Group PLC options	195
Transaction costs	138
Total purchase consideration	17,009

The total purchase consideration has been preliminarily allocated to acquired net tangible and identifiable intangible assets based on their estimated fair values as of April 17, 2008 as set forth below. The excess of the purchase price over the net tangible and identifiable intangible assets was recorded as goodwill and will not be deductible for tax purposes.

The preliminary allocation of the purchase price was based upon estimated fair values and assumptions and is subject to change pending completion of a comprehensive valuation process.

	Purchase Price Allocation
Assets	(millions of U.S. dollars)
Cash and cash equivalents	465
Accounts receivable, net of allowances	1,460
Prepaid expenses and other current assets	391
Deferred income taxes	93
Current assets	2,409
Computer hardware and other property, net	1,042
Computer software, net	1,100
Identifiable intangible assets, net	5,400
Goodwill	12,950
Other non-current assets	918
Total assets	23,819
Liabilities	
Short-term indebtedness	895
Accounts payable and accruals	1,497
Deferred revenue	926
Current portion of long-term debt and finance lease obligations	409
Current liabilities	3,727
Long-term debt and finance lease obligations	851
Other non-current liabilities	458
Deferred income taxes	1,774
Total liabilities	6,810
Total	17,009

See note 10 for further discussion regarding uncertain tax positions.

(continued)

EXHIBIT 7—
continued

NOTES TO
CONSOLIDATED
FINANCIAL
STATEMENTS
(UNAUDITED)

Intangible assets

The Company's preliminary estimates of the fair values of intangible assets acquired and their respective estimated useful lives as at April 17, 2008 are as set forth below. These values are subject to change and such changes may be material. To estimate fair value, the Company considered, among other factors, the intended future use of acquired assets as well as projected performance:

	Estimated Fair Value	Estimated Useful Life
	(millions of U.S. dollars)	
Trade names	2,000	Indefinite
Customer relationships	2,400	8-18 years
Other (databases, images and other)	1,000	5 years
Identifiable intangible assets	5,400	
Developed technology	1,100	5–10 years

"Customer relationships" represent the underlying relationships with existing customers. "Other" includes financial and media content, databases and images. "Developed technology" primarily represents acquired software which processes data and provides customers access to databases and subscription services, as well as applications sold directly to customers.

Leases

The estimated net favorable difference between the fair value of acquired leases and their contractual terms is $388 million. The individual values which comprise this amount will be amortized over the terms of the respective leases, and have been included as components of prepaid expenses and other current assets, other non-current assets, accounts payable and accruals, and other non-current liabilities as applicable. These estimates are subject to change and such changes may be material.

Deferred revenue

The carrying value of deferred revenue was reduced by $40 million to reflect the estimated fair value of customer contract obligations assumed. This adjustment reduced revenues and operating profit by $35 million in the three months ended June 30, 2008. As a result, revenues recognized from these agreements will be less than the amounts paid by the customer.

Mitchells & Butlers plc

From 1980 until 2008, eating out as a percentage of total UK food expenditures climbed from 12% to 32%, whereas beer consumed in pubs and restaurants declined from 37 million barrels annually to 16 million barrels.[1] As the UK market shifted from pubs with limited food offerings to pubs with expanded menus and midpriced/value-for-money restaurants, Mitchells & Butlers became the leading operator of managed pubs and pub restaurants in the UK. Through internal growth and acquisitions, it grew to 2,000 pubs, pub restaurants, and hotels in the UK and Germany and employed more than 40,000 people. The firm divided the trade food and beverage market (as opposed to the home market) into four quadrants based on location and percentage of liquor to food sales. Mitchells & Butlers operated chains of themed pubs and pub restaurants with strong brand profiles, primarily in three of those quadrants.

Local Pubs (upper left quadrant) are aimed at specific audiences: Sizzling Pub Co., Ember Inns, and Cornerstone for family and neighborhood appeal; Metro Professionals geared toward the contemporary, youthful, and urban crowd; and Scream, catering to students and sport enthusiasts. Pub Restaurants (upper right quadrant) target the growing residential casual market. The High Street and City Centre segments occupy the lower two quadrants and cater to the bar and food scene within the city.

	Drinks-led	Food-led
	Sizzling Pub Co.	Vintage Inns
	Ember Inns	Harvester
	Cornerstone	Toby Carvery
Residential	Metro Professionals	Crown Carveries
	Scream	Premium Country Dining Group
	Local Pubs:	**Pub Restaurants:**
	37% of pubs; 36% of sales	**40% of pubs; 40% of sales**
	Town Pubs	All Bar One
	O'Neill's	Browns
City Centre	Nicholson's and Classic Pubs	
	Music bars	
	High Street Pubs & Bars	**City Centre Restaurants**
	20% of pubs; 20% of sales	**3% of pubs; 4% of sales**

Mitchells & Butlers, 2008

The year 2008 was difficult for the UK economy, and it was the first full year of the restaurant and pub smoking ban in the UK. Despite those problems, Mitchells & Butlers took market share from competitors in every market segment in which it operated due to its efficient operations, volume purchases, attractive locations, well-designed buildings, and quality food. It also disposed of 82 smaller pubs and

---

1. Mitchells & Butlers annual report, 2008, p. 19. ONS (Family Spending Service); BBPA.

hotels with low growth opportunities and acquired 44 high-quality pub restaurant sites from Whitbread, a major competitor, which were to be converted to Mitchells & Butlers' industry-leading brands and formats during the first half of 2009.

In contrast, the UK's two largest pub owners, Punch Taverns, plc, and Enterprise Inns, plc, which combined own nearly one-third of the UK's 56,000 pubs, are in financial difficulty. Both firms borrowed heavily to expand, as did Mitchells & Butlers, but with the recession and decline in pub revenues, both are closing or selling hundreds of pubs.[2] In July 2009, the BBC reported that 52 pubs were closing each week throughout the UK.[3]

Mitchells & Butlers had strong operating performance during 2008. However, in 2007, it planned a property joint venture. To hedge interest rates on the anticipated borrowings and hedge real estate prices for the planned property acquisitions, Mitchells & Butlers entered into derivatives contracts. When the joint venture did not occur, Mitchells & Butlers closed the derivative contracts at a loss of £386 million ($550 million USD). In his letter to shareholders, chairman Drummond Hall apologized:

> It has been a very challenging year for the pub sector and Mitchells & Butlers. We delivered a strong operational performance despite the pressures resulting from the first year of the smoking ban, the acceleration in the rate of on-trade beer market volume declines and significant cost inflationary pressures. Unfortunately, we were an early casualty of the difficulties caused by the credit crunch. In January the Company announced that, following a rapid deterioration in the mark-to-market deficit on the financial hedges taken out in connection with last year's proposed property joint venture, it had closed out in cash the hedges no longer required at a pre-tax cost of £386 million. On behalf of all the members of the Board I want to express our deep regret for the loss that occurred and the effect it has had on your business.
>
> At that time, in the absence of a property joint venture, we announced that we would conduct a thorough strategic review to determine clearly and openly what the best options were for creating value for our shareholders. This review examined an extensive range of options. Its main conclusions were the following: our business model was robust, sustainable and powerful; the Company should extend its leadership in the pub eating-out market by continuing to pursue our successful value and volume strategy; the Board should investigate options to create value from the non-core assets including Lodges, Hollywood Bowl and Alex; the creation of value through a REIT should be pursued when the timing is appropriate; and the executive management were proven, respected and committed to shareholder value.
>
> Mitchells & Butlers' operational performance has been robust with operating profits maintained for the year ended, while current trading is resilient, reflecting an acceleration in the rate of market share gains. As a result of this performance, cash generation has been strong with net cash flow last year of £164m, before dividend payments but after amortisation of secured debt. Overall, since the end of January, net debt has reduced by £175m to £2,735m.
>
> We are also conserving cash by reducing current year expansionary capital expenditure to focus resources on the maintenance of the existing high amenity standards in the estate as well as implementing further cost efficiency measures in the business.

2. Martinez, Jennifer, *The Wall Street Journal*, April 16, 2009, p. B1 and B4.

3. BBC Online News, "UK is losing 52 pubs each week." July 22, 2009. http://news.bbc.co.uk/2/hi/business/8161793.stm

We will continue to seek value creative disposal opportunities. However, our ability to realise cash at acceptable values from the remaining non-core assets, as envisaged in the strategic review, has been significantly impacted by the prevailing conditions in the financial markets in recent months. We are not prepared to dispose of non-core assets for amounts materially below their fair value.

The settlement in January 2008 of the majority of the interest rate and inflation hedging arrangements that the Company entered into in July 2007 in respect of the proposed property joint venture resulted in a post-tax loss of £274m (£386m loss before tax). Of this, £145m (£204m before tax) was reported as an exceptional charge against income in 2007. A portion of the interest rate swaps were retained to provide an economic hedge against the future anticipated cash flows associated with an element of the Group's non-securitised debt as this forms part of the Company's core long-term debt structure. These swaps do not qualify for hedge accounting as defined in IAS 39. The reduction in fair value on these swaps was £17m after tax (£23m before tax) during the year.

That cost is also shown on the firm's cash flow statement (see Exhibit 4, sixth item from the bottom, 2008).

Fair Value Reporting

All UK quoted companies were required to adopt IFRS for years starting January 1, 2005, or later and all UK AIM companies were required to adopt IFRS for years starting January 1, 2007, or later.[4] Mitchells & Butlers, whose year ends September 30, adopted IFRS for its fiscal year ended September 30, 2006.

Under IAS 16, firms have the option to value property, plant, and equipment using either the cost model or the revaluation model. On September 30, 2007, Mitchells & Butlers adopted the revaluation model for freehold (owned) and long leasehold land and buildings and then revalued them at fair value. It continued to value short leasehold properties, fixtures, and furnishings at historic cost. The following are excerpts from IAS 16 that describe IFRS rules for the *cost model* and the *revaluation model*.

Cost model

Under the cost model, an item of property, plant and equipment shall be carried at its cost less any accumulated depreciation and any impairment losses (IAS 16: 30). Each part of an item of property, plant and equipment with a cost that is significant in relation to the total cost of the item shall be depreciated separately (IAS 16: 43). The impairment loss recognized in prior periods for an asset other than goodwill shall be reversed if, and only if, there has been a change in the estimates used to determine the asset's recoverable amount since the last impairment loss was recognized (IAS 36: 114). The increased carrying amount of an asset other than goodwill attributable to a reversal of an impairment loss shall not exceed the carrying amount that would have been determined (net of amortization or depreciation) had no impairment loss been recognized for the asset in prior years (IAS 36: 117).

Revaluation model

After recognition as an asset, an item of property, plant and equipment whose fair value can be measured reliably shall be carried at a revalued amount, being its fair value at the date of the revaluation less any subsequent accumulated depreciation

---

4. The London Stock Exchange operates two principal equity trading markets, the Main Market and AIM (Alternate Investments Markets). Larger firms trade on the Main Market; smaller firms trade on AIM.

and subsequent accumulated impairment losses. Revaluations shall be made with sufficient regularity to ensure that the carrying amount does not differ materially from that which would be determined using fair value at the end of the reporting period. (IAS 16: 31).

The fair value of land and buildings is usually determined from market-based evidence by valuation that is normally undertaken by professionally qualified appraisers. The fair value of items of plant and equipment is usually their market value determined by appraisal (IAS 16: 36).

When an item of property, plant and equipment is revalued, any accumulated depreciation at the date of revaluation is treated in one of the following ways: (a) restated proportionately with the change in the gross carrying amount of the asset so that the carrying amount of the asset after revaluation equals its revalued amount. This method is often used when an asset is revalued by means of applying an index to determine its depreciated replacement cost, or (b) eliminated against the gross carrying amount of the asset and the net amount restated to the revalued amount of the asset. This method is often used for buildings (IAS 36: 35).

If an asset's carrying amount is increased as a result of a revaluation, the increase shall be recognized in other comprehensive income and accumulated in equity under the heading of revaluation surplus. However, the increase shall be recognized in profit or loss to the extent that it reverses a revaluation decrease of the same asset previously recognized in profit or loss (IAS 36: 39).

If an asset's carrying amount is decreased as a result of revaluation, the decrease shall be recognized in profit or loss. However, the decrease shall be recognized in other comprehensive income to the extent of any credit balance existing in the revaluation surplus in respect to that asset. The decrease recognized in other comprehensive income reduces the amount accumulated in equity under the heading of revaluation surplus (IAS 36:40).

2008 Annual Report

Mitchells & Butlers financial statements are shown in Exhibits 1–4. The income statement in Exhibit 1 is different from U.S. GAAP financial statements and many other IFRS financial statements in that it has a separate column for exceptional items. Under U.S. GAAP, extraordinary items are shown net of tax, in a separate section of the income statement. IFRS does not allow firms to report extraordinary items, but many countries that adopted IFRS require firms to separately report exceptional items. Although IFRS rules prohibit extraordinary items and do not even mention exceptional items, exceptional items are commonly reported in the UK and France.[5]

Exhibit 5 includes several notes from Mitchells & Butlers' 2008 annual report. Note 9, Exceptional Items, explains the exceptional column in the income statement (Exhibit 1). Note 15, Property, Plant and Equipment, describes Mitchells & Butlers' revaluation of its freehold and long-leased properties, for which it adopted the IFRS Revaluation Model.

Note 20, Borrowings, describes how, on November 13, 2003, Mitchells & Butlers issued £1.9 billion of securitized debt backed by the majority of its UK pubs and restaurants. Note 21, Financial Instruments, includes a fair value section. Mitchells & Butlers' securitized debt has a £2.339 billion book value and a £2.087 billion fair

---

5. PriceWaterhouseCoopers, *Survey of 2,800 European financial statements, Presentation of income under IFRS: flexibility and consistency explored*, 2007. http://download.pwc.com/ie/pubs/presentation_of_income_under_ifrs.pdf.

value. Because IFRS rules require that Mitchells & Butlers report all derivatives at fair value, the firm reports a £52 billion loss on its interest rate swaps (a £1 million asset offset by a £53 million liability) and a £28 million loss on currency swaps. The text below the fair value table discloses that Mitchells & Butlers entered into interest rate swap contracts such that it receives quarterly floating rate interest payments based on LIBOR, and it pays a fixed rate of 4.8938% to its counterparty (based on a nominal value of £1.015 billion).

Note 27 reports cash flow from operations, which is the starting number in Exhibit 4, the firm's cash flow statement.

Required

1. Evaluate Mitchells & Butlers' reporting of exceptional items in its income statement (Exhibit 1) and in note 9 (Exhibit 5). Would it be preferable to omit that information or to only provide it as a note to the financial statements? Explain.

2. Why did Mitchells & Butlers adopt the revaluation model for its freehold and long-leasehold properties and land in 2007? Compare the relevance and reliability of the cost model versus the revaluation model for Mitchells & Butlers.

3. Based on your analysis of Mitchells & Butlers' exceptional items, revaluation model, and segment disclosures in note 3, do you expect the firm to report a profit for 2009? Do you expect it to report positive cash flows from operations? Explain.

4. Evaluate Mitchells & Butlers' use of securitization in 2003 and 2006 (note 20, Exhibit 5). Why did it issue floating rate notes but convert them to fixed rate debt with swaps?

	Notes	2008 52 weeks Before exceptional items and IAS 39 movements £m	Exceptional items and IAS 39 movements[a] £m	Total £m	2007 52 weeks Before exceptional items and IAS 39 movements £m	Exceptional items and IAS 39 movements[a] £m	Total £m
Revenue	1, 3	1,908	—	1,908	1,894	—	1,894
Operating costs before depreciation and amortisation	4, 9	(1,431)	(12)	(1,443)	(1,422)	(11)	(1,433)
Net profit arising on property disposals	9	—	6	6	—	27	27
EBITDA[b]		477	(6)	471	472	16	488
Depreciation, amortisation and impairment	4, 14, 15	(134)	(206)	(340)	(129)	(50)	(179)
Operating profit	3	343	(212)	131	343	(34)	309
Finance costs	9, 10	(174)	(205)	(379)	(153)	(221)	(374)
Finance revenue	10	7	—	7	6	—	6
Net finance income from pensions	10	3	—	3	11	—	11
Profit/(loss) before tax		179	(417)	(238)	207	(255)	(48)
Tax (expense)/credit	9, 11	(52)	114	62	(62)	100	38
Profit/(loss) for the financial period attributable to equity holders of the parent		127	(303)	(176)	145	(155)	(10)
Earnings/(loss) per ordinary share							
Basic	13	31.5p		(43.7)p	35.5p		(2.5)p
Diluted	13	31.1p		(43.7)p	34.4p		(2.5)p
Dividends							
Ordinary dividends							
Proposed or paid (pence)	12			4.55			14.25
Proposed or paid (£m)	12			18			57
Special dividends							
Paid (pence)	12			—			100.00
Paid (£m)	12			—			486

[a] Exceptional items and IAS 39 movements are explained in note 1 and analysed in notes 9 and 10.
[b] Earnings before interest, tax, depreciation, amortisation and impairment.

All activities relate to continuing operations.

	Notes	2008 £m	2007 £m
ASSETS			
Goodwill and other intangible assets	14	3	17
Property, plant and equipment	15	4,545	5,030
Lease premiums		10	11
Deferred tax asset	22	58	75
Derivative financial instruments	21	1	30
Total non-current assets		4,617	5,163
Inventories	16	39	38
Trade and other receivables	17	80	69
Current tax asset		3	—
Derivative financial instruments	21	—	79
Other cash deposits	28	2	—
Cash and cash equivalents	28	129	117
Total current assets		253	303
Non-current assets held for sale	18	114	6
Total assets		4,984	5,472
LIABILITIES			
Borrowings	20	(89)	(234)
Derivative financial instruments	21	(48)	(295)
Trade and other payables	19	(276)	(243)
Current tax liabilities		—	(18)
Total current liabilities		(413)	(790)
Borrowings	20	(2,755)	(2,317)
Derivative financial instruments	21	(33)	(47)
Pension liabilities	8	(23)	(18)
Deferred tax liabilities	22	(584)	(723)
Provisions	23	(1)	(1)
Total non-current liabilities		(3,396)	(3,106)
Total liabilities		(3,809)	(3,896)
Net assets attributable to equity holders of the parent		1,175	1,576
EQUITY			
Called up share capital	24,26	34	34
Share premium account	26	14	14
Capital redemption reserve	26	3	3
Revaluation reserve	26	697	828
Own shares held	26	(3)	(13)
Hedging reserve	26	(16)	20
Translation reserve	26	12	7
Retained earnings	26	434	683
Total equity		1,175	1,576

EXHIBIT 2

GROUP BALANCE SHEET, 27 SEPTEMBER 2008

EXHIBIT 3

GROUP STATEMENT
OF RECOGNIZED
INCOME AND
EXPENSE FOR THE
52 WEEKS ENDED
27 SEPTEMBER
2008

	Notes	2008 52 weeks £m	2007 52 weeks £m
Unrealised (loss)/gain on revaluation of the property portfolio	15	(166)	1,124
Tax credit/(charge) relating to movements in respect of revaluations	11	64	(292)
(Losses)/gains on cash flow hedges taken to equity	21	(20)	55
Actuarial (losses)/gains on defined benefit pension schemes	8	(35)	33
Tax on items recognised directly in equity	11	5	(23)
Tax credit in respect of change in tax rate	11	—	30
Income recognised directly in equity **Transfers to the income statement:**		(152)	927
On cash flow hedges	21	(30)	15
Tax on items transferred from equity	11	8	(5)
Net income recognised directly in equity		(174)	937
Loss for the financial period		(176)	(10)
Total recognised income and expense for the financial period attributable to equity holders of the parent		(350)	927

EXHIBIT 4

GROUP CASH FLOW
STATEMENT FOR THE
52 WEEKS ENDED
27 SEPTEMBER 2008

	Notes	2008 52 weeks £m	2007 52 weeks £m
Cash flow from operations	27	474	447
Interest paid		(171)	(151)
Interest received		7	6
Tax paid		(4)	(33)
Net cash from operating activities		306	269
Investing activities			
Purchases of property, plant and equipment		(192)	(252)
Acquisition of Whitbread pub restaurant sites		—	(8)
Purchases of intangibles (computer software)		(1)	(1)
Proceeds from sale of property, plant and equipment		82	162
Transfers to cash deposits with a maturity of greater than three months		(2)	—
Corporate restructuring costs		(3)	(4)
Net cash used in investing activities		(116)	(103)
Financing activities			
Purchase of own shares		(5)	(46)
Proceeds on release of own shares held		3	11
Repayment of principal in respect of securitised debt	20	(41)	(39)
Proceeds from other debt		320	192
Expenditure associated with refinancing		(11)	(4)
Derivative financial instruments closure costs	9	(386)	—

(continued)

Dividends paid	12	(58)	(538)
Net cash used in financing activities		(178)	(424)
Net increase/(decrease) in cash and cash equivalents	29	12	(258)
Cash and cash equivalents at the beginning of the financial period		117	375
Cash and cash equivalents at the end of the financial period		129	117

Cash and cash equivalents are defined in note 1.

The notes on pages 69 to 98 form an integral part of these financial statements.

EXHIBIT 4—
continued

GROUP CASH FLOW
STATEMENT FOR THE
52 WEEKS ENDED
27 SEPTEMBER 208

1. General information

Mitchells & Butlers plc (the 'Group') is required to prepare its consolidated financial statements in accordance with International Financial Reporting Standards as adopted by the European Union (IFRS) and in accordance with the Companies Act 1985.

The Group revalues its freehold and long leasehold land and buildings to fair value, which it reviews at least annually. Short leasehold properties, fixtures and fittings are held at deemed cost on transition to IFRS less depreciation and impairment provisions, which is also considered by the Group to be a reasonable approximation to their fair value. Non-current assets held for sale as at 27 September 2008 are held at their carrying value in accordance with the Group's policy or their net realisable value where this is lower. The Group's policy is to account for land held under both long and short leasehold contracts as operating leases, since it has no expectation that title will pass on expiry of the lease contracts.

Property, plant and equipment

Within property plant and equipment, freehold and long leasehold land and buildings have been revalued as at 27 September 2008 to fair value. Short leasehold properties, fixtures and fittings are held at deemed cost on transition to IFRS less depreciation and impairment provisions and non-current assets held for sale as at 27 September 2008 are held at their carrying value in accordance with the Group's policy or their net realisable value where this is lower. Surpluses which arise from the revaluation exercise are recorded directly within the revaluation reserve unless they are reversing a revaluation decrease which has been recognised in the income statement previously; in which case an amount equal to a maximum of that recognised in the income statement previously is recognised in income. Where the revaluation exercise gives rise to a deficit, this is reflected directly in the revaluation reserve to the extent that a surplus exists against the same asset. Any residual amount is then recognised against income.

Leases

i Operating leases

Leases in which substantially all the risks and rewards of ownership are retained by the lessor are classified as operating leases. Payments made under operating leases and sub-leases are charged to the income statement on a straight line basis over the period of the lease. Lease incentives are recognised as a reduction in the rental expense over the lease term.

Premiums paid on acquiring a new lease are spread on a straight line basis over the lease term. Such premiums are classified in the balance sheet as current or non-current prepayments, with the current portion being the element which relates to the following financial period.

EXHIBIT 5

NOTES TO THE
FINANCIAL
STATEMENTS
(SELECTED)

(continued)

EXHIBIT 5—
continued

NOTES TO THE
FINANCIAL
STATEMENTS
(SELECTED)

The Group's policy is to account for land held under both long and short leasehold contracts as operating leases, since it has no expectation that title will pass on expiry of the lease contracts.

ii Finance leases

Leases in which the Group assumes substantially all the risks and rewards of ownership are classified as finance leases. Property, plant and equipment acquired by way of finance lease are capitalised at the inception of the lease at an amount equal to the lower of their fair value and the present value of the minimum lease payments. The corresponding liability to the lessor is included in the balance sheet as a finance lease obligation. Lease payments are apportioned between the finance lease obligation and finance charges in the income statement so as to achieve a constant rate of interest on the remaining balance of the obligation.

5. Auditors' remuneration

	2008 52 weeks £m	2007 52 weeks £m
Audit of the financial statements	0.2	0.1
Audit of the Company's subsidiaries	0.4	0.4
	0.6	0.5
Other fees to auditors:		
– taxation and other services	0.1	0.1
– corporate finance services	0.2	0.5
	0.3	0.6

The auditors' fee for the audit of the parent company was £22,000 (2007 £21,000). Substantially all of the auditors' remuneration was paid in the UK.

9. Exceptional items

	2008 52 weeks £m	2007 52 weeks £m
Operating exceptional items		
Integration costs[a]	—	(4)
Corporate restructuring costs[b]	—	(7)
Strategic review costs[c]	(12)	—
	(12)	(11)
Profits on disposal of properties	19	39
Losses on disposal of properties	(13)	(12)
Net profit arising on property disposals	6	27
Impairment arising from the revaluation of the property portfolio[d]	(160)	(45)
Impairment arising on classification of non-current assets held for sale[e]	(46)	(5)
Total impairment	(206)	(50)
Total operating exceptional items	(212)	(34)
Exceptional finance costs		
Movement in fair value of derivative financial instruments closed out in the period[f] (note 10)	(182)	(204)
	(182)	(204)

(continued)

EXHIBIT 5—
continued

NOTES TO THE
FINANCIAL
STATEMENTS
(SELECTED)

Total exceptional items before tax	(394)	(238)
IAS 39 movements (note 10)	(23)	(17)
Total exceptional items and IAS 39 movements before tax	(417)	(255)
Tax credit relating to above items	88	74
Exceptional tax released in respect of prior years[g]	14	9
Tax credit in respect of change in tax rate[h]	—	17
Tax credit in respect of change in tax legislation[i]	12	—
	114	100
Total exceptional items and IAS 39 movements after tax	(303)	(155)

15. Property, plant and equipment

	Land and buildings £m	Fixtures, fittings and equipment £m	Total £m
Cost or valuation			
At 1 October 2006	3,267	906	4,173
Exchange differences	1	—	1
Additions	105	154	259
Revaluation	1,042	—	1,042
Disposals[a]	(37)	(79)	(116)
Impairment arising on classification of non-current assets held for sale	(2)	(3)	(5)
Classified as held for sale	(5)	(4)	(9)
At 29 September 2007	4,371	974	5,345
Exchange differences	4	2	6
Additions	159	108	267
Revaluation	(343)	—	(343)
Disposals[a]	(133)	(129)	(262)
Impairment arising on classification of non-current assets held for sale	(33)	(2)	(35)
Classified as held for sale	(104)	(41)	(145)
At 27 September 2008	**3,921**	**912**	**4,833**
Depreciation			
At 1 October 2006	97	209	306
Exchange differences	—	1	1
Provided during the year	21	101	122
Disposals[a]	—	(70)	(70)
Classified as held for sale	(4)	(3)	(7)
Revaluation	(37)	—	(37)
At 29 September 2007	77	238	315
Exchange differences	1	2	3
Provided during the year	23	106	129
Disposals[a]	(3)	(108)	(111)
Classified as held for sale	(16)	(15)	(31)
Revaluation	(17)	—	(17)

(continued)

EXHIBIT 5—
continued

NOTES TO THE
FINANCIAL
STATEMENTS
(SELECTED)

At 27 September 2008	**65**	**223**	**288**
Net book value			
At 27 September 2008	**3,856**	**689**	**4,545**
At 29 September 2007	4,294	736	5,030
At 1 October 2006	3,170	697	3,867

---

[a]Includes assets which are fully depreciated and have been removed from the fixed asset ledger.

Properties

A policy of valuing the majority of the Group's freehold and long leasehold land and buildings was adopted on 29 September 2007. Short leasehold properties and fixtures, fittings and equipment are held at deemed cost at transition to IFRS less depreciation and impairment, which is also considered by the Group to be a reasonable approximation to their fair value. Non-current assets held for sale are held at their carrying value in accordance with the Group's policy or their net realisable value where this is lower. The Group accounts for long leasehold land as an operating lease.

The freehold and long leasehold land and buildings were valued at market value, as at 27 September 2008 and 29 September 2007 by Colliers CRE plc, independent chartered surveyors and by Andrew Cox MRICS, Director of Property, Chartered Surveyor. The valuation was carried out in accordance with the provisions of RICS Appraisal and Valuation Standards ('The Red Book') assuming each asset is sold as part of the continuing enterprise in occupation individually as a fully operational trading entity. The market value has been determined having regard to factors such as current and future projected income levels, taking account of the location, the quality of the pub or restaurant and recent market transactions in the sector. Changes in these assumptions such as the valuation basis applied in comparable market transactions, or the income level generated by a pub could materially impact the valuation of the freehold and long leasehold land and buildings.

Included within property, plant and equipment are assets with a net book value of £3,974m (2007 £4,321m), which are pledged as security for the securitisation debt and over which there are certain restrictions on title.

On 19 September 2008, the Group announced that it had completed a deal to exchange 21 of its hotels (these were included within the 'Restaurants' operating segment, see note 3, segmental analysis, until the date of completion) for 44 individual pub restaurants owned by Whitbread PLC. The hotels, which were carried at net book value of £78m are included within disposals above. The pub restaurants acquired are included at their fair value of £85m within additions, including £3m of stamp duty land tax and £5m of costs which were directly related to the asset exchange. No profit or loss arose on the transaction and no cash proceeds were received.

Finance leases

The net book value of fixtures, fittings and equipment includes £2m (2007 £2m) in respect of assets held under finance leases. The assets are pledged as security for the finance lease liabilities.

(continued)

EXHIBIT 5—
continued

NOTES TO THE
FINANCIAL
STATEMENTS
(SELECTED)

Net book value[a]

The split of the net book value of land and buildings is as follows:

	2008 £m	2007 £m
Freehold	3,476	3,824
Leasehold:		
– unexpired term of more than 50 years	258	325
– unexpired term of 50 years or less	122	145
	3,856	4,294

[a] The carrying value of freehold and long leasehold land and buildings based on their historic cost (or deemed cost at transition to IFRS), is £3,331m and £298m respectively.

In addition to the above, premiums paid on acquiring a new lease are classified in the balance sheet as prepayments of rentals under the leases. At 27 September 2008 an amount of £11m (2007 £12m) was included in the balance sheet.

20. Borrowings

	2008			2007		
Group	Current liabilities £m	Non-current liabilities £m	Total £m	Current liabilities £m	Non-current liabilities £m	Total £m
Securitised debt[a,b]	43	2,296	2,339	40	2,316	2,356
Other borrowings[b]	46	458	504	192	—	192
Loan notes[c]	—	—	—	2	—	2
Finance leases (note 31)	—	1	1	—	1	1
Total borrowings	89	2,755	2,844	234	2,317	2,551

[a] This debt is secured as explained on page 85.
[b] Stated net of deferred issue costs.
[c] The loan notes repaid during the year were partially secured by a bank deposit. Their effective interest rate at 29 September 2007 was 6.03%.

	2008 £m	2007 £m
Analysis by year of repayment[a]		
Due within one year or on demand	89	234
Due between one and two years	243	43
Due between two and five years	1,446	517
Due after five years	1,066	1,757
Total borrowings	2,844	2,551

[a] The analysis by year of repayment is calculated on the basis that the Group's securitised loan notes are refinanced on the margin step-up dates, however, the Group has an unconditional right to continue to hold the individual loan note tranches through to their final maturity dates (the analysis of loan notes below includes the principal repayment periods).

(continued)

EXHIBIT 5—
continued

NOTES TO THE
FINANCIAL
STATEMENTS
(SELECTED)

Securitised debt

On 13 November 2003, a group company, Mitchells & Butlers Finance plc, issued £1,900m of secured loan notes in connection with the securitisation of the majority of the Group's UK pubs and restaurants business owned by Mitchells & Butlers Retail Ltd. The funds raised were mainly used to repay existing bank borrowings of £1,243m, pay issue costs of £23m and return £501m to shareholders by way of a special dividend.

On 15 September 2006 Mitchells & Butlers Finance plc completed the issue of £655m of further secured loan notes in the form of the A4, AB, C2 and D1 loan notes as detailed below. These were issued under substantially the same terms as the original securitisation in November 2003. The funds raised were mainly used to return £486m to shareholders by way of a special dividend and to provide long-term funding for the Whitbread pub restaurant sites acquired. As part of the issue, the original A1 and A3 loan note tranches were repaid and reissued as A1N and A3N loan notes to take advantage of market rates.

At 27 September 2008 the loan notes consisted of 10 tranches as follows:

Tranche	Initial principal borrowed £m	Interest	Principal repayment period (all by installments)	Effective interest rate %	Principal outstanding at 27 September 2008 £m	Expected WAL[c]
A1N	200	Floating	2011 to 2028	5.69[b]	200	2 years
A2	550	Fixed–5.57%	2003 to 2028	6.01	429	8 years
A3N	250[a]	Floating	2011 to 2028	5.92[b]	250[a]	2 years
A4	170	Floating	2016 to 2028	5.24[b]	170	5 years
AB	325	Floating	2020 to 2032	5.25[b]	325	5 years
B1	350	Fixed–5.97%	2003 to 2023	6.12	291	6 years
B2	350	Fixed–6.01%	2015 to 2028	6.12	350	16 years
C1	200	Fixed–6.47%	2029 to 2030	6.57	200	21 years
C2	50	Floating	2033 to 2034	5.44[b]	50	5 years
D1	110	Floating	2034 to 2036	5.50[b]	110	5 years
	2,555[a]				2,375[a]	

At 29 September 2007 the loan notes consisted of 10 tranches as follows:

Tranche	Initial principal borrowed £m	Interest	Principal repayment period (all by installments)	Effective interest rate %	Principal outstanding at 29 September 2007 £m	Expected WAL[c]
A1N	200	Floating	2011 to 2028	5.69[b]	200	3 years
A2	550	Fixed–5.57%	2003 to 2028	6.01	456	9 years
A3N	250[a]	Floating	2011 to 2028	5.92[b]	250[a]	3 years
A4	170	Floating	2016 to 2028	5.24[b]	170	6 years
AB	325	Floating	2020 to 2032	5.25[b]	325	6 years
B1	350	Fixed–5.97%	2003 to 2023	6.12	305	7 years
B2	350	Fixed–6.01%	2015 to 2028	6.12	350	17 years
C1	200	Fixed–6.47%	2029 to 2030	6.57	200	22 years

(continued)

EXHIBIT 5—
continued

NOTES TO THE
FINANCIAL
STATEMENTS
(SELECTED)

C2	50	Floating	2033 to 2034	5.44[b]	50	6 years
D1	110	Floating	2034 to 2036	5.50[b]	110	6 years
	2,555[a]				2,416[a]	

[a] Includes the fair value impact of £22m (2007 £45m) in respect of the currency swaps
[b] After the effect of interest rate swaps
[c] The expected remaining weighted average life ('WAL') is based on the amortisation profile of the individual note tranches calculated on the basis of the refinancing of the notes on the margin step-up dates. The Group has an unconditional right to continue to hold the individual note tranches through to their final maturity dates however. The margin step-up dates as at 27 September 2008 are set out below.

The notes are secured on the majority of the Group's property and future income streams therefrom. All of the floating rate notes are fully hedged using interest rate swaps which fix the interest rate payable.

Interest and margin is payable on the floating rate notes as follows:

Tranche	Interest	Margin	Margin step-up date	Post step-up margin
A1N	3 month LIBOR	0.18%	December 2010	0.45%
A3N	3 month $ LIBOR	0.18%	December 2010	0.45%
A4	3 month LIBOR	0.23%	September 2013	0.58%
AB	3 month LIBOR	0.24%	September 2013	0.60%
C2	3 month LIBOR	0.75%	September 2013	1.88%
D1	3 month LIBOR	0.85%	September 2013	2.13%

The overall cash interest rate payable on the loan notes is 5.7% after taking account of interest rate hedging and the cost of the provision of a financial guarantee provided by Ambac in respect of the Class A and AB notes.

The securitisation is governed by various covenants, warranties and events of default, many of which apply to Mitchells & Butlers Retail Ltd, the Group's main operating subsidiary. These include covenants regarding the maintenance and disposal of securitised properties and restrictions on its ability to move cash, by way of dividends for example, to other group companies. At 27 September 2008, Mitchells & Butlers Retail Ltd had cash and cash equivalents of £118m (2007 £91m) which were governed by the covenants associated with the securitisation. Of this amount £14m (2007 £9m), representing disposal proceeds, was held on deposit in a secured account ('restricted cash'). The use of this cash requires the approval of the securitisation trustee and may only be used for certain specified purposes such as capital enhancement expenditure and business acquisitions.

20. Borrowings

The carrying value of the securitised debt in the Group balance sheet at 27 September 2008 is analysed as follows:

	2008 £m	2007 £m
Principal outstanding at beginning of period	2,371	2,429
Principal repaid during the period	(41)	(39)
Exchange on translation of dollar loan notes	23	(19)
Principal outstanding at end of period	2,353	2,371
Deferred issue costs	(18)	(20)
Accrued interest	4	5
Carrying value at end of period	2,339	2,356

(continued)

EXHIBIT 5—
continued

NOTES TO THE
FINANCIAL
STATEMENTS
(SELECTED)

At 27 September 2008 the Group had the following undrawn committed borrowing facilities:

Undrawn committed borrowing facilities[a]	2008 £m	2007 £m
Unutilised facilities expire:		
Within one year	—	—
Between two and five years	86	108
	86	108

[a] In addition to the undrawn amounts against the £600m term and revolving credit facility the Group holds a £295m liquidity facility against the securitised loan notes, which is not available for any other purpose.

On 28 September 2006 the Group entered into a three year £300m revolving credit facility for general business purposes which incurred interest at LIBOR plus a margin. On 21 November 2007, Mitchells and Butlers plc entered into a further £400m facility expiring on 28 September 2009 which was used to fund the settlement of the derivative financial transactions relating to the aborted property joint venture. On 24 July 2008 the Group entered into a three year £600m term and revolving credit facility expiring on 30 November 2011, including a £300m revolving credit facility, for general business purposes which incurs interest at LIBOR plus a margin. The facility has been set at £600m initially, reducing to £550m from December 2008, £400m from December 2009 and £300m by December 2010. The drawings against the original £300m revolving credit facility and £400m facility were repaid using the proceeds of the new £600m medium-term facility and these facilities were cancelled. As at 27 September 2008 the Group had drawn an amount of £504m (net of deferred issue costs) against the £600m facility which forms part of the 'Other borrowings' balance.

21. Financial instruments

Fair values

Fair values of financial instruments are disclosed below:

	2008 Book value £m	2008 Fair value £m	2007 Book value £m	2007 Fair value £m
Primary financial instruments[a] held or issued to finance the Group's operations:				
Cash and cash equivalents	129	129	117	117
Other cash deposits	2	2	—	—
Other borrowings	(504)	(504)	(192)	(192)
Securitised debt (excluding interest rate and currency swaps)	(2,339)	(2,087)	(2,356)	(2,408)
Loan notes	—	—	(2)	(2)
Finance leases	(1)	(1)	(1)	(1)
Provisions	(1)	(1)	(1)	(1)
Derivative financial instruments held to manage the interest rate and currency profile: Interest rate swaps:				
– asset	1	1	75	75
– liability	(53)	(53)	(140)	(140)

(continued)

EXHIBIT 5—
continued

NOTES TO THE
FINANCIAL
STATEMENTS
(SELECTED)

Currency swaps[b]	(28)	(28)	(48)	(48)
Inflation swaps	—	—	(154)	(154)
Reverse gilt locks	—	—	34	34
	(2,794)	(2,542)	(2,668)	(2,720)

[a] Excludes working capital items such as trade receivables and payables as their carrying amount is considered to approximate to their fair value.

[b] Includes £22m (2007 £45m) relating to currency movements on the retranslation of the $418.75m A3N loan note, included within net debt (see note 20).

The various tranches of the securitised debt have been valued using period end quoted offer prices. As the securitised debt is traded on an active market, the market value represents the fair value of this debt. The fair value of interest rate and currency swaps is the estimated amount which the Group could expect to pay or receive on termination of the agreements. These amounts are based on quotations from counterparties which approximate to their fair market value and take into consideration interest and exchange rates prevailing at the balance sheet date. Other financial assets and liabilities are either short-term in nature or book values approximate to fair values.

27. Cash flow from operations

	2008 52 weeks £m	2007 52 weeks £m
Operating profit	131	309
Add back: operating exceptional items	212	34
Operating profit before exceptional items	343	343
Add back:		
Depreciation of property, plant and equipment	129	122
Amortisation of intangibles (computer software)	4	6
Amortisation of lease premiums	1	1
Cost charged in respect of share remuneration	4	8
Defined benefit pension cost less regular cash contributions	(2)	3
Operating cash flow before exceptional items, movements in working capital and additional pension contributions	479	483
Movements in working capital and pension contributions:		
(Increase)/decrease in inventories	(1)	4
(Increase)/decrease in trade and other receivables	(7)	3
Increase in trade and other payables	39	3
Movement in provisions	—	(2)
Additional pension contributions (note 8)	(24)	(40)
Cash flow from operations before exceptional items	486	451
Integration costs paid	—	(4)
Strategic review costs	(12)	—
Cash flow from operations	474	447

CASE 4.6

Barclays' Acquisition of Lehman Brothers

By the end of September 2007, there was no indication that questionable mortgages were a serious problem in the United States or abroad. On the contrary, the problems seemed both minor and in the past. HSBC Holdings plc wrote off $10.6 billion of sub-prime mortgage loans in March 2007, and New Century Financial Corporation filed for bankruptcy protection in April 2007. Those problems were small relative to the size of the world's booming economies, and by September the problems seemed to be over. On Friday, October 5, 2007, the Dow Jones Industrial Average and S&P 500 Average reached record highs.

The same day, Merrill Lynch announced a $5 billion write-down, primarily on subprime loans. Ten days later, Citigroup announced a $5.9 billion write-off, including $2.24 billion for mortgage-backed securities and consumer loans. The following week, the week of October 24, Merrill Lynch increased its write-down to $8.4 billion, including a $7.9 billion write-down for mortgage-related derivatives. Mr. Stanley O'Neal, chairman and CEO of Merrill Lynch since 2003, resigned on October 29, 2007. Two weeks later, on November 5, Citigroup announced an estimated $8 to $11 billion loss on its $55 billion subprime mortgage-related portfolio; Citigroup CEO Charles Prince resigned that same day.

U.S. markets stabilized until early March 2008, when rumors spread about liquidity problems and subprime mortgage losses at The Bear Stearns Companies (Bear Stearns). On Friday, March 14, 2008, Bear Stearns' common stock price dropped by half to $30 per share, but liquidity problems were so serious that Bear Stearns executives realized they would be unable to open for business the following Monday. That weekend, officials from Bear Stearns, JPMorgan Chase, the U.S. Treasury, and the New York Federal Reserve Bank officials arranged for JPMorgan to acquire Bear Stearns. The Federal Reserve Bank of New York provided a $30 billion nonrecourse loan backed by questionable mortgages; JPMorgan would pay $2 per share for Bear Stearns (later increased to $10 per share). *The Wall Street Journal* announced the acquisition Sunday evening, March 16, and the financial markets stabilized.[1]

Fannie Mae and Freddie Mac, the massive U.S. mortgage lenders and mortgage guarantors, also had serious financial problems. Fannie Mae's share price declined from about $30 in May to $7 on Friday, September 5, 2008, and Freddie Mac's shares fell from about $25 in May to $5 on September 5. On Sunday, September 7, the United States announced it had placed both organizations into conservatorship (similar to a Chapter 11 bankruptcy, but for government sponsored entities, or GSEs). The share price of both organizations fell to less than $1, yet financial markets rose on the news.

During the week beginning Monday, September 8, rumors swirled about Merrill Lynch, AIG, Washington Mutual, and Wachovia, but Lehman Brothers (Lehman), the giant investment bank, seemed in the most immediate danger. In May, Lehman's share price was near $40. By Thursday, September 11, its share price declined to nearly $4.

---

1. Paulson, Henry M. Jr., *On the Brink*, Business Plus, Hachette Book Group, New York, 2010, pp. 110–121.

During that weekend, the U.S. Treasury Department and the Federal Reserve Bank of New York searched frantically for a way to save Lehman, as financial markets were in turmoil.[2] The spread between U.S. Treasuries and the London Interbank Offering Rate (LIBOR) increased to 135 basis points by Friday, September 12. The following week, the spread rose to 300 basis points and then above 400 in early October.[3] Leading financial institutions were no longer lending to each other, and there were few financial institutions in the world qualified to acquire Lehman.

Citigroup, the world's largest and most profitable financial institution a year earlier, had collapsed under tens of billions of subprime mortgage losses; Bank of America was in the process of acquiring Merrill Lynch; JPMorgan acquired Bear Stearns earlier in the year and was about to acquire Washington Mutual; Wells Fargo was in the process of acquiring Wachovia. Of the international banks, only Barclays had avoided losses in complex, highly illiquid derivatives of questionable value. Barclays, however, was subject to UK banking authority regulations.

By the end of trading on Friday, September 12, it was clear that Lehman would not open for business the following week. On Monday, September 15, Lehman Brothers Holdings, Inc. (LBHI), the parent company of Lehman, commenced a voluntary bankruptcy proceeding under Title 11 of the U.S. Bankruptcy Code. That Friday, September 19, Lehman Brothers, Inc. (LBI), Lehman's highly profitable U.S. broker-dealer operations, filed its own bankruptcy petition.

That weekend, in extraordinarily complex and hurried negotiations, LBHI bankruptcy trustees reached an agreement to sell LBI to Barclays. Barclays agreed to pay approximately $1.75 billion for the LBI U.S. broker-dealer operations and to separately acquire approximately $47.4 billion in securities and assume approximately $45.5 billion in trading liabilities. However, because of turmoil in the securities markets, many of the assets and liabilities were illiquid, so their value was highly uncertain. Lehman recorded the assets and liabilities at fair value ("fair market value" in some legal responses), but in many instances fair values were not current (i.e., were "old" marks). On Saturday, September 20, shortly after midnight, the court approved the transaction and the deal closed Monday, September 22.[4]

Barclays Acquires LBI

Lehman Brothers had been one of the world's most profitable investment banks through 2007. Exhibit 1 shows LBHI's income statements from 2005 to 2007, with a breakdown of revenue and pre-tax income by region. Until 2007, most LBHI earnings were from its North American operations, which were the primary operations Barclays acquired.

Under U.S. GAAP and IFRS, firms must record the fair value of all identifiable intangible assets acquired in a business combination, such as Barclays' acquisition of LBI. The only identifiable intangible assets specifically excluded are the value of an in-place workforce and the value of potential future customers; they are included in goodwill (existing customers are usually included in "customer lists" or "customer relationships").

Exhibit 2 shows the business combination note from Barclays' 2008 annual report. Barclays was required to record all acquired assets and liabilities at fair value under IFRS Statement 3. Under both IFRS and U.S. GAAP, if the purchase price exceeds

---

2. Paulson, *On the Brink*.

3. Bloomberg.com, TED spread. http://www.bloomberg.com/apps/quote?ticker=.TEDSP:IND.

4. Reuters online, "Judge approves Lehman, Barclays pact," Sept. 20, 2008. http://www.reuters.com/article/idUSN1932554220080920.

fair value of identifiable tangible and intangible acquired assets, the difference is recorded as goodwill. If the fair value of identifiable tangible and intangible acquired assets exceeds the purchase price, the difference is recorded as a gain on acquisition. From Exhibit 2, Barclays recorded a total acquisition cost of £874 million ($1.85 per British pound). Barclays also recorded net assets acquired of £3,299 (including £888 of identifiable intangible assets), for a £2.262 billion gain on the acquisition.

For comparison, Exhibits 3, 4, and 5 show JPMorgan's acquisition of Bear Stearns, Washington Mutual, and Bank One, respectively. Exhibit 3 shows that JPMorgan recorded $761 million of goodwill from its Bear Stearns acquisition (i.e., JPMorgan paid $761 more than the fair value of Bear Stearns' assets). However, JPMorgan recorded no identifiable intangibles from the acquisition.

Exhibit 4 shows that JPMorgan also recorded no identifiable intangibles from its acquisition of Washington Mutual. Without assigning any value to identifiable intangible assets, JPMorgan still paid $9.968 billion less than the fair value of net assets it acquired. However, under U.S. GAAP, JPMorgan did not record that as a gain. At the time, U.S. GAAP and IFRS accounting rules differed for business combinations. The FASB and IASB had worked closely to produce nearly identical business combination standards, but the IASB implemented them in 2007 and the FASB delayed implementation until December 15, 2008.

JPMorgan first reduced the value of its acquired nonfinancial assets to zero before it could record a gain on the acquisition. JPMorgan then recorded the remaining excess of acquired assets over purchase price, $1.906 billion, as an extraordinary gain. In contrast, under IFRS rules, Barclays recorded its entire £2.262 billion gain as ordinary income without reducing the fair value of any acquired assets.

Exhibit 5 shows JPMorgan's 2004 Bank One acquisition, an acquisition under ordinary circumstances. JPMorgan recorded $8.665 billion of identifiable intangible assets and $34.16 billion of goodwill. Although JPMorgan did not disclose the breakdown of the acquired intangible assets, they almost certainly included customer lists and customer relationships.

The LHBI Bankruptcy Trustees' Lawsuit

On September 15, 2009, Lehman's Bankruptcy Trustees filed a motion under Federal Rule 60 of Civil Procedure for Relief asking that parts of the bankruptcy settlement be overturned. Lehman contended, in effect, that Barclays acted in bad faith in the purchase of certain assets and had aided and abetted certain fiduciary obligation breaches by Lehman executives. Exhibit 6 is an excerpt of the 36-page adversary complaint, filed November 16, 2009, alleging that Barclays acted in bad faith and that it encouraged certain Lehman executives to breach their fiduciary duties. The full document can be found at http://insuranceclaimsbadfaith.typepad.com/files/lehman-brothers-v.-barclays-capital-adversary-complaint-bankr.-s.d.n.y.-case-no.-09-01731-filed-november-16-2009.pdf.

In that complaint, Jones Day, one of the nation's leading law firms, alleges that LHBI attorneys provided the bankruptcy court with incomplete and misleading information. They claimed that Barclays and certain Lehman executives withheld crucial information from LBHI's law firm, Weil Gotshal & Manges, and Weil Gotshal's lead attorney, Harvey Miller, one of the nation's leading bankruptcy and corporate restructuring attorneys.

Most of the nation's leading corporate law firms have existed for 50–100 years. A rare exception is Boies, Schiller & Flexner, founded in 1997 by David Boies and Jonathan Schiller. For at least 35 years, David Boies has been widely regarded as one of the most brilliant and tireless attorneys in the nation. He is renowned for searching through hundreds of thousands of documents to find evidence or legal opinions to support his positions. He is widely known for devastating cross examinations and he represented former Vice President Al Gore in *Bush v. Gore*.

To defend against LBHI's charges, Barclays hired Boies, Schiller & Flexner. Exhibit 7 is the preliminary statement from Boise, Schiller & Flexner's 304-page response to the Jones Day 36-page complaint. Communications between a client and attorney are privileged in the United States, a privilege considered near sacred. However, by claiming that Mr. Miller had been mislead, Boies, Schiller & Flexner successfully argued that LHBI waived its attorney-client privilege, so that Mr. Boies was allowed to depose Mr. Miller; portions of that deposition are included in the Boise, Schiller & Flexner response. The full Boise, Schiller & Flexner response can be found at http://insuranceclaimsbadfaith.typepad.com/files/012910.barclaysmemorandum-bankr.-s.d.n.y.-case-nos.-08-13555-08-01420.-1.pdf.

Mr. Miller's 117-page deposition, with Mr. Boies examining, can be found at http://online.wsj.com/public/resources/documents/miller_deposition.pdf (pp. 1–30; includes other depositions). Also see Case 4.8.

Mr. Miller's deposition gives a highly detailed view of the confusion, uncertainty, and pace of the negotiations surrounding Barclay's acquisition.

Required

1. How would Barclays have computed the value of customer lists acquired in the Lehman Brothers acquisition? How would JPMorgan Chase have computed the $8.665 billion of intangible assets acquired in its Bank One acquisition? Explain in detail.

2. Why did JPMorgan record no identifiable intangible assets when it acquired Bear Stearns and Washington Mutual?

3. If a firm pays less than the fair value of acquired net assets and has a potential gain, does it have an incentive to record identifiable intangible assets at a high or a low value? Explain.

4. If a firm pays more than the fair value of acquired net assets and has potential goodwill, does it have an incentive to record identifiable assets at a high or low value? Explain.

5. How subjective is the valuation of identifiable intangible assets? Explain.

6. Identify all the alleged undervalued or excess assets transferred to Barclays and all the alleged overstated liabilities transferred to Barclays (Exhibit 6).

7. Evaluate the Boise, Schiller response (Exhibit 7). Does the response address all of the alleged undervalued or excess asset claims and all the alleged overstated liability claims? Explain.

8. Is it possible that Barclays substantially undervalued the identifiable assets it acquired from LBHI (for example, by tens of billions of U.S. dollars)? Explain. Is it possible that JPMorgan undervalued the identifiable assets it acquired from Bear Stearns and Washington Mutual by similar amounts? Explain.

EXHIBIT 1

LBHI
CONSOLIDATED
STATEMENT OF
INCOME

In millions, except per share data	Year ended November 30,		
	2007	**2006**	**2005**
Revenues			
Principal transactions	$9,197	$9,802	$7,811
Investment banking	3,903	3,160	2,894
Commissions	2,471	2,050	1,728
Interest and dividends	41,693	30,284	19,043
Asset management and other	1,739	1,413	944
Total revenues	59,003	46,709	32,420
Interest expense	39,746	29,126	17,790
Net revenues	19,257	17,583	14,630
Non-Interest Expenses			
Compensation and benefits	9,494	8,669	7,213
Technology and communications	1,145	974	834
Brokerage, clearance and distribution fees	859	629	548
Occupancy	641	539	490
Professional fees	466	364	282
Business development	378	301	234
Other	261	202	200
Total non-personnel expenses	3,750	3,009	2,588
Total non-interest expenses	13,244	11,678	9,801
Income before taxes and cumulative effect of accounting change	6,013	5,905	4,829
Provision for income taxes	1,821	1,945	1,569
Income before cumulative effect of accounting change	4,192	3,960	3,260
Cumulative effect of accounting change	—	47	—
Net income	$4,192	$4,007	$3,260
Net income applicable to common stock	$4,125	$3,941	$3,191

Geographic Operating Results

In millions	Year ended November 30,		
	2007	**2006**	**2005**
Europe and the Middle East			
Net revenues	$6,296	$4,536	$3,601
Non-interest expense	4,221	3,303	2,689
Income before taxes	2,075	1,233	912
Asia-Pacific			
Net revenues	3,145	1,809	1,650
Non-interest expense	1,831	1,191	872
Income before taxes	1,314	618	778

(continued)

EXHIBIT 1—
continued

LBHI
CONSOLIDATED
STATEMENT OF
INCOME

Americas				
	U.S.	9,634	11,116	9,270
	Other Americas	182	122	109
	Net revenues	9,816	11,238	9,379
	Non-interest expense	7,192	7,184	6,240
	Income before taxes	2,624	4,054	3,139
Total				
	Net revenues	19,257	17,583	14,630
	Non-interest expense	13,244	11,678	9,801
	Income before taxes	$6,013	$5,905	$4,829

EXHIBIT 2

BARCLAYS'
ACQUISITION OF
LEHMAN BROTHERS,
INC.

39 Acquisitions

The Group made the following material acquisitions in 2008:

		Acquisition date	Gains on acquisitions £m	Goodwill £m
Lehman Brothers North American businesses	(a)	22nd September 2008	2,262	—
Macquarie Bank Limited residential mortgage businesses	(b)	6th November 2008	52	—
Goldfish credit card UK businesses	(b)	31st March 2008	92	—
Expobank (100% of ordinary shares)	(c)	1st July 2008	—	243
Gains on acquisitions			2,406	

(a) Lehman Brothers North American businesses

On 22nd September 2008, the Group completed the acquisition of Lehman Brothers North American businesses.

The assets and liabilities of Lehman Brothers North American businesses after the acquisition, details of the purchase price and the gain on acquisition arising were as follows:

	Fair values £m
Assets	
Cash and balances at central banks	861
Trading portfolio assets	23,837
Loans and advances to customers	3,642
Available-for-sale financial investments	1,948
Other assets	41
Intangible assets[a]	888
Property, plant and equipment	886
Deferred tax asset	229
Total assets	**32,332**

(continued)

EXHIBIT 2—
continued

BARCLAYS'
ACQUISITION OF
LEHMAN BROTHERS
INC.

Liabilities	
Customer accounts	2,459
Derivative financial instruments	599
Repurchase agreements and cash collateral on securities lent	24,409
Other liabilities	1,049
Deferred tax liabilities	517
Total liabilities	**29,033**
Net assets acquired (excludes Obligation to be settled in shares)	**3,299**
Obligation to be settled in shares[b]	(163)
Acquisition cost	
Cash paid	834
Attributable costs	40
Total consideration	**874**
Gain on acquisition	**2,262**

The acquired assets and liabilities summarised in the table above do not represent the entire balance sheet of Lehman Brothers North American businesses, or of discrete business lines within those operations. For this reason it is not practical to reliably determine the carrying amount of the assets and liabilities in the pre-acquisition books and records of Lehman Brothers.

Notes

[a] Intangible assets included an amount of £636m relating to customer lists.

[b] Under the terms of the acquisition, the Group assumed an obligation to make payments to employees of the acquired business in respect of their pre-acquisition service provided to Lehman Brothers. This amount represents the equity-settled portion of that obligation and is recognised as a component of shareholders' equity.

Certain assets were received subsequent to the acquisition date, since it was first necessary to agree their status as assets of the Group with the relevant regulators, custodians, trustees, exchanges and bankruptcy courts. Such assets were initially classified within loans and advances. Once they were received, the related receivable was derecognised and the resulting asset recognized within the appropriate balance sheet category. In the table such assets are classified accordingly.

The initial accounting for the acquisition has been determined only provisionally. Any revisions to fair values that result from the conclusion of the acquisition process with respect to assets not yet received by the Group will be recognised as an adjustment to the initial accounting. Any such revisions must be effected within 12 months of the acquisition date and would result in a restatement of the 2008 income statement and balance sheet.

The excess of the fair value of net assets acquired over consideration paid resulted in £2,262 m of gain on acquisition.

It is impracticable to disclose the profit or loss of the acquired Lehman Brothers North American businesses since the acquisition date. The acquired business has been integrated into the corresponding existing business lines and there is no reliable basis for allocating post-acquisition results between the acquirer and the acquiree. Similarly, it is impracticable to disclose the revenue and profit or loss of the combined entity as though the acquisition date had been 1st January 2008. Only parts of Lehman Brothers US and Canadian businesses, and specified assets and liabilities, were acquired. There is no reliable basis for identifying the proportion of the pre-acquisition results of Lehman Brothers that relates to the business acquired by the Group.

EXHIBIT 3

JPMorgan's
Acquisition of
Bear Stearns

Note 2—Business changes and developments

Merger with The Bear Stearns Companies Inc.

Effective May 30, 2008, BSC Merger Corporation, a wholly owned subsidiary of JPMorgan Chase, merged with The Bear Stearns Companies Inc. ("Bear Stearns") pursuant to the Agreement and Plan of Merger, dated as of March 16, 2008, as amended March 24, 2008, and Bear Stearns became a wholly owned subsidiary of JPMorgan Chase. The merger provided the Firm with a leading global prime brokerage platform; strengthened the Firm's equities and asset management businesses; enhanced capabilities in mortgage origination, securitization and servicing; and expanded the platform of the Firm's energy business. The merger is being accounted for under the purchase method of accounting, which requires that the assets and liabilities of Bear Stearns be fair valued. The total purchase price to complete the merger was $1.5 billion.

The merger with Bear Stearns was accomplished through a series of transactions that were reflected as step acquisitions in accordance with SFAS 141. On April 8, 2008, pursuant to the share exchange agreement, JPMorgan Chase acquired 95 million newly issued shares of Bear Stearns common stock (or 39.5% of Bear Stearns common stock after giving effect to the issuance) for 21 million shares of JPMorgan Chase common stock. Further, between March 24, 2008, and May 12, 2008, JPMorgan Chase acquired approximately 24 million shares of Bear Stearns common stock in the open market at an average purchase price of $12.37 per share. The share exchange and cash purchase transactions resulted in JPMorgan Chase owning approximately 49.4% of Bear Stearns common stock immediately prior to consummation of the merger. Finally, on May 30, 2008, JPMorgan Chase completed the merger. As a result of the merger, each outstanding share of Bear Stearns common stock (other than shares then held by JPMorgan Chase) was converted into the right to receive 0.21753 shares of common stock of JPMorgan Chase. Also, on May 30, 2008, the shares of common stock that JPMorgan Chase and Bear Stearns acquired from each other in the share exchange transaction were cancelled. From April 8, 2008, through May 30, 2008, JPMorgan Chase accounted for the investment in Bear Stearns under the equity method of accounting in accordance with APB 18. During this period, JPMorgan Chase recorded reductions to its investment in Bear Stearns representing its share of Bear Stearns net losses, which was recorded in other income and accumulated other comprehensive income.

In conjunction with the Bear Stearns merger, in June 2008, the Federal Reserve Bank of New York (the "FRBNY") took control, through a limited liability company ("LLC") formed for this purpose, of a portfolio of $30 billion in assets acquired from Bear Stearns, based on the value of the portfolio as of March 14, 2008. The assets of the LLC were funded by a $28.85 billion term loan from the FRBNY, and a $1.15 billion subordinated loan from JPMorgan Chase. The JPMorgan Chase note is subordinated to the FRBNY loan and will bear the first $1.15 billion of any losses of the portfolio. Any remaining assets in the portfolio after repayment of the FRBNY loan, the JPMorgan Chase note and the expense of the LLC will be for the account of the FRBNY.

As a result of step acquisition accounting, the total $1.5 billion purchase price was allocated to the Bear Stearns assets acquired and liabilities assumed using their fair values as of April 8, 2008, and May 30, 2008, respectively. The summary computation of the purchase price and the allocation of the purchase price to the net assets of Bear Stearns are presented below. The allocation of the purchase price may be modified through May 30, 2009, as more information is obtained about the fair value of assets acquired and liabilities assumed.

(continued)

EXHIBIT 3—
continued

JPMORGAN'S
ACQUISITION OF
BEAR STEARNS

(in millions, except for shares (in thousands), per share amounts and where otherwise noted)

Purchase price		
Shares exchanged in the Share Exchange transaction (April 8, 2008)	95,000	
Other Bear Stearns shares outstanding	145,759	
Total Bear Stearns stock outstanding	240,759	
Cancellation of shares issued in the Share Exchange transaction	(95,000)	
Cancellation of shares acquired by JPMorgan Chase for cash in the open market	(24,061)	
Bear Stearns common stock exchanged as of May 30, 2008	121,698	
Exchange ratio	0.21753	
JPMorgan Chase common stock issued	26,473	
Average purchase price per JPMorgan Chase common share[a]	$45.26	
Total fair value of JPMorgan Chase common stock issued		$1,198
Bear Stearns common stock acquired for cash in the open market (24 million shares at an average share price of $12.37 per share)		298
Fair value of employee stock awards (largely to be settled by shares held in the RSU Trust)		242
Direct acquisition costs		27
Less: Fair value of Bear Stearns common stock held in the RSU Trust and included in the exchange of common stock		(269)
Total purchase price		1,496
Net assets acquired		
Bear Stearns common stockholders' equity	$6,052	
Adjustments to reflect assets acquired at fair value:		
Trading assets	(3,831)	
Premises and equipment	497	
Other assets	(235)	
Adjustments to reflect liabilities assumed at fair value:		
Long-term debt	504	
Other liabilities	(2,252)	
Fair value of net assets acquired excluding goodwill		735
Goodwill resulting from the merger		$761

Note 2–Business changes and development

Acquisition of the banking operations of Washington Mutual Bank

On September 25, 2008, JPMorgan Chase acquired the banking operations of Washington Mutual Bank ("Washington Mutual") from the Federal Deposit Insurance Corporation ("FDIC") for $1.9 billion. The acquisition expands JPMorgan Chase's consumer branch network into several states, including California, Florida and Washington, among others. The acquisition also extends the reach of the Firm's business banking, commercial banking, credit card, consumer lending and wealth management businesses. The acquisition was accounted for under the purchase method of accounting in accordance with SFAS 141.

The $1.9 billion purchase price was allocated to the Washington Mutual assets acquired and liabilities assumed using preliminary allocated values as of September 25, 2008, which resulted in negative goodwill. The initial allocation of the purchase price was presented on a preliminary basis at September 30, 2008, due to the short time period between the closing of the transaction (which occurred simultaneously with its announcement on September 25, 2008) and the end of the third quarter. In accordance with SFAS 141, noncurrent nonfinancial assets that are not held-for-sale, such as the premises and equipment and other intangibles, acquired in the Washington Mutual transaction were written down against the negative goodwill. The negative goodwill that remained after writing down the nonfinancial assets was recognized as an extraordinary gain. As a result of the refinement of the purchase price allocation during the fourth quarter of 2008, the initial extraordinary gain of $581 million was increased $1.3 billion to $1.9 billion. The computation of the purchase price and the allocation of the purchase price to the net assets acquired in the Washington Mutual transaction–based upon their respective values as of September 25, 2008, and the resulting negative goodwill–are presented below. The allocation of the purchase price may be modified through September 25, 2009, as more information is obtained about the fair value of assets acquired and liabilities assumed.

	(in millions)
Purchase price	
Purchase price	$1,938
Direct acquisition costs	3
Total purchase price	1,941
Net assets acquired	
Washington Mutual's net assets before fair value adjustments	$38,766
Washington Mutual's goodwill and other intangible assets	(7,566)
Subtotal	31,200
Adjustments to reflect assets acquired at fair value:	
Securities	(20)
Trading assets	(591)
Loans	(31,018)
Allowance for loan losses	8,216
Premises and equipment	680
Accrued interest and accounts receivable	(295)
Other assets	4,125

(continued)

Adjustments to reflect liabilities assumed at fair value:		
Deposits	(683)	
Other borrowed funds	68	
Accounts payable and other liabilities	(900)	
Long-term debt	1,127	
Fair value of net assets acquired		11,909
Negative goodwill before allocation to nonfinancial assets		(9,968)
Negative goodwill allocated to nonfinancial assets[a]		8,062
Negative goodwill resulting from the acquisition[b]		$(1,906)

(a) The acquisition was accounted for as a purchase business combination in accordance with SFAS 141. SFAS 141 requires the assets (including identifiable intangible assets) and liabilities (including executory contracts and other commitments) of an acquired business as of the effective date of the acquisition to be recorded at their respective fair values and consolidated with those of JPMorgan Chase. The fair value of the net assets of Washington Mutual's banking operations exceeded the $1.9 billion purchase price, resulting in negative goodwill. In accordance with SFAS 141, noncurrent, nonfinancial assets not held-for-sale, such as premises and equipment and other intangibles, were written down against the negative goodwill. The negative goodwill that remained after writing down transaction related core deposit intangibles of approximately $4.9 billion and premises and equipment of approximately $3.2 billion was recognized as an extraordinary gain of $1.9 billion.

(b) The extraordinary gain was recorded in Corporate/Private Equity.

EXHIBIT 4—
continued

JPMORGAN'S
ACQUISITION OF
WASHINGTON
MUTUAL BANK

Note 2–Business changes and developments

Merger with Bank One Corporation

Bank One Corporation merged with and into JPMorgan Chase (the "Merger") on July 1, 2004. As a result of the Merger, each outstanding share of common stock of Bank One was converted in a stock-for-stock exchange into 1.32 shares of common stock of JPMorgan Chase. JPMorgan Chase stockholders kept their shares, which remained outstanding and unchanged as shares of JPMorgan Chase following the Merger. Key objectives of the Merger were to provide the Firm with a more balanced business mix and greater geographic diversification. The Merger was accounted for using the purchase method of accounting, which requires that the assets and liabilities of Bank One be fair valued as of July 1, 2004. The purchase price to complete the Merger was $58.5 billion.

As part of the Merger, certain accounting policies and practices were conformed, which resulted in $976 million of charges in 2004. The significant components of the conformity charges comprised a $1.4 billion charge related to the decertification of the seller's interest in credit card securitizations, and the benefit of a $584 million reduction in the allowance for credit losses as a result of conforming the wholesale and consumer credit provision methodologies.

The final purchase price of the Merger has been allocated to the assets acquired and liabilities assumed using their fair values as of the merger date. The computation of the purchase price and the allocation of the purchase price to the net assets of Bank One–based on their respective fair values as of July 1, 2004–and the resulting goodwill are presented below.

EXHIBIT 5

JPMORGAN'S
ACQUISITION OF
BANK ONE

EXHIBIT 5—
continued

JPMORGAN'S
ACQUISITION OF
BANK ONE

(in millions, except per share amounts)	July 1, 2004	
Purchase price		
Bank One common stock exchanged	1,113	
Exchange ratio	1.32	
JPMorgan Chase common stock issued	1,469	
Average purchase price per JPMorgan Chase common share[a]	$39.02	
		$57,336
Fair value of employee stock awards and direct acquisition costs		1,210
Total purchase price		$58,546
Net assets acquired:		
Bank One stockholders' equity	$24,156	
Bank One goodwill and other intangible assets	(2,754)	
Subtotal	21,402	
Adjustments to reflect assets acquired at fair value:		
Loans and leases	(2,261)	
Private equity investments	(72)	
Identified intangibles	8,665	
Pension plan assets	(778)	
Premises and equipment	(417)	
Other assets	(267)	
Amounts to reflect liabilities assumed at fair value:		
Deposits	(373)	
Deferred income taxes	932	
Other postretirement benefit plan liabilities	(49)	
Other liabilities	(1,162)	
Long-term debt	(1,234)	
		24,386
Goodwill resulting from Merger[b]		$34,160

[a] The value of the Firm's common stock exchanged with Bank One shareholders was based on the average closing prices of the Firm's common stock for the two days prior to, and the two days following, the announcement of the Merger on January 14, 2004.

[b] Goodwill resulting from the Merger reflects adjustments of the allocation of the purchase price to the net assets acquired through June 30, 2005. Minor adjustments subsequent to June 30, 2005, are reflected in the December 31, 2005 Goodwill balance in Note 15 on page 114 of this Annual Report.

EXHIBIT 6

LBHI v. BARCLAYS CAPITAL INC., JONES DAY

Jones Day
Attorneys for Debtor
and Debtor in Possession

United States Bankruptcy Court
Southern District of New York

in re:
Lehman Brothers Holdings Inc., et al., Debtors
Lehman Brothers Holdings Inc., Plaintiff,

v.

Barclays Capital, Inc., Defendant

Case No. 08-13555 (JMP)

Adversary Complaint

Lehman Brothers Holdings Inc. ("LBHI" or "Debtor" and, collectively with its debtor and non-debtor affiliates, "Lehman"), by and through its undersigned counsel, as and for its Complaint against defendant Barclays Capital Inc. ("Barclays") alleges, on information and belief as follows:

Introduction

1. Prior to its bankruptcy, the family of Lehman companies constituted one of the largest investment banks in the world. Lehman's businesses included its North American broker-dealer operations, as well as other businesses and assets located around the globe. On September 15, 2008, LBHI commenced a voluntary proceeding under title 11 of the United States Code (the "Bankruptcy Code"), and other Lehman entities filed for bankruptcy shortly thereafter. Lehman Brothers Inc. ("LBI") filed its bankruptcy proceedings on September 19, 2008. LBI was the entity through which Lehman operated its North American broker-dealer business.

2. Right after LBHI's bankruptcy filing, certain Barclays and Lehman executives began negotiations for Barclays' purchase of Lehman's North American broker-dealer business and related support systems and assets as well as key pieces of real estate, including the flagship Lehman building at 745 Broadway, New York City. Barclays ultimately purchased these assets in a sale transaction negotiated, approved and executed within the span of just a few days (the "Sale Transaction"). The Court approved the Sale Transaction shortly after midnight on September 20, 2008, and the deal closed on Monday, September 22, 2008, just a week after LBHI had filed for bankruptcy and just three days after LBI's bankruptcy filing.

3. Since then, Lehman has learned (after taking Court-ordered Rule 2004 discovery) that, contrary to the terms expressed in the deal documents and the deal documents and the disclosures to the Court about the Sale Transaction, the Sale Transaction was secretly structured from the outset to give Barclays an immediate and enormous windfall profit. Certain Lehman executives knew, but did not reveal to others in Lehman management or to Lehman's attorneys, that Lehman negotiators had agreed to give Barclays an undisclosed $5 billion discount off the book value of the assets transferred to Barclays, and later agreed to undisclosed transfers of billions more in so-called "additional value" that Barclays demanded for no additional consideration. This windfall to Barclays was not disclosed to the Boards of Directors of LHI or LBI (the "Lehman Boards"). It was not disclosed to all Lehman executives involved in the Sale Transaction. It was not disclosed to Lehman's counsel charged with documenting the deal and describing it to the Court. It was not disclosed to the Court when the Sale Transaction was submitted for approval. And it was not approved by the Court.

(continued)

EXHIBIT 6—
continued

*LBHI v. BARCLAYS
CAPITAL INC.,
JONES DAY*

4. All disclosures made to the Lehman Boards and to the Court indicated the deal would be essentially a "was" as to assets with Barclays paying full equivalent value for the assets sold. The Asset Purchase Agreement (the "Asset Purchase Agreement") submitted to the Court for approval expressly stated that certain securities, a component of the purchase price, being sold to Barclays had a "book value" of about $70 billion as of September 16, 2008 when, in fact, this was a negotiated price and the book value of the securities was between $5 and $7 billion higher. In addition, in the days that followed the submission of the Sale Transaction to the court, the deal was modified in material ways, also to Barclays benefit, but the discount, and the modification, remained undisclosed.

5. For example, by Friday, September 19, 2008, when the Court's Sale Hearing commenced, certain Lehman officers involved in the Sale Transaction had already decided to deliver the undisclosed discount to Barclays by terminating a repurchase agreement entered into between Lehman's broker-dealer, LBI, and Barclays on September 18, 2008 (the "Repurchase Agreement"), thus enabling Barclays to keep approximately $5 to $7 billion in excess collateral, over and above the amount Barclays had advanced in the Repurchase Agreement. It was never disclosed to the Lehman Boards or the court that the Repurchase Agreement had thus been transformed from a temporary financing device for Lehman's Broker-dealer into a means effectively to transfer assets to Barclays at the undisclosed discounted price. The Repurchase Agreement had been described to the Court only as a means of providing temporary funding so the Lehman broker-dealer business could operate in an orderly fashion until LBI filed its own liquidation proceeding. Certain Lehman and Barclays executives, however, had decided that rather than mark down the value of the securities on Lehman's books to fit the undisclosed discount retroactively (their original plan for disguising the discount) the better way to deliver the discount to Barclay's (sic) would be to terminate the Repurchase Agreement, and let Barclays simply keep the excess collateral. Changing the deal in this way orchestrated an exchange of assets that were to be priced at between approximately $50 and $52 billion for a payment of only $45 billion, thereby delivering to Barclays an undisclosed discount of between $5 billion and $7 billion.

6. Under Sections 542 and 559 of the Bankruptcy Code, however, the termination of the Repurchase Agreement in this way obligated Barclays to return the value of excess collateral to the Lehman estate. Certain Lehman and Barclays negotiators tried to make this problem disappear by adding two seemingly innocuous paragraphs in a so-called "Clarification Letter" that was finalized and signed after the Court's Sale Order was entered. These provisions purported to rescind the Repurchase Agreement "ab initio" and to transform the excess value in the Repurchase Agreement into "Purchased Assets" under the Asset Purchase Agreement without the knowledge or authority of the Court. And the ramifications of these extraordinary post-hearing changes were not brought to the attention of the Lehman Boards, Lehman's creditors, or other parties of interest.

7. The undisclosed benefit to Barclays did not end there. On September 19, 2008, the day the Court held the Sale Hearing, and throughout the weekend, a scramble was going on inside Lehman to find billions more in assets to turn over to Barclays, without additional consideration or disclosure. In response to Barclays' demands, a small group of Lehman executives agreed to turn over approximately $5 billion in additional assets to Barclays, without additional consideration and without disclosure to the Court. These included approximately $800 million in so-called "15c3-3 assets" and approximately $1.9 billion worth of unencumbered assets contained in so-called "clearance boxes." Like the excess collateral in the Repurchase Agreement, these additional assets were added to the post-hearing Clarification Letter, but not submitted for Court approval. In addition, through the never-approved Clarification Letter, Barclays claims that approximately $2.3 billion in further assets, consisting of certain OCC margin deposits, were to be transferred to Barclays, also without consideration, disclosure or the Court's approval.

(continued)

EXHIBIT 6—
continued

*LBHI v. Barclays
Capital Inc.,
Jones Day*

8. Barclays' windfall was increased still further because of estimates of liabilities the Court was told Barclays would assume as part of the Asset Purchase Agreement were, in fact, inflated. These assumed liabilities included, *inter alia*, Barclays' purported agreement to pay (i) $2 billion in employee bonuses and (ii) between $1.5 and $2.25 billion in contract cure amounts. These assumed liabilities, which materially impacted the value of the sale, were deliberately inflated to make it appear the deal would provide a net benefit to Lehman. After the closing, Barclays in fact paid only about $1.738 billion of this $3.5-4.25 billion amount that had been described to the Court.

9. In the aggregate, these undisclosed, and unapproved, features of the Sale Transaction resulted in an embedded windfall to Barclays at the expense of Lehman of (i) between $5 and $7 billion of excess collateral under the Repurchase Agreement, (ii) approximately $2.7 billion in so-called "additional value" added to the deal while the Sale Hearing was in progress and indeed, after it had concluded, and (iii) approximately $2.3 billion in OCC margin deposits purportedly added after the Sale Hearing ended. In addition, Barclays failed to pay approximately $500 million of the bonuses it had agreed to pay, and paid only about $238 million of the $1.5 billion in cure liabilities that the Court had been told it would likely assume.

10. These undisclosed gains for Barclays, at Lehman's expense, were at least in part the result of self dealing and breaches of fiduciary duty owed to Lehman by certain Lehman officers aided and abetted by Barclays, which participated in the breaches of duty. Certain Lehman officers involved in negotiating and consummating the Sale Transaction, included officers who knew about but did not disclose the discount, had from the outset of negotiations been offered lucrative Barclays employment contracts, or were informed such contracts would be offered to them, conditioned on the closing of the Sale Transaction. Thus, coupled with the fact that an enormous body of assets was essentially given to Barclays, the Sale Transaction was not the product of arms length negotiations.

Boies, Schiller & Flexner LLP
Attorneys for Barclays Capital Inc.

United States Bankruptcy Court
Southern District of New York

in re:
Lehman Brothers Holdings Inc., et al., Debtors

in re:
Lehman Brothers Inc., Debtor

Case No. 08-13555 (JMP)
Case No. 08-01420 (JMP)

. . . In accordance with paragraph 1 of the stipulated amendment to the Scheduling Order dated October 27, 2009, this brief and its supporting materials are also submitted in support of Barclays' affirmative motion to enforce the Sale Order and the Purchase Agreement, and to require delivery of certain Purchased Assets not yet delivered by Seller (the "Undelivered Assets").[5]

Preliminary Statement

1. The fall of Lehman in September 2008 sent shock waves throughout the financial markets, and helped trigger the worst financial crisis since the Great Depression. With the encouragement and support of the Federal Reserve Bank of New York ("New York Fed"), the Securities and Exchange Commission ("SEC"), SIPC, the SIPC Trustee, and other independent parties, Barclays agreed to purchase the assets of the failed Lehman business. The Purchase Agreement provided for Barclays to acquire "all of the assets" used in the "Business," except specifically defined "Excluded Assets," with the "Business" defined as:

> the U.S. and Canadian investment banking and capital markets business of the Seller including the fixed income and equities cash trading, brokerage, dealing, trading and advisory business, investment banking operations, and LBI's business as a futures commission merchant.

2. The Court correctly approved this historic transaction (the "Sale"). In doing so, the Court helped provide some measure of stability to the growing panic throughout the world's financial markets. The Court's approval allowed the prompt transfer of over 72,000 customer accounts to Barclays, providing them with a solvent broker-dealer through which they could access their accounts, avoiding what might otherwise have been a "contagion" of even greater panic and uncertainty. It also preserved thousands of jobs. And, as the Court was told at the time, the Court's approval maximized the value to the Lehman estates of the "wasting assets" that were sold—avoiding potential losses in the "hundreds of billions of dollars."[6]

3. One year later—after the financial markets had stabilized—the Lehman Estates and the creditors' Committee filed motions asking the Court to modify its Sale Order and to rewrite the terms of the Purchase Agreement governing the Sale. The Movants do not challenge the fact that the Barclays acquisition was far better for the Lehman Estates and its creditors than the

(continued)

---

5. Where not otherwise defined herein, capitalized terms shall have the same meaning as provided in the Sale Order and the Purchase Agreement.

6. BCI Ex. 49 [Sept. 19, 2008 Hearing Tr.] at 102:3-103:11. Note: abbreviation for "Hearing Transcript."

EXHIBIT 7—
continued

*LBHI v. BARCLAYS
CAPITAL INC.,
BOISE SCHILLER*

incalculable losses posed by an LBI liquidation. Instead, they claim the deal was too good for Barclays, and therefore ask the Court to rewrite the terms of the Sale.

4. Indeed, the Rule 60 Motions are nothing more than a blatant attempt to *breach* both the Sale Order and the Purchase Agreement. The Debtor and the Trustee owe Barclays billions of dollars of assets that area *specifically identified* in the Purchase Agreement. The Debtor effectively admits that the Purchase Agreement entitles Barclays to these assets, but now asks the Court to rewrite the agreement, so that the Lehman Estates may avoid their contractual obligations. The Trustee takes a slightly different, but equally audacious approach: he offers strained contractual interpretations, but then argues that if the Court rejects those interpretations, the Court must *nullify* the contract, and impose a new one—one which was never discussed or agreed to, and to which Barclays never would have agreed.

5. The Court should reject these extraordinary requests. They are based upon a series of distortions and fictions. They also contradict well-established legal doctrines that absolutely bar the Movants' claims. The Court does not need an evidentiary hearing. As a matter of law, it should reject the Rule 60 Motions, should enforce the plain terms of the Purchase Agreement, and should order to Barclays of the Undelivered Assets.

**Both Weil Gotshal and Lazard Stand by Their Presentation to This Court
and Believe All Lehman Executives Acted in Good Faith.**

6. The two professionals who asked the Court to approve the Sale on behalf of the Debtor—Harvey Miller of Weil Gotshal & Manges ("Weil Gotshal") and Barry Ridings of Lazard—have reviewed the Debtor's Rule 60 Motion. They both *stand by their presentations to the Court* recommending approval of the Sale as the best deal for the estates. They also both believe the Lehman executives involved in the Sale *acted in good faith*.

7. Testifying on behalf of Weil Gotshal, Mr. Miller confirmed he had read the Rule 60 Motion filed by his client,[7] confirmed that he stood by his presentation to the Court and stated he had no basis for believing that anyone at Lehman acted in bad faith:

Q. Based on everything you know as of today, do you believe that your presentation to the Court on September 19 was fair and accurate and appropriate?

A. I believe that it was fair, accurate, and appropriate based upon the information which we were given and the assumption that everyone at Lehman was acting in good faith.

Q. And have you found anything since then that has led you to believe that the information that you were given was inaccurate or that the people at Lehman were not operating in good faith?

A. No.

   Id. At 59:18-60:7.

8. Mr. Ridings also confirmed that he had read the Rule 60 Motion, and emphatically stood by his support for the Sale: "I believe today that there was no other alternative; that [the Sale] was the best alternative at the time."[8] He also testified he had no reason to believe anyone at Lehman acted in bad faith:

Q. Have you become aware of anything since that hearing that has led you to believe that the information you received for Lehman was inaccurate in any way?

(continued)

---

7. BCI Ex. 87 [Miller Dep. Tr.] at 56:4-9. Note: abbreviation for "Deposition Transcript."

8. BCI Ex. 92 [Ridings Dep. Tr.] at 12:2-4.

EXHIBIT 7—
continued

*LBHI v. Barclays
Capital Inc.,
Boise Schiller*

A. I do not believe that Lehman gave me inaccurate information. They—in an unbelievable stressful period, they gave us whatever information they had. Remember, things were changing by the second.

Q. Do you have any reason to believe that those at Lehman who were dealing with Barclays that week were not acting in good faith?

A. I have no reason to believe that to be the case.

BCI Ex. 92 [Ridings Dep. Tr.] at 49:13-50:3.

9. Even the debtor's own CEO, Bryan Marsal, when asked whether he had any basis for believing anyone at Lehman breached their fiduciary duties in connection with the Sale, testified: "I don't have any evidence. I don't have facts one way or the other." BCI Ex. 84 [Marsal Dep. Tr.] at 76:15-16.

10. Everyone acted in good faith. The Movants complain that Barclays made employment offers to some of the top executives before the Closing, but the disinterested members of the Lehman Boards were told of this at the time, and approved the Sale.[9] It was understood that Barclays had to retain Lehman's top talent to keep the Business intact. Moreover, the lead Lehman negotiator, Bard McDade, would not discuss employment until after the Closing. He joined Barclays to help oversee the transition—but never accepted a bonus. The Movants' insinuations of "bad faith" are frivolous.

The Sale Was the Purchase of the Assets of a Business: It Was Neither Structured as a "Wash" Nor Represented to the Court To Be a "Wash."

11. In requesting approval for the Sale, Weil Gotshal presented the Court with an Asset Purchase Agreement ("APA") that made clear Barclays was acquiring "all of the assets" used in connection with the Business, other than specifically Excluded Assets. The APA did not provide total valuations for either the Purchased Assets or the Assumed Liabilities. It did provide initial estimates for many of the financial assets and liabilities in the trading portfolios, and these estimates showed Barclays was acquiring trading assets *in excess* of trading liabilities.[10]

12. The Debor's lawyers also presented the Court with a Sale Order which provided that to consummate the transaction, Barclays needed assurances that it was not taking on any liabilities to the Debtors (or anyone else) beyond those specifically set forth in the contract.[11] Neither the Purchase Agreement nor the Sale Order makes any finding, representation, or warranty as to any agreed *valuation* of the assets being acquired, or the liabilities being assumed. They say nothing about the deal being a "wash."

13. Yet the Movants base their Motions on the fictitious claim that sale was *required* to be a "wash"—with the values of the assets acquired by Barclays equal to the liabilities assumed by Barclays. That is false. Barclays never agreed to such a requirement, and never would have agreed to such a requirement.

14. Again, both Mr. Miller and Mr. Ridings—the two advisers of the Debtor who recommended that this Court approve the Sale—rejected this "wash" concept out of hand. Mr. Miller denied that the sale was presented to the Court as a "wash."

(continued)

---

9. BCI E. 104 [Minutes of the Sept. 16, 2008 LBHI/LBI Board Meeting].

10. *See* Fact Sect A(2), *ifra..*

11. BCI Ex. 16 [Sale Order] at . . .

Q *Did Weil Gotshal ever tell the Court, directly or indirectly, that the deal was going to be a wash?*

A *I don't believe so. I did not, certainly.*

Q *Did you in fact believe that the deal was going to be a wash?*

A *I hadn't—I did not hear the expression "wash" until very recently.*

·15. Mr. Ridings was equally dismissive of the Movants' assertion that the deal was somehow structured to be a "wash":

Q *Was the deal structured to be a precise wash Mr. Ridings?*

A *I do not think it was structured that way.*

BCI Ex. 92 [Ridings Dep. Tr.] at 17:5-10 (emphasis added) (objections omitted).

16. Given that the transaction was negotiated on an emergency basis in the middle of a financial crisis, such a guaranteed "wash" result would have been impossible.[12] Moreover, Barclays would not have agreed to it. It was important to both the Barclays Board and to its regulators that the transaction would, under Barclays' accounting, result in some measure of positive capital accretion. The result could of course not be guaranteed, but Barclay's negotiated in good faith to acquire assets and liabilities that it believed, as accounted for on its balance sheet, would result in some positive capital (or "negative goodwill").[13]

17. Barclays made no secret of this. Two days before this Court was asked to approve the sale, Barclays *publicly announced to the world*, in both a press release and a public conference call with analysts and investors, that it expected the deal to generate a day one accounting gain, and to result in a deal that would be "capital ratio accretive" in the amount of approximately $2 billion (post tax). Before the Sale Hearing took place, that same public information was emailed to over two dozen senior Lehman executives, as well as to Lazard and the Committee's advisors. There was nothing secret or even surprising about this fact. As Harvey Miller put it: "I assumed that Barclays was not making this acquisition for the purpose of taking a loss."[14]

18. Barry Ridings was even more emphatic: "If Barclays lost money on this transaction, it would have been the end of the U.S. capital markets."[15]

19. The creditors took note of the Barclays expectation of an acquisition gain, and some of them objected to it. At the Sale Hearing, at least two creditors objected to the fact that Barclays was buying assets at a "discount" and a "fire sale" price.[16] This Court correctly rejected those objections, holding that Barclays was the only viable alternative to a

(continued)

EXHIBIT 7—
continued

LBHI v. BARCLAYS
CAPITAL INC.,
BOISE SCHILLER

---

12. When asked how the sale could possibly be structured as a wash in these circumstances, the Debtor's CEO could only state that Barclays could have had a "cushion" (a spread between assets and liabilities—as was in fact the case under the APA), and then for there to be a contractual "true-up" provision. There was no such contractual true-up provision. Indeed, the Court was expressly told that the only thing remotely close to such a provision was being *removed* from the agreement. BCI Ex. 49 [Sept. 19, 2008 Hearing Tr.] at 47:7-10.

13. It was hardly unusual for a distressed sale in the middle of the financial crisis to result in negative goodwill (or positive capital) on the acquisition balance sheet. In March 2008, JP Morgan purchased Bear Stearns for $250 million, and initially recorded $10 billion of negative goodwill on the deal. Similarly, the Lloyds acquisition of HBOS generated over £11.2 billion of negative goodwill. *See* BCI Ex. 341 [Pfleiderer Report] at ¶

14. BCI Ex. 87 [Miller Dep. Tr.] at 64:20-64:6.

15. BCI ex. 92 [Ridings Dep. Tr.] at 25:24-26:2.

16. BCI Ex. 49 [Sept. 19, 2008 Hearing Tr.] at 173:24-174:8, 227:5-15.

EXHIBIT 7—
continued

*LBHI v. BARCLAYS
CAPITAL INC.,
BOISE SCHILLER*

potentially "disastrous" liquidation, and that the public interest and the interests of the Estates were best served by an immediate approval.[17]

20. Indeed, Mr. Ridings reviewed the accounting gain recorded by Barclays on the Sale, and confirmed that it was not inconsistent with his understanding of the Sale. He also emphatically stood by his proffered presentation to the Court, and his conclusion that the Sale to Barclays was unquestionably superior to the catastrophic liquidation it avoided:

Again, my testimony was that [the Sale] was the highest and best alternative that we had, and the alternative was liquidation. I was confident and remain confident that this transaction was better than a liquidation would have been.

Id. at 65:10-15 (emphasis added).[18]

Movants' Alleged "Secret Discount" Was Neither Secret Nor a Discount.

21. The Movants complain that there was a "secret discount" because the estimated "book value" of certain of the financial inventory set forth in the APA may have been less than the "marks" on Lehman's books. This complaint is a gross distortion. By the week of September 15, 2008, the Lehman "marks" for many of its financial assets were stale and overstated. Barclays did not agree with those marks, and did not want to accept those marks and then have to take an immediate write down after the Sale. Thus, the "discount" described throughout the Movants' Rule 60 Motions is not a discount *from* fair market value, but rather an attempt to adjust from stale Lehman marks *to* fair market value. As Harvey Miller testified I his deposition, "I wouldn't call that a discount."[19]

22. In any event, there is *nothing* "newly discovered" about this. Harvey Miller testified that there was a "persistent theme" throughout the negotiations that "Lehman was always aggressive on its marks."[20] Likewise, Barry Ridings of Lazard testified that "it was my understanding that throughout the week Barclays had said that the marks were not appropriate; that they were too high because they were no longer market or stale"[21]

23. There likewise is *nothing* "newly discovered" about the fact that certain Lehman finance executives described this discussion of the financial inventory as involving a "discount." One of the key emails on which the Movants rely to show the alleged "secret discount" *was sent to Lazard* on September 17, 2008—two days before the Sale Hearing at which Lazard appeared and testified in support of the Sale. As part of its "diligence," Lazard reviewed and responded to the email. In deposition, Barry Ridings of Lazard confirmed he was "intimately involved" in the negotiations, testified that "[t]here were no secret discussions," and agreed that "there's nothing secret" about Barclays believing Lehman marks were stale and overstated, since Barclays "said that all the time."[22]

24. Despite the foregoing, the Debtor's "special counsel" asserts that it was only during the 2004 discovery in August of 2009 that it was first "revealed" that Lehman understood

(continued)

---

17. BCI Ex. 49 [Sept. 19, 2008 Hearing Tr.] at 248:8-251:3.

18. *See also id.* at 12:15-17 (absent a sale to Barclays, "the prices of securities would have dropped by enormous amounts"); *id.* at 13:2-4 ("I believe today that there was no other alternative; that [the Barclays sale] was the best alternative at the time.").

19. BCI Ex. 87 [Miller Dep. Tr.] at 112:17-114:2.

20. BCI Ex. 87 [Miller Dep. Tr.] at 34:10-20.

21. BCI Ex. 92 [Ridings Dep. Tr.] at 29:15-19.

22. BCI Ex. 92 [Ridings Dep. Tr.] at 31:10-16, 38:14-23, 39:11-17.

EXHIBIT 7—
continued

*LBHI v. BARCLAYS
CAPITAL INC.,
BOISE SCHILLER*

the deal to involve a "five billion dollar discount" from the Lehman marks.[23] That is *false*. Right after the Sale, Bryan Marsal made a presentation to the Creditors' Committee which specifically described the Sale as involving the transfer of financial assets that had a "*$5.0 billion reduction*" that was "*negotiated*" from "*Lehman 'stale' marks*."[24] This was *the Debtor's* second description of the deal at the time of the Sale, as shared with the Committee. It was *not* discovered in August 2009.

25. Indeed, Mr. Philip Kruse, the corporate representative who testified on behalf of both LBHI and Alvarez & Marsal, *admitted* that there is *nothing new* about the alleged "$5 billion discount" described in the rule 60 Motion, and the $5 billion "reduction from "Lehman 'stale' marks" referred in the October 2008 Alvarez & Marsal presentation:

Q   And you recall there being a discount talked about in that motion?

A   Yes.

Q   Is that the same discount that's referred to on page 28 [of the October 8, 2008 Alvarez & Marsal report], the $5 billion reduction?

A   I believe it applies to the same pool of securities.

Q   *Is it different in any way?*

A   *Well, no.* Again, because it applies to the same group of securities, the repo collateral, I think it is the same concept being communicated.

    BCI Ex. 81 [Kruse Dep. Tr.] at 142:21-143:13 (objections omitted)(emphasis added).

26. Mr. Krause went on to claim that LBHI and Alvarez & Marsal did not pursue this issue at the time of the Sale because "we had different priorities." *Id.* at 242:2-242:7. The lawyers for the Creditors Committee likewise admitted they discussed "an overall theme" of "a $5 billion mismatch" with Weil Gotshal *before the Closing*.[25] But the Committee's financial advisers testified that they did not follow up because "*Barclays was good for the money*" and "*that's not the type of thing that you would run to the court with your hair on fire*."[26]

27. Finally, the Movants falsely claim that Barclays received a $5 billion discount through the "mechanism" of taking over the "repo" agreement that was in place between LBI and the New York Fed.[27] But it was the *New York Fed*, not Barclays or Lehman, which insisted that Barclays take over that repo position. There was nothing "secret" about it. Before the Sale was even approved, the New York Fed asked Barclays to advance *45 billion in cash* to LBI, and in exchange Barclays was supposed to receive securities that had previously been pledged to the New York Fed, and that were supposed to be worth approximately worth $49.7 billion.

28. But Barclays never actually received $49.7 billion in repo collateral. Close to 40 percent of the securities in the repo collateral that were actually transferred to Barclays (which was in substantial measure *different* from what the New York Fed had received, and from what Barclays had been promised) could not be valued by looking them up on a Bloomberg or similar terminal. They were illiquid and exceptionally difficult to value. The parties *knew* there was uncertainty as to these asset values, and *knew* that the stated "marks" were higher than the actual values. They also knew that the Purchase Agreement provided for "all" of these assets to be Purchased Assets.

(continued)

---

23. LBHI Br. . . . .

24. BCI Ex. 131 [Oct 8, 2008 Report by Alvarez & Marsal to Creditors' Committee] at p. 28.

25. BCI Ex. 88 . . .

26. BCI Ex. 58 . . .

27. Committee Br. . . . .

EXHIBIT 7—
continued

*LBHI v. BARCLAYS
CAPITAL INC.,
BOISE SCHILLER*

29. Ultimately, it took Barclays months to properly value the illiquid assets it received, after which it concluded that the fair value for accounting purposes of *all* of the Purchased Assets received in connection with the repo transaction was approximately $45.5 billion.[28] And that amount *overstates* what would have been realized in any attempted *liquidation* of those *illiquid* assets during September 2008. Thus, the repo collateral did not contain a discount—secret or otherwise.[29]

The Estimates for Compensation and Cure Payments Were Rough Estimates of Potential Exposure—as Weil Gotshal Explained to the Court.

30. The Movants claim the estimates relating to the "cure" and "comp" liabilities were "inflated" because they exceeded the accruals on certain provisional LBI balance sheets. But that fact was shared *before the Sale Hearing* with Weil Gotshal, Lazard, and Alvarez & Marsal. Harvey Miller told the Court the numbers being provided were *estimates* of *"potential exposure"* not precise accruals. Mr. Miller confirmed this in deposition: "The figures on comp and also the figure on the assumption of executor contracts was always a very contingent figure. Thus, nobody knew what contracts were going to be assumed and how many employees Barclays would ultimately keep."[30]

The Alleged "Additional Assets" Were Defined as Purchased Assets in the Plain Text of the Contract.

31. The "additional assets" about which Movants complain are described in *plain English* in the Clarification Letter, which Weil Gotshal helped draft, which Committee and Trustee professionals reviewed before the Closing, which was filed publicly in Court, and which the Debtor and the Trustee defended on appeal. The Clarification Letter plainly provided that Barclays was acquiring all assets used primarily in the Business that were not specifically excluded, including (a) all of the assets transferred to Barclays as part of its replacement of the New York Fed's repo loan to LBI (the "Repo Collateral"); (b) all of the assets in LBI's clearance boxes ("Clearance Box Assets"); (c) all of LBI's exchange-traded derivatives and any property held to secure those derivatives ("ETD Margin" or "Margin"), and (d) 769 million of securities from the Rules 15c3-3 account, *or* equivalent securities from outside of that account.[31]

32. There was nothing "secret" about any of this. The Debtor and the Trustee have failed to honor their written and court-ordered obligation to deliver certain of these assets, and the court should now order them to do so.

The Clarification Letter Was Clearly Approved by the Sale Order.

33. Recognizing that they cannot avoid their own clear agreement to the terms of the contact, the Movants try to argue that the contract governing this historic transaction—the contract they agreed to and defended on appeal—was somehow not "approved by the Court." That is preposterous. *This Court issued a Sale Order approving the Sale.* That Sale Order

(continued)

---

28. That amount includes everything (cash and securities) Barclays received in the December 2008 Settlement between the Trustee, Barclays, and JPMorgan Chase, which was approved by the Court at the request of the Trustee.

29. Prior to the Sale Hearing, Lehman itself had independently reached a similar conclusion concerning the original Fed rpo collateral—estimating that securities marked at $50.6 billion were worth closer to $45.4 billion. BCI Ex. 370 [Seery Decl.] at ¶ 7. Moreover, James Seery, a senior Lehman executive, emphasized to the Committee, *before the Sale Hearing*, the $5 billion difference between the marks on the repo collateral and the amount of the repo loan. BCI Ex. 370 [Seery Decl.] at ¶¶5-6.

30. BCI Ex. 87 [Miller Dep. Tr.] at 81:6-11.

31. BCE Ex. 5 . . .

EXHIBIT 7—
continued

*LBHI v. BARCLAYS
CAPITAL INC.,
BOISE SCHILLER*

approved the "Purchase Agreement," which the Order defined as including both the APA and the Clarification Letter—*i.e.,* a "letter agreement" that "may be subsequently modified or amended or clarified."[32] As the Court *was told* by Harvey Miller, there had been "major changes in the transaction," and the changes "weren't finalized until about a half hour ago."[33] As the court *was also told* by Weil Gotshal, those changes would be reflected in what Weil Gotshal called a "Clarification Letter." The Court *was also told* that this letter was still being finalized.[34]

34. Indeed, certain creditors objected to this lack of a "final" contract. One creditor objected at the Sale Hearing, arguing that the Court should not approve a sale governed by "a contract that's not complete."[35] The Court correctly rejected those objections, and accepted arguments of the Debtor, the SIPC Trustee, and government regulators that expedited approval was absolutely necessary for the Estate and for "the national interest."[36] The Court then approved the Sale through an Order approving the contemplated but not yet finalized Clarification Letter referenced by Weil Gotshal.

35. Moreover, the Clarification Letter actually narrowed what was in the APA: it *narrowed* the overall definition of Purchased Assets, and it *removed* from the list of Purchased Assets certain assets that had been specifically identified in the APA, but that Lehman was unable to deliver. It then described the Purchased Assets referenced above, which the parties had identified and agreed upon *before* the Sale Hearing, and that were worth *less* than the estimated value of the removed assets.

36. The Clarification Letter also provided that, instead of acquiring "short positions" that would partially hedge the "long positions," Barclays was to acquire an un-hedged portfolio, and was required to forgive its $45 billion repo loan. In other words, under the Clarification Letter, *Barclays paid over $45 billion in cash,* over and above the original "Cash Amount contemplated by the APA. This massive cash outlay in the middle of the financial crisis substantially increased the risk for Barclays.

37. The Movants obviously all believed, correctly, that the Clarification Letter was approved. In his recent deposition, Mr. Miller confirmed that the Clarification Letter reflected the terms that were agreed before the Sale Hearing, and that it was clearly part of the Purchase Agreement approved by this Court, as specified in the Sale Order:

Q   And did this Clarification Letter represent, in substance, the deal that the Court had approved Friday night or early Saturday morning?

A   In my view, yes.

   BCI EX. 87 [Miller Dep. Tr.] . . .

38. Mr. Miller further recalled there was actually a discussion after the Sale Hearing, but before the Closing, about going back to Court in connection with the Clarification Letter. The conclusion of that discussion was "it wasn't necessary" to go back to the Court for further approval because the Clarification Letter "did not change the deal that was presented to the Court." *Id.*

(continued)

---

32. BCI Ex. 16 . . .

33. BCI Ex. 49 . . .

34. *Id.* . . .

35. *Id.* . . .

36. *Id* . . .

EXHIBIT 7—
continued

*LBHI v. BARCLAYS
CAPITAL INC.,
BOISE SCHILLER*

39. No one disagreed with Weil Gotshal's conclusions. The Committee's representatives told Mr. Miller: "Everything's fine, and going forward, if it's okay with you, it's okay with us," and "if you guys are satisfied with it, we're satisfied."[37]

The Parties Did Not Agree Upon a Valuation Cap and Did Not Tell the Court There Was a "Valuation Cap."

40. The Movants disingenuously claim that the Clarification Letter was somehow subject to a "valuation cap" on the value of the Purchased Assets Barclays was entitled to receive. This claim has no merit. Neither the APA nor the Clarification Letter contains any "valuation cap" or any representation or warranty as to the final value of the assets being acquired. The nature of the financial assets being transferred to Barclays—many of them illiquid structured securities that were extremely difficult to value in the financial crisis—would have made such representations or warranties untenable. No one ever agreed to a "valuation cap" or even discussed it. Again, Mr. Miller flatly rejected this recent invention of the Movants:

Q Now, in this agreement, there are no values specified for any of the assets that are being transferred or the liabilities being assumed, correct?

A I believe that's correct.

Q Why is that?

A It was a purchase of the business and the assets that went with that business, to the extent not excluded.

Q *And those—and those assets that were being purchased were being purchased irrespective of what their value was, correct?*

A *Essentially, yes.*

    BCI Ex. 87 . . .

41. In sum, there is no "new evidence," there were no "secrets," and there was no bad faith. At bottom, Movants are just complaining that Barclays got too good a deal. But they ignore the enormous risks Barclays took, and they distort the nature of the acquisition gain Barclays recorded.

42. Barclays acquired the assets of a Business that was rapidly disintegrating; that Business included financial assets that were constantly changing, in both identity and value, due to Lehman's collapse and the crisis in the market; those assets were in many instances illiquid and carried stale marks; and the future of the Business was far from assured in the middle of the worst financial crisis in decades.

43. In that highly uncertain environment, Barclays intended, and publicly announced that the deal would have a day one accounting gain to provide some cushion against all the risks it was assuming.[38] Ultimately, as a result of taking those risks, Barclays announced a gain of $4.1 billion on the acquisition.[39] The Acquisition Balance Sheet reporting that gain *includes* over $3 billion of assets that the Lehman Movants have refused to deliver: thus it is absolutely false for the Movants to suggest to the Court that Barclays is seeking billions of dollars of assets *over and above* the gain that has already been recorded.

44. Moreover, over $2 billion of the Barclays accounting gain reflects intangible assets and other assets that were *not* financial trading assets, that would have been worthless to Lehman in a liquidation, and that Barclays is required to amortize against future earnings.

(continued)

---

37. BCI Ex. 87 . . .

38. BCI Ex. 110 . . .

39. *See* BCI Ex. 134 [Barclays Form 6-K] (announcing after tax gain of $2.2).

EXHIBIT 7—
continued

*LBHI V. BARCLAYS
CAPITAL INC.,
BOISE SCHILLER*

The Movants do not challenge any accounting gain from these assets. The balance of the gain can be attributed to the net value in the exchange-traded derivatives, which represented a serious risk to Barclays, as they contain both liabilities and assets, and there was scarcely any reliable information about them prior to the Closing. Neither side knew if there was significant net value there, but both sides knew they were included in the Sale, along with all associated margin. They also knew these assets carried risks: indeed, they subsequently caused over $800 million of losses to Barclays, which are not on the Acquisition Balance Sheet.

45. Thus, the accounting gain was *far from guaranteed*, given the uncertainty as to the values of the assets and liabilities in the deal. One thing *was* certain, however: had the deal turned out differently, such that the plain text of the Purchase Agreement caused Barclays to incur a loss because the assets were worth even less than feared, Barclays would not have had the right to come back to Court a full year later to ask for revised terms. The Movants should not have that right either. In addition to being grossly unfair and legally barred, the relief requested by Movants is contrary to public policy and decades of jurisprudence upholding the finality of bankruptcy sales: it would scare away future bidders in future bankruptcies, especially in a crisis, when those buyers are needed most.

46. In this brief, Barclays provides an exhaustive account of the facts relating to the Sale. That is provided in the interest of full disclosure and a complete record. But this dispute does not require an evidentiary hearing. It should be resolved summarily, *as a matter of law*.

47. *First*, the plain terms of the Purchase Agreement require immediate delivery to Barclays of the Undelivered Assets. The terms of the Purchase Agreement unambiguously entitle Barclays to those assets, and should be enforced. Indeed, the Debtor (who actually negotiated the contract) does not dispute the *meaning* of the contract—to the contrary, the *premise* of its Rule 60 Motion is that the plain terms of the Purchase Agreement entitle Barclays to the assets in question. As a matter of law, the Court should reject the strained contractual arguments of the Trustee, and order delivery of the Undelivered Assets.

48. *Second,* the law does not permit the extraordinary relief sought by the Movants. At the time of the Sale, the Movants *knew* the plain terms of the Clarification Letter. They *knew* that it provided for Barclays to acquire the entire Repo Collateral. They *knew* that the Repo Collateral had "marks" of over $49 billion. They *knew* Lehman finance executives characterized the deal as involving a $5 billion "reduction" or "discount" from "stale" marks. They *knew* the estimates of *potential exposure* for "cure" and "comp" were higher than the LBI accruals that were available. They *knew all of this* when they agreed to the terms of the Sale, and when the Lehman Movants sought this Court's approval of this historic transaction (to which the Committee did not object).

49. Moreover, by November of 2008, they *knew* that the amount of Barclays' actual cure payments was much less than estimated. The Lehman Movants then filed appellate briefs before the District Court advancing all of the positions Barclays argues here, including (a) "Barclays acted in *good faith*"; (b) the Clarification letter was *part of the approved Purchase Agreement*; (c) "[a]ll relevant facts regarding the Sale were disclosed to the Bankruptcy Court"; and (d) "[t]he only transaction available was the proposal by Barclays."[40] They maintained that position on appeal through the District Court's affirmation of the Sale Order in March of 2009. They are barred as a matter of law from changing these positions now.

50. Moreover, in December of 2008, the Trustee asked this Court to approve a settlement between Barclays, the Trustee, and JPMorgan Chase ("JPMorgan"), in which the Trustee *told this Court* that in the repo transaction, "LBI was to provide Barclays with $49.7 billion in

(continued)

---

40. BCI Ex. 33 . . .

EXHIBIT 7—
continued

*LBHI v. BARCLAYS
CAPITAL INC.,
BOISE SCHILLER*

securities in exchange for $45 billion in cash," and likewise told the court that since Barclays had not received the full amount of that Repo Collateral, it was entitled to the settlement in order to "achieve the intended economic outcome" of that transaction, and because the securities in the Repo Collateral were "contemplated to be transferred in the purchase agreement."[41] The Trustee's representative admitted in deposition that when he asked the court to approve this settlement, the Trustee did not know whether the full amount of the Repo Collateral (including what would be received in the settlement) exceeded the $47.3 billion "valuation cap" the Trustee now seeks to impose upon Barclays. The Trustee said *nothing at all* to the Court about that alleged valuation cap when he asked the Court to approve the December settlement. Nor did the Committee. For one simple reason: *none of them believed that such a valuation cap was part of the deal.*

51. The law does not permit the Movants to abandon their prior positions, and to launch a wholesale attack on Barclays to reclaim assets that they all knew were promised to Barclays in the Sale this Court approved. The mandate rule is an absolute bar to their claims: the District Court affirmed the Sale Order, and that mandate is the law of this case. In addition, the long-established legal doctrine of judicial estoppels, equitable estoppels, and waiver all exist precisely in order to prevent the kinds of *ex post* claims made by the Movants. There is no "new evidence" that could possibly justify evading these legal bars. Moreover, granting any of the relief Movants seek would set a terrible policy precedent that would discourage future potential acquirers of assets out of bankruptcy.

52. Neither Rule 60 nor the Bankruptcy Code can possibly support the claims made by Movants. Rule 60 does not permit the Court to rewrite the terms of a written contract. And the Bankruptcy Code provisions invoked by Movants have no application to a sale that was expressly approved by the Court. The Movants cite no case, and Barclays is not aware of one, where a Court has permitted a party to contend that a sale was "unauthorized" after that party obtained Court approval for the sale, agreed to the contract governing the sale, and successfully defended that contract on appeal.

53. As a matter of law, the court should summarily deny the Rule 60 Motions, and order the prompt delivery of all Undelivered Assets to Barclays.

---

41. BCI Ex. 29 [Trustee's Motion for Entry of Order Approving Settlement Agreement] at ¶¶ 7, 10; BCI Ex. 50 [Dec. 22, 2008 Hearing Tr.] at 22:3-6.

SECTION 5

FINANCIAL STATEMENT ANALYSIS

Harley-Davidson, Inc. (A)

Financial Crises, 2008–2009

A German inventor, Gottlieb Daimler, developed the first gas engine–motorized bicycle in 1885. Ten years later, the first crude motorcycle was produced in the United States. In 1901, William S. Harley, age 21, completed a blueprint drawing of an engine designed to fit on a bicycle. In 1903, he and Arthur Davidson produced the first Harley-Davidson® motorcycle in a 10-by-15 foot wooden shed with the words "Harley-Davidson Motor Company" scrawled on the door. Arthur Davidson's brother, Walter Davidson, joined the firm later that year. In 1906, the firm built a 28-by-80 foot factory and increased the number of staff to six full-time employees. The following year brought a variety of developments: William Davidson joined the firm, Harley-Davidson Motor Company was incorporated, and the shares were equally split between Mr. Harley and the three Davidson brothers.[1]

More than 200 companies began producing motorcycles in the United States in the early 1900s, including Thor, Pierce, Sears, Excelsior, Flying Merkel, Reading Standard, Iver Johnson, Ace, Cleveland, and Indian. By 1917, Harley-Davidson was a growing brand, but little distinguished its reputation from that of competitors. The company's big break came when the United States entered World War I: Harley-Davidson became the U.S. Army's primary motorcycle supplier. By 1918, half of the motorcycles the firm produced were sold to the Army. By the end of the war, the Army had purchased 20,000 motorcycles, most of them from Harley-Davidson, and hundreds of thousands of soldiers had become familiar with the brand. By 1920, Harley-Davidson was the world's largest motorcycle manufacturer, with more than 2,000 dealers in 67 countries.[2]

In 1941, the United States entered World War II, and Harley-Davidson shifted motorcycle production almost entirely to meet the needs of the military. By 1945, Harley had produced nearly 100,000 motorcycles for the military. Most of the millions of Americans who served in the Army were familiar with Harley-Davidson motorcycles. As Harley-Davidson sales grew, their competitors began to close their businesses. In 1953, Hendee Manufacturing, producer of the Indian motorcycles and the last remaining U.S. motorcycle manufacturer other than Harley-Davidson, closed its operations. For the next 49 years, Harley-Davidson was the only U.S. motorcycle manufacturer.

In 1953, Marlon Brando starred in the movie *The Wild One*, which established Harley's reputation for rebellion; in 1969, Peter Fonda and Dennis Hooper starred in *Easy Rider*, which cemented that reputation. By 2000, the 60th annual Black Hills Rally in Sturgis, South Dakota, drew 600,000 people to the town of 6,500. In 2003, more than 250,000 people went to Milwaukee, Wisconsin, to mark the end of the Open Road Tour and to celebrate Harley-Davidson's 100th anniversary. In 2008, the firm opened the Harley-Davidson Museum, where for $250 individuals can have

1. Harley-Davidson history, Harley-Davidson Web site. http://www.harley-davidson.com/wcm/Content/Pages/H-D_History/history.jsp.
2. Ibid.

their name and other information engraved on a 3-inch rivet embedded in a wall; for $1,500 they can buy an engraved 6-inch rivet embedded in a walkway.[3]

The Product

Throughout its history Harley-Davidson specialized in heavyweight motorcycles divided into four categories:

- Standard (emphasizes simplicity and cost)
- Performance (emphasizes handling and acceleration)
- Custom (emphasizes styling and individual owner customization)
- Touring (emphasizes comfort and amenities for long-distance travel)

In the United States, Harley-Davidson competes most heavily in the touring and custom segments of the heavyweight motorcycle market, which accounted for approximately 84%, 80%, and 79% of total heavyweight retail unit registrations in the United States during 2008, 2007, and 2006, respectively. In 1993, Harley-Davidson acquired a minority interest in Buell Motorcycle Company, a U.S. manufacturer of sport motorcycles (and purchased the remaining interest in 1998). During 2008, the heavyweight sector represented approximately 55% of total U.S. motorcycle registrations (on- and off-highway motorcycles and scooters), and Harley's share of that market ranged from 50.0% in 2006 to 46.3% in 2008.[4]

Financial Crises of 2008 and 2009

Harley Davidson Financial Services (HDFS) provides financing and insurance to both its dealers and retail customers. Those financing and insurance businesses have long been highly profitable. Most Harley-Davidson dealerships are housed in new, large, modern buildings that sell both motorcycles and a wide range of Harley-Davidson-branded products. Typically, a Harley-Davidson dealership is far larger and more upscale than dealers that sell motorcycles from Japan or Europe. In addition, although Harley Davidson motorcycles are often associated with rebellion and motorcycle gangs, a large percentage of Harley-Davidson owners are professionals:

> The average U.S. retail purchaser of a new Harley-Davidson motorcycle is a married male in his middle to late forties (nearly two-thirds of U.S. retail purchasers of new Harley-Davidson motorcycles are between the ages of 35 and 54) with a median household income of approximately $87,000. Nearly three-quarters of the U.S. retail sales of new Harley-Davidson motorcycles are to buyers with at least one year of education beyond high school, and 32% of the buyers have college/graduate degrees. Approximately 12% of U.S. retail motorcycle sales of new Harley-Davidson motorcycles are to female buyers.[5]

Because retail customers are relatively well-off and intensely loyal, credit losses have been minimal. HDFS's receivables from dealers are primarily for motorcycles and parts; most of those receivables are due within one year. Typically, HDFS retained the dealer receivables as investments and financed them through retained profits ($1.16 billion, $1.33 billion, and $1.34 billion of wholesale receivables in 2008, 2007, and 2006, respectively).

---

3. Ibid.

4. Harley-Davidson 2008 10-K, Item 1, Business, pp. 4–5.

5. 2008 company study, Harley-Davidson 2008 10-K, p. 8.

In contrast, HDFS securitized most of its retail customer receivables. However, the 2007 collapse of the subprime mortgage securitization market led to a near world-wide collapse in the entire securitization market in 2008. HDFS securitized and sold a normal issue of retail receivables in the first quarter of 2008, and that was HDFS's last securitized transaction until April 2009.

Harley-Davidson's Statement of Income (Exhibit 1) shows that revenues declined slightly from 2007 to 2008 ($5.726 billion to $5.594 billion), and gross profits from motorcycle sales dropped slightly more because of discounting ($2.114 billion to $1.931 billion). Financial Services operating income declined from $212 million in 2007 to $82.8 million in 2008 (Exhibit 5). Harley-Davidson also had $22.3 million of investment income in 2007 but only $4.95 million in 2008 (net of interest expense) because HDFS was unable to sell its securitized retail customer receivables. Exhibit 1 also includes Note 16: Earnings per Share.

As seen in Harley's Balance Sheet (Exhibit 2), Finance Receivables Held for Sale increased from a normal $781 million on December 31, 2007, to $2.444 billion on December 31, 2008. To finance the retail customer receivables it was unable to sell, Harley-Davidson increased its long-term debt from $980 million as of December 31, 2007, to $2.176 billion as of December 31, 2008. The last line of Exhibit 4 (Cash Flows from Operations) shows the dramatic change in net cash (used by) provided by operating activities for 2008 compared with 2007 and 2006.

In an April 16, 2009, *Fortune* article, Raymond James analyst Joseph Hovorka reported that in February 2008, 25–30% of HDFS customers were rated as subprime borrowers.[6] Such borrowers typically pay interest rates of 18–24%. In the past, HDFS securitized its retail receivables by transferring those receivables to a securitization trust. The trust then sold notes backed by those receivables to institutional investors. Typically, the notes equaled about 92–94% of the face value of receivables, and Harley-Davidson kept a 6–8% retained interest that would be paid to Harley-Davidson only after the trust repaid notes issued to institutional investors. Given the economic environment in early 2009, HDFS might be required to keep a far higher retained interest percentage of future securitizations.

Accruals and Allowances

In addition to Harley-Davidson's inability to securitize retail receivables, analysts were concerned about accruals and allowances. In the past, accruals often seemed conservative. Harley disclosed its significant 2008 accruals and allowances in the following Exhibits:

- Exhibit 5 provides information on the warranty and safety recall liability, and Exhibit 6 discloses the significant decline in operating income from Harley-Davidson financial services.

- Exhibit 7 discloses that on December 31, 2008, finance receivables held for investment, minus allowance for credit losses, plus investment in retained interests on finance receivable securitized and sold in earlier periods, equaled $2,195,563,000 ($1,378,461,000 current; $817,102,000 long term—see Exhibit 2). Exhibit 7 also discloses that a "lower of cost or market valuation adjustment (reduction) of $31,700,000 is included in its $2,443,965,000 of receivables held for sale."

---

6. Cendrowski, Scott, "Harley-Davidson: bears vs. bulls," *Fortune Magazine, Fortune Investor Daily*, April 16, 2009. Available at http://money.cnn.com/2009/04/16/pf/harley_davidson.fortune/index.htm.

- Exhibit 8 discloses information about securitization transactions, including the residual cash flows discount rate.
- Exhibit 9 provides information on Harley-Davidson's debt, including the debt issued to fund customer receivables.
- Exhibit 11 discloses allowance/reserve balances and write-offs for accounts receivable, finance receivables held for investment, and inventories.

Retiree Benefits

Exhibit 10 provides selected disclosures from Harley-Davidson's pension and post-retirement health-care benefits note. The following table compares Harley Davidson investment performance and investment allocation for 2008 with seven other major U.S. pension funds, ranked by estimated 2008 returns, from best to worst:

	Boeing	American Airlines	Dupont	JP Morgan Chase	Chevron	Lockheed Martin	UPS	Harley Davidson Health care	Pensions
Estimated returns									
Beginning assets	$50,439	$9,099	$22,618	$9,960	$7,918	$27,259	$17,954	$136	$1,068
Actual return	−$7,296	−$1,659	−$5,142	−$2,377	−$2,092	−$7,358	−$5,124	−$41	−$358
Estimated return	−14.5%	−18.2%	−22.7%	−23.9%	−26.4%	−27.0%	−28.5%	−30.1%	−33.5%
Asset allocation									
Equity	28%	37%	52%	36%	52%	49%	44%	72%	64%
Debt	55%	48%	31%	25%	34%	36%	31%	14%	23%
Real estate	4%		7%	7%	13%		25%		
Alternative	8%	11%		32%					
Global/emerging	5%	4%							
Cash/other			10%		1%	15%		14%	13%
Total	100%	100%	100%	100%	100%	100%	100%	100%	100%

Required

1. Does Harley-Davidson have adequate allowance/reserve balances in: (a) warranty and safety recall liability, (b) accounts receivable, (c) finance receivables held for investment, (d) finance receivables held for sale, and (e) inventories? Are these balances more or less adequate than in the past? Explain.

2. Is the "finance receivables held for investment" disclosure adequate? Explain.

3. Evaluate the change in Harley-Davidson's debt from 2007 to 2008.

4. Evaluate Harley-Davidson's pension and retiree health-care funds and their asset allocations (from the above table).

5. For 2009 and 2010, will Harley-Davidson (a) be able to continue its current level of operations, or (b) be required to reduce operations somewhat (10–15%) because of its inability to securitize retail receivables, or (c) be required to substantially reduce operations (more than 15%) because of its inability to securitize retail customer receivables? Explain.

EXHIBIT 1

CONSOLIDATED
STATEMENTS OF
INCOME AND NOTE
ON EARNINGS
PER SHARE

HARLEY-DAVIDSON, INC.

Years ended December 31, 2008, 2007 and 2006

	2008	2007	2006
	(in thousands, except per share amounts)		
Net revenue	$5,594,307	$5,726,848	$5,800,686
Cost of goods sold	3,663,488	3,612,748	3,567,839
Gross profit	1,930,819	2,114,100	2,232,847
Financial services income	376,970	416,196	384,891
Financial services expense	294,205	204,027	174,167
Operating income from financial services	82,765	212,169	210,724
Selling, administrative and engineering expense	984,560	900,708	846,418
Income from operations	1,029,024	1,425,561	1,597,153
Investment income	9,495	22,258	27,087
Interest expense	4,542	—	—
Income before provision for income taxes	1,033,977	1,447,819	1,624,240
Provision for income taxes	379,259	513,976	581,087
Net income	$654,718	$933,843	$1,043,153
Earnings per common share:			
Basic	$2.80	$3.75	$3.94
Diluted	$2.79	$3.74	$3.93
Cash dividends per common share	$1.29	$1.06	$0.81

16. Earnings Per Share

The following table sets forth the computation of basic and diluted earnings per share for the years ended December 31 (in thousands):

	2008	2007	2006
Numerator:			
Net income used in computing basic and diluted earnings per share	$654,718	$933,843	$1,043,153
Denominator:			
Denominator for basic earnings per share—weighted-average common shares	234,225	249,205	264,453
Effect of dilutive securities—employee stock compensation plan	252	677	820
Denominator for diluted earnings per share—adjusted weighted-average shares outstanding	234,477	249,882	265,273

Options to purchase 5.2 million, 1.4 million and 1.9 million weighted-average shares of common stock outstanding during 2008, 2007 and 2006, respectively, were not included in the Company's computation of dilutive securities because the exercise price was greater than the market price and therefore the effect would have been anti-dilutive.

EXHIBIT 2

CONSOLIDATED
BALANCE SHEETS

HARLEY-DAVIDSON, INC.

December 31, 2008 and 2007

	2008	2007
	(in thousands, except share amounts)	
ASSETS		
Current assets:		
Cash and cash equivalents	$593,558	$402,854
Marketable securities	—	2,475
Accounts receivable, net	296,258	181,217
Finance receivables held for sale	2,443,965	781,280
Finance receivables held for investment, net	1,378,461	1,575,283
Inventories	400,908	349,697
Deferred income taxes	123,327	103,278
Prepaid expenses and other current assets	141,404	71,230
Total current assets	5,377,881	3,467,314
Finance receivables held for investment, net	817,102	845,044
Property, plant and equipment, net	1,094,487	1,060,590
Prepaid pension costs	—	89,881
Goodwill	138,579	61,401
Deferred income taxes	288,240	54,376
Other long-term assets	112,336	78,000
	$7,828,625	$5,656,606
LIABILITIES AND SHAREHOLDERS' EQUITY		
Current liabilities:		
Accounts payable	$323,736	$300,188
Accrued liabilities	541,372	484,936
Short-term debt	1,738,649	722,447
Current portion of long-term debt	—	397,508
Total current liabilities	2,603,757	1,905,079
Long-term debt	2,176,238	980,000
Pension liability	484,003	51,551
Postretirement healthcare benefits	274,408	192,531
Other long-term liabilities	174,616	151,954
Shareholders' equity:		
Series A Junior participating preferred stock, none issued	—	—
Common stock, 335,653,577 and 335,211,201 shares issued in 2008 and 2007, respectively	3,357	3,352
Additional paid-in-capital	846,796	812,224
Retained earnings	6,458,778	6,117,567
Accumulated other comprehensive loss	(522,526)	(137,258)
	6,786,405	6,795,885
Less:		
Treasury stock (102,889,370 and 96,725,399 shares in 2008 and 2007, respectively), at cost	(4,670,802)	(4,420,394)
Total shareholders' equity	2,115,603	2,375,491
	$7,828,625	$5,656,606

HARLEY-DAVIDSON, INC.

Years ended December 31, 2008, 2007 and 2006

EXHIBIT 3

CONSOLIDATED
STATEMENTS OF
CASH FLOWS

	2008	2007	2006
		(in thousands)	
Net cash (used by) provided by operating activities (Note 2)	$(684,649)	$798,146	$761,780
Cash flows from investing activities:			
Capital expenditures	(232,169)	(242,113)	(219,602)
Origination of finance receivables held for investment	(608,621)	(514,359)	(411,757)
Collections on finance receivables held for investment	448,990	368,978	260,133
Collection of retained securitization interests	93,747	118,175	101,641
Purchase of marketable securities	—	(467,609)	(970,935)
Sales and redemptions of marketable securities	2,543	1,125,344	1,224,447
Acquisition of business, net of cash acquired	(95,554)	—	—
Other, net	(2,183)	2,789	(19,186)
Net cash (used by) provided by investing activities	(393,247)	391,205	(35,259)
Cash flows from financing activities:			
Proceeds from issuance of medium term notes	993,550	398,144	—
Repayment of medium-term notes	(400,000)	—	—
Net increase (decrease) in credit facilities and unsecured commercial paper	761,065	(16,247)	493,125
Net borrowings of asset-backed commercial paper	490,000	—	—
Repayment of senior subordinated debt	—	(30,000)	—
Dividends	(302,314)	(260,805)	(212,914)
Purchase of common stock for treasury	(250,410)	(1,153,439)	(1,061,968)
Excess tax benefits from share-based payments	320	3,066	18,933
Issuance of common stock under employee stock option plans	1,179	21,478	125,801
Net cash provided by (used by) financing activities	1,293,390	(1,037,803)	(637,023)
Effect of exchange rate changes on cash and cash equivalents	(24,790)	12,909	7,924
Net increase in cash and cash equivalents	190,704	164,457	97,422
Cash and cash equivalents:			
At beginning of period	402,854	238,397	140,975
At end of period	$593,558	$402,854	$238,397

EXHIBIT 4

CASH FLOWS FROM
OPERATIONS

From Note 2

	2008	2007	2006
Cash flows from operating activities:			
Net income	$654,718	$933,843	$1,043,153
Adjustments to reconcile net income to net cash provided by operating activities:			
Depreciation and amortization	222,191	204,172	213,769
Amortization of acquisition-related intangibles	20,090	—	—
Provision for employee long-term benefits	76,426	75,683	80,179
Contributions to pension and postretirement plans	(19,517)	(15,302)	(13,512)
Stock compensation expense	24,473	20,974	21,446
Loss (gain) on current year securitizations	5,370	(36,033)	(32,316)
Net change in wholesale finance receivables	99,373	22,816	(159,886)
Origination of retail finance receivables held for sale	(2,788,463)	(2,919,937)	(2,772,733)
Collections on retail finance receivables held for sale	507,106	110,756	112,131
Proceeds from securitization of retail finance receivables	467,722	2,486,780	2,303,562
Impairment of retained securitization interests	41,403	9,932	—
Lower of cost or fair market value adjustment on finance receivables held for sale	37,764	—	—
Provision for credit losses	39,555	11,252	5,962
Deferred income taxes	(49,428)	(60,529)	(39,768)
Foreign currency adjustments	2,892	(14,581)	(7,975)
Other, net	53,982	16,830	26,573
Changes in current assets and liabilities:			
Accounts receivable, net	(4,474)	(26,449)	(16,361)
Finance receivables – accrued interest and other	(7,149)	(19,680)	(23,442)
Inventories	(45,094)	(48,019)	(54,352)
Accounts payable and accrued liabilities	9,734	48,157	76,058
Other	(33,323)	(2,519)	(708)
Total adjustments	(1,339,367)	(135,697)	(281,373)
Net cash (used by) provided by operating activities	$(684,649)	$798,146	$761,780

EXHIBIT 5

NOTE 1,
SIGNIFICANT
ACCOUNTING
POLICIES, SELECTED

Finance Receivables Credit Losses – The allowance for finance credit losses on finance receivables held for investment is charged to earnings in amounts sufficient to maintain the allowance for uncollectible accounts at a level HDFS believes is adequate to cover the losses of principal in the existing portfolio. HDFS' periodic evaluation of the adequacy of the allowance is generally based on HDFS' past loan loss experience, known and inherent risks in the portfolio, the value of the underlying collateral and current economic conditions. HDFS' wholesale and other large loan charge-off policy is based on a loan-by-loan review which considers the specific borrower's ability to repay and the estimated value of any collateral. Retail loans are generally charged-off at 120 days contractually past due. All finance receivables accrue interest until either collected or charged-off. Accordingly, as of December 31, 2008 and 2007, all finance receivables are accounted for as interest-earning receivables.

Finance Receivables Held for Sale – U.S. retail motorcycle loans intended for securitization at origination are classified as finance receivables held for sale. These finance receivables held for sale in the aggregate are carried at the lower of cost or estimated fair value. Any amount by which cost exceeds fair value is accounted for as a valuation adjustment with an offset to other income. Cash flows related to finance receivables held for sale are included in cash flows from operating activities.

Asset-Backed Commercial Paper Conduit Facility – In December 2008, HDFS sold for legal purposes U.S. retail motorcycle finance receivables to a wholly-owned special purpose entity (SPE), which in turn issued debt to third-party bank-sponsored asset-backed commercial paper conduits. The SPE funded the purchase of the finance receivables from HDFS primarily with cash obtained through the issuance of the debt. HDFS is the primary and sole beneficiary of the SPE, and the finance receivables sale does not satisfy the requirements for accounting sale treatment under SFAS No. 140. Therefore, the assets and associated debt are included in the Company's financial statements. The assets of the SPE are restricted as collateral for the payment of the debt or other obligations arising in the transaction and are not available to pay other obligations or claims of the Company's creditors. At December 31, 2008, the SPE held $24.1 million of cash collections from the finance receivables held by the SPE restricted for payment on the outstanding debt. The assets of the SPE totaled $686.3 million at December 31, 2008 and are included primarily in cash, finance receivables held for sale and finance receivables held for investment in the Company's Consolidated Balance Sheet. The related asset-backed commercial paper conduit facility was $500.0 million at December 31, 2008 and is included in short-term debt in Company's Consolidated Balance Sheet.

Product Warranty and Safety Recall Campaigns – The Company currently provides a standard two-year limited warranty on all new motorcycles sold worldwide, except for Japan, where the Company provides a standard three-year limited warranty on all new motorcycles sold. The warranty coverage for the retail customer includes parts and labor and generally begins when the motorcycle is sold to a retail customer. The Company maintains reserves for future warranty claims using an estimated cost per unit sold, which is based primarily on historical Company claim information. Additionally, the Company has from time to time initiated certain voluntary safety recall campaigns. The Company reserves for all estimated costs

(continued)

EXHIBIT 5—
continued

NOTE 1,
SIGNIFICANT
ACCOUNTING
POLICIES, SELECTED

associated with safety recalls in the period that the safety recalls are announced. Changes in the Company's warranty and safety recall liability were as follows (000):

	2008	2007	2006
Balance, beginning of period	$70,523	$66,385	$43,073
Warranties issued during the period	52,645	54,963	56,008
Settlements made during the period	(71,737)	(66,422)	(57,267)
Safety recalls and changes to pre-existing warranty liabilities	13,112	15,597	24,571
Balance, end of period	$64,543	$70,523	$66,385

The liability for safety recall campaigns was $4.6 million, $3.7 million and $6.5 million at December 31, 2008, 2007 and 2006, respectively.

EXHIBIT 6

NOTE 6, FINANCIAL
SERVICES

HDFS is engaged in the business of financing and servicing wholesale inventory receivables and retail loans, primarily for the purchase of motorcycles and, as an agent, providing insurance and insurance-related programs primarily to Harley-Davidson and Buell dealers and their retail customers. HDFS conducts business principally in the United States and Canada and is responsible for all credit and collection activities for the Company's U.S. dealer receivables and its Canadian distributor receivables.

The condensed statements of operations relating to the Financial Services segment, for the years ended December 31, were as follows (in thousands):

	2008	2007	2006
Interest income	$290,083	$196,803	$167,504
Income from securitizations	13,439	97,576	111,177
Other income	73,448	121,817	106,210
Financial services income	376,970	416,196	384,891
Interest expense	136,763	81,475	59,761
Operating expenses	157,442	122,552	114,406
Financial services expenses	294,205	204,027	174,167
Operating income from financial services	$82,765	$212,169	$210,724

Financial Services interest income includes approximately $18.0 million, $27.7 million and $23.6 million of interest on wholesale finance receivables paid by HDMC to HDFS in 2008, 2007 and 2006, respectively. This interest was paid on behalf of HDMC's independent dealers as a way to manage seasonal increases in inventory. The offsetting cost of these interest incentives was recorded as a reduction to net revenue.

Income from securitizations includes losses on current year securitization transactions of $5.4 million during 2008, and gains of $36.0 million and $32.3 million during 2007 and 2006, respectively, and income on investment in retained securitization interests of $18.8 million, $61.6 million and $78.9 million during 2008, 2007 and 2006, respectively.

EXHIBIT 7

NOTE 7, FINANCE
RECEIVABLES

Finance receivables held for investment, net at December 31 for the past five years, were as follows (in thousands):

	2008	2007	2006	2005	2004
Wholesale					
United States	$1,074,377	$1,132,748	$1,206,753	$1,040,220	$870,640
Europe	—	86,947	66,421	59,960	73,231
Canada	89,859	108,756	65,538	50,097	51,945
Total wholesale	1,164,236	1,328,451	1,338,712	1,150,277	995,816
Retail					
United States	514,637	485,579	409,788	319,856	287,841
Canada	226,084	228,850	174,894	149,597	120,217
Total retail	740,721	714,429	584,682	469,453	408,058
	1,904,957	2,042,880	1,923,394	1,619,730	1,403,874
Allowance for credit losses	40,068	30,295	27,283	26,165	30,277
	1,864,889	2,012,585	1,896,111	1,593,565	1,373,597
Investment in retained securitization interests	330,674	407,742	384,106	349,659	282,187
	$2,195,563	$2,420,327	$2,280,217	$1,943,224	$1,655,784

Finance receivables held for sale at December 31 for the past five years were as follows (in thousands):

	2008	2007	2006	2005	2004
Retail					
United States	$2,443,965	$781,280	$547,106	$299,373	$456,516

Included in finance receivables held for sale at December 31, 2008 is a lower of cost or market valuation adjustment of $31.7 million.

At December 31, 2008, finance receivables of $649.8 million are restricted as collateral for the payment of $500.0 million short-term asset-backed commercial paper conduit facility debt, which is included in the Company's Consolidated Balance Sheet.

HDFS has cross-border outstandings to Canada as of December 31, 2008, 2007 and 2006 of $75.8 million, $92.2 million and $61.1 million, respectively.

HDFS provides wholesale financing to the Company's independent dealers. Wholesale loans to dealers are generally secured by financed inventory or property and are originated in the U.S. and Canada. Effective January 1, 2008, the finance receivables and related assets of the international wholesale operations located in Oxford, England were transferred at book value to Harley-Davidson Europe Ltd., a subsidiary of HDMC. Beginning in 2008, HDMC assumed responsibility for the collection of all wholesale receivables in Europe.

HDFS provides retail financial services to customers of the Company's independent dealers in the United States and Canada. The origination of retail loans is a separate and distinct transaction between HDFS and the retail customer, unrelated to the Company's sale of product to its dealers. Retail loans consist of secured promissory notes and installment loans. HDFS either holds titles or liens on titles to vehicles financed by promissory notes and installment loans. As of December 31, 2008 approximately 11% of gross outstanding finance receivables were originated in Texas and as of December 31, 2007 approximately 12% were originated in Canada.

(continued)

EXHIBIT 7—
continued

NOTE 7, FINANCE
RECEIVABLES

At December 31, 2008 and 2007, unused lines of credit extended to HDFS' wholesale finance customers totaled $941.9 million and $994.3 million, respectively. Approved but unfunded retail finance loans totaled $263.1 million and $458.4 million at December 31, 2008 and 2007, respectively.

Wholesale finance receivables are related primarily to motorcycles and related parts and accessories sales to independent dealers and are generally contractually due within one year. Retail finance receivables are primarily related to sales of motorcycles to the dealers' customers. On December 31, 2008, contractual maturities of finance receivables held for investment (excluding retained securitization interests) were as follows (in thousands):

	United States	Canada	Total
2009	$1,116,324	$117,177	$1,233,501
2010	33,496	29,261	62,757
2011	37,066	32,781	69,847
2012	41,036	36,723	77,759
2013	45,447	41,140	86,587
Thereafter	315,644	58,862	374,506
Total	$1,589,013	$315,944	$1,904,957

As of December 31, 2008, all finance receivables due after one year were at fixed interest rates.

The allowance for finance credit losses on finance receivables held for investment is comprised of individual components relating to wholesale and retail finance receivables. Changes in the allowance for finance credit losses on finance receivables held for investment for the years ended December 31 were as follows (in thousands):

	2008	2007	2006
Balance at beginning of year	$30,295	$27,283	$26,165
Provision for finance credit losses	39,555	11,252	5,962
Charge-offs, net of recoveries	(29,782)	(8,240)	(4,844)
Balance at end of year	$40,068	$30,295	$27,283

The carrying value of retail and wholesale finance receivables contractually past due 90 days or more at December 31 for the past five years were as follows (in thousands):

	2008	2007	2006	2005	2004
United States	$23,678	$6,205	$4,476	$2,574	$1,906
Canada	1,275	1,759	1,561	1,442	994
Europe	—	386	452	283	3,688
Total	$24,953	$8,350	$6,489	$4,299	$6,588

EXHIBIT 8

NOTE 8,
SECURITIZATION
TRANSACTIONS

During 2008, 2007 and 2006, the Company sold $540.0 million, $2.53 billion and $2.33 billion, respectively, of retail motorcycle loans through securitization transactions utilizing QSPEs (see Note 1). These sales resulted in cash proceeds of $467.7 million, $2.49 billion and $2.30 billion during 2008, 2007 and 2006, respectively. The Company retains an interest in excess cash flows, subordinated securities and cash reserve account deposits, collectively referred to as investment in retained securitization interests (a component of finance receivables held for investment in the Company's Consolidated Balance Sheets). The Company retains servicing rights and receives annual servicing fees approximating 1% of the outstanding securitized retail loans. HDFS serviced $3.25 billion and $4.67 billion of securitized retail loans as of December 31, 2008 and 2007, respectively. The total investment in retained securitization interests received in connection with securitizations during the year for the last three years is disclosed under non-cash investing activities in Note 2. In conjunction with current and prior year sales, HDFS had investments in retained securitization interests of $330.7 million and $407.7 million at December 31, 2008 and 2007, respectively.

The Company's investment in retained securitization interests, excluding servicing rights, is subordinate to the interests of securitization trust investors. Such investors have priority interests in the cash collections on the retail loans sold to the securitization trust (after payment of servicing fees) and in the cash reserve account deposits. These priority interests ultimately could impact the value of the Company's investment in retained securitization interests. Investors do not have recourse to the assets of HDFS for failure of the obligors on the retail loans to pay when due. The investment in retained securitization interests is recorded at fair value. Key assumptions in the valuation of the investment in retained securitization interests and in calculating the gain or loss on current year securitizations are credit losses, prepayments and discount rate.

At the date of the transaction, the following weighted-average key assumptions were used to calculate the loss on the securitization completed in 2008 and the gain on securitizations completed in 2007 and 2006:

	2008	2007	2006
Prepayment speed (Single Monthly Mortality)	2.00%	2.27%	2.47%
Weighted-average life (in years)	1.95	1.97	1.96
Expected cumulative net credit losses	4.25%	3.73%	2.84%
Residual cash flows discount rate	12.00%	12.00%	12.00%

As of December 31, 2008 and 2007, respectively, the following weighted-average key assumptions were used to value the investment in retained securitization interests:

	2008	2007
Prepayment speed (Single Monthly Mortality)	1.88%	2.17%
Weighted-average life (in years)	2.09	2.07
Expected cumulative net credit losses	4.63%	3.89%
Residual cash flows discount rate	17.89%	12.00%

Expected cumulative net credit losses are a key assumption in the valuation of the investment in retained securitization interests. As of December 31, 2008, 2007 and 2006, respectively, weighted-average expected net credit losses for all active securitizations were 4.63%, 3.89% and 2.99%. The table on the next page summarizes, as of December 31, 2008, 2007 and 2006, respectively, expected weighted-average cumulative net credit losses by year of securitization, expressed as a percentage of the original balance of loans securitized for all securitizations completed during the years noted.

(continued)

EXHIBIT 8—
continued

NOTE 8,
SECURITIZATION
TRANSACTIONS

Expected weighted-average cumulative net credit losses (%) as of:	Loans securitized in				
	2008	2007	2006	2005	2004
December 31, 2008	4.50%	4.66%	4.78%	4.66%	3.66%
December 31, 2007	—	3.88%	4.00%	4.13%	3.48%
December 31, 2006	—	—	3.00%	3.15%	2.93%

For the years ended December 31, 2008 and 2007, the Company recorded an impairment charge of $41.4 and $9.9 million, respectively, related to its investment in retained securitization interests. The investment in retained securitization interests is recorded at fair value, which is based on the present value of future expected cash flows using the Company's best estimate of key assumptions for credit losses, prepayment speed and discount rates that, in management's judgment, reflect the assumptions marketplace participants would use. During 2008 and 2007, the fair value of certain retained securitization interests was lower than the amortized cost, which indicated impairment. These impairments were considered permanent and as a result the investment in retained securitization interests has been appropriately written down to fair value. The decline in fair value below cost was due to higher projected credit losses and an increased discount rate in the fourth quarter of 2008 from 12% to 18%. During the year ended December 31, 2007, the higher actual and anticipated credit losses were partially offset by a slowing in actual and expected prepayment speeds. These charges were recorded as a reduction of financial services income.

Detailed below at December 31, 2008 and 2007, is the sensitivity of the fair value to immediate 10% and 20% adverse changes in the weighted-average key assumptions for the investment in retained securitization interests (dollars in thousands):

	2008	2007
Carrying amount/fair value of retained interests	$330,674	$407,742
Weighted-average life (in years)	2.09	2.07
Prepayment speed assumption (monthly rate)	**1.88%**	**2.17%**
Impact on fair value of 10% adverse change	$(5,700)	$(7,900)
Impact on fair value of 20% adverse change	$(11,300)	$(15,400)
Expected cumulative net credit losses	**4.63%**	**3.89%**
Impact on fair value of 10% adverse change	$(36,400)	$(36,400)
Impact on fair value of 20% adverse change	$(72,700)	$(72,700)
Residual cash flows discount rate (annual)	**17.89%**	**12.00%**
Impact on fair value of 10% adverse change	$(8,600)	$(7,500)
Impact on fair value of 20% adverse change	$(16,800)	$(14,700)

These sensitivities are hypothetical and should not be considered to be predictive of future performance. Changes in fair value generally cannot be extrapolated because the relationship of change in assumption to change in fair value may not be linear. Also, in this table, the effect of a variation in a particular assumption on the fair value of the retained interest is calculated independently from any change in another assumption. In reality, changes in one factor may contribute to changes in another, which may magnify or counteract the sensitivities. Furthermore, the estimated fair values as disclosed should not be considered indicative of future earnings on these assets.

(continued)

EXHIBIT 8—
continued

NOTE 8,
SECURITIZATION
TRANSACTIONS

The table below provides information regarding certain cash flows received from and paid to all motorcycle loan securitization trusts during the years ended December 31, 2008 and 2007 (in thousands):

	2008	2007
Proceeds from new securitizations	$467,722	$2,486,780
Servicing fees received	43,049	45,478
Other cash flows received on retained interests	132,594	162,556
10% clean-up call repurchase option	(150,240)	(90,506)

Managed retail motorcycle loans consist of all retail motorcycle installment loans serviced by HDFS including those held by securitization trusts and those held by HDFS. As of December 31, 2008 and 2007, managed retail motorcycle loans totaled $6.03 billion and $5.80 billion, respectively, of which $3.25 billion and $4.67 billion, respectively, were securitized. The principal amount of managed retail motorcycle loans 30 days or more past due was $339.1 million and $324.9 million at December 31, 2008 and 2007, respectively. The principal amount of securitized retail motorcycle loans 30 days or more past due was $225.0 million and $291.3 million at December 31, 2008 and 2007, respectively. Managed loans 30 days or more past due exclude loans reclassified as repossessed inventory. Credit losses, net of recoveries, of the managed retail motorcycle loans were $138.7 million, $106.5 million and $68.1 million during 2008, 2007 and 2006, respectively. Securitized retail motorcycle loan credit losses, net of recoveries, were $107.9 million, $93.9 million and $63.5 million during 2008, 2007 and 2006, respectively.

EXHIBIT 9

NOTE 9, DEBT

Debt with a contractual term less than one year is generally classified as short-term debt and consisted of the following as of December 31 (in thousands):

	2008	2007
Unsecured commercial paper	$1,238,649	$722,447
Asset-backed commercial paper conduit facility	500,000	—
	$1,738,649	$722,447

Debt with a contractual term greater than one year is generally classified as long-term debt and consisted of the following as of December 31 (in thousands):

	2008	2007
Unsecured commercial paper	$177,800	$120,171
Bank borrowings		
Credit facilities	390,932	256,531
Unsecured notes		
3.63% Medium-term notes due in 2008 ($400.0 million par value)	—	397,508
5.00% Medium-term notes due in 2010 ($200.0 million par value)	209,684	203,747
5.25% Medium-term notes due in 2012 ($400.0 million par value)	399,643	399,551
6.80% Medium-term notes due in 2018 ($1,000.0 million par value)	998,179	—
Gross long-term debt	2,176,238	1,377,508
Less: current portion of long-term debt	—	(397,508)
Long-term debt	$2,176,238	$980,000

(continued)

EXHIBIT 9—
continued

NOTE 9, DEBT

The Company has classified $568.7 million and $376.7 million related to its unsecured commercial paper and its Global Credit Facilities as long-term debt as of December 31, 2008 and 2007. This amount has been excluded from current liabilities because it is supported by the Global Credit Facilities and is expected to remain outstanding for an uninterrupted period extending beyond one year from the balance sheet date.

Commercial paper maturities may range up to 365 days from the issuance date. The weighted-average interest rate of outstanding commercial paper balances was 1.96% and 4.61% at December 31, 2008 and 2007, respectively. The December 31, 2008 and 2007 weighted-average interest rates include the impact of interest rate swap agreements.

In July 2008, the Company and HDFS entered into a $950.0 million 364-day facility and a $950.0 million three-year facility (collectively, "Global Credit Facilities") to replace existing credit facilities. The Global Credit Facilities, which total $1.90 billion, are committed facilities and are primarily used to support HDFS' unsecured commercial paper program and to fund HDFS' lending activities and other operations. Borrowings under the Global Credit Facilities bear interest at various variable rates, which may be adjusted upward or downward depending on whether certain criteria are satisfied. As a result of the Global Credit Facilities, HDFS may issue unsecured commercial paper in the aggregate equal to the unused portion of the Global Credit Facilities.

During December 2008, HDFS entered into agreements with a bank-sponsored asset-backed commercial paper conduit facility resulting in proceeds of $500.0 million. Unless earlier terminated or extended by the mutual agreement of HDFS and the lenders, the loan and servicing agreement will expire on March 31, 2009, at which time HDFS will be obligated to repay the $500.0 million advance in full. The weighted average interest rate of the outstanding asset-backed commercial paper facility was 6.97% at December 31, 2008. The December 31, 2008 weighted average interest rate includes the impact of interest rate swap agreements.

HDFS' Medium Term Notes (collectively "the Notes") provide for semi-annual interest payments and principal due at maturity. At December 31, 2008 and 2007, the Notes included a fair value adjustment increasing the balance by $9.7 million and $1.3 million, respectively, due to interest rate swap agreements designated as fair value hedges. The effect of the interest rate swap agreements is to convert the interest rate on a portion of the Notes from a fixed to a floating rate, which is based on 3-month LIBOR. Unamortized discounts on the Notes reduced the balance by $2.2 million and $0.5 million at December 31, 2008 and 2007, respectively.

HDFS has a revolving credit line with the Company whereby HDFS may borrow up to $210.0 million at market rates of interest. As of December 31, 2008 and 2007, HDFS had no borrowings owed to the Company under the revolving credit agreement.

The Company and HDFS have entered into a support agreement wherein, if required, the Company agrees to provide HDFS certain financial support to maintain HDFS' fixed-charge coverage at 1.25 and minimum net worth of $40.0 million. Support may be provided either as capital contributions or loans at the Company's option. No amount has ever been provided to HDFS under the support agreement.

HDFS and the Company are subject to various operating and financial covenants related to the Global Credit Facilities, asset-backed commercial paper conduit facility and Notes. The more significant covenants are described below.

(continued)

EXHIBIT 9—
continued

NOTE 9, DEBT

The covenants limit the Company's and HDFS' ability to:

Incur certain additional indebtedness;

Assume or incur certain liens;

Participate in a merger, consolidation, liquidation or dissolution; and

Purchase or hold margin stock under the financial covenants of the Global Credit Facilities and the asset-backed commercial paper conduit facility, the debt to equity ratio of HDFS and its consolidated subsidiaries cannot exceed 10.0 to 1.0 and the Company must maintain an interest ratio coverage of 2.5 to 1.0. The minimum required HDFS consolidated tangible net worth is $300.0 million. No financial covenants are required under the Notes.

At December 31, 2008 and 2007, HDFS and the Company remained in compliance with all of these covenants.

EXHIBIT 10

NOTE 12,
POSTRETIREMENT
BENEFITS
(SELECTED)

Obligations and Funded Status:

The information following provides detail of changes in the benefit obligations, changes in the fair value of plan assets and funded status as of the Company's December 31, 2008 and September 30, 2007 measurement dates (000):

	Pension and SERPA		Postretirement Healthcare Benefits	
	2008	2007	2008	2007
Change in benefit obligation				
Benefit obligation, beginning of period	$1,033,635	$976,712	$332,139	$324,985
Effects of change in measurement date	21,974	—	5,765	—
Service cost	51,363	51,647	13,078	12,880
Interest cost	68,592	59,762	21,640	19,579
Plan amendments	1,685	3,604	—	—
Actuarial losses (gains)	36,861	(32,179)	13,934	(11,814)
Plan participant contributions	6,920	7,019	952	464
Benefits paid, net of Medicare Part D subsidy	(42,747)	(32,930)	(19,758)	(13,955)
Special retiree benefits	—	—	4,881	—
Benefit obligation, end of period	1,178,283	1,033,635	372,631	332,139
Change in plan assets:				
Fair value of plan assets, beginning of period	1,067,865	982,102	136,080	119,829
Effects of change in measurement date	15,210	—	2,808	—
Actual return on plan assets	(357,793)	110,670	(41,045)	16,251
Company contributions	1,103	1,004	18,414	13,467

(continued)

EXHIBIT 10—
continued

NOTE 12,
POSTRETIREMENT
BENEFITS
(SELECTED)

Plan participant contributions	6,920	7,019	952	464
Benefits paid	(42,747)	(32,930)	(20,603)	(13,931)
Fair value of plan assets, end of period	690,558	1,067,865	96,606	136,080
Fourth quarter contributions	—	1,207	—	3,094
Funded status of the plans, December 31	(487,725)	35,437	(276,025)	(192,965)
Amounts recognized in the Consolidated Balance Sheets, December 31:				
Accrued benefit liability (other current liabilities)	$(3,722)	$(2,893)	$(1,617)	$(434)
Accrued benefit liability (other long-term liabilities)	(484,003)	(51,551)	(274,408)	(192,531)
Prepaid benefit cost (other long-term assets)	—	89,881	—	—
Net amount recognized	$(487,725)	$35,437	$(276,025)	$(192,965)

Benefit Costs:

Components of net periodic benefit costs for the years ended December 31 (in thousands):

	Pension and SERPA			Postretirement Healthcare Benefits		
	2008	2007	2006	2008	2007	2006
Service cost	$51,363	$51,647	$48,829	$13,078	$12,880	$12,944
Interest cost	68,592	59,762	52,625	21,640	19,579	16,074
Expected return on plan assets	(88,061)	(80,835)	(76,415)	(11,232)	(9,984)	(9,112)
Amortization of unrecognized:						
Prior service cost (credit)	6,158	6,691	6,997	(1,123)	(1,123)	(1,123)
Net loss	6,414	11,675	17,640	5,501	6,938	6,515
Special retiree benefits	—	—	—	4,881	—	—
Net periodic benefit cost	$44,466	$48,940	$49,676	$32,745	$28,290	$25,298

As discussed in Note 4, the Company recorded a restructuring reserve of $4.8 million related to postretirement healthcare benefits which is included as special retiree benefits in the table above.

Amounts included in accumulated other comprehensive income, net of tax, at December 31, 2008 which have not yet been recognized in net periodic benefit cost are as follows (in thousands):

	Pension and SERPA	Postretirement Healthcare Benefits	Total
Prior service cost (credit)	$19,939	$(4,307)	$15,632
Net actuarial loss	404,307	107,385	511,692
	$424,246	$103,079	$527,325

(continued)

EXHIBIT 10—
continued

NOTE 12,
POSTRETIREMENT
BENEFITS
(SELECTED)

Assumptions:

Weighted-average assumptions used to determine benefit obligations as of December 31, 2008, September 30, 2007 and September 30, 2006 and weighted-average assumptions used to determine net periodic benefit cost for the years ended December 31, 2008, September 30, 2007 and September 30, 2006 are as follows:

	Pension and SERPA			Postretirement Healthcare Benefits		
	2008	2007	2006	2008	2007	2006
Assumptions for benefit obligations:						
Discount rate	6.10%	6.30%	5.90%	6.10%	6.30%	5.90%
Rate of compensation	3.66%	4.00%	3.33%	n/a	n/a	n/a
Assumptions for net periodic benefit cost:						
Discount rate	6.30%	5.90%	5.50%	6.30%	5.90%	5.50%
Expected return on plan assets	8.50%	8.50%	8.50%	8.50%	8.50%	8.50%
Rate of compensation increase	4.00%	3.31%	3.20%	n/a	n/a	n/a

EXHIBIT 11

CONSOLIDATED
VALUATION AND
QUALIFYING
ACCOUNTS

HARLEY-DAVIDSON, INC.

Years ended December 31, 2008, 2007 and 2006

	2008	2007	2006
		(in thousands)	
Accounts receivable—allowance for doubtful accounts			
Balance at beginning of period	$9,016	$9,435	$8,492
Provision charged to expense	3,061	365	863
Reserve adjustments	2,985	(1,028)	80
Write-offs, net of recoveries	(5,983)	244	—
Balance at end of period	$9,079	$9,016	$9,435
Finance receivables held for investment—allowance for credit losses			
Balance at beginning of period	$30,295	$27,283	$26,165
Provision charged to expense	39,555	11,252	5,962
Write-offs, net of recoveries	(29,782)	(8,240)	(4,844)
Balance at end of period	$40,068	$30,295	$27,283
Inventories—allowance for obsolescence[1]			
Balance at beginning of period	$16,307	$15,282	$16,669
Provision charged to expense	37,840	11,695	6,516
Reserve adjustments	(353)	1,116	(910)
Write-offs, net of recoveries	(24,963)	(11,786)	(6,993)
Balance at end of period	$28,831	$16,307	$15,282
Deferred tax assets—valuation allowance			
Balance at beginning of period	—	—	—
Allowance for operating loss carryforwards	$42,218	—	—
Balance at end of period	$42,218	—	—

[1] Inventory obsolescence reserves deducted from cost determined on first-in first-out (FIFO) basis, before deductions for last-in, first-out (LIFO) valuation reserves.

Harley-Davidson, Inc. (B), February 2010

Harley-Davidson Motorcycle Trust 2007-3

Harley-Davidson had long provided motorcycle loans to its customers. It securitized those motorcycle receivables and then sold notes backed by the receivables to institutional investors. Exhibit 1 includes selected portions of Harley-Davidson Motorcycle Trust 2007-3, a typical Harley-Davidson securitization prior to the first quarter of 2008. From the first page of Exhibit 1, the prospectus is an offering to sell $782,000,000 of notes, backed by $782,000,294.05 of motorcycle receivables (last page of Exhibit 1).[1]

The bottom portion of the first page of Exhibit 1 describes how investors are protected by credit enhancement. That protection includes a reserve fund into which Harley-Davidson or an affiliate will deposit $1,955,000.74 in cash and a yield enhancement fund into which Harley-Davidson or an affiliate will deposit $27,386,672.85 in cash. That $29,341,673.59 of cash, plus the $782,000,294.05 of motorcycle receivables, will provide investors with a 3.75% cushion above the principal value of the notes ($782,000,000). Investors are also protected by an excess interest rate spread. The trust paid an average interest rate of slightly above 6% on the notes it issued (first page, Exhibit 1) and the trust received an average interest rate of 10.748% on the motorcycle receivables it owned.

Securitizations such as Harley-Davidson Motorcycle Trust 2007-3 were highly beneficial to institutional investors who bought the receivables-backed notes issued by the trust. At a time when U.S. Treasury securities paid interest rates of about 4%, these notes paid interest rates of about 6%; there had been few if any instances of Harley-Davidson receivables-backed notes ever failing to repay principal or failing to make all interest payments on time.

The securitizations were also highly advantageous to Harley-Davidson. It received about 96.25% of the face value of its receivables when they were securitized. It also bore no risk if the receivables were uncollectible, other than its initial 3.75% cash deposit. In addition, with the excess spread between what the trust paid to note holders and what the trust collected from motorcycle borrowers, the Harley-Davidson Motorcycle Trust usually received more in interest that it paid out. After deducting servicing and other fees, the excess was returned to Harley-Davidson. In nearly all of its securitizations, Harley-Davidson received both its initial cash deposit and additional funds from the excess spread when the securitization pool closed.

Legally, the securitization was a sale and it was treated as a sale for accounting purposes. Neither the receivables nor the receivables-backed notes appeared on Harley-Davidson's balance sheet. However, as the credit crises worsened throughout the world in early 2008, the securitization market came to a halt. Harley-Davidson sold a small securitization issue in the first quarter of 2008 but was unable to securitize or sell receivables during the remainder of 2008.

---

1. Prospectus Supplement to Prospectus, dated August 22, 2007, Harley-Davidson Motorcycle Trust 2007-3. http://www.sec.gov/Archives/edgar/data/1114926/000110465907065058/a07-22516_5424b5.htm.

Harley-Davidson's 2009 income statement (Exhibit 2) shows that revenues declined in both 2008 and 2009 because Harley-Davidson could no longer fund everyone who wanted to buy a Harley-Davidson motorcycle. Harley-Davidson's interest expense also increased. As shown in its balance sheet (Exhibit 3), long-term debt rose dramatically as Harley-Davidson was forced to borrow to fund its motorcycle credit sales. In 2008, Harley-Davidson reported the $2,443,965,000 of receivables it was unable to sell as "Finance receivables held for sale." In early 2009, as it became apparent that it would be unable to sell those receivables, Harley-Davidson reclassified the receivables as $3,621,048,000 of "Finance receivables held for investment." Exhibit 4 provides additional information about finance receivables held for sale and finance receivables held for investment, as does Exhibit 5, Harley-Davidson's 2009 Cash Flow from Operating Activities.

Harley-Davidson Motorcycle Trust 2009-4

In 2009, Harley-Davidson was once again able to securitize its receivables, but at far less advantageous terms. Exhibit 4 provides selected information from Harley-Davidson Motorcycle Trust 2009-4. As seen on the first page of the prospectus, the notes pay interest rates about twice that of similar-maturity U.S. Treasury securities.[2] The trust retains only a 1% reserve fund, which is a smaller reserve fund than Trust 2007-3.[3] Far more important, $562,499,000 of notes that will pay an average interest rate of well under 2% (first page, Exhibit 4) will be backed by $720,305,230.29 of motorcycle receivables that pay an average of 11.221% (last page, Exhibit 4). In addition, as seen at the bottom of the diagram in Exhibit 4, Harley-Davidson or its affiliates must purchase the $39,831,000 of class C notes to be issued by the trust. As a result, Harley-Davidson receives cash equal to only about 71% of the face value of the receivables it transfers into the trust. In comparison, Harley-Davidson received about 96% of the face value of receivables it transferred into trust 2007-3.

Furthermore, the securitizations no longer qualify as a sale of receivables. Instead, the motorcycle receivables must be reported as assets on Harley-Davidson's balance sheet as "receivables held for investment." The notes issued by the trust must also be included as liabilities on Harley-Davidson's balance sheet.

Required

1. What is more important, that Harley-Davidson must not report the trust's receivables and liabilities on its own balance sheet, or the fact that Harley-Davidson now is able to borrow only about 71% of the value of its receivables instead of more than 96% prior to the credit crises of 2008–2010? Explain.

2. Explain the effects on Harley-Davidson's financial statements (Exhibits 2–5).

3. Explain the effects on Harley-Davidson's market value, including the effects on its ability to increase or even maintain motorcycle credit sales.

---

2. Prospectus Supplement to Prospectus, dated November 23, 2009, Harley-Davidson Motorcycle Trust 2009-4. http://www.sec.gov/Archives/edgar/data/1114926/000110465909067539/a09-34142_4424b5.htm.

3. Ibid., p. S-7.

EXHIBIT 1

HARLEY-DAVIDSON
MOTORCYCLE TRUST
2007-3

PROSPECTUS SUPPLEMENT
(To Prospectus Dated August 22, 2007)

Harley-Davidson Motorcycle Trust 2007-3
Issuing Entity

$782,000,000 Motorcycle Contract Backed Notes

Harley-Davidson Customer Funding Corp.
Depositor

Harley-Davidson Credit Corp.
Seller, Servicer and Sponsor

The notes will represent obligations of Harley-Davidson Motorcycle Trust 2007-3 only, and will not represent obligations of or interests in Harley-Davidson Financial Services, Inc., Harley-Davidson Credit Corp., Harley-Davidson Customer Funding Corp., Harley-Davidson, Inc. or any of their respective affiliates. The notes are motorcycle contract backed notes issued by the issuing entity. Payments on the notes will be made monthly on the 15th day of each month, or if the 15th is not a business day, on the business day immediately following the 15th, beginning September 17, 2007. The assets securing the notes are fixed rate, simple interest, conditional sales contracts or promissory notes and security agreements relating to the purchase of new or used motorcycles. This prospectus supplement may be used to offer and sell the notes only if accompanied by the prospectus.

Consider carefully the risk factors beginning on page S-23 in this prospectus supplement and on page 9 of the prospectus.

The issuing entity will issue the following classes of notes:

	Principal Amount	Interest Rate	Final Scheduled Payment Date	Price to Public	Underwriting Discount	Proceeds to Issuer
Class A-1 Notes	$120,000,000	5.5942%	September 2008	100.000000%	0.10%	99.900000%
Class A-2a Notes	$65,000,000	5.34%	September 2010	99.994939%	0.14%	99.854939%
Class A-2b Notes	$120,000,000	LIBOR + 0.25%	September 2010	100.000000%	0.14%	99.860000%
Class A-3 Notes	$230,000,000	LIBOR + 0.35%	June 2012	100.000000%	0.17%	99.830000%
Class A-4 Notes	$174,660,000	5.52%	November 2013	99.989082%	0.21%	99.779082%
Class B Notes	$50,832,000	6.04%	August 2014	99.989277%	0.30%	99.689277%
Class C Notes	$21,508,000	6.91%	May 2015	99.970091%	0.35%	99.620091%
Total	$782,000,000			$781,965,757	$1,364,560	$780,601,197

The Class A-2b notes and the Class A-3 notes are floating rate notes. All other notes are fixed rate notes. The interest rate on the floating rate notes will be based on one-month LIBOR. The issuing entity will enter into an interest rate swap with respect to each class or tranche of floating rate notes with JPMorgan Chase Bank, National Association as the swap counterparty.

Credit Enhancement:

- Reserve fund with an initial deposit of $1,955,000.74.
- Yield supplement account with an initial deposit of $27,386,672.85.
- Subordination of the Class B notes and Class C notes to the Class A notes and subordination of the Class C notes to the Class B notes as described in this prospectus supplement.
- Excess spread.

(continued)

EXHIBIT 1—
continued

HARLEY-DAVIDSON
MOTORCYCLE TRUST
2007-3

SUMMARY OF TRANSACTION STRUCTURE AND FLOW OF FUNDS

This structural summary briefly describes certain major structural components, the relationship among the parties, the flow of proceeds from the issuance of the notes and certain other material features of the transaction. This structural summary does not contain all of the information that you need to consider in making your investment decision. You should carefully read this entire prospectus supplement and the accompanying prospectus to understand all the terms of this offering.

Harley-Davidson Customer Funding Corp., the depositor, will purchase from Harley-Davidson Credit Corp. a pool of motorcycle conditional sales contracts or promissory notes and security agreements purchased by Harley-Davidson Credit Corp. from Eaglemark Savings Bank and, to a limited extent, certain Harley-Davidson® motorcycle dealers. Harley-Davidson Customer Funding Corp. then will sell the contracts to Harley-Davidson Motorcycle Trust 2007-3. The following chart illustrates the use of proceeds from investors by the issuing entity and the depositor to purchase the contracts.

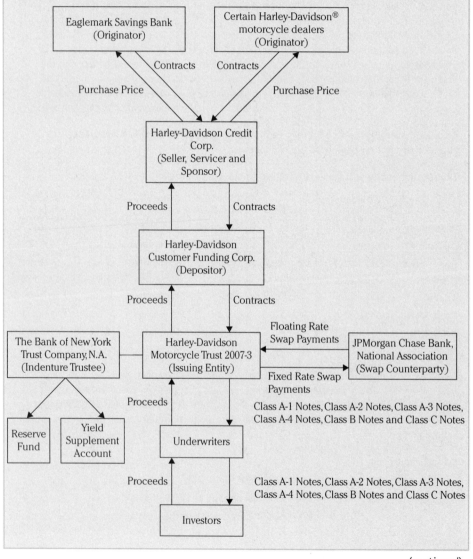

(continued)

EXHIBIT 1—
continued

HARLEY-DAVIDSON
MOTORCYCLE TRUST
2007-3

The Contracts and Other Assets of the Issuing Entity

The primary assets of the issuing entity will be a pool of fixed rate, simple interest conditional sales contracts and promissory notes and security agreements relating to the retail purchase of new or used motorcycles manufactured by one or more subsidiaries of Harley-Davidson, Inc. (including Buell Motorcycle Company, LLC, a wholly-owned subsidiary of Harley-Davidson, Inc. ("*Buell*")) or certain other manufacturers. Harley-Davidson, Inc. and its subsidiaries are collectively referred to herein as "Harley-Davidson." See "*Other Manufacturers*" in the prospectus. The contracts were or will be originated indirectly by the seller primarily through Eaglemark Savings Bank, a wholly-owned subsidiary of Harley-Davidson Credit Corp., and, to a limited extent, through Harley-Davidson® motorcycle dealers.

The issuing entity's assets also include:

- Security interests in the motorcycles securing the contracts;
- Proceeds, if any, from certain insurance policies and debt cancellation agreements with respect to such motorcycles;
- Payments received from the swap counterparty and due under the interest rate swap agreement; and
- Amounts on deposit in various accounts.

The Contracts

The issuing entity's main source of funds for making payments on the notes will be collections on the contracts. The contracts transferred to the issuing entity will be selected from contracts in the seller's portfolio based on the criteria specified in the transfer sale agreement. The obligors on the contracts are located in the 50 states of the United States, the District of Columbia, U.S. Territories and military bases.

On the closing date, pursuant to the sale and servicing agreement, the depositor will transfer, and the issuing entity will acquire, contract with the characteristics set forth below as of the close of business on the cutoff date.

In addition to the purchase of contracts from the issuing entity in connection with the servicer's exercise of its "clean-up call" option as described above under "*Optional Redemption*," contracts will be purchased from the issuing entity by the depositor if certain representations and warranties concerning the characteristics of the contracts are breached, and by the servicer if certain servicing covenants are breached.

No contract will have a scheduled maturity later than October 2014. However, an obligor can generally prepay its contract at any time without penalty.

Composition of the Contracts (as of the cutoff date)

Aggregate Principal Balance	$782,000,294.05
Number of Contracts	50,520
Average Principal Balance	$15,479.02
Weighted Average Contract Interest Rate	10.748%
(Range)	4.027% to 25.976%
Weighted Average Original Term (in months)	73.55
(Range)	12 to 84
Weighted Average Remaining Term (in months)	72.44
(Range)	3 to 84
Weighted Average FICO® Score	692

(continued)

EXHIBIT 1—
continued

HARLEY-DAVIDSON
MOTORCYCLE TRUST
2007-3

Geographic Concentration (as of the cutoff date)

State	Principal Balance Concentration
Texas	9.38%
California	7.46%
Florida	5.48%
Pennsylvania	5.29%
Ohio	5.09%

No other state represented more than 5.00% of the aggregate principal balance of the contracts as of the cutoff date.

EXHIBIT 2

CONSOLIDATED
STATEMENTS
OF INCOME

HARLEY-DAVIDSON, INC.

Years ended December 31, 2009, 2008 and 2007

	2009	2008	2007
	(In thousands, except per share amounts)		
Revenue:			
Motorcycles and related products	$4,287,130	$5,578,414	$5,726,848
Financial services	494,779	376,970	416,196
Total revenue	4,781,909	5,955,384	6,143,044
Costs and expenses:			
Motorcycles and related products cost of goods sold	2,900,934	3,647,270	3,612,748
Financial services interest expense	283,634	136,763	81,475
Financial services provision for credit losses	169,206	39,555	11,252
Selling, administrative and engineering expense	979,384	1,060,154	1,012,008
Restructuring expense and asset impairment	224,278	12,475	—
Goodwill impairment	28,387	—	—
Total costs and expenses	4,585,823	4,896,217	4,717,483
Operating income	196,086	1,059,167	1,425,561
Investment income	4,254	11,296	22,258
Interest expense	21,680	4,542	—
Income before provision for income taxes	178,660	1,065,921	1,447,819
Provision for income taxes	108,019	381,686	513,976
Income from continuing operations	70,641	684,235	933,843
Loss from discontinued operations, net of tax	(125,757)	(29,517)	—
Net (loss) income	$(55,116)	$654,718	$933,843

EXHIBIT 3

CONSOLIDATED
BALANCE SHEETS

HARLEY-DAVIDSON, INC.

December 31, 2009 and 2008

	2009	2008
	(in thousands, except share amounts)	
ASSETS		
Current assets:		
Cash and cash equivalents	$1,630,433	$568,894
Marketable securities	39,685	—
Accounts receivable, net	269,371	265,319
Finance receivables held for sale	—	2,443,965
Finance receivables held for investment, net	1,436,114	1,378,461
Inventories	323,029	379,141
Assets of discontinued operations	181,211	238,715
Deferred income taxes	179,685	123,327
Prepaid expenses and other current assets	282,421	128,730
Total current assets	4,341,949	5,526,552
Finance receivables held for investment, net	3,621,048	817,102
Property, plant and equipment, net	906,906	1,056,928
Goodwill	31,400	60,131
Deferred income taxes	177,504	288,240
Other long-term assets	76,711	79,672
	$9,155,518	$7,828,625
LIABILITIES AND SHAREHOLDERS' EQUITY		
Current liabilities:		
Accounts payable	$162,515	$303,277
Accrued liabilities	514,084	503,466
Liabilities of discontinued operations	69,535	77,941
Short-term debt	189,999	1,738,649
Current portion of long-term debt	1,332,091	—
Total current liabilities	2,268,224	2,623,333
Long-term debt	4,114,039	2,176,238
Pension liability	245,332	484,003
Postretirement healthcare liability	264,472	274,408
Other long-term liabilities	155,333	155,040
Commitments and contingencies (Note 17)		

(continued)

EXHIBIT 3—
continued

CONSOLIDATED
BALANCE SHEETS

Shareholders' equity:		
Series A Junior participating preferred stock, none issued	—	—
Common stock, 336,800,970 and 335,653,577 shares issued in 2009 and 2008, respectively	3,368	3,357
Additional paid-in-capital	871,100	846,796
Retained earnings	6,324,268	6,458,778
Accumulated other comprehensive loss	(417,898)	(522,526)
	6,780,838	6,786,405
Less:		
Treasury stock (102,487,275 and 102,889,730 shares in 2009 and 2008, respectively), at cost	(4,672,720)	(4,670,802)
Total shareholders' equity	2,108,118	2,115,603
	$9,155,518	$7,828,625

EXHIBIT 4

NOTE 6, FINANCE
RECEIVABLES

HARLEY-DAVIDSON, INC.

Finance receivables held for investment, net at December 31 for the past five years were as follows (in thousands):

	2009	2008	2007	2006	2005
Wholesale					
United States	$787,891	$1,074,377	$1,132,748	$1,206,753	$1,040,220
Europe	—	—	86,947	66,421	59,960
Canada	82,110	89,859	108,756	65,538	50,097
Total wholesale	870,001	1,164,236	1,328,451	1,338,712	1,150,277
Retail					
United States	3,835,235	514,637	485,579	409,788	319,856
Canada	256,658	226,084	228,850	174,894	149,597
Total retail	4,091,893	740,721	714,429	584,682	469,453
	4,961,894	1,904,957	2,042,880	1,923,394	1,619,730
Allowance for credit losses	150,082	40,068	30,295	27,283	26,165
	4,811,812	1,864,889	2,012,585	1,896,111	1,593,565
Investment in retained securitization interests	245,350	330,674	407,742	384,106	349,659
	$5,057,162	$2,195,563	$2,420,327	$2,280,217	$1,943,224

Finance receivables held for sale at December 31 for the past five years were as follows (in thousands):

	2009	2008	2007	2006	2005
Retail					
United States	$—	$2,443,965	$781,280	$547,106	$299,373

EXHIBIT 5

CASH FLOWS
FROM OPERATING
ACTIVITIES

HARLEY-DAVIDSON, INC.

The reconciliation of net (loss) income to net cash provided by (used by) operating activities of continuing operations is as follows (in thousands):

	2009	2008	2007
Cash flows from operating activities:			
Net (loss) income	$(55,116)	$654,718	$933,843
Loss from discontinued operations	(125,757)	(29,517)	—
Income from continuing operations	70,641	684,235	933,843
Adjustments to reconcile net income to net cash provided by operating activities:			
Depreciation	246,344	220,755	204,172
Provision for employee long-term benefits	118,201	76,426	75,683
Contributions to pension and postretirement plans	(233,224)	(19,517)	(15,302)
Stock compensation expense	17,576	24,473	20,974
Loss (gain) on off-balance sheet securitizations	—	5,370	(36,033)
Net change in wholesale finance receivables	332,167	99,373	22,816
Origination of retail finance receivables held for sale	(1,180,467)	(2,788,463)	(2,919,937)
Collections on retail finance receivables held for sale	919,201	507,106	110,756
Proceeds from securitization of retail finance receivables	—	467,722	2,486,780
Impairment of retained securitization interests	45,370	41,403	9,932
Lower of cost or fair market value adjustment on finance receivables held for sale	5,895	37,764	—
Goodwill and other impairments	46,410	—	—
Pension and postretirement healthcare plan curtailment and settlement expense	37,814	—	—
Provision for credit losses	169,206	39,555	11,252
Deferred income taxes	6,931	(46,729)	(60,779)
Foreign currency adjustments	(22,234)	2,892	(14,581)
Other, net	76,445	53,978	23,977
Changes in current assets and liabilities:			
Accounts receivable, net	8,809	2,710	(26,399)
Finance receivables–accrued interest and other	(3,360)	(7,149)	(19,680)
Inventories	85,472	(42,263)	(48,019)
Accounts payable and accrued liabilities	(239,009)	45,998	41,210
Restructuring reserves	65,988	2,149	—
Derivative instruments	4,711	(11,962)	3,492
Other	30,123	(3,855)	(6,011)
Total adjustments	538,369	(1,292,264)	(135,697)
Net cash provided by (used by) operating activities of continuing operations	$609,010	$(608,029)	$798,146

EXHIBIT 6

HARLEY-DAVIDSON
MOTORCYCLE TRUST
2009-4

PROSPECTUS SUPPLEMENT
(To Prospectus Dated November 23, 2009)

Harley-Davidson Motorcycle Trust 2009-4
Issuing Entity

$562,499,000 Motorcycle Contract Backed Notes

Harley-Davidson Customer Funding Corp.
Depositor

Harley-Davidson Credit Corp.
Seller, Servicer and Sponsor

The notes will represent obligations of Harley-Davidson Motorcycle Trust 2009-4 only, and will not represent obligations of or interests in Harley-Davidson Financial Services, Inc., Harley-Davidson Credit Corp., Harley-Davidson Customer Funding Corp., Harley-Davidson, Inc. or any of their respective affiliates. The notes are motorcycle contract backed notes issued by the issuing entity. Payments on the notes will be made monthly on the 15th day of each month, or if the 15th is not a business day, on the business day immediately following the 15th, beginning January 15, 2010. The assets securing the notes are fixed rate, simple interest, conditional sales contracts or promissory notes and security agreements relating to the purchase of new or used motorcycles. This prospectus supplement may be used to offer and sell the offered notes only if accompanied by the prospectus.

On the closing date, the Class A notes will be "eligible collateral" under and as defined in the Term Asset-Backed Securities Loan Facility, or "TALF", established by the Federal Reserve Bank of New York. Investors seeking to obtain a loan under TALF should consult their legal and financial advisors to determine the eligibility and other requirements under TALF.

Consider carefully the risk factors beginning on page S-18 in this prospectus supplement and on page 8 of the prospectus.

The issuing entity will issue the classes of notes described below:

	Principal Amount	Interest Rate	Final Scheduled Payment Date	Price to Public	Underwriting Discount	Proceeds to Depositor
Class A-1 Notes	$142,000,000	0.28603%	December 2010	100.00000%	0.125%	99.87500%
Class A-2 Notes	$162,000,000	1.16%	October 2012	99.99392%	0.200%	99.79392%
Class A-3 Notes	$154,000,000	1.87%	February 2014	99.98248%	0.280%	99.70248%
Class A-4 Notes	$42,000,000	2.40%	July 2014	99.98081%	0.380%	99.60081%
Class B Notes	$22,668,000	3.19%	September 2014	99.98242%	0.500%	99.48242%
Class C Notes	$39,831,000	4.57%	June 2017	—	—	—
Total	$562,499,000			$522,619,125	$1,205,640	$521,413,485

The issuing entity will also issue a class of certificates that represent fractional, undivided interests in the issuing entity, do not bear interest and are not being offered hereby, but instead will initially be issued to the depositor or one of its affiliates.

The Class C notes will not be purchased by the underwriters but will be acquired by the depositor and/or be sold to one or more affiliates of the depositor. See "*Underwriting*" in this prospectus supplement.

Credit Enhancement:

- Reserve fund.
- Subordination of the Class B notes, Class C notes and the certificates to the Class A notes, subordination of the Class C notes and the certificates to the Class B notes and subordination of the certificates to the Class C notes as described in this prospectus supplement.
- Excess spread.

(continued)

EXHIBIT 6—
continued

HARLEY-DAVIDSON
MOTORCYCLE TRUST
2009-4

SUMMARY OF TRANSACTION STRUCTURE AND FLOW OF FUNDS

This structural summary briefly describes certain major structural components, the relationship among the parties, the flow of proceeds from the issuance of the notes and certificates and certain other material features of the transaction. This structural summary does not contain all of the information that you need to consider in making your investment decision. You should carefully read this entire prospectus supplement and the accompanying prospectus to understand all the terms of this offering.

Harley-Davidson Customer Funding Corp., the depositor, will purchase from Harley-Davidson Credit Corp. a pool of motorcycle conditional sales contracts or promissory notes and security agreements purchased by Harley-Davidson Credit Corp. from Eaglemark Savings Bank and, to a limited extent, certain Harley-Davidson® motorcycle dealers. Harley-Davidson Customer Funding Corp. then will sell the contracts to Harley-Davidson Motorcycle Trust 2009-4. The following chart illustrates the use of proceeds from investors by the issuing entity and the depositor to purchase the contracts.

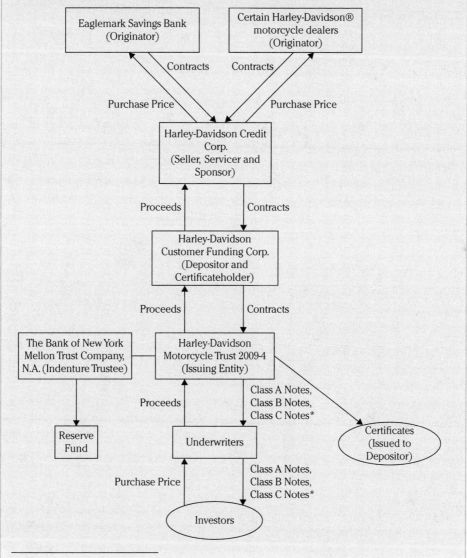

*Class C Notes will not be purchased by the underwriters but will be acquired by the depositor and/or be sold to one or more affiliates of the depositor.

(continued)

EXHIBIT 6—
continued

HARLEY-DAVIDSON
MOTORCYCLE TRUST
2009-4

No contract will have a scheduled maturity later than November 15, 2016. However, an obligor can generally prepay its contract at any time without penalty.

Composition of the Statistical Pool of Contracts (as of the cutoff date)

Aggregate Principal Balance	$720,305,230.29
Number of Contracts	59,809
Average Principal Balance	$12,043.43
Weighted Average Contract Interest Rate	11.221%
(Range)	1.000% to 24.250%
Weighted Average Original Term (in months)	74
(Range)	24 to 84
Weighted Average Remaining Term (in months)	60
(Range)	3 to 84
Weighted Average FICO® Score(1)	713
FICO® Score less than 640(2) (3)	11.16%
FICO® Score not available(3)	0.14%
No Down Payment(3)	9.85%
Down Payment less than 10%(3) (4)	5.32%
Used Motorcycle at Origination(3)	22.73%

(1) As of origination. Weighted Average FICO® Score is calculated excluding contracts for which no FICO® score was available.

(2) Excludes contracts for which no FICO® score was available.

(3) As a percentage of aggregate principal balance of the statistical pool of contracts.

(4) Does not include contracts with down payments not more than $200 less than 10% of the sales price of the motorcycle and related parts and accessories. Excludes contracts with no down payment.

Geographical Concentration of the Statistical Poll of Contracts (as of the statistical cutoff date)

State	Principal Balance Concentration
Texas	12.28%
California	8.32%
Florida	7.45%
North Carolina	7.31%

No other state represented more than 5.00% of the aggregate principal balance of the statistical pool of contracts as of the statistical cutoff date.

Apple Inc. and Retrospective Adoption of Revenue Recognition Rules

Many sales include arrangements with multiple deliverables; some goods or services are delivered immediately, whereas others are provided later, in a different accounting period. Examples include the following: sale of heavy equipment that includes maintenance and parts for three years; sale of a computer system that includes hardware, software, and software updates for three years; and sale of copiers (with imbedded software) that includes software updates for three years.

The revenue recognition principles established by SEC Staff Accounting Bulletin 104 (SAB 104) apply to sales with multiple deliverables. These four principles are (1) persuasive evidence of an arrangement exists; (2) delivery has occurred or services have been rendered; (3) the seller's price to the buyer is fixed or determinable, and (4) collectability is reasonably assured.

In the first example, revenue can usually be recognized for heavy equipment when the equipment is delivered. However, revenue for maintenance or parts must be recognized pro rata over the next three years because the service and parts will be delivered over that three-year period, not at contract inception. In the second example, revenue can usually be recognized for hardware and software at the beginning of the contract, when they are delivered, but not for software updates, which are provided later. Similarly, revenue can usually be recognized for the copying equipment when delivered, but software update revenue would be recognized over the three-year update period, unless it is immaterial.

In each instance, firms must allocate the total sales price between the multiple elements in a reasonable way. The most reliable way might be to use the firm's own history of selling items separately. Suppose a firm sells heavy equipment and also offers three-year maintenance contracts on equipment it sells and on equipment sold by competitors. The maintenance contract price may be a percentage of the original cost of the equipment, adjusted for usage or age. If the firm has evidence that it routinely sells service contracts on equipment bought elsewhere and that it routinely sells equipment without maintenance contracts, then the firm has support for the selling price of both the equipment and the maintenance contract. If the firm sells equipment bundled with a maintenance contract at a discount, it can use historical selling prices for equipment and maintenance contracts to allocate the discounted revenue to the separate elements.

The firm might also consider prices its competitors charge for the separate elements or use its best judgment to allocate revenue to each element in a multiple element sale. However, some firms that sell software bundled with updates or support seemingly allocate too much revenue to the initial software component and too little to the subsequent support or maintenance. That practice lets firms recognize too much revenue at the start of the contract period. Later, when the firm incurs high support or maintenance costs, it has minimal revenue to offset those expenses.

ACS 985-605 (SOP 97-2)

In response, the American Institute of Certified Public Accountants (AICPA) issued ASC 985-605, Statement of Position 97-2 (SOP 97-2), in 1997. Under ASC 985-605, if a multiple element sale includes software that is more than incidental to the sale, a vendor must have vendor-specific objective evidence (VSOE) of the selling price of each element in the sale (i.e., evidence it had sold each item separately and that the sales were more than occasional or incidental).

Without VSOE, firms had two options. If the cost of the future service was highly uncertain, the firm was required to defer all revenue until the contract was complete. In most cases, however, firms provided services gradually; in those instances, firms were required to use the subscription method (i.e., recognize the entire selling price evenly over the contract period).

Although it was difficult to completely satisfy ASC 985-605's VSOE requirements, many firms assumed they could avoid using the subscription method if their deviations from ASC 985-605 were immaterial. However, when the Public Company Accounting Oversight Board (PCAOB) began reviewing auditing firms in 2004, one of its main findings was that companies were not meeting ASC 985-605's VSOE requirement. The PCAOB noted that some companies had only occasional sales of items in a multiple-element sale or even sales that seemed contrived. The PCAOB further noted that selling prices of different items fluctuated too much relative to each other to be deemed reliable.

As a result, some firms were required to restate their financial statements to show far lower revenues and profits than in the past. In many instances that change made financial statements highly misleading; in other instances, the change made it difficult for firms that were economically profitable to obtain funding. For example, a firm might sell software that included updates for a three-year period. The software might be far more valuable than the updates, but without VSOE the firm was required to use subscription accounting.

To avoid subscription accounting, firms went to great lengths to establish VSOE. This trend was particularly true for companies that sold high-value products that contained software deemed more than incidental to the product. Some customers will agree to a total price for a multiple-element sale but want that price allocated to individual elements in some way for internal purposes. Because that could have caused the selling firm to violate ASC 985-605, many firms had revenue recognition specialists who were required to approve the contract terms before the selling company could accept the order. That procedure clearly interfered with a firm's business practices, but the FASB seemed unwilling to change VSOE rules.

The iPhone

In 2007, Apple began selling its iPhone, a product with highly sophisticated imbedded software. Apple decided to offer customers free software updates over an unspecified period. At the time, Apple probably had little idea of the cost or even the extent of these software updates, or the eventual popularity of the iPhone. Because it was offering the software at no cost, Apple had no VSOE for the price of the software updates. As a result, Apple adopted the subscription model and decided to spread iPhone revenue evenly over 24 months. If Apple sold an iPhone for $480 it recognized $20 of revenue the first month and recorded $460 as deferred (unearned) revenue.

As iPhone sales grew, deferred revenues grew past $12 billion, and it was apparent that software update costs would be trivial relative to deferred revenues. Apple's 2009 10-K for the period ending September 30, 2009, included the following balance sheet and note disclosures about current and non-current deferred revenue:

Current liabilities:		
Accounts payable	$5,601	$5,520
Accrued expenses	3,376	3,719
Deferred revenue	10,305	4,853
Total current liabilities	19,282	14,092
Deferred revenue—non-current	4,485	3,029
Other non-current liabilities	2,252	1,421
Total liabilities	26,019	18,542

Note 4–Consolidated Financial Statement Details

The following tables show the Company's consolidated financial statement disclosures as of September 26, 2009 and September 27, 2008 (in millions) about current and non-current deferred costs associated with the above deferred revenues:

Other Current Assets

	2009	2008
Deferred costs under subscription accounting-current	$3,703	$1,931
Vendor non-trade receivables	1,696	2,282
Inventory component prepayments-current	309	475
Other current assets	1,176	1,134
Total other current assets	$6,884	$5,822

Other Assets

	2009	2008
Deferred costs under subscription accounting-non-current	$1,468	$1,089
Inventory component prepayments-non-current	844	208
Deferred tax assets-non-current	259	138
Capitalized software development costs, net	106	67
Other assets	974	433
Total other assets	$3,651	$1,935

Possibly in response to Apple's financial reports, in October 2009 the FASB issued two Accounting Software Updates: ASC 605-25–ASU 2009-13, Revenue Recognition (Topic 605) *Multiple-Deliverable Revenue Arrangements* and ASU 2009-14, Software (Topic 985) *Certain Revenue Arrangements That Include Software Elements*. These two ASCs incorporated the software recognition portion of ASC 985-605 with an acceptable hierarchy of revenue recognition rules for multiple-element sales that include software. The hierarchy is (1) vendor-specific objective evidence of fair value (VSOE), (2) third-party evidence of selling price (TPE), and (3) best estimate of the selling price (ESP). Although VSOE is still the preferred method, a company's own best estimate of the separate selling prices (ESP) is acceptable, so effectively, VSOE is now nearly irrelevant.

Apple Retrospectively Adopts New Revenue Recognition Rules

ASC 605-25 and ASC 985-605 are effective for new multiple-element sales entered into in fiscal years beginning on or after June 15, 2010. Most U.S. firms have a December 31 year end, so those firms are not required to use the new rules in their sales contracts until January 1, 2011. However, companies had the option to adopt the new rules immediately and apply them retrospectively, that is, restate prior periods as if the new rules had always been in effect.

Apple issued its 10-K for the year ending September 30, 2009, on October 27, 2009. On January 25, 2010, Apple issued its 10-Q for the three months ended December 31, 2009, and also issued an amended (revised) 10-K (10-K/A) on that date that restated its prior financial results to reflect the new revenue recognition rules.

Exhibit 1 is an explanatory note at the beginning of Apple's 2009 10-K/A (Amendment No. 1) that explains why it is restating its financial statements. Exhibit 2, an excerpt from Note 1 to that 10-K/A, explains Apple's new revenue recognition for arrangements with multiple deliverables. This note explains that Apple is deferring $25 of revenue for each iPhone sale for free software updates, and it explains the rationale.

Exhibit 3 provides restated balance sheets as of September 26, 2009, and September 27, 2008, and provides restated income statements for the years ended September 26, 2009, September 27, 2008, and September 29, 2007. For each of the five statements, Apple shows an "As Reported" column, an "Adjustments" column, and an "As Amended" column.

Required

1. Should the FASB have overturned the software revenue recognition portion within ASC 985-605? As part of your explanation, consider whether firms will now have too much flexibility to manipulate revenues.

2. Is Apple's explanation for why it adopted the new rules retrospectively clear (Exhibit 1)? Is it valid?

3. Is Apple's explanation of how it implemented the new rules clear (Exhibit 2)? Is the new revenue recognition/deferral method reasonable?

4. Explain the changes to Apple's 2008 and 2009 balance sheets and its 2007, 2008, and 2009 income statements (Exhibit 3). Do the restated financial statements better reflect Apple's financial condition?

5. Why are there no revised statements of cash flows in Note 2 of the 2009 10-K/A (Exhibit 3)?

EXHIBIT 1

EXPLANATORY
NOTE, APPLE INC.
2009 10-K/A
(AMENDMENT 1)

Explanatory Note

Apple Inc. (the "Company") is filing this Amendment No. 1 to the Annual Report on Form 10-K (the "Form 10-K/A") to amend its Annual Report on Form 10-K for the year ended September 26, 2009, which was filed with the Securities and Exchange Commission ("SEC") on October 27, 2009 (the "Original Filing" and together with the Form 10-K/A, the "Form 10-K"). As amended by this Form 10-K/A, the Form 10-K reflects the Company's retrospective adoption of the Financial Accounting Standards Board's ("FASB") amended accounting standards related to revenue recognition for arrangements with multiple deliverables and arrangements that include software elements ("new accounting principles"). The new accounting principles permit prospective or retrospective adoption, and the Company elected retrospective adoption. The Company adopted the new accounting principles during the first quarter of 2010, as reflected in the Company's financial statements included in its Quarterly Report on Form 10-Q for the quarter ended December 26, 2009, which was filed with the SEC on January 25, 2010. The new accounting principles significantly change how the Company accounts for certain revenue arrangements that include both hardware and software elements as described further below.

Under the historical accounting principles, the Company was required to account for sales of both iPhone and Apple TV using subscription accounting because the Company indicated it might from time-to-time provide future unspecified software upgrades and features for those products free of charge. Under subscription accounting, revenue and associated product cost of sales for iPhone and Apple TV were deferred at the time of sale and recognized on a straight-line basis over each product's estimated economic life. This resulted in the deferral of significant amounts of revenue and cost of sales related to iPhone and Apple TV. Costs incurred by the Company for engineering, sales, marketing and warranty were expensed as incurred. As of September 26, 2009, based on the historical accounting principles, total accumulated deferred revenue and deferred costs associated with past iPhone and Apple TV sales were $12.1 billion and $5.2 billion, respectively.

The new accounting principles generally require the Company to account for the sale of both iPhone and Apple TV as two deliverables. The first deliverable is the hardware and software delivered at the time of sale, and the second deliverable is the right included with the purchase of iPhone and Apple TV to receive on a when-and-if-available basis future unspecified software upgrades and features relating to the product's software. The new accounting principles result in the recognition of substantially all of the revenue and product costs from sales of iPhone and Apple TV at the time of sale. Additionally, the Company is required to estimate a standalone selling price for the unspecified software upgrade right included with the sale of iPhone and Apple TV and recognizes that amount ratably over the 24-month estimated life of the related hardware device. For all periods presented, the Company's estimated selling price for the software upgrade right included with each iPhone and Apple TV sold is $25 and $10, respectively. The adoption of the new accounting principles increased the Company's net sales by $6.4 billion, $5.0 billion and $572 million for 2009, 2008 and 2007, respectively. As of September 26, 2009, the revised total accumulated deferred revenue associated with iPhone and Apple TV sales to date was $483 million; revised accumulated deferred costs for such sales were zero.

(continued)

EXHIBIT 1—
continued

EXPLANATORY
NOTE, APPLE INC.
2009 10-K/A
(AMENDMENT 1)

The Company had the option of adopting the new accounting principles on a prospective or retrospective basis. Prospective adoption would have required the Company to apply the new accounting principles to sales beginning in fiscal year 2010 without reflecting the impact of the new accounting principles on iPhone and Apple TV sales made prior to September 2009. Accordingly, the Company's financial results for the two years following adoption would have included the impact of amortizing the significant amounts of deferred revenue and cost of sales related to historical iPhone and Apple TV sales. The Company believes prospective adoption would have resulted in financial information that was not comparable between financial periods because of the significant amount of past iPhone sales; therefore, the Company elected retrospective adoption. Retrospective adoption required the Company to revise its previously issued financial statements as if the new accounting principles had always been applied. The Company believes retrospective adoption provides the most comparable and useful financial information for financial statement users, is more consistent with the information the Company's management uses to evaluate its business, and better reflects the underlying economic performance of the Company. Accordingly, the Company has revised its financial statements for 2009, 2008 and 2007 in this Form 10-K/A to reflect the retrospective adoption of the new accounting principles. There was no impact from the retrospective adoption of the new accounting principles for 2006 and 2005. Those years predated the Company's introduction of iPhone and Apple TV.

EXHIBIT 2

NOTE 1, APPLE INC.
2009 10-K/A

Note 1—Summary of Significant Accounting Policies

Revenue Recognition

Revenue Recognition for Arrangements with Multiple Deliverables

For multi-element arrangements that include tangible products that contain software that is essential to the tangible product's functionality and undelivered software elements that relate to the tangible product's essential software, the Company allocates revenue to all deliverables based on their relative selling prices. In such circumstances, the new accounting principles establish a hierarchy to determine the selling price to be used for allocating revenue to deliverables as follows: (i) vendor-specific objective evidence of fair value ("VSOE"), (ii) third-party evidence of selling price ("TPE"), and (iii) best estimate of the selling price ("ESP"). VSOE generally exists only when the Company sells the deliverable separately and is the price actually charged by the Company for that deliverable.

For both iPhone and Apple TV, the Company has indicated it may from time-to-time provide future unspecified software upgrades and features free of charge to customers. The Company has identified two deliverables generally contained in arrangements involving the sale of iPhone and Apple TV. The first deliverable is the hardware and software essential to the functionality of the hardware device delivered at the time of sale, and the second deliverable is the right included with the purchase of iPhone and Apple TV to receive on a when-and-if-available basis future unspecified software upgrades and features relating to the product's essential software. The Company has allocated revenue between these two deliverables using the relative selling price method. Because the Company has neither VSOE nor TPE for the two deliverables the allocation of revenue has been based on the Company's ESPs. Amounts allocated to the delivered hardware and the related essential software are recognized at the time of sale provided the other conditions for revenue recognition have been met. Amounts allocated to the unspecified software upgrade rights are deferred and recognized on a straight-line basis over the 24-month estimated life of the related hardware. All product cost of sales, including estimated warranty costs, are generally recognized at the time of sale. Costs for engineering and sales and marketing are expensed as incurred.

(continued)

EXHIBIT 2—
continued

NOTE 1, APPLE INC.
2009 10-K/A

For all periods presented, the Company's ESP for the software upgrade right included with each iPhone and Apple TV sold is $25 and $10, respectively. The Company's process for determining its ESP for deliverables without VSOE or TPE considers multiple factors that may vary depending upon the unique facts and circumstances related to each deliverable. The Company believes its customers, particularly consumers, would be reluctant to buy unspecified software upgrade rights related to iPhone and Apple TV. This view is primarily based on the fact that upgrade rights do not obligate the Company to provide upgrades at a particular time or at all, and do not specify to customers which upgrades or features will be delivered in the future. Therefore, the Company has concluded that if it were to sell upgrade rights on a standalone basis, such as those included with iPhone and Apple TV, the selling price would be relatively low. Key factors considered by the Company in developing the ESPs for iPhone and Apple TV upgrade rights include prices charged by the Company for similar offerings, the Company's historical pricing practices, the nature of the upgrade rights (e.g., unspecified and when-and-if-available), and the relative ESP of the upgrade rights as compared to the total selling price of the product. In addition, when developing ESPs for products other than iPhone and Apple TV, the Company may consider other factors as appropriate including the pricing of competitive alternatives if they exist, and product-specific business objectives.

EXHIBIT 3

NOTE 2, APPLE INC.
2009 10-K/A

Note 2–Retrospective Adoption of New Accounting Principles

In September 2009, the FASB amended the accounting standards related to revenue recognition for arrangements with multiple deliverables and arrangements that include software elements. In the first quarter of 2010, the Company adopted the new accounting principles on a retrospective basis. The Company believes retrospective adoption provides the most comparable and useful financial information for financial statement users, is more consistent with the information the Company's management uses to evaluate its business, and better reflects the underlying economic performance of the Company. The financial statements and notes to the financial statements presented herein have been adjusted to reflect the retrospective adoption of the new accounting principles. Note 1, "Summary of Significant Accounting Policies" under the subheadings *"Basis of Presentation and Preparation"* and *"Revenue Recognition"* of this Form 10-K provides additional information on the Company's change in accounting resulting from the adoption of the new accounting principles and the Company's revenue recognition accounting policy.

(continued)

EXHIBIT 3—
continued

NOTE 2, APPLE INC.
2009 10-K/A

The following tables present the effects of the retrospective adoption of the new accounting principles to the Company's previously reported Consolidated Balance Sheets as of September 26, 2009 and September 27, 2008 (in millions, except share amounts):

	September 26, 2009		
	As Reported	Adjustments	As Amended
Current assets:			
Cash and cash equivalents	$5,263	$—	$5,263
Short-term marketable securities	18,201	—	18,201
Accounts receivable, less allowance of $52	3,361	—	3,361
Inventories	455	—	455
Deferred tax assets	2,101	(966)	1,135
Other current assets	6,884	(3,744)	3,140
Total current assets	36,265	(4,710)	31,555
Long-term marketable securities	10,528	—	10,528
Property, plant and equipment, net	2,954	—	2,954
Goodwill	206	—	206
Acquired intangible assets, net	247	—	247
Other assets	3,651	(1,640)	2,011
Total assets	$53,851	$(6,350)	$47,501
Current liabilities:			
Accounts payable	$5,601	$—	$5,601
Accrued expenses	3,376	476	3,852
Deferred revenue	10,305	(8,252)	2,053
Total current liabilities	19,282	(7,776)	11,506
Deferred revenue–non-current	4,485	(3,632)	853
Other non-current liabilities	2,252	1,250	3,502
Total liabilities	26,019	(10,158)	15,861
Commitments and contingencies			
Shareholders' equity:			
Common stock, no par value; 1,800,000,000 shares authorized; 899,805,500 shares issued and outstanding	8,210	—	8,210
Retained earnings	19,538	3,815	23,353
Accumulated other comprehensive income	84	(7)	77
Total shareholders' equity	27,832	3,808	31,640
Total liabilities and shareholders' equity	$53,851	$(6,350)	$47,501

(continued)

EXHIBIT 3—
continued

NOTE 2, APPLE INC.
2009 10-K/A

	September 27, 2008		
	As Reported	Adjustments	As Amended
Current assets:			
Cash and cash equivalents	$11,875	$—	$11,875
Short-term marketable securities	10,236	—	10,236
Accounts receivable, less allowance of $47	2,422	—	2,422
Inventories	509	—	509
Deferred tax assets	1,447	(403)	1,044
Other current assets	5,822	(1,902)	3,920
Total current assets	32,311	(2,305)	30,006
Long-term marketable securities	2,379	—	2,379
Property, plant and equipment, net	2,455	—	2,455
Goodwill	207	—	207
Acquired intangible assets, net	285	—	285
Other assets	1,935	(1,096)	839
Total assets	$39,572	$(3,401)	$36,171
Current liabilities:			
Accounts payable	$5,520	$—	$5,520
Accrued expenses	3,719	505	4,224
Deferred revenue	4,853	(3,236)	1,617
Total current liabilities	14,092	(2,731)	11,361
Deferred revenue–non-current	3,029	(2,261)	768
Other non-current liabilities	1,421	324	1,745
Total liabilities	18,542	(4,668)	13,874
Commitments and contingencies			
Shareholders' equity:			
Common stock, no par value; 1,800,000,000 shares authorized; 888,325,973 shares issued and outstanding	7,177	—	7,177
Retained earnings	13,845	1,284	15,129
Accumulated other comprehensive income/(loss)	8	(17)	(9)
Total shareholders' equity	21,030	1,267	22,297
Total liabilities and shareholders' equity	$39,572	$(3,401)	$36,171

(continued)

EXHIBIT 3—
continued

NOTE 2, APPLE INC.
2009 10-K/A

The following tables present the effects of the retrospective adoption of the new accounting principles to the Company's previously reported Consolidated Statements of Operations for the years ended September 26, 2009, September 27, 2008, and September 29, 2007 (in millions, except share amounts):

	Fiscal Year Ended September 26, 2009		
	As Reported	Adjustments	As Amended
Net sales	$36,537	$6,368	$42,905
Cost of sales	23,397	2,286	25,683
Gross margin	13,140	4,082	17,222
Operating expenses:			
Research and development	1,333	—	1,333
Selling, general and administrative	4,149	—	4,149
Total operating expenses	5,482	—	5,482
Operating income	7,658	4,082	11,740
Other income and expense	326	—	326
Income before provision for income taxes	7,984	4,082	12,066
Provision for income taxes	2,280	1,551	3,831
Net income	$5,704	$2,531	$8,235
Earnings per common share:			
Basic	$6.39	$2.83	$9.22
Diluted	$6.29	$2.79	$9.08
Shares used in computing earnings per share:			
Basic	893,016	—	893,016
Diluted	907,005	—	907,00

(continued)

EXHIBIT 3—
continued

NOTE 2, APPLE INC.
2009 10-K/A

	Fiscal Year Ended September 27, 2008		
	As Reported	Adjustments	As Amended
Net sales	$32,479	$5,012	$37,491
Cost of sales	21,334	2,960	24,294
Gross margin	11,145	2,052	13,197
Operating expenses:			
Research and development	1,109	—	1,109
Selling, general and administrative	3,761	—	3,761
Total operating expenses	4,870	—	4,870
Operating income	6,275	2,052	8,327
Other income and expense	620	—	620
Income before provision for income taxes	6,895	2,052	8,947
Provision for income taxes	2,061	767	2,828
Net income	$4,834	$1,285	$6,119
Earnings per common share:			
Basic	$5.48	$1.46	$6.94
Diluted	$5.36	$1.42	$6.78
Shares used in computing earnings per share:			
Basic	881,592	—	881,592
Diluted	902,139	—	902,139

(continued)

EXHIBIT 3—
continued

NOTE 2, APPLE INC.
2009 10-K/A

	Fiscal Year Ended September 29, 2007		
	As Reported	Adjustments	As Amended
Net sales	$24,006	$572	$24,578
Cost of sales	15,852	574	16,426
Gross margin	8,154	(2)	8,152
Operating expenses:			
Research and development	782	—	782
Selling, general and administrative	2,963	—	2,963
Total operating expenses	3,745	—	3,745
Operating income	4,409	(2)	4,407
Other income and expense	599	—	599
Income before provision for income taxes	5,008	(2)	5,006
Provision for income taxes	1,512	(1)	1,511
Net income	$3,496	$(1)	$3,495
Earnings per common share:			
Basic	$4.04	$—	$4.04
Diluted	$3.93	$—	$3.93
Shares used in computing earnings per share:			
Basic	864,595	—	864,595
Diluted	889,292	—	889,292

Merrill Lynch & Co., Inc.

Background

On January 6, 1914, Charles Merrill opened Charles E. Merrill & Co. Five months later, he convinced Edmund C. Lynch to join him, and they opened an office at 7 Wall Street. The following year they renamed the firm Merrill, Lynch & Co. At the time, an associate noted, "Merrill could imagine the possibilities; Lynch imagined what might go wrong in a malevolent world."[1]

Almost from the start, the firm operated a retail brokerage firm and an investment bank. Over the years, it dabbled in various industries, including a film company in 1921 later sold to Joseph P. Kennedy and Cecil B. DeMille and renamed RKO Pictures, as well a stake in the retail market through a controlling interest in Safeway Stores, the grocery chain. By 1928, Mr. Merrill was concerned about the speculative stock market boom, and he advised brokerage clients to "take advantage of present high prices and put your financial house in order."[2]

In 1930, as the depression worsened, Merrill, Lynch & Co. decided to devote itself to investment banking and sold its retail brokerage business to E. A. Pierce. Mr. Merrill focused on Safeway Stores and built it into the nation's third-largest grocery store chain. In 1932, Mr. Merrill founded *Family Circle*, the first grocery store point-of-sale magazine. Mr. Lynch died in 1938 at the age of 52. Mr. Merrill, out of respect to his partner, dropped the comma in the firm's name.[3]

Merrill Lynch reacquired its brokerage business in 1940 by merging with E. A. Pierce & Cassatt. The following year the firm merged with Fenner & Beane, and the new firm, Merrill Lynch, Pierce, Fenner & Beane, became the world's largest securities house, with offices in 93 cities. In 1964, it acquired C. J. Devine and became a fixed income securities dealer. In 1976, the firm created Merrill Lynch Asset Management and in 1978 acquired White, Weld & Co., an old-line international investment banking house. By 1988, Merrill Lynch topped the list of firms that handle U.S. and global debt and equity underwriting for the first time; in 1997, Merrill Lynch became the first financial services firm to manage more than $1 trillion in client assets.[4]

Merrill Lynch—A Transition in Power and Focus

In 2000, Merrill Lynch was a highly diversified financial institution, but it still relied primarily on retail brokerage, investment banking, and wealth management. Merrill Lynch grew rapidly during the Internet boom, but as the Internet bubble collapsed, Merrill Lynch agreed to pay $200 million toward settlement of a lawsuit alleging Merrill Lynch and 11 other firms defrauded investors by issuing overly optimistic ratings on Internet firms. Additionally, rapidly growing on-line brokerage firms were taking business from Merrill Lynch's highly profitable retail brokers.

---

1. Timeline: History of Merrill Lynch, Reuters, New York, September 15, 2008. http://www.reuters.com/article/idUSN1546989520080915.

2. Ibid.

3. Ibid.

4. Ibid.

On July 22, 2002, Merrill Lynch announced that E. Stanley O'Neal would replace David H. Komansky as chairman and chief executive officer. Mr. O'Neal, Merrill Lynch's CFO before being promoted to president and chief operating officer in 2001, had a reputation as a hard-driving executive who drastically cut Merrill's costs in response to the business downturn.

Merrill Lynch had a proprietary trading group when Mr. O'Neal took over, but it lagged far behind that of Goldman Sachs. Merrill Lynch also lagged far behind Lehman Brothers in the rapidly expanding residential mortgage securitization market. Mr. O'Neal quickly began to move Merrill Lynch into those faster-growing and more profitable markets. From 2005 through January 2007, Merrill Lynch acquired at least 10 residential and commercial mortgage-related businesses, including the $1.3 billion acquisition of subprime mortgage lender First Franklin Financial Corporation on December 31, 2005.

On August 3, 2007, Merrill Lynch announced record earnings of $4.297 billion for the six-month period ended June 30, 2007, and increased its six-month dividend from $.50 to $.70 per share (Exhibit 1). Merrill Lynch's balance sheet (Exhibit 2) showed that the firm also acquired an additional $4.573 billion of its own common stock (treasury stock) during the first six months of 2007, an indication of Merrill Lynch's confidence in its future prospects.

For financial reporting, Merrill Lynch divides its firm into two business segments, Global Markets and Investment Banking (GMI) and Global Wealth Management (GWM) (see Exhibit 3). GMI's largest segment, Fixed Income, Currencies and Commodities (FICC), includes most of Merrill's proprietary trading groups. For the first six months of 2007, FICC generated $5.4 billion of net revenues, up 45% from the previous year, the highest net revenue of any unit in either business segment. The increases were driven primarily by strong growth in net revenues from trading credit products, interest rate products, and commodities. The increases were partially offset by a revenue decline in the structured finance and investments business, which included mortgage-related activities.

Revenues from mortgage-related activities for the first six months of 2007 declined from 2006, primarily because of the difficult environment for the origination and securitization of U.S. subprime mortgage loans. In 2007, New Century Financial Corporation, one of the nation's largest mortgage finance companies, declared bankruptcy. Others were in financial difficulty, and some large financial institutions were closing their mortgage finance units.

Fair Value Reporting

In 2006, the Financial Accounting Standards Board issued ASC 820 (FAS 157, *Fair Value Measurements*), and in early 2007 it issued ASC 825-10 (FAS 159, *The Fair Value Option for Financial Assets and Financial Liabilities*). Those two standards had three primary effects on U.S. corporations, as follows.

Standard terms and a standard definition

Over the past 20 years, the Financial Accounting Standards Board (FASB) gradually replaced historical cost with fair value for certain assets and liabilities. That change was often haphazard, so by 2006, the United States had dozens of rules requiring firms to use *fair value, fair market value,* or some other term for a measure of an asset or liability's current value. In addition, the FASB had a wide range of ways to measure fair value, so fair value for one asset might be computed differently than fair value for a different asset. ASC 820 (FAS 157) replaced all of the various terms with one, *fair value,* and provided one definition for how fair value should be measured for all assets and liabilities:

> *Fair value is the price that would be received to sell an asset or paid to transfer a liability in an orderly transaction between market participants at the measurement date.*

One previous FASB definition, still in use by the International Financial Accounting Standards Board (IASB), the U.S. Internal Revenue Service, and various business valuation groups is a variant of the following:

> *Fair value (or fair market value) is the amount for which an asset could be exchanged, or a liability settled, between knowledgeable, willing parties, in an arm's length transaction.*

Although the two definitions appear nearly identical, they are not. The FASB fair value definition is an exit price—the price a hypothetical market participant would pay for a firm's asset, or the price that must be paid to a hypothetical market participant to assume a firm's liabilities. If a firm has an asset that is highly valuable for its own purposes, but worthless to anyone else, the asset's fair value is zero. Similarly, if a firm owns an asset it has no use for, but the asset is valuable to a hypothetical market participant, the fair value is what a hypothetical market participant would pay. In contrast, the second definition is more general; fair value (or fair market value) is usually considered to be the value to the asset's owner, which is an entry price.

Fair value option

ASC 825-10 (FAS 159) gives firms an option to value most financial assets and liabilities at fair value. To facilitate hedging, ASC 825-10 (FAS 159) gives firms the option to value their own liabilities, including long-term debt (bonds), at fair value. Suppose a firm's trading assets include long-maturity fixed income securities whose fair value fluctuates with interest rates. Also suppose a firm finances those assets with its own fixed-rate debt and elects the fair value option for that debt (trading assets were valued at fair value, or marked-to-market, long before ASC 820). If interest rates increase, the fair value of the fixed-income asset (the investment) declines for a loss; the fair value of the firm's own debt also declines, but for an offsetting gain (because the present value of the debt is less), so the firm has a reasonable hedge without the need to justify it under complex FASB hedging rules. If interest rates decline, the fair value of the fixed-income assets rise for a gain, and the fair value of the firm's debt also rises for an offsetting loss; again, the firm has a reasonable hedge.

Although that offset can provide a reasonable hedge, some analysts worried that if a firm elected fair value reporting for its own debt, and then suffered financial difficulties, the debt's fair value would decline because of the credit risk, with no offsetting increase in the value of the firm's fixed-income assets. The firm would report a gain on the fair value of its liabilities but would lack the cash to acquire the debt at the lower market price. In effect, analysts worried that firms in financial distress could report misleading gains, or smaller losses, if they elected the fair value option for their own debt.

Disclosures

The third significant change was to greatly expand the disclosures for items reported at fair value. Although firms were not required to use fair value reporting until January 1, 2008, many large financial institutions, including Merrill Lynch, Goldman Sachs, and Citigroup, elected early adoption of both ASC 820 (FAS 157) and ASC 825-10

(FAS 159), so those three firms used the new fair value rules for all of 2007. Exhibit 4 is Merrill Lynch's fair value note for the second quarter 2007.

As part of the fair value disclosure, firms must separate those assets and liabilities measured at fair value into three measurement categories: level 1, level 2, and level 3. Exhibit 4 provides definitions and examples for each of the three levels. Level 1 measurements are quoted prices for identical assets or liabilities in active markets. Level 2 measurements are based on quoted prices for identical or similar assets or liabilities in markets that are not active, on quoted prices for similar assets or liabilities in active markets, or model inputs that are observable either directly or indirectly for substantially the full term of the asset or liability. Level 3 measurements are based on prices or valuation techniques that require inputs that are both unobservable and significant to the overall fair value measurement. They reflect management's own belief about an unidentified market participant's assumptions.

Merrill Lynch Fair Value Note, Second Quarter, 2007

Fair value disclosures

Many firms and analysts were concerned that unsophisticated investors would unnecessarily worry that level 3 assets and liabilities were highly risky. However, as shown in the first table of Exhibit 4, Merrill Lynch had few assets and liabilities measured using level 3 inputs (millions—totals not provided in Exhibit 4):

Level 1 assets:	$97,775
Level 1 liabilities:	$60,960
Level 2 assets:	$469,675
Level 2 liabilities:	$382,122
Level 3 assets:	$16,037
Level 3 liabilities:	$6,654

In addition to disclosing asset and liability fair values by measurement level, firms must also disclose additional details about their assets and liabilities measured using level 3 inputs. Exhibit 4 includes two tables that reconcile changes in level 3 assets and liabilities. The first is for the three-month period ended June 29, 2007; the second is for the six-month period ended June 29, 2007.

Companies worried that unsophisticated investors would be mislead by "total realized and unrealized gains or (losses)" disclosed in those schedules. For example, Merrill Lynch had $603 million of level 3 gains for the three months ended June 30, 2007, and $909 million of level 3 gains for the six months ended June 30, 2007. However, assets and liabilities measured using level 3 inputs are often hedged against assets and liabilities measured using level 2 or level 1 inputs, so gains or losses on assets or liabilities measured using level 3 inputs are nearly meaningless without supplemental information. No early adopting firm provided that supplemental information, as there was no requirement to provide it.

If a firm elects the fair value option for any of its assets or liabilities, ASC 825-20 (FAS 159) requires the firm to report additional information about those assets or liabilities. The primary items for which Merrill elected fair value were: (1) fixed-rate investment securities previously classified as available-for-sale (AFS) and (2) some of Merrill Lynch's own long-term debt.

Without the fair value option, firms report the fair value of AFS securities on their balance sheet but defer gains or losses in "other comprehensive income (OCI)" until the securities are sold. If a firm elects the fair value option for any AFS securities, as Merrill Lynch did (only for some of the AFS securities, which is permitted under ASC 825-20), then when the firm records those investments at fair value at the end of each quarter, it immediately recognizes gains or losses on its income statement instead of deferring them to OCI until they are sold. However, when a firm first adopts fair value reporting, unrealized gains or losses in OCI are transferred to retained earnings—they never appear on the firm's income statement.

Fair value option disclosures

Merrill Lynch elected the fair value option for some of its assets and liabilities. It discloses information about those assets and liabilities in the last three tables of Exhibit 4, in a section titled "Fair Value Option." The first table shows carrying value prior to adoption and carrying value after adoption, as of December 30, 2006, the date Merrill made its election for existing assets and liabilities under the fair value option. Prior to adoption, the AFS securities for which Merrill elected the fair value option had an unrealized loss in its OCI section of retained earnings. Upon election of the fair value option for those AFS securities, the unrealized loss was transferred to retained earnings without first appearing on Merrill's income statement.

The second table shows fair value gains and losses by category for the three- and six-month periods ended June 29, 2007 (primarily AFS securities and Merrill Lynch's own debt); the changes in value appear on Merrill's income statement for the three- and six-month periods ending June 29, 2007. For example, the fair value of investment securities increased by $218 million in the first three months of 2007. Of that $218 million gain, Merrill reported $210 million in principal transactions revenue and $8 million in other revenue. The fair value of Merrill Lynch's long-term borrowings declined by $985 million in the first three months of 2007, possibly because interest rates increased or possibly because of a slight increase in Merrill's credit risk. The entire $985 million gain appeared in principal transactions revenue.

The third table shows, as of June 29, 2007, the total fair value and principal amount due at maturity for assets and liabilities for which Merrill elected the fair value option. The fair value of long-term borrowings is $37,473 million in the third table, as opposed to the $10,337 million carrying value as of December 30, 2006, in the first fair value option table. That is because when Merrill Lynch acquires new financial assets and liabilities that qualify for the fair value option, it can elect the fair value option for those assets and liabilities on the acquisition date. Merrill Lynch elected the fair value option for at least $27 billion of newly issued long-term borrowings during the first six months of 2007. If it retired some of its debt that had been recorded at fair value in the previous quarter, then the amount of new debt for which Merrill Lynch elected the fair value option was more than $27 billion.

October, 2007

By the end of 2006, U.S. firms had dominant positions in most institutional finance markets. In early 2007, several mortgage finance companies, including New Century Financial Corp., declared bankruptcy. Several large banks, including HSBC, also announced substantial write-offs for bad mortgages. However, by the end of September 2007, no major U.S. financial institution had significant bad mortgage write-offs, and there was little concern that mortgages were a serious problem in the United States or abroad. On Friday, October 5, 2007, the Dow Jones Industrial Average (14,066.01) and the S&P 500 Average (1557.59) reached all-time highs. That same day, Merrill Lynch announced it would take a $5 billion write-down, primarily on subprime loans and other complex fixed-income derivatives.

Ten days later, Citigroup announced a $5.9 billion write-off, including $2.24 billion for mortgage-backed securities and consumer loans. The following week, October 24, Merrill Lynch increased its write-down to $8.4 billion, including $7.9 billion for mortgage-related derivatives. Mr. O'Neal resigned as chairman and CEO of Merrill Lynch on October 29, 2007. Two weeks later, on November 5, 2007, Citigroup announced significant declines since September 30 in the fair value of approximately $55 billion of U.S. subprime mortgage-related securities. Citigroup estimated the additional decline in Principal transaction revenues ranged from $8 billion to $11 billion. Charles Prince, Citigroup's chairman and CEO, resigned that day.

November, 2007, to December 31, 2008

On November 15, 2007, three weeks after Mr. O'Neal's resignation, Merrill selected John A. Thain, one of the most widely mentioned candidates, as its chairman. Mr. Thain, an MIT electrical engineer and Harvard MBA, rose to chief financial officer at Goldman Sachs at age 37, the youngest person to hold that position in the firm's history. The CFO position is one of the most powerful roles within Goldman's executive group. At most investment firms, the CFO's office has little expertise in complex financial instruments and limited control over powerful traders that are paid far more. At Goldman, the CFO is one of the six most senior executives in the firm, and the office of the CFO employs approximately 20 people with doctorate degrees in physics, mathematics, and similar fields. At Goldman, if the CFO asks Trading to reduce its positions, they do so, unless they can convince the CFO the investments are worth the risk.

Mr. Thain had been a candidate for chairman of Goldman, but when he lost out to another candidate, in December 2003 he accepted the CEO position at the New York Stock Exchange (NYSE). Mr. Thain quickly corrected many serious problems at the NYSE. To address competition with the AMEX and several European exchanges, he made numerous acquisitions, culminating with the purchase of Euronext in March 2007.

When Mr. Thain began work as Merrill's CEO, he quickly began to install Goldman's sophisticated control systems. However, there was considerable uncertainty about the value of Merrill's assets and liabilities. The market for subprime and Alt-A mortgage-backed derivatives was collapsing, and it was unclear how much of those securities Merrill owned. For its third quarter 2007, Merrill announced a $2.24 billion after-tax loss, but year-to-date, Merrill still had a $2.1 billion after-tax profit. For the fourth quarter 2007, Merrill reported a $9.8 billion after-tax loss and a $7.8 billion after-tax loss for the year.

For the first-quarter 2008, Merrill reported a $1.96 billion after-tax loss; by the second-quarter 2008, it reported a year-to-date $6.62 billion after-tax loss. On September 15, 2008, in response to the continual losses at Merrill, Mr. Thain agreed to a $50 billion buyout offer from Bank of America, a 70% premium over Merrill's stock price. On October 12, 2008, Merrill Lynch accepted $10 billion of TARP (Troubled Asset Relief Program) funds. For third-quarter 2008, Merrill reported a $14.5 billion year-to-date loss.

In mid-December 2008, shortly before Bank of America's acquisition of Merrill closed and a month earlier than it customarily paid bonuses, Merrill gave approximately $3.2 billion in bonuses to employees. Merrill then announced an after-tax loss for the year of $27.6 billion (Exhibit 5). In response, Bank of America requested and received an additional $20 billion of TARP funds to complete the acquisition, and a federal government backstop for an extra $118 billion of assets. On January 22, 2009, after a 15-minute meeting with Bank of America CEO Ken Lewis, Mr. Thain resigned from Merrill Lynch.

Financial Information

Exhibits 6 through 9 contain Merrill Lynch's balance sheets, cash flow statements, statements of owners' equity, and statements of comprehensive (loss)/income for the year ended December 31, 2008. Exhibit 10 contains segment information from Merrill Lynch's 2008 Management Discussion and Analysis form, and Exhibit 11 contains Note 3: Fair Value.

Required

1. Explain Merrill Lynch's fair value and fair value option notes (Exhibits 4 and 11).

2. Why did Merrill Lynch elect the fair value option for only some of its available-for-sale securities ($8.723 billion carrying value prior to adoption, Exhibit 4, first Fair Value Option table, column 1)?

3. Explain the 2008 $7.617 billion of "Net unrealized losses on investment securities available-for-sale" in Exhibit 9, Statements of Comprehensive (Loss)/Income.

4. The third from the last table in Exhibit 11 shows that in 2008, Merrill Lynch included a $15.938 billion gain in "Principal Transactions" (column 1) and $1.709 billion in "Other Revenues" (column 2) because the fair value of its long-term borrowings decreased. That table also shows that in 2007 Merrill included additional gains of $3.857 billion in "Principal Transactions" (column 4) and $1.182 billion in "Other Revenues," (column 5) because the fair value of its long-term borrowings decreased (a total of $22.686 billion for the two years). Explain these gains. Were they real?

5. The last page of Exhibit 11 shows that at year-end 2008, Merrill had $62.244 billion at face value ($49.521 billion at fair value) of its own debt for which it elected the fair value option. On that same page Merrill states:

   The changes in the fair value of liabilities for which the fair value option was elected that was attributable to changes in Merrill Lynch credit spreads were estimated gains of $5.1 billion for the year ended December 31, 2008.

   The following are yields on various fixed-income securities:

	Dec. 31, 2008	Dec. 31, 2007
10-year Treasury notes	2.25%	4.04%
Moody's seasoned Aaa corporate bond yield	5.05	5.49
Moody's seasoned Baa corporate bond yield	8.43	6.65

   Is Merrill's statement that its gain from the increase in its credit spreads was $5.1 billion reasonable? Explain.

6. What was Merrill's total pre-tax loss for the 18-month period June 30, 2007, to December 31, 2008? Did you adjust for the effects of AFS securities and the fair value election for Merrill Lynch's own debt? Why, or why not.

7. Suppose you were restructuring Merrill Lynch. Which segments of Merrill Lynch are profitable? As part of your analysis, estimate Merrill Lynch's total losses

from its "Principal Transactions" from June 30, 2007, through December 31, 2008. Include an explanation of the $7.617 billion of unrecognized losses from "Net unrealized losses on available-for-sale securities" in Exhibit 8. Also include an explanation of the $17.647 billion realized gains in "Principal Transactions" and "Other Revenues" for 2008 and $5.039 billion for 2007 in the first Fair Value Option table of Exhibit 11. Revenues for Principles transactions are reported as a separate line item on Merrill's income statements (Exhibits 1 and 5). Most revenues for principles transactions are included in FICC in Notes 3 and 10, Business Segments. Expenses are also shown in Notes 3 and 10, although not by business segment.

8. Suppose the fair value of the assets and liabilities on Merrill Lynch's December 31, 2008, balance sheet (Exhibit 6) are valid. What was Merrill Lynch's value on that date?

9. Evaluate the quality of Merrill's Business Segment disclosures.

10. Did the new fair value rules in ASC 820 (FAS 157) and the new fair value option rules in ASC 825-10 (FAS 159) cause or contribute to Merrill's problems? Explain in detail.

11. What were Bank of America's primary risks when it acquired Merrill Lynch? Explain.

EXHIBIT 1

MERRILL LYNCH
& CO. INCOME
STATEMENT,
JUNE 30, 2007

MERRILL LYNCH & CO., INC. AND SUBSIDIARIES
Condensed Consolidated Statements of Earnings (Unaudited)

	For the Six Months Ended	
(in millions, except per share amounts)	June 29, 2007	June 30, 2006
Net Revenues		
Principal transactions	$6,282	$3,168
Commissions	3,483	3,102
Investment banking	3,052	2,244
Managed accounts and other fee-based revenues	2,765	3,452
Revenues from consolidated investments	264	290
Other	1,802	1,665
Subtotal	17,648	13,921
Interest and dividend revenues	27,633	18,354
Less interest expense	25,699	16,130
Net interest profit	1,934	2,224
Total Net Revenues	19,582	16,145
Non-Interest Expenses		
Compensation and benefits	9,646	9,730
Communications and technology	964	882
Brokerage, clearing, and exchange fees	656	525
Occupancy and related depreciation	542	490
Professional fees	470	396
Advertising and market development	359	335
Office supplies and postage	115	114
Expenses of consolidated investments	102	192
Other	610	539
Total Non-Interest Expenses	13,464	13,203
Earnings before income taxes	6,118	2,942
Income tax expense	1,821	834
Net earnings	$4,297	$2,108
Preferred stock dividends	124	88
Net earnings applicable to common stockholders	$4,173	$2,020
Earnings per common share		
Basic	$4.98	$2.28
Diluted	$4.50	$2.07
Dividend paid per common share	$0.70	$0.50

EXHIBIT 2

MERRILL LYNCH
& CO. BALANCE
SHEET, JUNE 30,
2007

MERRILL LYNCH & CO., INC. AND SUBSIDIARIES
Condensed Consolidated Balance Sheets (Unaudited)

(dollars in millions)	June 29, 2007	December 29, 2006
ASSETS		
Cash and cash equivalents	$38,755	$32,109
Cash and securities segregated for regulatory purposes or deposited with clearing organizations	18,410	13,449
Securities financing transactions		
Receivables under resale agreements (includes $99,774 measured at fair value in 2007 in accordance with SFAS No. 159)	261,266	178,368
Receivables under securities borrowed transactions	187,355	118,610
	448,621	296,978
Trading assets, at fair value (includes securities pledged as collateral that can be sold or repledged of $86,653 in 2007 and $58,966 in 2006)		
Equities and convertible debentures	60,780	48,527
Contractual agreements	42,868	32,100
Corporate debt and preferred stock	41,349	32,854
Mortgages, mortgage-backed, and asset-backed	34,513	44,401
Non-U.S. governments and agencies	18,565	21,075
U.S. Government and agencies	16,296	13,086
Municipals and money markets	5,980	7,243
Commodities and related contracts	4,438	4,562
	224,789	203,848
Investment securities ($3,384 measured at fair value in 2007; SFAS No. 159)	86,439	83,410
Securities received as collateral	48,048	24,929
Other receivables		
Customers (net of allowance for doubtful accounts of $37 in 2007 and $41 in 2006)	56,091	49,427
Brokers and dealers	29,825	18,900
Interest and other	23,593	21,054
	109,509	89,381
Loans, notes, and mortgages (net of allowances for loan losses of $435 in 2007 and $478 in 2006) (includes $1,244 measured at fair value in 2007 in accordance with SFAS No. 159)	73,465	73,029
Separate accounts assets	12,605	12,314
Equipment and facilities (net of accum dep and amort of $5,205 in 2007 and $5,213 in 2006)	2,713	2,924
Goodwill and other intangible assets	3,644	2,457
Other assets	9,326	6,471
Total Assets	$1,076,324	$841,299

(continued)

EXHIBIT 2—
continued

MERRILL LYNCH
& CO. BALANCE
SHEET, JUNE 30,
2007

(dollars in millions, except per share amount)	June 29, 2007	December 29, 2006
LIABILITIES		
Securities financing transactions		
Payables under repurchase agreements ($100,752 at fair value in 2007; SFAS No. 159)	$306,816	$222,624
Payables under securities loaned transactions	71,879	43,492
	378,695	266,116
Short-term borrowings	20,064	18,110
Deposits	82,801	84,124
Trading liabilities, at fair value		
Contractual agreements	55,289	38,434
Equities and convertible debentures	32,230	23,268
Non-U.S. governments and agencies	12,409	13,385
U.S. government and agencies	10,461	12,510
Corporate debt and preferred stock	6,362	6,323
Commodities and related contracts	2,736	3,606
Municipals, money markets and other	937	1,336
	120,424	98,862
Obligation to return securities received as collateral	48,048	24,929
Customers payables	55,951	49,414
Brokers and dealers payables	40,763	24,282
Interest and other payables	41,661	36,096
	138,375	109,792
Liabilities of insurance subsidiaries	2,702	2,801
Separate accounts liabilities	12,605	12,314
Long-term borrowings ($37,473 measured at fair value in 2007; SFAS No. 159)	226,016	181,400
Junior subordinated notes (related to trust preferred securities)	4,403	3,813
Total Liabilities	1,034,133	802,261
STOCKHOLDERS' EQUITY		
Preferred Stockholders' Equity (liquidation $30,000/share)	4,624	3,145
Common Stockholders' Equity		
Shares exchangeable into common stock	39	39
Common stock (par value $1.331/3 per share)	1,672	1,620
Paid-in capital	21,611	18,919
Accumulated other comprehensive loss (net of tax)	(630)	(784)
Retained earnings	36,566	33,217
	59,258	53,011
Less: Treasury stock, at cost (2007—395,341,397 shares; 2006—350,697,271 shares)	21,691	17,118
Total Common Stockholders' Equity	37,567	35,893
Total Stockholders' Equity	42,191	39,038
Total Liabilities and Stockholders' Equity	$1,076,324	$841,299

Business Segments

Our operations are currently organized into two business segments: GMI and GWM. GMI provides full service global markets and origination products and services to corporate, institutional, and government clients around the world. GWM creates and distributes investment products and services for individuals, small- and mid-size businesses, and employee benefit plans.

Results for the six months ended June 30, 2006 include one-time compensation expenses, as follows: $1.4 billion in GMI, $281 million in GWM and $109 million in MLIM.

Revenues and expenses associated with inter-segment activities are recognized in each segment. In addition, revenue and expense sharing agreements for joint activities between segments are in place, and the results of each segment reflect their agreed-upon apportionment of revenues and expenses associated with these activities.

The following segment results represent the information that is used by our management in its decision-making processes. Prior period amounts have been reclassified to conform to the current period presentation.

Global Markets and Investment Banking

GMI's Results of Operations (dollars in millions)	Three Months Ended			Six Months Ended		
	June 29, 2007	June 30, 2006	% Inc.	June 29, 2007	June 30, 2006	% Inc.
Global Markets						
FICC	$2,618	$1,691	55%	$5,419	$3,749	45%
Equity Markets	2,148	1,863	15	4,534	3,450	31
Total Global Markets net revenues	4,766	3,554	34	9,953	7,199	38
Investment Banking						
Debt Origination	479	401	19	1,070	829	29
Equity Origination	547	315	74	910	552	65
Strategic Advisory Services	397	296	34	796	553	44
Total Investment Banking net revenues	1,423	1,012	41	2,776	1,934	44
Total GMI net revenues	6,189	4,566	36	12,729	9,133	39
Non-interest expenses before one-time compensation expenses	4,087	3,101	32	8,284	6,083	36
One-time compensation expenses	—	—		—	1,369	N/M
Pre-tax earnings	$2,102	$1,465	43	$4,445	$1,681	164
Pre-tax profit margin	34.0%	32.1%		34.9%	18.4%	

N/M = Not Meaningful.

During the second quarter of 2007, each of GMI's major business lines — Fixed Income, Currencies and Commodities ("FICC"); Equity Markets; and Investment Banking — generated very strong net revenues compared with the second quarter of 2006. GMI's net revenues increased 36% from the 2006 second quarter, to $6.2 billion. Pre-tax earnings were $2.1 billion, 43% higher than the prior-year period, driven by strong revenue growth and continued focus on expenses. The pre-tax profit margin was 34.0%, up from 32.1% in the year-ago quarter.

(continued)

For the first six months of 2007, GMI's net revenues were a record at $12.7 billion, an increase of 39% from the first half of 2006, driven by strong revenues in nearly every major line of business. Pre-tax earnings were a record $4.4 billion, 164% higher from the prior-year period. Pre-tax profit margin was 34.9%, compared with 18.4% in the first half of 2006. Excluding the impact of the $1.4 billion of one-time compensation expenses recognized by GMI in the first quarter of 2006, GMI's pre-tax earnings for the first six months of 2006 were $3.1 billion, and the pre-tax profit margin was 33.4%. A detailed discussion of GMI's net revenues follows:

Fixed Income, Currencies and Commodities (FICC)

FICC net revenues include principal transactions and net interest profit (which we believe should be viewed in aggregate to assess trading results), commissions, revenues from principal investments, fair value adjustments on investments that are held for capital appreciation and/or current income, and other revenues.

In the second quarter of 2007, FICC net revenues were $2.6 billion, up 55% from the second quarter of 2006, reflecting increased diversity and depth across asset classes and regions. These increases were driven primarily by strong growth in net revenues from trading credit products, interest rate products and commodities. These increases were partially offset by a revenue decline in the structured finance and investments business, which includes mortgage-related activities.

Revenues from mortgage-related activities for both the second quarter of 2007 and the first six months of 2007 declined from the prior year periods resulting primarily from a difficult environment for the origination, securitization and trading of sub-prime mortgage loans and securities in the United States.

Equity Markets

Equity Markets net revenues include commissions, principal transactions and net interest profit (which we believe should be viewed in aggregate to assess trading results), revenues from equity method investments, fair value adjustments on private equity investments that are held for capital appreciation and/or current income, and other revenues.

In the second quarter of 2007, Equity Markets net revenues were $2.1 billion, up 15% over the year-ago quarter with strong performances in nearly every major revenue category. The increase was driven by record net revenues in equity-linked trading and financing and services, as well as significant growth in revenues from our cash and proprietary trading businesses. These increases were partially offset by a revenue decline in our private equity business.

Investment Banking

Investment Banking net revenues for the second quarter of 2007 were $1.4 billion, up 41% from the year-ago quarter. The substantial increase was driven by strong revenue growth in equity origination, debt origination and merger and acquisition advisory services.

Origination

Origination revenues represent fees earned from the underwriting of debt, equity and equity-linked securities as well as loan syndication fees. Origination revenues in the second quarter of 2007 were $1.0 billion, up 43% from the year-ago quarter. Equity origination set a new revenue record at $547 million, up 74% from the 2006 second quarter. Debt origination revenues were also strong at $479 million, up 19% from the year-ago quarter. The increase in revenues for debt and equity origination compared to the prior year quarter was primarily related to an increase in deal volume.

(continued)

EXHIBIT 3—
continued

MERRILL LYNCH
& CO. GMI AND
GWM BUSINESS
SEGMENTS, 10-Q,
MARCH 31, 2007

EXHIBIT 3—
continued

MERRILL LYNCH
& CO. GMI AND
GWM BUSINESS
SEGMENTS, 10-Q,
MARCH 31, 2007

Strategic Advisory Services

Strategic advisory services revenues, which include merger and acquisition and other advisory fees, were $397 million in the second quarter of 2007, an increase of 34% over the year-ago quarter as overall deal volume increased. Year-to-date strategic advisory services revenues increased 44% from the year-ago period, to $796 million, on higher activity and an increase in our share of completed merger and acquisition volume.

Global Wealth Management

GWM Results of Operations (dollars in millions)	For the Three Months Ended			For the Six Months Ended		
	June 29, 2007	June 30, 2006	% Inc.	June 29, 2007	June 30, 2006	% Inc.
GPC						
Fee-based revenues	$1,602	$1,443	11%	$3,141	$2,815	12%
Transactional and origination revenues	1,007	881	14	1,910	1,757	9
Net interest profit and related hedges[1]	587	533	10	1,191	1,060	12
Other revenues	117	77	52	214	133	61
Total GPC net revenues	3,313	2,934	13	6,456	5,765	12
GIM						
Total GIM net revenues	305	139	119	566	243	133
Total GWM net revenues	3,618	3,073	18	7,022	6,008	17
Non-interest expenses before one-time compensation expenses	2,607	2,344	11	5,169	4,637	11
One-time compensation expenses	—	—		—	281	N/M
Pre-tax earnings	$1,011	$729	39	$1,853	$1,090	70
Pre-tax profit margin	27.9%	23.7%		26.4%	18.1%	
Total Financial Advisors[2]	16,200	15,520		16,200	15,520	

N/M = Not Meaningful.

(1) Includes interest component of non-qualifying derivatives which are included in other revenues on the Condensed Consolidated Statements of Earnings.

(2) Includes 170 and 140 Financial Advisors associated with the Mitsubishi UFJ joint venture at the end of 2Q07 and 2Q06, respectively.

GWM is comprised of GPC and GIM. Our share of the after-tax earnings of BlackRock are included in the GIM portion of GWM revenues for the three- and six-month periods ended June 29, 2007, but not the three- and six-month periods ended June 30, 2006, when our asset management activities were reported in the former MLIM segment.

GWM generated record net revenues of $3.6 billion for the second quarter of 2007, up 18% from the year-ago quarter, reflecting strong growth in both GPC and GIM businesses. Pre-tax earnings were $1.0 billion, up 39% from the year-ago period, and the pre-tax profit margin was a record 27.9%, compared with 23.7% in the second quarter of 2006.

GWM's net inflows of client assets into annuitized-revenue products were $12 billion for the second quarter of 2007 and $28 billion for the first half of 2007. Assets in annuitized-revenue products ended the quarter at $668 billion, up 19% from the year-ago quarter. Total

(continued)

EXHIBIT 3—
continued

MERRILL LYNCH
& CO. GMI AND
GWM BUSINESS
SEGMENTS, 10-Q,
MARCH 31, 2007

client assets in GWM accounts were $1.7 trillion, up 14% from the year-ago quarter. Total net new money was $9 billion for the second quarter of 2007 and $24 billion for the first six months of 2007.

The value of client assets in GWM accounts at June 29, 2007 and June 30, 2006 follows:

	June 29, 2007	June 30, 2006
Assets in client accounts:	(dollars in billions)	
U.S.	$1,550	$1,370
Non-U.S.	153	124
Total	$1,703	$1,494

On January 29, 2007, we announced that we had entered into a definitive agreement with First Republic Bank ("First Republic") to acquire all of the outstanding common shares of First Republic in exchange for a combination of cash and stock for a total transaction value of $1.8 billion. First Republic is a private banking and wealth management firm focused on high-net-worth individuals and their businesses. The transaction is expected to close in the third quarter of 2007, pending necessary regulatory approval. The shareholders of First Republic approved this transaction on July 26, 2007. The results of operations of First Republic will be included in GWM.

Global Private Client (GPC)

GPC's second quarter 2007 net revenues were $3.3 billion, up 13% from the year-ago quarter. The increase in GPC's net revenues was driven by all major revenue categories.

Financial Advisor headcount reached 16,200 at the end of the second quarter of 2007, a net increase of 680 FAs since the second quarter of 2006, as GPC continued to successfully execute its strategy for recruiting and training high-quality FAs.

A detailed discussion of GPC's revenues follows:

Fee-based revenues

Fee-based revenues primarily consist of portfolio service fees that are derived from accounts that charge an annual fee based on net asset value (generally billed quarterly in advance based on prior quarter asset values), such as Merrill Lynch Consults® (a separately managed account product) and Unlimited Advantage® (a fee-based brokerage account). Fee-based revenues also include fees from insurance products and taxable and tax-exempt money market funds, as well as fixed annual account fees and other account-related fees, and commissions related to distribution fees on mutual funds.

GPC's fee-based revenues were $1.6 billion in the second quarter of 2007, up 11% from the prior year. These increases reflect continued growth in assets in annuitized-revenue products and higher market values.

Transactional and origination revenues

Transactional and origination revenues include certain commission revenues, such as those that arise from agency transactions in listed and OTC equity securities, insurance products, and mutual funds. These revenues also include principal transactions which primarily represent bid-offer revenues on government bonds and municipal securities, as well as new issue revenues which include selling concessions on newly issued debt and equity securities, including shares of closed-end funds.

Transactional and origination revenues were $1.0 billion in the second quarter of 2007, up 14% from the year-ago quarter, driven primarily by increased origination activity.

(continued)

EXHIBIT 3—
continued

MERRILL LYNCH
& CO. GMI AND
GWM BUSINESS
SEGMENTS, 10-Q,
MARCH 31, 2007

Net interest profit and related hedges

Net interest profit (interest revenues less interest expenses) and related hedges include GPC's allocation of the interest spread earned in our banking subsidiaries for deposits, as well as interest earned, net of provisions for loan losses, on margin, small- and middle-market business and other loans, corporate funding allocations, and the interest component of non-qualifying derivatives.

GPC's net interest profit and related hedge revenues were $587 million in the second quarter of 2007, up 10% from the year-ago quarter. The increase reflects higher spreads on deposits due to a year-over-year increase in short-term interest rates.

Other revenues

GPC's other revenues were $117 million in the second quarter of 2007, up 52% from the year-ago quarter. The increase was primarily due to additional revenues from the distribution of mutual funds and higher foreign exchange gains.

Global Investment Management (GIM)

GIM includes revenues from the creation and management of hedge fund and other alternative investment products for clients, as well as our share of net earnings from our ownership positions in other investment management companies, including BlackRock.

GIM's second quarter 2007 revenues of $305 million were up 119% from the year-ago quarter. The increase in net revenues was primarily due to the inclusion of revenues from our ownership position in BlackRock.

Merrill Lynch Investment Managers

On September 29, 2006, Merrill Lynch merged MLIM with BlackRock in exchange for a total of 65 million common and preferred shares in the newly combined BlackRock, representing an economic interest of approximately half. Following the merger, the MLIM business segment ceased to exist, and under the equity method of accounting, an estimate of the net earnings associated with Merrill Lynch's ownership position in BlackRock is recorded in the GIM portion of the GWM segment. For the second quarter of 2006, MLIM's net revenues were $630 million, and its pre-tax earnings were $240 million. For the first six months of 2006, MLIM's net revenues were $1.2 billion, and its pre-tax earnings were $353 million. Excluding the impact of the $109 million of one-time compensation expenses recognized by MLIM in the first quarter of 2006, MLIM's pre-tax earnings for the first six months of 2006 were $462 million.

EXHIBIT 4

MERRILL LYNCH
& CO. FAIR VALUE
NOTE, 10-Q,
MARCH 31, 2007

Note 3. Fair Value of Financial Instruments

Merrill Lynch early adopted the provisions of SFAS No. 157 and SFAS No. 159 in the first quarter of 2007.

Fair Value Measurements

SFAS No. 157 defines fair value, establishes a framework for measuring fair value, establishes a fair value hierarchy based on the quality of inputs used to measure fair value and enhances disclosure requirements for fair value measurements. SFAS No. 157 nullifies the guidance provided by EITF 02-3 that prohibits recognition of day one gains or losses on derivative transactions where model inputs that significantly impact valuation are not observable. In addition, SFAS No. 157 prohibits the use of block discounts for large positions of unrestricted financial instruments that trade in an active market and requires an issuer to incorporate changes in its own credit spreads when determining the fair value of its liabilities.

(continued)

EXHIBIT 4—
continued

MERRILL LYNCH
& CO. FAIR VALUE
NOTE, 10-Q,
MARCH 31, 2007

Fair Value Hierarchy

In accordance with SFAS No. 157, we have categorized our financial instruments into a three-level fair value hierarchy. The fair value hierarchy gives the highest priority to quoted prices in active markets for identical assets or liabilities (Level 1) and the lowest priority to unobservable inputs (Level 3). If the inputs used to measure the financial instruments fall within different levels of the hierarchy, the categorization is based on the lowest level input that is significant to the fair value measurement of the instrument. Financial assets and liabilities recorded on the Condensed Consolidated Balance Sheets are categorized based on the inputs to the valuation techniques as follows:

Level 1.   Financial assets and liabilities whose values are based on unadjusted quoted prices for identical assets or liabilities in an active market (examples include active exchange-traded equity securities, listed derivatives, most U.S. Government and agency securities, and certain other sovereign government obligations).

Level 2.   Financial assets and liabilities whose values are based on quoted prices in markets that are not active or model inputs that are observable either directly or indirectly for substantially the full term of the asset or liability. Level 2 inputs include the following:

   a) Quoted prices for similar assets or liabilities in active markets (for example, restricted stock);

   b) Quoted prices for identical or similar assets or liabilities in non-active markets (examples include corporate and municipal bonds, which trade infrequently);

   c) Pricing models whose inputs are observable for substantially the full term of the asset or liability (examples include most over-the-counter derivatives, including interest rate and currency swaps); and

   d) Pricing models whose inputs are derived principally from or corroborated by observable market data through correlation or other means for substantially the full term of the asset or liability (examples include certain residential and commercial mortgage related assets, including loans, securities and derivatives).

Level 3.   Financial assets and liabilities whose values are based on prices or valuation techniques that require inputs that are both unobservable and significant to the overall fair value measurement. These inputs reflect management's own assumptions about the assumptions a market participant would use in pricing the asset or liability (examples include certain private equity investments, certain residential and commercial mortgage related assets (including loans, securities and derivatives), and long-dated or complex derivatives including certain foreign exchange options and long dated options on gas and power).

(continued)

EXHIBIT 4—
continued

MERRILL LYNCH
& CO. FAIR VALUE
NOTE, 10-Q,
MARCH 31, 2007

The following table presents Merrill Lynch's fair value hierarchy for those assets and liabilities measured at fair value on a recurring basis as of June 29, 2007.

(dollars in millions)	Fair Value Measurements on a Recurring Basis as of June 29, 2007				
	Level 1	Level 2	Level 3	Netting Adj[1]	Total
Assets:					
Securities segregated for regulatory purposes or deposited with clearing organizations	$534	$6,102	$—	$—	$6,636
Receivables under resale agreements	—	99,774	—	—	99,774
Trading assets, excluding contractual agreements	87,681	86,611	3,648	—	177,940
Contractual agreements[2]	4,572	216,321	6,601	(180,645)	46,849
Investment securities	2,974	58,519	5,784	—	67,277
Loans, notes and mortgages	—	1,240	4	—	1,244
Other assets[3]	14	1,108	—	(262)	860
Liabilities:					
Payables under repurchase agreements	$—	$100,752	$—	$—	$100,752
Trading liabilities, excluding contractual agreements	55,760	6,702	—	—	62,462
Contractual agreements[2]	5,200	236,006	6,372	(189,616)	57,962
Long-term borrowings[4]	—	38,184	282	—	38,466
Other payables—interest and other[3]	—	478	—	—	478

(1) Represents counterparty and cash collateral netting.

(2) Includes $4.0 billion and $2.7 billion of derivative assets and liabilities, respectively, that are included in commodities and related contracts on the Condensed Consolidated Balance Sheet.

(3) Primarily represents certain derivatives used for non-trading purposes.

(4) Includes bifurcated embedded derivatives carried at fair value.

The following tables provide a summary of changes in fair value of Merrill Lynch's Level 3 assets and liabilities for the three and six months ended June 29, 2007. As required by SFAS No. 157, when the inputs used to measure fair value fall within different levels of the hierarchy, the level within which the fair value measurement is categorized is based on the lowest level input that is significant to the fair value measurement in its entirety. Thus, a Level 3 fair value measurement may include inputs that are observable (Levels 1 and 2) and unobservable (Level 3). Gains and losses for such assets and liabilities categorized within the Level 3 table below may include changes in fair value that are attributable to both observable inputs (Levels 1 and 2) and unobservable inputs (Level 3). Further, it should be noted that the following tables do not take into consideration the effect of offsetting Level 1 and 2 financial instruments entered into by Merrill Lynch that economically hedge certain exposures to the Level 3 positions.

(*continued*)

EXHIBIT 4—
continued

MERRILL LYNCH
& CO. FAIR VALUE
NOTE, 10-Q,
MARCH 31, 2007

Level 3 Financial Assets and Liabilities
Three Months Ended June 29, 2007

(dollars in millions)	Beginning Balance	Total Realized and Unrealized Gains or (Losses) Included in Income			Total Realized and Unrealized Gains or (Losses) Included in Income	Purchases, Issuances and Settlements	Transfers In (Out)	Ending Balance
		Principal Transactions	Other Revenue	Interest				
Assets:								
Trading assets	$2,324	$259	$—	$32	$291	$483	$550	$3,648
Contractual agreements, net	(1,357)	416	5	1	422	249	915	229
Investment securities	5,922	(295)	185	5	(105)	568	(601)	5,784
Loans, notes and mortgages	6	—	(5)	—	(5)	(1)	4	4
Liabilities:								
Long-term borrowings	—	—	—	—	—	—	282	282

Level 3 Financial Assets and Liabilities
Six Months Ended June 29, 2007

(dollars in millions)	Beginning Balance	Total Realized and Unrealized Gains or (Losses) Included in Income			Total Realized and Unrealized Gains or (Losses) Included in Income	Purchases, Issuances and Settlements	Transfers In (Out)	Ending Balance
		Principal Transactions	Other Revenue	Interest				
Assets:								
Trading assets	$2,021	$253	$—	$28	$281	$503	$843	$3,648
Contractual agreements, net	(2,030)	571	5	6	582	807	870	229
Investment securities	5,117	(430)	480	5	55	1,204	(592)	5,784
Loans, notes and mortgages	7	—	(9)	—	(9)	(2)	8	4
Liabilities:								
Long-term borrowings	—	—	—	—	—	—	282	282

The following table provides the portion of gains or losses included in income for the three and six months ended June 29, 2007 attributable to unrealized gains or losses relating to those Level 3 assets and liabilities still held at June 29, 2007.

Unrealized Gains or (Losses) for Level 3 Assets and Liabilities
Still Held at June 29, 2007

(dollars in millions)	Three Months Ended June 29, 2007				Six Months Ended June 29, 2007			
	Principal Transactions	Other Revenue	Interest	Total	Principal Transactions	Other Revenue	Interest	Total
Trading assets	$234	$—	$32	266	$203	$—	$28	$231
Contractual agreements, net	336	5	1	342	460	—	6	466
Investment securities	(295)	189	5	(101)	(430)	396	5	(29)
Loans, notes and mortgages	—	1	—	1	—	3	—	3

(continued)

EXHIBIT 4—
continued

MERRILL LYNCH
& CO. FAIR VALUE
NOTE, 10-Q,
MARCH 31, 2007

The following table shows the fair value hierarchy for those assets and liabilities measured at fair value on a non-recurring basis as of June 29, 2007.

(dollars in millions)	Fair Value Measurements on a Non-Recurring Basis as of June 29, 2007			
	Level 1	Level 2	Level 3	Total
Loans, notes, and mortgages[1]	$—	$943	$38	$981
Other assets	—	27	—	27

(1) These loans include Held-for-Sale loans and certain impaired Held-for-Investment loans where the fair value is below cost.

For the assets and liabilities measured at fair value on a non-recurring basis at June 29, 2007, the losses recorded in the Condensed Consolidated Statement of Earnings for the three and six months ended June 29, 2007 were, $54 million and $10 million, respectively.

Fair Value Option

SFAS No. 159 provides a fair value option election that allows companies to irrevocably elect fair value as the initial and subsequent measurement attribute for certain financial assets and liabilities. Changes in fair value for assets and liabilities for which the election is made will be recognized in earnings as they occur.

The following table presents a summary of eligible financial assets and financial liabilities for which the fair value option was elected on December 30, 2006 and the cumulative-effect adjustment to retained earnings recorded in connection with the initial adoption of SFAS No. 159.

(dollars in millions)	Carrying Value Prior to Adoption	Transition Adjustments to Retained Earnings Gain/(Loss)	Carrying Value After Adoption
Assets:			
Investment securities[1]	$8,723	$(268)	$8,732
Loans, notes, and mortgages[2]	1,440	2	1,442
Liabilities:			
Long-term borrowings[3]	$10,308	$(29)	$10,337
Pre-tax cumulative-effect of adoption		$(295)	
Deferred tax benefit		110	
Cumulative effect of adoption of the fair value option		$(185)	

(1) Merrill Lynch adopted the fair value option for certain fixed rate securities in its treasury liquidity portfolio previously classified as available-for-sale securities as management modified its investment strategy and economic exposure to interest rate risk by eliminating long-term fixed rate assets in its liquidity portfolio and replacing them with floating rate assets. These securities were carried at fair value in accordance with SFAS No. 115 prior to the adoption of SFAS No. 159. An unrealized loss of $172 million, net of tax, related to such securities was reclassified from accumulated other comprehensive loss to retained earnings.

(2) Merrill Lynch adopted the fair value option for certain automobile and corporate loans because the loans are risk managed on a fair value basis.

(3) Merrill Lynch adopted the fair value option for certain positions, which are risk managed on a fair value basis and for which the fair value option eliminates the need to apply hedge accounting under SFAS No. 133.

(continued)

EXHIBIT 4—
continued

MERRILL LYNCH
& CO. FAIR VALUE
NOTE, 10-Q,
MARCH 31, 2007

The following table provides information about where in the Condensed Consolidated Statement of Earnings changes in fair values, for which the fair value option has been elected, are included for the three and six month periods ended June 29, 2007.

(dollars in millions)	Changes in Fair Value for the Three Months Ended June 29, 2007, for Items Measured at Fair Value Pursuant to Fair Value Option			Changes in Fair Value for the Six Months Ended June 29, 2007, for Items Measured at Fair Value Pursuant to Fair Value Option		
	Gains Principal Transactions	Gains Other Revenues	Total Changes in Fair Value	Gains Principal Transactions	Gains Other Revenues	Total Changes in Fair Value
Assets:						
Receivables under resale agreements[1]	$6	$—	$6	$5	$—	$5
Investment securities	210	8	218	210	21	231
Loans, notes and mortgages[2]	—	20	20	2	40	$42
Liabilities:[3]						
Payables under repurchase agreements[1]	$7	$—	$7	$17	$—	$17
Long-term borrowings	985	—	985	838	—	838

The following table presents difference between fair values and aggregate contractual principal amounts of loans, notes and mortgages and long-term borrowings, for which the fair value option has been elected.

(dollars in millions)	Fair Value at June 29, 2007	Principal Due Upon Maturity	Difference
Assets			
Loans, notes and mortgages[1]	$1,244	$1,473	$(229)
Liabilities			
Long-term borrowings[2]	37,473	38,872	$(1,399)

EXHIBIT 5

MERRILL LYNCH
& CO. INCOME
STATEMENT,
DECEMBER 31,
2008

MERRILL LYNCH & CO., INC. AND SUBSIDIARIES
Consolidated Statements of (Loss)/Earnings

(dollars in millions, except per share amounts)	Year Ended Last Friday in December		
	2008 (52 weeks)	2007 (52 weeks)	2006 (52 weeks)
Revenues			
Principal transactions	$(27,225)	$(12,067)	$7,248
Commissions	6,895	7,284	5,985
Managed accounts and other fee-based revenues	5,544	5,465	6,273
Investment banking	3,733	5,582	4,648
Earnings from equity method investments	4,491	1,627	556
Other	(10,065)	(2,190)	2,883
Subtotal	(16,627)	5,701	27,593
Interest and dividend revenues	33,383	56,974	39,790
Less interest expense	29,349	51,425	35,571
Net interest profit	4,034	5,549	4,219
Gain on merger	—	—	1,969
Revenues, net of interest expense	(12,593)	11,250	33,781
Non-interest expenses			
Compensation and benefits	14,763	15,903	16,867
Communications and technology	2,201	2,057	1,838
Brokerage, clearing, and exchange fees	1,394	1,415	1,096
Occupancy and related depreciation	1,267	1,139	991
Professional fees	1,058	1,027	885
Advertising and market development	652	785	686
Office supplies and postage	215	233	225
Other	2,402	1,522	1,383
Payment related to price reset on common stock offering	2,500	—	—
Goodwill impairment charge	2,300	—	—
Restructuring charge	486	—	—
Total non-interest expenses	29,238	24,081	23,971
Pre-tax (loss)/earnings from continuing operations	(41,831)	(12,831)	9,810
Income tax (benefit)/expense	(14,280)	(4,194)	2,713
Net (loss)/earnings from continuing operations	(27,551)	(8,637)	7,097
Discontinued operations:			
Pre-tax (loss)/earnings from discontinued operations	(141)	1,397	616
Income tax (benefit)/expense	(80)	537	214
Net (loss)/earnings from discontinued operations	(61)	860	402
Net (loss)/earnings	$(27,612)	$(7,777)	$7,499

(continued)

Preferred stock dividends	**2,869**	270	188
Net (loss)/earnings applicable to common stockholders	**$(30,481)**	$(8,047)	$7,311
Basic (loss)/earnings per common share from continuing operations	**$(24.82)**	(10.73)	7.96
Basic (loss)/earnings per common share from discontinued operations	**(0.05)**	1.04	0.46
Basic (loss)/earnings per common share	**$(24.87)**	(9.69)	8.42
Diluted (loss)/earnings per common share from continuing operations	**$(24.82)**	$(10.73)	$7.17
Diluted (loss)/earnings per common share from discontinued operations	**(0.05)**	1.04	0.42
Diluted (loss)/earnings per common share	**$(24.87)**	$(9.69)	$7.59
Dividend paid per common share	**$1.40**	$1.40	$1.00

EXHIBIT 5—
continued

MERRILL LYNCH & CO. INCOME STATEMENT, DECEMBER 31, 2008

MERRILL LYNCH & CO., INC. AND SUBSIDIARIES
Consolidated Balance Sheets

(dollars in millions, except per share amounts)	December 26, 2008	December 28, 2007
ASSETS		
Cash and cash equivalents	$68,403	$41,346
Cash and securities segregated for regulatory purposes or deposited with clearing organizations	32,923	22,999
Securities financing transactions		
Receivables under resale agreements (includes $62,146 in 2008 and $100,214 in 2007 measured at fair value in accordance with SFAS No. 159)	93,247	221,617
Receivables under securities borrowed transactions (includes $853 in 2008 measured at fair value in accordance with SFAS No. 159)	35,077	133,140
	128,324	354,757
Trading assets, at fair value (includes securities pledged as collateral that can be sold or repledged of $18,663 in 2008 and $45,177 in 2007)		
Derivative contracts	89,477	72,689
Corporate debt and preferred stock	30,829	37,849
Equities and convertible debentures	26,160	60,681
Mortgages, mortgage-backed, and asset-backed	13,786	28,013
Non-U.S. governments and agencies	6,107	15,082
U.S. Government and agencies	5,253	11,219
Municipals, money markets and physical commodities	3,993	9,136
	175,605	234,669

EXHIBIT 6

MERRILL LYNCH & CO. BALANCE SHEET, DECEMBER 31, 2008

(continued)

EXHIBIT 6—
continued

MERRILL LYNCH &
CO. BALANCE
SHEET,
DECEMBER 31,
2008

Investment securities (includes $2,770 in 2008 and $4,685 in 2007 measured at fair value in accordance with SFAS No. 159) (includes securities pledged as collateral that can be sold or repledged of $2,557 in 2008 and $16,124 in 2007)	57,007	82,532
Securities received as collateral, at fair value	11,658	45,245
Other receivables		
Customers (net of allowance for doubtful accounts of $143 in 2008 and $24 in 2007)	51,131	70,719
Brokers and dealers	12,410	22,643
Interest and other	26,331	23,487
	89,872	116,849
Loans, notes and mortgages (net of allowances for loan losses of $2,072 in 2008 and $533 in 2007) (includes $979 in 2008 and $1,149 in 2007 measured at fair value in accordance with SFAS No. 159)	69,190	94,992
Equipment and facilities (net of accumulated depreciation and amortization of $5,856 in 2008 and $5,518 in 2007)	2,928	3,127
Goodwill and other intangible assets	2,616	5,091
Other assets	29,017	18,443
Total Assets	$667,543	$1,020,050

CONSOLIDATED BALANCE SHEETS

(dollars in millions, except per share amounts)	December 26, 2008	December 28, 2007
LIABILITIES		
Securities financing transactions		
Payables under repurchase agreements (includes $32,910 in 2008 and $89,733 in 2007 measured at fair value in accordance with SFAS No. 159)	$92,654	$235,725
Payables under securities loaned transactions	24,426	55,906
	117,080	291,631
Short-term borrowings (includes $3,387 in 2008 measured at fair value in accordance with SFAS No. 159)	37,895	24,914
Deposits	96,107	103,987
Trading liabilities, at fair value		
Derivative contracts	71,363	73,294
Equities and convertible debentures	7,871	29,652
Non-U.S. governments and agencies	4,345	9,407
U.S. Government and agencies	3,463	6,135
Corporate debt and preferred stock	1,318	4,549
Municipals, money markets and other	1,111	551
	89,471	123,588

(continued)

EXHIBIT 6—
continued

MERRILL LYNCH &
CO. BALANCE
SHEET,
DECEMBER 31,
2008

Obligation to return securities received as collateral, at fair value	11,658	45,245
Other payables		
Customers	44,924	63,582
Brokers and dealers	12,553	24,499
Interest and other	32,918	44,545
	90,395	132,626
Long-term borrowings (includes $49,521 in 2008 and $76,334 in 2007 measured at fair value in accordance with SFAS No. 159)	199,678	260,973
Junior subordinated notes (related to trust preferred securities)	5,256	5,154
Total Liabilities	647,540	988,118

COMMITMENTS AND CONTINGENCIES

STOCKHOLDERS' EQUITY

Preferred Stockholders' Equity (liquidation preference of $30,000 per share; issued: 2008 — 244,100 shares; 2007 — 155,000 shares; liquidation preference of $1,000 per share; issued: 2008 and 2007 — 115,000 shares; liquidation preference of $100,000 per share; issued: 2008 — 17,000 shares)	8,605	4,383
Common Stockholders' Equity		
Shares exchangeable into common stock	—	39
Common stock (par value $1.331/3 per share; authorized: 3,000,000,000 shares; issued: 2008 — 2,031,995,436 shares; 2007 — 1,354,309,819 shares)	2,709	1,805
Paid-in capital	47,232	27,163
Accumulated other comprehensive loss (net of tax)	(6,318)	(1,791)
(Accumulated deficit) / retained earnings	(8,603)	23,737
	35,020	50,953
Less: Treasury stock, at cost (2008 — 431,742,565 shares; 2007 — 418,270,289 shares)	23,622	23,404
Total Common Stockholders' Equity	11,398	27,549
Total Stockholders' Equity	20,003	31,932
Total Liabilities and Stockholders' Equity	$667,543	$1,020,050

EXHIBIT 7

MERRILL LYNCH &
CO. STATEMENT OF
CASH FLOWS,
DECEMBER 31,
2008

(dollars in millions)	Year Ended Last Friday in December		
	2008	2007	2006
Cash flows from operating activities:			
Net (loss)/earnings	$(27,612)	$(7,777)	$7,499
Adjustments to reconcile net (loss)/earnings to cash provided by (used for) operating activities			
Gain on merger	—	—	(1,969)
Gain on sale of MLIG	—	(316)	—
Depreciation and amortization	886	901	523
Share-based compensation expense	2,044	1,795	3,156
Payment related to price reset on common stock offering	2,500	—	—
Goodwill impairment charge	2,300	—	—
Deferred taxes	(16,086)	(4,924)	(360)
Gain on sale of Bloomberg L.P. interest	(4,296)	—	—
Loss (earnings) from equity method investments	306	(1,409)	(421)
Other	13,556	160	1,045
Changes in operating assets and liabilities:			
Trading assets	59,064	(29,650)	(55,392)
Cash and securities segregated for regulatory purposes or deposited with clearing organizations	(6,214)	(8,886)	(1,019)
Receivables under resale agreements	128,370	(43,247)	(15,346)
Receivables under securities borrowed transactions	98,063	(14,530)	(26,126)
Customer receivables	19,561	(21,280)	(9,562)
Brokers and dealers receivables	10,236	(3,744)	(6,825)
Proceeds from loans, notes, and mortgages held for sale	21,962	72,054	41,317
Other changes in loans, notes, and mortgages held for sale	2,700	(86,894)	(47,670)
Trading liabilities	(34,338)	23,878	9,554
Payables under repurchase agreements	(143,071)	13,101	29,557
Payables under securities loaned transactions	(31,480)	12,414	24,157
Customer payables	(18,658)	14,135	13,795
Brokers and dealers payables	(11,946)	113	4,791
Trading investment securities	3,216	9,333	(867)
Other, net	(31,588)	2,411	6,400
Cash provided by (used for) operating activities	39,475	(72,362)	(23,763)

(continued)

EXHIBIT 7—
continued

MERRILL LYNCH &
CO. STATEMENT OF
CASH FLOWS,
DECEMBER 31,
2008

Cash flows from investing activities:

Proceeds from (payments for):

Maturities of available-for-sale securities	7,250	13,362	13,222
Sales of available-for-sale securities	29,537	39,327	16,176
Purchases of available-for-sale securities	(31,017)	(58,325)	(31,357)
Proceeds from the sale of discontinued operations	12,576	1,250	—
Equipment and facilities, net	(630)	(719)	(1,174)
Loans, notes, and mortgages held for investment	(13,379)	5,113	(681)
Other investments	1,336	(5,049)	(6,543)
Transfer of cash balances related to merger	—	—	(651)
Acquisitions, net of cash	—	(2,045)	—
Cash provided by (used for) investing activities	5,673	(7,086)	(11,008)

Cash flows from financing activities:

Proceeds from (payments for):

Commercial paper and short-term borrowings	12,981	6,316	9,123
Issuance and resale of long-term borrowings	70,194	165,107	87,814
Settlement and repurchases of long-term borrowings	(109,731)	(93,258)	(42,545)
Deposits	(7,880)	9,884	4,108
Derivative financing transactions	543	848	608
Issuance of common stock	9,899	4,787	1,838
Issuance of preferred stock, net	9,281	1,123	472
Common stock repurchases	—	(5,272)	(9,088)
Other common stock transactions	(833)	(60)	539
Excess tax benefits related to share-based compensation	39	715	531
Dividends	(2,584)	(1,505)	(1,106)
Cash (used for) provided by financing activities	(18,091)	88,685	52,294
Increase in cash and cash equivalents	27,057	9,237	17,523
Cash and cash equivalents, beginning of period	41,346	32,109	14,586
Cash and cash equivalents, end of period	$68,403	$41,346	$32,109

Supplemental Disclosure of Cash Flow Information:

Income taxes paid	$1,518	$1,846	$2,638
Interest paid	30,397	49,881	35,685

EXHIBIT 8

CHANGES IN OWNERS' EQUITY, DECEMBER 31, 2008

	Amounts			Shares		
(dollars in millions)	2008	2007	2006	2008	2007	2006
Preferred Stock, net						
Balance, beginning of year	$4,383	$3,145	$2,673	257,134	104,928	89,685
Issuances	10,814	1,615	374	172,100	165,000	12,000
Redemptions	(6,600)	—	—	(66,000)	—	—
Shares (repurchased) re-issuances	8	(377)	98	211	(12,794)	3,243
Balance, end of year	$8,605	$4,383	$3,145	363,445	257,134	104,928
Common Stockholders' Equity						
Shares Exchangeable into Common Stock						
Balance, beginning of year	$39	$39	$41	2,552,982	2,659,926	2,707,797
Exchanges	(39)	—	(2)	(2,544,793)	(106,944)	(47,871)
Balance, end of year	—	39	39	8,189	2,552,982	2,659,926
Common Stock						
Balance, beginning of year	1,805	1,620	1,531	1,354,309,819	1,215,381,006	1,148,714,008
Capital issuance and acquisition[1][2]	648	122	—	486,166,666	91,576,096	—
Preferred stock conversion	236	—	—	177,322,917	—	—
Shares issued to employees	20	63	89	14,196,034	47,352,717	66,666,998
Balance, end of year	2,709	1,805	1,620	2,031,995,436	1,354,309,819	1,215,381,006
Paid-in Capital						
Balance, beginning of year	27,163	18,919	13,320			
Capital issuance and acquisition[1][2]	11,544	4,643	—			
Preferred stock conversion	6,970	—	—			
Employee stock plan activity and other	(553)	1,962	2,351			
Amortization of employee stock grants	2,108	1,639	3,248			
Balance, end of year	47,232	27,163	18,919			

Accumulated Other Comprehensive Loss:			
Foreign Currency Translation Adjustment (net of tax)			
Balance, beginning of year	**(441)**	(430)	(507)
Translation adjustment	**(304)**	(11)	77
Balance, end of year	**(745)**	(441)	(430)
Net Unrealized Gains (Losses) on Investment Securities Available-for-Sale (net of tax)			
Balance, beginning of year	**(1,509)**	(192)	(181)
Net unrealized losses on available-for-sale securities	**(7,617)**	(2,460)	(15)
Adjustment to initially apply SFAS 159[3]	**—**	172	4
Other adjustments[4]	**3,088**	971	—
Balance, end of year	**(6,038)**	(1,509)	(192)
Deferred Gains (losses) on Cash Flow Hedges (net of tax)			
Balance, beginning of year	**83**	2	(3)
Net deferred (losses) gains on cash flow hedges	**(2)**	81	5
Balance, end of year	**81**	83	2
Defined benefit pension and postretirement plans (net of tax)			
Balance, beginning of year	**76**	(164)	(153)
Net gains	**306**	240	—
Minimum pension liability adjustment	**—**	—	(76)
Adjustment to apply SFAS 158 change in measurement date[3]	**2**	—	—
Adjustment to initially apply SFAS 158[3]	**—**	—	65
Balance, end of year	**384**	76	(164)
Balance, end of year	**(6,318)**	(1,791)	(784)

(continued)

EXHIBIT 8 —continued
CHANGES IN OWNERS' EQUITY, DECEMBER 31, 2008

Year Ended Last Friday in December

(dollars in millions)	Amounts 2008	2007	2006	Shares 2008	2007	2006
(Accumulated deficit) Retained Earnings						
Balance, beginning of year	23,737	33,217	26,824			
Net (loss) earnings	(27,612)	(7,777)	7,499			
Preferred stock dividends declared	(2,869)	(270)	(188)			
Common stock dividends declared	(1,853)	(1,235)	(918)			
Adjustment to initially apply SFAS 157	—	53				
Adjustment to apply SFAS 158 change in measurement date	(6)	—	—			
Adjustment to initially apply SFAS 159	—	(185)	—			
Adjustment to initially apply FIN 48	—	(66)	—			
Balance, end of year	(8,603)	23,737	33,217			
Treasury Stock, at cost						
Balance, beginning of year	(23,404)	(17,118)	(7,945)	(418,270,289)	(350,697,271)	(233,112,271)
Shares repurchased	—	(5,272)	(9,088)	—	(62,112,876)	(116,610,876)
Shares reacquired from employees and other(5)	(363)	(1,014)	(89)	(16,017,069)	(5,567,086)	(1,021,995)
Share exchanges	145		4	2,544,793	106,944	47,871
Balance, end of year	(23,622)	(23,404)	(17,118)	(431,742,565)	(418,270,289)	(350,697,271)
Total Common Stockholders' Equity	$27,549	$35,893	$11,398			
Total Stockholders' Equity	$31,932	$39,038	$20,003			

(1) The 2008 activity relates to the July 28, 2008 public offering and additional shares issued to Davis Selected Advisors and Temasek Holdings.

(2) The 2007 activity relates to the acquisition of First Republic Bank and to additional shares issued to Davis Selected Advisors and Temasek Holdings.

(3) This adjustment is not reflected on the Statement of Comprehensive (Loss)/Income.

(4) Other adjustments primarily relate to income taxes, policyholder liabilities and deferred policy acquisition costs.

(5) Share amounts are net of reacquisitions from employees of 19,057,068, 12,490,283 shares and 6,622,887 shares, in 2008, 2007 and 2006, respectively.

See Notes to Consolidated Financial Statements.

EXHIBIT 9

STATEMENTS OF
COMPREHENSIVE
(LOSS)/INCOME,
DECEMBER 31,
2008

(dollars in millions)	Year Ended Last Friday in December		
	2008	2007	2006
Net (Loss)/Earnings	**$(27,612)**	$(7,777)	$7,499
Other Comprehensive (Loss) Income			
Foreign currency translation adjustment:			
Foreign currency translation gains (losses)	**694**	(282)	(366)
Income tax (expense) benefit	**(998)**	271	443
Total	**(304)**	(11)	77
Net unrealized gains (losses) on investment securities available-for-sale:			
Net unrealized losses arising during the period	**(11,916)**	(2,291)	(16)
Reclassification adjustment for realized losses/ (gains) included in net (loss)/earnings	**4,299**	(169)	1
Net unrealized losses on investment securities available-for-sale	**(7,617)**	(2,460)	(15)
Adjustments for:			
Policyholder liabilities	—	4	1
Income tax benefit	**3,088**	967	3
Total	**(4,529)**	(1,489)	(11)
Deferred gains (losses) on cash flow hedges:			
Deferred gains (losses) on cash flow hedges	**240**	162	9
Reclass adjustment for realized losses (gains) included in net earnings	**(241)**	(30)	(2)
Income tax (expense) benefit	**(1)**	(51)	(2)
Total	**(2)**	81	5
Defined benefit pension and postretirement plans:			
Minimum pension liability adjustment	—	—	(110)
Net actuarial gains	**489**	353	
Prior service cost	**(4)**	6	
Reclassification adjustment for realized losses included in net (loss)/earnings	**(5)**	23	—
Income tax (expense) benefit	**(174)**	(142)	34
Total	**306**	240	(76)
Total Other Comprehensive Loss	**(4,529)**	(1,179)	(5)
Comprehensive (Loss)/Income	**$(32,141)**	$(8,956)	$7,494

EXHIBIT 10

MERRILL LYNCH &
CO. SEGMENT
INFORMATION,
DECEMBER 31,
2008

Business Segments

Our operations are organized into two business segments: GMI and GWM. We also record revenues and expenses within a "Corporate" category. Corporate results primarily include unrealized gains and losses due to interest rate hedges on certain debt. In addition, Corporate results for the year ended December 26, 2008 included expenses of $2.5 billion for the payment to Temasek, $0.5 billion associated with the ARS repurchase program, and $0.7 billion of litigation accruals recorded in 2008. Net revenues and pre-tax losses recorded within Corporate for 2008 were $1.1 billion and $2.6 billion, respectively, compared with net revenues and pre-tax losses of negative $103 million and $116 million, respectively, in the prior year.

The following segment results represent the information that is relied upon by management in its decision-making processes. Revenues and expenses associated with inter-segment activities are recognized in each segment. In addition, revenue and expense sharing agreements for joint activities between segments are in place, and the results of each segment reflect their agreed-upon apportionment of revenues and expenses associated with these activities. Segment results are presented from continuing operations only.

Global Markets and Investment Banking

The Global Markets division consists of the FICC and Equity Markets sales and trading activities for investor clients and on a proprietary basis, while the Investment Banking division provides a wide range of origination and strategic advisory services for issuer clients.

GMI Results of Operations

(dollars in millions)	2008	2007	%Change 2008 vs. 2007
Global Markets			
FICC	$(37,423)	$(15,873)	N/M%
Equity Markets	7,668	8,286	(7)
Total Global Markets revenues, net of interest expense	(29,755)	(7,587)	N/M
Investment Banking			
Origination:			
Debt	931	1,550	(40)
Equity	1,047	1,629	(36)
Strategic Advisory Services	1,317	1,740	(24)
Total Investment Banking revenues, net of interest expense	3,295	4,919	(33)
Total GMI revenues, net of interest expense	(26,460)	(2,668)	N/M
Non-interest expenses before restructuring charge	14,753	13,677	8
Restructuring charge	331	—	N/M
Pre-tax loss from continuing operations	$(41,544)	$(16,345)	N/M
Pre-tax profit margin	N/M	N/M	
Total full-time employees	9,700	12,300	

GMI recorded negative net revenues and a pre-tax loss from continuing operations in 2008 of $26.5 billion and $41.5 billion, respectively, as the difficult market conditions that existed during the year contributed to net losses in FICC and lower net revenues in Equity Markets and Investment Banking. The 2008 pre-tax loss was primarily driven by the net write-downs

(continued)

EXHIBIT 10—
continued

MERRILL LYNCH &
CO. SEGMENT
INFORMATION,
DECEMBER 31,
2008

within FICC that are discussed below, as well as a $2.3 billion impairment charge related to goodwill. Partially offsetting these losses was a net gain of approximately $5.1 billion recorded by GMI during 2008 due to the impact of the widening of Merrill Lynch's credit spreads on the carrying value of certain of our long-term debt liabilities.

GMI's 2007 net revenues were negative $2.7 billion; $16.3 billion in continuing operations pre-tax loss. The 2007 loss was mainly due to net write-downs within FICC, including $20.9 billion for U.S. ABS CDOs and residential mortgage-related exposures and $3.1 billion for valuation adjustments against guarantor counterparties. GMI's 2007 net revenues included a net gain of $1.9 billion due to the impact of the widening of Merrill Lynch's credit spreads on the carrying value of certain of our long-term debt liabilities.

Fixed Income, Currencies and Commodities (FICC)

During 2008, FICC was adversely impacted by extremely difficult market conditions, particularly during the second half of the year. Such conditions included the continuing deterioration in the credit markets, lower levels of liquidity, reduced price transparency, asset price declines, increased volatility and severe market dislocations, particularly following the default of a major U.S. broker-dealer and the U.S. Government's conservatorship of certain GSEs.

In 2008, FICC recorded approximately $10.2 billion of net write-downs related to U.S. ABS CDOs, about $4.4 billion of which related to the sale of U.S. super senior ABS CDOs conducted during the third quarter. In addition, as a result of the deteriorating environment for financial guarantors, FICC also recorded credit valuation adjustments related to hedges with financial guarantors of negative $10.4 billion. FICC's net revenues were also adversely impacted by net losses related to our U.S. banks' investment securities portfolio of $4.1 billion and certain of our U.S. sub-prime, U.S. Alt-A and Non-U.S. residential mortgage-related exposures aggregating approximately $4.6 billion. FICC also recognized net write-downs related to leveraged finance loans and commitments of approximately $4.2 billion and $1.9 billion of net write-downs related to commercial real estate. These losses were partially offset by a $2.6 billion foreign currency gain related to currency hedges of our U.K. deferred tax assets recognized in quarter four of 2008 and a net gain of approximately $3.7 billion related to the impact of the widening of our credit spreads on the carrying value of certain of our long-term debt liabilities. In addition, net revenues for most other FICC businesses declined from 2007, as the environment for those businesses was materially worse than the prior-year.

In 2007, FICC net revenues were negative $15.9 billion as strong revenues in global currencies and global rates were offset by declines in the global credit and structured finance and investments businesses. FICC's 2007 net revenues included net writedowns of approximately $20.9 billion due to U.S. ABS CDOs and residential mortgage-related exposures and $3.1 billion related to valuation adjustments against guarantor counterparties, which were partially offset by a net benefit of approximately $1.2 billion due to the impact of the widening of our credit spreads on the carrying value of certain of our long-term debt liabilities.

Equity Markets

Equity Markets net revenues for 2008 were $7.7 billion compared with $8.3 billion in the prior-year period. Net revenues in 2008 included a gain of $4.3 billion from the sale of the investment in Bloomberg L.P. as well as a gain of $1.4 billion related to changes in the carrying value of certain of our long-term debt liabilities. These gains were more than offset by declines from other equity products, including cash and global equity-linked products. In addition, private equity recorded negative net revenues of $2.1 billion in 2008 as compared with net revenues of $0.4 billion in 2007.

(continued)

EXHIBIT 10—
continued

MERRILL LYNCH &
CO. SEGMENT
INFORMATION,
DECEMBER 31,
2008

For 2007, Equity Markets net revenues were a record $8.3 billion, driven by our equity-linked business, up nearly 80%, global cash equity trading business, up over 30%, and global markets financing and services business, which includes prime brokerage, up over 45%. Equity Markets 2007 net revenues included a gain of about $700 million related to changes in the carrying value of certain of our long-term debt liabilities.

Investment Banking

For 2008, Investment Banking net revenues were $3.3 billion, down 33% from a record $4.9 billion in the prior-year period, as the difficult market conditions that existed in 2008 resulted in lower industry-wide transaction volumes across all product lines.

Origination

For 2008, origination revenues were $2.0 billion, down 38% from the year-ago period. Debt and equity originations were down 40% and 36%, respectively, compared with 2007, primarily reflecting lower industry-wide transaction volumes in 2008.

Strategic Advisory Services

Strategic advisory services net revenues, which include merger and acquisition and other advisory fees, were $1.3 billion in 2008, a decrease of 24% from the prior-year. The decline was primarily due to lower industry-wide transaction activity, which reflected the high level of volatility in the global financial markets, economic uncertainty and a lack of available liquidity in the credit markets.

Global Wealth Management

GWM, our full-service retail wealth management segment, provides brokerage, investment advisory and financial planning services. GWM is comprised of GPC and GIM.   GPC provides a full range of wealth management products and services to assist clients in managing all aspects of their financial profile principally through our FA network. GIM includes our interests in creating and managing wealth management products, including alternative investment products for clients. GIM also includes our share of net earnings from our ownership positions in other investment management companies, including BlackRock.

GWM Results of Operations

(dollars in millions)	2008	2007	% Change 2008 vs. 2007
GPC			
Fee-based revenues	**$6,171**	$6,278	(2)%
Transactional and origination revenues	**3,313**	3,887	(15)
Net interest profit and related hedges[1]	**2,337**	2,318	1
Other revenues	**288**	416	(31)
Total GPC revenues, net of interest expense	**12,109**	12,899	(6)
GIM			
Total GIM revenues, net of interest expense	**669**	1,122	(40)
Total GWM revenues, net of interest expense	**12,778**	14,021	(9)
Non-interest expenses before restructuring charge	**10,277**	10,391	(1)
Restructuring charge	**155**	—	N/M
Pre-tax earnings from continuing operations	**$2,346**	**$3,630**	(35)
Pre-tax profit margin	**18.4%**	25.9%	
Total full-time employees	**29,400**	31,000	
Total Financial Advisors	**16,090**	16,740	

(continued)

EXHIBIT 10—
continued

MERRILL LYNCH &
CO. SEGMENT
INFORMATION,
DECEMBER 31,
2008

For 2008, GWM's net revenues were $12.8 billion, down 9% from the prior-year, due to declines in transactional and origination revenues. GWM recorded $2.3 billion of pre-tax earnings from continuing operations, down 35% from the prior-year. The pre-tax profit margin was 18.4%, down from 25.9% in the prior-year period. Excluding the impact of the $155 million restructuring charge, GWM's pre-tax earnings were $2.5 billion, a decline of 31% from 2007. On the same basis, the pre-tax profit margin was 19.6%.

GWM's net revenues in 2007 were $14.0 billion, reflecting strong growth in both GPC's and GIM's businesses. GWM generated $3.6 billion of pre-tax earnings from continuing operations.

Global Private Client

GPC's 2008 net revenues were $12.1 billion, down 6% from the prior year, driven by lower transactional and origination revenues, resulting from reduced client and origination activity in a challenging market environment. Financial Advisor headcount was 16,090 at the end of 2008, a decrease of 650 FAs.

Fee-Based Revenues

GPC generated $6.2 billion of fee-based revenues in 2008, down 2% from 2007, reflecting lower asset levels in annuitized fee-based products resulting from market declines, partially offset by the inclusion of fee-based accounts from First Republic, which was acquired in September 2007.

The value of client assets in GWM accounts at year-end 2008 and 2007 were as follows:

(dollars in billions)	2008	2007
Assets in client accounts:		
U.S.	$1,125	$1,586
Non-U.S.	122	165
Total	$1,247	$1,751
Assets in Annuitized-Revenue Products	$466	$655

Total client assets in GWM accounts were $1.2 trillion, down from $1.8 trillion in 2007. Total net new money was negative $12 billion for 2008 and was adversely affected by client reaction to persistent volatility and significantly negative market movements during the year. GWM's net inflows of client assets into annuitized-revenue products were $11 billion for 2008. Assets in annuitized-revenue products ended 2008 at $466 billion, down from $655 billion in 2007. The decrease in total client assets and assets in annuitized-revenue products in GWM accounts during 2008 was primarily due to market depreciation.

Transactional and Origination Revenues

Transactional and origination revenues were $3.3 billion in 2008, down 15% from the prior-year due to lower client transaction and origination volumes amidst increasingly challenging market conditions.

Net Interest Profit and Related Hedges

Net interest profit (interest revenues less interest expenses) and related hedges include GPC's allocation of the interest spread earned in our banking subsidiaries for deposits, as well as interest earned, net of provisions for loan losses, on securities-based loans, mortgages, small- and middle-market business and other loans, corporate funding allocations, and the interest component of non-qualifying derivatives.

Other Revenues

For 2008, other revenues were down 31% to $288 million, primarily due to lower gains on sales of mortgages and markdowns on certain alternative investments.

(continued)

EXHIBIT 10—
continued

MERRILL LYNCH
& CO. SEGMENT
INFORMATION,
DECEMBER 31,
2008

Global Investment Management

GIM includes revenues from the creation and management of hedge fund and other alternative investment products for clients, as well as our share of net earnings from our ownership positions in other investment management companies, including BlackRock.

GIM's 2008 revenues were $669 million, down 40% from the year-ago period, primarily due to lower revenues from our investments in investment management companies.

EXHIBIT 11

MERRILL LYNCH
& CO. NOTE 3,
FAIR VALUE,
DECEMBER 31,
2008

Fair Value Measurements

Fair Value Hierarchy

As required by SFAS No. 157, when the inputs used to measure fair value fall within different levels of the hierarchy, the level within which the fair value measurement is categorized is based on the lowest level input that is significant to the fair value measurement in its entirety. For example, a Level 3 fair value measurement may include inputs that are observable (Levels 1 and 2) and unobservable (Level 3). Therefore gains and losses for such assets and liabilities categorized within the Level 3 table below may include changes in fair value that are attributable to both observable inputs (Levels 1 and 2) and unobservable inputs (Level 3). Further, the following tables do not take into consideration the effect of offsetting Level 1 and 2 financial instruments entered into by Merrill Lynch that economically hedge certain exposures to the Level 3 positions.

A review of fair value hierarchy classifications is conducted on a quarterly basis. Changes in the observability of valuation inputs may result in a reclassification for certain financial assets or liabilities. Level 3 gains and losses represent amounts incurred during the period in which the instrument was classified as Level 3. Reclassifications impacting Level 3 of the fair value hierarchy are reported as transfers in/out of the Level 3 category as of the beginning of the quarter in which the reclassifications occur.

Recurring Fair Value

The following tables present Merrill Lynch's fair value hierarchy for those assets and liabilities measured at fair value on a recurring basis as of December 26, 2008 and December 28, 2007, respectively.

(dollars in millions)	Fair Value Measurements on a Recurring Basis as of December 26, 2008				
	Level 1	Level 2	Level 3	Netting Adj[(1)]	Total
Assets:					
Securities segregated for regulatory purposes or deposited with clearing organizations	$1,421	$10,156	$—	—	$11,577
Receivables under resale agreements	—	62,146	—	—	62,146
Receivables under securities borrowed transactions	—	853	—	—	853
Trading assets, excluding derivative contracts	30,106	33,902	22,120	—	86,128
Derivative contracts	8,538	1,239,225	37,325	(1,195,611)	89,477
Investment securities	2,280	29,254	3,279	—	34,813
Securities received as collateral	9,430	2,228	—	—	11,658
Loans, notes and mortgages	—	690	359	—	1,049
Other assets[(2)]	—	8,046	—	—	8,046

(continued)

EXHIBIT 11—
continued

MERRILL LYNCH
& CO. NOTE 3,
FAIR VALUE,
DECEMBER 31,
2008

Liabilities:

Payables under repurchase agreements	$—	$32,910	$—	—	$32,910
Short-term borrowings	—	3,387	—	—	3,387
Trading liabilities, excluding derivative contracts	14,098	4,010	—	—	18,108
Derivative contracts	8,438	1,254,158	35,018	(1,226,251)	71,363
Obligation to return securities received as collateral	9,430	2,228	—	—	11,658
Long-term borrowings[3]	—	41,575	7,480	—	49,055
Other payables — interest and other[2]	10	741	—	(79)	672

(1) Represents counterparty and cash collateral netting.

(2) Primarily represents certain derivatives used for non-trading purposes.

(3) Includes bifurcated embedded derivatives carried at fair value.

Level 3 trading assets primarily include U.S. asset-backed collateralized debt obligations ("U.S. ABS CDOs") of $9.4 billion, corporate bonds and loans of $5.0 billion and auction rate securities of $3.9 billion.

Level 3 derivative contracts (assets) primarily relate to derivative positions on U.S. ABS CDOs of $5.8 billion, $23.6 billion of other credit derivatives that incorporate unobservable correlation, and $7.9 billion of equity, currency, interest rate and commodity derivatives that are long-dated and/or have unobservable correlation.

Level 3 investment securities primarily relate to certain private equity and principal investment positions of $2.6 billion.

Level 3 derivative contracts (liabilities) primarily relate to derivative positions on U.S. ABS CDOs of $6.1 billion, $22.3 billion of other credit derivatives that incorporate unobservable correlation, and $4.8 billion of equity derivatives that are long-dated and/or have unobservable correlation.

Level 3 long-term borrowings primarily relate to structured notes with embedded equity derivatives of $6.3 billion that are long-dated and/or have unobservable correlation.

	Fair Value Measurements on a Recurring Basis as of December 28, 2007				
(dollars in millions)	Level 1	Level 2	Level 3	Netting Adj[1]	Total
Assets:					
Securities segregated for regulatory purposes or deposited with clearing organizations	$1,478	$5,595	$84	$—	$7,157
Receivables under resale agreements	—	100,214	—	—	100,214
Trading assets, excluding derivative contracts	71,038	81,169	9,773	—	161,980
Derivative contracts	4,916	522,014	26,038	(480,279)	72,689
Investment securities	2,240	53,403	5,491	—	61,134
Securities received as collateral	42,451	2,794	—	—	45,245
Loans, notes and mortgages	—	1,145	63	—	1,208
Other assets[2]	7	1,739	—	(24)	1,722

(continued)

EXHIBIT 11—
continued

MERRILL LYNCH
& CO. NOTE 3,
FAIR VALUE,
DECEMBER 31,
2008

Liabilities:

Payables under repurchase agreements	$—	$89,733	$—	$—	$89,733
Trading liabilities, excluding derivative contracts	43,609	6,685	—	—	50,294
Derivative contracts	5,562	526,780	35,107	(494,155)	73,294
Obligation to return securities received as collateral	42,451	2,794	—	—	45,245
Long-term borrowings[3]	—	75,984	4,765	—	80,749
Other payables — interest and other[2]	2	287	—	(13)	276

Level 3 Assets and Liabilities as of December 28, 2007

Level 3 trading assets primarily include corporate bonds and loans of $5.4 billion and U.S. ABS CDOs of $2.4 billion, of which $1.0 billion was sub-prime related.

Level 3 derivative contracts (assets) primarily relate to derivative positions on U.S. ABS CDOs of $18.9 billion, of which $14.7 billion is sub-prime related, and $5.1 billion of equity derivatives that are long-dated and/or have unobservable correlation.

Level 3 investment securities primarily relate to certain private equity and principal investment positions of $4.0 billion, as well as U.S. ABS CDOs of $834 million that are accounted for as trading securities under SFAS No. 115.

Level 3 derivative contracts (liabilities) primarily relate to derivative positions on U.S. ABS CDOs of $25.1 billion, of which $23.9 billion relates to sub-prime, and $8.3 billion of equity derivatives that are long-dated and/or have unobservable correlation.

Level 3 long-term borrowings primarily relate to structured notes with embedded long-dated equity and currency derivatives.

The following tables provide a summary of changes in fair value of Merrill Lynch's Level 3 financial assets and liabilities for the years-ended December 26, 2008 and December 28, 2007, respectively.

		Level 3 Financial Assets and Liabilities Year Ended December 26, 2007						
		Total Realized and Unrealized Gains or (Losses) Included in Income			Total Realized and Unrealized Gains or (Losses) Included in Income	Purchases, Issuances and		
(dollars in millions)	Beginning Balance	Principal Transactions	Other Revenue	Interest		Settlements	Transfers In (Out)	Ending Balance
Assets:								
Securities segregated for regulatory purposes or deposited with clearing organizations	$84	$—	$—	$1	$1	$(79)	$(6)	$—
Trading assets	9,773	(5,460)	—	122	(5,338)	10,114	7,571	22,120
Derivative contracts, net	(9,069)	(11,955)	—	5	(11,950)	26,187	(2,861)	2,307
Investment securities	5,491	(1,021)	(1,535)	—	(2,556)	426	(82)	3,279
Loans, notes and mortgages	63	—	(105)	(8)	(113)	399	10	359
Liabilities:								
Long-term borrowings	$4,765	$5,582	$285	$—	$5,867	$1,198	$7,384	$7,480

(continued)

EXHIBIT 11—
continued

MERRILL LYNCH
& CO. NOTE 3,
FAIR VALUE,
DECEMBER 31,
2008

Net losses in principal transactions for 2008 were due primarily to losses of $15.5 billion related to U.S. ABS CDOs and the termination and potential settlement of related hedges with monoline guarantor counterparties, of which $12.6 billion was realized as a result of the sale of these assets to Lone Star during the third quarter. These losses were partially offset by $4.8 billion in gains related to long-term borrowings with equity and commodity related embedded derivatives.

The increase in Level 3 trading assets and net derivative contracts for the year-ended December 26, 2008 due to purchases, issuances and settlements is primarily attributable to the recording of assets for which the exposure was previously recognized as derivative liabilities (total return swaps) at December 28, 2007. During 2008, Merrill Lynch recorded certain of these trading assets as a result of consolidating certain SPEs that held the underlying assets on which the total return swaps were referenced. The increase in trading assets was partially offset by the sale of U.S. ABS CDO assets to Lone Star during the third quarter of 2008. As a result of the Lone Star transaction, certain total return swaps that were in a liability position were terminated, resulting in an increase in purchases, issuances and settlements for derivative contracts, net.

The Level 3 net transfers in for trading assets primarily relates to decreased observability of inputs on certain corporate bonds and loans. The net transfers on Level 3 derivative contracts were primarily due to the impact of counterparty credit valuation adjustments for U.S. ABS CDO positions as well as other net credit derivative contracts that incorporate unobservable correlation and that were in a net liability position at December 26, 2008. The Level 3 net transfers in for long-term borrowings were primarily due to decreased observability of inputs on certain long-dated equity linked notes.

The loss in other revenue is due to net losses of $1.0 billion on private equity investments in quarter four, 2008.

	Level 3 Financial Assets and Liabilities Year Ended December 28, 2007							
		Total Realized and Unrealized Gains or (Losses) Included in Income			Total Realized and Unrealized Gains or (Losses) Included in Income	Purchases, Issuances and Settlements	Transfers In (Out)	Ending Balance
(dollars in millions)	Beginning Balance	Principal Transactions	Other Revenue	Interest				
Assets:								
Securities segregated for regulatory purposes or deposited with clearing organizations	$—	$(5)	$—	$1	$(4)	$—	$88	$84
Trading assets	2,021	(4,180)	—	46	(4,134)	2,945	8,941	9,773
Derivative contracts, net	(2,030)	(7,687)	4	25	(7,658)	465	154	(9,069)
Investment securities	5,117	(2,412)	518	8	(1,886)	3,000	(740)	5,491
Loans, notes and mortgages	7	—	(18)	—	(18)	(5)	79	63
Liabilities:								
Long-term borrowings	$—	$524	$7	$—	$531	$2,203	$3,093	$4,765

The following tables provide the portion of gains or losses included in income for the years ended December 26, 2008, and December 28, 2007, attributable to unrealized gains or losses relating to those Level 3 assets and liabilities still held at December 26, 2008, and December 28, 2007, respectively.

(continued)

EXHIBIT 11—
continued

MERRILL LYNCH
& CO. NOTE 3,
FAIR VALUE,
DECEMBER 31,
2008

| | Unrealized Gains or (Losses) for Level 3 Assets and Liabilities Still Held | | | | | | | |
| | Year Ended December 26, 2008 | | | | Year Ended December 28, 2007 | | | |
(dollars in millions)	Principal Transactions	Other Revenue	Interest	Total	Principal Transactions	Other Revenue	Interest	Total
Assets:								
Securities segregated for regulatory purposes or deposited with clearing organizations	$—	$—	$1	$1	$(5)	$—	$1	$(4)
Trading assets	(4,945)	—	83	(4,862)	(4,205)	—	4	(4,201)
Derivative contracts, net	114	—	5	119	(7,826)	(2)	25	(7,803)
Investment securities	(964)	(1,523)	—	(2,487)	(2,412)	428	8	(1,976)
Loans, notes and mortgages	—	(94)	(8)	(102)	—	1	—	1
Liabilities:								
Long-term borrowings	$5,221	$285	$—	$5,506	$524	$7	$—	$531

Net unrealized losses in principal transactions for the year-ended December 26, 2008 were primarily due to approximately $2.9 billion of net losses on U.S. ABS CDO related assets and liabilities. These losses were largely offset by $4.8 billion of gains on long-term borrowings with equity and commodity related embedded derivatives.

The loss in other revenue is primarily related to net losses of $1.0 billion on private equity investments primarily during the fourth quarter of 2008.

Non-recurring Fair Value

Certain assets and liabilities are measured at fair value on a non-recurring basis and are not included in the tables above. These assets and liabilities primarily include loans and loan commitments held for sale and reported at lower of cost or fair value and loans held for investment that were initially measured at cost and have been written down to fair value as a result of an impairment. The following table shows the fair value hierarchy for those assets and liabilities measured at fair value on a non-recurring basis as of December 26, 2008 and December 28, 2007, respectively.

| | Non-Recurring Basis as of December 26, 2008 | | | | Losses Year Ended December 26, 2008 |
(dollars in millions)	Level 1	Level 2	Level 3	Total	
Assets:					
Loans, notes and mortgages	$—	$4,386	$6,727	$11,113	$(6,555)
Goodwill	—	—	—	—	(2,300)
Liabilities:					
Other liabilities	$—	1,258	$67	$1,325	$(653)

| | Non-Recurring Basis as of December 28, 2007 | | | | Losses Year Ended December 28, 2007 |
(dollars in millions)	Level 1	Level 2	Level 3	Total	
Assets:					
Loans, notes and mortgages	$—	$32,594	$7,157	$39,751	$(1,304)
Liabilities:					
Other liabilities	$—	$666	$—	$666	$(502)

Loans, notes, and mortgages include held for sale loans that are carried at the lower of cost or fair value and for which the fair value was below the cost basis at December 26, 2008, and/or

(continued)

EXHIBIT 11—
continued

MERRILL LYNCH
& CO. NOTE 3,
FAIR VALUE,
DECEMBER 31,
2008

December 28, 2007. It also includes certain impaired held for investment loans where an allowance for loan losses has been calculated based upon the fair value of the loans or collateral. Level 3 assets as of December 26, 2008, primarily relate to U.K. and other European residential and commercial real estate loans of $4.6 billion that are classified as held for sale where there continues to be significant illiquidity in the loan trading and securitization markets. The fair value of Level 3 loans was calculated primarily by a fundamental cash flow valuation analysis. This cash flow analysis includes cumulative loss and prepayment assumptions derived from multiple inputs including mortgage remittance reports, property prices and other market data. In addition, independent third party bids received on loans are also considered for valuation purposes. Level 3 assets as of December 28, 2007, primarily related to residential and commercial real estate loans that are classified as held for sale in the U.K. of $4.1 billion.

Goodwill with a carrying value of $2.3 billion was written down in its entirety, resulting in a related $2.3 billion impairment charge. This impairment charge is primarily related to the Fixed Income, Currencies and Commodities ("FICC") reporting unit within the GMI business segment. The fair value was estimated by considering Merrill Lynch's market capitalization as determined by the Bank of America acquisition price, price-to-earnings and price-to-book multiples, and discounted cash flow analyses.

Other liabilities include amounts recorded for loan commitments at lower of cost or fair value where the funded loan will be held for sale, particularly leveraged loan commitments in the U.S.

Fair Value Option

SFAS No. 159 provides a fair value option election that allows companies to irrevocably elect fair value as the initial and subsequent measurement attribute for certain financial assets and liabilities. Changes in fair value for assets and liabilities for which the election is made will be recognized in earnings as they occur. SFAS No. 159 permits the fair value option election on an instrument by instrument basis at initial recognition of an asset or liability or upon an event that gives rise to a new basis of accounting for that instrument. As discussed above, certain of Merrill Lynch's financial instruments are required to be accounted for at fair value under SFAS No. 115 and SFAS No. 133, as well as industry level guidance. For certain financial instruments that are not accounted for at fair value under other applicable accounting guidance, the fair value option has been elected.

The following tables provide information about where in the Consolidated Statements of (Loss)/Earnings changes in fair values of assets and liabilities, for which the fair value option has been elected, are included for the years ended December 26, 2008 and December 28, 2007, respectively.

	Changes in Fair Value for the Year Ended December 26, 2008, for Items Measured at Fair Value Pursuant to Fair Value Option			Changes in Fair Value for the Year Ended December 28, 2007, for Items Measured at Fair Value Pursuant to Fair Value Option		
(dollars in millions)	Gains/ (losses) Principal Transactions	Gains/ (losses) Other Revenues	Total Changes in Fair Value	Gains/ (losses) Principal Transactions	Gains Other Revenues	Total Changes in Fair Value
Assets:						
Receivables under resale agreements	$190	$—	$190	$124	$—	$124
Investment securities	(1,637)	(923)	(2,560)	234	43	277
Loans, notes and mortgages	(87)	(11)	(98)	(2)	73	71
Liabilities:						
Payables under repurchase agreements	$(54)	$—	$(54)	$(7)	$—	$(7)
Short-term borrowings	(438)	—	(438)	—	—	—
Long-term borrowings[1]	15,938	1,709	17,647	3,857	1,182	5,039

(1) Other revenues primarily represent fair value changes on non-recourse long-term borrowings issued by consolidated SPEs.

(continued)

EXHIBIT 11—
continued

MERRILL LYNCH
& CO. NOTE 3,
FAIR VALUE,
DECEMBER 31,
2008

Resale and repurchase agreements:

Merrill Lynch elected the fair value option on a prospective basis for certain resale and repurchase agreements. The fair value option election was made based on the tenor of the resale and repurchase agreements, which reflects the magnitude of the interest rate risk. The majority of resale and repurchase agreements collateralized by U.S. government securities were excluded from the fair value option election as these contracts are generally short-dated and therefore the interest rate risk is not considered significant. Amounts loaned under resale agreements require collateral with a market value equal to or in excess of the principal amount loaned resulting in minimal credit risk for such transactions.

Securities borrowed transactions:

Merrill Lynch elected the fair value option for certain Japanese government bond borrowings for Q2 2008.

Investment securities:

At December 26, 2008, investment securities primarily represented non-marketable convertible preferred shares for which Merrill Lynch has economically hedged a majority of the position with derivatives.

Loans, notes and mortgages:

Merrill Lynch elected the fair value option for automobile and certain corporate loans because the loans are risk managed on a fair value basis. The change in the fair value of loans, notes, and mortgages for which the fair value option was elected that was attributable to changes in borrower-specific credit risk was $77 million for the year ended December 26, 2008, and was not material for the year ended December 28, 2007.

Short-term and long-term borrowings:

Merrill Lynch elected the fair value option for certain short-term and long-term borrowings that are risk managed on a fair value basis, including structured notes, and for which hedge accounting under SFAS No. 133 had been difficult to obtain. The majority of the fair value changes on long-term borrowings is from structured notes with coupon or repayment terms that are linked to the performance of debt and equity securities, indices, currencies or commodities. The majority of gains in 2008 and 2007 are offset by losses on derivatives that economically hedge these borrowings and that are accounted for at fair value under SFAS No. 133. *The changes in the fair value of liabilities for which the fair value option was elected that was attributable to changes in Merrill Lynch credit spreads were estimated gains of $5.1 billion for the year ended December 26, 2008.* The changes in the fair value of liabilities for which the fair value option was elected that were attributable to changes in Merrill Lynch credit spreads were estimated gains of $2.0 billion for the year ended December 28, 2007. Changes in Merrill Lynch specific credit risk are derived by isolating fair value changes due to changes in Merrill Lynch's credit spreads as observed in the secondary cash market.

The following tables present the difference between fair values and the aggregate contractual principal amounts of receivables under resale agreements, receivables under securities borrowed transactions, loans, notes, and mortgages and long-term borrowings for which the fair value option has been elected as of December 26, 2008, and December 28, 2007, respectively.

(continued)

EXHIBIT 11—
continued

MERRILL LYNCH
& CO. NOTE 3,
FAIR VALUE,
DECEMBER 31,
2008

(dollars in millions)	Fair Value December 26, 2008	Principal Due Upon Maturity	Difference
Assets:			
Receivables under resale agreements	$62,146	$61,466	$680
Receivables under securities borrowed transactions	853	853	—
Loans, notes and mortgages	979	1,326	(347)
Liabilities:			
Long-term borrowings[1]	$49,521	$62,244	$(12,723)

(1) The majority of the difference relates to the impact of the widening of Merrill Lynch's credit spreads, the change in fair value of non-recourse debt, and zero coupon notes issued at a substantial discount from the principal amount.

(dollars in millions)	Fair Value December 28, 2007	Principal Due Upon Maturity	Difference
Assets:			
Receivables under resale agreements	$100,214	$100,090	$124
Loans, notes and mortgages[1]	1,149	1,355	(206)
Liabilities:			
Long-term borrowings[2]	$76,334	$81,681	$(5,347)

SECTION 6

VALUATION

CASE 6.1

Anheuser-Busch and the 2008 Acquisition Bid

George Schneider established the Bavarian Brewery in St. Louis, Missouri, in 1852. Eberhard Anheuser acquired the brewery in 1860 and renamed it E. Anheuser & Co. A year later Adolphus Busch married Mr. Anheuser's daughter, and by 1864 Mr. Busch had joined his father-in-law's brewery.[1] In 1876, the firm introduced Budweiser beer, and in 1879 changed the company name to Anheuser-Busch Brewing Association. The following year Mr. Anheuser died, and Adolphus Busch became president. As the firm grew, it introduced Michelob in 1896, its premium-priced beer. When Adolphus Busch died in 1913, his son, August A. Busch Sr., became president.[2]

In 1920, the National Prohibition Act against alcohol was passed, and Anheuser-Busch entered a wide range of markets, including ice cream, barley malt syrup, ginger ale, root beer, corn syrup, truck and bus bodies, refrigerated cabinets, and nonalcoholic Budweiser. When Prohibition ended in 1933, Anheuser-Busch resumed beer production and introduced the Budweiser Clydesdale horses.[3]

August A. Busch Sr. died in 1934, and his son, Adolphus Busch III, became president; when he died in 1946, August A. Busch Jr. became president. His son, August A. Busch III, became president in 1974, and in 2002 Patrick Stokes was named president and CEO. In 2006, when August A. Busch III's son 42-year-old August A. Busch IV had gained enough experience, he became president and CEO.[4]

By 2006, Anheuser-Busch had long been the largest U.S. brewing company, with a market share of about 50%. Anheuser-Busch, Budweiser, Michelob, and the Clydesdales were among the best-known brand names in the United States. Anheuser-Busch had long been the largest Super Bowl advertiser, and its ads were among the most popular, particularly those involving the Clydesdales. August A. Busch III and his son, August A. Busch IV, were prominently featured in many ads that emphasized Anheuser-Busch's long family tradition. Although Anheuser-Busch was a publicly traded firm, it projected an image of family ownership.

Anheuser-Busch also developed one of the strongest distributor networks of any industry in the world. Alcohol sales are regulated by each state in the United States, but some version of a three-tier distribution is used in most states. Typically, a brewer (or winemaker or alcohol distiller) must sell to a distributor, who then sells to retail establishments such as liquor stores, supermarkets, bars, and restaurants. In some states, the state acts as the distributor; in other states, the state is both the distributor and retailer. However, most states make exceptions for brew pubs, which are both breweries and retail establishments.

Anheuser-Busch was by far the largest liquor producer in the United States, and its distributors were among the wealthiest and most prominent businessmen and businesswomen in their region. Many were personal friends of August A. Busch II,

1. Historical Timeline, Anheuser-Busch Web site, http://www.anheuser-busch.com/History.html.
2. Ibid.
3. Ibid.
4. Ibid.

August A. Busch III, or August A. Busch IV, and nearly all of them were active in charitable, civic, and political activities.

For example, Cindy McCain, wife of U.S. Senator and former presidential candidate John S. McCain III, is chair of the board and controlling shareholder of Hensley Beverage Company, the Phoenix-based Anheuser-Busch distributor, which was started by her father.[5] She is widely known for civic and charitable activities and is said to have a net worth of between $100 and $200 million. Yusef Jackson, his brother Jonathan Jackson, and a third partner own a Chicago Anheuser-Busch Distributorship. Yusef and Jonathan Jackson are sons of former presidential candidate Rev. Jesse Jackson and brothers of U.S. Representative Jesse Jackson Jr.

Anheuser-Busch, 2008

Anheuser-Busch was the most prominent firm in St. Louis and Missouri and the Busch family was easily the most prominent family there as well. The firm was almost an extension of the family. The firm's relationship with its distributors and customers had been established through some of the most innovative and memorable advertising over the past 50 years. The firm offered tours of its breweries that ended with free beer for adults and free soft drinks for children. Anheuser-Busch also leased Grant's Farm, a large wildlife preserve near St. Louis, from the Busch family. Grant's Farm was open to the public at no charge and Grant's Farm tours also ended with free Anheuser-Busch beverages for adults and soft drinks for children.

In 1953, Anheuser-Busch acquired the St. Louis Cardinals. The Cardinals were intertwined with Anheuser-Busch advertising for many years and were the second-most successful major league baseball team during the period they were owned by Anheuser-Busch (after the New York Yankees). However, company executives grew concerned that fans of opposing teams might stop buying Anheuser-Busch products, so in 1996 the firm sold the Cardinals. Anheuser-Busch also expanded into other areas, such as Sea World and Busch Gardens, in a separately operated entertainment division.

Although the entertainment division operated separately from the brewery division, Sea World and Busch Gardens had hospitality centers that offered free beer samples. Anheuser-Busch was widely known as an attractive employer. Salaries were well above average, layoffs were extremely rare, turnover was low, and employees received two free cases of beer each month. By 2008, Anheuser-Busch had been run by the founding family for 148 years, and its civic and charitable activities, strong distributor relations, and excellent employee relations were far more common to a family-controlled firm than one controlled by the public. However, by 1994 Anheuser-Busch had 265,804,242 common voting shares outstanding.[6] August A. Busch III owned 1,587,506 shares (0.6%); James B. Orthwein, a company director and great-grandson of Adolphus Busch, owned 1,301,703 shares (0.5%).[7] Various other members of the Busch family were beneficiaries of various trusts that owned shares, but by 2007 Busch family members probably owned no more than 4% of the firm and they did not always act as a group.

---

5. About Hensley, Hensley & Co. Phoenix/Henley Beverage Company Web site, http://www.abwholesaler.com/hensley/AboutUs/AboutUs.

6. Anheuser-Busch 1993 10-K, p. 1.

7. Anheuser-Busch 19993 Proxy Statement, p. 10.

Consolidation in the Brewing Industry

In the 1800s, most European countries and the United States had hundreds or thousands of breweries serving small local regions. As transportation became less expensive and more reliable, smaller breweries were acquired or went out of business, particularly in the United States, which lacked breweries with long histories and unique flavors (by the 1800s, many European breweries had been in continuous operation for hundreds of years). By 1980, the U.S. brewing industry consisted of a few very large breweries (Anheuser-Busch, Millers Brewing Company, and Schlitz Brewing Company), 10–20 regional breweries, and 60–70 local breweries.[8]

In 1985, Sam Adams Brewing Company began selling beer in Boston and it was named the best beer in the United States. That started a new tradition of local breweries, but most are small and some are no more than one- or two-location brew pubs. As regional brands disappeared, the industry became dominated by large breweries; by 2000, Anheuser-Busch was easily the world's largest brewery.

Beginning in 2000, however, with the exception of Anheuser-Busch, the worldwide brewing industry began to consolidate. Firms such as AmBev (Brazil), Interbrew (Belgium), Heineken (Germany), SAB (South African Brewing, South Africa), Carlsberg (Denmark), S&N (Scottish & Newcastle, Scotland, United Kingdom) were involved in a series of increasingly larger mergers. By 2008, InBev (Belgian, but controlled by Brazilians) was the world's largest brewer; SABMiller was second; Anheuser-Busch was third; and Heineken was fourth. Exhibit 1 includes a list of significant brewery acquisitions from 2000 to 2005.[9]

Although Anheuser-Busch acquired a few small brands, such as Rolling Rock from InBev in 2006, Anheuser-Busch primarily acquired noncontrolling equity interests in strong national breweries such as Grupo Modelo S.A. (Corona, Mexico) and Tsingtao (China).

InBev's Unsolicited Cash Bid for Anheuser-Busch

On June 12, 2008, Anheuser-Busch confirmed that InBev had made an unsolicited $46.3 billion ($65 per share) bid for Anheuser-Busch. A Bloomberg article speculated that "InBev's acquisition strategy, which relies on cutting costs, might clash with the culture of Anheuser-Busch, known for close relationships with distributors and expensive marketing. After taking over as president of InBev's Labatt Brewing Co. in 2004, Brito (InBev's Carlos Brito) fired staff and closed a brewery."[10] On June 20, 2008, Anheuser-Busch announced that Carlos Fernandez G., chairman and CEO of Mexican brewer Grupo Modelo, resigned immediately as a member of the board of directors of Anheuser-Busch, apparently in anticipation of a fight for control of the company.[11]

---

8. Beer Info, "The history of Beer and Brewing in the United States." http://www.beerinfo.com/index. php/pages/beerhistory.html.

9. Heyder, Matthias, Oliver Ebneth, and Ludwig Theuvsen, Financial Market Reactions to International Mergers & Acquisitions in the Brewing Industry: An Event Study Analysis, 47th Annual Conference of the GEWISOLA (German Association of Agricultural Economists), Freising/Weihenstephan, Germany, September 26–28, 2007, p. 7.

10. Stanford, Duan D., "InBev offers $46.3 billion in cash for Anheuser-Busch," Bloomberg.com, June 12, 2008. http://www.bloomberg.com/apps/news?pid=20601087&refer=home&sid=aYMWoV9Yp9g8.

11. Press release, SEC Form 8-K, Exhibit 99.1, June 20, 2008. http://www.sec.gov/Archives/edgar/data/310569/000106880008000254/ex99.htm.

On June 26, 2008, Anheuser-Busch issued a press release calling the InBev bid inadequate.[12] The following day, June 27, 2008, Anheuser Busch issued a series of proxy statements, one of which included a detailed PowerPoint-like strategic plan in support of the company's position that the InBev bid was too low.[13]

That strategic plan stated that Anheuser-Busch had more than $1 billion in planned savings, the majority of which would occur in 2008 and 2009, although it was unclear whether those were one-time costs or annual cost savings. The plan also stated that Anheuser-Busch had already revised its employee incentive programs, would offer an early retirement program in the third quarter of 2008 with a targeted reduction in employment of 10–15%, and would have zero overhead growth.[14]

The strategic plan also emphasized Anheuser-Busch's partnerships with leading brands in other countries. Those arrangements often gave Anheuser-Busch exclusive rights to sell a partner's beer in the United States and required that partner to sell Anheuser-Busch in its home country.[15] Many analysts considered that strategy to be far too cautious to compete with Anheuser-Busch's far more aggressive competitors.

The strategic plan concluded with an evaluation of InBev's offer of $65 per share, which InBev claimed was at 12 times earnings before interest, taxes, depreciation, and amortization (EBITDA). Anheuser-Busch argued that based on 2007 actual results the offer was at 11.5 times EBITDA and only 11.5 times 2008 estimated EBITDA. The plan contrasted that offer with recent acquisitions in the consumer goods markets, such as 12.9 times EBITDA for Heineken's acquisition of S&N, 15.4 for Pepsi's acquisition of Quaker, 15.7 for Nestlé's acquisition of Purina, and 18.4 for Mars's acquisition of Wrigley.[16]

An academic article on consolidation in the brewing industry found that acquisitions at above 10.0 times EBITDA usually resulted in a stock price decline for the acquirer, whereas acquisitions below 10.0 times EBITDA usually resulted in a stock price increase for the acquirer.[17]

After numerous press releases by InBev and Anheuser-Busch, InBev and Anheuser-Busch issued a joint press release announcing a merger on July 14, 2008. InBev had increased its offer to $70 per share in cash, or $52 billion, and Anheuser-Busch's board of directors had unanimously approved the offer.[18]

Valuation of Anheuser-Busch

Analysts had varying views of the acquisition. Many believed the price was too high, particularly for an all-cash bid. Exhibits 2–4 show Anheuser-Busch's 2007 income statements, balance sheets, and statements of cash flows. From Exhibit 2, Anheuser-Busch's 2007 income statement, both revenues and net income grew gradually but steadily from 2005 to 2007. Net income was slightly above $2.1 billion in 2001 and was nearly $2.0 billion in 2006. Many analysts expected that InBev would be able to increase net income after tax by at least $700 million through aggressive cost cutting.

12. Press release, SEC Form 8-K, Exhibit 99.1, June 26, 2008. http://www.sec.gov/Archives/edgar/data/310569/000134100408001501/ex99-1.htm.

13. Strategic Plan, Def A14A, Exhibit 99.3 dated June 27, 2008. http://www.sec.gov/Archives/edgar/data/310569/000095013708008937/c27852exv99w3.htm.

14. Ibid., pp. 15–26.

15. Ibid., pp. 30–35.

16. Ibid., pp. 47–48.

17. Heyder, Matthias, et al.

18. Press Release, Form 8-K, Exhibit 99.2, July 14, 2008, Leuven, Belgium, and July 13, 2008, St. Louis, Missouri. http://www.sec.gov/Archives/edgar/data/310569/000095013708009320/c30929exv99.htm.

From Exhibit 3, Anheuser-Busch's 2007 balance sheet, Anheuser-Busch reported $4.019 billion of investments in affiliated companies. Those were primarily for the firm's investments in Grupo Modelo and Tsingtao. The following section from Anheuser-Busch's Management Discussion and Analysis section of its 2007 10-K, and a portion of Note 2 to that 10-K, explain the Grupo Modelo Investment's fair value:

Other Matters

Fair value of modelo investment

The economic benefit of the company's Modelo investment can be measured in two ways: through equity income, which represents Anheuser-Busch's pro rata share in the net earnings of Modelo; and by the excess of the fair market value of the investment over its cost. The excess of fair market value over the company's cost, based on Grupo Modelo's closing stock price on the Mexican stock exchange (Bolsa) at December 31, 2007, was $8.7 billion. Although this amount is appropriately not reflected in the company's income statement or balance sheet, it represents economic value to Anheuser-Busch and its shareholders.

2. International Equity Investments

Grupo modelo

Anheuser-Busch owns a 35.12% direct interest in Grupo Modelo, S.A.B. de C.V. (Modelo), Mexico's largest brewer and producer of the Corona brand, and a 23.25% direct interest in Modelo's operating subsidiary Diblo, S.A. de C.V. (Diblo). The company's direct investments in Modelo and Diblo give Anheuser-Busch an effective (direct and indirect) 50.2% equity interest in Diblo. Anheuser-Busch holds nine of 19 positions on Modelo's board of directors (with the Controlling Shareholders Trust holding the other 10 positions) and also has membership on the audit committee. Anheuser-Busch does not have voting or other effective control of either Diblo or Modelo and consequently accounts for its investments using the equity method. The total cost of the company's investments was $1.6 billion. The carrying values of the Modelo investment were $3.6 billion and $3.4 billion, respectively, at December 31, 2007 and 2006. Included in the carrying amounts of the Modelo investment is goodwill of $540.1 million and $536.6 million, respectively. Changes in goodwill during 2007 and 2006 are primarily due to changes in exchange rates between the U.S. dollar and Mexican peso.

Analysts expected that InBev might sell Anheuser-Busch's investments in Grupo Modelo and Tsingtao to help pay for the acquisition. They also speculated that InBev might sell Anheuser-Busch's entertainment division. Exhibit 6 provides information on Anheuser-Busch's business segments, although it was unclear what the entertainment segment might sell for.

The balance sheets also show that Anheuser-Busch had $1.002 billion of underfunded retiree benefit costs, which was less than the $1.192 billion underfunding in 2006. Anheuser-Busch's pension plan was underfunded by $184.3 million in 2007 and $465.8 million in 2006; nearly all of the $1.002 billion retiree benefit underfunding for 2007 was from the firm's retiree health-benefit fund, which had no assets. The following is the firm's explanation of that obligation from Note 5 to its 2007 10-K:

The following table details the components of the company's obligation for its single-employer defined benefit retirement health care and life insurance plans as of December 31 (in millions). As of December 31, 2007 and 2006, respectively, $69.6 million and $64.3 million of the company's obligation was classified as current. Retirement health care and insurance benefits obligations are unfunded; therefore no assets are associated with the plans.

	2007	2006
Benefit obligation, beginning of year	$791.8	$654.3
Service cost	26.8	24.3
Interest cost	45.3	36.9
Actuarial loss	29.5	140.2
Plan amendments	0.3	—
Benefits paid	(71.7)	(68.7)
Plan participants' contributions	2.6	2.4
Medicare Part D subsidy	2.6	2.4
Benefit obligation, end of year	$827.2	$791.8

From Exhibit 4, Anheuser Busch's 2007 statements of cash flow, the firm reported stock repurchases of $620.4 million in 2005, $745.9 million in 2006, and $2.707 billion in 2007. The firm also reported that it received $161.4 million in 2005, $143.5 million in 2006, and $304.8 million from the sale of stock through employee stock purchase and savings plans, and through the exercise of employee stock options. Exhibit 6 provides selected information on Anheuser-Busch's outstanding employee stock options, which almost certainly vest and are exercisable immediately upon change of control, such as the pending InBev acquisition.

On November 12, 2008, Anheuser-Busch issued a press release announcing that a majority of shares voted to approve the InBev acquisition at a price of $70 per share in cash.[19] On November 18, 2008, InBev issued a press release announcing it completed its acquisition of Anheuser-Busch for a price of US$70 per share in cash for an aggregate of US$52 billion. The press release also announced that the firm had changed its name to Anheuser-Busch InBev.[20]

Required

1. Was the $52 billion purchase price too high? Explain.

2. How did the value of Anheuser-Busch's equity investments influence your answer to 1? Explain.

3. How did the value of Anheuser-Busch's entertainment division influence your answer to 1? Explain.

4. Did the unfunded retiree health-care liability influence your answer to 1? Explain.

5. Did the outstanding employee stock options influence your answer to 1? Explain.

6. Which assets could InBev sell to help pay for the acquisition? Estimate the cash it could receive for the sale of those assets.

7. Is Anheuser-Busch's explanation of its Grupo Modelo investment clear? Explain.

---

19. Press Release, Form 8-K, Exhibit 99.1, dated November 12, 2008. http://www.sec.gov/Archives/edgar/data/310569/000095013708013648/c47620exv99w1.htm

20. Press Release dated November 18, 2008: Form 8-K, Exhibit 99.1 filed November 24, 2008. http://www.sec.gov/Archives/edgar/data/310569/000095013708013967/c47821exv99w1.htm.

EXHIBIT 1

CONSOLIDATION
IN THE BREWING
INDUSTRY

Date	Acquirer	Target	EBITDA Multiple
20-Mar-00	S&N	Kronenbourg	9.9
3-Nov-00	Carlsberg	Feldschlösschen	8.6
11-Feb-01	Heineken	Schörghuber	9.1
25-May-01	Interbrew	Bass	9.7
13-Jul-01	Interbrew	Diebels	8.3
6-Aug-01	Interbrew	Becks	13.0
29-Nov-01	SAB	BevCo	6.5
1-Feb-02	Heineken	Bravo	9.7
14-Feb-02	S&N	Hartwall	10.1
18-Mar-02	Heineken	Molson Brazil	13.7
30-May-02	SAB	Miller	9.1
5-Jun-02	Heineken	Karlsberg	10.8
12-Sep-02	Heineken	Al Ahram	8.0
15-Nov-02	Interbrew	Gilde	8.6
14-Jan-03	Heineken	CCU	11.3
28-Apr-03	S&N	Bulmer	9.8
2-May-03	Heineken	BBAG	10.2
13-May-03	S&N	Centralcer	11.4
13-May-03	SABMiller	Peroni	12.6
8-Sep-03	Interbrew	Lion	11.4
11-Sep-03	Interbrew	Apatinska Pivara	6.3
18-Sep-03	Interbrew	Spaten	9.9
7-Jan-04	Interbrew	Oriental Brewery	10.7
20-Jan-04	Carlsberg	Holsten	9.1
19-Feb-04	Carlsberg	Orkla	8.6
3-Mar-04	Interbrew	Ambev	11.5
12-Aug-04	Interbrew	SunInterbrew	11.0
16-Sep-04	SABMiller	Lion Nathan China	10.3
3-Jan-05	InBev	SunInterbrew	8.8
19-Jul-05	SABMiller	Bavaria	10.0
16-Aug-05	Heineken	Taranov	11.8
	Average		10.0

From: Heyder, Matthias, Oliver Ebneth, and Ludwig Theuvsen, Financial Market Reactions to International Mergers & Acquisitions in the Brewing Industry: An Event Study Analysis, 47th Annual Conference of the GEWISOLA (German Association of Agricultural Economists), Freising/Weihenstephan, Germany, September 26–28, 2007, p. 7.

EXHIBIT 2

ANHEUSER-BUSCH
STATEMENTS OF
INCOME

Year ended December 31 (in millions, except per share)	2007	2006	2005
Gross sales	$18,988.7	$17,957.8	$17,253.5
Excise taxes	(2,303.0)	(2,240.7)	(2,217.8)
Net sales	16,685.7	15,717.1	15,035.7
Cost of sales	(10,836.1)	(10,165.0)	(9,606.3)
Gross profit	5,849.6	5,552.1	5,429.4
Marketing, distribution and administrative expenses	(2,982.1)	(2,832.5)	(2,837.5)
Gain on sale of distribution rights	26.5	—	—
Litigation settlement	—	—	(105.0)
Operating income	2,894.0	2,719.6	2,486.9
Interest expense	(484.4)	(451.3)	(454.5)
Interest capitalized	17.4	17.6	19.9
Interest income	3.9	1.8	2.4
Other income/(expense), net	(8.2)	(10.8)	2.7
Income before income taxes	2,422.7	2,276.9	2,057.4
Provision for income taxes	(969.8)	(900.5)	(811.1)
Equity income, net of tax	662.4	588.8	498.1
Net income	$2,115.3	$1,965.2	$1,744.4

The footnotes . . . of this report are an integral component of the company's consolidated financial statements.

EXHIBIT 3

ANHEUSER-BUSCH
BALANCE SHEETS

Year ended December 31 (in millions, except per share)	2007	2006
Assets		
Current Assets		
Cash	$283.2	$219.2
Accounts receivable	805.2	720.2
Inventories	723.5	694.9
Other current assets	212.6	195.2
Total current assets	2,024.5	1,829.5
Investments in affiliated companies	4,019.5	3,680.3
Plant and equipment, net	8,833.5	8,916.1
Intangible assets, including goodwill of $1,134.6 and $1,077.8, respectively	1,547.9	1,367.2
Other assets	729.6	584.1
Total Assets	$17,155.0	$16,377.2

EXHIBIT 3—
continued

ANHEUSER-BUSCH
BALANCE SHEETS

Liabilities and Shareholders Equity

Current Liabilities

Accounts payable	**$1,464.5**	$1,426.3
Accrued salaries, wages and benefits	**374.3**	342.8
Accrued taxes	**106.2**	133.9
Accrued interest	**136.4**	124.2
Other current liabilities	**222.4**	218.9
Total current liabilities	**2,303.8**	2,246.1
Retirement benefits	**1,002.5**	1,191.5
Debt	**9,140.3**	7,653.5
Deferred income taxes	**1,314.6**	1,194.5
Other long-term liabilities	**242.2**	152.9
Shareholders Equity		
Common stock, $1.00 par value, authorized 1.6 billion shares	**1,482.5**	1,473.7
Capital in excess of par value	**3,382.1**	2,962.5
Retained earnings	**17,923.9**	16,741.0
Treasury stock, at cost	**(18,714.7)**	(16,007.7)
Accumulated nonowner changes in shareholders equity	**(922.2)**	(1,230.8)
Total Shareholders' Equity	**3,151.6**	3,938.7
Commitments and contingencies	**—**	—
Total Liabilities and Shareholders' Equity	**$17,155.0**	$16,377.2

The footnotes . . . of this report are an integral component of the company's consolidated financial statements.

EXHIBIT 4

ANHEUSER-BUSCH
STATEMENTS OF
CASH FLOWS

Year ended December 31 (in millions)	2007	2006	2005
Cash Flow from Operating Activities			
Net Income	**$2,115.3**	$1,965.2	$1,744.4
Adjustments to reconcile net income to cash provided by operating activities:			
Depreciation and amortization	**996.2**	988.7	979.0
Stock compensation expense	**135.9**	122.9	134.1
Decrease in deferred income taxes	**(65.9)**	(45.8)	(39.1)
Gain on sale of business	**(42.5)**	—	(15.4)
Undistributed earnings of affiliated companies	**(249.1)**	(341.8)	(288.0)
Other, net	**73.2**	(168.6)	136.6
Operating cash flow before the change in working capital	**2,963.1**	2,520.6	2,651.6
(Increase)/Decrease in working capital	**(23.5)**	188.8	50.3
Cash provided by operating activities	**2,939.6**	2,709.4	2,701.9

(continued)

EXHIBIT 4—
continued

ANHEUSER-BUSCH
STATEMENTS OF
CASH FLOWS

Cash Flow from Investing Activities			
Capital expenditures	**(870.0)**	(812.5)	(1,136.7)
New business acquisitions	**(155.7)**	(101.0)	—
Proceeds from sale of business	**41.6**	—	48.3
Cash used for investing activities	**(984.1)**	(913.5)	(1,088.4)
Cash Flow from Financing Activities			
Increase in debt	**1,708.2**	334.8	100.0
Decrease in debt	**(265.0)**	(663.3)	(456.0)
Dividends paid to shareholders	**(932.4)**	(871.6)	(800.8)
Acquisition of treasury stock	**(2,707.1)**	(745.9)	(620.4)
Shares issued under stock plans	**304.8**	143.5	161.4
Cash used for financing activities	**(1,891.5)**	(1,802.5)	(1,615.8)
Net increase/(decrease) in cash during the year	**64.0**	(6.6)	(2.3)
Cash, beginning of year	**219.2**	225.8	228.1
Cash, end of year	**$283.2**	$219.2	$225.8

The footnotes . . . of this report are an integral component of the company's consolidated financial statements.

EXHIBIT 5

ANHEUSER-BUSCH
NOTE 13, BUSINESS
SEGMENTS

The company categorizes its operations into four business segments: U.S. beer, international beer, packaging and entertainment. The U.S. beer segment consists of the company's U.S. beer manufacturing and import operations; company-owned beer wholesale operations; vertically integrated rice, barley and hops operations; and a short-haul transportation business. The international beer segment consists of the company's overseas beer production and marketing operations, which include company-owned operations in China and the United Kingdom, administration of contract and license brewing arrangements and equity investments. Principal foreign markets for sale of the company's products are China, the United Kingdom, Canada, Mexico and Ireland. The company attributes foreign sales based on the location of the distributor purchasing the product. The packaging segment is composed of the company's aluminum beverage can and lid manufacturing, aluminum recycling, label printing and glass manufacturing operations. Cans and lids are produced for both the company's U.S. beer operations and external customers in the U.S. soft drink industry. The entertainment segment consists of the company's SeaWorld, Busch Gardens and other adventure park operations.

Following is Anheuser-Busch business segment information for 2007, 2006 and 2005 (in millions). Intersegment sales are fully eliminated in consolidation. No single customer accounted for more than 10% of sales. General corporate expenses, including net interest expense and stock compensation expense, are not allocated to the operating segments. In 2007, the company changed management reporting responsibility for certain administrative and technology support costs from Corporate to the U.S. beer segment. 2006 and 2005 segment results have been updated to conform to this reporting convention. Corporate results for 2005 have been recast for the retrospective adoption of FAS 123R, which had no impact on the company's four operating segments. **[Note: 2005 results not included in this exhibit.]**

(continued)

EXHIBIT 5—*continued*

ANHEUSER-BUSCH NOTE 13, BUSINESS SEGMENTS

2007	U.S. Beer	International Beer	Packaging	Entertainment[1]	Corporate & Eliminations	Consolidated
Income Statement Information						
Gross sales	$14,158.7	1,351.7	2,632.8	1,272.7	(427.2)	$18,988.7
Net sales – intersegment	$3.2	0.6	931.9	—	(935.7)	$—
Net sales – external	$14,106.1	1,097.5	1,700.9	1,272.7	508.5	$16,685.7
Depreciation and amortization	$749.0	49.8	68.9	103.0	25.5	$996.2
Income before income taxes	$2,784.0	93.3	175.8	262.7	(893.1)	$2,422.7
Equity income, net of tax	$2.3	660.1	—	—	—	$662.4
Net income	$1,728.4	717.9	109.0	162.9	(602.9)	$2,115.3
Balance Sheet Information						
Total assets	$8,142.0	5,880.8	772.6	1,548.3	811.3	$17,155.0
Equity method investments	$93.9	3,925.6	—	—	—	$4,019.5
Goodwill	$21.2	1,343.3	21.9	288.3	—	$1,674.7
Foreign-located fixed assets	$4.5	544.4	—	—	—	$548.9
Capital expenditures	$554.4	59.2	72.4	169.4	14.6	$870.0

2006	U.S. Beer	International Beer	Packaging	Entertainment	Corporate & Eliminations[1]	Consolidated
Income Statement Information						
Gross sales	$13,394.2	1,235.6	2,562.3	1,178.5	(412.8)	$17,957.8
Net sales – intersegment	$2.8	—	896.4	—	(899.2)	—
Net sales – external	$11,388.2	998.2	1,665.9	1,178.5	486.3	$15,717.1
Depreciation and amortization	$715.1	51.2	76.9	99.0	46.5	$988.7
Income before income taxes	$2,709.2	76.7	145.0	232.8	(886.8)	$2,276.9
Equity income, net of tax	$3.4	585.4	—	—	—	$588.8
Net income	$1,683.1	633.0	89.9	144.3	(585.1)	$1,965.2
Balance Sheet Information						
Total assets	$7,988.3	5,350.6	781.5	1,479.1	777.7	$16,377.2
Equity method investments	$67.8	3,604.6	—	—	—	$3,672.4
Goodwill	$21.2	1,283.0	21.9	288.3	—	$1,614.4
Foreign-located fixed assets	$4.2	517.7	—	—	—	$521.9
Capital expenditures	$516.7	36.9	55.9	157.6	45.4	$812.5

Note 1: Corporate assets principally include cash, marketable securities, deferred charges and certain fixed assets. Eliminations impact only gross and intersegment sales. External net sales reflect the reporting of pass-through beer delivery costs reimbursed by independent wholesalers of $423.5 million, $370.9 million and $340.1 million in 2007, 2006 and 2005, respectively.

EXHIBIT 6

NOTE 6,
STOCK-BASED
COMPENSATION

STOCK OPTIONS

Under the terms of the company's stock option plans, officers, certain other employees and nonemployee directors may be granted options to purchase the company's common stock at a price equal to the closing market price per the New York Stock Exchange Composite Tape on the date the options are granted. The company issues either new shares or treasury shares when options are exercised under employee stock compensation plans. Under the plans for the board of directors, shares are issued exclusively from treasury stock. The company's stock option plans provide for accelerated exercisability on the occurrence of certain events relating to a change in control, merger, sale of substantially all company assets or complete liquidation of the company. At December 31, 2007, 2006 and 2005, a total of 137 million, 115 million and 121 million shares of common stock were designated for future issuance under existing stock option plans, respectively.

Following is a summary of stock option activity and pricing for the years shown (options in millions).

	Options Outstanding	Wtd. Avg. Exercise Price	Options Exercisable	Wtd. Avg. Exercise Price
Balance, December 31, 2004	91.8	$43.93	64.1	$40.92
Granted	11.4	$43.83		
Exercised	(5.9)	$25.48		
Canceled	(0.8)	$49.38		
Balance, December 31, 2005	96.5	$45.01	71.5	$44.06
Granted	9.5	$46.34		
Exercised	(4.9)	$27.43		
Canceled	(1.1)	$48.64		
Balance, December 31, 2006	100.0	$45.97	80.3	$45.89
Granted	**10.1**	**$51.86**		
Exercised	**(9.3)**	**$35.71**		
Canceled	**(0.3)**	**$48.52**		
Balance, December 31, 2007	**100.5**	**$47.49**	**81.1**	**$47.18**

The fair values of options granted during the last three years follow (in millions, except per option).

	2007	2006	2005
Fair value of each option granted	**$10.73**	$9.73	$8.81
Total number of options granted	**10.1**	9.5	11.4
Total fair value of options granted	**$108.4**	$92.4	$100.4

InBev and the Anheuser-Busch Acquisition

Jorge Paulo Lemann was born in Brazil in 1939 to Swiss immigrants. Mr. Lemann, a 1961 Harvard College graduate and world-ranked tennis player, was Swiss national tennis champion in 1962 and the Brazilian national champion five times between 1967 and 1976.[1] Additionally, in 1971 Mr. Lemann founded Banco de Investimentos Garantia SA. Carlos Sicupira and Marcel Telles joined Garantia, eventually became partners at the firm, and the three of them grew Garantia into Brazil's most prestigious investment bank.[2]

In 1989, Mr. Lemann, Mr. Sicupira, and Mr. Telles gained control of Copanhia Cervejaria Brahma, one of Brazil's two largest brewers, and Mr. Telles became the brewer's CEO. Mr. Telles, in collaboration with his partners, eliminated company cars, luxurious offices, and the executive dining room. He also introduced incentive performance systems throughout the firm. In 1998, following heavy trading losses from the Asian financial crises, the three partners sold their investment bank to CreditSuisse for $675 million.[3] The following year, however, Brahma acquired brewer Companhia Antarctica Paulista in Brazil's largest-ever corporate takeover. The combined firm, renamed AmBev, controlled 70% of the Brazilian beer market.[4]

In 2004, InterBrew, a Belgium brewery that ranked as the second-largest beer company in the world, acquired AmBev, the fifth-largest brewing company in the world. The combined firm, renamed InBev, and headquartered in Belgium, surpassed Anheuser-Busch to become the world's largest brewing company. Although InterBrew was the acquirer, Mr. Lemann, Mr. Sicupira, and Mr. Telles retained a significant equity interest in InBev. Mr. Carlos Brito, a Brazilian citizen and Stanford MBA, had served as AmBev's CEO since 2003. He was named InBev's North American zone president. In 2005, when Mr. Lemann, Mr. Sicupira, and Mr. Telles gained a controlling interest in InBev, Mr. Brito was named InBev's president.[5]

InBev Acquires Anheuser-Busch

In early June 2008, InBev made an unsolicited $46.3 billion bid for Anheuser-Busch ($65 per share). InBev had a reputation as an innovative marketer and cost-cutter; Anheuser-Busch had a paternalistic reputation. Employees—from brewery workers to executives—were highly compensated, and each employee received two free cases of Anheuser-Busch products each month. Anheuser-Busch had one of the strongest distribution networks of any industry in the world. Anheuser-Busch distributors

1. University of Illinois Foundation, "Donors pledge $14 million for Brazilian Studies Institute at Illinois," Press release, February 20, 2009. http://www.uif.uillinois.edu/storydetail.aspx?id=906.

2. Alumni Achievement Awards, 2009, Harvard Business School, Alumni.

3. Hynds, Tim, "If takeover happens, A-B faces big changes," siouxcityjournal.com, May 28, 2008.

4. Romero, Simon, "International Business; Internet takeovers fuel a big surge in acquisitions in Brazil," *The New York Times*, April 11, 2000. http://www.nytimes.com/2000/04/11/business/international-business-internet-takeovers-fuel-big-surge-acquisitions-brazil.html?pagewanted=1

5. "New leadership for InBev," InBev press release, December 27, 2005. http"//www.ab-inbev.com/go/media/global_presss_releases/press_releases_archive.cfm?theYear=2005.

were among the wealthiest business owners in their respective regions, and both Anheuser-Busch and its distributors were widely known for their charitable and civic contributions. Anheuser-Busch also had many of the most popular and innovative advertisements in the United States. Anheuser-Busch was usually the Super Bowl's heaviest advertiser, and those advertisements were among the most popular.

If InBev acquired Anheuser-Busch, there was little question it would cut costs. The only question was whether InBev would overpay, given the worldwide recession. After a series of press releases from Anheuser-Busch arguing the price was too low and from InBev arguing the price was fair, the two firms issued a July 14, 2008, joint press release announcing that Anheuser-Busch agreed to be acquired for $70 per share in cash, or $52 billion.[6]

Many analysts considered the price too high. Anheuser-Busch's 2007 net income before tax was only $2.42 billion (Exhibit 1) and its 2007 cash flow from operations only $2.94 billion (Exhibit 2). However, the $2.42 before tax income in Exhibit 1 includes "Equity income net of tax" of $662.4 million, primarily from Anheuser-Busch's 50% ownership in Mexican brewer Grupo Modelo, producers of Corona beer. Anheuser-Busch's 2007 10-K reported that interest was worth approximately $9 billion. Anheuser-Busch also owned two divisions that InBev could sell: Busch Entertainment division, owner of Sea World and Busch Gardens, and a producer of metal beverage containers (Exhibit 3). In addition, Anheuser-Busch owned several smaller breweries that InBev could sell.

InBev's Rights Offering

Exhibits 4, 5, and 6 show InBev's income statement, balance sheet, and statement of cash flows from its 2007 annual report (in Euros). To help pay for the acquisition, InBev announced in a 720-page prospectus dated November 23, 2008, that it would sell additional shares through a rights offering. Each shareholder of record as at the closing of Euronext Brussels on November 24, 2008 (the record date) would receive one right for each share owned. On that date, InBev's approximate share price was EUR 20.

For every five rights, shareholders were granted the right to purchase eight additional shares of InBev at a price of EUR 6.45 per new share. As of December 31, 2007, InBev had 615,043,509 shares outstanding, which would have allowed shareholders to purchase 984,069,614 additional shares at a total cost of 6,347,249,013 euro. In its 2008 annual report, InBev disclosed that on December 16, 2008, it issued 986,109,272 new Anheuser-Busch InBev shares. In exchange, InBev received aggregate consideration of $6.36 billion euro (virtually all rights holders exchanged their rights, and the required cash payment, for additional Anheuser-Busch InBev shares).

Anheuser-Busch InBev Cost Cuts

Exhibit 7 shows Anheuser-Busch InBev's reporting of the Anheuser-Busch acquisition. Anheuser-Busch InBev almost immediately began making changes at Anheuser-Busch. On January 14, 2009, it sent a letter to its suppliers stating that on February 1, 2009, it would extend payment terms from 30 days to 120 days. That letter asked suppliers to notify Anheuser-Busch InBev in writing if they were unable to conduct business under the new terms. Specifically, the letter stated the following: "If you are not able to work with the change in payment terms, we may have to consider an alternative supplier. . . . While we recognize these terms may be difficult for some of our

---

6. Press Release, Form 8-K, Exhibit 99.2, July 14, 2008, Leuven, Belgium, and July 13, 2008, St. Louis, Missouri.

suppliers, they are consistent with standards used by other multinational companies, and we hope we will be able to continue working together."[7]

In February, 2009, the *St. Louis Post Dispatch* reported that Anheuser-Busch would no longer support a St. Louis American Legion post of World War II veterans. Long-time Anheuser-Busch CEO August A. Busch had been a member of that post, and each September 29, the date of his death, a rifle guard lays a wreath at his grave.[8] Anheuser-Busch also replaced luxurious executive offices with cubicles, cut salaries, and began a series of firmwide layoffs.

Emerson, a major St. Louis corporation that supplies equipment to the brewing industry, issued an internal memo dated April 14, 2009. That memo stated that Emerson would no longer buy Anheuser-Busch products. It also mentioned that "numerous St. Louis not-for-profits have lost all or most of their Anheuser-Busch funding—United Way, Boy Scouts, Girl Scouts, and the list goes on!" Anheuser-Busch President Dave Peacock said his company was "surprised and disappointed" about Emerson's decision and called the memo an "inaccurate portrayal of us as a company. . . .We are continuing to make substantial contributions to St. Louis and elsewhere. . . . In February, we announced a $2.5 million donation to the University of Missouri-St. Louis (and $2 million to the St. Louis United Way)."[9]

In April 2009, Anheuser-Busch InBev notified NBC it would cut advertising spending for the Olympic broadcasts by about half and would no longer remain the exclusive beer advertiser during the Olympics.[10]

Since Prohibition, U.S. states have generally required a three-tier alcoholic beverage distribution system. In most instances, alcohol producers (brewers, distillers, and wineries), alcohol distributors, and alcohol retailers must be separately owned (in some states the state acts as the distributor or the retailer). Those rules protect small distributors and retailers from being driven out of business by large brewers or distillers. On March 10, 2010, Anheuser-Busch InBev sued the Illinois Liquor Control Commission for rejecting its plan to buy the 70% of City Beverage, a Chicago-based Anheuser-Busch distributor, it does not now own. In its suit, Anheuser-Busch InBev argued that the Illinois rule violates the U.S. Constitution's Commerce Clause by limiting interstate commerce. The brewer labeled the rule a form of "protectionism" designed to help local companies at the expense of those based outside the state.[11]

Anheuser-Busch InBev Asset Sales

During 2009, Anheuser-Busch InBev issued several press releases announcing asset sales. On May 7, 2009, Anheuser-Busch InBev announced it agreed to sell Oriental Brewery, South Korea's second largest brewery, to an affiliate of Kohlberg Kravis Roberts for US$1.8 billion (InBev owned Oriental Brewery prior to its acquisition

---

7. CSP, A-B Extends Payment Terms for suppliers, CSP Information Group, January 23, 2009. http://www.cspnet.com/ME2/Audiences/dirmod.asp?sid=&nm=&type=Publishing&mod=Publications:: Article&mid=8F3A7027421841978F18BE895F87F791&tier=4&id=E86D76D9E94E42E797987B0684E3C2D2& AudID=4AD8BF14480842378CC24C182A48D9D7.

8. McWilliams, Jeremiah, "Anheuser-Busch drops cash donations to local American Legion Post, says it remains committed to military." *St. Louis Post Dispatch*, May 29, 2009.

9. Volkmann, Kelsey, "Emerson boycotts Anheuser-Busch," *St. Louis Business Journal,* April 16, 2009.

10. Klayman, Ben, and Paul Tomasch, "AB InBev to cut Olympic TV ad spending in half-source," Reuters, April 29, 2009. http://www.reuters.com/article/idUSN2941828220090429.

11. Lowe, Zach, "Anheuser-Busch HIres Skadden in suit against Illinois regulators," *The AmLaw Daily,* March 11, 2010.

of Anheuser-Busch).[12] On July 1, 2009, Anheuser-Busch InBev announced it would sell four metal beverage container manufacturing plants to Ball Corporation for US$577 million. On October 7, 2009, it announced it would sell Busch Entertainment Corporation to Blackstone Capital Partners V L.P. for a cash payment of US$2.3 billion and a right to participate in Blackstone's return on its initial investment, capped at US$400 million. On October 15, 2009, Anheuser-Busch InBev announced it would sell its Central European Operations to CVC Capital Partners for an enterprise value of approximately US$2.231 billion and an additional right to participate in CVC's return on its capital estimated to be as much as US$800 million, contingent on CVC's return on its initial investment. Exhibit 8 summarizes those disposals.

Anheuser-Busch InBev 2009

Many analysts believed InBev overpaid for Anheuser-Busch, particularly given the serious recession at the time of the acquisition. Although the recession continued for at least a year after the acquisition, through asset sales, cost cutting, extended payment terms, and other actions, Anheuser-Busch InBev avoided selling its 50% interest in Grupo Modelo, Mexico's dominant brewer and a major brand throughout the United States. On March 9, 2009, broker Evolution Securities speculated that Anheuser-Busch InBev might acquire the remaining 50% interest of Grupo Model for $10.8 billion.[13]

Exhibits 9, 10, and 11 are Anheuser-Busch InBev's 2009 income statement, balance sheet, and statement of cash flows. For the year ending December 31, 2009, InBev changed its financial reporting units from euros to U.S. dollars and its functional currency from the euro to U.S. dollars because its largest segment is in the United States. However, because it is headquartered in Belgium, the firm follows International Financial Reporting Standards (IFRS), not U.S. GAAP.

Exhibit 12 shows Note 8, Non-Recurring Items, and Exhibit 13 shows Note 5, Segment Disclosures. Anheuser-Busch InBev also disclosed the following 2009 and 2008 debt repayment schedules in Note 24 of its 2009 annual report:

Terms and debt repayment schedule at 31 December 2009 Million US dollar	Total	1 year or less	1–2 years	2–3 years	3–5 years	More than 5 years
Secured bank loans	83	30	22	16	15	—
Unsecured bank loans	20,175	1,559	5,648	427	12,416	125
Unsecured bond issues	28,513	387	819	3,784	6,684	16,839
Secured other loans	20	14	—	—	6	—
Unsecured other loans	223	19	104	14	26	60
Finance lease liabilities	50	6	4	4	1	35
	49,064	2,015	6,597	4,245	19,148	17,059

12. "InBev taps K.K.R. to buy South Korea brewer," Private Equity, *The New York Times*, April 27, 2009. http://dealbook.blogs.nytimes.com/2009/04/27/inbev-taps-kkr-to-buy-south-korea-brewer-reports-say/.

13. "Deals, Mexico, AB InBev to buy Modelo this year: broker Evolution," Reuters, March 9, 2010.

Terms and debt repayment schedule at 31 December 2008 Million US dollar	Total	1 year or less	1–2 years	2–3 years	3–5 years	More than 5 years
Secured bank loans	107	50	11	16	30	—
Unsecured bank loans	50,553	10,723	11,441	14,003	14,261	125
Unsecured bond issues	8,432	520	604	1,035	1,309	4,964
Secured other loans	7	—	—	2	4	1
Unsecured other loans	174	4	33	32	64	41
Finance lease liabilities	53	4	8	2	4	35
	59,326	**11,301**	**12,097**	**15,090**	**15,672**	**5,166**

Required

1. Did Anheuser-Busch InBev overpay for Anheuser-Busch? In your analysis, consider:

   a. The rights offering.

   b. Anheuser-Busch InBev's current value compared to InBev's value prior to the acquisition.

   c. Potential future cost savings.

   d. Potential gains from being able to sell InBev brands through Anheuser-Busch's distributors.

   e. Potential loss of market share in the United States from lower advertising expenditures and possible adverse reactions to other cost cuts.

   f. Potential gains from entering the distribution market.

2. Is Anheuser-Busch InBev in danger of being unable to repay its debt? Explain.

3. Is Anheuser-Busch InBev capable of acquiring Grupo Modelo in 2010? Explain.

4. Evaluate InBev's performance in integrating and transforming Anheuser-Busch.

Year ended December 31 (in millions, except per share)	2007	2006	2005
Gross sales	$18,988.7	$17,957.8	$17,253.5
Excise taxes	(2,303.0)	(2,240.7)	(2,217.8)
Net sales	16,685.7	15,717.1	15,035.7
Cost of sales	(10,836.1)	(10,165.0)	(9,606.3)
Gross profit	5,849.6	5,552.1	5,429.4
Marketing, distribution and administrative expenses	(2,982.1)	(2,832.5)	(2,837.5)
Gain on sale of distribution rights	26.5	—	—
Litigation settlement	—	—	(105.0)
Operating income	2,894.0	2,719.6	2,486.9
Interest expense	(484.4)	(451.3)	(454.5)
Interest capitalized	17.4	17.6	19.9
Interest income	3.9	1.8	2.4
Other income/(expense), net	(8.2)	(10.8)	2.7
Income before income taxes	2,422.7	2,276.9	2,057.4
Provision for income taxes	(969.8)	(900.5)	(811.1)
Equity income, net of tax	662.4	588.8	498.1
Net income	$2,115.3	$1,965.2	$1,744.4

The footnotes . . . of this report are an integral component of the company's consolidated financial statements.

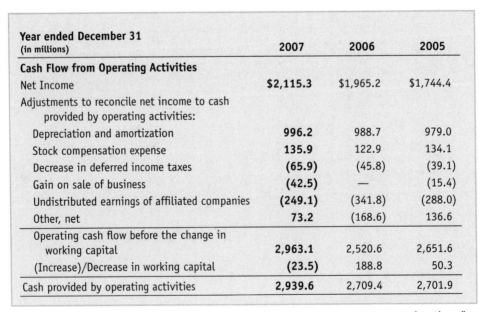

Year ended December 31 (in millions)	2007	2006	2005
Cash Flow from Operating Activities			
Net Income	$2,115.3	$1,965.2	$1,744.4
Adjustments to reconcile net income to cash provided by operating activities:			
Depreciation and amortization	996.2	988.7	979.0
Stock compensation expense	135.9	122.9	134.1
Decrease in deferred income taxes	(65.9)	(45.8)	(39.1)
Gain on sale of business	(42.5)	—	(15.4)
Undistributed earnings of affiliated companies	(249.1)	(341.8)	(288.0)
Other, net	73.2	(168.6)	136.6
Operating cash flow before the change in working capital	2,963.1	2,520.6	2,651.6
(Increase)/Decrease in working capital	(23.5)	188.8	50.3
Cash provided by operating activities	2,939.6	2,709.4	2,701.9

(continued)

EXHIBIT 2—
continued

ANHEUSER-BUSCH
STATEMENT OF
CASH FLOWS, 2007

Cash Flow from Investing Activities

Capital expenditures	(870.0)	(812.5)	(1,136.7)
New business acquisitions	(155.7)	(101.0)	—
Proceeds from sale of business	41.6	—	48.3
Cash used for investing activities	(984.1)	(913.5)	(1,088.4)

Cash Flow from Financing Activities

Increase in debt	1,708.2	334.8	100.0
Decrease in debt	(265.0)	(663.3)	(456.0)
Dividends paid to shareholders	(932.4)	(871.6)	(800.8)
Acquisition of treasury stock	(2,707.1)	(745.9)	(620.4)
Shares issued under stock plans	304.8	143.5	161.4
Cash used for financing activities	(1,891.5)	(1,802.5)	(1,615.8)
Net increase/(decrease) in cash during the year	64.0	(6.6)	(2.3)
Cash, beginning of year	219.2	225.8	228.1
Cash, end of year	$283.2	$219.2	$225.8

The footnotes . . . of this report are an integral component of the company's consolidated financial statements.

EXHIBIT 3

ANHEUSER-BUSCH
NOTE 13, BUSINESS
SEGMENTS

The company categorizes its operations into four business segments: U.S. beer, international beer, packaging and entertainment. The U.S. beer segment consists of the company's U.S. beer manufacturing and import operations; company-owned beer wholesale operations; vertically integrated rice, barley and hops operations; and a short-haul transportation business. The international beer segment consists of the company's overseas beer production and marketing operations, which include company-owned operations in China and the United Kingdom, administration of contract and license brewing arrangements and equity investments. Principal foreign markets for sale of the company's products are China, the United Kingdom, Canada, Mexico and Ireland. The company attributes foreign sales based on the location of the distributor purchasing the product. The packaging segment is composed of the company's aluminum beverage can and lid manufacturing, aluminum recycling, label printing and glass manufacturing operations. Cans and lids are produced for both the company's U.S. beer operations and external customers in the U.S. soft drink industry. The entertainment segment consists of the company's SeaWorld, Busch Gardens and other adventure park operations.

Following is Anheuser-Busch business segment information for 2007 (in millions). Intersegment sales are fully eliminated in consolidation. No single customer accounted for more than 10% of sales. General corporate expenses, including net interest expense and stock compensation expense, are not allocated to the operating segments. In 2007, the company changed management reporting responsibility for certain administrative and technology support costs from Corporate to the U.S. beer segment. **[Note: 2005 and 2006 results not included in this Exhibit.]**

(continued)

EXHIBIT 3—
continued

ANHEUSER-BUSCH
NOTE 13, BUSINESS
SEGMENTS

2007	U.S. Beer	International Beer	Packaging	Entertainment	Corporate & Eliminations[1]	Consolidated
Income Statement Information						
Gross sales	$14,158.7	1,351.7	2,632.8	1,272.7	(427.2)	$18,988.7
Net sales – intersegment	$3.2	0.6	931.9	—	(935.7)	—
Net sales – external	$12,106.1	1,097.5	1,700.9	1,272.7	508.5	$16,685.7
Depreciation and amortization	$749.0	49.8	68.9	103.0	25.5	$996.2
Income before income taxes	$2,784.0	93.3	175.8	262.7	(893.1)	$2,422.7
Equity income, net of tax	$2.3	660.1	—	—	—	$662.4
Net income	$1,728.4	717.9	109.0	162.9	(602.9)	$2,115.3
Balance Sheet Information						
Total assets	$8,142.0	5,880.8	772.6	1,548.3	811.3	$17,155.0
Equity method investments	$93.9	3,925.6	—	—	—	$4,019.5
Goodwill	$21.2	1,343.3	21.9	288.3	—	$1,674.7
Foreign-located fixed assets	$4.5	544.4	—	—	—	$548.9
Capital expenditures	$554.4	59.2	72.4	169.4	14.6	$870.0

EXHIBIT 4

INBEV INCOME
STATEMENT, 2007

For the year ended 31 December Million euro	Notes	2007	2006
Revenue		**14,430**	**13,308**
Cost of sales		(5,936)	(5,477)
Gross profit		**8,494**	**7,831**
Distribution expenses		(1,713)	(1,551)
Sales and marketing expenses		(2,134)	(2,115)
Administrative expenses		(990)	(1,075)
Other operating income/(expenses)	6	263	133
Profit from operations before non-recurring items		**3,920**	**3,223**
Restructuring (including impairment losses)	7	(43)	(139)
Business and asset disposal	7	393	(19)
Disputes	7	24	64
Profit from operations		**4,294**	**3,129**
Finance cost	10	(713)	(639)
Finance income	10	115	166
Net finance cost		**(598)**	**(473)**
Share of result of associates		1	1
Profit before tax		**3,697**	**2,657**
Income tax expense	11	(649)	(531)
Profit		**3,048**	**2,126**
Attributable to:			
Equity holders of InBev		2,198	1,411
Minority interests		850	715

459

EXHIBIT 5

INBEV BALANCE
SHEET, 2007

As at 31 December Million euro	Notes	2007	2006
Assets			
Non-current assets			
Property, plant and equipment	12	6,629	6,301
Goodwill	13	13,834	12,305
Intangible assets	14	1,250	1,265
Investments in associates		31	13
Investment securities	15	163	40
Deferred tax assets	16	663	857
Employee benefits	24	7	6
Trade and other receivables	18	583	695
		23,160	21,482
Current assets			
Investment securities	15	179	223
Inventories	17	1,119	1,017
Income tax receivable		306	213
Trade and other receivables	18	2,570	2,571
Cash and cash equivalents	19	1,324	626
Assets held for sale	20	41	114
		5,539	4,764
Total assets		28,699	26,246
Equity and liabilities			
Equity			
Issued capital	21	474	473
Share premium	21	7,450	7,412
Reserves	21	292	715
Retained earnings	21	5,409	3,662
Equity attributable to equity holders of InBev		13,625	12,262
Minority interests	21	1,285	880
		14,910	13,142
Non-current liabilities			
Interest-bearing loans and borrowings	23	5,185	5,146
Employee benefits	24	624	753
Deferred tax liabilities	16	468	637
Trade and other payables	27	315	241
Provisions	26	512	448
		7,104	7,225
Current liabilities			
Bank overdrafts	19	80	90
Interest-bearing loans and borrowings	23	1,438	1,204
Income tax payable		570	372
Trade and other payables	27	4,410	3,919
Provisions	26	187	253
Liabilities held for sale	20	—	41
		6,685	5,879
Total equity and liabilities		28,699	26,246

EXHIBIT 6

INBEV STATEMENT
OF CASH FLOWS,
2007

For the year ended 31 December Million euro	2007	2006
Operating activities		
Profit	3,048	2,126
Depreciation, amortization and impairment	1,030	1,093
Impairment losses on receivables & inventories	49	24
Additions/(reversals) in provisions & employee benefits	136	173
Net finance cost	598	473
Loss/(gain) on sale of property, plant and equipment and intangible assets	(43)	(94)
Loss/(gain) on sale of subsidiaries	(354)	8
Loss/(gain) on assets held for sale	(12)	—
Equity-settled share-based payment expense	53	49
Income tax expense	649	531
Other non-cash items included in profit	30	23
Share of result of associates	(1)	(1)
Cash flow from operating activities before changes in working capital and provisions	**5,183**	**4,405**
Decrease/(increase) in trade and other receivables	(17)	(307)
Decrease/(increase) in inventories	(69)	1
Increase/(decrease) in trade and other payables	356	437
Use of provisions	(363)	(440)
Cash generated from operations	**5,090**	**4,096**
Interest paid	(623)	(452)
Interest received	44	55
Dividends received	1	1
Income tax paid	(448)	(413)
Cash flow from operating activities	**4,064**	**3,287**
Investing activities		
Proceeds from sale of property, plant and equipment	134	93
Proceeds from sale of intangible assets	7	69
Proceeds from sale of other assets	407	30
Repayments of loans granted	7	12
Sale of subsidiaries, net of cash disposed of	422	3
Acquisition of subsidiaries, net of cash acquired	(190)	(1,531)
Purchase of minority interests	(1,152)	(740)
Acquisition of property, plant and equipment	(1,481)	(1,266)
Acquisition of intangible assets	(100)	(114)
Acquisition of other assets	(404)	(16)
Payments of loans granted	(8)	(21)
Cash flow from investing activities	**(2,358)**	**(3,481)**
Financing activities		
Proceeds from the issue of share capital	84	82
Purchase of treasury shares	(600)	(59)
Proceeds from borrowings	6,544	6,429
Repayment of borrowings	(6,178)	(5,549)

(continued)

EXHIBIT 6—
continued

INBEV STATEMENT
OF CASH FLOWS,
2007

Cash net finance costs other than interests	(44)	(75)
Payment of finance lease liabilities	(7)	(3)
Dividends paid	(769)	(617)
Cash flow from financing activities	**(970)**	**208**
Net increase/(decrease) in cash and cash equivalents	**736**	**14**
Cash and cash equivalents less bank overdrafts at beginning of year	536	552
Effect of exchange rate fluctuations	(28)	(30)
Cash and cash equivalents less bank overdrafts at end of year	**1,244**	**536**

EXHIBIT 7

2009 ANHEUSER-
BUSCH INBEV
ANNUAL REPORT,
NOTE 6,
ACQUISITIONS OF
SUBSIDIARIES

In 2009, the company completed the purchase price allocation in compliance with IFRS 3. IFRS 3 requires the acquirer to retrospectively adjust the provisional amounts recognized at the acquisition date to reflect new information obtained about facts and circumstances that existed as of the acquisition date. The following table summarizes the final purchase price allocation of the Anheuser-Busch business with adjustments being retrospectively applied as of 18 November 2008:

Million US dollar	Provisional Allocation (Reported)	Adjustments	Final Purchase Price Allocation (Adjusted)
Non-current assets			
Property, plant and equipment	11,143	(3)	11,140
Intangible assets	21,867	(36)	21,831
Investment in associates	7,075	3	7,078
Trade and other receivables	196	(19)	177
Current assets			
Income tax receivable	320	—	320
Inventories	1,230	(35)	1,195
Trade and other receivables	1,264	(10)	1,254
Cash and cash equivalent	494	—	494
Assets held for sale	21	—	21
Non-controlling interest	(48)	—	(48)
Non-current liabilities			
Interest-bearing loans and borrowings	(6,274)	(14)	(6,288)
Employee benefits	(1,720)	26	(1,694)
Trade and other payables	—	(75)	(75)
Provisions	(146)	—	(146)
Deferred tax liabilities	(11,838)	(493)	(12,331)
Current liabilities			
Trade and other payables	(3,167)	(32)	(3,199)
Net identified assets and liabilities	**20,417**	**(688)**	**19,729**
Goodwill on acquisition	32,235	688	32,923
Consideration paid in cash	**52,652**	**—**	**52,652**

(continued)

EXHIBIT 7—
continued

2009 ANHEUSER-
BUSCH INBEV
ANNUAL REPORT,
NOTE 6,
ACQUISITIONS OF
SUBSIDIARIES

Given the nature of the adjustments, the impact to the consolidated income statement as of 31 December 2008 is immaterial.

The transaction resulted in 32.9 billion US dollar of goodwill allocated primarily to the US business. The factors that contributed to the recognition of goodwill include the acquisition of an assembled workforce and the premiums paid for cost synergies expected to be achieved in Anheuser-Busch. Management's assessment of the future economic benefits supporting the recognition of this goodwill is in part based on expected savings through the implementation of AB InBev best practices such as, among others, a zero based budgeting program and initiatives that are expected to bring greater efficiency and standardization to brewing operations, generate cost savings and maximize purchasing power. Goodwill also arises due to the recognition of deferred tax liabilities in relation to the fair value adjustments on acquired intangible assets for which the amortization does not qualify as a tax deductible expense.

The valuation of the property, plant and equipment, intangible assets, investment in associates, interest bearing loans and borrowings and employee benefits and other assets and liabilities are based on the current best estimates of AB InBev's management, with input from third parties.

The majority of the intangible asset valuation relates to brands with indefinite life. The valuation of the brands with indefinite life is based on a series of factors, including the brand history, the operating plan and the countries in which the brands are sold. The brands with indefinite life include the Budweiser family (including Bud and Bud Light), the Michelob brand family, the Busch brand family and the Natural brand family and have been fair valued for a total amount of 21.4 billion US dollar. Distribution agreements and favorable contracts have been fair valued for a total amount of 439m US dollar. These are being amortized over the term of the associated contracts ranging from 3 to 18 years.

EXHIBIT 8

ANHEUSER-BUSCH
INBEV ANNUAL
REPORT, NOTE 6,
DISPOSALS OF
SUBSIDIARIES

2009 Disposals

The table below summarizes the impact of disposals on the Statement of financial position of AB InBev for 31 December 2009 and 2008:

Million US dollar	2009 Oriental Brewery	2009 Busch Entertainment	2009 Central Europe	2009 Other disposals	2009 Total disposals	2008 Total disposals
Non-current assets						
Property, plant and equipment	—	(1,889)	(595)	—	(2,484)	(3)
Goodwill	—	—	(166)	—	(166)	—
Intangible assets	—	(470)	(39)	(1)	(510)	(1)
Investment securities	—	—	(1)	—	(1)	—
Deferred tax assets	—	—	(5)	—	(5)	—
Trade and other receivables	—	(3)	(15)	(1)	(19)	—
Current assets						
Income tax receivable	—	—	(3)	—	(3)	—
Inventories	—	(33)	(75)	(1)	(109)	(1)
Trade and other receivables	—	(82)	(138)	3	(217)	(3)

(continued)

EXHIBIT 8—
continued

ANHEUSER-BUSCH
INBEV ANNUAL
REPORT, NOTE 6,
DISPOSALS OF
SUBSIDIARIES

Cash and cash equivalents	(75)	—	(334)	(7)	(416)	—
Assets held for sale	(1,396)	—	—	(58)	(1,454)	—
Non-current liabilities						
Interest–bearing loans and borrowings	—	—	1	—	1	—
Trade and other payables	—	—	5	—	5	—
Provisions	—	—	4	—	4	—
Deferred tax liabilities	—	—	8	—	8	—
Current liabilities						
Bank overdrafts	43	—	13	—	56	—
Interest–bearing loans and borrowings	—	—	—	4	4	—
Income tax payable	—	—	21	—	21	—
Trade and other payables	—	195	190	1	386	3
Provisions	—	—	5	—	5	—
Liabilities held for sale	159	—	—	60	219	—
Net identifiable assets and liabilities	**(1,269)**	**(2,282)**	**(1,124)**	**0**	**(4,675)**	**(5)**
Loss/(gain) on disposal	(428)	—	(1,088)	(1)	(1,517)	4
Net cash received from last years' disposal	—	—	—	—	—	(46)
Consideration received, satisfied in cash	**(1,697)**	**(2,282)**	**(2,212)**	**(1)**	**(6,192)**	**(47)**
Cash disposed of	32	—	322	7	361	—
Cash to be received	225	—	374	—	599	—
Net cash inflow	**(1,440)**	**(2,282)**	**(1 516)**	**6**	**(5,232)**	**(47)**

On 24 July 2009, AB InBev announced that it completed the sale of Oriental Brewery to Kohlberg Kravis Roberts & Co. L.P. for 1.8 billion US dollar of which 1.5 billion US dollar was cash and 0.3 billion US dollar was received as an unsecured deferred payment. As a result of the sale, AB InBev recorded a capital gain of approximately 428m US dollar.

On 1 December, AB InBev completed the sale of its indirect wholly owned subsidiary of Busch Entertainment Corporation, to an entity established by Blackstone Capital Partners V L.P. for up to 2.7 billion US dollar. The purchase price was comprised of a cash payment of 2.3 billion US dollar and a right to participate in Blackstone Capital Partners' return on initial investment, which is capped at 400m US dollar. There was no capital gain recorded on this transaction as the selling price equaled the net carrying value at the date of disposal.

On 2 December, the company completed the sale of the Central European operations to CVC Capital Partners for an enterprise value of 2.2 billion US dollar, of which 1.6 billion US dollar was cash, 448m US dollar was received as a unsecured deferred payment obligation with a six-year maturity and 165m US dollar represents the value to non-controlling interest. The company also received additional rights to a future payments estimated up to 800m US dollar contingent on CVC's return on initial investments. As a result of the sale, AB InBev recorded a capital gain of approximately 1.1 billion US dollar.

EXHIBIT 9

ANHEUSER-BUSCH
INBEV INCOME
STATEMENT, 2009

Consolidated income statement

For the year ended 31 December
Million US dollar

	Notes	2009	2008
Revenue		**36,758**	**23,507**
Cost of sales		(17,198)	(10,336)
Gross profit		**19,560**	**13,171**
Distribution expenses		(2,671)	(2,725)
Sales and marketing expenses		(4,992)	(3,510)
Administrative expenses		(2,310)	(1,478)
Other operating income/(expenses)	7	661	440
Profit from operations before non-recurring items		**10,248**	**5,898**
Restructuring (including impairment losses)	8	(153)	(457)
Fair value adjustments	8	(67)	(43)
Business and asset disposal (including impairment losses)	8	1,541	(38)
Disputes	8	—	(20)
Profit from operations		**11,569**	**5,340**
Finance cost	11	(4,291)	(1,701)
Finance income	11	501	288
Non-recurring finance cost	8	(629)	(187)
Net finance cost		**(4,419)**	**(1,600)**
Share of result of associates	16	513	60
Profit before tax		**7,663**	**3,800**
Income tax expense	12	(1,786)	(674)
Profit		**5,877**	**3,126**
Attributable to:			
Equity holders of AB InBev		4,613	1,927
Non-controlling interest		1,264	1,199
Basic earnings per share	23	2.91	1.93
Diluted earnings per share	23	2.90	1.93

Consolidated statement of comprehensive income

For the year ended 31 December
Million US dollar

	2009	2008
Profit	**5,877**	**3,126**
Other comprehensive income:		
Exchange differences on translation of foreign operations (gains/(losses))	2,468	(4,212)
Cash flow hedges		
Recognized in equity	729	(2,311)
Removed from equity and included in profit or loss	478	(22)
Removed from equity and included in the initial cost of inventories	(37)	25
Actuarial gains/(losses)	134	(372)
Other comprehensive income, net of tax	**3,772**	**(6,892)**

(continued)

Total comprehensive income	9,649	(3,766)
Attributable to:		
Equity holders of AB InBev	8,168	(4,690)
Non-controlling interest	1,481	924

EXHIBIT 9—
continued

ANHEUSER-BUSCH
INBEV INCOME
STATEMENT, 2009

Consolidated statement of financial position

EXHIBIT 10

ANHEUSER-BUSCH
INBEV BALANCE
SHEET, 2009

As at 31 December Million US dollar	Notes	2009	2008 Adjusted[1]	2008 Reported[2]
ASSETS				
Non-current assets				
Property, plant and equipment	13	16,461	19,671	19,674
Goodwill	14	52,125	50,244	49,556
Intangible assets	15	23,165	23,637	23,673
Investments in associates	16	6,744	6,871	6,868
Investment securities	17	277	239	239
Deferred tax assets	18	949	932	932
Employee benefits	25	10	8	8
Trade and other receivables	20	1,941	1,315	1,334
		101,672	102,917	102,284
Current assets				
Investment securities	17	55	270	270
Inventories	19	2,354	2,868	2,903
Income tax receivable		590	580	580
Trade and other receivables	20	4,099	4,126	4,136
Cash and cash equivalents	21	3,689	2,936	2,936
Assets held for sale	22	66	51	51
		10,853	10,831	10,876
Total assets		112,525	113,748	113,160
EQUITY AND LIABILITIES				
Equity				
Issued capital	23	1,732	1,730	1,730
Share premium		17,515	17,477	17,477
Reserves		623	(3,247)	(3,247)
Retained earnings		10,448	6,482	6,482
Equity attributable to equity holders of AB InBev		30,318	22,442	22,442
Non-controlling interest		2,853	1,989	1,989
		33,171	24,431	24,431

(continued)

EXHIBIT 10—
continued

ANHEUSER-BUSCH
INBEV BALANCE
SHEET, 2009

Non-current liabilities				
Interest-bearing loans and borrowings	24	47,049	48,039	48,025
Employee benefits	25	2,611	2,983	3,009
Deferred tax liabilities	18	12,495	12,569	12,076
Trade and other payables	28	1,979	1,763	1,688
Provisions	27	966	796	796
		65,100	**66,150**	**65,594**
Current liabilities				
Bank overdrafts	21	28	765	765
Interest-bearing loans and borrowings	24	2,015	11,301	11,301
Income tax payable		526	405	405
Trade and other payables	28	11,377	10,238	10,206
Provisions	27	308	458	458
		14,254	**23,167**	**23,135**
Total equity and liabilities		**112,525**	**113,748**	**113,160**

The accompanying notes are an integral part of these consolidated financial statements.

EXHIBIT 11

ANHEUSER-BUSCH
INBEV STATEMENT
OF CASH FLOWS,
2009

For the year ended 31 December Million US dollar	2009	2008[1]
OPERATING ACTIVITIES		
Profit	5,877	3,126
Depreciation, amortization and impairment	2,818	1,912
Impairment losses on receivables, inventories and other assets	167	149
Additions/(reversals) in provisions and employee benefits	188	572
Net finance cost	4,419	1,600
Loss/(gain) on sale of property, plant and equipment and intangible assets	(189)	(56)
Loss/(gain) on sale of subsidiaries, associates and assets held for sale	(1,555)	(33)
Equity-settled share-based payment expense	208	63
Income tax expense	1,786	674
Other non-cash items included in the profit	24	(12)
Share of result of associates	(513)	(60)
Cash flow from operating activities before changes in working capital and use of provisions	**13,230**	**7,935**
Decrease/(increase) in trade and other receivables	149	201
Decrease/(increase) in inventories	301	(388)
Increase/(decrease) in trade and other payables	337	364
Pension contributions and use of provisions	(548)	(490)
Cash generated from operations	**13,469**	**7,622**

(continued)

Interest paid	(2,908)	(975)
Interest received	132	126
Dividends received	—	1
Income tax paid	(1,569)	(1,241)
CASH FLOW FROM OPERATING ACTIVITIES	**9,124**	**5,533**
INVESTING ACTIVITIES		
Proceeds from sale of property, plant and equipment and of intangible assets	327	228
Proceeds from sale of assets held for sale	877	76
Proceeds from sale of associates	936	13
Sale of subsidiaries, net of cash disposed of	5,232	47
Acquisition of subsidiaries, net of cash acquired	(608)	(51,626)
Purchase of non-controlling interest	(38)	(853)
Acquisition of property, plant and equipment and of intangible assets	(1,713)	(2,652)
Net proceeds/(acquisition) of other assets	227	(114)
Net repayments/(payments) of loans granted	29	3
CASH FLOW FROM INVESTING ACTIVITIES	**5,269**	**(54,878)**
FINANCING ACTIVITIES		
Net proceeds from the issue of share capital	76	9,764
Net purchase of treasury shares	—	(797)
Proceeds from borrowings	27,834	56,425
Payments on borrowings	(39,627)	(11,953)
Cash net finance costs other than interests	(62)	(632)
Payment of finance lease liabilities	(4)	(6)
Dividends paid	(1,313)	(2,922)
CASH FLOW FROM FINANCING ACTIVITIES	**(13,096)**	**49,879**
Net increase/(decrease) in cash and cash equivalents	**1,297**	**534**
Cash and cash equivalents less bank overdrafts at beginning of year	2,171	1,831
Effect of exchange rate fluctuations	193	(194)
Cash and cash equivalents less bank overdrafts at end of year	**3,661**	**2,171**

EXHIBIT 11— *continued*

ANHEUSER-BUSCH INBEV STATEMENT OF CASH FLOWS, 2009

EXHIBIT 12

NON-RECURRING
ITEMS, 2009

8. NON-RECURRING ITEMS

IAS 1 *Presentation of financial statements* requires material items of income and expense to be disclosed separately. Non-recurring items are items, which in management's judgment, need to be disclosed by virtue of their size or incidence in order for the user to obtain a proper understanding of the financial information. The company considers these items to be of significance in nature, and accordingly, management has excluded these from their segment measure of performance as noted in Note 5 *Segment Reporting*.

The non-recurring items included in the income statement are as follows:

Million US dollar	2009	2008
Restructuring (including impairment losses)	(153)	(457)
Fair value adjustments	(67)	(43)
Business and asset disposal (including impairment losses)	1,541	(38)
Disputes	—	(20)
Impact on profit from operations	**1,321**	**(558)**
Non-recurring finance cost	(629)	(187)
Non-recurring taxes	29	145
Non-recurring non-controlling interest	(35)	16
Net impact on profit attributable to equity holders of AB InBev	**686**	**(584)**

The 2009 restructuring charges of (153)m US dollar primarily relate to the Anheuser-Busch integration, organizational alignments and outsourcing activities in the global headquarters, Western Europe and Asia Pacific. These changes aim to eliminate overlap or duplicated processes and activities across functions and zones. These one time expenses as a result of the series of decisions will provide us with a lower cost base besides a stronger focus on AB InBev's core activities, quicker decision-making and improvements to efficiency, service and quality.

IFRS fair value adjustments, recognized in 2009 for a total of (67)m US dollar, relates to the non-recurring employee benefit expenses in accordance with IFRS 2, following the change in vesting conditions on certain shared-based payment plans.

2009 business and asset disposals resulted in a non-recurring income of 1 541m US dollar mainly representing the sale of assets of InBev USA LLC (also doing business under the name Labatt USA) to an affiliate of KPS Capital Partners, L.P. (54m US dollar), the sale of the Korean subsidiary Oriental Brewery to an affiliate of Kohlberg Kravis Roberts & Co. L.P. (428m US dollar) and the sale of the Central European operations to CVC Capital Partners (1,088m US dollar), next to other costs linked to divestitures.

During the 4th quarter of 2009, AB InBev used the proceeds from the disposals to prepay part of the senior facilities that financed the acquisition of Anheuser-Busch. The prepayments resulted in the recognition of 629m US dollar non-recurring finance cost comprised of 474m US dollar hedging losses as interest rate swaps hedging the re-paid parts of the facilities are no longer effective, 145m US dollar accelerated accretion expenses and 10m US dollar loss on hedges that are no longer effective due to the sale of the Central European operations to CVC Capital Partners.

(continued)

EXHIBIT 12—
continued

NON-RECURRING
ITEMS, 2009

The 2008 non-recurring restructuring charges include 182m US dollar costs which mainly result of organizational alignments and outsourcing of activities in Western Europe, the global headquarters and Asia Pacific, next to a 195m US dollar provision in relation to the integration of Anheuser-Busch. The 2008 restructuring charges also include an impairment loss of 80m US dollar related to the restructuring of AB InBev's integrated distribution network ("CafeIn") in France.

IFRS fair value adjustments, recognized in 2008 for a total of (43)m US dollar, related to the non-recurring impact of revaluing the inventories of Anheuser-Busch in line with IFRS.

Business and asset disposals in 2008 resulted in a net loss of 38m US dollar and was partly related to losses recognized in connection with the above mentioned reorganization in France (10m US dollar). Next to that, additional losses related to business and asset disposals of previous years were booked in 2008.

Profit from operations as at 31 December 2008 was negatively affected by provisions for disputes of 20m US dollar.

In connection with the combination with Anheuser-Busch, the company recognized a non-recurring financial expense of 187m US dollar in 2008. This expense comprised 119m US dollar relating to the commitment fees for the syndicated senior facilities and equity bridge facilities and the underwriting and arrangement fees for the equity bridge facility. In addition, a 68m US dollar loss was recognized for ineffectiveness of the hedging on the Anheuser-Busch financing prior to the closing of the acquisition. All the above amounts are before income taxes. The 2009 non-recurring items as at 31 December decreased income taxes by 29m US dollar, the non-recurring items as at 31 December 2008 decreased income taxes by 145m US dollar.

The non-controlling interest on the non-recurring items amounts to (35)m US dollar in 2009 versus 16m US dollar in 2008.

5. Segment reporting

Segment information is presented by geographical segments, consistent with the information that is available and evaluated regularly by the chief operating decision maker. AB InBev operates its business through seven zones. Regional and operating company management is responsible for managing performance, underlying risks, and effectiveness of operations. Internally, AB InBev management uses performance indicators such as normalized profit from operations (normalized EBIT) and normalized EBITDA as measures of segment performance and to make decisions regarding allocation of resources. These measures are reconciled to segment profit in the tables presented (figures may not add up due to rounding).

Million US dollar, except volume (million his) and full time equivalents (FTE in units)	North America		Latin America North		Latin America South	
	2009	2008	2009	2008	2009	2008
Volume	135	27	110	102	33	34
Revenue	15,486	3,753	7,649	7,664	1,899	1,855
Cost of goods sold	(7,525)	(1,586)	(2,487)	(2,634)	(735)	(782)
Distribution expenses	(792)	(499)	(781)	(916)	(166)	(145)
Sales and marketing expenses	(1,694)	(430)	(1,016)	(837)	(182)	(191)
Administrative expenses	(636)	(155)	(551)	(418)	(73)	(72)
Other operating income/(expenses)	54	(4)	243	208	(12)	11
Normalized profit from operations (EBIT)	4,894	1,079	3,056	3,067	731	676
Non-recurring items (refer note 8)	62	(220)	109	(27)	(7)	(4)
Profit from operations (EBIT)	4,956	859	3,165	3,040	724	672
Net finance cost	(567)	(97)	(353)	(590)	(92)	(43)
Share of result of associates	514	57	—	—	—	1
Profit before tax	4,903	819	2,811	2,450	632	630
Income tax expense	(1,519)	(151)	(521)	(303)	(184)	(189)
Profit	3,384	668	2,290	2,147	448	441
Normalized EBITDA	5,868	1,308	3,492	3,540	875	808
Non-recurring items	62	(220)	109	(27)	(7)	(4)
Non-recurring impairment	—	—	—	—	—	—
Depreciation, amortization and impairment	(974)	(229)	(437)	(473)	(144)	(132)
Net finance costs	(567)	(97)	(353)	(590)	(92)	(43)
Share of results of associates	514	57	—	—	—	1
Income tax expense	(1,519)	(151)	(521)	(303)	(184)	(189)
Profit	3,384	668	2,290	2,147	448	441
Normalized EBITDA margin in %	37.9%	34.9%	45.7%	46.2%	46.1%	43.6%
Segment assets	72,222	69,633	16,221	12,052	3,766	3,841
Intersegment elimination						
Non-segmented assets						
Total assets						
Segment liabilities	5,250	6,075	3,819	2,470	785	763
Intersegment elimination						
Non-segmented liabilities						
Total liabilities						
Gross capex	342	318	499	615	155	285
Additions to/(reversals of) provisions	(24)	157	53	88	3	6
FTE	19,597	21,871	28,460	28,517	7,780	7,554

Western Europe		Central and Eastern Europe		Asia Pacific		Global export and holding companies		Consolidated	
2009	2008	2009	2008	2009	2008	2009	2008	2009	2008
33	34	40	46	53	37	5	5	409	285
4,312	4,754	2,492	3,267	1,985	1,494	2,936	720	36,758	23,507
(1,962)	(2,232)	(1,194)	(1,693)	(1,052)	(812)	(2,243)	(597)	(17,198)	(10,336)
(457)	(592)	(241)	(410)	(142)	(99)	(93)	(64)	(2,671)	(2,725)
(798)	(943)	(485)	(660)	(542)	(333)	(275)	(116)	(4,992)	(3,510)
(389)	(345)	(171)	(176)	(142)	(101)	(349)	(211)	(2,310)	(1,478)
(107)	(144)	(121)	(132)	36	26	568	475	661	440
599	498	281	196	144	175	543	207	10,248	5,898
(56)	(275)	(1)	(10)	(47)	(22)	1,261		1,321	(558)
543	223	279	186	96	153	1,805	207	11569	5,340
(299)	(504)	(37)	(97)	(10)	(9)	(3,061)	(260)	(4,419)	(1,600)
(1)	—	—	1	—		1		513	60
244	(281)	243	90	86	144	(1,256)	(52)	7,663	3,800
(73)	130	(48)	(42)	(76)	(72)	636	(47)	(1,786)	(674)
171	(151)	195	48	10	72	(620)	(99)	5,877	3,126
983	948	599	571	349	341	870	295	13,037	7811
(56)	(275)	(1)	(11)	(47)	(22)	1,290		1,350	(560)
—	—	—	1	—		(29)		(29)	1
(384)	(450)	(319)	(374)	(206)	(166)	(326)	(88)	(2,789)	(1,912)
(299)	(504)	(37)	(97)	(10)	(9)	(3,061)	(260)	(4,419)	(1,600)
(1)	—	—	1	—		1		513	60
(73)	130	(48)	(42)	(76)	(72)	636	(47)	(1,786)	(674)
171	(151)	195	48	10	72	(620)	(99)	5,877	3,126
22.8%	19.9%	24.1%	17.5%	17.6%	22.8%	—	—	35.5%	33.2%
5,889	6,169	2,484	3,804	3,549	5,344	4,189	8,210	108,320	109,053
								(2,089)	(1,308)
								6,294	5415
								112,525	113,160
3,067	2,577	418	722	1,143	1,108	3,134	1,389	17,616	15,104
								(2,089)	(1,308)
								96,998	99,364
								112,525	113,160
246	537	175	503	224	282	67	79	1,708	2,619
59	142	—	19	47	22	69	33	207	467
7,551	8,965	10,588	16,054	40,859	41,588	1,654	12,050	116,489	136,599

Koss Corporation and Unauthorized Financial Transactions

In 1953, John C. Koss founded the Koss Corporation and began renting televisions to hospital patients. Several years later he teamed up with a friend, Martin Lange, to develop audio products. In 1958, they began building a model 390 stereo phonograph (record player) and a model SP-3 stereophone in Mr. Koss's basement. The phonograph offered few advantages over existing products, but the SP-3, the world's first stereo headphone, was an immediate success.[1]

In 1962, Koss introduced the Pro4 stereophone, an even higher-quality headset that became the recording industry standard. Music sensations such as Tony Bennett and the Beatles were photographed using the Pro4. In 1969, a Pro4 was installed on Air Force One. By 1983, Koss employed more than 850 people in locations throughout the world. In 1991, John C. Koss retired from active management, and his oldest son, Michael J. Koss, became president and CEO.[2]

Unauthorized Financial Transactions

On December 21, 2009, Lisa Cohen, managing general partner of Barrington Capital LLC, a small Barrington, Illinois, hedge fund, noticed an announcement that Koss Corporation had requested a halt in the trading of its shares until it could learn the extent and effect of unauthorized financial transactions. Ms. Cohen immediately downloaded Koss's press release (Exhibit 1). Aside from the notice about unauthorized transactions, a halt in trading, and the fact that Koss's CFO was on unpaid administrative leave pending the outcome of its investigation, the press release contained only a standard disclaimer about forward-looking statements.

Ms. Cohen next downloaded Koss's 2009 proxy statement (excerpts in Exhibit 2) and learned that Koss was still controlled by the founding family. John C. Koss Sr., the founder, and his son, Michael, were board members, along with four executives from medium-size Midwest manufacturing firms. Koss appeared to be a highly stable firm in terms of board membership and executive leadership. Three nonfamily directors had been on the board for between 22 and 31 years; the fourth joined in 2006. Nonfamily executives had been with the firm for between 9 and 18 years. Ms. Cohen had an associate download Koss's annual financial statements for the years ended June 30, 2005 through 2009 (Exhibits 3 and 4), and the three months ended September 30, 2009 (Exhibit 5 and 6).

The following day, December 22, 2009, the Milwaukee *Journal Sentinel* quoted a federal criminal complaint charging Koss's CFO, Sujata Sachdeva, with spending hundreds of thousands of dollars at high-end clothing stores. The complaint alleged that the spending came to light when American Express contacted Koss CEO Michael J. Koss and informed him the CFO was paying down her balances with large wire transfers from a Koss bank account. According to the complaint, spending included $1,358,322

---

1. Koss corporate history, Koss museum. http://www.koss.com/koss/kossweb.nsf/kmuseum?openform.
2. Ibid.

at Valentina, $670,000 at Au Courant, and $649,000 at Zita, three clothing boutiques north of Milwaukee. The article mentioned a possible $4.5 million embezzlement, a very large amount for a firm with 2009 revenue of only $38.2 million.[3]

Ms. Cohen's first thought was that cash was overstated, but a quick glance at Koss's September 30, 2009, balance sheet (Exhibit 5) showed that overstated cash was not a major problem. She assumed the unauthorized transactions must have reduced cash on Koss's balance sheet. The cash withdrawals would have been offset with some combination of debits that (1) overstated asset accounts, (2) increased expense accounts, (3) increased loss accounts, (4) increased owners' equity—other comprehensive losses, (5) decreased revenues, or (6) understated liabilities. Other comprehensive income did not appear on Koss's balance sheets, and Koss's 2009 10-K did not mention other comprehensive income, so Ms. Cohen ruled out item 4. Koss's income statements also showed no losses, so Ms. Cohen assumed Koss had overstated asset accounts, understated liability accounts, offset the cash withdrawals by increasing expenses or reducing revenues, or some combination of those problems.

Given that investors often over- or underreact to this type of news, Ms. Cohen assumed she might have an opportunity to either short Koss's stock or place a large buy order when trading resumed. Two days later, December 24, 2009, Koss issued a press release stating that unauthorized transactions since 2006 might exceed $20 million, but those losses might be offset by insurance or asset recoveries (Exhibit 7A). At that point, Ms. Cohen decided on a target price for when Koss resumed trading. If the stock traded at 20% above her target price, she would short the shares; if it traded at 20% below her target price, she would buy shares.

On January 4, 2010, Koss issued a press release stating that unauthorized transactions since 2005 may have exceeded $31 million (Exhibit 7B), which gave Ms. Cohen even more confidence in her decision and led to a change in her target price. On January 11, 2010, trading resumed. The price quickly dropped from about $5.50 per share ($81.2 million market value) when trading was suspended to about $4.10 per share ($60.5 million market value). Trading volume was about 110,000 shares on that day; within three days Ms. Cohen established her investment position and then waited for price changes or additional news.

On January 15, 2010, *The Business Journal of Milwaukee* published an interview with Valentina's owner:[4]

> *"You find yourself dumbfounded," Valentina owner Tony Chirchirillo said of the news. "We never expected anything like this."* . . . *She seemed to be "a very nice person" who placed special orders for designer gowns and garments that cost between $2,000 and $8,000, he said.*
>
> *Chirchirillo said he and his wife, Cheryl, and daughter, Gina Frakes, who run the store, assumed "she came from money" and that her job at Koss, plus her husband Ramesh Sachdeva's position as a prominent pediatrician, provided the spending money.*
>
> *The Chirchirillos . . . are now planning the future of the business with the "devastating" loss of their biggest customer. . . . "It threw everything upside down," Chirchirillo said.*

---

3. Romell, Rick, "American Express alerted Koss about executive's spending spree," *Milwaukee Wisconsin Journal Sentinel,* December 22, 2009. http://www.jsonline.com/business/79905827.html.

4. Kirchen, Rich, "Fall from grace: Most shocked by Sachdeva's embezzlement case," *The Business Journal of Milwaukee,* January 15, 2010. http://milwaukee.bizjournals.com/milwaukee/stories/2010/01/18/story2.html?b=1263790800^2737281&page=2.

The Milwaukee division of the FBI issued a January 20, 2010, press release announcing that a grand jury returned an indictment charging Sujata Sachdeva with six counts of wire fraud. The press release included the following additional information:[5]

> *The indictment also seeks the forfeiture of property alleged to have been purchased with the proceeds of Sachdeva's fraud should she be convicted in this matter. Among this property is her residence located in Mequon, Wisconsin, a 2007 Mercedes Benz, and clothing, jewelry, art objects, and household items seized from Sachdeva's home and two storage units she maintained in Milwaukee. In addition, the indictment seeks the forfeiture of various items of clothing, jewelry, art objects, and other items currently in the possession of five merchants in the Milwaukee area, as well as a hand-carved door and a vacation ownership interest in a resort property.*

That same day the Milwaukee *Journal Sentinel* article reported that a mental plea was likely:[6]

> *Stephen E. Kravit, a well-known Milwaukee criminal defense attorney and former federal prosecutor who is not connected to the case, said the short length of the indictment is an indication that prosecutors expect Sachdeva to try to work out a plea agreement rather than go to trial.*
>
> *"Normally, the prosecutors would have laid out way more charges if they expected it to go to trial," Kravit said. A plea agreement would put Sachdeva in a more favorable position for sentencing, he said.*
>
> *Asked whether he would seek a plea bargain, Hart (Michael F. Hart, Mrs. Sachdeva's defense attorney) said only, "These are early stages of an ongoing process."*
>
> *The "unusual behaviors" Hart cited Wednesday include Sachdeva's apparent practice of buying expensive clothing and then leaving it at the shops or placing it in storage.*
>
> *A federal search warrant made public this week detailed a huge cache of goods— including 461 boxes of shoes, 34 fur coats and 65 racks of clothing—allegedly stored by Sachdeva in rented space in the Third Ward. Merchants also have acknowledged that they stored paid-for clothing for Sachdeva.*
>
> *"It is unusual to say the least to buy items of clothing and never pick them up from the store," Hart said. "Does that sound like rational behavior to you?"*

In a January 29, 2010, court hearing, Mrs. Sachdeva pleaded not guilty to accusations that she embezzled $31 million. According to the *Journal Sentinel,*[7]

> *Sachdeva's husband, pediatrician and Children's Hospital of Wisconsin executive Ramesh Sachdeva, also was present Friday, sitting in the third row at the back of the small courtroom. After the hearing, he shook hands with two FBI agents and Jacobs (prosecutor, Assistant U.S. Attorney Matt Jacobs) and said, "Thank you." . . .*
>
> *Jacobs said later that he believed it was simple courtesy that prompted Ramesh Sachdeva to thank the prosecutor and the FBI agents.*
>
> *"I think he's appreciative that we're treating his wife in a professional way," Jacobs said.*

5. Department of Justice Press Release, U.S. Attorney's Office, Eastern District of Wisconsin, January 20, 2010. http://milwaukee.fbi.gov/dojpressrel/pressrel10/mw012010.htm.

6. Hajewski, Doris, and Rick Romell, "Mental plea in Koss case likely," *Journal Sentinel,* January 20, 2010. http://www.jsonline.com/business/82194642.html.

7. Hajewski, Doris, and Rick Romell, "Former Koss executive pleads not guilty to embezzlement," *Journal Sentinel,* March 30, 2010. http://www.jsonline.com/business/83040142.html.

On February 16, 2010, Koss issued a press release (Exhibit 7C) announcing that its Form 10-Q for the six months ended December 31, 2009, did not contain financial statements. The press release stated that "the absence of such unauthorized transactions can be expected to result in improved cash flow from operations in the future." It also mentioned class action law suits against various Koss executives and directors. Although the 10-Q omitted financial statements, it did mention that law officials had seized more than 25,000 items and released preliminary estimates of the amounts of the unauthorized transactions since 2005:

FY 2005:	$2,195,477
FY 2006:	$2,227,669
FY 2007:	$3,160,310
FY 2008:	$5,040,968
FY 2009:	$8,485,937
Q1 FY 2010:	$5,326,305
Q1 FY 2010:	$4,917,005

On February 24, 2010, Koss issued a press release (Exhibit 7D) stating that a law suit had been filed against Michael Koss, John Koss Sr., the other Koss directors, Sujata Sachdeva, Grant Thornton LLP, and Koss Corporation (as a nominal defendant). By the end of March Koss's stock price increased to $5.86 per share, for a market valuation of $86.5 million.

Required

1. Why was Ms. Cohen not concerned that cash was overstated?

2. Which asset accounts might be overstated? How difficult would it be to overstate them? What would be the effect on Koss's value if assets were overstated?

3. Which liability accounts might be understated? How difficult would it be to understate them? What would be the effect on Koss's value if liabilities were understated?

4. Which expense accounts might be overstated? How difficult would it be to overstate them? What would be the effect on Koss's value if expenses were overstated?

5. How difficult would it be to understate revenues? What would be the effect on Koss's value if revenues were understated?

6. Of the possible errors (asset or expense overstatements, liability or revenue understatements), which is the most likely error? Which is least likely? Why?

7. What is the likely effect of the pending lawsuits on Koss Corporation's value? Explain.

8. Did the alleged embezzlement likely start in 2005, or earlier? Explain.

9. Was stability in Koss's management and board a strength or weakness in terms of corporate governance? Explain.

10. Evaluate Koss's compensation structure for its executives and its board. Did that compensation structure influence corporate governance? Explain.

EXHIBIT 1

KOSS
CORPORATION, SEC
FORM 8-K FILING,
DECEMBER 21,
2009

NEWS RELEASE

4129 NORTH PORT WASHINGTON AVENUE, MILWAUKEE, WI 53212 / 414 964-5000 /
WWW.KOSS.COM

FOR IMMEDIATE RELEASE   CONTACT: Michael J. Koss
December 21, 2009   President & CEO
                                                                         (414) 964-5000
                                                                         mjkoss@koss.com

Trading of Koss Corporation Stock Halts

Milwaukee, Wisconsin:

Koss Corporation (NASDAQ SYMBOL: KOSS), the U.S. based high-fidelity stereophone leader,
requested today that NASDAQ immediately halt trading of its securities after discovering
information regarding certain unauthorized transactions. The Board of Directors appointed
a special committee of independent directors to lead an internal investigation involving the
unauthorized transactions and determine the effect, if any, on Koss' financial statements.
NASDAQ halted trading of Koss Corporation stock today. Law enforcement is also assisting
Koss Corporation with this matter. Sujata Sachdeva, Vice President of Finance and Secretary
of Koss Corporation, was placed on unpaid administrative leave pending the results of this
investigation.

Koss Corporation markets a complete line of high-fidelity stereophones, speaker-phones,
computer headsets, telecommunications headsets, active noise canceling stereophones,
wireless stereophones, and compact disc recordings of American Symphony Orchestras on the
Koss Classics label.

This press release contains forward-looking statements. These statements relate to future
events or our future financial performance. In some cases, you can identify forward-looking
statements by terminology such as "may," "will," "should," "forecasts," "expects," "plans,"
"anticipates," "believes," "estimates," "predicts," "potential," or "continue" or the negative
of such terms and other comparable terminology. These statements are only predictions.
Actual events or results may differ materially. In evaluating forward-looking statements,
you should specifically consider various factors that may cause actual results to vary from
those contained in the forward-looking statements, such as general economic conditions,
in particular, consumer demand for the Company's and its customers' products, competitive
and technological developments, foreign currency fluctuations, and costs of operations.
Shareholders, potential investors and other readers are urged to consider these factors
carefully in evaluating the forward-looking statements and are cautioned not to place
undue reliance on such forward-looking statements. The forward-looking statements made
herein are only made as of the date of this press release and the Company undertakes no
obligation to publicly update such forward-looking statements to reflect subsequent events
or circumstances. In addition, such uncertainties and other operational matters are discussed
further in the Company's quarterly and annual filings with the Securities and Exchange
Commission.

EXHIBIT 2

KOSS
CORPORATION, SEC
FORM 8-K FILING,
DECEMBER 21,
2009

PROPOSAL 1. ELECTION OF DIRECTORS

The By-Laws of the Company provide that the number of directors on the Board of Directors of the Company (the "Board") will be no fewer than five and no greater than twelve. We had six directors during fiscal year 2009 and will also elect six directors for fiscal year 2010. Each director elected will serve until the next Annual Meeting of Stockholders and until the director's successor is duly elected, or until his prior death, resignation, or removal. The six nominees that receive the most votes will be appointed to serve on our Board for the next year.

Information as to Nominees

The following identifies the nominees for the six director positions and provides information as to their business experience for the past five years. Each nominee is presently a director of the Company:

John C. Koss, 79, has served continuously as Chairman of the Board of the Company or its predecessors since 1958. Previously, he served as Chief Executive Officer from 1958 until 1991. He is the father of Michael J. Koss (the Company's Vice Chairman, President, Chief Executive Officer, Chief Financial Officer, and Chief Operating Officer, and a nominee for director of the Company), and the father of John Koss, Jr. (the Company's Vice President–Sales).

Thomas L. Doerr, 65, has been a director of the Company since 1987. In 1972, Mr. Doerr co-founded Leeson Electric Corporation and served as its President and Chief Executive Officer until 1982. The company manufactures industrial electric motors. In 1983, Mr. Doerr incorporated Doerr Corporation as a holding company for the purpose of acquiring established companies involved in distributing products to industrial and commercial markets. Currently, Mr. Doerr serves as President of Doerr Corporation.

Michael J. Koss, 55, has held various positions at the Company since 1976, and has been a director of the Company since 1985. He was elected President, Chief Operating Officer, and Chief Financial Officer of the Company in 1987, Chief Executive Officer in 1991, and Vice-Chairman in 1998. He is the son of John C. Koss (the Company's Chairman of the Board) and the brother of John Koss, Jr. (the Company's Vice President–Sales). Michael J. Koss is also a director of STRATTEC Security Corporation.

Lawrence S. Mattson, 77, has been a director of the Company since 1978. Mr. Mattson is the retired President of Oster Company, a division of Sunbeam Corporation, which manufactures and sells portable household appliances.

Theodore H. Nixon, 57, has been a director of the Company since 2006. Since 1992, Mr. Nixon has been the Chief Executive Officer of D.D. Williamson, which is a manufacturer of caramel coloring used in the food and beverage industries. Mr. Nixon joined D.D. Williamson in 1974 and was promoted to President and Chief Operating Officer in 1982. Mr. Nixon is also a director of the non-profit Center for Quality of Management.

John J. Stollenwerk, 69, has been a director of the Company since 1986. Mr. Stollenwerk is the Chairman of the Allen-Edmonds Shoe Corporation, an international manufacturer and retailer of high quality footwear. He is also a director of Allen-Edmonds Shoe Corporation, Badger Meter, Inc., U.S. Bancorp, and Northwestern Mutual Life Insurance Company.

The Company expects that the "Koss Family" (John C. Koss, Michael J. Koss, and John Koss, Jr.), who beneficially own approximately 73.13% of the outstanding Common Stock, will vote "for" the election of all nominees named above to the Board of Directors.

(continued)

EXHIBIT 2—
continued

KOSS
CORPORATION, SEC
FORM 8-K FILING,
DECEMBER 21,
2009

THE BOARD OF DIRECTORS RECOMMENDS THAT STOCKHOLDERS VOTE "FOR" THE ELECTION OF ALL NOMINEES NAMED ABOVE TO THE BOARD OF DIRECTORS.

Board Committees (Selected)

The Board has appointed the following standing committees for auditing and accounting matters, executive compensation and board nominations. Each member of these committees is "independent" as defined in Nasdaq Marketplace Rule 4200.

> **Audit Committee.** The Audit Committee, which is composed of Mr. Doerr, Mr. Mattson Mr. Nixon, and Mr. Stollenwerk, reviews and evaluates the effectiveness of the Company's financial and accounting functions, including reviewing the scope and results of the audit work performed by the independent accountants and by the Company's internal accounting staff. The Audit Committee met three times during the fiscal year ended June 30, 2009. The independent accountants were present at two of these meetings to discuss their audit scope and the results of their audit. For more information about the Audit Committee meetings, see the "Audit Committee Report." The Audit Committee is governed by a written charter approved and adopted by the Board, which charter was attached as Appendix A to the proxy materials, dated August 31, 2007, for the annual meeting held on October 10, 2007 for the fiscal year ended June 30, 2007.

> **Audit Committee Financial Expert.** The Board has determined that Mr. Mattson is an "Audit Committee Financial Expert" as that term is defined in Item 407(d)(5)(ii) of Regulation S-K promulgated by the Securities and Exchange Commission (the "SEC").

Attendance at Board and Committee Meetings

During the fiscal year ended June 30, 2009, the Board held four meetings. Every incumbent director attended 75% or more of the total of (i) all meetings of the Board, plus (ii) all meetings of the committees on which they served during their respective terms of office.

Attendance at Annual Meetings

All of the members of the Board, Mr. John C. Koss, Mr. Michael J. Koss, Mr. Doerr, Mr. Mattson, Mr. Stollenwerk and Mr. Nixon, attended last year's annual meeting held on October 08, 2008. The Company has no formal written policy regarding attendance at annual meetings of the Company, but strongly encourages all directors to make attendance at all annual meetings a priority.

Independence of the Board

Each of Mr. Doerr, Mr. Mattson, Mr. Nixon, and Mr. Stollenwerk, is "independent" as such term is defined in Nasdaq Marketplace Rule 4200. These independent directors constitute a majority of the Board, as required under Nasdaq Marketplace Rule 4350(c).

Code of Ethics

The Board approved and adopted a Code of Ethics for the Company's directors, officers, and employees, which is attached as Exhibit 14 to the Company's Annual Report on Form 10-K for the fiscal year ended June 30, 2004.

Executive Officers

Information is provided below with respect to the executive officers of the Company. Each executive officer is elected annually by the Board of Directors and serves for one year or until his or her successor is appointed.

(continued)

EXHIBIT 2—
continued

Koss
Corporation, SEC
Form 8-K Filing,
Dec. 21, 2009

Name	Age	Positions Held	Current Position Held Since
Michael J. Koss	55	President, Chief Operating Officer, Chief Financial Officer, Chief Executive Officer	1987 (Chief Executive Officer since 1991)
John Koss, Jr.	52	Vice President – Sales	1988
Sujata Sachdeva	45	Vice President – Finance, Secretary	1992
Declan Hanley	62	Vice President – International Sales	1994
Lenore E. Lillie	50	Vice President – Operation	1998
Cheryl Mike	57	Vice President – Human Resources and Customer Service	2001

Beneficial Ownership of Company Securities

Security Ownership by Nominees and Management. The following table sets forth, as of August 1, 2009, the number of shares of Common Stock "beneficially owned" (as defined under applicable regulations of the SEC), and the percentage of such shares to the total number of shares outstanding, for all nominees, for each executive officer named in the Summary Compensation Table (*see* "Executive Compensation and Related Matters—Summary Compensation Table"), for all directors and executive officers as a group, and for each person and each group of persons who, to the knowledge of the Company as of June 30, 2009, were the beneficial owners of more than 5% of the outstanding shares of Common Stock.

Name and Business Address (1)	Number of Shares Beneficially Owned (2)	Percent of Outstanding Common Stock (3)
John C. Koss (4)	1,404,476	38.05%
Michael J. Koss (5)	999,976	27.09%
John Koss, Jr. (6)	295,142	8.00%
Thomas L. Doerr	0	*
Lawrence S. Mattson	0	*
Theodore H. Nixon	2,480	*
John J. Stollenwerk	13,551	*
Sujata Sachdeva (7)	35,785	*
Declan Hanley (8)	60,000	1.63%
Lenore E. Lillie (9)	58,984	1.60%
Cheryl Mike (10)	40,494	1.10%
All directors and executive officers as a group (11 persons) (11)	2,910,888	78.86%
Koss Family Voting Trust, John C. Koss, Trustee (12)	1,216,785	32.96%
Koss Employee Stock Ownership Trust ("KESOT") (13)	339,258	9.19%
Royce and Associates, LLC (14)	370,723	10.04%

(*continued*)

EXHIBIT 2—
continued

KOSS
CORPORATION, SEC
FORM 8-K FILING,
DEC. 21, 2009

(4) Includes the following shares which are deemed to be "beneficially owned" by John C. Koss: (i) 61,732 shares owned directly or by his spouse; (ii) 1,216,785 shares as a result of his position as trustee of the Koss Family Voting Trust; (iii) 124,300 shares as a result of his position as co-trustee of the John C. and Nancy Koss Revocable Trust; and (iv) 1,659 shares by reason of the allocation of those shares to his account under the Koss Employee Stock Ownership Trust ("KESOT") and his ability to vote such shares pursuant to the terms of the KESOT — *see* "Executive Compensation and Related Matters — Other Compensation Arrangements—Employee Stock Ownership Plan and Trust."

(5) Includes the following shares which are deemed to be "beneficially owned" by Michael J. Koss: (i) 538,380 shares owned directly or by reason of family relationships; (ii) 73,696 shares by reason of the allocation of those shares to his account under the KESOT and his ability to vote such shares; (iii) 111,034 shares as a result of his position as an officer of the Koss Foundation; (iv) 85,000 shares with respect to which he holds options which are exercisable within 60 days of August 1, 2009; and (v) 339,258 shares which are held by the KESOT (*see* Note (9), below). The 73,696 shares allocated to Michael J. Koss' KESOT account, over which he holds voting power, are included within the aforementioned 339,258 shares but are counted only once in his individual total.

(6) Includes the following shares which are deemed to be "beneficially owned" by John Koss, Jr.: (i) 247,642 shares owned directly or by reason of family relationships; (ii) 47,500 shares with respect to which he holds options which are exercisable within 60 days of August 1, 2009; and (iii) 53,495 shares by reason of the allocation of those shares to his account under the KESOT and his ability to vote such shares.

[Notes 7–10 not included.]

(11) This group includes 11 people, all of whom are listed on the accompanying table. To avoid double-counting: (i) the 339,258 total shares held by the KESOT and deemed to be beneficially owned by Michael J. Koss as a result of his position as a KESOT Trustee (*see* Note (5), above) include shares allocated to the KESOT accounts of John C. Koss, Michael J. Koss, John Koss, Jr., Ms. Sachdeva, Ms. Lillie, and Ms. Mike, in the above table but are included only once in the total; and (ii) the 1,216,785 shares deemed to be beneficially owned by John C. Koss as a result of his position as trustee of the Koss Family Voting Trust (*see* Note (4), above) are included in his individual total share ownership and are included only once in the total.

(12) The Koss Family Voting Trust was established by John C. Koss. The sole trustee is John C. Koss. The term of the Koss Family Voting Trust is indefinite. Under the Trust Agreement, John C. Koss, as trustee, holds full voting and dispositive power over the shares held by the Koss Family Voting Trust. All of the 1,216,785 shares held by the Koss Family Voting Trust are included in the number of shares shown as beneficially owned by John C. Koss (*see* Note (4), above).

(13) The KESOT holds 339,258 shares. Authority to vote these shares is vested in KESOT participants to the extent shares have been allocated to individual KESOT accounts. All 339,258 of these KESOT shares are also included in the number of shares shown as beneficially owned by Michael J. Koss (*see* Note (5), above). Michael J. Koss and Cheryl Mike (the Company's Vice President of Human Resources) serve as Trustees of the KESOT and, as such, they share dispositive power with respect to (and are therefore each deemed under applicable SEC rules to be beneficially own) all 339,258 KESOT shares.

SUMMARY COMPENSATION TABLE

The following table presents certain summary information concerning compensation paid or accrued by the Company for services rendered in all capacities during the fiscal year ended June 30, 2009 for (i) the Chief Executive Officer ("CEO") of the Company, and (ii) each of the other six executive officers of the Company (determined as of the end of the last fiscal year) whose total annual salary and bonus exceeded $75,000 (collectively, including the CEO, the "Named Executive Officers").

(*continued*)

EXHIBIT 2—*continued*

KOSS CORPORATION, SEC FORM 8-K FILING, DEC. 21, 2009

Name & Principal Position	Year	Salary ($)	Bonus ($)	Stock Awards ($)	Option Awards ($)(1)	Non-Equity Incentive Plan Compensation ($)	Nonqualified Deferred Compensation Earnings ($)	All Other Compensation ($)	Total ($)
John C. Koss (2)	2009	150,000	0	0	0	82,795	0	34,447	267,242
Chairman of the Board	2008	150,000	0	0	0	213,433	0	37,612	401,045
Michael J. Koss (3)	2009	295,000	0	0	0	115,913	0	39,594	450,507
Chief Executive Officer	2008	280,500	0	0	192,995	298,807	0	59,251	831,553
John Koss, Jr. (4)	2009	200,000	0	0	0	0	0	35,122	235,122
Vice President–Sales	2008	190,000	0	0	96,499	46,555	0	39,912	372,966
Sujata Sachdeva (5)	2009	145,000	0	0	0	11,851	0	16,883	173,734
Vice President–Finance	2008	137,000	0	0	18,160	28,717	0	22,585	206,462
Declan Hanley (6)	2009	131,346	0	0	0	264,581	0	30,746	426,673
Vice President–International Sales	2008	110,114	0	0	18,160	286,345	0	32,722	447,341
Lenore Lillie (7)	2009	140,000	0	0	0	11,442	0	22,115	173,557
Vice President–Operations	2008	130,000	0	0	18,160	27,250	0	23,994	199,404
Cheryl Mike (8)	2009	95,000	0	0	0	7,764	0	15,060	117,824
Vice President–Human Resources & Cust. Service	2008	90,000	0	0	18,160	18,865	0	28,513	155,538

DIRECTOR COMPENSATION

The Company uses cash-based incentive compensation to attract and retain qualified candidates to serve on the Board. In setting director compensation, the Company considers the significant amount of time that Directors expend in fulfilling their duties to the Company as well as the skill-level required by the Company of members of the Board.

Cash Contributions Paid to Non-employee Board Members

Directors who are not also employees of the Company receive an annual retainer of $10,000, plus $2,000 per director for each board meeting attended, $1,000 per director for each committee meeting attended, $2,000 per year for the audit committee chair to review statements with the audit partner, and $1,000 per year for other committee chairs for service for each remaining committee.

DIRECTOR COMPENSATION TABLE								
Name	Year	Fees Earned or Paid in Cash ($)	Stock Awards ($)	Options Awards ($)	Non-Equity Incentive Plan Compensation ($)	Nonqualified Deferred Compensation Earnings ($)	All Other Compensation ($)	Total ($)
John C. Koss (1)	2009	0	0	0	0	0	0	0
Thomas L. Doerr	2009	24,000	0	0	0	0	0	24,000
Michael J. Koss (2)	2009	0	0	0	0	0	0	0
Lawrence S. Mattson	2009	23,000	0	0	0	0	0	23,000
Theodore H. Nixon	2009	21,000	0	0	0	0	0	21,000
John J. Stollenwerk	2009	23,000	0	0	0	0	0	23,000

(1) John C. Koss did not receive additional compensation for his service as a member of our Board.

(2) Michael J. Koss did not receive additional compensation for his service as a member of our Board.

EXHIBIT 3

KOSS CORPORATION, CONSOLIDATED BALANCE SHEETS, YEARS ENDED JUNE 30, 2005 TO 2009

	2009	2008	2007	2006	2005
Assets					
Current Assets:					
Cash	$1,664,407	$3,322,873	$4,187,682	$6,146,580	$5,218,698
Accounts receivable	$8,679,606	$10,148,646	$7,938,913	$6,819,852	$8,763,968
Inventories	$9,763,158	$9,374,344	$9,923,544	$10,522,605	$7,595,803
Prepaid expense	$179,549	$504,806	$403,983	$418,818	$1,129,939
Deferred income taxes	$720,121	$783,995	$1,124,799	$1,365,547	$857,840
Income taxes receivable	$0	$0	$291,251	$0	$0
Total current assets	$21,006,841	$24,134,664	$23,870,172	$25,273,402	$23,566,248
Equipment and Leasehold Improvements at cost:					
Leasehold improvements	$1,783,946	$1,766,842	$1,748,816	$1,706,484	$1,662,506
Machinery, equipment, furniture, and fixtures	$2,650,158	$2,488,657	$2,464,050	$3,444,111	$5,068,368
Tools, dies, molds, and patterns	$11,371,402	$9,605,720	$11,656,951	$11,898,074	$11,198,723
	$15,805,506	$13,861,219	$15,869,817	$17,048,669	$17,929,597
Less—accumulated depreciation	$11,729,308	$11,114,852	$13,302,678	$14,011,121	$14,935,897
	$4,076,198	$2,746,367	$2,567,139	$3,037,548	$2,993,700
Deferred Income Taxes	$1,237,727	$1,066,853	$423,928	$672,823	$315,531
Other Assets	$2,149,586	$2,029,123	$2,312,304	$2,457,840	$2,365,982
Total Assets	$28,470,352	$29,977,007	$29,173,543	$31,441,613	$29,241,461
Liabilities and Stockholders' Investment					
Current Liabilities					
Accounts payable	$1,810,466	$2,950,721	$1,371,152	$1,870,256	$3,012,736
Accrued liabilities	$1,153,089	$1,808,467	$2,282,155	$2,149,102	$1,841,862
Dividends payable	$479,876	$480,395	$476,459	$4,202,591	$486,918
Income taxes payable	$175,568	$347,507	$0	$927,528	$692,538
Total current liabilities	$3,618,999	$5,587,090	$4,129,766	$9,149,477	$6,034,054
Deferred Compensation	$1,095,961	$1,047,482	$989,153	$992,830	$961,165
Derivative Liability	$125,000	$125,000	$125,000	$125,000	$125,000
Stockholders Investment:					
Common stock	$2,049,384	$1,649,408	$1,104,200	$541,782	$18,728
Retained earnings	$21,581,008	$21,568,027	$22,825,424	$20,632,524	$22,102,514
Total Stockholders' Investment	$23,630,392	$23,217,435	$23,929,624	$21,174,306	$22,121,242
Total Liabilities plus Equity	$28,470,352	$29,977,007	$29,173,543	$31,441,613	$29,241,461

EXHIBIT 4

KOSS CORPORATION, STATEMENTS OF INCOME AND CASH FLOWS, YEARS ENDED JUNE 30, 2005 TO 2009

CONSOLIDATED STATEMENTS OF INCOME

	2009	2008	2007	2006	2005
Net sales	$38,184,150	$46,943,293	$46,201,858	$50,891,637	$40,286,691
Cost of goods sold	$24,917,013	$29,151,791	$28,284,981	$31,095,377	$25,216,760
Gross profit	$13,267,137	$17,791,502	$17,916,877	$19,796,260	$15,069,931
Selling, general, and administrative expense	$10,653,243	$10,792,064	$10,066,385	$10,063,871	$8,544,383
Income from operations	$2,613,894	$6,999,438	$7,850,492	$9,732,389	$6,525,548
Other income (expense)					
Royalty income	$258,333	$291,667	$324,996	$341,918	$805,485
Interest income	$15,503	$119,464	$169,227	$169,047	$64,795
Interest expense	$0	$0	$0	$0	
Income before income tax provision	$2,887,730	$7,410,569	$8,344,715	$10,243,354	$7,395,828
Provision for income taxes	$911,062	$2,916,280	$3,188,195	$4,021,163	$2,902,001
Net income	$1,976,668	$4,494,289	$5,156,520	$6,222,191	$4,493,827

CONSOLIDATED STATEMENTS OF CASH FLOWS

	2009	2008	2007	2006	2005
Cash Flows From Operating Activities					
Net Income	$1,976,668	$4,494,289	$5,156,520	$6,222,191	$4,493,827
Adjustments to reconcile net income to net cash provided by operating activities					
Change in allowance for doubtful accounts	$77,007	($58,164)	($222,491)	$572,688	$155,324
(Gain) loss on disposal	$0	($149,775)	$0	$116	$0
Depreciation and amortization	$817,957	$961,605	$973,802	$955,166	$1,103,951
Stock compensation expense	$399,996	$545,052	$562,680	$523,194	$0
Deferred income taxes	($107,000)	($302,121)	$489,643	($864,999)	($61,875)
Cash surrender value	($195,463)	($193,533)	($181,787)	($169,181)	($177,641)
Deferred compensation	$48,479	$58,329	($3,677)	$31,665	($24,100)
Net changes in operating assets and liabilities	($639,018)	($18,553)	($1,867,504)	($1,444,503)	$2,251,161
Net cash provided by operating activities	$2,378,626	$5,337,129	$4,907,186	$5,826,337	$7,740,647
Cash Flows from Investing Activities					
Sale of investments	$75,000	$25,000	$250,000	$0	$0
Proceeds from sale of certain Bi-Audio assets	$0	$700,000	$0	$0	$0
Acquisition of equipment and and leasehold improvements	($2,147,866)	($1,179,344)	($426,070)	($921,807)	($1,170,494)
Net cash used in investing activities	($2,072,866)	($454,344)	($176,070)	($921,807)	($1,170,494)

(continued)

EXHIBIT 4—*continued*

KOSS CORPORATION, STATEMENTS OF INCOME AND CASH FLOWS, YEARS ENDED JUNE 30, 2005 TO 2009

Cash Flows from Financing Activities					
Tax benefit of non-qualified stock options	$0	($286,200)	$288,630	$691,660	$104,749
Dividends paid to stockholders	($1,920,586)	($5,591,850)	($5,641,556)	($1,932,483)	($1,923,938)
Purchase of common stock	($43,640)	($1,283,413)	($1,837,655)	($6,605,451)	($2,217,371)
Exercise of options	$0	$1,413,869	$500,566	$3,869,626	$577,188
Net cash used in financing activities	($1,964,226)	($5,747,594)	($6,690,015)	($3,976,648)	($3,459,372)
Net (decrease) increase in cash	($1,658,466)	($864,809)	($1,958,899)	$927,882	$3,110,781
Cash at beginning of period	$3,322,873	$4,187,682	$6,146,580	$5,218,698	$2,110,917
Cash at end of period	$1,664,407	$3,322,873	$4,187,681	$6,146,580	$5,221,698

EXHIBIT 5

KOSS CORPORATION, CONSOLIDATED BALANCE SHEETS, THREE MONTHS ENDED SEPT. 30, 2008 AND 2009

CONDENSED CONSOLIDATED BALANCE SHEETS	September 30, 2009 (Unaudited)	June 30, 2009
ASSETS		
Current Assets:		
Cash	$2,847,643	$1,664,407
Accounts receivable	10,280,462	8,679,606
Inventories	10,371,604	9,763,158
Deferred income taxes	720,121	720,121
Other current assets	920,153	179,549
Total current assets	25,139,983	21,006,841
Property and equipment, net	4,364,028	4,076,198
Deferred income taxes	1,237,727	1,237,727
Other assets	2,160,586	2,149,586
Total Assets	$32,902,324	$28,470,352
LIABILITIES AND STOCKHOLDERS' INVESTMENT		
Current Liabilities:		
Line of credit	$2,750,000	$—
Accounts payable	2,428,020	1,810,466
Accrued liabilities	1,935,695	1,153,089
Dividends payable	479,876	479,876
Income tax payable	287,681	175,568
Total current liabilities	7,881,272	3,618,999
Deferred compensation	1,095,961	1,095,961
Derivative liability	125,000	125,000
Stockholders' investment	23,800,091	23,630,392
Total Liabilities & Stockholders' Investments	$32,902,324	$28,470,352

See accompanying notes to the condensed consolidated financial statements.

EXHIBIT 6

KOSS
CORPORATION,
STATEMENTS OF
INCOME AND CASH
FLOWS, 3 MONTHS
ENDED SEPTEMBER
30, 2008 AND 2009

KOSS CORPORATION AND SUBSIDIARIES
CONDENSED CONSOLIDATED STATEMENTS OF INCOME
(Unaudited)

Three months ended September 30	2009	2008
Net sales	$10,796,853	$11,486,034
Cost of goods sold	6,679,562	7,085,574
Gross profit	4,117,291	4,400,460
Selling, general and administrative expense	3,188,800	2,998,527
Income from operations	928,491	1,401,933
Other income (expense)		
Royalty income	—	58,333
Interest income	—	14,053
Income before income tax provision	928,491	1,474,319
Provision for income taxes	362,112	560,555
Net income	$566,379	$913,764

See accompanying notes to the condensed consolidated financial statements.

KOSS CORPORATION AND SUBSIDIARIES
CONDENSED CONSOLIDATED STATEMENTS OF CASH FLOWS
(Unaudited)

Three months ended September 30	2009	2008
CASH FLOWS FROM OPERATING ACTIVITIES:		
Net income	$566,379	$913,764
Adjustments to reconcile net income to net cash by operating activities:		
Depreciation and amortization	252,107	289,899
Net changes in operating assets and liabilities	(1,363,103)	980,370
Net cash used in provided by operating activities	(544,617)	2,184,033
CASH FLOWS FROM INVESTING ACTIVITIES:		
Acquisition of equipment	(542,271)	(941,493)
Net cash used in investing activities	(542,271)	(941,493)
CASH FLOWS FROM FINANCING ACTIVITIES:		
Proceeds from line of credit	2,750,000	—
Dividends paid	(479,876)	(480,395)
Net cash provided by (used in) financing activities	2,270,124	(480,395)
Net increase in cash	1,183,236	762,145
Cash at beginning of period	1,664,407	3,322,873
Cash at end of period	$2,847,643	$4,085,018

EXHIBIT 7

Koss Corporation Press Releases, December 24, 2009, and January 4, February 16, and February 24, 2010

A. December 24, 2009

Koss Terminates V.P. of Finance and Warns That Financial Statements are Unreliable Since At Least 2006.

December 24, 2009 — Milwaukee, Wisconsin: Koss Corporation (NASDAQ SYMBOL:KOSS), the U.S. based high-fidelity stereophone leader, announced that following the discovery of unauthorized financial transactions, Sujata Sachdeva, the Company's Vice President of Finance and Secretary, has been terminated. Ms. Sachdeva served as the Company's Principal Accounting Officer. Also, two members of the Company's accounting staff who served under Ms. Sachdeva were placed on unpaid administrative leave.

The scope of the Company's previously disclosed internal investigation of unauthorized financial transactions has been expanded to include fiscal years since 2006 and to the present. Preliminary estimates indicate that the amount of unauthorized transactions since fiscal year 2006 through the present may exceed $20 million, but at this point the Company and its advisors cannot assess the potential impact on its financial statements or identify the extent that specific fiscal periods may be affected. Nor can the Company and its advisors yet assess the extent of the possible offsets through insurance, asset recoveries and other mechanisms related to the unauthorized transactions. As a result, the Company has concluded that its previously issued financial statements at least since the end of its 2006 fiscal year should no longer be relied upon. The Company plans to restate its financial statements for such periods as further investigation indicates.

The Company's internal investigation, supervised by an independent committee of the board of directors, including the committee's independent counsel and forensic accountants, is continuing, as are efforts to recover merchandise related to the unauthorized transactions. The Company continues to work with law enforcement and regulatory authorities.

B. January 4, 2010

Koss Corporation's Investigation Expands as Grant Thornton is Dismissed as the Independent Auditors

Milwaukee, Wisconsin: Koss Corporation (NASDAQ SYMBOL: KOSS), the U.S. based high-fidelity stereophone leader, announced that the scope of the Company's previously disclosed internal investigation of unauthorized financial transactions by Sujata Sachdeva, the Company's former Vice President of Finance and Secretary, has been expanded to include fiscal years since 2005 through the present. Preliminary estimates indicate that the amount of unauthorized transactions since fiscal year 2005 through the present has exceeded $31 million, but at this point the Company and its advisors cannot assess the potential impact on its financial statements or identify the extent that specific fiscal periods may be affected. Nor can the Company and its advisors yet assess the extent of the possible offsets through insurance, asset recoveries and other mechanisms related to the unauthorized transactions. As a result, the Company has concluded that its previously issued financial statements at least since the end of its 2005 fiscal year should no longer be relied upon. The Company plans to restate its financial statements for at least the last three fiscal years as further investigation indicates.

On December 31, 2009, upon a recommendation from Koss Corporation's Audit Committee and approved by the Board of Directors, Koss dismissed Grant Thornton LLP as its independent auditors. None of Grant Thornton's audit reports of Koss Corporation's financial statements, including the ones for the past two fiscal years, contained an adverse opinion, a disclaimer of opinion, nor were they qualified or modified as to uncertainty, scope, or accounting principles. The Company is currently evaluating candidates to serve as its independent auditors and anticipates receiving a recommendation from the Audit Committee within the next week.

(continued)

EXHIBIT 7—
continued

KOSS CORPORATION
PRESS RELEASES,
DEC. 24, 2009, AND
JAN. 4, FEB. 16,
AND FEB. 24, 2010

The Company's internal investigation, supervised by an independent committee of the Board of Directors, including the committee's independent counsel and forensic accountants, is continuing, as are efforts to recover merchandise related to the unauthorized transactions. The Company continues to work with law enforcement and regulatory authorities.

C. February 16, 2010

Restatement Delays Koss Q2 Financial Results

Milwaukee, Wisconsin: Koss Corporation (NASDAQ SYMBOL: KOSS), the U.S. based high-fidelity stereophone leader, announced that its quarterly report on Form 10-Q for the period ended December 31, 2009 filed with the SEC today did not include unaudited consolidated financial statements due to delays relating to the previously disclosed unauthorized transactions by its former Vice President of Finance and Secretary, Sujata Sachdeva. The Company intends to amend its SEC filing to include the quarterly unaudited financial statements promptly after the restatements of the Company's previously issued consolidated financial statements are completed. The Company anticipates restating its financial statements for at least fiscal years 2008 and 2009, and the quarter ending September 30, 2009. The Company has discussed with its independent auditor, Baker Tilly, a preliminary schedule to file restated consolidated financial statements possibly as early as April 2010. In any event, although the Company cannot predict with certainty when these financial statements will be available, it expects that these financial statements will be available no later than June 2010.

The Company did report that the total amount of unauthorized transactions that occurred from October 2009 through December 2009 remains at approximately $5 million, which is consistent with amounts previously reported by the Company. The Company further reported that this $5 million amount is included in the total estimated amount of $31.5 million of unauthorized transactions that occurred since fiscal year 2005.

"The Company has continued to operate in the normal course of business despite the disruption resulting from the discovery of the unauthorized transactions," Michael J. Koss, President and CEO said today. "We believe that the elimination of these unauthorized transactions will enhance our future operating results."

"Over 25,000 items have now been seized by law enforcement authorities," Michael Koss continued. "The Company intends to vigorously pursue proceeds from the sale of these items as well as from insurance coverage, potential claims against third parties, and tax refunds."

The Company anticipates that its current liquidity and cash flow from operations will meet its cash requirements for operations, including the additional investigation costs related to the unauthorized transactions, and new product development. After discovering the unauthorized transactions, the Company's cash and cash equivalents have increased since December 31, 2009. The unauthorized transactions adversely affected the Company's cash flow from operations. But the Company noted that the absence of such unauthorized transactions can be expected to result in improved cash flow from operations in the future.

The Company reported that as of December 31, 2009 and leading up through today, the outstanding balance on the Company's credit facility with Harris, N.A. was approximately $5.9 million. The Company does not anticipate drawing additional amounts on the credit facility to support the Company's short term cash requirements.

In terms of legal proceedings relating to the unauthorized transactions, the Company reported the following:
- On January 11, 2010, the Company received a letter from a law firm stating that it represented a shareholder and demanding that the Company's Board of Directors

(continued)

EXHIBIT 7—
continued

KOSS CORPORATION
PRESS RELEASES,
DEC. 24, 2009, AND
JAN. 4, FEB. 16,
AND FEB. 24, 2010

investigate and take legal action against all responsible parties to ensure compensation for the Company's losses stemming from the unauthorized transactions. The Company's legal counsel has responded preliminarily to the letter indicating that the Board of Directors will determine the appropriate course of action after an independent investigation is completed.

- On January 15, 2010, a class action complaint was filed in federal court in Wisconsin against the Company, the Company's President and CEO Michael Koss, and Ms. Sachdeva. The suit alleges violations of Section 10(b), Rule 10b-5 and Section 20(a) of the Exchange Act relating to the unauthorized transactions and requests an award of compensatory damages in an amount to be proven at trial.

- On January 26, 2010, the SEC's Division of Enforcement advised the Company that it obtained a formal order of investigation in connection with the unauthorized transactions. The Company immediately brought the unauthorized transactions to the SEC staff's attention when they were discovered in December 2009, and is cooperating fully with the ongoing SEC investigation.

D. February 24, 2010

Koss Receives Notice of Non-Compliance with NASDAQ Continued Listing Requirements

Milwaukee, Wisconsin: Koss Corporation (NASDAQ SYMBOL: KOSS), the U.S. based high-fidelity stereophone leader, received notice from The NASDAQ Stock Market that because Koss's Form 10-Q for the period ended December 31, 2009 contained no financial statements, it is incomplete and does not comply with Listing Rule 5250(c)(1), which requires the timely filing of periodic financial statements. Koss has 60 calendar days, or until April 20, 2010, to submit a plan to regain compliance. If the compliance plan is accepted, NASDAQ can grant an exception of up to 180 calendar days from the filing's due date, or until August 16, 2010, to regain compliance. If the compliance plan is not accepted, Koss will have the opportunity to appeal that decision to a NASDAQ hearings panel.

As previously disclosed, because of certain previously reported unauthorized financial transactions, Koss is restating its previously issued financial statements for the fiscal years ended 2008 and 2009, for all quarterly periods during those fiscal years, and for the period ended September 30, 2009. Koss's unaudited consolidated quarterly financial statements for the period ended December 31, 2009 were not available to be included in Koss's quarterly report on Form 10-Q filed on February 16, 2010. Although Koss cannot predict with certainty when the restated consolidated financial statements will be available, Koss anticipates that the restated consolidated financial statements will be available as early as April 2010 but no later than June 2010. The quarterly report on Form 10-Q for the period ended December 31, 2009 will be amended to include the unaudited consolidated quarterly financial statements promptly after the restated consolidated financial statements are available.

On February 16 and 18, 2010, separate shareholder derivative suits were filed in Milwaukee County Circuit Court in connection with the previously disclosed unauthorized transactions. The first suit names as defendants Michael Koss, John Koss Sr., the other Koss directors, Sujata Sachdeva, Grant Thornton LLP, and Koss Corporation (as a nominal defendant); the second suit names the same parties except Grant Thornton LLP. Among other things, both suits allege various breaches of fiduciary and other duties, and seek recovery of unspecified damages and other relief. See *Ruiz v. Koss, et al.*, Circuit Court, Milwaukee County, Wisconsin, No. 10CV002422 (February 16, 2010) and *Mentkowski v. Koss, et al.*, Circuit Court, Milwaukee County, Wisconsin, No. 10CV002290 (February 18, 2010).

Sunbelt Beverage Corp. and Fair Value Litigation

Sunbelt Beverage, a wholesale liquor distributor, was a division of McKesson Corporation until 1988, when McKesson decided to exit the industry. McKesson sold a majority of Sunbelt's stock to a group of investors that included the private investment firm Weiss, Peck, and Greer (WPG); several members of the Merinoff family, who had been involved in the wholesale alcohol distribution industry for at least three generations; and former McKesson vice chairman Ray Hermann.[1]

In 1991, Sunbelt acquired certain alcohol distribution rights in Florida held by Jane Goldring, whose family had been in the wholesale liquor business for four generations (the shares were owned by Ms. Goldring but controlled by her husband through an irrevocable trust). (Note: Sometimes the court case refers to Goldring as "she," sometimes as "he." Sometimes the court refers to "the Merinoffs" and sometimes to "Merinoff." This case uses the court terminology in both instances.)[2] In exchange, Goldring received 54,000 shares of Sunbelt. In 1994, WPG sought to sell its controlling interest in Sunbelt, and McKesson wished to sell its remaining interest. WPG asked Goldring if he was interested in acquiring the majority interest held by WPG and McKesson. Goldring declined but expressed an interest in purchasing some number of additional Sunbelt shares. WPG then contacted members of the Merinoff family, who agreed to acquire the shares owned by WPG and McKesson, except for the additional shares Goldring wished to acquire.[3]

Under a stock purchase agreement dated March 31, 1994 (1994 agreement), the Merinoffs and several of their associates gained the right to acquire Sunbelt stock from WPG and McKesson over a three-year period, subject to a formula that would be used to calculate the share price for each round of purchases (WPG formula). At the same time, Goldring acquired additional Sunbelt shares through a share purchase agreement (1994 shareholder agreement) and agreed to use the WPG formula as the basis for computing the put or call price on those shares should certain triggering events occur. That increased Goldring's Sunbelt investment to 120,000 shares, or approximately 14.9%.[4]

In 1994, as now, most U.S. states regulate the importation (from other states and countries) and sale of alcoholic beverages through a three-tier distribution system. Suppliers (brewers, winemakers, and distillers) can generally sell only to licensed in-state wholesalers such as Sunbelt; wholesalers generally can sell only to licensed in-state liquor retailers such as bars, restaurants, and liquor stores.

---

1. Chandler, William B., III, *In re Sunbelt Beverage Corp. Shareholder Litigation Consolidated Civil Action No. 16089-CC,* Court of Chancery of the State of Delaware, February 15, 2010, pp. 1–4.

2. Ibid., p. 4.

3. Ibid., pp. 1–5.

4. Ibid. Judge Chandler noted in footnote 1 that there was an apparent discrepancy in the number of shares Goldring owned, but since the two parties agreed that she owned 120,000 shares, he would not probe more deeply into Goldring's share ownership (p. 20).

The Dispute

Soon after the Merinoff family gained control of Sunbelt, the firm faced several difficulties, including the loss of a key product line in Florida and South Carolina. However, by 1997 it overcame those difficulties and posted record profits.

Throughout the spring and summer of 1997, an exchange of letters and conversations occurred between the Merinoffs and Goldring in which Merinoff expressed an interest in acquiring Goldring's shares. Golding was not interested in selling, especially at what he deemed an extremely undervalued offer price; however, Goldring suggested an exchange could be made in which Goldring would acquire full rights to certain segments of Sunbelt's operations in exchange for Merinoff acquiring Goldring's shares. In addition, Goldring offered to purchase the entirety of the Sunbelt stock she did not already own at the same purchase price the Merinoffs had offered. No Sunbelt shareholder accepted Goldring's offer.[5]

In the summer of 1997, Sunbelt and Young's Market, then the largest wholesale alcohol distributor in California, were deliberating a proposed stock swap whereby each company would acquire 15% of the other firm. Goldring learned of the proposed stock swap through the grapevine and commented to the Merinoffs that the transaction would greatly enhance the value of both firms. Merinoff informed Goldring that the transaction with Young was dependant on Goldring's 15% share in Sunbelt being the stock exchanged (in a 2001 deposition, Vern Underwood, president, chairman, and CEO of Young's Market, stated he was indifferent as to where the shares came from). Merinoff also mentioned his recollection that Goldring verbally agreed to relinquish her shares to Merinoff at his request, at a price determined by the WPG formula. Hermann also sent a letter to Goldring stating his recollection of this agreement.[6]

1997 Fairness Opinion

On July 31, 1997, McKesson and WPG sold their last remaining shares of Sunbelt stock to the Merinoffs at the WPG formula price of $45.83 per share. The following week, August 6, 1997, Sunbelt's board of directors met to discuss the proposed stock swap with Young's Market and the promises Goldring purportedly made to relinquish her stock at Merinoff's request (as well as her denial of having made any such promises). The board also authorized Sunbelt's officers to obtain a fairness opinion for the proposed $45.83 per share offering price for Goldring's shares.[7]

Between Friday, August 8, 1997, and Friday, August 15, 1997, Mark Penny of Hempstead & Co. conducted a valuation of Sunbelt and prepared a fairness opinion for the proposed cash-out at $45.83 per share (Hempstead specializes in corporate valuations, fairness opinions, economic damages, and similar valuations). During that same week, Penny was simultaneously working on and traveling for another project.[8]

Following widely accepted valuation methods, Penny prepared Sunbelt valuations using three separate methods: (a) income approach, (b) market approach, and (c) asset approach.[9] Under the income approach, the valuation specialist estimated

5. Ibid., p. 6.

6. Ibid., pp. 7–8.

7. Ibid., p. 8.

8. Ibid., pp. 8–9.

9. Hitchner, James R., *Financial Valuation, Application and Models*, 2nd edition, John Wiley & Sons, Hoboken, NJ, 2006.

Sunbelt's future cash flows and discounted them at Sunbelt's estimated cost of capital. Under the market approach, the valuation specialist considered estimated values of similar guideline public companies and/or prices in similar guideline public transactions (sales of privately held firms) to estimate the value of the subject firm. Under the asset approach, the valuation specialist estimated the fair market value of the firm's individual assets. Using those methods, Penny computed the following values:[10]

Discounted cash flows (income approach)	$36.68 per share
Prior transactions, Sunbelt stock (market approach)	$45.83 per share
Asset-based approach	$33.57 to $37.06 per share

Based on those calculations, Penny issued a fairness opinion that $45.83 was a fair price for each share of Sunbelt stock. On August 18, 1997, Penny presented his fairness opinion to Sunbelt's board, which then issued two authorizations. First, it issued a call on Goldring's shares per the 1994 shareholder's agreement, which specified the call would be at the WPG formula price ($45.83 per share). Second, it issued a freeze-out merger at the same $45.83 WPG formula price (under a freeze-out merger, a corporation's majority owners form a second corporation that then merges with the original corporation. Merger terms require the minority shareholders of the original corporation to accept cash for their shares). That merger became effective August 22, 1997.[11]

Goldring's Lawsuit

In a September 9, 1997, letter to Sunbelt, Goldring demanded appraisal of her shares under Delaware law, and on December 12, 1997, she filed her appraisal action in the Delaware Court of Chancery seeking a determination of the statutory fair value of her stock plus interest, fees, expenses, and costs. The U.S. District Court for the Southern District of New York compelled Goldring to participate in arbitration that Sunbelt sought pursuant to the 1994 Shareholder Agreement (under mediation, parties attempt to reach an agreement but are not compelled to do so; under arbitration, the arbitrator hands down a binding decision after hearing testimony from both parties).[12]

> *The New York arbitration hearing was conducted from October 1, 2001 through October 4, 2001. On December 18, 2001, the arbitration panel held that the Call and the Merger were attempts to eliminate Goldring as a minority shareholder without notice and without legal justification and to obtain her stock at a formula price, and that the Call was neither valid nor supported in law or in fact. The panel also held that it found no persuasive evidence that Goldring had ever promised she would relinquish her shares to Merinoff upon request, at the WPG Formula price or at any other price.*"[13]

Following the conclusion of the New York Arbitration (which ended December 18, 2001), the presiding Delaware Chancery judge, Chandler, conducted a three-day trial on April 14, 16, and 17, 2009. At the trial, both sides presented valuations prepared by expert witnesses. Goldring's witness was Richard S. Ruback, Willard Prescott Smith Professor of Corporate Finance at the Harvard Business School; Sunbelt's witness was Robert Reilly, a managing director of Willamette Management Associates,

---

10. Chandler, p. 9.

11. Ibid., p. 9.

12. Ibid., p. 10.

13. Ibid., p. 10.

a well-known Chicago-headquartered valuation consulting firm. The results of Ruback's valuations were as follows:[14]

Discounted cash flow analysis	$114.04 per share
Comparable transactions analysis	$104.16 per share

The results of Reilly's valuations were as follows:[15]

Discounted cash flow analysis	$36.30 per share
Sunbelt stock transactions	$45.83 per share
Asset-based approach	$42.12 per share

Judge Chandler's Analysis

Judge Chandler's analysis considers both a fairness action and a statutory appraisal action. The fairness action required both fair dealing and a fair price, but under Delaware law the fair price is closely related to fair value under the statutory appraisal. Judge Chandler placed the burden of demonstrating that the merger was fair on Sunbelt because it did not use fairness devices such as a special negotiating committee of disinterested and independent directors or a majority-of-the-minority shareholder vote provision.[16]

Fair dealing

In Chandler's decision, he made it clear that he felt the defendants' tactics were designed to force Goldring into relinquishing her shares through a "coordinated attack" of alleged promises made by Goldring to sell her shares back to Merinoff upon the Merinoffs' request. When this tactic failed, defendants issued the call on Goldring's shares priced at the WPG formula based on the terms of the shareholder agreement. The defendants also approved a "squeeze-out merger, devoid of procedural protections" as a last-ditch effort to obtain the shares in case the court or arbitration panel held the call to be unjustified.

Chandler further went on to say that the process was clearly unfair. The lack of procedural protections in the merger failed to ensure arm's-length bargaining or to provide a fair valuation procedure for the shares in question. There was no protection for Goldring against becoming a "drastically disadvantaged minority shareholder."

According to Chandler's report, the fairness opinion obtained for the proposed merger was $45.83 per share. However, Chandler felt the fairness opinion itself was suspicious; a one-week preparation in which the lead appraiser was simultaneously working on at least one other project while traveling cross-country seriously jeopardized the amount of legitimate research and effort required to "fairly" value Sunbelt's shares. Chandler noted the convenience with which the "fairness opinion" justified the WPG formula price of $45.83 per share and reiterated the lack of fairness in the process.[17]

Fair Value and Statutory Appraisal
WPG Formula

Chandler opined on the use of the WPG Formula to determine the fair share price as well. He remained unconvinced that any of the proof offered by the defendants

---

14. Ibid., p. 11.
15. Ibid., pp. 11–12.
16. Ibid., p. 12.
17. Ibid., pp. 13–14.

represented a valid argument for the use of the WPG Formula. He concluded that the Formula price was irrelevant to the determination of fair value of Goldring's shares, and declined to give it any weight in the determination of Sunbelt's fair value at the time of the merger.[18] He did, however, go on to evaluate the specific nature of the formula.[19]

Judge Chandler then criticized the WPG Formula for relying far too heavily on Sunbelt's book value. He did not believe Sunbelt was in an industry—wholesale alcohol distribution—that merited much, if any, use of book value in determining a firm's fair value. Companies in that industry rely primarily on agreements and good relationships with suppliers and customers. He contrasted that with industries such as coal or the steel industry, which derive far more of their value from the use and maintenance of physical assets, arguably justifying valuation driven by book value. In wholesale alcohol distribution, however, goodwill and other intangibles should heavily influence company value, which the WPG Formula ignored.[20]

Judge Chandler also mentioned that Ruback's examination demonstrated that the WPG Formula gave a value approximately one third that of the market value of twelve companies in SIC Code 514. In response, Sunbelt argued that Goldring had agreed to the WPG Formula in the 1994 Shareholder Agreement. However, Judge Chandler rejected that argument because Goldring only agreed to use the WPG Formula in the event of a valid put or call but no valid put or call ever occurred.[21]

Market approach

In the market approach (or guideline public company approach), the valuation specialist uses the implied market value of publicly traded firms in the same or similar industry as the subject company to estimate the value of the subject company. A subset of the market approach is the transaction approach, whereby the valuation specialist considers prices paid in purchases of similar companies in a similar time period to estimate the value of the subject company. For example, the market value of a similar firm, or a recent sale of a similar firm, might imply a price-earnings ratio of 8.5 to 1, an EBITDA ratio of 5.5 to 1, a market value-to-book value ratio of 1.5 to 1, and a market value-to-sales ratio of 1.2 to 1. The valuation consultant might determine that in a particular industry EBITDA is the most reliable ratio to use when applying the market-comparable method.

As of 1997, there were no publicly traded wholesale liquor distributors in the United States, so the guideline public company approach was inapplicable.[22] Ruback then deferred to the market transaction method. In general, transaction data is not publicly available but can be purchased from third-party data providers. Unfortunately, transaction data is limited, inconsistent, incomplete, and often noncomparable. For example, the database may provide the selling price for one company, the state in which it was located, and its revenues but not its net income. For another company, the database may provide only the selling price and net income.

Furthermore, there are typically few transactions in any particular industry, and the transactions with data available often involve firms whose size, markets, and geographic locations are drastically different from those of the subject company.

---

18. Ibid., pp. 15–16
19. Ibid., p. 19–20.
20. Ibid., p. 20.
21. Ibid., pp. 22–23.
22. Ibid., p. 4.

Those transactions may also have occurred far earlier or later than the subject transaction. As a result, this method is usually quite subjective. Litigating parties nearly always disagree on the results of this method, and litigators often ridicule the results the opposing side computed using this method. However, the market transaction method is the method most commonly used by private equity firms when deciding whether or not to acquire a firm. The method is inherently subjective, but is often considered a sound method of valuing a business.

Goldring proposed to apply a weight of 50% to the results determined by Ruback's comparable transactions method. Initially, Ruback valued Sunbelt at $149.69 per share using the comparable transactions method. Sunbelt argued that Ruback's analysis, since it was based on sales/purchases, included the implied value of synergies that would likely occur after the acquisitions; therefore, the analysis should be omitted. Ruback argued that implied synergies likely did not influence the determined values, but he still reduced the results of his comparable transactions method valuation to $104.16 per share to account for possible synergies.[23]

Judge Chandler affirmed that Goldring correctly noted that Delaware courts have used the comparable transactions approach when determining the fair value of companies and affirmed that Sunbelt correctly noted that Delaware courts have expressed reservations when using that approach. Sunbelt also accurately recognized that the burden of proof on the question of whether the comparables are truly comparable lies with the party making that assertion (which is no different from the burden of proof lying with the party using the discounted cash flow approach or any other approach).[24]

Judge Chandler then expressed reservations regarding Ruback's use of comparables transactions because of differences in size between those companies and Sunbelt and differences across product lines and geography (both of which introduce differences across regulatory regimes; each state regulates sales within that state, and some states have different regulators for different types of liquor). In addition, Judge Chandler was influenced by two Sunbelt criticisms of Ruback's analysis.[25]

Sunbelt argued that Ruback failed to properly include real estate payments in his valuations and also failed to consider postclosing adjustments. Some sale prices are far higher than others because the sale includes valuable real estate. In addition, the sale of a business often includes a postclosing adjustment, where the purchase price is adjusted upward or downward because of information obtained after the closing date. Sometimes a database includes information about the value of real estate included in a transaction, and sometimes it does not. Similarly, occasionally a database includes postclosing adjustments about a sale, but usually it does not. Rarely is it possible to determine whether real estate and postclosing adjustments were omitted because there were none, or because the information was unavailable. As a result, it is impossible to know whether a particular market comparables valuation is seriously flawed, so the method is always subject to criticism.[26]

Ruback argued that he used a median approach to compensate for any shortcomings related to specific companies or transactions. In response, the defendants' attorney argued that Ruback's comment was "academic doubletalk." While Judge Chandler disagreed with that comment, he did agree that the failure to account for the mentioned issues (size, product lines, geography, real estate, and

23. Ibid., p. 24.
24. Ibid., p. 24.
25. Ibid., p. 25.
26. Ibid., pp. 24–25.

postclosing adjustment) made the market comparables approach too unreliable. As a result, he attached no weight to Ruback's comparables analysis.[27]

Income approach

In the income approach, the valuation specialist estimates the firm's future cash flows and then discounts them to their present value by applying a discount rate, or expected rate of return. Parties rarely agree about either estimated cash flows or discount rates, both of which are highly subjective. In the case of Sunbelt, however, management had prepared projected financial statements and cash flows in anticipation of the Young's Market stock-swap transaction, which was unrelated to the disputed price for Goldring's shares. Both parties' valuation experts agreed to use those projections but disagreed on the appropriate discount rate.[28] The experts disagreed as to the appropriate small stock risk premium, and they disagreed as to whether a company-specific risk premium was appropriate.

Selecting a discount rate may be the most complex and controversial issue in finance, both theoretically and from a practitioner's view. The discount rate gained theoretical support in 1964 and 1965, with the publication of the Sharpe-Lintner Capital Asset Pricing Model (CAPM).[29] However, the CAPM is a highly sophisticated set of simultaneous equations in expectations form. The practical implementation of the CAPM is a simple one-factor linear regression model sometimes called the market model. There is no mathematical relation between the CAPM and the market model and little theoretical support for the market model.

The market model has been tested tens of thousands of times by academics and practitioners. The risk measure from that model (beta) is so unreliable that in 1992 and 1993 two highly respected University of Chicago finance professors, Eugene Fama and Kenneth French, published two articles suggesting that after adjustments for size and book value, the market model beta had a near zero correlation with future stock returns. That lack of observed correlation led to conjecture that simple market comparable valuation method, as discussed in the previous section, may be superior to discounted cash flow analysis.[30]

Small firm risk premium

In general, expected rates of return appear to be higher for smaller firms, probably to compensate investors for the greater risk inherent in smaller firms and the lack of liquidity in their stocks. Adding a small firm risk premium to the discount rate adjusts for the inherently greater risk by increasing the discount rate.

Ibbotson Associates, now owned by Morningstar, sells a commercial database that provides a table of small stock risk premiums. Firms are divided into deciles (tenths) based on firm size. Ibbotson supplies a risk premium for each decile, and the risk premium consistently increases as firm size decreases. Academic studies usually show that smaller firms have higher risk premiums, but the relation between size

---

27. Ibid., p. 27.

28. Ibid., p. 27.

29. Sharpe, W., "Capital asset prices: A theory of market equilibrium under conditions of risk," *The Journal of Finance*, 19, 1964, pp. 425–442; Lintner, J., "The valuation of risk assets and the selection of risky-investments in stock portfolios and capital budgets," *Review of Economics and Statistics*, 47, 1965, pp. 13–37.

30. Fama, E., and K. French,. "The cross-section of expected stock returns." *The Journal of Finance*, 67, 1992, pp. 427–465; Fama, E., and K. French, "Common risk factors in the returns on stocks and bonds," *Journal of Financial Economics*, 33, 1993, pp. 3–56.

and risk premium is not nearly as consistent as the relation reported by Ibbotson. Academic studies have also been unable to find consistent size/risk premium relationships by industry. In addition, academic studies have not found consistent size/risk premium relationships over time.

Initially, Ibbotson provided premiums only by decile for New York Stock Exchange firms. Over the years, as demand for more detailed risk measures arose, Morningstar/Ibbotson expanded its database to firms whose market capitalization was as low as $1.4 million and extended the precision of its premiums, first to 60 general SIC codes in 2000 and then to 500 specific SIC codes in 2005.[31] There is widespread disagreement as to whether any risk premium is objective enough to be valid. There is nothing approaching consensus among either academics or practitioners that Morningstar/Ibbotson risk premiums are superior to other methods or that their breakdown by firm size and industry is reliable or valid.[32] It is also unclear how Morningstar/Ibbotson computes its risk premiums, although it seems likely it is partially based on the market model. Firm's executives do sometimes publish research, and those studies often discuss beta, but it is unclear to what extent the published research reflects Ibbotson's commercial product.[33] From the prospective of users, Morningstar/Ibbotson risk premiums are, in effect, provided by a black box.

Both Ruback and Reilly used Morningstar/Ibbotson risk premiums, and Judge Chandler seemed to accept the Morningstar/Ibbotson risk premiums as valid. However, the two valuation consultants differed on two issues. First, they disagreed on the market value decile to which Sunbelt should be assigned. If it was in decile 10, as Reilly claimed, it would have a higher discount rate; if it was in decile 9/10, as Ruback claimed, it would have a lower discount rate. In addition, Reilly assigned a company-specific risk measure to Sunbelt, which increased the discount rate; Ruback did not.[34]

Ruback chose a premium of 3.47%, which was the value Ibbotson used for companies in the 9th and 10th deciles of equity capitalization. Reilly chose a premium of 5.78%, which was the value Ibbotson used for companies in the 10th decile of equity. Judge Chandler argued that the use of Ibbotson was circular. If a valuation analyst decides a firm is in the 9th decile, a lower discount rate will apply, valuation will be higher, and the firm will be in the 9th decile. If an analyst decides a firm is in the 10th decile, a higher discount rate will apply, valuation will be lower, and the firm will be in the 10th decile.[35] Judge Chandler decided to rely on how Ibbotson said to use its table. The instructions stated that the 9th/10th decile premium of 3.47% was a weighted balance between a 2.65% 9th decile premium and a 10th decile premium of 5.78%. Given that Sunbelt seemed to be somewhere between the 9th and 10th decile, Judge Chandler accepted the 3.47% discount rate.

Company-specific risk premium

Valuation experts sometimes apply an additional premium to the discount rate to adjust for the additional (or reduced) risk associated with the subject company. Reilly assigned a company-specific risk premium to Sunbelt, which increased the discount rate; Ruback did not.

31. Hitchner, pp. 171–173.

32. Pratt, Shannon P., and Roger J. Grabowski, *Cost of Capital, Applications and Examples,* 3rd edition, John Wiley & Sons, Inc., Hoboken, NJ, 2008.

33. Ibbotson, Roger G., and Peng Chen, *Stock Market Returns in the Long Run: Participating in the Real Economy.* http://corporate.morningstar.com/ib/documents/MethodologyDocuments/IBBAssociates/StockMarketReturns.pdf.

34. Chandler, pp. 27–35.

35. Ibid., p. 29.

Reilly applied a 3% company-specific risk premium. He argued that a company-specific risk premium was appropriate because of the at-will termination of supplier agreements, both between suppliers and wholesalers and between wholesalers and retailers, and because of competition in the industry. However, Judge Chandler dismissed the application of a company specific risk premium to Sunbelt. He cited Vice Chancellor Strine's decision: "even though courts may approve the use of these premiums, the company-specific risk premium often seems like the device experts employ to bring their final results in line with their clients' objectives, when other valuation inputs fail to do the trick." Judge Chandler then stated that "Proponents of a company-specific risk premium thus not only bear a burden of proof but also must overcome some level of baseline skepticism founded upon judges' observations over time of how parties have employed the quantitative tool of a company-specific risk premium. Here, defendants have completely failed to clear this hurdle. I believe the use of a company-specific risk premium in this case is unwarranted."[36]

Subchapter S Conversion

Both parties experts adjusted their valuations upward by 26% because Sunbelt converted to an "S" corporation at the time the freeze-out merger occurred on August 22, 1997 (an "S" corporation structure is generally more favorable to investors than a "C" corporation). However, Judge Chandler argued that under Delaware law, Goldring was entitled to what had been taken from her—shares in a "C" corporation (not shares in an "S" corporation). As a result, Judge Chandler assigned no weight to either party's expert's adjustments for Sunbelt's conversion to an S corporation.[37]

Judge Chandler's Opinion

Court's valuation of Sunbelt and determination of appropriate remedy

Chandler had rejected the comparable transactions analysis used by Ruback, the WPG formula, and the adjustments based on Sunbelt's postmerger conversion to S corporation status. Instead, he used the discounted cash flow method used by both experts to value Sunbelt. He drew on financial inputs provided by Sunbelt and agreed to by both valuation experts. He also approved the discount rates employed by Ruback and valued Sunbelt at the time of the merger at $114.04 per share.[38]

Additional consideration, fees and costs

Goldring sought a shift of attorney fees and costs in her favor, and defendants opposed the shift and proposed a shift in Sunbelt's favor. Chandler awarded Goldring all court costs and expert witness fees incurred in the litigation process but declined shifting attorney's fees. Chandler determined the total costs to be awarded to Goldring to be all court costs and the expert fees of $841,763. Chandler denied awarding attorney's fees on the basis that, according to American Rule, ". . . the defendants' action must rise to a high level of egregiousness." Chandler did not feel the defendants' actions qualified as egregious as the use of the WPG formula represented a legal issue upon which parties could reasonably disagree, even though it was not ultimately a determining factor in the case.[39]

---

36. Ibid., pp. 32–33.
37. Ibid., pp. 36–37.
38. Ibid., p. 38.
39. Ibid., pp. 39–42.

Required

1. How subjective was Judge Chandler's opinion with respect to:

    a. Rejecting the WPG formula?

    b. Rejecting comparable transactions analysis?

    c. Accepting the Morningstar/Ibbotson risk premiums?

    d. Accepting Ruback's small firm premium and rejecting Reilly's?

    e. Rejecting the specific-risk premium?

    f. Rejecting the Subchapter S conversion premium?

2. Valuation methods described in this case are widely used in impairment tests, fairness opinions, economic damage calculations, and the purchase and sale of securities, entire companies, and other assets. How subject to criticism are those methods?

3. What, if anything, could a valuation expert do to lessen the criticisms raised by Judge Chandler and prepare to defend against similar criticisms raised by most cross-examining attorneys?

4. Are the risk premiums provided by Morningstar/Ibbotson more objective than the comparable transactions analysis used by Ruback? Explain.

SECTION 7

BACKGROUND NOTES

Fair Value Reporting

In 2006 and 2007, the FASB issued three related financial accounting standards that substantially moved U.S. accounting away from historical cost and toward fair value accounting: (1) ASC 820 (FAS 157, *Fair Value Measurements*), (2) ASC 825 (FAS 159, *The Fair Value Option for Financial Assets and Financial Liabilities*), and (3) ASC 805 (FAS 141(Revised), *Business Combinations*). This note discusses ASC 820 and ASC 825, which became effective November 15, 2007 (with possible early adoption). A separate note, *Business Combination Accounting*, discusses ASC 805, which became effective December 15, 2008.

Fair Value Definition

Prior to ASC 820, at least 67 accounting rules dealt with fair value, fair market value, or market value. Those rules defined fair value various ways and described numerous ways to compute fair value. To standardize the subject, ASC 820 explicitly defined fair value as follows:

> *Fair value is the price that would be received to sell an asset or paid to transfer a liability in an orderly transaction between market participants at the measurement date.*[1]

ASC 820, *Fair Value*, emphasizes that this is an exit price: the price a hypothetical market participant would pay for an asset or the amount paid to a hypothetical market participant to assume a liability. ASC 820 also revised 28 other financial reporting rules so they all use the term *fair value* and define and compute it the same way. Those revisions substantially changed U.S. fair value reporting.

ASC 825, *Fair Value Option,* significantly expanded U.S. fair value accounting, so it is crucial that financial statement users understand the complex and often subtle changes to U.S. and international financial reporting. The International Accounting Standards Board (IASB) issues IFRS rules that have been adopted by over 100 countries. The IASB and FASB have worked together on many issues, including fair value. The IASB has incorporated much of ASC 820 and ASC 825 and, indirectly, measurement levels 1, 2, and 3. The IASB has not revised its fair value definition, so the current IASB definition is not an exit price.

> *Fair value is the amount for which an asset could be exchanged, or a liability settled, between knowledgeable, willing parties in an arm's length transaction.*[2]

Although the FASB and IFRS fair value definitions are brief, both organizations provide considerable guidance on measuring the fair value of various assets and liabilities in a wide range of settings.

ASC 820, *Fair Value*—Basics

Orderly transaction

The ASC 820 fair value definition states that fair value is estimated assuming an orderly transaction. It later explains that it assumes exposure to the market for a

---

1. FAS 157, *Fair Value*, par 5, Financial Accounting Standards Board, September 2006.
2. IAS 32, *Financial Instruments: Presentation*, par. 11, Revised December 2003.

normal period prior to the measurement date, rather than a forced sale. Suppose the asset being valued is a Chicago office building as of October 15, 2010. If Chicago office buildings that sold around that date had been on the market for an average of ten months, then the value of the office building would be its expected selling price on October 15, 2010, if it had been offered for sale ten months earlier. Although that may seem speculative, it is a typical way that real estate appraisers value a building for estate tax valuation, divorce settlements, or business disputes.

Principal or most advantageous market

ASC 820's definition assumes that the hypothetical transaction occurs in the principal market, typically the market with highest trading or transaction volume. For example, in the United States, investors can trade the shares of hundreds of companies on several different exchanges. Nearly all large U.S. firms are primarily traded on the New York Stock Exchange or the NASDAQ. The ASC 820 definition assumes the transaction occurs on the NYSE or NASDAQ, not the far smaller Philadelphia Exchange. In the absence of a principal market, the definition assumes that transactions occur in the most advantageous market: the market that maximizes the amount received for an asset or minimizes the amount paid to assume a liability.

Initial fair value

An asset's initial fair value includes transportation costs but not transaction costs. For real estate, transaction costs include surveys, legal fees, appraisal fees, and real estate commissions. For the acquisition of an entire business, transaction costs include finder's fees and the costs of attorneys, accountants, investment bankers, and valuation consultants. Fair value must also consider any restrictions on an asset's use or sale. Land might have a restrictive covenant that half the property must remain undeveloped. As another example, an acquired firm might have property for which a third party has an option to acquire part of that property at a fixed price or at a price established by formula.

Assets

The fair value of a group of assets is the greater of its in-use value or in-exchange value. A factory's in-use value is the factory's value to a hypothetical market participant who would use that facility for manufacturing operations. The factory's in-exchange value is the total it would receive by selling the assets separately to two or more hypothetical market participants. Suppose a factory consists of highly valuable land, a building in poor repair, and production equipment that could be sold to another manufacturer. The factory's highest value might be to sell the equipment to a manufacturer and sell the land and building to a buyer who would demolish the building and develop the land for other purposes. In this case, the in-exchange value of the equipment and the land (including the building) would probably be greater than the in-use value as a manufacturing facility.

On the other hand, suppose the land is not particularly valuable, the building is in excellent condition, and machines are installed on expensive foundations that make them highly efficient. The in-use value of the factory would likely be far higher than the sum of the fair value of the land and building to one market participant, and the fair value of the equipment, which would need to be transported to and installed at a site owned by a second market participant.

Liabilities

The fair value of a liability must include a discount for non-performance risk—the risk that the creditor will not repay the liability in full, or will not repay on time. For example, if a firm bought bonds for $100 million that now have a market value of $30 million, it might seem obvious that the owner of the bonds should record a $70 million loss and report their value as $30 million.

However, ASC 825, which is discussed below, also gives firms that issue debt the option of reporting their own liabilities at fair value. Consider the bonds discussed in the previous paragraph. Suppose a firm decides to value $100 million (face value) of its own debt at fair value. The firm encounters financial difficulty and the market value of its debt declines from $100 million to $30 million during a fiscal year. That firm would debit its bond payable account for $70 million, credit a gain account for $70 million, and its balance sheet would show a bond liability of only $30 million. The result would be higher profits (or smaller losses), lower liabilities, and a lower debt-to-equity ratio than if the firm had not elected fair value for its own debt. Although the market value of its bonds is only $30 million, the firm is in financial difficulty, so it will be unable to buy the bonds for $30 million.

Possible day-one gains

Under the FASB's definition, a firm might record a gain or loss on the date it acquires an asset. In the case of marketable securities, many securities firms operate in both retail markets and inter-dealer (broker-to-broker) markets. A money center bank might enter into a derivatives contract with a manufacturing client that will provide a hedge for an expected purchase the client intends to make in foreign currency. The bank sets the terms of the derivatives contract such that it expects to earn a profit on the transaction. If the bank has the ability to transfer the contract to another financial institution in the inter-dealer market at an immediate profit (i.e., an exit price that will provide the bank with an immediate profit), then under the ASC 820 fair value definition, the bank should record a day-one gain.

It also is possible that a company acquiring another firm might record a day-one gain. When one firm acquires another, the acquirer must value the acquired assets and liabilities at their fair value. As discussed in ASC 805, *Business Combinations* (FAS 141(R)), if the net fair value at exit price of the acquired assets and liabilities exceeds the consideration paid, then the acquirer records an immediate gain.

Valuation techniques

In ASC 820, the FASB uses terms, classifications, and methods that have been used in the valuation industry for years (see *Business Valuation*). ASC 820 describes three general valuation classifications that are standard in the valuation industry. They are the income approach, the market approach, and the cost approach (called the asset approach in business valuation). However, with respect to fair value, the cost approach does not refer to "historical cost" as used by accountants for hundreds of years; it refers to summing the fair values of each of a firm's individual assets.

The income approach includes discounted cash flow methods such as net present value and excess earnings associated with a particular asset or group of assets. It also includes capitalization of earnings, whereby either current net income or cash flow is divided by a capitalization rate, which effectively capitalizes earnings in perpetuity. Usually, net income (or cash flow) is adjusted for unusual or non-recurring items and for accounting methods that differ from economic reality. These methods rely on an estimate for net income (or cash flow) and an estimate for a capitalization rate (a discount rate, adjusted for estimated growth).

The market method involves comparisons with similar firms that were recently acquired in an arms-length transaction. This method may include private transactions that are available only from proprietary databases and the market value of similar publicly traded firms, where the financial statements and price per share are public information. For example, similar privately held firms may have been sold at a price (or publicly traded firms may have a market value) of between two and five times net income, one and two times revenues, and two and three times net asset value. A valuation specialist would select the ratio that seemed most appropriate in the circumstances. The analyst might adjust the selected ratio because the firm being valued differs from firms to which it is being compared.

In the cost (asset) method, a valuation consultant estimates the fair value of individual assets. When testing for impairment, the cost method is usually used only when there is substantial doubt as to whether the firm is a going concern. The cost method is also used for firms in liquidation or in danger of entering liquidation, and to value individual assets in an acquisition (at their fair value).

Assets with no intended use

Previously, when one firm bought another, the acquirer ignored assets it did not intend to use. They were, effectively, valued at zero. Under ASC 820, such assets must be valued at their exit price, which is their value to a hypothetical market participant. For example, when Mars acquired Wrigley Wm. Jr. Inc., it almost certainly acquired chewing gum recipes it did not intend to use. Under ASC 820, Mars should record those recipes at their fair value and then amortize them over a useful life.

Venture capital, private equity, and hedge fund investments

One of the most significant changes in ASC 820 is that most venture capital, private equity, and hedge fund investments must be recorded at fair value. Venture capital and private equity investments are nearly always highly illiquid, as are many hedge fund investments. Prior to ASC 820, venture capital and private equity investments were recorded at the price of the most recent transaction, which could remain unchanged for extended periods. They rarely changed the recorded value of their investments until the investee firm obtained an additional funding round or went public.

The fair value requirement has a significant effect on investment firms. They nearly always receive a management fee based on the net asset value (NAV) of their investments, and an incentive fee based on gains from their investments (carried interest, or carry). When they valued their investments at the most recent transaction price, that value was objective, even though it may have differed significantly from what the investment could be sold for. Under fair value, the computed value of an investment may be highly subjective and considerably higher than in the past. As a result, the fee based on NAV is far more subjective and subject to challenge, and the carried interest is also far more subjective.

ASC 820—Fair Value Hierarchy

One of the most significant and controversial sections of ASC 820 is its fair value hierarchy. ASC 820 classifies the inputs used to value assets and liabilities as either observable or unobservable. Observable inputs are prices (e.g., the market price of Google's stock or a bushel of wheat), interest rates or yields, inflation rates, and other variables that can be observed by someone other than whoever values the asset or liability. They can be readily verified and reliably measured.

Variables such as projected cash flows, equity discount rates, and market multiples of "comparable firms" are unobservable inputs. They require judgment by whoever values an asset or liability. A third party can observe the numbers a valuation consultant used, but they are not observable because they cannot be observed in a newspaper, database, or price feed. The inputs may be highly relevant, but they are less reliable than variables such as market prices, interest rates, and interest yields.

Level 1 inputs

Level 1 inputs are quoted prices in active markets for identical assets or liabilities. They include quoted security prices that an institutional investor might obtain from an end-of-day pricing vendor. However, not all prices provided by an end-of-day pricing vendor are level 1 inputs. For example, a mutual fund (investment company) or other investment management firm (investment adviser) may own hundreds of different securities for its clients. Those firms use pricing vendors who provide them with a data feed of security prices as of the close of trading each day. Although a price feed would appear to provide level 1 inputs, that is not necessarily the case.

Some securities are actively traded; the price an end-of-day price vendor provides for those firms may be the price at which that security traded in the last minute before the market closed. The price could also be the midpoint of the bid and ask prices where there were many offers to buy and sell large quantities of the security when the market closed. There may also have been a small difference between the bid and ask prices. In these cases, the provided security price is clearly a level 1 input. One other change in ASC 820 is that in the past, the fair value of an asset was the bid price. Now it should be the most representative price, which can be the bid price, the ask price, or something in between.

Other securities may not have traded in the last hour, that day, or in the past several days. The bid and ask quantities could only be for a few hundred shares, and there could be a large difference between the bid and ask price. Because there is no recent price near the end of a trading day, exchanges or pricing vendors estimate the value of many thinly traded securities as of the end of a trading day. These are called "indicative" prices; in some instances they are highly reliable, in other instances they are rough estimates. In these instances, the end-of-day indicative price would be a level 2 input or a level 3 input. Pricing vendors may be unwilling to specify whether an end-of-day price is a level 1, a level 2, or a level 3 price.

Level 2 inputs

Level 2 inputs are observable inputs other than quoted market prices in active markets for the asset being valued. This includes quoted prices for identical or similar assets in inactive markets and quoted prices in active markets for similar assets. In some cases, level 2 inputs may be market multiples based on similar companies. However, the FASB has not yet clarified its position on market multiples for similar companies. In most instances, those inputs will probably be considered unobservable inputs and will be level 3 inputs.

The prices for mortgage interests backed by sub-prime mortgages are one example of securities that were classified as level 2 inputs and are now classified as level 3 inputs. There were active markets for some derivatives backed by sub-prime mortgages. As discussed in the following section, some major financial institutions elected to adopt ASC 820 for fiscal year 2007. Many of those financial institutions seem to have classified their sub-prime mortgage-backed derivatives as level 2 inputs prior to September 2007 because they were priced relative to similar assets in an active market.

Level 3 inputs

Level 3 inputs are unobservable. They are a firm's own assumptions or assumptions used by a valuation specialist hired by a firm. Because fair values are exit prices, these inputs are actually a firm's own assumptions about a hypothetical, unidentified market participant's assumptions.

ASC 820—Fair Value Disclosures

Balance sheet disclosures

A balance sheet line item that is entirely measured at fair value must be identified as such. A balance sheet line item may contain some assets (liabilities) measured at fair value and some assets (liabilities) measured at other than fair value. In that instance, the line item must state that some items are measured at fair value and some items are measured at other than fair value, and must clearly state the fair value amount.

Note disclosures

Firms must explain their valuation methods in a note to their financial statements. This may sound useful, but a major financial institution has hundreds or thousands of valuation methods that they apply to tens of thousands of investments. As a result, the note explanations in 2007 10-Q and 10-K statements are, of necessity, highly general.

Firms must also show assets and liabilities measured at fair value by level, with a breakdown by major asset and liability class. For level 3 inputs, firms must also include a reconciliation that includes the following:

- Beginning and ending balances by major asset and liability class (level 3 only)
- Gains and losses by major asset and liability class (level 3 only)
- Transfers in and out of level 3

For the 2007 10-Q and 10-K statements, the level 3 reconciliations seemed to cover only some asset and liability classes and some reconciliations seemed incomplete or incorrect. That may have been because this was the first time firms prepared those reconciliations or because of the turmoil in the sub-prime mortgage market. Some firms had massive portfolios of these derivatives. At the beginning of 2007, most sub-prime mortgage-backed derivatives appeared to be classified as level 2 assets or liabilities, but as the year progressed, most wound up in level 3.

ASC 825—The Fair Value Option

At specified election dates, ASC 825 allows entities to choose to measure eligible items at fair value. The fair value option applies to most financial assets and liabilities and to certain firm commitments and other items.

Financial assets

Prior to ASC 825, entities were required to report on their balance sheet the fair value of securities classified as available-for-sale. However, gains or losses were included in owners' equity as comprehensive income until the securities were sold. Under ASC 825 firms can elect the fair value option for some or all of their available-for-sale securities. They may also elect the fair value option for held-to-maturity fixed income securities and for joint ventures.

When one firm owned more than 20% but less than 50% of another, the investment was usually recorded using the equity method. Under ASC 825, firms may elect fair value reporting for such investments, but they must still disclose in a note the results from using the equity method.

Financial liabilities

As discussed earlier, one of the most controversial issues in ASC 825 is that firms may elect the fair value option for their own liabilities. Suppose a firm has $20 billion of bonds payable at face value. If the firm encounters serious financial problems, the market value of those bonds might decline to $10 billion. If the firm elected the fair value option for its own bonds payable, the firm would debit the bond payable account for $10 billion and credit a gain account for $10 billion. The result would be a fair value gain and a significant improvement in the firm's debt-to-equity ratio.

Similarly, if the firm's financial condition improved and the bonds increased in value from $10 million to $18 million, the firm would report an $8 million loss. The firm would also show a worsening debt-to-equity ratio.

Other items that qualify for the fair value election

ASC 825 permits the fair value for a number of items that are not financial assets or liabilities but that involve only financial instruments or cash. This list is far from complete, and it will almost certainly expand as firms attempt to comply with ASC 825.

- A written loan commitment
- A firm commitment that involves only financial instruments, such as a forward contract for a loan commitment
- The rights and obligations under an insurance contract that is not a financial instrument but that can be settled by paying a third party to assume the insurance contract
- The rights and obligations under a warranty because a warranty can be settled by paying a third party to assume the warranty
- An airline's obligations for frequent flier miles because that obligation can be settled by paying another airline cash to assume the liability

Financial assets and liabilities that do not qualify for the fair value option

Some financial assets and liabilities do not qualify for the fair value option because they are governed by other accounting rules.

- An investment in a subsidiary that must be consolidated under business combination rules
- An investment in a variable interest entity that must be consolidated
- Pension benefits and other post-retirement benefits (such as retiree health-care plans)
- Financial assets and liabilities that are classified as leases
- Financial instruments that are classified as shareholders' equity (such as convertible debt with a non-contingent beneficial conversion feature—that is, convertible debt that can be converted to equity)

Election dates

Firms had the option to elect the fair value option during their first reporting in 2007. A few large financial institutions made that election, but most reporting entities did not. Aside from that early election, firms had the option to elect the fair value option in their first reporting period after November 15, 2007. For most firms, that was the first quarter, 2008.

Firms that elected to adopt fair value (ASC 820) early could elect the fair value option (ASC 825) early for any existing qualifying financial asset, qualifying financial liability, or other qualifying asset during the first eligible reporting period. Once a firm elected the fair value option for a qualifying item, it could not discontinue fair value reporting for that item. If the firm did not elect the fair value option for a qualified item during that first reporting period, it could never elect the fair value option for that item. However, whenever a firm acquired a new financial asset, financial liability, or other item that qualified for the fair value option, it could elect the fair value option during the first quarter of ownership.

Item-by-item election and documentation

Current U.S. hedge accounting rules are incredibly complex, and they require extensive documentation. In the past several years, dozens of firms restated their financial statements because they failed to meet the documentation or other hedging rules. In most cases, although the accounting failed to satisfy the hedge accounting rules, the differences between the financial statements as originally issued and as restated were usually immaterial.

ASC 825 attempts to simplify those rules by letting firms use the fair value election to hedge certain transactions. One way FAS facilitates hedging is by letting entities elect the fair value option on an item-by-item basis. Suppose a firm owns $50 million of "June 30, 2012, 4 ⅞% U.S. Treasury notes" that were previously classified as available-for-sale securities. Under ASC 825, it could elect the fair value option for $27,535,100 of those notes and retain available-for-sale reporting for the rest of the Treasury notes. Thereafter, it could no longer elect fair value for the remaining Treasury notes, but if it acquired another $10 million of those same notes, it could elect the fair value for all or some of the newly acquired notes during the reporting period in which they were acquired.

ASC 825 also facilitates hedging by placing almost no documentation requirements on fair value reporting. The only requirement is that the documentation must comply with a firm's own internal controls. This is in stark contrast to the extensive documentation required under other hedge accounting rules.

ASC 825—Disclosures

ASC 825 adds two primary disclosure requirements to those required by ASC 820. First, a firm must provide a note disclosure that explains why it elected the fair value option for each major asset class. Second, if a firm elects the fair value option for some items in a group but not for others, it must explain why. Given the extensive financial assets, liabilities, and other qualifying items held by major investment firms, these explanations are highly general. The following are typical explanations from firms that elected early adoption of ASC 820 and ASC 825.

> *Merrill Lynch adopted the fair value option for certain automobile and corporate loans because the loans are risk managed on a fair value basis.*[3]

---

3. Merrill Lynch 10-Q, Quarter 1, 2007, Note 3. Fair Value of Financial Instruments.

Merrill Lynch adopted the fair value option for certain positions, which are risk managed on a fair value basis and for which the fair value option eliminates the need to apply hedge accounting under SFAS no. 133.[4]

The Company has elected the fair value option for our United States and United Kingdom portfolios of fixed income securities purchased under agreements to resell, and fixed income securities sold under agreements to repurchase (and nonrelated non-collateralized short-term borrowings) because these positions are managed on a fair value basis.[5]

---

4. Ibid.
5. Citigroup 10-Q, Quarter 1, 2007, Note 16. Fair Value.

Business Combinations

Fair Value

In 2006 and 2007, the FASB issued three related financial accounting standards that substantially shifted U.S. accounting from historical cost to fair value accounting: (1) ASC 820 (FAS 157), *Fair Value Measurements*, (2) ASC 825 (FAS 159), *The Fair Value Option for Financial Assets and Financial Liabilities*, and (3) ASC 805 (FAS 141(Revised)), *Business Combinations*.

Prior to ASC 820, at least 67 different accounting rules dealt with some type of fair value, fair market value, or market value. Those rules defined fair value in a variety of ways and described numerous ways to compute fair value. To bring order to the area, ASC 820 explicitly defined fair value as follows:

> *Fair value is the price that would be received to sell an asset or paid to transfer a liability in an orderly transaction between market participants at the measurement date.*[1]

That definition is an exit price. It is the price a hypothetical market participant would pay for an asset, or the amount paid to a hypothetical market participant to assume a liability.

Suppose an asset is worth a great deal to the acquiring firm because of some specific need or advantage. Fair value is the lower value to a hypothetical market participant, not its higher value to the acquirer. Conversely, if the acquired asset is worth less to the acquiring firm than to a hypothetical market participant, the fair value is its higher value. In fact, if the acquiring firm has no use for an asset, its fair value is still its value to a hypothetical market participant. ASC 820 provided specific examples of how to compute fair value in a variety of circumstances for a wide range of assets and liabilities. It also revised 28 existing accounting rules to make them more uniform. They all use the term fair value, define fair value the same way, and compute it the same way.

Background

Businesses invest in other firms in a variety of ways, from simply buying a few hundred shares through a broker to the acquisition of an entire company. Accounting for investments in other firms has varied over the years and varies with the percentage of ownership. In the past, if a firm bought less than 20% of the equity in another firm, that investment was reported at original cost and the value usually remained unchanged until the sale of the security. More recently, such investments are adjusted to fair value at the end of each accounting period.

Investments of between 20% and 49.9% are usually accounted for using the equity method if the investor has the ability to influence the investee company's operating or financial decisions (ASC 323). The investment is recorded at cost, adjusted downward for dividends received (a return of capital) and upward (downward) for the investor's proportionate share of the investee's net income (loss). ASC 825 gives firms a choice of using the equity method or reporting the investment at fair value.

---

1. ASC 820, *Fair Value Measurements*.

Business Combinations

When one firm owns more than 50% of the voting rights of another, the investor has majority control unless other investors have been granted the right to block certain actions, such as acquisitions or sale of the firm. Such investments are called acquisitions and must be accounted for using business combination accounting rules. The general rule under ASC 805, *Business Combinations,* is that firms must record the assets and liabilities of the acquired firm at their fair value, partially limited by the consideration paid.

Suppose a firm pays $1 million cash for 100% of the common stock of a firm with no liabilities and two assets, one with a $300,000 book value and a $400,000 fair value and the other with a $500,000 book value and a $600,000 fair value ($800,000 total book value; $1 million total fair value). According to ACS 805, the acquirer must debit the assets at their fair values. The firm credits cash for $1 million and the transaction is complete. Later sections of this note discuss more common situations in which consideration paid exceeds or is less than fair value of acquired assets and liabilities.

ACS 805 (FAS 141(R)), Overview

ACS 805 (FAS 141(R), *Business Combinations*) revised FAS 141 to make acquisition accounting consistent with fair value accounting.[2] The accounting method used for business combinations is now called the "acquisition method" (instead of the purchase method).

ACS 805 considers the following:

- Determine if a business combination occurred
- Identify the acquirer
- Determine the acquisition date
- Measure the fair value of consideration paid
- Measure the fair value of acquired assets and liabilities
  - Measure the fair value of acquired tangible assets and liabilities
  - Measure the fair value of acquired identifiable intangible assets and liabilities
  - Evaluate in-process R&D
  - Measure the fair value of any non-controlling interest (minority interest)
- Determine gain for bargain purchase (gain)
- Determine goodwill
- Identify the differences between ACS 805 and IFRS 3 (as revised in 2007)

Determine If a Business Combination Occurred

ACS 805 does not apply to the following transactions:

- Joint ventures
- Acquisition of an asset or group of assets that does not constitute a business
- A combination between entities or businesses under common control
- A combination between not-for-profit organizations or the acquisition of a for-profit business by a not-for-profit organization

---

2. ACS 805 applies to business combinations whose acquisition date is on or after the beginning of the first annual reporting period beginning on or after December 15, 2008.

Identify the Acquirer

ACS 805 provides the following guidance on how to identify which firm is the acquirer and which is the acquiree:

- The acquirer is usually the entity that transfers the cash or other assets or incurs the liabilities.
- The acquirer is usually the combining entity whose former management dominates the management of the combined entity.
- In a reverse acquisition, the entity that issues the equity is the acquiree. For example, if a privately held business wishes to go public by acquiring a publicly traded corporation, the publicly traded firm issues equity, but for accounting purposes it is the acquiree. In such cases, the acquirer is usually the entity whose owners as a group receive the largest share of voting rights.

Determine the Acquisition Date

The acquisition date is the date on which the acquirer obtains control of the acquiree.

Measure the Fair Value of Consideration Paid

For several reasons, the acquirer must measure the fair value of consideration paid for the acquisition. First, the amount paid must be disclosed to shareholders. Second, if consideration includes the transfer of any of the acquirer's assets, the acquirer must record a gain (loss) on the transfer of those assets if their fair value exceeds (is less than) their book value. Finally, the acquirer must record goodwill if the fair value of consideration paid exceeds the fair value of net assets acquired, or must record a gain if the fair value of consideration paid is less than the fair value of net assets acquired.

Consideration paid for an acquisition may consist of the following items:

- Cash
- Fair value of the acquirer's own securities
- Fair value of tangible or intangible assets transferred by the acquirer
- Fair value of contractual contingencies
- Fair value of non-contractual contingencies if it is more likely than not that they will occur (i.e., more than a 50% probability of occurring)

Under ACS 805, transaction costs are expensed immediately and planned restructuring costs are expensed in the period ending immediately after the acquisition.

Cash

Cash payments are usually straightforward. If they are deferred for more than one year, they are recorded at their present value.

Fair value of the acquirer's own securities

When a firm issues its own securities to pay for all or part of an acquisition, the securities should be recorded at their fair value on the acquisition date. The fair value of equity securities of a publicly traded company is usually their closing market price on the acquisition date.

Employee stock options issued to the acquiree firm's employees

The acquired firm's employees often own employee stock options in their firm. Because the acquired firm will no longer have its own equity securities, the acquirer typically replaces the acquired firm's outstanding employee stock options (both vested and non-vested) with employee stock options in the acquired firm. If those newly issued employee stock options are issued for prior services at the acquired firm, then the fair value of the newly issued employee stock options are recorded as consideration paid for the acquired firm.

If acquirer's employee stock options are issued to retain employees of the acquired firm, then they are not part of the acquisition cost. They must be recorded as employee compensation expense after the acquisition date.

Fair value of tangible and intangible assets transferred by the acquirer

When one firm acquires another, it occasionally pays for all or part of the acquisition by transferring some of its own assets to the acquiree. For example, one firm may acquire a second firm's subsidiary by transferring land to the second firm. The acquirer would record the fair value of the land on the acquisition date as consideration paid and would record a gain (loss) if the fair value exceeded (was less than) the land's book value.

Fair value of contractual contingencies

Acquisitions often include contingent consideration clauses in the purchase agreement. ACS 805 includes contingent consideration as part of the acquisition cost and treats contractual contingencies different from non-contractual contingencies. The buyer must estimate the probable outcome of contractual contingencies and, if it is more likely than not that the liabilities will be incurred, recognize them as liabilities incurred with the acquisition.

Suppose the acquired firm had accounts receivable of $150 million and a $10 million offsetting allowance for uncollectible accounts (net receivables of $140 million). One contractual clause might require that the buyer pay the seller 80% of the amount collected over $140 million. Another contractual clause might require the seller to refund to the buyer 100% of the amount collected less than $135 million. The fair value of this two-part contract could be either a contingent asset or a contingent liability, depending on the most probable outcome.

Fair value of non-contractual contingencies

Other contingencies might exist, not because of contract, but because of potential legal liability or the threat of asset expropriations in another country. Under ACS 805, the buyer must estimate the probable outcome of non-contractual contingencies and recognize (record) them at their fair value only if it is more likely than not that they will occur (>50% probability).

Transaction costs

When one firm acquires another, ASC 805 requires that transaction costs such as finder's fees and payments to attorneys, accountants, investment bankers, and valuation specialists be expensed immediately because they would have no value to a market participant. If a market participant were to acquire the firm, it would need to pay its own legal, accounting, and investment banking fees.

Planned restructuring costs

Suppose an acquirer plans to restructure an acquired business as soon as the acquisition is complete. Under ACS 805, the planned restructuring is not part of the acquisition because a market participant might not wish to restructure the firm.

Suppose a buyer pays $120 million for a firm that has $100 million of assets at fair value and no liabilities. The acquirer also plans to restructure the acquired business at a projected cost of $10 million once the acquisition is complete. The restructuring is recorded as an expense in the period ending immediately after the acquisition. The two entries will be as follows:

Assets	$100,000,000	
Goodwill	$20,000,000	
Cash		$120,000,000
Acquisition date journal entry		
Restructuring expenses	$10,000,000	
Restructuring Reserve		$10,000,000

Recorded in the first period ending after the acquisition date

Measure the Fair Value of Acquired Assets and Liabilities

Measure the fair value of acquired liabilities and tangible assets

Under ACS 805, acquired liabilities and tangible assets are measured at their fair values, so ASC 820, *Fair Values*, offers primary guidance on measuring the value of acquired tangible assets and liabilities.

ASC 820 is discussed in detail in a separate note, *Fair Value Reporting* (Case 7.1): However, an acquirer may need to use several specialists to value the acquired firm's assets and liabilities. If the acquired firm has complex, thinly traded debt securities, the acquirer may need to hire a derivatives specialist to value them. The firm may also need to hire an equipment appraiser to value acquired equipment, a real estate appraiser to value acquired land and buildings, and a business valuation specialist to value the overall business.

Measure the fair value of acquired identifiable intangible assets

Under 141(R), the purchaser must also record the cost of acquired identifiable intangible assets at their fair value. Exhibit 1 lists identifiable intangible assets that ACS 805 indentifies as examples of ones that must be capitalized at Fair Value. Because Fair Value is the estimated price a hypothetical market participant would pay, it is irrelevant whether the acquirer intends to use the assets. For example, Mars recently acquired the Wm Wrigley Jr. Company. Wrigley almost certainly owns dozens of discontinued chewing gum recipes that Mars has no intention using. If hypothetical market participants would pay for the recipes, then Mars would be required record them at Fair Value.

As seen in Exhibit 1, the list of identifiable intangibles that must be capitalized in an acquisition is extensive (valuation specialists have identified at least 100 types of intangible assets that can be capitalized). The FASB mentions only two identifiable intangible assets that cannot be capitalized. First, purchasers cannot capitalize the value of an assembled (in-place) workforce. Second, purchasers cannot capitalize the value of potential future sales or future customers even if it seems likely the acquired firm will obtain those future sales or future customers. When an acquisition is complete, the purchaser must do the following:

1. assign a fair value to each of the acquired firm's identifiable intangibles,
2. establish an amortization period for identifiable intangible assets with a finite life (trademarks, newspaper mastheads, and Internet domain names do not have finite lives), and
3. establish an amortization method (usually straight-line).

U.S. Tax Courts have been active in valuations for decades. Many of their decisions involve intangible asset valuation for estate tax disputes. The Public Company Accounting Oversight Board (PCAOB) has also been involved in valuation. During the first two years that the PCAOB inspected auditing firms, one of its most common findings was that auditors failed to adequately test the work of valuation specialists. However, as discussed in a separate note, *Business Valuation* (Case 7.3), both the calculated values and estimated lives of nearly every asset are highly subjective. In many instances, valuation specialists have wide discretion in assigning a fair value and estimated life to both tangible and intangible assets. Over the years, many valuation firms have developed ways to assign values and estimated lives to the intangibles listed in Exhibit 1 that are usually accepted by the IRS, accounting firms, and the SEC.

Evaluate in-process R&D

Research and development costs are expensed in the United States, except for development expenses for technologically feasible software. Legal and filing fees to obtain a patent are capitalized and amortized, as are fair values of patents obtained through an acquisition. When one firm acquires another, items such as patents obviously must be capitalized, but the acquirer must also capitalize patents applied for, blueprints, formulas, and specifications or designs for new products or processes. The acquirer must capitalize specific in-process research projects if they are relatively far along in the development process and if it seems likely they have a future value.

Until recently, most in-process research and development projects at acquired firms were expensed. For example, in 2000, Cisco Systems Inc. expensed $1.37 billion of acquired in-process R&D costs. Under ACS 805, if acquired in-process R&D has value to a hypothetical market participant, the acquirer must capitalize it at fair value even if the R&D is too far from completion to qualify as an asset under previous rules and even if the purchaser has no intention of using it.

Measure the fair value of any non-controlling interest

When one firm acquires another, the acquirer may buy less than 100% of the acquired firm's equity. The equity not owned by the acquirer was formerly called the minority interest but, for accounting purposes, is now called a non-controlling interest. The non-controlling interest is sometimes valued at its pro-rata share of equity ownership. Suppose a firm purchases 80% of the equity in a firm whose net assets have a $10 million fair value. For simplicity, assume the acquirer pays $8 million for the 80% interest. The minority interest is valued at its pro-rata share of equity (20%), or $2 million. The journal entry is as follows:

Assets at fair value	$10,000,000	
Cash		$8,000,000
Minority interest		$2,000,000

Under ACS 805, the equity owned by others is called a non-controlling interest and is recorded at its fair value. For years, valuation consultants, U.S. tax courts, and civil courts have struggled with ways to value minority interests. The most thoroughly litigated and developed area is federal estate tax law, where heirs of the deceased and the IRS attempt to establish the fair value of non-controlling interests in privately held firms.

There are numerous reasons why a non-controlling interest is worth less than a controlling interest, although heirs to controlling interests have occasionally convinced tax courts that a controlling interest is less valuable than a non-controlling interest. For example, suppose one individual, the controlling interest, owns 60% of a firm and another individual, the non-controlling interest, owns 40% of the firm. The individual with the controlling interest can become president of the firm at a high salary and can hire friends and relatives at high salaries. All of those individuals can travel on business to attractive locations, can attend seminars in exclusive resorts, and can drive expensive company owned cars.

Because the controlling interest has ways to withdraw value from the firm other than dividends, the controlling interest can avoid paying dividends to both the controlling and non-controlling interest. That can make the non-controlling interest so unattractive that the controlling interest can sometimes acquire the non-controlling interest at a very low price. As a result, for privately held firms, courts and valuation experts often assign lack-of-control discount to a non-controlling interest in the 20% range.

It is less common to apply a lack-of-control discount to the non-controlling interest of an acquired firm. Generally, the SEC will not object to a 15% lack-of-control discount to the non-controlling interest, although accounting firms are often reluctant to approve such discounts.

Determine Gain for Bargain Purchase

Under ACS 805, an acquisition can produce a gain in one of two ways:

1. By acquiring a firm for less than the fair value of its assets, or
2. By acquiring less than 100% of the equity, so there is a non-controlling interest, and then applying a lack-of-control discount to the non-controlling interest.

Gain from acquiring a firm at less than the fair value of its assets

Under ACS 805 acquisitions are recorded at fair value. Suppose a firm pays $8 million for 100% of the equity in a company with two assets, one with a $6 million fair value and the second with a $4 million fair value. Since ACS 805 requires that acquirers record acquired assets and liabilities at fair value; the excess of fair value over consideration transferred is recorded as a gain:

Asset 1	$6,000,000	
Asset 2	$4,000,000	
Cash		$8,000,000
Gain on acquisition		$2,000,000

Gain from recording a non-controlling interest discount

Consider the example in the earlier section in which the buyer acquired 80% of a firm's equity for $8 million and the acquired firm had a fair value of $10 million. Under ACS 805, the non-controlling interest is recorded at fair value. With a 15% lack-of-control discount (non-controlling interest discount), the acquirer records the non-controlling interest at $1.7 million ($2 million × .85), so the acquirer records a $300,000 gain as follows:

Assets at fair value	$10,000,000	
Cash		$8,000,000
Minority interest		$1,700,000
Gain on acquisition		$300,000

Step acquisition

Before considering the complete rule for measuring either the gain on an acquisition or goodwill, we must consider acquirers who own equity in the acquired firm prior to the acquisition date. Suppose the acquiree owns 30% of the equity interest in another firm and later obtains a controlling interest by acquiring another 40%. This is called a combination in stages. On the second acquisition date, the previous 30% ownership interest is recorded at its new fair value. Suppose the 30% interest consisted of one million shares valued $30 million using the equity method. If the fair value of the acquired firm at acquisition date is $40 per share, the acquirer records a $10 million gain on its initial 30% interest.

Rule for measuring a gain on acquisition

The gain on an acquisition equals:

1. the fair value of net assets acquired, minus
2. the sum of:
   a. the fair value of consideration transferred, plus
   b. the fair value of the non-controlling interest, plus
   c. the acquisition date fair value of acquirer's previous equity interest of a combination in stages

If 1 minus 2 is positive, the acquirer records that amount as a gain. If it is negative, the acquirer records that amount as goodwill, as described in the next section.

Measure Goodwill

If the acquirer pays more than the fair value of identifiable acquired net assets, that difference is recorded as goodwill, an unidentifiable intangible asset that is a residual value.

Rule for measuring goodwill

Goodwill equals (a) the sum of (1) the fair value of consideration transferred, plus (2) the fair value of the non-controlling interest, plus (3) the acquisition date fair value of acquirer's previous equity interest of a combination in stages, minus (B) the fair value of net assets acquired. If that number is negative, the acquirer records a gain, as described in the previous section.

Suppose an acquirer pays $12 million for a firm with two assets, one with a $6 million fair value and a second with a $4 million fair value. The firm records the difference as goodwill, as follows:

Asset 1	$6,000,000	
Asset 2	$4,000,000	
Goodwill	$2,000,000	
Cash		$12,000,000

Goodwill disclosures

Under ACS 805, the acquirer must provide a qualitative description of factors that comprise goodwill. As mentioned earlier in this note, two intangible assets that cannot be recognized by the acquirer are the value of an assembled workforce and the value of potential customers or future sales. Those two unrecognized intangible assets are almost always mentioned as components of goodwill. Other goodwill components for strategic buyers are potential synergies from combining corporate headquarters, eliminating duplicate computer systems, and reducing the cost of audit and legal services.

Assigning goodwill to business units

An acquirer often separates the acquired firm into two or more reporting segments. When that occurs, the acquirer must allocate goodwill to each reporting unit as follows:

1. Compute the fair value of the individual acquired assets and liabilities to obtain the fair value of net assets by segment.
2. Compute total goodwill, as described above, using the fair value of net assets by segment from step 1.
3. Compute the fair value of each segment of the acquired firm as an operating business. For each segment, this value should exceed the fair value of the segment's net assets from step 1.
4. For each segment, take the segment fair value (as an operating business) from step 3, and subtract that net asset fair value (as individual assets and liabilities) from step 1. Call these differences "excess value" by segment. They are a measure of how much each segment's fair value exceeds the fair value of its individual assets and liabilities.
5. Sum the excess value from step 4 of each segment to obtain total excess value (this should be equal to or greater than goodwill or there is a problem—see below).
6. Divide goodwill by total excess value to obtain a percentage.
7. Multiply the ratio from step 6 by each segment's excess value. The result is goodwill for each business segment, which must be tested for impairment at least annually and whenever it seems likely that a business segment's goodwill has been impaired.

Suppose a firm with two operating segments is acquired for $10 million cash. Segment A has a $6 million fair value as an operating business, and the fair value of its individual assets and liabilities is $3 million ($3 million excess value). Segment B has a $5 million fair value as an operating business, and the fair value of its individual assets is $3 million ($2 million excess value). The summary journal entry is as follows:

Fair value of net assets, Segment A	$3 million	
Fair value of net assets, Segment B	$3 million	
Goodwill	$4 million	
Cash		$10 million

Total excess value is $5 million ($3 million for segment A; $2 million for segment B), so the percentage of goodwill to total excess value is 80% (step 6). Segment A is assigned $2,400,000 goodwill ($3 million × 80% excess value); Segment B is assigned $1,600,000 ($2 million × 80%).

Suppose, instead, the fair value of segment A as an operating business is $5 million and the fair value of segment B as an operating business is $4 million (and as in the previous example, the fair value of segment A's individual assets and liabilities is $3 million, and the fair value of segment B's individual assets and liabilities is also $3 million). The $9 million fair value of the two acquired business segments as operating businesses is less than the $10 million paid for them. Therefore, the acquirer must record an immediate impairment loss of $1 million. This would be a rare occurrence unless the acquirer discovered problems with the acquired business after it was acquired.

Goodwill impairment test

Prior to FAS 141, firms amortized goodwill over a period of not more than 40 years. Under ACS 805, each year, and whenever the acquired firm or one of its segments may have declined in value, the acquirer must test the acquisition for goodwill impairment. For example, in the above example with $4 million of recorded goodwill, assume that immediately after the acquisition the acquired firm lost a major customer and the firm's value declined from $10 million to $9 million. The acquirer would debit a loss account for $1 million and credit goodwill impairment (a contra-asset account to goodwill) for $1 million.

Identify the Differences Between ACS 805 and IFRS 3 (as revised in 2007)

The IASB and FASB worked closely to produce two similar business combination standards. The primary difference between ACS 805 and IFRS 3 (as revised in 2007) is that IFRS 3 (as revised in 2007) lets issuers record any non-controlling interest in the acquired firm at either its proportionate share of equity ownership or at fair value of the non-controlling interest; under ACS 805, the non-controlling interest must be measured at its fair value.

Another difference between business combination reporting under U.S. Generally Accepted Accounting Principles (GAAP) and IFRS is a result of their different fair value definitions. As mentioned, under ASC 820, fair value is defined as

> *Fair value is the price that would be received to sell an asset or paid to transfer a liability in an orderly transaction between market participants at the measurement date.*

Under IFRS, fair value is defined as

> *Fair value is the amount for which an asset could be exchanged, or a liability settled, between knowledgeable, willing parties in an arm's length transaction.*[3]

In practice, it appears these different definitions will have little practical effect.

---

3. IAS 32, *Financial Instruments: Presentation*, paragraph 11, International Accounting standards Board, Revised December 2003.

		EXHIBIT 1
Trademarks	Licensing or royalty agreements	PARTIAL LIST OF IDENTIFIABLE INTANGIBLE ASSETS THAT MUST BE CAPITALIZED IN AN ACQUISITION— ACS 805, *BUSINESS COMBINATIONS*
Trade dress (unique color, shape, package, etc.)	Advertising or service contracts	
Newspaper mastheads	Operating lease agreements[4]	
	Construction permits	
Internet domain names		
Noncompetition agreements	Franchise agreements	
	Operating and broadcast rights	
Customer lists	Servicing contracts	
Order or production backlog	Employment contracts[5]	
Customer contracts	Use rights such as drilling, timber	
Non-contractual customer relations		
	Patented technology	
Plays, operas, ballets	Computer software	
Books, magazines, other literary works	Unpatented technology	
Musical works, such as compositions, lyrics	Databases	
Pictures, photographs	Trade secrets, formulas, and recipes	
Video and AV material, films, TV shows		

4. If an operating lease is at a favorable rate relative to the market, its bargain component must be recorded as an asset at its fair value. If the operating lease is at an unfavorable rate relative to the market, its excess cost component must be recorded as a liability at its fair value.

5. An employment contract may be an asset or a liability, depending on its cost relative to fair value. Under special circumstances, several other identifiable intangibles in the above list can also be either an asset or liability.

Business Valuation

Since ancient times, business owners have used business valuation methods, in various forms and levels of complexity, to make critical decisions about the purchase and sale of businesses (and business interests) and about gifting businesses and business interests to their heirs. American economist Irving Fisher began writing on interest rates and their application to valuation theory in the 1890s, and in 1930, he published his classic work, *The Theory of Interest.*[1] Since then, valuation has become a subject widely taught in economics and business courses throughout the world.

For at least 50 years, business owners have routinely used the outcomes of discounted cash flow (DCF) analysis to aid them in investment decisions such as whether to buy a new machine or whether a business for sale is worth its offering price. More recently, private equity firms have earned huge profits as a result of their ability to identify and acquire undervalued businesses, improve their operations, and sell them at optimal times. Those private equity firms typically use five, six, or more different valuation methods in each decision because, for most decisions, each valuation method has different strengths and weaknesses.

As businesses, investment banks, and private equity firms began to rely on the results of valuation methods more prevalently, one characteristic remained constant; the individual valuation specialist's judgment and experience were still the overarching determinants of both the valuation methods implemented and the investment-specific modifications made to the methods. Any oversight or guidance came from a valuation firm's executives or policies.

A particular firm may have established preferred ways to compute DCF or to calculate certain ratios, and it may prefer some valuation methods over others; however, there was no authoritative regulation regarding which valuation methods valuation specialists should consider, what they should include in their reports, or even whether to issue a report at all. Because of business valuation's historically discretionary and subjective nature, the practice of regulating business valuation may seem unfathomable to some; nevertheless, regulation has gradually expanded into the realm of business valuation. In general, the IRS governs valuations performed for a tax purposes, and various de facto regulations govern valuations performed for external, third-party purposes.

IRS

In 1959, the IRS published Revenue Ruling 59-60 (Rev. Rul. 59-60, 1959-1 C.B. 237 IRC Sec. 2031); the ruling is still widely used today as a benchmark for the validity of a business valuation. The ruling states,

The following (eight) factors, although not all-inclusive, are fundamental and require careful analysis in each case:

a. The nature of the business and the history of the enterprise from its inception

b. The economic outlook in general and the condition and outlook of the specific industry in particular

---

1. Irving Fisher, *The Theory of Interest*, Macmillan, New York, 1930.

c. The book value of the stock and the financial conditions of the business

d. The earning capacity of the company

e. The dividend-paying capacity

f. Whether or not the enterprise has goodwill or other intangible value

g. Sales of the stock and the size of the block of stock to be valued

h. The market price of stocks of corporations engaged in the same or a similar line of business having their stocks actively traded in a free and open market, either on an exchange or over-the-counter

Although the above eight factors leave significant room for a specialist's discretion, tax courts often judge, at least partially, the quality of a business valuation on whether the valuation report discusses each of those eight factors.

Valuations for External Purposes

Business valuations are not limited to internal purposes, such as to aid business owners in decision making or to aid the IRS in business income tax determination. Businesses, business interests, and business assets are also valued for a wide range of external purposes, including the following instances, among others:

- Divorce settlements
- Estate taxes
- Loan collateral
- Business disputes
- Tax planning
- Charitable contributions
- Employee stock ownership plans (ESOPs)
- Solvency or insolvency opinions
- Minority or non-controlling interest valuations
- Employee benefit plans
- Buy/sell agreements
- Liquidation value in bankruptcy

Often, the instances listed above involve litigation; despite the present lack of definitive valuation regulation, many courts give credence to de facto regulation, or valuation standards developed by reputable valuation professional associations and followed by their members.

De Facto Regulation

The Appraisal Foundation

Whereas *valuation* is the process of valuing a business or intangible asset (or an ownership interest in a business or intangible asset), *appraisal* is the process of valuing specialized tangible assets such as real estate, art, coins, machinery and equipment, jewelry, antiques, or other collectibles. In 1987, eight different appraisal groups came together to form The Appraisal Foundation (TAF).

In response to rampant real estate lending fraud in the savings and loan industry, the U.S. Congress passed Title XI of the Financial Institutions Recovery, Reform, and Enforcement Act in 1989. The act required that federal interests in real estate-related transactions be protected by having appraisals performed on real estate-related transactions that are (1) in writing, (2) performed in accordance with uniform standards, and (3) performed by competent individuals.

As part of the Act, Congress gave TAF the authority to establish the Uniform Standards of Professional Appraisal Practice (USPAP) to govern real estate-related transactions involving the federal government. Congress also gave TAF authority to set training and certification standards for real estate appraisers who value federal interests in real estate-related transactions. However, TAF's authority does not extend to business valuation in general—only to valuations performed on real estate in which the federal government has an interest.

The American Society of Appraisers and the National Association of Certified Valuation Analysts

The American Society of Appraisers (ASA), one of the eight founding (and funding) organizations of The Appraisal Foundation, is the largest multidisciplinary appraisal organization in the United States. The ASA comprises several disciplines, including real property (land and buildings), gems and jewelry, machinery and technical specialties, and personal property. By U.S. statute, USPAP applies only to real estate transactions; however, the ASA requires that its members use USPAP standards for appraisals performed in all disciplines. In addition, the ASA also has a specific business valuation section comprising education, testing, and certification rules regarding business valuations. ASA Business Valuation section members must follow the section's Business Valuation Standards, its Principles of Appraisal Practice and Code of Ethics, and the USPAP standards. A second organization, the National Association of Certified Valuation Analysts (NACVA), also has its own educational, testing, and certification rules, and its members must follow the NACVA business valuation and ethics standards.

Neither the U.S. Congress nor any individual state government requires that business valuations follow USPAP, and no governmental agency has authorized either the ASA or the NACVA to set authoritative business valuation rules, ethical rules, or licensing standards. However, recent court rulings seem to have adopted USPAP standards as a de facto regulation regarding business valuations, and the courts often give credence to certifications by ASA, NACVA, and similar organizations. One example is a 2002 United States Tax Court ruling concerning the fair value of Kohler, Inc. stock for estate tax determination purposes, where the United States Tax Court held:

> *Although Dr. Hakala (the IRS expert witness) has a doctorate from the University of Minnesota and is a Chartered Financial Analyst, he is not a member of the American Society of Appraisers nor the Appraisal Foundation. Dr. Hakala's report also was not submitted in accordance with the Uniform Standards of Professional Appraisal Practice (USPAP). Dr. Hakala did not provide the customary USPAP certification, which assures readers that the appraiser has no bias regarding the parties, no other persons besides those listed provided professional assistance, and that the conclusions in the report were developed in conformity with USPAP.[2]*

Public Company Accounting Oversight Board (PCAOB)

The Public Company Accounting Oversight Board (PCAOB) was created by the U.S. Congress as part of the Sarbanes-Oxley Act to oversee the work of public accounting firms that audit publicly traded corporations. Although, technically, the PCAOB

---

2. See Exhibit 1 for USPAP's requirement for a Certification.

is a private, nonprofit corporation, the board is controlled by the U.S. Securities and Exchange Commission (SEC). The SEC appoints the five PCAOB Board members, and it approves the PCAOB budget each year. After budget approval, the PCAOB then funds itself by billing service fees to publicly traded corporations and to certified public accounting (CPA) firms subject to the Act's oversight.

To comply with ASC 805 (formerly FAS 141 (R)), corporations acquiring other businesses must compute the fair value of the acquired businesses' individual assets and liabilities. Corporations also must test goodwill for impairment at least annually, and they must also test goodwill and other long-lived assets for impairment whenever it seems likely impairment may exist. Corporations often employ third-party valuation specialists to determine and assign values to the individual assets and liabilities in the acquisition and to test for impairment.

A common deficiency the PCAOB noted in its audit inspections was the auditors' failure to provide evidence they had evaluated the assumptions and methods used by valuation specialists. This finding was so prevalent that some auditors and valuation specialists were concerned that (a) the PCAOB expected auditors to effectively conduct their own valuations (even though the Sarbanes-Oxley Act prohibits CPA firms from auditing their own valuation work) and (b) the PCAOB preferred certain valuation methods over others and would challenge the work of valuation specialists who did not use PCAOB-preferred methods.

The Financial Accounting Standards Board (FASB)

In 2007, ASC 820 (FAS 157) established a prevailing definition for fair value. The standard describes in detail how to compute fair value, and the FASB retrospectively applied this definition to 28 prior standards. ASC 820 extends much of the valuation terminology and methodology to U.S. Generally Accepted Accounting Principles (GAAP).

Valuation methods

First, ASC (820) adopts the valuation practice's concept of three distinct valuation methodologies: the market approach, the income approach, and the cost approach (often called the asset approach, but the cost/asset approach does not refer to historical cost as used by accountants for hundreds of years. Instead, it refers to the fair value of individual assets and liabilities).

The market approach refers to methods such as the guideline public company method and the market transaction method. In the guideline public company method, a valuation specialist determines a value for a business by identifying publicly traded companies that are comparable to the subject company. The valuation specialist then applies certain financial ratios (called "multiples") of the guideline companies to the subject company (e.g., price-to-earnings multiple, price-to-book multiple, or price-to-sales multiple). In the market transaction method, the specialist identifies and analyzes privately held companies that are similar to the subject company and determines a value for the business based on the selling prices of those similar businesses.

The income approach comprises methods such as discounted cash flow valuation, excess earnings valuation, and capitalization of earnings (e.g., current year earnings discounted into perpetuity by dividing those earnings by a discount rate).

The cost or asset approach is typically used for asset-intensive businesses or businesses in financial distress or in liquidation. This approach determines a value for the business by estimating the current market value of a firm's individual assets less, its liabilities.

Discounts and premiums

Another concept the FASB adopted from the valuation practice is the application of discounts and premiums to the indicated value of a business. The valuation practice has historically applied a discount to the indicated value of the non-controlling business interest (interest comprising less than 50% ownership) because the non-controlling interest holder's interest is often subject to the decision making of the controlling interest holder. Conversely, valuation specialists typically assign a control premium to the controlling interest. The average discount for lack of control (DLOC) is approximately 20% for non-controlling interests in privately held companies, but it may range from approximately 10% to 45%. For publicly traded companies, the discount generally does not exceed 15%.

Another common discount is a discount for lack of marketability (DLOM). Valuation specialists often apply DLOMs to the indicated values of smaller businesses because interests in smaller businesses are harder to transfer than interests in larger, publicly traded companies. Valuation specialists typically assign DLOMs in the range of 5–45%.

Valuation specialists also may apply a key employee discount if the success of the business is dependent on "key" employees who might voluntarily leave the firm, die, or be incapacitated. The discount reflects the diminished value of the business if those employees were to voluntarily leave the firm, die, or be incapacitated. Key employee discounts often range between 10% and 20%, but they can be greater if the business's reliance on these employees is significant.

When a valuation specialist assigns more than one discount to an indicated business value, the discounts are multiplicative and they are usually applied in a certain order. *Enterprise discounts* (discounts that applied to an entire business, which is also called the enterprise value) are applied before *interest discounts* (applied solely to the interest being valued, such as a non-controlling interest in a business). Key employee and lack of marketability discounts are enterprise discounts; a lack of control discounts is an interest discount.

Suppose a valuation specialist computes a firm's indicated value as $20 million based on either a market approach or an income approach, as discussed above. Then suppose that a valuation specialist determines that three discounts are applicable when valuing a non-controlling interest in that firm—a 10% key employee discount, a 20% lack of marketability discount, and a 25% non-controlling interest discount (with the non-controlling interest discount applied to a 10% minority equity interest in the company).

The order of application of enterprise discounts is irrelevant because the discounts are multiplicative. If the specialist first applies the 10% key employee discount, the adjusted value becomes $18 million; then, after applying the 20% lack of marketability discount, the adjusted value becomes $14.4 million. Next, the specialist makes adjustments for the specific interest being valued, which in this case is the 10% non-controlling interest. The specialist first computes the value of a 10% interest before the lack-of-control discount, as follows: $14.4 million × 10% = $1.44 million. The non-controlling or lack-of-control discount is 25%, or: $1.44 million × 25% = $0.36 million. The 10% non-controlling interest is, therefore: $1.44 million − $0.36 million = $1.08 million.

Conversely, the interest-level discount for lack of control translates to a control premium for the controlling interest. The indicated value of the 90% controlling interest without considering the control premium is: $14.4 million enterprise value × 90% interest = $12.96 million. Considering the control premium, the controlling interest is: $12.96 million + $.36 million control premium = $13.32 million, and the total value of the firm is $1.08 million (non-controlling interest) + $13.32 million (controlling interest) = $14.4 million.

Uniform Standards of Professional Appraisal Practice (USPAP)

The USPAP Business Appraisal (valuation) Standards consist of a certification requirement (Exhibit 1), standards for developing a business valuation (Standard 9, Exhibit 2), and standards for reporting the results of a valuation (Standard 10, Exhibit 3).

American Society of Appraisers (ASA) Business Valuation Standards

The ASA provides Business Valuation Standards on its Web page; the eight sections are shown below. As with the USPAP Standards, the ASA Standards are relatively general in nature and brief (20 pages for the eight sections).

BVS-I   General Requirements for Developing a Business Valuation

BVS-II   Financial Statement Adjustments

BVS-III   Asset-Based Approach to Business Valuation

BVS-IV   Income Approach to Business Valuation

BVS-V   Market Approach to Business Valuation

BVS-VI   Reaching a Conclusion of Value

BVS-VII   Valuation Discounts and Premiums

BVS-VIII   Comprehensive Written Business Valuation Report

Summary

As businesses' needs for fair value calculations in financial reporting increase, business owners' use of independent third-party valuation specialists will likely increase as well. Additionally, as private equity firms must now value their investments at fair value for financial reporting purposes, many of them use third-party valuations to avoid litigation.

The practice of business valuation is, and always has been, highly subjective, and there are no overarching standards governing its application. The PCAOB and IRS provide some inspection of valuation work, but the inspections are generally high level and seem to be primarily in response to seriously flawed valuations. Several valuation and appraisal professional organizations promulgate standards their members must adhere to, but the organizations rarely investigate member compliance unless non-compliance is obvious.

Despite the inherent subjectivity and lack of oversight in the field, increasing transparency requirements for financial reporting—especially in regard to fair value—will likely increase the reliance on work performed by independent third-party valuation specialists. Increasing transparency requirements will also likely lead to audit firms more closely scrutinizing the valuations performed by third-party valuation specialists, including evaluating the specialists' underlying assumptions.

EXHIBIT 1

USPAP
CERTIFICATION

Standards Rule 10-3[3]

I certify that, to the best of my knowledge and belief:

- The statements of fact contained in this report are true and correct.
- The reported analyses, opinions, and conclusions are limited only by the reported assumptions and limiting conditions and are my personal, impartial, and unbiased professional analyses, opinions, and conclusions.
- I have no (or the specified) present or prospective interest in the property that is the subject of this report, and I have no (or the specified) personal interest with respect to the parties involved.
- I have no bias with respect to the property that is the subject of this report or to the parties involved with the assignment.
- My engagement in this assignment was not contingent upon developing or reporting predetermined results.
- My compensation for completing this assignment is not contingent upon the development or reporting of a predetermined value or direction in value that favors the cause of the client, the amount of the value opinion, the attainment of a stipulated result, or the occurrence of a subsequent event directly related to the intended use of this appraisal.
- My analyses, opinions, and conclusions were developed, and this report has been prepared, in conformity with the *Uniform Standards of Professional Appraisal Practice*.
- No one provided significant business and/or intangible asset appraisal assistance to the person signing this certification. (If there are exceptions, the name of each individual providing significant business and/or intangible asset appraisal assistance must be stated.)

3. Material in this exhibit is from Appraisalfoundation.org, Standard 10, *Business Appraisal Reporting*, 10-3, *Certification*, USPAP 2008–2009.

EXHIBIT 2

STANDARD 9

Business Appraisal, Development
Standard 9: *Business Appraisal, Development*

In developing an appraisal of an interest in a business enterprise or intangible asset, an appraiser must identify the problem to be solved, determine the scope of work necessary to solve the problem, and correctly complete the research and analyses necessary to produce a credible appraisal.[4]

Standard Rule 9-1

In developing an appraisal of an interest in a business enterprise or intangible asset, an appraiser must:

a) be aware of, understand, and correctly employ those recognized approaches, methods and procedures that are necessary to produce a credible appraisal;

b) not commit a substantial error of omission or commission that significantly affects an appraisal; and

c) not render appraisal services in a careless or negligent manner, such as by making a series of errors that, although individually might not significantly affect the results of an appraisal, in the aggregate affect the credibility of those results.

Standards Rule 9-2

a) identify the client and other intended users;

b) identify the intended use of the appraiser's opinion and conclusion[5];

c) identify the standard and definition of value and the premise of value[6];

d) identify the effective date of the appraisal;

e) identify the characteristics of the subject property that are relevant to the standard (type) and definition of value and intended use of the appraisal, including:

   i. the subject business enterprise or intangible asset, if applicable;

   ii. the interest in the business enterprise, equity, asset, or liability to be valued[7];

   iii. all buy-sell and option agreements, investment letter stock restrictions, restrictive corporate charter or partnership agreement clauses, and similar features or factors that may have an influence of value;

   iv. the extent to which the interest contains elements of control[8];

   v. the extent to which the interest is marketable and/or liquid;

f) identify any extraordinary assumptions necessary in the assignment;

g) identify any hypothetical conditions necessary in the assignment; and

h) determine the scope of work necessary to produce credible assignment results in accordance with the scope of work rule.

---

4. Material in this exhibit is from Appraisalfoundation.org, Standard 9, *Business Appraisal, Development*.

5. Such as for loan collateral or business dispute.

6. Standard of value means, for example, fair value, fair market value, or investment value. Definition of value does not seem to be defined in USPAP; premise of value means value as a going concern or liquidation value.

7. Such as 40% of the equity.

8. Such as lack of control or control.

(continued)

EXHIBIT 2—
continued

STANDARD 9

Standards Rule 9-3

In developing an appraisal of an equity interest in a business enterprise with the ability to cause liquidation, an appraiser must investigate the possibility that the business enterprise may have a higher value by liquidation of all or part of the enterprise than by continued operation as is. If liquidation of all or part of the enterprise is the indicted premise of value, an appraisal of any real property or personal property to be liquidated may be appropriate.

Standards Rule 9-4

In developing an appraisal of an interest in a business enterprise or intangible asset, an appraiser must collect and analyze all information necessary for credible assignment results.

a) An appraiser must develop value opinion(s) and conclusion(s) by use of one or more approaches that are necessary for credible assignment results.

b) An appraiser must, when necessary for credible assignment results, analyze the effect on value, if any, of:

  i. The nature and history of the business enterprise or intangible asset;

  ii. Financial and economic conditions affecting the business enterprise or intangible asset, its industry, and the general economy;

  iii. Past results, current operations, and future prospects of the business enterprise;

  iv. Past sales of capital stock or other ownership interests in the business enterprise or intangible asset being appraised;

  v. Sales of capital stock or other ownership interests in similar business enterprises;

  vi. Prices, terms, and conditions affecting past sales of similar ownership interests in the asset being appraised or a similar asset; and

  vii. Economic benefit of tangible and intangible assets.

c) An appraiser must, when necessary for credible assignment results, analyze the effect on value, if any, of buy-sell and option agreements, investment letter stock restrictions, restrictive charter or partnership agreement clauses, and similar features or factors that may influence value.

d) An appraiser must, when necessary for credible assignment results, analyze the effect on value, if any, of the extent to which the interest appraised contains elements of ownership control and is marketable and/or liquid.

Standards Rule 9-5

In developing an appraisal of a business enterprise or intangible asset, an appraiser must:

a) reconcile the quality and quantity of data available and analyzed within the approaches, methods, and procedures used; and

b) reconcile the applicability and relevance of the approaches, methods and procedures used to arrive at the value conclusion.

EXHIBIT 3

Standard 10

Business Appraisal, Reporting (except Standard 10-3)

Standard 10: Business Appraisal, Reporting

In reporting the results of an appraisal of an interest in a business enterprise or intangible asset, an appraiser must communicate each analyses, opinion, and conclusion in a manner that is not misleading.[9]

Standard Rule 10-1

Each written or oral appraisal report for an interest in a business enterprise or intangible asset must:

a) clearly and accurately set forth the appraisal in a manner that will not be misleading;

b) contain sufficient information to enable the intended user(s) to understand the report, and;

c) clearly and accurately disclose all assumptions, extraordinary assumptions, hypothetical conditions, and limiting conditions used in the assignment.

Standards Rule 10-2

Each written appraisal report for an interest in a business enterprise or intangible asset must be prepared in accordance with one of the following options and prominently state which option is used: Appraisal Report or Restricted Use Appraisal Report.

a) The content of an Appraisal Report must be consistent with the intended use of the appraisal and, at a minimum:

    i. state the identity of the client and any other intended users, by name or type;

    ii. state the intended use of the appraisal;

    iii. summarize information sufficient to identify the business or intangible asset and the interest appraised;

    iv. state the extent to which the interest appraised contains elements of ownership control;

    v. state the extent to which the interest appraised lacks elements of marketability and/ or liquidity, including the basis for that determination;

    vi. state the standard (type) and definition of value and the premise of value and cite the source of the definition;

    vii. state the effective date of the appraisal and the date of the report;

    viii. summarize the scope of work used to develop the appraisal;

    ix. summarize the information analyzed, the appraisal procedures followed, and the reasoning that supports the analyses, opinions, and conclusions; exclusion of the market approach, asset-based (cost) approach, or income approach must be explained;

    x. clearly and conspicuously:

       a. state all extraordinary assumptions and hypothetical conditions; and

       b. state that their use might have affected the assignment results; and

    xi. include a signed certification in accordance with Standards Rule 10-3.

---

9. Material in this exhibit is from Appraisalfoundation.org, Standard 10, *Business Appraisal, Reporting*.

(continued)

b) The content of a Restricted Use Appraisal Report must be consistent with the intended use of the appraisal and, at a minimum:

   i. state the identity of the client, by name or type and state a prominent use restriction that limits use of the report to the client and warns that the appraiser's opinions and conclusions set forth in the report may not be understood properly without additional information in the appraiser's work file[10];

   ii. state the intended use of the appraisal;

   iii. state information sufficient to identify the business or intangible asset and the interest appraised;

   iv. state the extent to which the interest appraised contains elements of ownership control, including the basis for that determination;

   v. state the extent to which the interest appraised lacks elements of marketability and/or liquidity, including the basis for that determination;

   vi. state the standard (type) of value and the premise of value, and cite the source of its definitions;

   vii. state the effective date of the appraisal and the date of the report;

   viii. state the scope of the work used to develop the appraisal;

   ix. state the appraisal procedures followed, state the value opinion(s) and conclusion(s) reached, and reference the work-file; exclusion of the market approach, asset-based (cost) approach, or income approach must be explained;

   x. clearly and conspicuously:

      a. state all extraordinary assumptions and hypothetical conditions; and

      b. state that their use might have affected the assignment results; and

   xi. include a signed certification in accordance with Standards Rule 10-3.

Standard Rule 10-3 (See Exhibit 1)

Standards Rule 10-4

To the extent that is both possible and appropriate, an oral appraisal report for an interest in a business enterprise or intangible asset must address the substantive matters set forth in Standards Rule 10-2(a).

---

10. Most business valuations are Restricted Use Appraisal Reports and contain this statement.

EXHIBIT 3—
continued

Standard 10

INDEX